The Gendered Society

Second Canadian Edition
Michael S. Kimmel
& Jacqueline Holler

OXFORD
UNIVERSITY PRESS

OXFORD
UNIVERSITY PRESS

Oxford University Press is a department of the University of Oxford.
It furthers the University's objective of excellence in research, scholarship,
and education by publishing worldwide. Oxford is a registered trade mark of
Oxford University Press in the UK and in certain other countries.

Published in Canada by
Oxford University Press
8 Sampson Mews, Suite 204,
Don Mills, Ontario M3C 0H5 Canada

www.oupcanada.com

Library and Archives Canada Cataloguing in Publication
Kimmel, Michael S., author
The gendered society / Michael S. Kimmel, Jacqueline
Holler. —Second Canadian edition.

Includes bibliographical references and index.
ISBN 978-0-19-900822-3 (paperback)

1. Sex role—Textbooks. 2. Sex differences (Psychology)—
Textbooks. 3. Gender identity—Textbooks. 4. Sex discrimination—
Textbooks. 5. Equality—Textbooks. I. Holler, Jacqueline,
1964-, author II. Title.

HQ1075.K55 2016   305.3   C2016-904356-8

Cover image: tattywelshie/Getty Images

2 3 4 — 20 19 18 17

Contents

Part 2 Gendered Identities, Gendered Institutions

Part 3 Gendered Interactions

Preface

Since the first edition of this text (now more than five years old!), gender studies have become an even more urgent and central theme of our time. Gender, it seems, is "having a moment." Some of the most important national conversations are ones in which gender takes a front seat, whether those discussions are of missing and murdered Aboriginal women (and men) or sexual violence as experienced on university campuses or at the hands of once-adored media figures. A mere decade ago, those who raised such topics were often greeted with barely veiled impatience—or even eye-rolling. But today, increasing numbers of us seem to be acknowledging that gender matters. While there is still a long way to go to combat *all* forms of discrimination and inequality in Canadian society, our growing willingness to engage with the issue is heartening—and long overdue.

I have heard from many readers and users of the book, and I thank everyone who has contacted me. Rewriting the first edition has transformed it significantly, particularly in the second half of the book. I have been guided by reviewer comments and by my own sense of needed changes.

The growth in gender studies and the explosion of research in the field makes any text like this an exercise in selection. Choosing what to highlight—and what to include at all—is painful and challenging. But I hope that readers will find the changes helpful, and I look forward to hearing your comments.

Acknowledgements

On this second edition, once again, I had the privilege of working with an excellent team at Oxford. Lisa Peterson, Suzanne Clark, and Jodi Lewchuk were tremendously helpful in the planning stages, and Developmental Editor Tanuja Weerasooriya was both helpful and monumentally patient through the long process of revision. Shelly Stevenson proved an effective and incredibly cheerful copy editor. Thank you to all of you!

At UNBC, Sarah Blawatt served as my very capable research assistant; I thoroughly enjoyed our discussions about new directions in gender studies. My graduate and undergraduate students have continued to challenge and inform my thinking, and I thank all of them. It is an honour to be able to work with so many engaged and thoughtful students.

Finally, as ever, I must thank my children, Helga and Urs, for their patience and for their fine company. To them I dedicate whatever is valuable in the work I have done.

Jacqueline Holler
2016

Introduction
Human Beings: An Engendered Species

Daily, we hear how men and women are different. We hear that we come from different planets. They say we have different brain chemistries, different brain organization, and different hormones. They say our different anatomies lead to different destinies. They say we have different ways of knowing, listen to different moral voices, and have different ways of speaking and hearing each other.

You'd think we were different species, like, say, lobsters and giraffes, or Martians and Venusians. In his bestselling book and on his popular website, pop psychologist John Gray informs us that not only do women and men communicate differently, but also they "think, feel, perceive, react, respond, love, need, and appreciate differently."[1] It's a miracle of cosmic proportions that we ever understand one another!

This **interplanetary theory** of complete and universal *gender difference* is also typically the way we explain another universal phenomenon: *gender inequality*. Gender is not simply a system of classification, by which biological males and biological females are sorted, separated, and socialized into equivalent sex roles. Gender also expresses the near-universal inequality between women and men. When we speak about gender, we also speak about hierarchy, power, and inequality, not simply difference.

Therefore, the two tasks of any study of gender are to explain both difference and inequality or, to be alliterative, *difference* and *dominance*. Every general explanation of gender must address two central questions along with their ancillary derivative questions.

First: *Why is it that virtually every single society differentiates people based on gender?* Why are women and men perceived as different in every known society? What are the differences that are perceived? Why is gender at least one—if not the central—basis for the division of labour?

Second: *Why is it that virtually every known society is also based on **male dominance**?* Why do most societies divide social, political, and economic resources unequally between the genders? Moreover, why is it that men almost always get more? Why is a gendered division of labour often an unequal division of labour? Why are women's tasks and men's tasks valued differently?

It is clear, as we shall see, that there are dramatic differences among societies regarding the types of gender differences, the levels of gender inequality, and the amount of violence (implied or real) that are necessary to maintain both systems of difference and domination. Nevertheless, the basic facts remain; *virtually every society known to us is founded upon assumptions of gender difference and the politics of gender inequality.*

On these axiomatic questions, two basic schools of thought prevail: **biological determinism** and **differential socialization**. We know them as "nature" and "nurture," and the question of which is dominant has been debated for a century in classrooms, at dinner parties, by political adversaries, and among friends and families. Are men and women different because they are "hardwired" to be different, or are they different because they've been taught to be? Is biology destiny?

Most of the arguments about gender difference begin, as will this book, with biology (in Chapter 2). Women and men *are* biologically different, after all. Our reproductive anatomies are different, and so are our reproductive destinies. Our brain structures differ; our brain chemistries differ. Our musculature is different. Different levels of different hormones circulate through our different bodies. Surely, these add up to fundamental, intractable, and universal differences, and these differences provide the foundation for male domination, don't they?

The answer is an unequivocal maybe, or, perhaps more accurately, yes and no. Very few people would suggest that there are no differences between males and females. What social scientists call **sex differences** refer precisely to that catalogue of anatomical, hormonal, chemical, and physical differences between women and men. Nevertheless, even here, as we shall see, there are enormous ranges of femaleness and maleness. Though our musculature differs, plenty of women are physically stronger than many men. Though on average our chemistries are different, it's not an all-or-nothing proposition—women do have varying levels of androgens, and men have varying levels of estrogen in their systems. Although our brain structure may be differently lateralized, males and females both do tend to use both sides of their brain. Additionally, it's far from clear that these biological differences automatically and inevitably lead men to dominate women. Could we not imagine, as some writers already have, a culture in which women's biological abilities to bear and nurse children might be seen as the expression of such ineffable power—the ability to create life—that strong men wilt in impotent envy?

In fact, in order to underscore this issue, most social and behavioural scientists now use the term **gender** in a different way than we use the term **sex**. Sex refers to the biological apparatus, the male and the female—our chromosomal, chemical, anatomical organization. Gender refers to the meanings that are attached to those differences within a culture. Sex is male and female; gender is masculinity and femininity—what it means to be a man or a woman. Whereas biological sex varies little (though much more than we once thought, as discussed in Chapter 2), gender varies enormously. What it means to possess the anatomical configuration of male or female means very different things depending on where you are, who you are, and when you are living.

It fell to anthropologists to detail some of those differences in the meanings of masculinity and femininity. What they documented is that gender means different things to different people—that it varies cross-culturally. (We discuss and review the anthropological evidence in Chapter 4.) Some cultures, like that of mainstream North America, encourage men to be stoic and to prove their masculinity through strength and competition. Other cultures prescribe a more relaxed definition of masculinity, based on civic participation, emotional responsiveness, and the collective provision for the community's needs. Moreover, some cultures encourage women to be decisive and competitive, whereas others insist that women are naturally passive, helpless, and dependent. What it meant to be a man or a woman in seventeenth-century France and what it means among Aboriginal peoples in the Australian outback at the turn of the twenty-first century are so far apart that comparison is difficult, if not impossible. *The differences between two cultures are often greater than the differences between the two genders.* If the meanings of gender vary from culture to culture and vary within any one culture over historical time, then understanding gender must employ the tools of the social and behavioural sciences and history.

The other reigning school of thought that explains both gender difference and gender domination is *differential socialization*—the "nurture" side of the equation. Men and women are different because we are taught to be different. From the moment of birth, males and females are treated differently. Gradually we acquire the traits, behaviours, and attitudes that our culture defines as "masculine" or "feminine." We are not necessarily born different: We become different through this process of socialization.

Nor are we born biologically predisposed toward gender inequality. Domination is not a trait carried on the Y chromosome; it is the outcome of the different cultural valuing of men's and women's experiences. Consequently, the adoption of masculinity and femininity implies the adoption of "political" ideas that what men do is culturally more important than what women do.

Developmental psychologists have also examined the ways in which the meanings of masculinity and femininity change during the course of a person's life. The issues confronting a man about proving himself and feeling successful will change, as will the social institutions in which he will attempt to enact those experiences. The meanings of femininity are subject to parallel changes, for example, among prepubescent girls, women in child-bearing years, and post-menopausal women, as they are different for women entering the labour market and those retiring from it.

Although we typically cast the debate in terms of *either* biological determinism or differential socialization—nature versus nurture—it may be useful to pause for a moment to observe what characteristics they have in common. Both schools of thought share two fundamental assumptions. First, both "nature lovers" and "nurturers" see women and men as markedly different from each other—truly, deeply, and irreversibly different. (Nurture does allow for some possibility of change, but it still argues that through the process of socialization males and females become dramatically different from each other.) Additionally, both schools of thought assume that the differences *between* women and men are far greater and more decisive (and worthy of analysis) than the differences that might be observed *among* men or *among* women. Therefore, both "nature lovers" and "nurturers" subscribe to some version of the interplanetary theory of gender.

Second, both schools of thought assume that gender domination is the inevitable outcome of gender difference, that difference causes domination. To the biologists, it may be because pregnancy and lactation make women more vulnerable and in need of protection, or because male musculature makes men more adept hunters, or because testosterone makes them more aggressive with other men and with women, too. Or it may be that men have to dominate women in order to maximize their chances to pass on their genes. On the "nurture" side, psychologists of "gender roles" tell us that, among other things, men and women are taught to devalue women's experiences, perceptions, and abilities and to overvalue those of men.

We argue in this book that both of these propositions are false—or at least incomplete. First, we hope to show that the differences *between* women and men are not nearly as great as are the differences *among* women or *among* men. Many perceived differences turn out to be differences based less on gender than on the social positions people occupy. Second, we argue that gender difference is the product of gender inequality, and not the other way around. In fact, gender difference is the chief outcome of gender inequality, because it is through the idea of difference that inequality is legitimated. As one sociologist put it, "the very creation of difference is the foundation on which inequality rests."[2]

Using what social scientists have come to call a **social constructionism** approach—discussed further in Chapter 5—we make the case that neither gender difference nor gender inequality is inevitable in the nature of things nor, more specifically, in the nature of our bodies. Neither difference—nor domination—is explainable solely by reference to differential socialization of boys and girls into sex roles typical of men and women.

When proponents of both nature and nurture positions assert that gender inequality is the inevitable outcome of gender difference, they take, perhaps inadvertently, a political position that assumes that inequality may be lessened or that its most negative effects may be ameliorated, but that it cannot be eliminated—precisely because it is based upon intractable differences. On the other hand, to assert, as we do, that the exaggerated gender differences that we see are not as great as they appear and that they are the result of inequality allows a far greater political latitude. By eliminating gender inequality, we will remove the foundation upon which the entire edifice of gender difference is built. What will then remain of gender difference is unknown. Will gender eventually disappear? No one knows the answer, of course; but as we discuss in our conclusion, the world of gender is already changing from one built on binary distinction and hierarchy to one that values plurality and egalitarianism.

Making Gender Visible for Both Women and Men

A dramatic transformation in thinking about gender has occurred within a generation or two. In particular, five decades of work by feminist scholars, both in traditional disciplines and in women's studies, have made us aware of the centrality of gender in shaping social life. We now know that gender is one of the central organizing principles around which social life revolves.

In the past 50 years, feminist scholars focused most of their attention on women—on what Catharine Stimpson has called the "omissions, distortions, and trivializations" of women's experiences—and the spheres to which they have historically been consigned (like private life and the family).[3] Women's history sought to rescue from obscurity the lives of significant women who had been ignored and to examine the everyday lives of ordinary women in the past. Feminist scholarship accordingly brought to academic attention both the lives of women and the role of gender in constructing (and constraining) the lives of individuals of both sexes. Women's Studies programs brought these key insights— and many more—to both academic publishing and the classroom.

Despite the fact that feminist scholars have been studying both women *and gender* for many years, it is not unusual to find, in courses on history of gender, psychology of gender, or sociology of gender, that the classroom is populated almost entirely by women. It's as if only women had gender and were therefore interested in studying it. Though more and more (brave) men are enrolling in women's studies classes, they remain a minority in courses dealing with gender. We need to integrate men into our curriculum and classrooms, because masculinity currently flies below many people's radar.

Of course, men are far from invisible. They are ubiquitous in universities and professional schools and in the public sphere in general—not to mention in every subject in the university curriculum! Nevertheless, when we study men, we often study them as political leaders, military heroes, scientists, writers, artists. They are often invisible *as men*. What is the impact of gender on the lives of famous men? How does masculinity play a part in the lives of great artists, writers, athletes, politicians, etc.? How does masculinity play out in the lives of "ordinary" men—in factories and on farms, in union halls and large corporations?[4]

Gender, like race and class, plays out in everyone's life, male or female. These attributes affect not only people who are marginalized by racial, class, or gender inequality, but to those who enjoy privilege. Therefore, "whiteness" can (and must) be analyzed in terms of race just as can the experiences and identities of **racialized** people. When we talk about "class," it doesn't only apply to lower or working classes. Moreover, masculinity is just as much about gender as femininity is.

Still, the very processes that confer **privilege** to one group and not another group are often invisible to those upon whom that privilege is conferred. Invisibility is a luxury. Only white people in our society have the luxury not to think about race; and only men have the luxury to pretend that gender does not matter.

Consider another example of how power is so often invisible to those who have it. You've probably noticed that Canadian e-mail addresses, like those of most people in the world, end with a country code (in our case, .ca). If you were writing to someone in South Africa, you'd put .za at the end, .jp for Japan, .uk for England (United Kingdom), and .de for Germany (Deutschland). However, when you write to people in the United States, the e-mail address ends with .edu for an educational institution, .org for an organization, .gov for a federal government office, and .com or .net for commercial Internet providers. Why is it that the United States doesn't have a country code? From the point of view of the United States, a powerful and influential nation, all other countries are "other" and accordingly need to be named, marked, and noted. Once again, privilege is invisible.

The **invisibility of privilege** means that many men, like many white people, become defensive and angry when confronted with the statistical realities or the human consequences of racism or sexism. Because privilege is invisible, those who have it may not even believe they have it; or they may view an end to privilege as a fundamental attack on their rights.

The continued invisibility of masculinity also means that the gendered standards that are held up as the norm appear to us to be gender-neutral. The illusion of gender neutrality has serious consequences for both women and men. It means that men can maintain the fiction that they are being measured by "objective" standards; for women, it means that they are being judged by someone else's yardstick. At the turn of the twentieth century, the great sociologist Georg Simmel underscored this issue when he wrote:

> We measure the achievements and the commitments . . . of males and females in terms of specific norms and values; but these norms are not neutral, standing above the contrasts of the sexes; they have themselves a male character. . . . The standards of art and the demands of patriotism, the general mores and the specific social ideas, the equity of practical judgements and the objectivity of theoretical knowledge, . . . —all these categories are formally generically human, but are in fact masculine in terms of their actual historical formation . . . it is a fact that in the historical life of our species there operates the equation: objective = male.[5]

Simmel's theoretical formulation echoes in our daily interactions. When a female professor makes a statement such as, "Men are privileged in North American society," students might respond by saying, "Of course, you'd say that. You're biased." They'd see such a normative statement as revealing the inherent biases of gender, a case of special pleading. However, when a man says it—an objective fact, transmitted by an objective professor—they'll probably take notes. Similarly, a white professor's statements on race privilege might be taken more seriously by students than the same comments made, say, by an Aboriginal colleague.

Such equations of "objective = male" (or "objective = white") have enormous practical consequences in every arena of our lives, from the elementary school classroom to professional and graduate schools and in every workplace we enter. As Simmel writes, "Man's *position of power* does not only assure his relative superiority over the woman but it assures that his standards become generalized as generically human standards that are to govern the behaviour of men and women alike."[6]

The Current Debate

North Americans, at this moment, are having a debate about masculinity—but we don't know it. For example, what gender comes to mind when you read about the following current North American problems: "teen violence," "gang violence," "suburban violence," "drug violence," "violence in the schools"? Additionally, what gender comes to mind along with the words "suicide bomber" or "terrorist hijacker"?

Most likely, you've imagined men. Moreover, not just any men—but younger men, in their teens and twenties, and relatively poorer men, from the working class or lower middle class. Nevertheless, how do our social commentators discuss these problems? Do they note that the problems of youth and violence are really problems of young *men* and violence? Do they ever mention that everywhere ethnic nationalism sets up shop, young men are the shopkeepers? Do they ever mention masculinity at all?

No. Listen, for example, to the voice of one expert, asked to comment on the brutal 1998 murder of Matthew Shepard, a gay 21-year-old college student at the University of Wyoming. After being reminded that young men account for 80–90 per cent of people arrested for "gay-bashing" crimes, the reporter quoted a sociologist as saying, "[t]his youth variable tells us they are working out identity issues, making the transition away from home into adulthood."[7] Aside from the offensiveness of linking brutal violence to "working out identity issues," what about addressing this "*youth* variable"—what had been a variable about age and gender was transformed into a variable only about age. Gender simply disappeared. That is the sound of silence, what invisibility looks like.

Now, imagine that these were all women—all the ethnic nationalists, the militias, the gay-bashers. Would that not be *the* story, the *only* story? Would not a gender analysis be at the centre of every single story? Would we not hear from experts on female socialization, frustration, anger, PMS, and everything else under the sun? The ubiquity of men as perpetrators of these incidents, however, earns nary a word.

Take one final example. What if it had been young girls who opened fire on their classmates in Taber, Alberta; in Pearl, Mississippi; in Jonesboro, Arkansas; in Winnenden, Germany; or in Springfield, Oregon? What if nearly all the children who died were boys? Do you think that the social outcry would demand that we investigate the "inherent violence" of a particular culture; or would they simply express dismay that young "people" have too much access to guns? In these cases, no one seemed to mention that the young boys who actually committed those crimes were simply doing—albeit in dramatic form at a younger age—what American men have been taught to do for centuries when they are upset and angry. Men don't get mad; they get even. Moreover, very few mentions are made of the targeting of girls in school shootings. (The gender of violence is explored in Chapter 13.)

We believe that until we make gender visible for both women and men, our culture will not know how to address problems such as school shootings and terrorist attacks. That's not to say that all we have to do is address masculinity. These issues are complex, requiring analyses of the political economy of global economic integration, of the transformation of social classes, of urban poverty and hopelessness, and of racism. However, if we ignore masculinity—if we let it remain invisible—we will never completely understand society's problems, let alone resolve them.

Gender and Power: Hegemonic Masculinity and Emphasized Femininity

When we use the term "gender," then, it is with the explicit intention of discussing both masculinity and femininity. However, even these terms are inaccurate because they imply that there is only one simple definition of masculinity and only one simple definition of femininity. One of the important elements of a social-constructionist approach is to explore the differences *among* men and *among* women, because, as it turns out, these are often more decisive than the differences between women and men.

Within any one society at any one moment, several meanings of masculinity and femininity coexist. Simply put, not all North American men and women are the same. Our experiences are also structured by class, race, ethnicity, age, sexuality, and region. Each of these axes modifies the others. Just because we make gender visible doesn't mean that we make these other organizing principles of social life invisible. Imagine, for example, an older, black, gay man in Toronto and a young, white, heterosexual farm boy in Manitoba. Wouldn't they have different definitions of masculinity? Alternatively, imagine a 22-year-old middle-class, Asian-Canadian, heterosexual woman in Vancouver and an elderly, poor, white, Scots-Canadian lesbian in Halifax. Wouldn't their ideas about what it means to be a woman be somewhat different?

Consider that gender varies across cultures, over historical time, among men and women within any one culture, and during the life course. This being so, can people really speak of masculinity or femininity as though they were constant, universal essences, common to all women and to all men? If not, gender must be seen as an ever-changing fluid assemblage of meanings and behaviours. In that sense, we must speak of *masculinities* and *femininities* and consequently recognize the different definitions of masculinity and femininity that we construct. By pluralizing the terms, we acknowledge that masculinity and femininity mean different things to different groups of people at different times.

At the same time, we can't forget that not all masculinities and femininities are created equal. North American men and women must also contend with a particular definition that is held up as the model against which we are expected to measure ourselves. We therefore come to know what it means to be a man or a woman in our culture by setting our definitions in opposition to a set of "others"—racial minorities, sexual minorities. For men, the classic "other" is, of course, women. It feels imperative to most men that they make it clear—eternally, compulsively, decidedly—that they are unlike women. Robert McElvaine calls this the "notawoman" definition of manhood, linking it to both competition among men and the deprecation of all things feminine.[8]

Nevertheless, one form of masculinity reigns supreme. For most men, this is the **hegemonic** definition—the one that is held up as the model for all. Hegemonic masculinity is not defined simply as a rejection of the feminine. Indeed, we might say that in contemporary North American society, the "manly" man is defined against both the boy, the immature and powerless child, and the "fag," the effeminate sexual "other." For R.W. Connell, **hegemonic masculinity** is "constructed in relation to various subordinated masculinities as well as in relation to women."[9] The sociologist Erving Goffman once described this hegemonic definition of masculinity like this:

> In an important sense there is only one complete unblushing male in America: a young, married, white, urban, northern, heterosexual, Protestant, father, of college education, fully employed, of good complexion, weight, and height, and a recent record in sports. . . . Any male who fails to qualify in any one of these ways is likely to view himself—during moments at least—as unworthy, incomplete, and inferior.[10]

Goffman's definition makes it clear that like any ideal, the ideal of hegemonic masculinity is unattainable, based as it is on a version of virtually impossible competitive success. Even if a man manages to attain the status of Goffman's "unblushing male," he cannot remain young, fit, and employed forever. Not surprisingly, most of our ideals of hegemonic masculinity are media images—like the Marlboro Man—who can remain fixed in their stoic and perfect performance of masculinity without ever growing old, getting weak, feeling doubt, or losing control of their emotions, families, or careers.

Given the power of hegemonic masculinity and the growth, in modern societies, of protest and counterculture identities, we should not be surprised that not everyone subscribes to the ideals of hegemonic masculinity. Indeed, particular resistant forms of masculinity, including queer, skinhead, punk, emo, and female/trans masculinities contest the power of the hegemonic stereotype while sometimes reinforcing many of its definitions

Independent, stoic, rugged, almost always alone, the Marlboro Man was introduced in the 1950s to counter the idea that filtered cigarettes were "feminine."[11] This emblem of American hegemonic masculinity became one of the most successful and recognizable images in the history of advertising, making Marlboro the top brand of cigarettes in the world. This suggests that while masculinity may vary from culture to culture, there are key attributes that appeal across cultures.

of manhood, particularly the "notawoman" definition. Hegemonic masculinity is accordingly an enormously powerful ideal despite, or because of, its unattainable and exaggerated quality.

There is no "hegemonic" version of femininity, according to R.W. Connell, because hegemonic masculinity arose through competition among men within patriarchal societies. In a sense, this made masculinity more important, in many societies, than femininity. We've all heard the exhortation "Be a man," but how many of us have ever used, or heard, the phrase "Be a woman"? What would that even mean? In fact, in most societies the transition to womanhood is perceived as much more natural and simple than the comparable transition for men. Masculinity must be earned, femininity simply grown into.

This does not mean that women face no gendered expectations, or that their lot is somehow easier. Indeed, women also have to contend with an exaggerated ideal of femininity, which Connell calls **emphasized femininity**. Emphasized femininity is organized around (real or apparent) compliance with gender inequality and is "oriented to accommodating the interests and desires of men." One sees emphasized femininity in "the display of sociability rather than technical competence, fragility in mating scenes, compliance with men's desire for titillation and ego-stroking in office relationships, acceptance of marriage and child care as a response to labour-market discrimination against women."[12] Emphasized femininity exaggerates gender difference as a strategy of "adaptation to men's power" stressing empathy and nurturance; "real" womanhood is described as "fascinating," and women are advised that they can wrap men around their fingers by knowing and playing by the "rules."

Emphasized femininity (compliance with the desires and interests of men) is used here to sell Kelpidine Chewing Gum.

In one research study, an eight-year-old boy captured emphasized femininity eloquently:

> If I were a girl, I'd have to attract a guy wear makeup; sometimes. Wear the latest style of clothes and try to be likable. I probably wouldn't play any physical sports like football or soccer. I don't think I would enjoy myself around men in fear of rejection or under the pressure of attracting them.[13]

Gender Differences as "Deceptive Distinctions"

The existence of multiple masculinities and femininities dramatically undercuts the idea that the gender differences we observe are due solely to differently gendered people occupying gender-neutral positions. Moreover, that these masculinities and femininities are arrayed along a hierarchy, and measured against one another, buttresses the argument that domination creates and exaggerates difference.

The interplanetary theory of gender assumes that, whether through biology or socialization, women act like women, no matter where they are, and that men act like men, no matter where they are. Psychologist Carol Tavris argues that such binary thinking leads to what philosophers call the "law of the excluded middle," which, as she reminds us, "is where most men and women fall in terms of their psychological qualities, beliefs, abilities, traits, and values."[14] It turns out that many of the differences between women and men that we observe in our everyday lives are actually **deceptive distinctions**: not *gender* differences at all, but rather differences that are the result of being in different positions or in different arenas. It's not that gendered individuals occupy these ungendered positions, but rather that the *positions themselves* elicit the behaviours we see as gendered. The sociologist Cynthia Fuchs Epstein calls these "deceptive distinctions" because, although they appear to be based on gender, they are actually based on something else.[15]

Take, for example, the well-known differences in communication patterns observed by Deborah Tannen in her bestselling book, *You Just Don't Understand*. Tannen argues that men employ the competitive language of hierarchy and domination to get ahead; women create webs of inclusion with softer, more embracing language that ensures that everyone feels okay. When couples communicate, women talk more, using language to create intimacy while their husbands speak less and use language instrumentally. To understand the opposite sex, Tannen argues, one must understand its "genderlect."[16]

However, it turns out that men and women use language differently in different situations. The very same men who are silent at home may be more verbal at work, where they are in positions of dependency and powerlessness, and need to use conversation to maintain a relationship with their superiors; and their wives are just as capable of using language competitively to maximize their position in a corporate hierarchy. Education and class may also be a more important determinant of language use than gender. When he examined the recorded transcripts of women's and men's testimony in trials, anthropologist William O'Barr concluded that the witnesses' occupation was a more accurate predictor of their use of language than was gender. "So-called women's language is neither characteristic of all women, nor limited only to women," O'Barr writes. If women use "powerless" language, it may be due "to the greater tendency of women to occupy relatively powerless social positions" in society.[17] Communication differences turn out to be "deceptive distinctions" because rarely do we observe the communication patterns of dependent men and executive women.

We could take another example from the world of education, explored in Chapter 7. Aggregate differences in girls' and boys' scores on standardized math tests have led people to speculate that whereas males have a natural propensity for arithmetic figures, females have a "fear of math." If you couple this with their "fear of success" in the workplace, you might find that women manage money less effectively—with less foresight, less calculation, less care. The popular writer Colette Dowling, author of the bestselling 1981 book *The Cinderella Complex*, interviewed 65 women in their late 50s about money matters and found that only two had *any* investment plans for their retirements. Broke and bankrupt after several bestsellers, and single again herself, Dowling argues that this relates to "conflicts with dependency. Money savvy is connected with masculinity in our culture," she told an interviewer. "That leaves women with the feeling that if they want to take care of themselves and are good at it, the quid pro quo is they'll never hook up with a relationship." Because of ingrained femininity, women end up shooting themselves in the foot.[18]

However, such assertions fly in the face of all available research, argues financial expert Jane Bryant Quinn, herself the author of a bestseller about women and money. "It *is* more socially acceptable for women not to manage their money," she told the same interviewer. "But the Y chromosome is not a money management chromosome. In all the studies, if you control for earnings, age, and experience, women are the same as men. At 23, out in the working world staring at a [retirement] plan, they are equally confused. But if those women quit working, they will know less and less about finance, while the man, who keeps working, will know more and more."[19] In sum, our *experience*, not our *gender*, predicts how we'll handle our retirement investments.

What about those enormous gender differences that some observers have found in the workplace (the subject of Chapter 8)? Men, we hear, are competitive social climbers who seek advancement at every opportunity; women are co-operative team-builders who shun competition and may even suffer from a "fear of success." However, a pioneering study by Rosabeth Moss Kanter indicated that gender mattered far less than opportunity. When women had the same opportunities, networks, mentors, and possibilities for advancement, they behaved just as the men did. Women were unsuccessful because they lacked opportunities, not because they feared success; when men lacked opportunities, they behaved in stereotypically "feminine" ways.[20]

Finally, take our experiences in the family, examined in Chapter 6. Here, again, we assume that women are socialized to be nurturing and maternal, men to be strong and silent, relatively emotionally inexpressive arbiters of justice—that is, we assume that women do the work of "mothering" because they are socialized to do so. Again, sociological research suggests that our behaviour in the family has somewhat less to do with gender socialization than with the family situations in which we find ourselves.

Research by sociologist Kathleen Gerson, for example, found that gender socialization was not very helpful in predicting women's family experiences. Only slightly more than half the women who were primarily interested in full-time motherhood were, in fact, full-time mothers; and only slightly more than half the women who were primarily interested in full-time careers had them. It turned out that marital stability, husband's income, women's workplace experiences, and support networks were far more important than gender socialization in determining which women ended up full-time mothers and which did not.[21]

On the other side of the ledger, research by sociologist Barbara Risman found that despite a gender socialization that downplays emotional responsiveness and nurturing, most single fathers are perfectly capable of "mothering." Single fathers do not hire female workers to do the typically female tasks around the house: They do those tasks themselves. In fact, Risman found few differences between single fathers and mothers (single or married) when it came to what they did around the house, how they acted with their children, or even in their children's emotional and intellectual development—a finding that led Risman to argue that "men can mother and that children are not necessarily better nurtured by women than by men."[22]

These findings also shed a very different light on other research. For example, some recent researchers found significant differences in the amount of stress that women and men experience on an everyday basis. According to the researchers, women reported higher levels of stress and lower numbers of "stress-free" days than did men. David Almeida and Ronald Kessler sensibly concluded that this was not a biologically based difference, a signal of women's inferiority in handling stress, but rather (as discussed further in Chapter 6) an indication that women had more stress in their lives, because they had to juggle more family and work issues than did men.[23]

Based on all this research, you might conclude, as does Risman, that "if women and men were to experience identical structural conditions and role expectations, empirically observable gender differences would dissipate."[24] Still, there *are* some differences between women and men, after all. Nevertheless, this research suggests that those differences are not as great, decisive, or impervious to social change as we once thought. It is the task of this book to explore those areas where there appear to be gender differences (but where there are in fact few or no differences) as well as the areas where gender differences are significant and decisive.

The Meaning of Mean Differences

Few of the differences between women and men are "hardwired" into all males to the exclusion of all females, or vice versa. Although we can readily observe differences between women and men in rates of aggression, physical strength, math or verbal achievement, caring and nurturing, or emotional expressiveness, it is not true that *all* males and *no* females are aggressive, physically strong, and adept at math and science. Neither can we say that *all* females and *no* males are caring and nurturing, verbally adept, or emotionally expressive. What we mean when we speak of gender differences are **mean differences**, differences in the average scores obtained by women and men.

These mean scores tell us something about the differences between the two groups, but they tell us nothing about the distributions themselves, the differences *among* men or *among* women. Sometimes these distributions can be enormous: There are large numbers of caring or emotionally expressive men and of aggressive and physically strong women. (See Figure 1.1.) In fact, in virtually all of the research that has been done on the attributes associated with masculinity or femininity, the differences *among* women and *among* men are far greater than the mean differences *between* women and men. We tend to focus on the mean differences, but they may tell us far less than we think they do.

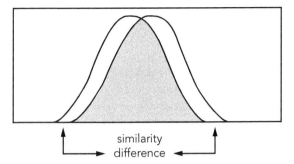

similarity
difference

Figure 1.1 Schematic rendering of the overlapping distributions of traits, attitudes, and behaviours by gender.

Although mean differences might obtain on many characteristics, these distributions suggest far greater similarity between women and men and far greater variability among men and among women.

What we think mean differences tell us, of course, is that women and men are different, from different planets. This is the interplanetary theory of gender difference—that the observed mean differences between women and men are decisive and that they come from the fact that women and men are biologically so different.

For example, even the idea that we are from different planets—that our differences are deep and intractable—has a political dimension: To call the "other" sex the "opposite" sex obscures the many ways we are alike. As the anthropologist, Gayle Rubin, points out:

> Men and women are, of course, different. But they are not as different as day and night, earth and sky, yin and yang, life and death. In fact from the standpoint of nature, men and women are closer to each other than either is to anything else—for instance mountains, kangaroos, or coconut palms . . . Far from being an expression of natural differences, exclusive gender identity is the suppression of natural similarities.[25]

The interplanetary theory of gender difference is important not because it's right—in fact, it is wrong far more often than it is right—but because, as a culture, we seem desperately to want it to be true. That is, the real sociological question about gender is not the sociology of gender differences, which explains the physiological origins of gender difference. Rather, the real sociology-of-knowledge question explores why gender difference is so important to us, why we cling to the idea of gender difference so tenaciously, and why we shell out millions of dollars for books that "reveal" the deep differences between women and men, but will probably never buy a book that says, "Hey, we're all Earthlings!"

That, however, is the message of this book. Virtually all available research from the social and behavioural sciences suggests that women and men are not from Venus and Mars, but from planet Earth. We're not opposite sexes, but neighbouring sexes—we have far more in common with each other than we have differences.

Difference and Domination: Individuals in a Gendered Society

Whether we believe that gender difference is biologically determined or is a cultural formation, the interplanetary theory of gender difference assumes that gender is a property of individuals, that is, that gender is a component of one's identity. However, this is only half the story. We believe that individual boys and girls become gendered—that is, we learn the "appropriate" behaviours and traits that are associated with hegemonic masculinity and emphasized femininity—and then we each, individually, negotiate our own path in a way that feels right to us. In a sense, we each "cut our own deal" with the dominant definitions of masculinity and femininity. That's why we are so keenly attuned to, and so vigorously resist, gender stereotypes—because we believe that they do not actually encompass our experiences.

Nevertheless, we do not cut our own deal by ourselves in gender-neutral institutions and arenas. The social institutions of our world—workplace, family, school, and politics—are also gendered institutions, sites where the dominant definitions are reinforced and reproduced, and where "deviants" are disciplined. We become gendered selves in a **gendered society**.

When we say that we live in a gendered society, we imply that the organizations of our society have evolved in ways that reproduce both the differences between women and men and the domination of men over women. Institutionally, we can see how the structure of the workplace is organized around demonstrating and reproducing masculinity: The temporal organization and the spatial organization of work both depend upon the separation of spheres (distance between work and home and the fact that women are the primary child-care providers).

As with the invisibility of gendered identity, assuming **institutional gender neutrality** actually serves to maintain the gender politics of those institutions. Additionally, it underscores the way we often assume that if you allow individuals to express a wider range of gender behaviours, they'll be able to succeed in those gender-neutral institutions. We assume, then, that the best way to eliminate gender inequality in higher education or in the workplace is to promote sameness—that is, we're unequal only because we're different.

This, however, creates a political and personal dilemma for women in gendered institutions. It's a no-win proposition for women when they enter the workplace, the military, politics, or sports—arenas that are already established to reproduce and sustain masculinity. To the extent that they become "like men" in order to succeed, they are seen as having sacrificed their femininity. Yet to the extent to which they refuse to sacrifice their femininity, they are seen as different, and gender discrimination is therefore legitimate as the sorting of different people into different slots.[26] Women who succeed are punished for abandoning their femininity—rejected as potential partners, labelled as "dykes," left off the invitation lists. Consequently, gender inequality creates a double bind for women—a double bind that is based on the assumption of gender difference and the assumption of institutional gender neutrality.

Both difference and domination are produced and reproduced in our social interactions, in the institutions in which we live and work. Though the differences between us are not as great as we often assume, they become important in our expectations and observations. This book examines those differences—those that are real and important—and seeks to reveal those that are neither real nor important. We will explore the ways in which gender inequality provides the foundation for assumptions of gender difference. Finally, we will endeavour to show the impact of gender on our lives—how we become gendered people living gendered lives in a gendered society.

Summary

Despite the persistence of the interplanetary theory of gender difference, men and women are more similar than different. Gender difference exists, of course, but it is neither complete nor absolute. Still, virtually every human society is founded upon assumptions of gender differences; most have also exhibited gender inequality in the form of male dominance. The frequency of both gender difference and gender inequality is often explained using arguments of biological determinism versus differential socialization, or "nature versus nurture."

While science provides evidence of significant biological differences between the sexes, definitions of gender differences vary greatly among cultures. This suggests that biological determinism ("nature") can't fully explain gender difference or domination. Developmental psychology provides ample evidence of differential socialization ("nurture"), suggesting that men and women are different because they are socialized to be different. While the differential socialization argument contests biological determinism, both arguments assume that men and women are dramatically different and that their differences produce gender inequality or domination. Nevertheless, men and women are not so dramatically different—and, what's more, this book argues that their differences do not produce inequality, but rather are produced by inequality.

To examine how inequality produces gender difference, we need to make gender visible in the way that feminist scholars have been doing it for the past 50 years. It's particularly important to stop acting as though only women have gender. We need to study masculinity to understand how some of our social norms are really "masculine norms," based on the yardstick of "universal" man. We also need to understand masculinity to assess truly some of the most important issues we face, most notably violence.

When we study masculinity and femininity, though, we need to keep in mind that there is not just one form or "essence" of manliness or womanliness that exists everywhere at all times. To be sure, each society holds up one version that is "hegemonic." R.W. Connell coined the term "hegemonic masculinity" to describe the version of masculinity most celebrated in a culture at a given time. For Connell, the feminine counterpart is "emphasized femininity," defined as a kind of exaggerated compliance with the desires of men and the system of gender inequality. So then, emphasized femininity and hegemonic masculinity are a kind of recipe for manliness and womanliness; though the recipe's ingredients vary from culture to culture, and change over time, the basic idea is that there is a recipe to which men and women need to adhere. Though not everyone in North American society—or any society—adheres to hegemonic masculinity, this gender ideology remains a force to be reckoned with in any society, organizing forms of masculinity in a continuum or hierarchy.

While we see hegemonic masculinity and emphasized femininity as powerful gender ideologies, it's important to recognize that many of the differences we attribute to being "masculine" or "feminine" may actually be "deceptive distinctions," that is, the result of being in different situations rather than of different genders. Many so-called "gender" differences—in language use, in financial habits, or in family roles—may be the result of different experiences rather than gender differences per se. That is, when men are in "female" situations, they act more "like women"—and vice versa. This doesn't mean that gender differences don't exist, but it does mean that we need to use caution when we analyze gender difference.

Another reason we need to use caution when discussing gender differences is that we are generally talking about mean differences—differences between "average" men and "average" women. There are probably greater differences among men and women than between them, as Figure 1.1 suggests.

Finally, many of the gender differences we see around us are not the result of some intractable difference between the masculine and the feminine, but the outcome of individual people trying to make their lives in a gendered society. To understand gender differences, we therefore need to understand the way in which institutions and organizations are gendered—the way that they reproduce the differences between men and women and reinforce the idea of gender inequality. When we look at gendered institutions, as we do in the second part of this book, we can see how institutions, far from being gender-neutral, have been set up according to a set of gendered "rules." Therefore, even though we may not be from Mars or from Venus, when we engage with the institutions that constitute our social worlds, we come up against those rules—rules that make the "gendered society." In the pages that follow, we explore that gendered society through an examination of gender differences, an exploration of gender inequality and the way it creates difference, and an assessment of the impact of gender on our lives.

Questions for Critical Thinking

1. Can you think of examples of hegemonic masculinity or emphasized femininity in your own life or community?
2. How does the "invisibility of privilege" operate? How might you experience privilege based on gender, class, ethnicity, ability, and/or sexuality? When you think of "a Canadian citizen," what picture do you see?
3. Why do you think the interplanetary theory of gender difference appeals so strongly to people?

Key Terms

biological determinism
deceptive distinctions
differential socialization
emphasized femininity
gender
gendered society
hegemonic
hegemonic masculinity
institutional gender neutrality

interplanetary theory
invisibility of privilege
male dominance
mean differences
privilege
racialized
sex
sex differences
social constructionism

Part 1

Explanations of Gender

2

Ordained by Nature
Biology Constructs the Sexes

You may drive nature out with a pitchfork; she will nevertheless come back.

—Horace (65–8 BC)

It is not human nature we should accuse but the despicable conventions that pervert it.

—Denis Diderot (1713–84)

What is human nature? That's an ancient and thorny question. It's no simpler to understand the "nature" of men and women as gendered beings. Still, many people claim, with Sigmund Freud, "anatomy is destiny." Though it's not clear that Freud ever intended that this statement be taken literally, many researchers believe that the differences in male and female anatomy provide the basis for observable differences between men and women.

Biological explanations hold a place of prominence in our explanations of both gender *difference* and gender *inequality*. First, because they are based on "objective scientific facts," the arguments of natural scientists are extraordinarily persuasive. Second, biological explanations seem to accord with our own observations: Women and men *seem* so different to us most of the time—so different, in fact, that we often appear to be from different planets.

There's also a certain conceptual tidiness to biological explanations, because the social arrangements between women and men (gender inequality) seem to stem directly and inevitably from the differences between us. Biological arguments can be used to argue that inequality is inevitable, or that "genes hold culture on a leash," as E.O. Wilson famously stated.[1]

This chapter will explore some of the biological evidence that is presented to demonstrate the natural, biologically based differences between the sexes and the ways in which social and political arrangements (inequality) directly flow from those differences. Biological differences can tell us much about the ways in which men and women behave. The search for such differences can also tell us a lot about our culture—about what we want so desperately to believe, and why we want to believe it.

Biological Differences, Then and Now

The idea of essential origins of the differences between women and men is not new. What is new, at least for the past few centuries, is that scientists have come to play the central role in exploring the natural differences between males and females.

Prior to the nineteenth century, most explanations of gender difference had been the province of theologians. God had created man and woman for different purposes, and those reproductive differences were decisive. These theological explanations continued to have meaning well into the nineteenth century when, for example, the American abolitionist preacher Reverend John Todd warned against women's suffrage, which would "reverse the very laws of God."[2]

By the late eighteenth century, however, scientists were beginning to join the debate. After 1750, European anatomists—few of whom were women—published drawings of the male and female skeletons that exaggerated the pelvises of women and the crania of men, therefore arguing for the sexes' "natural" suitedness to their social roles.[3]

The debate intensified later in the nineteenth century under the influence of Darwin and the emerging science of evolutionary biology. In his path-breaking work *On the Origin of Species* (1859), Darwin posed several questions. How do certain species come to be the way they are? Why is there such astonishing variety among those species? Why do some species differ from others in some ways and remain similar in other ways? He answered these questions with the law of natural selection. Species adapt to their changing environments. Those species that adapt well to their environments are reproductively successful, that is, their adaptive characteristics are passed on to the next generation, whereas those that are less adaptive do not pass on their characteristics. Within any one species, a similar process occurs, and those individuals who are best suited to their environment pass on their genes to the next generation. Species are always changing, always adapting.

Such an idea was heretical to those who believed that God had created all species, including human beings, intact and unchanging. Moreover, Darwin did believe that just as the species of the lower animal world show intrinsic sex differences, so, too, do human beings. "Woman seems to differ from man in mental disposition, chiefly in her greater tenderness and lesser selfishness," he wrote in *The Descent of Man*. Men's competitiveness, ambition, and selfishness "seem to be his natural and unfortunate birthright. The chief distinction in the intellectual powers of the two sexes is shown by man's attaining to a higher eminence, in whatever he takes up, than can woman—whether requiring deep thought, reason, or imagination, or merely the uses of the senses and the hands."[4]

No sooner had the biological differences between women and men been established as scientific fact than writers and critics declared all efforts to challenge social inequality and discrimination against women to be in violation of the "laws of nature." Many writers argued that women's efforts to enter the public sphere—to seek employment, to vote, and to enter colleges—were misguided because they placed women's social and political aspirations over the purposes for which their bodies had been designed. Women were not to be *excluded* from voting, from the labour force, or from higher education as much as they were, as the Reverend Todd put it, "to be exempted from certain things which men must endure."[5] This position was best summed up by a participant at an 1880 women's suffrage debate (Sacramento, California):

I am opposed to woman's sufferage [*sic*] on account of the burden it will place upon her. Her delicate nature has already enough to drag it down. Her slender frame, naturally weakened by the constant strain attendant upon her nature is too often racked by diseases that are caused by a too severe tax upon her mind. The presence of passion, love, ambition, is all too potent for her enfeebled condition, and wrecked health and early death are all too common.[6]

Social scientists quickly jumped on the biological bandwagon—especially social Darwinists, who shortened the time span necessary for evolution from millennia to one or two generations and who extended Darwin's range from ornithology to human beings. In their effort to legitimize social science by allying it with natural law, social Darwinists applied Darwin's theory in ways its originator had never imagined, distorting his ideas about natural selection to claim decisive biological differences among races, nations, families, and, of course, between women and men. For example, the eminent French sociologist Gustav LeBon wrote in 1879:

In the most intelligent races, as among the Parisians, there are a large number of women whose brains are closer in size to those of gorillas than to the most developed of male brains. . . . All psychologists who have studied the intelligence of women . . . recognize today that they represent the most inferior forms of human evolution and that they are closer to children and savages than to an adult civilized man. They excel in fickleness, inconstancy, absence of thought and logic, and incapacity to reason. Without doubt, there exist some distinguished women, very superior to the average man, but they are as exceptional as the birth of any monstrosity, as, for example, of a gorilla with two heads.[7]

Arguments about sexual difference were linked to assertions of the inevitability of racial and gendered inequality. "How did woman first become subject to man as she is now all over the world?" asked James Long (in an 1852 New York newspaper editorial). "By her nature, her sex, just as the negro is and always will be, to the end of time, inferior to the white race, and therefore, doomed to subjection; but happier than she would be in any other condition, just because it is the law of her nature."[8] Doomed to subjection to men of her own race, a white woman was still assured she had a role to play in upholding racial hierarchy. In Canada, "woman's nature" was yoked to the mission of populating the nation with the "right" sort of people. For Sophie Bevan, who wrote a letter to the (London) *Times* after a tour of North America, Canada would be lost to racial and class inferiors "unless we can induce the right sort of British women to emigrate"; were such women to fail in their mission, she warned, "we shall not have the Colonies peopled with our own race or speaking our own mother tongue."[9]

Biological arguments therefore became tied up not only with women's proper role but also with the hierarchical relationships among races and classes. The field of **eugenics** developed in the nineteenth century and spread its influence to Canada in the early twentieth century. Eugenics united feminists with social conservatives and progressives in the pursuit of biological improvement. Admired Canadians like Emily Murphy and J.S. Woodsworth were fellow travellers of the movement. Adhered to by many, though discredited because of Nazi atrocities committed in its name, eugenics had significant influence in Canada, particularly in the West. British Columbia and Alberta enacted legislation permitting the involuntary sterilization of the "mentally defective" (a blanket term that covered many forms of disability and mental illness). Ultimately, between 1929 and 1972, more than 2,800 people were sterilized in this manner. Although Aboriginal people were only between 2 and 3 per cent of the population, they represented 6 per cent of the cases presented to the board that approved involuntary sterilization. Moreover, 70 per cent of Aboriginal people whose cases were presented to the board were ultimately sterilized, compared with approximately 47 per cent of cases involving those of Eastern and Western European descent. Women, teenagers, and young adults were also overrepresented among those sterilized. Shockingly, eugenics legislation in the West was only repealed in the 1970s. In 1996, Leilani Muir won a judgment against the province of Alberta for wrongful sterilization, which was followed by a class-action suit brought by survivors of similar medical "treatment."[10]

The discrediting of such historical (if recent!) forms of **biological determinism** should make us cautious about the conclusions we draw from biology. Nonetheless, past misconceptions of scientists and misuses of scientific knowledge shouldn't cancel out the continuing importance and interest of research on biological difference. Today, serious biological arguments generally draw their evidence from three areas of research: evolutionary theory—from sociobiology to "evolutionary psychology"; brain research; and endocrinological research on sex hormones—before birth and again at puberty.

The Evolutionary Imperative: From Social Darwinism to Sociobiology and Evolutionary Psychology

Evolutionary biologists since Darwin have abandoned the more obviously political intentions of the social Darwinists, but the development of the new field of **sociobiology** in the 1970s revived evolutionary arguments. Edward O. Wilson, a Harvard entomologist specializing in ants, helped to found this school of thought, which studies the biological basis of social behaviour in all animals, including human beings. All creatures, Wilson argued, "obey" the "biological principle," and all temperamental differences (personalities, cultures) derive from the biological development of creatures undergoing the pressure of evolutionary selection. The natural differences that result are the source of the social and political arrangements we observe today. Eventually, he confidently predicted, the social sciences and humanities would "shrink to specialized branches of biology."[11]

One of the major areas that sociobiologists have stressed is the differences in male and female sexuality, which they believe to be the natural outgrowth of centuries of evolutionary development. Evolutionary success requires that all members of a species consciously or unconsciously desire to pass on their genes. Therefore, males and females develop reproductive "strategies" to ensure that our own genetic code passes on to the next generation. Sociobiologists accordingly suggest that the differences and inequality we observe between women and men today have come from centuries of advantageous evolutionary choices. As Wilson's fellow sociobiologist Richard Dawkins put it, "[F]emale exploitation begins here."[12]

Take, for example, the size and the number of the reproductive cells themselves. Add to that the differential **parental investment** required to produce a healthy offspring, and—presto!—you have the differences between male and female sexual behaviour at a typical dorm party this weekend. "He" produces billions of tiny sperm; "she" produces one gigantic ovum. For the male, reproductive success depends upon his ability to fertilize a large number of eggs. Therefore, males have a "natural" propensity toward promiscuity. By contrast, females require only one successful mating before their egg can be fertilized. What's more, females must invest a far greater amount of energy in gestation and lactation and have a much higher reproductive "cost." Females, therefore, tend to be monogamous, choosing the male who will make the best parent.

From this theory, it's a simple matter to extrapolate in simplistic manners to the behaviour of modern men and women. This is particularly true when sociobiological research is digested by popular media. "A woman seeks marriage to monopolize not a man's sexuality, but, rather, his political and economic resources, to ensure that her children (her genes) will be well provided for," writes journalist Anthony Layng. As sociobiologist Donald Symons puts it, women and men have different "sexual psychologies" that drive women to be "more choosy and more hesitant," while men are "less discriminating, more aggressive, and have a greater taste for variety of partners."[13]

Other evolutionary arguments examine different aspects of the differences and inequality between men and women. For example, the separation of masculine and feminine spheres seems to have a basis far back in evolutionary time. Lionel Tiger and Robin Fox emphasize the social requirements for the evolutionary transition to a hunting-and-gathering society. First, the hunting band must have solidarity and co-operation, which require bonding among the hunters. Women's biology—especially their menstrual cycle—puts them at a significant disadvantage for such consistent co-operation, and the presence of women would disrupt the co-operation necessary among the men and insinuate competition and aggression. Women also are possessed of a "maternal instinct." Consequently, it would make sense for men to hunt and for women to remain back home raising the children. For Tiger, male bonding through the hunt produces the basis of human society, with effects that persist to this day.[14] Fair enough for early humans—but does that mean that separate spheres are actually "in our genes"? Yes, writes Edward O. Wilson, "In hunter-gatherer societies, men hunt and women stay at home. This strong bias persists in most agricultural and industrial societies, and, on that ground alone, appears to have a genetic origin. . . . My own guess is that the genetic bias is intense enough to cause a substantial division of labour in the most free and most egalitarian of future societies."[15]

Other evolutionary arguments have examined such behaviours as interspecies violence and aggression. As we shall see in Chapter 13, some sociobiologists have argued that rape is "natural," a result of men's failed competition for mates. The breathless interpretive rush from male scorpion flies to human rapists is one example of sociobiology's biological determinism.

The newest incarnation of sociobiology is called **evolutionary psychology**, which explains psychological traits, including differences between women and men, as evolutionary adaptations. One key insight of evolutionary psychology is clear: Our brains did evolve under vastly different conditions from those we live in today. Millions of years of evolution preceded what we think of as human history, and we are creatures produced by that dimly understood period. Comparisons with other primates, as well as theories on hominid evolution, can help us understand many behaviours, from language use to play, from grandmothering to the choice of sexual partners. The key word here, however, is "help." Too often, however, evolutionary psychology falls into the reductionist patterns of sociobiology: men are aggressive, controlling, and managing by nature, while women are "programmed to be passive."[16]

According to evolutionary psychologists, these differences lead us to completely different contemporary mating strategies. Psychologist David Buss surveyed more than 10,000 people from 37 different cultures around the world and found strikingly similar things about what women and men want in a mate. It can't be culturally specific if they all agree, can it? In every society, females placed a high premium on signs of economic prosperity, whereas men placed their highest premium on youth and beauty, whose signal traits were large breasts and ample hips (i.e., signs of fertility). Does it interest you that although these traits were important, the single trait most highly valued by *both* women and men was love and kindness?[17] This suggests that when we choose mates, we are acting on a complex set of impulses derived at least as much from our cultural influences as from the demands of our genes. The best evolutionary psychology acknowledges this while insisting that we understand the evolutionary roots of behaviour as motivating significant sex differences. For example, Margo Wilson and Martin Daly write about the evolutionary roots of a number of features of male dominance, most notably "a sexually proprietary male psychology." Instead of offering reductive statements about women's psychological adaptation and consequent passivity, Wilson and Daly offer an analysis that recognizes that men and women might have distinctly different and conflicting interests—a key concept in evolutionary psychology—with women nowhere nearly so monogamous or passive as simplistic accounts might suggest.[18]

Indeed, studying women from an evolutionary perspective yields interesting questions that trouble the conventional narratives of monogamy on which sociobiology's view of women was built. Women are the only primate females who do not have specified periods of **estrus**. They are potentially sexually receptive at any time of their reproductive cycle, including when they are incapable of conception. Some have suggested that women's "concealed ovulation" is a unique feature, suggesting that women's evolutionary "strategy" may be not selectivity but promiscuity. More recently, Christopher Ryan and Cacilda Jethá have argued that women's selectivity is an innovation traceable to agricultural societies; they claim that our view of prehistoric hunter-gatherers has been "Flintstoneized"— coloured by our own sexual and social arrangements.[19]

This may not be so far-fetched. One recent study found that women reported that their partners increased their attentiveness and "monopolization" behaviour—calling them often to check on their whereabouts, for example—just as they began to ovulate. The women, however, found that they fantasized far more about cheating on their partners at the same time. (They reported no increase whatsoever in sexual thoughts about their partners—so much for their evolutionary predisposition toward fidelity.) Although this suggests that the men had good reason to be more guarding and jealous, it also suggests that women "instinctively want to have sex with as many men as possible to ensure the genetic quality of their offspring, whereas men want to ensure that their own genes get reproduced," according to a journalist reporting on the story.[20] Equally selfish genes and equally a "war between the sexes"—but, nonetheless, one with a completely different interpretation. The variation in possible interpretations of evolutionary evidence should give us pause.

Do the arguments of evolutionary psychology and sociobiology make sense? Can we explain human behaviour by recourse to biology? Critics say no. Ultimately, these theories may tidily describe the intricate mating rituals of fruit flies or brown birds or *seem* applicable to an urban singles bar or the dating dynamics of high school and college students, but the neatness of their explanations may obscure the distinctions between human behaviours and those of other organisms. Anne Fausto-Sterling notes the tendency of many sociobiologists to reason backward from human categories, like rape, adultery, and slavery, to non-human organisms, consequently obscuring the meanings and causes of these categories.[21]

Sociobiologists have been (sometimes unfairly) criticized for their inability to locate the genetic imperative for specific behaviours or for exaggerating the nature of genetic predisposition. Biologist Richard Lewontin, a passionate critic of sociobiology, argues that, "no evidence at all is presented for a genetic basis of these characteristics (religion, warfare, co-operation) and the arguments for their establishment by natural selection cannot be tested, since such arguments postulate hypothetical situations in human prehistory that are uncheckable." As well, fellow evolutionary biologist Stephen Jay Gould denies that there is "any direct evidence for genetic control of specific human social behaviour." "Genes don't cause behaviours," writes the neuroprimatologist Robert Sapolsky. "Sometimes, they influence them."[22]

Sociobiological arguments have also been condemned for selective use of species when making comparisons between animal and human behaviours. Which species should we use as the standard of measurement? Among chimpanzees and gorillas, for example, females usually leave home and transfer to new tribes, leaving the males at home with their mothers. Among baboons, macaques, and langurs, however, males are the ones to leave home to seek their fortune elsewhere. There are other species, however. For example, baboons seem to be female-dominant, with females determining the stability of the group and deciding which males are trustworthy enough to be their "friends." Then there is the female chimpanzee. She has sex with lots of different males, often up to 50 times a day during peak estrus. She flirts, seduces, and does everything she can to attract males—whom she then abandons and moves on to the next customer. Bonobos, with chimps our closest primate relatives, are remarkably communal, generous, and gender-egalitarian—and very promiscuous.

Sociobiologists have also tended to ignore same-sex sexual behaviour among primates, although sexual contact with same-sex others is "part of the normal sexual repertoire of all animals, expressed variously during the lifetime of an individual."[23] In fact, same-sex sexual contact is ubiquitous in the animal kingdom—ranging from bighorn sheep and giraffes—both of whom have what can be described only as gay orgies—to dolphins, whales, manatees, and Japanese macaques and bonobos, who bond through "lesbian" sexual choices. Regardless, few posit a natural predisposition toward homosexuality. "Simple-minded analogies between human behaviour and animal behaviour are risky at best," writes neurobiologist Simon LeVay.[24]

Sociobiology has often been used—particularly by media commentators—to provide us with what Rudyard Kipling called a "just-so story"—an account that uses some evidence to tell us how, for example, an elephant got its trunk or a tiger its stripes. "Just-so stories" are children's fables, understood by the reader to be fictions, but convenient, pleasant, and, ultimately, useful fictions. Evolutionary psychology, though a relatively new field, has overcome many of the limitations of sociobiology, but remains committed to relatively monocausal explanations. While critiquing, perhaps justly, the sometimes fuzzy understandings of pure cultural determinists, evolutionary psychologists can be as determinist as any.

Does this mean that these fields have no value? Not at all. To be sure, human beings are not fruit flies. We *are*, however, the products of our biology and of millions of years of evolution. Nature undoubtedly plays a role, though few scientists would today claim that it produces anything stronger than a tendency that interacts with cultural influences to produce behaviour. As Richard Bribiescas states in his recent "evolutionary history" of men, "are men the product of nature or nurture? The answer is yes."[25] Both nature and nurture form us. The difficulty comes in interpreting the evidence, which has too often been yoked to simplistic—and, frankly sexist—biological determinism.

Testing the Gendered Brain: Sex Differences in Spatial and Verbal Skills

Gender differences on standardized tests have been the subject of debate for decades. At the turn of the twentieth century, women scored higher than men did on comprehensive examinations at New York University. Because scientists "knew" that women were not as smart as men were, some other explanation had to be sought. "After all, men are more intellectual than women, examination papers or no examination papers," commented the dean of the college, R. Turner. "Women have better memories and study harder, that's all. In tasks, requiring patience and industry, women win out. But when a man is both patient and industrious he beats a woman any day." (It is interesting to see that women's drive, ambition, and industriousness were used against them but that men were not faulted for impulsiveness, impatience, and laziness.) In the 1920s, when IQ tests were invented, women scored higher on those tests as well. As a result, the experimenters changed the questions.[26]

This early debate over women's intellectual fitness has been replaced by a discussion that debates not just aptitude but gender roles. For example, in 2005, then-president of Harvard University, Lawrence Summers, suggested in a speech that the underrepresentation of women in **sciences, technology, engineering, and mathematics (STEM)** might be the result of men's innately greater representation at the highest levels of mathematical ability. The controversy that followed led to Summers's resignation from his position in early 2006; in the aftermath, however, conservative commentator Christine Hoff Sommers argued that persistent gender differences in *interests* (which she traces to innate tendencies) are the cause of women's underrepresentation in STEM.[27]

Sommers refrained from arguing that women were less skilled in mathematics. Test scores have continued, however, to show gender differences in relation to certain abilities, generally summarized as verbal, visuospatial, and quantitative. In a recent international literacy study, fourth-grade girls were found to outperform boys significantly in all

33 countries in which the study was conducted. Similar results were found for 15-year-olds in a 2002 Programme for International Student Assessment (PISA) study. In Canada, 2003 PISA assessments of 15-year-olds revealed girls' significantly superior performance in reading (the gap persisted in the 2006 and 2009 measurements). Moreover, the difference between boys' and girls' averages is large—equivalent to one full grade level.[28] In the 2009 assessment, the reading average for girls was 40.54 points above the boys' average, and there was a statistically significant difference in all 63 participating countries. The gap in mathematical performance is relatively small by comparison; the boys' advantage is 8.64 points. Moreover, there is substantial variation in math scores from nation to nation. In some, such as Sweden, girls outperform boys by a small margin; in others, such as Colombia, the gap is large, with boys outperforming girls by 33.32 points.[29]

Mathematical abilities are not one ability but many. Differences in these abilities begin to appear early in life and persist into adulthood, though they are not always significant. Still, girls tend to outperform boys in all subjects, including math, until senior high school. Is this because puberty somehow impairs girls' development, or is it because senior-high math introduces advanced geometry and calculus, which demand superior visuospatial skills? Both arguments have been advanced. Sex differences do not appear on all mathematical tests, nor even on all spatial tasks. For example, there are small to non-existent differences between males and females when it comes to geometry tests. Some of the greatest gender differences, however, emerge when young adults are asked to perform mental rotation tasks that require a subject to imagine what a three-dimensional object looks like when rotated. Much has been made of this male advantage, because visuospatial tasks are considered central to success in science, math, and engineering. Young men perform these tasks significantly better, on average, than young women, and women exposed to testosterone in utero may perform them better than do non-exposed women.[30]

It is also true that males outnumber females at the genius end of the mathematical spectrum. Indeed, it seems that there is simply greater variability in male test scores; men outnumber women at *both* ends of the spectrum. Twenty years ago, boys outnumbered girls 13:1 among those precocious (gifted) 13-year-olds with SAT math scores of more than 700. (The SAT is the standard university admissions test used in the US.) Now there are only 2.8 boys for every girl in this group; still a distinct advantage for boys "at the genius end," but a dramatic change from the situation in the late 1980s.[31]

Faced with evidence from standardized testing, many people, including some scholars, are tempted to biological explanations: "[B]oys are better at math, and girls are better at reading." There is, however, strong reason to doubt this simple platitude. First, what are we to make of the fact that boys, until recently, continued to outperform girls on the verbal component of the SAT? Clearly, what is meant by "verbal" ability can vary.

Moreover, as can be seen from the data above, the "gap" in mathematical performance is far from stable and consistent across cultures. In fact, it is ever-changing and inconsistent. What's more, girls simultaneously have the *largest* advantage in reading, and the *smallest* disadvantage in math scores. For example, if one were to take the massive Colombian gap in math scores as evidence of these girls' hyperfeminine cognition, one would have to contend with the fact that Colombian girls score relatively poorly in reading.

In addition, what should one make of the fact that the differences between boys and girls on these assessments are dwarfed by the gaps from country to country? Shanghai-China, for example, enjoys average math scores that are more than 35 points higher than any other country has, and reading scores that are similarly high. (In case you're wondering, Canada's scores are significantly above the average, but we still lag well behind China.) Would anyone seriously argue that the huge gaps among countries represent some innate difference in aptitude?

Even the much-vaunted male spatial advantage seems to ask more questions than it answers. Why do males perform better on rotation of 3D objects, but not on tasks that require mentally folding paper, which are also "visuospatial"? Why do women perform better on at least one spatial task, remembering object locations?[32] (No jokes about finding the TV remote, please.)

We are left with a bewildering number of studies that seem to confirm the existence of some sex or gender differences, but raise more questions than they answer. Do differences that emerge in early childhood reflect "nature" or "nurture"? In addition, what is the role of culture? How might having greater parental encouragement toward spatially oriented outdoor play (or indoor play, for example with Lego) affect boys' generally superior visuo-spatial abilities? We know, for example, that playing video games enhances a number of cognitive skills, especially spatial ones. In a study at the University of Toronto, the largest differences in performances on a spatial task were not between men and women, not be-tween sciences students and arts students, but between gamers and non-gamers. Given that boys play more of the action games that seem to enhance spatial ability most, the effects of play are a logical source for the differences we see in young adults.

What is more, these differences are extremely malleable. The same U of T study showed that just 10 hours of play with an action video game could make a tremendous difference: "[f]emales showed larger improvements than males, such that prior gender differences were virtually eliminated."[33] In fact, many test-score differences seem to change in relatively short time periods—as reflected both in SAT scores (US) and in provincial skills assessments (Canada).[34] We know also that test performance is vulner-able to immediate and short-term fluctuations. For example, scholars have discovered the phenomenon called **stereotype threat**: reminding women of stereotypes about their mathematical ability immediately lowers their performance and even alters their brain activation.[35] And having a math-anxious female teacher for a given year can depress girls' math achievement.[36]

All of this being the case, why do we rush to claim that differences on test scores reflect innate ability rather than the effect of a lifetime of cultural conditioning? Ad-ditionally, why do we assume that test scores can explain complex phenomena such as the underrepresentation of women in a given field of employment? Obviously, when we assess gender differences in cognition, we should remain aware that the topic is as com-plex as the human brain and human society themselves. In the words of one careful recent metastudy,

> Just as there are many related questions about sex differences in test scores and career choices, there are many variables that work together to present a level of complexity that is inherent in understanding complicated questions about the way people think and behave. . . . There is no single factor by itself that has been shown to determine sex differences in science and math. Early experience, biological

constraints, educational policy, and cultural context each have effects, and these effects add and interact in complex and sometimes unpredictable ways.[37]

Ultimately, we need to assess gender differences in cognitive ability in a way that respects complexity and avoids simplistic "sound-bite" stereotypes.

"His" Brain and "Her" Brain

As we've seen, discussions of cognitive gender differences have often explained them as the result of men's and women's different brains. Focusing on the brain to explain cognitive and other differences between women and men has a long history. The late nineteenth century was the first heyday of brain research, as researchers explored that spongy and gelatinous three-pound blob in order to discover the differences between whites and blacks, Jews and non-Jews, immigrants and "normal" or "real" Americans, criminals and law-abiding citizens. For example, the great sociologist Emile Durkheim succumbed to such notions when he wrote, "with the advance of civilization the brain of the two sexes has increasingly developed differently. . . . [T]his progressive gap between the two may be due both to the considerable development of the male skull and to a cessation and even a regression in the growth of the female skull." Another researcher argued that the brain of the average "grown-up Negro partakes, as regards his intellectual faculties, of the nature of the child, the female, and the senile White." These findings, obviously, satisfied sexist and racist assumptions.[38]

Contemporary brain research has moved beyond craniology, and in recent years has been able to study images of living brains rather than merely dissecting dead ones. While overall brain size and intelligence remain a topic of debate,[39] much of the past research focused on three areas: the differences between right hemisphere and left hemisphere; the ways in which males and females use different parts of their brains for similar functions; and the differences in the tissue that connects those hemispheres. More recently, differences in brain volume have been studied; men have larger absolute brain volume, but there is also variation in the volume of various regions of the brain, along with distinctions in brain density.[40]

The right and left hemispheres of the brain appear to be associated with different cognitive functions and abilities. Right-hemisphere dominance is associated with visual and spatial abilities, such as the ability to conceive of objects in space. Left-hemisphere dominance is associated with more practical functions, such as language and reading skills. Norman Geschwind and Peter Behan observed that sex differences begin in the womb when the male fetus begins to secrete testosterone that washes over the brain, selectively attacking parts of the left hemisphere and slowing its development. Therefore, according to Geschwind, males tend to develop "superior right hemisphere talents, such as artistic, musical, or mathematical talent." Geschwind argued that men's brains are more **lateralized**, with one half dominating over the other, whereas women's brains are less lateralized, with both parts interacting more than in men's.[41] However, Ruth Bleier reanalyzed Geschwind and Behan's data and found that in more than 500 fetal brains from 10 to 44 weeks of gestation, the authors had found no significant sex differences—this despite the much-trumpeted testosterone bath.[42]

In contrast to Geschwind, Buffery and Gray found that female brains were more lateralized than male brains, which, they argued, interfered with spatial functioning, and made women less capable at spatial tasks. That same year, neuroscientist Jerre Levy found that female brains were *less* lateralized than male brains, and so he argued that *less* lateralization interferes with spatial functioning.[43] Given these contradictory findings, perhaps it is not surprising that the nature and existence of gendered lateralization remain highly controversial.[44]

However, what if it's not the differences between the hemispheres, or even that males and females use the same hemispheres differently? Perhaps it's the structural connections *between* the hemispheres. Some researchers have explored the bundle of fibres known as the corpus callosum (CC) that connects the two hemispheres and carries information between them. A sub-region of this connecting network, the splenium, was found by one study of 14 brains to be significantly larger and more bulbous in shape in females, consequently affecting visual and spatial functioning. However, subsequent research failed to confirm this finding. What's more, in magnetic resonance imaging (MRI) tests on living men and women, small or no differences were found between women and men.[45]

Nevertheless, that didn't stop popular writers from dramatic and facile extrapolation. *Time* magazine claimed that women's wider CCs were "possibly the basis for women's intuition." As well, *The New York Times* science editor claimed that women's big CCs discredited "feminist ideologues" who linked girls' poor math performance to environmental factors. In *The Wonder of Girls* (2002), Michael Gurian claims that only females with "boys' brains" can grow up to be architects because girls' brains are organized to promote nurturing, love, and caring for children.[46] In this manner, enormously complicated research is boiled down through popular culture to become definitive "proof" of gender stereotype. The CC's function and structure are still not perfectly understood, the visual identification of a "tubular" or "bulbous" CC isn't as straightforward as it might seem, and recent research has demonstrated that there are no significant differences in CC size once sex differences in brain size are taken into account; nonetheless, the popular stereotype of the "sexed brain" remains.[47]

One of the most recent brain-sex studies to make a splash is Louanne Brizendine's popular study *The Female Brain*, a bestseller already translated into many languages and sold around the world. Despite Brizendine's credentials, this book (not peer-reviewed) offered questionable data such as the canard that women used 20,000 words per day against men's 7,000. Withdrawn from subsequent editions, this erroneous claim nonetheless exemplifies the sloppiness that characterizes what Cordelia Fine calls "our crude attempts to locate social pressures in the brain."[49] Unfortunately, the "20,000 words-per-day" statistic is still being repeated in the media.[50] Some errors apparently appeal to us more than others do—enough to persist a decade after their first appearance!

If these arguments rest on flimsy evidence and flimsier interpretations, why do they persist? Neuroscientist Lise Eliot suggests that the answer relates to our desire to justify current social arrangements:

Research findings about sex differences have been distorted and exploited by nonscientists to an extraordinary degree—perhaps second only to research on weight loss. Beginning with the wildly popular 1992 book *Men Are from Mars, Women Are from Venus*, public discourse has been saturated with faulty factoids about men, women, boys, and girls that have settled deeply into society's collective understanding of gender roles. From education and parenting to corporate leadership and marital harmony, so-called scientific findings about the male and female brain have been used to validate various stereotypical practices that are discriminatory to both sexes.[51]

Accordingly, we might laugh at Brizendine's assertion that the female brain is "a high performance emotion machine," but this "neurosexism," as Fine calls it, is no laughing matter. She points out that the **palliative system justification motive** allows us to justify and rationalize existing social arrangements. At their best, studies of the sexed brain offer intriguing food for thought; at their worst, as Fine warns, theories of brain sex offer "a tidy justification for accepting the status quo with clear conscience."[52]

Estrogen and Testosterone: Hormonal Bases for Gender Differences

The term "hormone," despite its ubiquity in contemporary culture, is only about one hundred years old. The word means "I excite" or "I arouse" and is a relic of a very important discovery: that certain secretions are chemical messengers that produce responses in the body. There are many hormones, but we are here concerned with those that produce or influence the differences between the sexes.

Sex differentiation faces its most critical events at two different phases of life, fetal development and puberty. During fetal development, the primary sex characteristics are determined by a combination of genetic inheritance and the biological development of the embryo that will become a boy or a girl. Then, during puberty, the bodies of boys and girls are transformed by a flood of sex hormones that causes the development of all the secondary sex characteristics. Breast development for girls, lowering of voices for boys, the development of facial hair for boys, and the growth of pubic hair for both are among puberty's most obvious signs.

The effects of hormones in producing these transformations are obvious. Much research has gone farther to explore the complex effects of hormones in shaping other real or purported areas of gender difference, from sexual expression to aggression to emotion. Summarizing his reading of this research, sociologist Steven Goldberg writes that because "men and women differ in their hormonal systems" and "every society demonstrates patriarchy, male dominance, and male attainment," it is logical to conclude that "the hormonal renders the social inevitable."[53]

We've all heard the arguments about how testosterone, the male sex hormone, is not only the driving force in the development of masculinity in males but also the biological basis of human aggression, which is why males are more prone to violence than women. While there may be some validity to this, we should remember that women and men have both testosterone *and* estrogen, although typically in dramatically different amounts. On average, men do have about 10 times the testosterone level that women have, but the level among men varies greatly, and some women have levels higher than those of some men. Men also have about twice as much estrogen as do post-menopausal women.

Testosterone levels also vary from culture to culture and from man to man, and often in surprising ways. For example, a finger-length study was conducted at the University of Bath (UK) in 2004. (As further discussed below, relative ring–index finger length is thought to correlate with prenatal hormone exposure.) In the study, male "hard" scientists unexpectedly had significantly higher levels of estrogen and lower testosterone levels than did male social scientists. Female social scientists were also found to have higher-than-average testosterone levels. Interesting research, but surely not proof, as one online news source trumpeted, that male scientists aren't so manly after all![54]

This perception of testosterone as the "masculinity hormone" pervades the media and less-careful research. In recent years, research has suggested correlations between levels of testosterone and body mass, baldness, self-confidence, and even the ability and willingness to smile. Some wildly inflated claims about the effects of testosterone have led to both popular misconceptions and a variety of medical interventions to provide remedies. In one recent book, for example, psychologist James Dabbs proclaims, "testosterone increases masculinity," which was translated by a journalist into the equation that "lust is a chemical" as he looked forward to his "biweekly encounter with a syringe full of manhood." Of course, today men can purchase testosterone patches or AndroGel, a product that seems to promise masculinity in a tube.[55]

Although the claims made for testosterone are often ridiculous—ministering less to science and more to men's fears of declining potency—there are some experiments on the testosterone–aggression relationship that appear convincing. Males have higher levels of testosterone and higher rates of aggressive behaviour than females do. What's more, if you increase the level of testosterone in a normal male, his level of aggression will increase. Castrate him—or at least a rodent proxy of him—and his aggressive behaviour will cease entirely. Though this might lead one to think that testosterone is the cause of the aggression, Stanford neurobiologist Robert Sapolsky warns against such leaps of logic. He explains, "testosterone isn't causing aggression; it's exaggerating the aggression that's already there."[56]

It turns out that testosterone has what scientists call a "permissive effect" on aggression, enabling it rather than causing it. What's more, testosterone is produced *by* aggression, so that the correlation between the two, in fact, may have the opposite direction than previously thought. In his thoughtful book *Testosterone and Social Structure*, Theodore Kemper notes several studies in which testosterone levels were linked to men's experiences. In studies of tennis players, medical students, wrestlers, nautical competitors, parachutists, and officer candidates, winning and losing determined levels of testosterone. The levels of the winners rose dramatically, whereas those of the losers dropped or remained the same. Kemper suggests that testosterone levels rise when men experience either *dominance*, "elevated social rank that is achieved by overcoming others in a competitive confrontation," or *eminence*, where elevated rank "is earned through socially valued and approved accomplishment." Significantly, men's testosterone levels prior to either dominance or eminence could not predict the outcome of competition; experiencing success was what led to the elevation of their testosterone levels. (These same experiences lead to increases in women's testosterone levels as well.)[57]

As we have seen, men's experiences of aggression, competition, success, and failure alter their levels of testosterone. There are also huge variations in normal testosterone levels within individual men, among men in industrialized nations, and between men in industrialized nations and men in other parts of the world (whose average levels, for unknown reasons, are much lower). We simply don't know what a globally "normal" level of testosterone might be and what causes the vast variations. We also don't know what an optimal level of testosterone might be, given the mixed effects of the hormone and its apparent potential to increase risks of certain illnesses.

Despite this, some therapists prescribe testosterone for men as a sort of chemical tonic. Happy consumers swear by the results, and some therapists have even diagnosed a malady called "andropause" or "male menopause," treatable by hormone-replacement therapy for men. Health Canada's 2002 approval of Androgel was trumpeted as bringing relief to the "one million Canadian men [who] have testosterone insufficiency," described as a "medical condition linked to depressed mood and fatigue, reduced lean body mass and muscle strength, decreased bone density—which can lead to osteoporosis—lower interest in sex, and erectile dysfunction." Despite the documented horrors of this widespread "pathology," few Canadians were able to either identify the medical condition (andropause) associated with low testosterone or the condition's many symptoms. Fortunately, Solvay Pharma's educative efforts seem to have convinced physicians, at least if the claim that 46 per cent of polled physicians treat andropause can be believed.[58]

Meanwhile, body builders, athletes, and men seeking fat loss consume testosterone in the form of anabolic steroids. Testosterone in this form is a controlled substance, and its distribution or purchase without a prescription is illegal. Moreover, as most Canadians know, anabolic steroid use is banned in amateur sport. In 1988, one of Canada's greatest track athletes of all time, Ben Johnson, was stripped of his Olympic gold medal after testing positive for stanozolol, a steroid taken orally. Such steroids remain widely available across Canada despite their illicit status.

Testosterone's effect on male sexual drive has been discussed almost as much as its effects on aggression and muscle mass. Clearly, testosterone has some effect: castrate a male guinea pig, and he stops mounting females. Administer testosterone, and he embraces his old role with enthusiasm. However, some intact male guinea pigs, in one classic experiment, showed much less interest in mating than others, despite similar levels of the manly hormone. Moreover, when the unenthusiastic breeders received more testosterone, they didn't get any sexier. As has been proved by experiments on men with normal levels of testosterone, having more of the hormone doesn't necessarily equal a stronger sex drive. (There is, however, some evidence that testosterone increases sex drive in men with extremely low levels as the result of various traumas or disorders.)[59]

Despite its reputation as the "masculinity hormone," testosterone is now seen as a panacea for women. Low testosterone levels have been linked to low libido in women, despite little understanding of what might constitute a "normal" female libido. Barbara Sherwin of McGill University has also conducted research linking testosterone to increased libido in women. Though Sherwin currently focuses on estrogen and its relationship to cognition, her research on the positive effects of testosterone supplementation has encouraged physicians to add a "tiny dose" of testosterone to estrogen-based hormone replacement regimes for women, as *The New York Times* reported.[60]

Some have also suggested that competition and aggression in women are linked to testosterone. Patricia Schreiner-Engel, for example, has found higher testosterone levels in successful executive women than in homemakers. She even suggested that Queen Elizabeth I, England's sixteenth-century "Virgin Queen," may have been a "High-T" woman![61] Once again, the assumption is that extra "T" made Schreiner-Engle's executive women competitive and successful, while it is more likely that their testosterone levels rose with their experience of success.

As Natalie Angier writes, "the male body gave birth to hormone research, but the female body reared it to maturity."[62] The first sex hormone isolated, in 1929, was one of many forms of estrogen. (The first hormones isolated, epinephrine and secretin, were discovered at the turn of the century.) Estrogen remains, of course, the hormone most associated with women. (Interestingly, when the male and female sex hormones were named, male hormones, including testosterone, received the name "androgens," roughly translatable as "man-builder." The female equivalent was termed estrogen or "estrus-builder.")

Like men's testosterone levels, women's estrogen levels naturally fluctuate. Through a woman's menstrual cycle, they rise and decline in relatively standard ways. This has led to interesting studies regarding estrogen's role in cognition and sexual desire throughout a woman's monthly cycle.

By far the greatest interest in estrogen, however, has come from its precipitous decline in post-menopausal women. These women, by the middle of the twentieth century, were diagnosed as "estrogen-deficient." In the late twentieth century, North American women by the millions were prescribed "estrogen replacement therapy" (ERT), which promised women an end to the symptoms of menopause along with protection from heart disease, improvement in mental clarity, and, not least, a more youthful appearance. "Never before [had] a drug regimen been proposed on such a scale," writes Angier.[63] In 2002, the US National Institutes of Health prematurely halted a long-term trial of ERT because of alarming evidence that it significantly increased women's risk of heart disease, invasive breast cancers, stroke, and blood clots.[64]

Since then, ERT has been prescribed more cautiously; we still need to know more about how estrogen works. Are women over 50 actually "estrogen-deficient"? Why do women outside North America seem to need replacement therapy so much less than we do? Much attention is now being paid to the perimenopause, the time preceding the cessation of menstruation, which some researchers believe may begin as early as the age of 35. Once again, the culprit is estrogen. This time, declining levels aren't the problem, but perhaps, an erratic and surging supply of the hormone.

Research on premenstrual syndrome (PMS) has provided yet another example of the way that hormones work—or are presumed to work—within the female body. During the days just before menstruation, some women seem to exhibit symptoms of dramatic and wildly unpredictable mood changes, outbursts of violence, anger, and fits of crying. Alec Coppen and Neil Kessel studied 465 women and observed that they were more irritable and depressed during the premenstrual phase than during mid-cycle. Such behaviours have led physicians to label these symptoms "premenstrual syndrome." Under the name "Premenstrual Dysphoric Disorder" PMS was included in an appendix to the fourth edition of the *Diagnostic and Statistical Manual of Mental Disorders* (*DSM-IV*) of the American Psychiatric Association, which guides physicians (and insurance companies) in treating illnesses. In the fifth edition (*DSM-V*), PMDD appears in the main body of the text—a sign of what the APA considers "strong scientific evidence" for the existence of the disorder.

Despite the relative rarity of pathological PMS, the term has entered popular culture, so that any woman who is irritable on a given day is said to be "PMSing." Young women now refer to the period of their menstruation (or immediately preceding it) as "Shark Week," a reference to the aggression and foul mood that supposedly herald or accompany the menses. PMS has even been used as a criminal defence strategy. Two British women, arguing that PMS is a form of temporary insanity, have used PMS as a successful defence in their trials for the murders of their male partners. If testosterone is seen as the "manly hormone," estrogen is seen as the emotional centre that makes women not only cuddlier than men but also occasionally hysterical. This phenomenon is accepted by many women, and society as a whole, as just a "natural" part of being a woman.

Recently, a firestorm was ignited when University of Toronto researchers published a study that found no clear relationship between women's moods and their menstrual cycles. The researchers noted that the estimated incidence of "true" PMS ranges from 1.3 per cent to 9 per cent, but that many scholars and members of the public alike believe there is a "well-defined PMS occurring in the female population as a whole." Through a systematic review, the researchers established that there is no clear evidence in support of "a specific premenstrual negative mood change occurring with any regularity in the general population."[65] Could the idea of widespread PMS be another "just-so story"? It seems likely.

Still, research on the "sex hormones" makes it clear that they have important effects throughout our lives. Once again, these effects are too often oversimplified in ways that ignore the complexity of human behaviour, sexuality, and health itself. We need to understand mood, sexuality, and behaviour as complex admixtures of *many* influences, including the hormonal.

"As Nature Made Him?"

One of the most famous cases that purports to prove how biological sex is the sole foundation for gender identity concerned a Manitoba boy, Bruce Reimer. In 1966, Bruce and his identical twin, Brian, underwent cauterization circumcisions in a Winnipeg hospital. Brian's circumcision went smoothly, but Bruce's went terribly wrong, and his penis was nearly burned off. His distraught parents brought him to Johns Hopkins University Medical Center where, at the age of 21 months and under the aegis of Dr John Money, he was surgically "transformed" into a girl. Throughout the next decades, the newly named "Brenda" was faced with several more aggressive (or abusive) surgical procedures, annual visits to Dr Money's clinic, and massive doses of female sex hormones, while her parents struggled to conceal Bruce's story and raise Brenda as a girl—and not just "a" girl, but a very frilly, feminine, and dainty girl at that. (Even though Brenda described herself as a tomboy as a child, Brenda's mother was determined that her "daughter" be "polite and quiet" and "ladylike.")

This case, known as the "John/Joan" case, was the most famous of Dr Money's career. However, behind the scenes, things were difficult for the twins. Despite being poster children for Money's claims that gender identity can be changed, both twins grew up depressed and unhappy. Eventually, Brenda's situation was revealed to a sexologist, Dr Milton Diamond at the University of Hawaii, a long-time foe of John Money's unorthodox ideas and practices. Under Diamond's supervision, Brenda reclaimed his male gender identity, renamed himself "David," and became the man he said he felt he always was. "Suddenly it all made sense why I felt the way I did," he told a journalist who eventually wrote a best-selling book about his life. "I wasn't some sort of weirdo. I wasn't crazy." David eventually married and adopted three children. His story, passionately told by journalist John Colapinto, became a book, *As Nature Made Him: The Boy Who Was Raised as a Girl* (2000) and a TV documentary. Colapinto argues forcefully that David's case demonstrates that nature trumps nurture, that biology is destiny, and that meddling with "Mother Nature" is always disastrous. The case "provides stark evidence that a person's brain predetermines sexual identity—not one's anatomy or social environment" was how a writer in the *Los Angeles Times* put it, and this is how the story has been cemented in the public imagination: as proof that biology determines gender.[66]

Yet is the case that simple, that no matter how much tinkering one does, nature always trumps nurture? Any scientist should be wary of generalizing from a single case—especially a case with so many other factors that might have influenced the outcome. How would you feel about yourself, and your gender identity, if you were constantly being dragged to some hospital every few months throughout your early childhood, had your testicles removed while your damaged penis was left intact, and had your genitals poked and prodded and surgically "repaired." How would you feel if everyone paid an inordinate amount of attention to your genitalia and *every aspect of your behaviour* without ever telling you why? Drs Money and Diamond believed that a child without a complete penis could not possibly be a boy, and that a girl must be feminine: demur, restrained, and dressed in frilly clothes. Dr Money "coached" the children on appropriate gender behaviour in ways that seem to us bizarre to say the least. Despite their apparent belief in gender malleability, the doctors were rigid and doctrinaire in what they thought "appropriate" for boys and girls.

Were our gender roles more elastic, we wouldn't try so obsessively to coerce such behaviours from our children, who express far more variability than our norms about proper gender behaviour. Surely, our gender identity is the result of a complex interaction of genetics, brain chemistry, hormones, and our immediate familial environment, nestled within a more general social and cultural milieu. No *one* cause of something so complex and variable as gender identity could possibly be extracted, especially from one complex and deeply troubling case. What *is* clear is the tragic outcome for both brothers (and their parents); Brian, who was severely mentally ill, died of an overdose of his anti-schizophrenia medication in 2002, David of a self-inflicted gunshot wound in 2004. (Their father was an alcoholic and their mother was clinically depressed.)[67]

Gay Brains, Gay Genes, or Gay Hormones?

In the twentieth century, biological research emerged as central in the demonstration of the fundamental and irreducible differences between homosexuals and heterosexuals. In the 1970s, German researcher Gunter Dorner (director of the Institute for Experimental Endocrinology at Humboldt University in Berlin) and his associates claimed to have found that homosexual men possess a "predominantly female-differentiated brain," which is caused by a "deficiency" of androgen during the hypothalamic organizational phase in prenatal life. This deficiency may be activated to homosexual behaviour by normal or about-normal androgen levels in adulthood.[68]

In the 1990s, with homosexual rights a topic of great interest and activism, "gay-brain" studies attempted to locate homosexuality in the brain structure itself. Hoping that science can demonstrate "the origins of sexual orientation at a cellular level," Simon LeVay examined the brain tissues of 41 deceased people. These brains were treated and compared. Three of the four sections revealed no differences, but a fourth section, the anterior hypothalamus, a region about the size of a grain of sand, was found to be different among the groups. LeVay found that the size of this area among the presumably heterosexual men was approximately twice the size of that area for the women and the purportedly gay men.[69]

Several problems in his experiments give us pause, however. LeVay and his colleagues failed to measure the cell number or density because "of the difficulty in precisely defining the neurons belonging to INAH-3," the area of the brain involved. A number of the "homosexual" men (5 of the 19) and of the women (2 of the 6) appeared to have areas of the brain as large as those of the presumed heterosexual men. In addition, in three of the presumed heterosexual men, this area of the brain was actually very small. What's more, the sources of his data were widely varied. All the "gay" men in his sample died of AIDS, a disease known to affect the brain. (Reduced testosterone occurs among AIDS patients, and this alone may account for the different sizes.) All the brains of the "gay" men were preserved in a formaldehyde solution that was of a different strength than the solution in which the brains of the heterosexual men were preserved, because of the fears of HIV transmission, although there was no effort to control for the effect of the formaldehyde on the organs. It is possible that what LeVay may have been measuring was the combined effect of HIV infection and preservation in high densities of formaldehyde solution on post-mortem brain structure, rather than differences in brain structure between living heterosexuals and homosexuals. Efforts to replicate LeVay's findings failed, and one researcher went further, suggesting, "INAH-3 is not necessary for sexual behaviour in men, whether they chose men or women as their partners."[70]

Also in the 1990s, researchers found that the brains of male transsexuals more closely resembled the brains of women than of heterosexual, "normal" men. Dutch scientists at the Netherlands Institute for Brain Research examined the hypothalamus sections of 42 autopsied men and women, 6 of whom were known to be transsexuals, and 9 of whom were gay men, whereas the rest were presumed to be heterosexual. Again, they found that the hypothalamus in the transsexual men and women was smaller than in the heterosexual or homosexual men. Although they were careful *not* to interpret their findings in terms of sexual orientation because the heterosexual and homosexual men's brains were similar, they did take their research to signal sex differences because the male transsexuals were men who felt themselves to be women. However, the brain difference may also be a result of transsexual surgery and the massive amounts of female hormones that the male transsexuals took, which might have had the effect of shrinking the hypothalamus, just as the surgery and hormones also resulted in other anatomical changes (loss of facial and body hair, breast growth, etc.). Again, these results were broadly publicized and accepted by the public as "proof" that both gender and sexuality are "written in the brain." A recent MRI study of 48 heterosexual men and women and 24 male-to-female transsexuals (non-hormone using) found *no evidence* of feminization of transsexual brain structure. This study has received little media attention.[71]

After 2000, MRI technology furthered neuroscience's move from neuroanatomical to brain functioning studies. Studies now focused on imaging living brains at work. A group of Swedish researchers exposed heterosexual men and women and gay men to chemicals derived from male and female sex hormones and recorded which parts of the brain were most visibly stimulated on a PET scan. When the subjects were presented with testosterone, the part of the brain most closely associated with sexual activity (the hypothalamus) was triggered, but only among women and gay men. When presented with estrogen, by contrast, the heterosexual men responded strongly in the hypothalamus. Gay men also responded to estrogen, though in different brain regions. Lesbians responded similarly to both estrogen and testosterone. Although the response among journalists was a collective "Eureka! The gay brain," the researchers themselves were far more circumspect. Lead researcher Ivanka Savic told a reporter "We cannot tell if the different pattern is cause or effect. The study does not give any answer to these crucial questions."[72]

Two members of the same team performed more research that measured brain asymmetry using MRI imaging in a group of 90 heterosexual and homosexual men and women. The functional connection of subjects' brains was also measured using PET scans that assessed blood flow during rest while breathing unscented air (no sexy hormones this time!). The researchers found that the brains of gay men resembled those of heterosexual women, while lesbian women's brains more closely resembled those of straight men. Again, the implications were unclear—unfortunately, the media didn't see it that way.[73]

"You can't assume that because you find a structural difference in the brain that it was caused by genes," says researcher Marc Breedlove, arguing that behaviour itself shapes the brain. "You don't know how the difference got there." Another adds that we "are still unsure whether these signs are causes or effects."[74] The mad rush to identify the brain's control over every aspect of human behaviour cheapens the value of basic research and, at its worst, provides support for tired stereotypes and questionable social policy.

Another attempt to show that sexual orientation has its basis in biology involves the so-called gay gene. Research on pairs of monozygotic twins (twins born from a single fertilized egg that splits in utero) suggested that identical twins have a statistically far higher likelihood of having similar sexualities (either both gay or both straight) than do dizygotic twins (twins born from two separate fertilized eggs). One genetic study involved 85 pairs of twins in the 1940s and 1950s. All 40 pairs of monozygotic twins studied shared the same sexual orientation; if one twin was heterosexual, the other was also; if one twin was homosexual, so, too, was the other twin. Such data were so perfect that subsequent scientists have doubted their validity, but other studies in the 1980s seemed to confirm the findings of this initial study.[75]

After 2000, these studies were revisited. Sociologists Peter Bearman and Hannah Bruckner examined all the studies that purported that opposite-sex twins are more likely to be gay than twins who are of the same sex. They concluded that there are no hormonal connections whatever and that the level of sex stereotyping in early childhood socialization is a far better predictor of behavioural outcome than whether or not one has a twin of the opposite sex. Predicting sexual orientation from that evidence is sort of like predicting penis size from shoe size—there's not even a correlation, but if there were, it would be specious.[76] Most recently, the largest-ever twin study was conducted in Sweden, involving more than 3,800 pairs of twins. While there seemed to be some role for genetics, the researchers found far more influence exerted by other factors. Interestingly, the "genetic effect" for women was much smaller than for men.[77]

The quest for a genetic link to homosexuality was predated by research on the relationship between hormones and homosexuality, which began almost as soon as "sex hormones" were identified. In the 1970s, Dorner and his associates argued that low levels of testosterone during fetal development, a rather tepid hormonal bath, would predispose males toward homosexuality. If rats did not receive enough of their appropriate sex hormone during fetal development, "then something would go wrong with the formation of the centres and with later sexual behaviour," reported two journalists. "Adult rats would behave in ways like members of the opposite sex. They would become, in a sense, 'homosexual.'"[78]

Could prenatal stress account for a disposition toward homosexuality? In another series of studies, Dorner and his colleagues argued that more homosexual men are born during wartime than during peacetime. Their evidence for this claim was that a high proportion of the 865 men treated for venereal disease in six regions of the German Democratic Republic were born between 1941 and 1947. They theorized that because prenatal stress leads to a "significant decrease in plasma testosterone levels" among rat fetuses, which also leads to increased bisexual or homosexual behaviours among the adult rats, why not among humans? Dorner theorized that war leads to stress, which leads to a lowering of androgens in the male fetuses, which encourages the development of a homosexual orientation. Based on this trajectory, Dorner concluded that the prevention of war "may render a partial prevention of the development of sexual deviation."[79]

The most interesting recent research on the relationship between prenatal hormones and sexual orientation has been carried out by University of California at Berkeley psychologist Marc Breedlove and his students. Breedlove is a far more careful researcher than most and is far more cautious in the claims he makes. Breedlove measured the lengths of the index and ring fingers (second and fourth digits) then calculated the ratios between them for both heterosexual women and lesbians and for gay and heterosexual men. It's now accepted that finger length serves as a marker for the effect of prenatal androgens. Breedlove found that the ratio between those two fingers was more "masculine" among lesbians than among heterosexual women (i.e., the lesbians' index fingers were significantly shorter than their ring fingers). He found no differences between gay and straight men (both were equally "masculine"). However, another study did find significant differences between the two, with gay men's finger ratios being somewhat more "masculine" than those of heterosexual men.[80]

Breedlove believed that the difference between lesbians and heterosexual women was due to the effect of increased prenatal androgens among the lesbians—therefore rendering them more "masculine." This corresponds with traditional stereotypes that suggest that homosexuality is related to gender nonconformity. Nevertheless, one must be careful about overstating these stereotypes, because Breedlove found the exact opposite among men. Breedlove also found a relationship between birth order and sexual orientation for men. The greater the number of older brothers a man had, the higher the likelihood that he would be homosexual. In fact, subsequent researchers have suggested that each additional elder brother that a man has increases the likelihood that he will be gay by about 30 per cent. Breedlove hypothesized that this also was the result of prenatal androgenization of subsequent children.

Although this might not appear controversial at first blush, it corresponds with other studies that find that gay men's levels of testosterone are significantly *higher* than are those of heterosexual men. That is, gay men are more "real men" than are straight men. (Other research supporting gay men's "hypermasculinity" includes studies that find that gay men's penis size is greater than that of straight men, despite the fact that gay men undergo puberty a bit earlier and are therefore slightly shorter than straight men; and that gay men report significantly higher amounts of sexual behaviour.) "This calls into question all of our cultural assumptions that gay men are feminine," said Breedlove in an interview.[81]

This sort of research does give us pause. Brock University psychologist Anthony Bogaert did a similar study in which he found that there was no effect on sexual orientation by unrelated siblings in the same household (they had to be biological) but that older brothers who did not live with a person did influence the chances of that person's being gay. This seems to rule out socialization effects (older non-related brothers "recruiting" the youngest through sexual coercion) or the outcome of seemingly harmless sexual play.[82]

Clearly, there is some evidence for biological factors in sexual orientation, particularly in men. Still, neither a gay brain, gay gene, nor gay hormone explanation fully satisfies, and we would be well advised to consider multiple factors, both biological and cultural, when we ponder what makes us gay—or what makes us straight.

Hormonal and Chromosomal Abnormalities: Research on Intersex People

Much of the research on the biological basis of sex difference has been done by inference—that is, by examining cases of chromosomal abnormality or cases where hormones did not work "properly," therefore giving a fetus too much of the "wrong" hormone or too little of the "right" one. These and other conditions result in some degree of sexual ambiguity, whether apparent at birth or evident only later in life. Once described as "hermaphrodites," people affected by hormonal and chromosomal abnormalities are now described as **intersex/intersexuals** and account for as many as 1.7 per cent of all births.[83]

In the twentieth century, it became possible to "correct" the structural differences sometimes seen in intersex children using both surgery and hormone therapy. By 1969, when Christopher Gordon and Ronald Dewhurst published *The Intersexual Disorders*, a uniform approach had developed; ambiguous children were "assigned" to the sex judged appropriate. Despite consensus on the need to correct the abnormalities of these children, they were seen as an appropriate research group—in some ways an ideal group—through which to study "normal" sex differences. After all, if a baby girl's genitals were masculinized, perhaps she would exhibit other signs of masculinity, consequently "proving" that nature trumped nurture.

In some of the more celebrated research on fetal hormone development, Money and Ehrhardt reported on girls who had **androgenital syndrome** (AGS)—a preponderance of male hormones (androgens) in their systems at birth—and on another set of girls whose mothers had taken progestins during pregnancy. All 25 girls had masculine-appearing genitalia and had operations to "correct" their genitals. The AGS girls also were given constant cortisone treatments to enable their adrenal glands to function properly. Money and Ehrhardt's findings were interesting. The girls and their mothers reported a higher frequency of tomboy behaviour in these girls. They enjoyed vigorous outdoor games and sports, preferred toy cars and guns to dolls, and attached more importance to career plans than to marriage. However, they showed no more aggression or fighting than other girls did. Later research seemed to confirm the notion that "prenatal androgen is one of the factors contributing to the development of temperamental differences between and within the sexes."[84]

Appearances, however, can be deceiving. Anne Fausto-Sterling argues that several problems make Ehrhardt and her colleagues' research less convincing than it at first may seem. The research suffered from "insufficient and inappropriate" controls: Cortisone is a powerful drug, the AGS girls underwent calamitous surgery (including **clitoridectomy**), and there weren't any independent measures of the effects. Further, the "method of data collection [was] inadequate" because it was based entirely on interviews with parents and children, without impartial direct observation of the reported behaviours. Finally, "the authors [did] not properly explore alternative explanations of their results," such as parental expectations and differential treatment of their supposedly very "different" children.[85]

Androgenital syndrome is now more commonly described as **congenital adrenal hyperplasia** (CAH), an enzyme disorder that impairs normal hormonal development and produces—in (chromosomal) females—masculinization or ambiguous genitalia. CAH is one of the most common causes of intersexuality. Though CAH girls have the potential to bear children, their genitals may look more like those of boys than those of "normal" girls. How else are they "like boys"? Between 1968 and 2000, according to Fausto-Sterling, approximately one dozen studies "looked for evidence of unusual masculinity in CAH girls." Such evidence included activity and masculine play, mathematical ability, and, of course, sexual orientation toward women.[86] Parents reported that CAH girls really enjoyed playing with boys' toys and showed decidedly masculine affective styles. However, does that mean that there was "something in them that's innately male," as John Stossel (libertarian television celebrity and advocate of biological determinism) claimed?[87] Methodological weaknesses and fragile results mark these studies. Although there is some evidence that girls with CAH have a visuospatial advantage, methodological issues make the evidence inconclusive. Finally, CAH girls seem to have little difficulty with their gender identity, according to multiple studies. In one recent study, though mothers reported that their CAH daughters exhibited "masculinized" play, the girls themselves were happy and comfortable with their gender. The masculinized brains and genitals of CAH girls do not seem to correlate with masculine gender identity.[88]

A genetically male group of intersexuals are those affected by **androgen insensitivity syndrome (AIS)**, a defect on the X chromosome that impairs androgen reception, preventing the fetus from responding to the famous "testosterone bath" that converts it into an unambiguous boy. Then, because AIS children appear female at birth, their parents raise them as girls. At puberty, they develop characteristically feminine bodies, often with larger-than-normal breasts. AIS girls and women call into question many of the stereotypes about androgens and behaviour. In many cases, they find out about their condition only when they fail to menstruate—or, as in the case of Spanish hurdler María Martínez-Patiño, when they fail a sex test at an athletic competition.[89] Are AIS girls more masculine than one might expect? Are they more likely to experience problems in gender identity? No. Indeed, as María writes, "having had my womanliness tested—literally and figuratively—I suspect I have a surer sense of my femininity than many women."

A famous case of genetically male but "feminized" children comes from two relatively isolated villages in the Dominican Republic that seemed to produce a larger-than-expected set of genetically male hermaphrodites for at least three generations. These babies were born with internal male structures but with sex organs that resembled a clitoris more than they did a penis. Moreover, the testes had not descended at all. Their condition was the result of an extremely rare deficiency in a steroid, 5-alpha reductase. Eighteen of these babies, raised as girls, were studied by a team of researchers from Cornell University.[90]

These children had relatively uneventful childhoods, during which they played and acted like other little girls, but their adolescence became somewhat more traumatic. They failed to develop breasts and noticed a mass of tissue in their groins that turned out to be testicles beginning a descent. At puberty, their bodies began to produce a significant amount of testosterone, which made their voices deepen, their muscles develop, and facial hair appear. Suddenly, these youngsters were no longer like the other girls! Consequently, all but one of them switched and became males. One remained a female, determined to marry and have a sex-change operation. (Another decided he was a male but continued to wear dresses and act as a female.) All the others were successful in making the transition; they became men, found typically masculine jobs (as woodchoppers, farmers, and miners), and married women.

However, they didn't do it alone. While the other villagers had made fun of them, calling them *guevadoces* ("eggs [testicles] at twelve") or *machihembra* ("first woman, then man"), after they made the move to become males, their neighbours were more encouraging and offered advice and gifts to ease the transition. Moreover, one might argue that these children had a less fixed relationship between early gender development and adolescent gender patterns precisely because of their ambiguous genital development. After three generations, villagers might have come to assume that a girl does not always develop into a woman. Anthropologist Gilbert Herdt argues that such "gender polymorphic" cultures have the ability to deal with radical gender changes across the life cycle far more easily than do "gender dimorphic" cultures, such as the United States, where we expect everyone to be either male or female for his or her entire life.[91]

In fact, research on intersexuality suggests that while our biology has important effects, those effects are not easy to separate from the cultural contexts in which we grow into men and women. Intersex people and their experiences do not prove the primacy of biology—or, conversely, its irrelevance. Indeed, the history of research and intervention on intersexuals suggests, rather, that we all need the same things: respect, fair and ethical treatment, and caution when entering the borderlands of biological sex.

The Politics of Biological Essentialism

Biological arguments for sex differences have historically tended to be politically conservative, suggesting that the social arrangements between women and men—including social, economic, and political discrimination based on sex—are actually the inevitable outcome of nature working in its mysterious ways. Political attempts to legislate changes in the gender order or efforts to gain civil rights for women or for gay men and lesbians have always been met with **biological essentialism**: Don't fool with Mother Nature! For example, sociologist Steven Goldberg, in his book *The Inevitability of Patriarchy*, argues that because male domination is ubiquitous and eternal, it simply has to be based on biological origins. There is simply too much coincidence for it to be social. Feminism, Goldberg argues, is therefore a war with nature:

> Women follow their own physiological imperatives. . . . In this, and every other society [men] look to women for gentleness, kindness, and love, for refuge from a world of pain and force. . . . In every society basic male motivation is the feeling that the women and children must be protected. . . . [T]he feminist cannot have it both ways: If she wishes to sacrifice all this, all that she will get in return is the right to meet men on male terms. She will lose.[92]

Unequal social arrangements are, in the end, ordained by nature.[93]

Still, the evidence—occasionally impressive, often uneven—is far from convincing. If male domination is natural, based on biological imperatives, why, asks sociologist Cynthia Fuchs Epstein, must it be coercive, held in place by laws, traditions, customs, and the constant threat of violence for any woman who dares step out of line? Why would women want to enter male spheres, like colleges and universities, politics and the labour force, the professions, and the military, for which they are clearly biologically ill-suited?

Ironically, in the past decade, conservatives who argue that biological bases account for both sex differences and sexuality differences have been joined by some women and some gay men and lesbians, who have adopted an essentialism of their own. Some feminists, for example, argue that women should be pleased to claim "the intuitive and emotional strengths given by their right-hemisphere, in opposition to the over-cognitive, left-hemisphere-dominated, masculine nature."[94]

Similarly, research on the biological bases of homosexuality suggests a dramatic shifting of positions. Gay-brain research may have shed little light on the etiology of sexual orientation, but it has certainly generated significant political heat. In a way, the promotion of gay essentialism has become seen as a political strategy to normalize gayness. "It points out that gay people are made this way by nature," observes Robert Bray, the director of public information of the National Gay and Lesbian Task Force. "It strikes at the heart of people who oppose gay rights and who think we don't deserve our rights because we're choosing to be the way we are." Michael Bailey and Richard Pillard, the authors of one of the gay twin studies, opined in a *New York Times* op-ed essay that a "biological explanation is good news for homosexuals and their advocates." "If it turns out, indeed, that homosexuals are born that way, it could undercut the animosity gays have had to contend with for centuries," added a cover story in *Newsweek*. Such an understanding would "reduce being gay to something like being left-handed, which is in fact all that it is," commented gay journalist and author Randy Shilts in the magazine. Moreover, Simon LeVay, whose research sparked the debate, hoped that homophobia would dissipate as the result of this research, because its basis in prejudice about the unnaturalness of homosexual acts would vanish. Gays would become "just another minority," just another ethnic group, with an identity based on primordial characteristics.[95]

This political implication is not lost on conservatives, who took up the social constructionist, "nurture" theory of sexual orientation as firmly as they argued for intractable biologically based differences between women and men. Such thinking leads to the politically volatile though scientifically dubious "conversion" movement that holds that, through intensive therapy, gay men and lesbians can become happy and "healthy" heterosexuals.[96]

Conclusion

Biological research holds significant sway over our thinking about the two fundamental questions in the study of gender: the *differences* between women and men and the gendered *inequalities* that are evident in our social lives. Still, there are many problems with the research on biological bases for gender difference and more and greater problems with the extrapolation of those differences to the social world of gender inequality. Consider the problem of what we might call "anthropomorphic hyperbole." Simon LeVay writes that, "Genes demand instant gratification."[97] What are we to make of such an obviously false statement? Genes do not "demand" anything. Which genes is he talking about anyway? Some genes simply control such seemingly unimportant and uninteresting things as eye colour or the capacity to differentiate between sweet and sour tastes. Others wait patiently for decades until they can instruct a man's hair to begin to fall out. Still others are so undemanding that they may wait patiently for several generations, until another recessive mate is found after multiple attempts at reproduction. Genes may play a role in the sexual decision-making of a species or even of individual members of any particular species; they do so only through an individual's interaction with his or her environment. They cannot possibly control any particular decision made by any particular individual at any particular time. With whom you decide to have sex this weekend—or even whether you *do* have sex—is not determined by your genes, but rather by you.

Another problem in biological research has been the casual assumption that causation always moves from physiology to psychology. Just because one finds a correlation between two variables doesn't permit one to speculate about the causal direction. As biologist Ruth Hubbard argues:

> If a society put half its children into short skirts and warns them not to move in ways that reveal their panties, while putting the other half into jeans and

overalls and encouraging them to climb trees, play ball, and participate in other vigorous outdoor games; if later, during adolescence, the children who have been wearing trousers are urged to "eat like growing boys" while the children in skirts are warned to watch their weight and not get fat; if the half in jeans runs around in sneakers or boots, while the half in skirts totters about on spike heels, then these two groups of people will be biologically as well as socially different.[98]

We know, then, what we *cannot* say about the biological bases for gender difference and gender inequality. What then *can* we say? We can say that biological differences provide the raw materials from which we begin to create our identities within culture, within society. "Biological sexuality is the necessary precondition for human sexuality," writes historian Robert Padgug. "But biological sexuality is only a precondition, a set of potentialities, which is never unmediated by human reality, and which becomes transformed in qualitatively new ways in human society."[99]

We seem to want desperately to believe that the differences between women and men are significant and traceable to biological origins in a simple line of causation. However, a better way to understand the influence of biology on our natures is through Anne Fausto-Sterling's simile that each of us is like a Russian nesting doll, with the smallest "doll" representing our being at the cellular level, the next doll our organism, etc. The largest "doll" is our own history as human beings. According to Fausto-Sterling, each one of these dolls is important and can be examined as significant, but each doll on its own is hollow: "Only the complete assembly makes sense."[100]

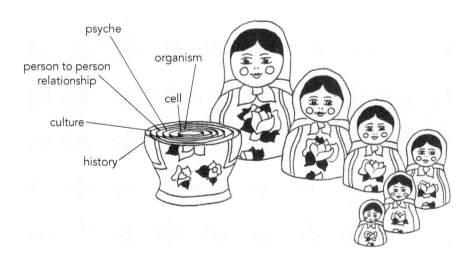

Figure 2.1 Anne Fausto-Sterling unpacks sex and gender.

Source: Drawing by Erica Warp for Anne Fausto-Sterling. Copyright 2000 Anne Fausto-Sterling, *Sexing the Body*. Reprinted by permission of Basic Books, a member of the Perseus Books Group.

The Russian doll:

Is there some easy way to envision the double-sided process that connects the production of gendered knowledge about the body on the one surface to the materialization of gender within the body on the other? While no metaphor is perfect, Russian nesting dolls have always fascinated me. As I take apart each outer doll, I wait expectantly to see if there is a smaller one within. As the dolls get tinier and tinier, I marvel at the delicacy of the craft that produces successively smaller dolls. . . .

I find the Russian nesting doll useful for envisioning the various layers of human sexuality, from the cellular to the social and historical. . . . Academics can take the system apart for display or to study one of the dolls in more detail. But each individual doll is hollow. Only the complete assembly makes sense. Unlike its wooden counterpart, the human nesting doll changes shape with time. Change can happen in any of the layers, but since the entire assembly has to fit together, altering one of the component dolls requires the interlinked system—from the cellular to the institution—to change.

While social and comparative historians write about the past to help us understand why we frame the present in particular ways (the outermost doll), analysts of popular culture, literary critics, and anthropologists tell us about our current culture (the second largest doll). They analyze our aggregate behaviours, think about how individuals and institutions interact, and chronicle social change. Other sociologists and psychologists think about individual relationships and individual development (the third largest doll), while some psychologists write about the mind or psyche (the fourth doll in). As the location (or as some would prefer, activity) that links events that occur outside the body to those that occur inside the organism (the second smallest doll), the mind plays an important and peculiar function. The brain is a key organ in the transfer of information from outside the body in and back again. And neuroscientists of many stripes try not only to understand how the brain works as an integrated organ but also how its individual cells function. Indeed, cells make the final, tiny doll found within the organism. In different organs, cells specialize for a variety of functions, They also work as systems, their history and immediate surroundings stimulating signals for particular genes—to contribute (or not) to cellular activities.

Using Russian nesting dolls as a framework suggests that history, culture, relationships, psyche, organism, and cell are each appropriate locations from which to study the formation and meanings of sexuality and gender. Developmental systems theory, whether applied to the assembled doll or to its subunits, provides the scaffolding for thought and experiment. Assembling the smaller dolls into a single large one requires the integration of knowledge derived from very different levels of biological and social organization. The cell, the individual, groups of individuals organized in families, peer groups, cultures, and nations and their histories all provide sources of knowledge about human sexuality. We cannot understand it well unless we consider all of these components. To accomplish such a task, scholars would do well to work in interdisciplinary groups. And while it is not reasonable, for example, to ask all biologists to become proficient in feminist theory, it *is* reasonable to ask each group of scholars to understand the limitations of knowledge obtained from a single discipline. Only non-hierarchical, multidisciplinary teams can devise more complete (or what Sandra Harding calls "less false") knowledge about human sexuality.[101]

How do we make sense of our totalities? How we do that, how we create identities out of our experiences, how we understand those experiences, and the choices we make— these are the province of social science, which tries to explore the remarkable diversity of human experience. Although biological studies can suggest to us the basic building blocks of experience and identity, it is within our cultures, our societies, and our families that those building blocks are assembled into the astonishingly diverse architecture that constitutes our lives.

Summary

Theories of "essential" gender difference predate modern science, but have been mainly the province of scientists since the nineteenth century. Today, theories of biological sex difference focus on three areas of research: evolutionary theory, brain research, and endocrinology.

The influence of Darwinian evolutionary theory strengthened biological determinism through the theory that men and women had evolved for different functions and that parallel evolution had produced gender roles, which were therefore "natural." Under the influence of **social Darwinism**, late-nineteenth-century scientific arguments about the nature of men and women became both sexist and racist. By the early twentieth century, these perspectives were forged into the eugenics movement, which, along with social Darwinism, was discredited after the Second World War. In the 1970s, evolutionary theory spawned the new field of sociobiology, which studies the biological basis of social behaviour. The key insights of sociobiology relate to differences in male and female sexual strategies, which sociobiologists see as reflective of evolution. Sociobiologists stress the distinct imperatives of men and women; men seek to maximize reproductive opportunities, while women are more discriminating and cautious. Other sociobiologists have explained such phenomena as the division of labour (Wilson) and male bonding (Tiger).

More recently, evolutionary psychology has explained psychological traits, including differences between men and women, as the result of evolutionary adaptation. Mating strategies have been of particular interest to evolutionary psychologists, but the field has yielded insights in a wide variety of areas. Evolutionary psychology is better than sociobiology at accounting for the different and sometimes conflicting interests of men and women in mating; however, it has sometimes fallen into similar reductive reasoning.

Criticisms of evolutionary theory, particularly sociobiology, include its teleological tendency to reason backward from human behaviours and categories to animal models or "causes"; the failure to locate genetic coding for specific behaviours; selective use of comparator species; and an exaggeration of the nature of genetic predisposition. Evolutionary theorists, whether sociobiologists or evolutionary psychologists, accordingly offer informative but incomplete readings of human—gendered—nature.

Brain studies emerged from nineteenth-century social science and gender-related differences in testing in the twentieth century. Studies of the gendered brain developed into two related areas of study. The first examines sex differences in verbal and spatial skills. Persistent sex differences have been found in visuospatial ability, which seems to be stronger, on average, in males, and verbal ability, which seems to be stronger in girls. Moreover, there seems to be simply more variability among males. These findings may indicate the presence of brain-based sex differences, but many questions remain. Most notably, the visuospatial gap appears to be narrowing, at least in Canada, while the verbal gap remains strong. This suggests that these cognitive abilities, whatever their foundation in biology, are highly susceptible to cultural influence. The most careful recent research sees cognitive gender differences as the result of many factors.

The second area of brain study focuses on the brain's structure and function, studying right-left hemisphere differences, use of different parts of the brain for similar functions, and differences in the tissue that connects the hemispheres. The male brain has been viewed as more lateralized, with one side dominant over the other, than a woman's brain, which is more "integrated." The discussion has sometimes been impaired by changing understandings of lateralization or the location of brain functions, and the implications of males' greater lateralization (if it exists) are not clear, although it has been presumed to explain males' visuospatial advantage. Other studies have focused on the use of parts of the brain, arguing that men and women use parts of the brain differently. Finally, the corpus callosum (CC) and its hindmost part, the splenium, have been seen as key to the structural differences between the male and female brains. In all of these areas, limited or even fallacious findings have been transformed into media claims of "male" and "female" brains, reinforcing crude gender stereotypes.

Hormones, discovered and named in the twentieth century, are the focus of the third major area of sex-difference research. Testosterone, which is thought of as the "masculinity hormone" in popular culture, has many effects, but its functions, normal levels, and effects are confusing and only now beginning to be well understood. While testosterone is clearly linked to aggression, it seems not to cause but to enable it. The hormone's relationship to libido is even less clear. This has not prevented outrageous claims and the creation of "andropause," a so-called medical condition found among no-longer-young men who are suffering from a "deficiency" of testosterone. Though women are now being encouraged to "add a dash of testosterone" to their hormone regimens, the most important hormone for women is estrogen. Estrogen has been studied for its relationship to cognition and to sexual desire, but most of the interest in estrogen relates to menopause, when women naturally undergo a precipitous drop in hormone levels. In North America in the late twentieth century, millions of women underwent ERT to "correct" this condition, at least until 2002 when the US National Institutes of Health cautioned women concerning the risk of hormone therapy. More recently, research has examined the "perimenopause," another time of hormonal turbulence preceding the menopause itself. PMS, another effect of hormonal fluctuation, was "discovered" in the 1980s and is now listed in the *DSM-V* of the American Psychiatric Association. Women, like men, are therefore now seen as greatly influenced (in mood, health, and behaviour) by their sex hormones. Hormones *are* important, but too often, their effects are grossly oversimplified.

Research on the possible biological origins of homosexuality has focused on brain structure, a "gay gene," and hormonal influences. Experiments identified structural differences between the brains of homosexual men and those of "straight" men, and between the brains of male transsexuals and non-transsexual heterosexual men. However, these studies have suffered from some methodological problems; in fact, recent scholarship has suggested that there are no significant structural differences. MRI-based studies of processing have revealed some distinctions, but their implications are unknown. The search for a gay gene or hormonal causation has deployed twin studies, which have yielded very scant evidence of a genetic connection. There is, however, some evidence that male homosexuality tends to cluster in families and that having older brothers predisposes a boy to homosexuality—neither of which claims proves pure biological causation.

Some sex-difference research has studied intersex people—those with hormonal or chromosomal abnormalities causing some degree of sexual ambiguity. Intersexuals were once known as hermaphrodites, though this term has a more restrictive definition and has now fallen from use. Intersexuality (broadly defined) affects as many as 1.7 per cent of the population and is expressed in a range of ways reflective of the different disorders that produce it. Since the 1960s, intersex people have been subjected to dramatic interventions, often from infancy onward, to "normalize" their sex and gender. They have also been seen as ideal subjects for the study of biological sex differences. Though there is some evidence that hormonal masculinization of girls in utero may make them more "masculine" as children, these findings seem superficial and militate against girls' own apparent comfort with their gender identities. Intersexuals do not "prove" that the essence of gender is biology.

Assertions of the biological bases for gender differences often have been linked to a conservative political agenda. However, this is changing, with some feminists and gay activists arguing determinist points of view and anti-gay conservatives becoming social constructionists, at least with regards to sexual orientation. Often when we argue about these theories, we seem to be arguing about politics and the present. We want to believe that the differences between men and women are significant and that they can be traced to biology. While biology is important, Anne Fausto-Sterling's metaphor of the Russian stacking dolls tells us that we are the sum of all our parts, of which our biology is only one.

Questions for Critical Thinking

1. What are the strengths of evolutionary explanations of gender difference and gender inequality? In your opinion, what can they explain (or help explain)? What behaviours and traits can they *not* explain?
2. Is women's underrepresentation in science, technology, engineering, and math (STEM) careers the result of biological differences between men and women?

3. Do you believe (with Simon LeVay) that the discovery of a biological basis for homo-sexuality would increase acceptance of homosexuals?
4. Assessing all of the evidence presented in this chapter regarding biology and sex difference, what evidence do you consider compelling? What arguments do you consider weak or unsupported?

Key Terms

androgen insensitivity syndrome (AIS)
androgenital syndrome (AGS)
biological determinism
biological essentialism
clitoridectomy
congenital adrenal hyperplasia (CAH)
estrus
eugenics

evolutionary psychology
intersex/intersexuals
lateralized
palliative system justification motive
parental investment
sciences, technology, engineering, and mathematics (STEM)
social Darwinism
sociobiology
stereotype threat

3

"So *That* Explains It"
Psychoanalytic and Developmental Perspectives on Gender

Upon no subject has there been so much dogmatic assertion based on so little scientific evidence, as upon male and female types of mind.

—John Dewey, "Is Coeducation Injurious to Girls?" (1911)

There's a famous cartoon of two babies, a boy and a girl, standing together. They're both holding open their diapers and peering down at their genitals. The caption reads, "So *that* explains the difference in our salaries." The cartoon adopts a popular idea about the theories of Sigmund Freud, the founder of **psychoanalysis**. As we saw at the beginning of the previous chapter, Freud claimed, "anatomy is destiny." He believed that the anatomical differences between males and females led them toward different personalities. However, he did not believe that such differences were biologically programmed into males and females at birth. On the contrary, Freud saw his work as challenging those who held that the body contained all the information it needed at birth to become an adult man or woman. He believed that the observed differences between women and men were traceable to our different experiences from infancy onward, especially in the ways we were treated in our families.

Of course, biology did play some role here: Freud and his followers believed that visible anatomical differences were decisive in the development of the child and especially that sexual energy, located in the body, propelled the child's experiences that determined gender identity. In a sense, Freud's ideas provide a bridge between biological or anatomical explanations of gender and theories of social construction. Throughout the twentieth century and into the twenty-first, scholars have continued to explore the psychological and developmental processes that produce gendered men and women.

Freud's Theory of Psychosocial Development

Freud proposed a theory of individual gender development in which each individual passes through a number of stages on his or her path to adult gender identity. These stages are set into motion by two factors: the composition or structure of the psyche and the realities of life.

Freud's model of the psyche comprises four elements: **id**, **ego**, **super-ego**, and the **external world**. These together form the basic architecture of the self, and each has a decisive role to play in the formation of personality. The id represents our desire to satisfy our basic animal needs. The id "knows" only that it wants gratification but has neither morality nor the means to acquire what it wants. Freud called the id "a cauldron filled with seething excitations."[1] Unfortunately, the external world offers limited possibilities for instinctual gratification; the id's desires are constantly thwarted. How we cope with those frustrations determines personality development.

The ego, the rational, problem-solving portion of our personality, must discipline the id, tame it, and seek possible sources of gratification for it. Another part of the psyche, the super-ego, is the seat of morality, and it assists the ego in selecting effective strategies toward socially approved goals. Ego and super-ego are therefore the brokers between the id and the external world. From these four elements, individuals fashion their psychological constitution: their drives for gratification, the limited possibilities offered by the world, the moralizing inner voice that tells us we do not deserve constant gratification, and the rational strategist that tries to keep all these forces in balance. These different components of the self emerge gradually through a child's development.

Freud believed that in the womb we are all sensuously content. Regardless, birth expels us from this enveloping Eden; hungry and alone, we can take nothing for granted. Now the infant transfers gratification to the mother's breast, seeking pleasure through ingesting food. This Freud calls the "oral stage." However, just as the ego accommodates itself to this source of gratification, it's removed by weaning. In the next stage, the "anal

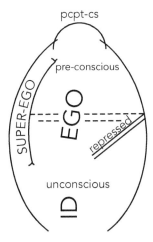

Figure 3.1 A recreation of Freud's own diagram of the organization of the human personality, as presented in a lecture in the 1930s. Note the relatively small size of the conscious part of the personality!

Source: *New Introductory Lectures on Psycho-Analysis* (London: The Hogarth Press and the Institute for Psycho-Analysis, 1993).

stage," gratification is achieved not by taking food in but through urination and defecation. Disappointingly, no sooner do we discover the joys of excretory creation then we are toilet-trained, forced to repress that source of gratification until it's convenient for grown-ups. Finally, after oral denial and anal repression, we reach what Freud calls the "genital stage." Now here's where gender comes in.

Until now, both boys and girls experience roughly the same things. However, at this stage, our paths diverge sharply as we "become" either masculine or feminine. This critical moment is called the **Oedipal crisis**, after Sophocles' play *Oedipus, the King*. The resolution of the Oedipal crisis is vital—the boy learns to desire sex with women and to identify as a man. This is crucial in Freudian theory: *The boy achieves gender identity and sexual orientation at the same moment in time.* During the Oedipal stage, the boy desires sexual union with his mother, but he also realizes that he is in competition with his father for her affections. The little boy sexualizes his fear of the father, believing that if he were to compete sexually with his father, his father would castrate him. The boy's ego resolves this state of **castration anxiety** by transferring the boy's identification from mother to father. Consequently, the boy must break the identification with his mother, repudiate her, and identify with his father. This is a great shock—the mother has been the source of warmth and love and is the object of his desire; the father has been a more distant source of authoritarian power and is the source of the boy's terror. Nevertheless, by identifying with the father the little boy ceases being "feminine" (identified with the mother) and becomes masculine, as he simultaneously becomes heterosexual. Almost literally, as the 1930s popular song put it, he will "want a girl just like the girl that married dear old Dad."

For girls, Freud believed, the Oedipal crisis is complementary but not nearly as traumatic. Girls retain their identification with the mother but must renounce their sexual desire for her in the phallic stage, developing what Swiss psychoanalyst Carl Jung named the **Electra complex**. Freud believed that women experience **penis envy**. The little girl understands that her only chance for sexual gratification is to retain her identification with the mother and to be sexually possessed by a man who can satisfy her so that she can have a baby, which will be her source of feminine gratification. In the process, she transfers the location of sexual gratification from the clitoris (an "atrophied penis," in Freud's terms) to the vagina, that is, she develops feminine, passive sexuality. Again, gender identity and sexual orientation go hand-in-hand. (Freud did acknowledge that his "insight into these developmental processes in girls is unsatisfactory, incomplete, and vague"—given how it was really an effort to derive some complementary comparison with boys' development and was not a theory of girls' development itself.[2])

Three issues are worth noting in this account of gender identity and sexuality. First, *Freud dislocates gender and sexuality from the realm of biology*. Nothing is inevitable about males' becoming masculine or females' becoming feminine. Gender and sexuality are accomplished within the family, Freud argues, not activated by internal biological clocks.

Second, *Freud links gender identity to sexual orientation*, making homosexuality a developmental *gender* issue rather than an issue of immorality, sin, or biological anomaly. Homosexuals are simply those who either have failed to renounce identification with the mother in favour of the father (gay men) or have failed to retain their ties of identification to the mother (lesbians). (This idea, of course, also served as the basis for therapeutic interventions designed to "cure" homosexuals by encouraging gender-appropriate behaviours.)

Third, *Freud restates with new vigour traditional gender stereotypes* as if they were the badges of successful negotiation of this perilous journey. A boy must be the sexual initiator and scrupulously avoid all feminine behaviours, lest he be seen as having failed to identify with the father. A girl must become sexually passive, wait for a man to be attracted to her, so that she can be fulfilled as a woman by becoming a mother.

It's important to remember that though Freud saw homosexuality as the failure of the child to identify adequately with the same-sex parent and therefore a problem of gender identity development, he did not believe in either the criminal persecution or psychiatric treatment of homosexuals. In fact, when Freud was contacted by a woman whose son was homosexual, he patiently explained why he did not think her son needed to be "cured":

> Homosexuality is assuredly no advantage, but it is nothing to be ashamed of, no vice, no degradation; it cannot be classified as an illness; we consider it to be a variation of the sexual function. . . . Many highly respectable individuals of ancient and modern times have been homosexuals, several of the greatest men among them. . . . It is a great injustice to persecute homosexuality as a crime—and a cruelty too. . . . What analysis can do for your son runs in a different line. If he is unhappy, neurotic, torn by conflicts, inhibited in his social life, analysis may bring him harmony, peace of mind, full efficiency, whether he remains homosexual or gets changed.[3]

It took another 40 years before the American Psychiatric Association declassified homosexuality as a mental illness, so Freud's opinion on this one wasn't as influential as were some of the other aspects of his theory!

Still, many popular stereotypes about homosexuality continue to rely on Freudian theories of gender development. Many people believe that homosexuality is a form of gender nonconformity; that is, effeminate men and masculine women are seen in the popular mind as likely or "latent" homosexuals, whereas masculine men's and feminine women's gender-conforming behaviour leads others to expect them to be heterosexual. In fact, we often believe we can "read" someone's sexual orientation by observing his or her gender-stereotypic behaviour, as if remarkably masculine men or truly feminine women couldn't possibly be gay or lesbian.

Freud's theories have been subject to considerable debate and controversy. He based his theories about the sexuality of women on a very small sample of upper-middle-class women in Vienna, all of whom were suffering from psychological difficulties that brought them to treatment with him in the first place. Initially, Freud believed that many of his patients' psychological issues were the result of traumatic childhood sexual experiences, including incest. He published a paper asserting this claim but retracted it in the face of his colleagues' derision. Many people believe that Freud's theory of girls' development is profoundly flawed as a result, because it rested at least in part on the theory that when women told him of sexual experiences with their fathers, they were expressing their Oedipal (or Electran) desires rather than describing reality.[4]

Freud's theories of male development were based on even fewer clinical cases and on his own recollections of his childhood and his dreams. These are not the

Hollywood Goes Freudian: Transgender, Sexual Repression, and Murder

The degree to which Freudian ideas of psychosexual development—including the Oedipus complex and repression—became "mainstream" can be judged from the many Hollywood films that address the topic. Freud probably wouldn't have agreed with the way in which gender and sexual development are portrayed in these films, however. One of the most common horror-film motifs of the past 40 years has been what Carol Glover calls "the notion of a killer propelled by psychosexual fury, more particularly a male in gender distress."

To list all of the movies—even the Hollywood ones—that draw from this notion would be impossible. Everyone agrees, however, on the first: Alfred Hitchcock's 1960 horror classic *Psycho*, which established at least two genres—the psycho-thriller and the slasher film. *Psycho* features numerous elements now so iconic that they are reproduced and referenced throughout popular culture; among these, the "shower scene" is probably most familiar.

As you probably already know, *Psycho* told the story of Norman Bates, a motel owner so dominated by and obsessed with his deceased mother that he has split his personality into two parts: one the arrested boy and the other the domineering, sexually repressive mother.

When a lone woman (Janet Leigh as "Marion") fleeing her home with embezzled funds stays at the Bates Motel, Norman becomes attracted to her. The "Mother" part of his personality, which Norman "channels" through donning his mother's clothes, must therefore, kill the object of his desire—hence the shower scene. However simplistic this view is of the effects of "inappropriate" parenting, it did strike a chord, which left even Hitchcock, according to Glover, "bewildered by the [film's] unprecedented success."

In the years that followed, many films relied upon what was, at the time, the dominant mode of understanding gender identity and sexual development. In 1980, Brian de Palma released his own tribute to *Psycho*, *Dressed to*

Paramount/William Creamer/The Kobal Collection at Art Resource, NY

Janet Leigh in the famous "shower scene" from *Psycho* (1960).

most reliable scientific methods, and his tendency to make sexuality the driving force of all individual development and all social and group processes may tell us more about his own life, and perhaps contemporary Vienna, than about other societies and cultures.

Kill. Starring Michael Caine as New York psychiatrist Dr Elliott, the film told the story of knife murders committed by the mysterious "Bobbi," a transgender (female-to-male) patient undergoing therapy with Dr Elliott. The ultimate revelation that Elliott *was* Bobbi was the shock ending to the drama. Helpfully, the film provides a culminating psychiatric evaluation; Dr Elliott, a psychiatrist explains, experienced gender confusion, but his "masculine" personality rebelled against the idea of seeking reassignment. At the same time, his "feminine" side (Bobbi) became jealous of and murdered women to whom Elliott was attracted. (Still following this?) Regardless of the cinematic merits of either *Dressed to Kill* or *Psycho*, they have been accused of cementing in the public mind simplistic and derogatory perceptions of non-gender-conforming people. As Barbara Creed suggests, "while [such films] might present a critique of a culture fearful of changes in traditional sex roles, they also equate cross-dressing and transsexuality with monstrousness."

Indeed, it might be argued that for many years, trans individuals were *most* commonly seen on screen in such "monstrous" roles. In her 2009 doctoral dissertation, Joelle Ruby Ryan describes being in a conference hotel elevator with several male-bodied but female-attired individuals; when the elevator stopped for a male passenger, he grimaced and would not enter. Afterward, Ryan writes, "internally I wondered: how do cultural codes that present gender-transgressive people as insane psychopaths, deviant killers, and monstrous, murdering machines function in the culture at large?"

Though Freudian understandings of sexual development have lost much of their influence, Freudian cinema studies remain potent. What's more, reductive interpretations of Freud's theories continue to inform Hollywood film. Slasher films continue to rely upon *Psycho*'s stereotypes. The 1983 film *Sleepaway Camp,* a B-grade slasher movie, has become a cult favourite for its "shocker" ending, which features—you guessed it—the revelation that the murderer "Angela" is actually a boy who was raised as a girl. Successful enough to have spawned numerous sequels, the film has generated legions of fans and controversy over its portrayal of the transgender woman. While the *Sleepaway* franchise may not be high art, even critically acclaimed movies like 1999's *American Beauty* cannot resist the trope. In that movie, the protagonist Lester is murdered by a neighbour unable to come to terms with his own repressed homosexual desires.

These readings of gender and sexuality are interesting for what they suggest about our culture and the way it grapples with difference. However, they also misrepresent the origins and nature of nonconforming gender and sexuality, and hide some troubling realities. Ruby lists more than 35 movies featuring transgender killers between 1960 and 2005. Not until 1999's *Boys Don't Cry* did Hollywood represent more accurately the relationship of transgender people with violence. That is, though there are no clear cases of transgender killers on record, transgender people are hundreds of times more likely to fall victim to murder.[5]

Although many today question Freud's theories on methodological, political, or theoretical grounds, there is no question that these theories have had a remarkable impact on contemporary studies and on popular assumptions about the relationship among gender identity, sexual behaviour, and sexual orientation.

Sex-Role Theories

Freud's theory that "normal" gender identity and sexual preference were successfully acquired—or not—in childhood proved enormously influential. Freudian psychoanalytic theory spawned several different traditions in psychology. As we shall see in this section, some psychologists used various statistical tests to measure more precisely the differences between males and females at certain ages, forming the basis for **sex-role theory**, which analyzed individuals' socialization into appropriate gender roles and identities.

In the early 1930s, just three decades after Freud initially developed his theories, Lewis Terman, a psychology professor at Stanford University, and his associate, Catherine Cox Miles, tried to codify masculinity and femininity into their component parts—traits, attitudes, and behaviours.[6]

Terman and Miles utilized a broad range of empirical measures to test gender identity and constructed a continuum from masculinity to femininity, along which any individual could be placed (according to answers on the Terman/Miles **M-F test**). As a result of inventories like the M-F test, gender identity came to be associated with a particular bundle of attitudes, traits, and behaviours that could be seen as indicators of "successful" gender acquisition. When embraced by social science in the 1940s, these inventories became the basis for sex-role theory.

The M-F test was perhaps the single most widely used means to determine successful acquisition of (or "deviation from") gender identity and was used until the 1960s. (The final edition of *Sex and Personality* appeared in 1968.) As late as 1978, McGill researchers reported that it successfully differentiated male from female subjects when administered to students in Montreal—despite what we might see as the US-centric character of some of its questions (see below).[7] Here is a small sample of the questions on the M-F test. (If you want to keep your own score on these few items—to make sure that your own gender identity is progressing "normally"—you should score it the way that Terman and Miles suggested in 1936: If your response is "masculine," you will see it indicated by a "+"; if feminine, it scores a "−." Interesting how these little value judgments creep into scientific research!)

Gendered Knowledge: In the following completion items, there are right and wrong answers—it was assumed that the more "masculine" would know the right answer to questions 2, 3, and 5 and that the more "feminine" would know the answers to items 1 and 4.

1. Things cooked in grease are boiled (+), broiled (+), fried (−), roasted (+).
2. Most of our anthracite coal comes from Alabama (−), Colorado (−), Ohio (−), Pennsylvania (+).
3. The "Rough Riders" were led by Funston (−), Pershing (−), Roosevelt (+), Sheridan (−).
4. Red goes best with black (−), lavender (+), pink (+), purple (+).
5. The proportion of the globe covered by water is about 1/8 (−), 1/4 (−), 1/2 (−), 3/4 (+).

Gendered Feelings: The test also included a variety of stimuli thought to provoke certain emotions. Respondents were to answer whether these things caused (a) a lot, (b) some, (c) little, or (d) none of the expected emotion. For example:

• Does being called lazy; seeing boys make fun of old people; seeing someone cheat on an exam make you ANGRY?

- Does being lost; deep water; graveyards at night; Negroes [this is actually on the list!] make you AFRAID?
- Does a fly caught on sticky fly paper; a man who is cowardly and can't help it; a wounded deer make you feel PITY?
- Does boys teasing girls; indulging in "petting"; not brushing your teeth; being a Bolshevik make you feel that a person is WICKED?

To score this section, give yourself a minus (–) for every answer in which you said the thing caused a lot of the emotion, except for the answer, "being a Bolshevik," which was obviously serious enough for men to get very emotional about. On all others, including being afraid of "Negroes," however, high levels of emotion were scored as feminine.

Gendered Occupations, Appearances, and Books: The test also included possible careers and their obvious sex-typing, such as librarian, auto racer, forest ranger, florist, soldier, and music teacher. There were lists of character traits (loud voices, men with beards, and tall women) that those tested were asked to like or dislike, and a list of children's books (for example, *Robinson Crusoe*, *Rebecca of Sunnybrook Farm*, *Little Women*, and *Biography of a Grizzly*) that they either liked, didn't like, or had not read.

Gendered People: There was a list of famous people whom one either liked, disliked, or did not know (Bismarck, Lenin, Florence Nightingale, and Jane Addams). (Obviously, not having read a book or not knowing about a famous person could be seen as gender confirming or non-confirming.)

There were also questions about what you might like to draw if you were an artist (ships or flowers); what you might like to write about if you were a newspaper reporter (accidents or theatre); and where you might like to travel if you had plenty of money (hunt lions in Africa or study social customs). Finally, the test included some self-reporting about the respondent's own behaviours and attitudes. Such "yes" or "no" items (here listed with the scoring of a "yes" answer) included:

- Do you rather dislike to take your bath? (+)
- Are you extremely careful about your manner of dress? (–)
- Do people ever say you talk too much? (+)
- Have you ever been punished unjustly? (+)
- Have you ever kept a diary? (–)

The research by Terman and Miles enabled a new generation of psychologists to construct a continuum between masculinity and femininity, along which any individual could be located. If a boy or girl exhibited "gender-appropriate" traits and attitudes, parents could be reassured that their child was developing normally. If, however, the child scored too high on the "inappropriate" side of the continuum, intervention strategies might be devised to facilitate the adoption of more appropriate behaviours. Artistic boys would be pushed toward rough-and-tumble play; tomboys would be forced into frilly dresses to read quietly instead of climbing a tree. Despite the apparent interest in both boys' and girls' "normal" development, however, there was much greater focus on male development. Behind these interventions lay the spectre of the sissy, the homosexual male, who, Terman and Miles and other psychologists believed, had gender identity problems. As another psychologist, George W. Henry, wrote in 1937:

> In a large majority of . . . cases the tendencies to homosexuality as shown by attitude and behaviour can be observed in early childhood. . . . To the extent that his interests, attitude and behaviour are out of harmony with his actual sex he is likely to meet with circumstances which will accentuate his deviation. Boys appear to be somewhat more vulnerable than girls and if they show undue feminine tendencies special care should be exercised to give them opportunity to develop masculine characteristics.[8]

By the 1950s, **social psychologists** were seeking to clarify the social requirements for both masculine and feminine sex roles. These scholars elaborated and extended original classifications of the M-F scale offered by Terman and Miles.[9] In the years after the Second World War, for example, some psychologists hypothesized that the propensity toward fascism and Nazism stemmed from distorted assertions of gender identity. The authors of *The Authoritarian Personality* posited a typology of behaviours, based on the M-F scale, a scale that suggested that femininity and masculinity could describe both an internal psychological identification and an external behavioural manifestation. Their typology, accordingly, created four possible combinations instead of two:

Internal Psychological Organization

		Masculine	Feminine
External Behavioural Manifestation	Masculine	MM	MF
	Feminine	FM	FF

Two of the cells, upper left and lower right, would be considered "gender-appropriate"—males and females whose internal psychological identification matches their external behaviours. However, those males whose scores placed them in the upper right cell—internally feminine, externally masculine—also scored highest on measures of racism, authoritarianism, and hypermasculinity. The authors proposed that such attitudes were the means for those who were insecure about their masculinity to cover up their insecurities—by more rigid adherence to the most traditional norms. This became known as the "masculinity overcompensation thesis."[10]

A recent effort to revisit this thesis found that American men who felt that their masculinity was more "threatened" would overcompensate. In 2005, Rob Willer conducted an experiment with 111 undergraduates at Cornell University. Using a questionnaire, he purported to be testing their gender identities, but instead randomly assigned them to either feminine or masculine groups. He then surveyed the participants through "political" and "car-buying" survey packets. Male participants who were told that they were "feminine" were more likely to support the Iraq War, oppose gay marriages, and state their interest in purchasing an SUV—all of which had been identified with masculinity by students in an earlier survey. Interestingly, while male students' responses were altered by the (fake) gender identity "diagnosis," female students were apparently unfazed by being

told they were "masculine." While Willer himself has urged caution in interpreting the results, other studies have confirmed overcompensation. For example, one study published
in 2007 found that young men who received bogus "feminine identity" feedback were
more likely to perceive effeminate (though not masculine) gay men with hostility, fear,
and discomfort.[11]

A second trajectory that coincided with sex-role studies was sociological, based on the
work of Harvard sociologist Talcott Parsons and others who sought to establish the societal necessity for masculinity and femininity. Parsons argued that society had two types of
major functions, production and reproduction, and that these required two separate institutional systems, the occupational system and the kinship system, which, in turn, required
two types of roles. **Instrumental roles** (occupational) demanded rationality, autonomy,
and competitiveness; **expressive roles** (kinship) demanded tenderness and nurturing so
that the next generation could be socialized. In this way, Parsons shifted the emphasis of
sex-role identity development away from the "need" of the infant to become either masculine or feminine to the need of society for individuals to fill specific slots. Fortunately,
Parsons argued, we had two different types of people who were socialized to assume these
two different roles.

Parsons suggested, however, that the allocation of roles to males and females did not
always work smoothly. For example, in Western societies, the isolation of the nuclear
family and the extended period of childhood meant that boys remained identified with
the mother for a very long time. What's more, the separation of spheres meant that girls
had their appropriate role model immediately before them, whereas boys did not have
adequate role models. Therefore, he argued, boys' break with the mother and their need to
establish their individuality and masculinity often were accompanied by violent protest
against femininity, and angry repudiation of the feminine became a way for the boy to
purge himself of feminine identification. This, Parsons suggests, has some negative consequences, including a **cult of compulsive masculinity**:

> Western men are peculiarly susceptible to the appeal of an adolescent type of as-
> sertively masculine behaviour and attitudes which may take various forms. They
> have in common a tendency to revolt against the routine aspects of the primar-
> ily institutionalized masculine role of sober responsibility, meticulous respect
> for the rights of others, and tender affection toward women. Assertion through
> physical prowess, with an endemic tendency toward violence and hence the mili-
> tary ideal, is inherent in the complex and the most dangerous potentiality.[12]

For the girl, Parson theorized, the process is somewhat different. Because she remains
identified with the mother, she has an easier time. Her rebellion and anger come from recognizing "masculine superiority." She may express the aggression that would invariably
follow upon such frustration by rebelling against the feminine role altogether.

By the 1970s, sex-role theory was, itself, facing significant critical scrutiny. Some
thinkers found the binary model between roles, system needs, and males and females
just a bit too facile and convenient, as well as politically conservative. Others stressed the
coercive nature of these roles: If they were natural and met readily evident needs, why did
so many people rebel against them, and why did they need to be so rigorously enforced?

Two significant challenges came from social psychologists themselves. Sandra Bem and others explored the *content* of sex roles. The Bem Sex Role Inventory (BSRI) tested adult respondents on their perception of 60 different attributes, 20 of which were coded as "feminine," 20 as "masculine," and 20 more as "fillers." Bem's **gender schema theory** argued that we learn a gender identity, which becomes the basis for our individual views (schemas) of gender. As we grow and become adults, we evaluate our gender performances with regard to our **gender schemas**, which are also reinforced by society. She discovered that the most psychologically well-adjusted and intelligent people were those who fell in between the polar oppositions of masculinity and femininity. In her initial studies, Bem therefore claimed that **androgyny**, "the combined presence of socially valued, stereotypic, feminine, and masculine characteristics," best described the healthily adjusted individual.

Subsequent studies failed to confirm the validity of these measures, and androgyny was discredited as a kind of wishy-washy non-personality, rather than the synthesis of the best of both worlds. Twenty years after her initial studies, Bem noted that the scale "reproduces . . . the very gender polarization that it seeks to undercut."[13] Gender schema theory nonetheless provides further understanding of how gender is learned by individuals, how society influences that learning, and how individuals can vary in their adherence to rigid gender norms.

Whereas proponents of androgyny challenged the content of sex-role theory, Joseph Pleck challenged the form. In a series of articles that culminated in his book *The Myth of Masculinity*, Pleck advanced the idea that the problem was not that men were having a hard time fitting into a rational notion of masculinity but rather that the role itself was internally contradictory and inconsistent. Pleck assessed and commented on what he called the **male sex role identity** (MSRI) model, arguing that the male sex role itself was the source of strain, anxiety, and male problems.

Psychology was consequently transformed from the vehicle that would help problematic men adapt to their rational sex role into the vehicle by which men had been fed a pack of lies about masculinity. The sex-role system itself was the problem. In its place, Pleck proposed the **male sex role strain** model (MSRS):

1. Sex roles are operationally defined by sex-role stereotypes and norms.
2. Sex roles are contradictory and inconsistent.
3. The proportion of individuals who violate sex roles is high.
4. Violating sex roles leads to social condemnation.
5. Violating sex roles leads to negative psychological consequences.
6. Actual or imagined violation of sex roles leads individuals to over conform to them.
7. Violating sex roles has more severe consequences for males than females.
8. Certain characteristics prescribed by sex roles are psychologically dysfunctional.
9. Each gender experiences sex-role strain in its work and family roles.
10. Historical changes cause sex-role strain.

The net effect of this new model is to shift the understanding of problems from the men themselves to the roles that they are forced to play.[14] Subsequent research has explored the grappling with these contradictory role specifications by different groups of men and the problematic behaviours (such as sexual risk taking) that they use to reconcile contradictory role demands.[15]

However, problems remain with sex-role theory that even these two ambitious efforts could not resolve. For one thing, when psychologists discussed the "male" sex role or the "female" sex role, they posited a single, monolithic entity, a "role," into which all boys and all girls were placed. However, there are a variety of different "masculinities" or "femininities" depending on class, race, ethnicity, age, sexuality, religion, and region. If all boys or all girls were to receive the same socialization to the appropriate sex role, differences in the construction of black masculinity, Aboriginal femininity, rural masculinity, or middle-aged gay masculinity would all be effaced. Sex-role theory is unable to account for the differences *among* men or *among* women because it always begins from the normative prescriptions of sex *roles*, rather than the experiences of men and women themselves.

A second problem with sex-role theory is that it obscures power. When we say that boys become masculine and girls become feminine in roughly similar ways, we posit a false equivalence between the two. "Men don't have power," writes pop therapist Warren Farrell, "men and women have roles."[16] Still, despite what men and women may *feel* about their situation, men, as a group, have more power in our society than women as a group. In addition, some men—privileged by virtue of race, class, ethnicity, sexuality, etc.—have power over other men. Any adequate explanation of gender must account not only for gender difference but also for male domination. Theories of sex roles cannot do so.[17]

This theoretical inadequacy stems from the sorting process in the first place. Sex-role theorists see boys and girls sorted into two separate categories. However, constructions of gender are *relational*—we understand what it means to be a man or a woman in relation to the dominant models as well as to one another. Those who also are marginalized by race, class, ethnicity, age, and sexuality, for example, measure their gender identities against those of the dominant group.

Finally, sex-role theory assumes that only individuals are gendered. However, gender is more than an attribute of individuals; gender organizes and constitutes the field in which those individuals move. The institutions of our lives—families, workplaces, schools—are themselves gendered institutions, organized to reproduce the differences and the inequalities between women and men. If one wants to understand the lives of people in any situation, the French philosopher Jean-Paul Sartre once wrote, one "must inquire first into the situation surrounding [them]."[18]

Cognitive Development Theory

As theorists of sex roles attempted to clarify the manner in which individuals learn and fulfil their sex roles, some developmental psychologists sought to chart the sequences or stages of gender and sexual development in children. **Cognitive development theory** locates the trigger of gender development and gender identity formation in early to mid-childhood. Lawrence Kohlberg, a psychologist who taught at Harvard and the University of Chicago, developed this theory based on Swiss psychologist Jean Piaget's model of cognitive development, which delineated the tasks and mental processes appropriate to children of various ages.[19] Kohlberg argued that children learned gender roles according to their characteristic modes of cognition at different ages. Psychologists of this school accordingly argue that children are born more or less gender neutral; that is, no important biological differences between boys and girls at birth explain later gender differences. As they grow, children process new information through "cognitive filters" that enable them to interpret information about gender.

One of the central developmental tasks of early childhood, Kohlberg argued, is to label oneself as either male or female. The point in time at which children learn "I am a boy" or "I am a girl" is a point after which self-identification seems fixed. The decision is *cognitive*, part of the pattern of mental growth in the organism. Even by age two, children have relatively stable and fixed understandings of themselves as gendered, and this categorization, Kohlberg argues, "is basically a cognitive reality judgment rather than a product of social rewards, parental justifications, or sexual fantasies." (Note the dig at Freud.) Things, persons, and activities are labelled, "this is appropriate to who I am" or "this is not appropriate to who I am."[20]

It is not until age five or six that most children have the cognitive machinery to recognize gender as an attribute of the person and not the result of the material props that we use to display gender (purses, for example). At that point, children begin to develop **gender constancy**—the idea that gender identity is permanent and unchanging—and cannot be changed simply because, for instance, one "inappropriately" holds a purse.

The child therefore becomes capable of socializing him- or herself by subjecting behaviour to analysis based on gender appropriateness. Because so many aspects of behaviour depend on gender identity, acquiring an irreversible filter is necessary for human development and is to be expected in all societies.

Because there is no "natural" relationship between gender identity and gender roles, the young child who "knows" his or her gender possesses a label with very little content. However, the label is used to organize the new things that are experienced. This is done by observing who (in gender terms) leaves the house to go to work, who is in charge of the labour of the household, and who plays with cars or dolls (or at least whom the child sees playing with these toys in the media). In addition, all children hear verbal exhortations of what boys do/don't do and what girls do/don't do. Children naturally tend to imitate models of behaviour, even if that imitation is not reinforced, and this includes the vast amount of gender-typical behaviour that is performed in front of them. Children swim in an ocean of gendered conduct, and it is terribly difficult to swim against the tide.[21]

Cognitive learning theory provides information on how children learn to navigate the prescriptions of a gendered society, but it takes that society for granted. Moreover, it overlooks how acquisition of gender identity may begin early, but continues throughout the life cycle.

Feminist and Other Challenges to Psychoanalysis and Developmental Psychology

As we have seen, Freud's key insights concerned the construction of gender identity and sexual orientation within the context of the family. This theory of psychosexual development offered a great challenge to biological explanations of gender. Freud stressed the universality of sex differences but argued that such differences were produced—learned by children in interactions with their families and the larger society. He didn't see anything inevitable about becoming either masculine or feminine, nor about becoming heterosexual. Sexual orientation and gender identity were achievements. Obviously, these theories had significant implications for feminism, which has also argued against the inevitability of society's arrangements regarding gender.

Many women have dismissed Freud's arguments because he argued that their development was the result of their coming to terms with the shame that would naturally follow from the realization that they did not have penises. What's more, Freud asserted that female development required the repudiation of the clitoris, the source of sexual agency and pleasure, for the more "mature" sexuality of vaginal receptivity.

No sooner had Freud published his theories than his own women followers challenged the centrality of penis envy in girls' development. One of these followers was Melanie Klein, an Austrian-born psychoanalyst who worked, unlike Freud, largely with children. Klein developed **object-relations theory**, which examines the development of the self in interaction with others. In her studies of female development, she shifted emphasis away from penis envy toward girls' relationships with their mothers. Indeed, she suggested, until the Oedipal crisis, children of both sexes existed in a **primary feminine phase**, identified strongly with their mothers.

German psychoanalyst Karen Horney also contested Freud's views of female development. Though Horney did not identify herself as a feminist, she pointed out that "the actual social subordination of women" provided the context for women's development. As Horney put it:

> It is the male who experiences the penis as a valuable organ and he assumes that women also must feel that way about it. But a woman cannot really imagine the sexual pleasure of a penis—she can only appreciate the social advantages its possessor has.[22]

Perhaps women had "privilege envy" rather than any envy to do with the body.

In fact, Horney (and eventually Klein) argued, perhaps Freud had it backward. Perhaps women did not have penis envy as much as men had **womb envy**. Women, after all, can produce babies. No matter what men do, they cannot create life. Austrian-American psychologist Bruno Bettelheim and several others suggested that the origins of women's subordination stemmed from men's fears of women's reproductive powers; these researchers pointed to male initiation rituals that imitated birth as an indication of ritual appropriation masking significant envy.[23]

Another line of analysis has been to reverse Freud's initial proposition. In other words, psychologists asked *men* how they see themselves as *superior* to women rather than asking *women* why they see themselves as *inferior* to men. Several feminist writers such as Nancy Chodorow, Lillian Rubin, Dorothy Dinnerstein, and Jessica Benjamin have posed that question. Freud argued that the final achievement of gender development was individual autonomy—freedom from dependency on the mother and therefore freedom from the need for group identification. Autonomy was achieved in the boy's renunciation of identification with his mother and subsequent identification with his father. In *The Reproduction of*

Mothering, Chodorow argued that Freud inadvertently revealed the sources of men's sense of superiority and, therefore, of male domination.[24]

What if, she argued, we were to suggest that the capacities for intimacy, connection, and community were healthy adult experiences? That would mean that the stage *before* the Oedipal crisis—when both boys and girls are deeply attached to their mother—was crucial. What happens is that boys lose that capacity for connection and intimacy in the break with the mother and the shift to the father, whereas girls retain that capacity. What's more, such a shift is so traumatic for boys—and yet so necessary in our culture—that they must demonstrate constantly that they have successfully achieved it. Masculinity comes to be defined as the distance between the boy and his mother, between himself and being seen as a "mama's boy" or a sissy. As a result, he must spend a significant amount of time and energy devaluing all things feminine—including girls, his mother, femininity, and, of course, all emotions associated with femininity. Male domination requires it. As Chodorow puts it:

> A boy, in his attempt to gain an elusive masculine identification, often comes to define his masculinity in largely negative terms, as that which is not feminine or involved with women. There is an internal and external aspect to this. Internally, the boy tries to reject his mother and deny his attachment to her and the strong dependency on her that he still feels. He also tries to deny the deep personal identification with her that has developed during his early years. He does this by repressing whatever he takes to be feminine inside himself, and, importantly, by denigrating whatever he considers to be feminine in the outside world.

Consequently, Freud provided a decidedly "feminist" reading of male domination. He just didn't know it, so fixated was he on the break with the mother as the crucial moment in *human* development.[25]

Kohlberg's ideas have also come under critical scrutiny from feminist scholars. Feminist critiques connected not with Kohlberg's theories of gender acquisition discussed above, but with his related work on moral reasoning and the stages of cognitive and moral development. Kohlberg's stages proceeded from very concrete and practical rules to the application of universal ethical principles. Nevertheless, when girls and boys were evaluated, girls seemed "arrested" at the third stage of moral development, a stage that stresses mutual interpersonal expectations and relationships. (Kohlberg argued that this difference followed logically from the more remote and abstracted nature of the boy's relationship with his father, compared with the girl's more interdependent relationship with her mother.)

Carol Gilligan, one of Kohlberg's students, believed the different types of moral reasoning shouldn't be hierarchically ranked. In her path-breaking book *In a Different Voice*, Gilligan suggested that such stages appear only when men's lives are regarded as the norm. In her interviews with Harvard women undergraduates, Gilligan found very different criteria for moral decision-making. She heard another moral voice besides the **ethic of justice**—that abstract, universal, ethical paradigm Kohlberg proposed as the final stage of moral development. There is also an **ethic of care**, stressing intimacy and connectedness, that seems to be followed more often by women.[26]

Gilligan's work unleashed a broad controversy among feminist psychologists that has continued to ripple through the larger culture. Gilligan's work *seemed* to support arguments that women and men are fundamentally, irretrievably, and irreconcilably different. Other work building on that premise followed quickly, including works on cognition and epistemology and popular works that emphasized differences between women's and men's linguistic and mythical spheres.[27]

Ironically, groups that sought to exclude women from various arenas attempted to use Gilligan's arguments to legitimate discrimination. If women and men were so obviously different, their reasoning went, then excluding women from certain positions would not be discrimination, but rather really a way to honour and respect differences. Historically, men who argued against extending rights to women made exactly the same case that Gilligan made. Here, for example, is the nineteenth-century pessimist philosopher Arthur Schopenhauer, from his famous essay *On Women* (1851): "women have more pity, and therefore show more human love and sympathy for the unhappy, than men; while in the matter of justice, honesty, and conscientiousness, they are behind them." Two US military training institutes cited the differences between women and men as justifications for excluding women from their state-supported corps of cadets, and fire departments sought to exclude women from entering their ranks. Given that the legal code requires the indifferent application of the law and adherence to abstract principles, one might have also predicted a move to exclude women from serving as judges.[28]

Gilligan herself was more circumspect, deploring efforts to use her findings "to rationalize oppression." What she found is that "educationally advantaged North American males have a strong tendency to focus on issues of justice when they describe an experience of moral conflict and choice; two-thirds of the men in our studies exhibited a 'justice focus.' One-third of the women we studied also showed a justice focus. But one-third of the women focused on care, in contrast to only one of the 46 men." Moreover, "one-third of both females and males articulate justice and care concerns with roughly equal frequency." The psychological patterns Gilligan observed, she argued, are "not based on any premise of inherent differences between the sexes, but solely on the different nature of their experiences." To extrapolate from these data to claim that *men* and *women* differ on moral voices would be to distort her findings into stereotypes. She writes:

The title of my book was deliberate; it reads, "in a *different* voice," not "in a *woman's* voice." In my introduction, I explain that this voice is not identified by gender but by theme. Noting as an empirical observation the association of this voice with women, I caution the reader that "this association is not absolute, and the contrasts between male and female voices are presented here to highlight a distinction between two modes of thought and to focus a problem of interpretation rather than to represent a generalization about either sex." In tracing development, I "point to the interplay of these voices within each sex and suggest that their convergence marks times of crisis and change." No claims, I state, are made about the origins of these voices or their distribution in a wider population, across cultures or time (p. 2). Thus, the care perspective in my rendition is neither biologically determined nor unique to women. It is, however, a moral perspective different from that currently embedded in psychological theories and measures, and it is a perspective that was defined by listening to both women and men describe their own experience.[29]

Gilligan's articulation of this "different moral perspective" has been enormously influential within North America and around the world, not least in the field of legal studies. In a 1990 lecture at the Osgoode Hall Law School, Madam Justice Bertha Wilson, Canada's first female Supreme Court judge, cited Gilligan's research to argue that perhaps women judges and lawyers might "succeed in infusing the law with an understanding of what it means to be fully human."[30] Still, subsequent research has failed to replicate consistent binary gender differences in ethics; most researchers "report no average differences in the kind of reasoning men and women use in evaluating moral dilemmas, whether it is care-based or justice-based."[31] Moreover, many feminists, including legal scholar Catharine MacKinnon, have condemned the essentialism and danger inherent in Gilligan's work. Despite these criticisms, a generation of feminists has used Gilligan's work as a touchstone. Finally, and most importantly, her insistence that the ethic of care not be considered a shabby second to justice-based reasoning has changed views of moral reasoning, regardless of thin evidence of consistent gender differences.

Feminist psychologists have raised important questions and exposed an androcentric bias in the psychological literature of gender identity and development. With men as the normative standard against which both men and women were evaluated, women always seemed to be coming up short. As Gilligan demonstrated, when psychologists began to shift their framework and to listen closely to the voices of women, new patterns of development emerged. This bias also had consequences in the lives of real people. For example, the *Diagnostic and Statistical Manual of Mental Disorders, Fifth Edition* (DSM-V), published by the American Psychiatric Association, is the diagnostic bible of mental illness professionals. For some time, the DSM-V has listed such mental illnesses as "Premenstrual Dysphoric Disorder" (PMDD), its version of PMS, despite controversy over the existence, nature, causation and prevalence of the disorder. Psychologist Paula Caplan suggested that the DSM-V instead should consider adding a new set of diagnoses, including "Delusional Dominating Personality Disorder" (DDPD) to classify sexist behaviour as symptomatic of mental illness. She also asks us to consider the "John Wayne syndrome" or the "macho personality disorder." Her tongue-in-cheek quiz to identify DDPD (see Figure 3.2, p. 67) goes a long way toward exposing the gender biases in those ostensibly gender-neutral manuals.

Developmental Differences

So what are the real psychological differences between women and men? Developmental psychologists have pointed to some significant differences between males and females that emerge as we grow. Yet even these are mean differences; once again, there is more variation *among* men and *among* women than there is *between* women and men. When psychologists Eleanor Maccoby and Carol Jacklin surveyed more than 1,600 empirical studies from 1966 to 1973, they found only four areas with significant and consistent sex

DO YOU RECOGNIZE THIS MAN?*

A quiz you'll never see in *Cosmo* and *Redbook*

Men who meet at least six of the following criteria may have Delusional Dominating Personality Disorder! Warning: DDPD is pervasive, profound, and a maladaptive organization of the entire personality! (Check as many as apply.)

1. Is he . . .

❏ unable to establish and maintain meaningful interpersonal relationships?

❏ unable to identify and express a range of feelings in himself (typically accompanied by an inablility to identify accurately the feelings of other people)?

❏ unable to respond appropriately and empathically to the feelings and needs of close associates and intimates (often leading to the misinterpretation of signals from others)?

❏ unable to derive pleasure from doing things for others?

2. Does he . . .

❏ use power, silence, withdrawal, and/or avoidance rather than negotiation in the face of interpersonal conflict or diffculty?

❏ believe that women are responsible for the bad things that happen to him, while the good things are due to his own ablilities, achievements, or efforts?

❏ inflate the importance and achievements of himself, males in general, or both?

❏ categorize spheres of functioning and sets of behavior rigidly according to sex (like believing housework is women's work)?

❏ use a gender-based double standard in interpreting or evaluating situations or behavior (considering a man who makes breakfast sometimes to be extraordinarily good, for example, but considering a woman who sometimes neglects to make breakfast deficient)?

❏ feel inordinately threatened by women who fail to disguise their intelligence?

❏ display any of the following delusions:

• the delusion that men are entitled to the services of any woman with whom they are personally associated;

• the delusion that women like to suffer and be orderd around;

• the delusion that physical force is the best method of solving interpersonal problems;

• the delusion that men's sexual and aggressive impulses are uncontrollable;

the delusion that pornography and erotica are identical;

• the delusion that women control most of the world's wealth and/or power but do little of the world's work;

• the delusion that existing inequalities in the distribution of power and wealth are a product of the survival of the fittest and that, therefore, allocation of greater social and economic rewards to the already privileged are merited.

3. Does he have . . .

❏ a pathological need to affirm his social importance by displaying himself in the company of females who meet any three of these criteria:

• are conventionally physically attractive; *or*

• are younger;

• are shorter;

• weigh less;

• appear to be lower on socioeconomic criteria; *or*

• are more submissive . . . than he is?

❏ a distorted approach to sexuality, displaying itself in one or both of these ways:

• a pathological need for flattery about his sexual performance and/or the size of his genitalia;

• an infantile tendency to equate large breasts on women with their sexual attractiveness.

❏ emotionally uncontrolled resistance to reform efforts that are oriented toward gender equity?

The tendency to consider himself a "New Man" neither proves nor disproves that the subject fits within this diagnostic category.

Some women also fit many of these criteria, either because they wish to be as dominant as men or because they feel men should be dominant.

Freely adapted, with permission, from *They Say You're Crazy:*
How the World's Most Powerful Psychiatrists Decide Who's Normal (Addison-Wesley, 1995) by Paula J. Caplan.

Figure 3.2 Hypothetical diagnostic tool for Delusional Dominating Personality Disorder (DDPD) by Paula J. Caplan.

differences: (1) verbal ability (advantage: girls); (2) visuospatial ability (advantage: boys); (3) mathematical ability (boys again!); (4) and levels of aggression (consistently higher among boys). They tested the validity of many other beliefs about sex and personality, and concluded, "there are many popular beliefs about the psychological characteristics of the two sexes that have proved to have little or no basis in fact."[32] More than 30 years later, when psychologist Janet Hyde reviewed 46 meta-analyses—studies that reviewed *all* the available studies on a certain topic—in a sort of "meta-meta-analysis," she found that the size of the gender difference for 78 per cent of all the traits, attitudes, and behaviours measured by these studies was "small or close to zero." Hyde therefore advanced the **gender similarities hypothesis**, claiming, "males and females are similar on most, but not all, psychological variables."[33]

Interestingly, some recent research suggests that men and women may be growing less alike exactly where one would expect them to be *more* alike—in the most modern and apparently gender-egalitarian cultures. Psychologist David P. Schmitt and his research team have analyzed thousands of personality tests taken by men and women in more than 55 countries around the world. They found that higher levels of human development—including long and healthy life, equal access to knowledge and education, and economic wealth—were the main nation-level predictors of larger sex difference in personality. They also state that the variation is almost entirely due to variation in *male* personality traits. That is, men are more stereotypically "masculine" in gender-egalitarian cultures. Based on this finding, they propose that "natural" or inherent differences in personality are now free to emerge: that men are free to be more competitive and risk taking, for example.[34] However, the assumption that modern post-industrial societies are a realm of gender freedom is an odd one; and even if we accept that, a much more logical interpretation of these findings is at hand. Might the increase in gender egalitarianism itself be at the root of this growing divergence? As women's and men's domains are increasingly similar, as many commentators have noted, men seek to distinguish themselves more effectively from women. (The phenomenon of masculinity threat might be employed here.) Whatever the case, it is clear that the differences between men and women are more complex than once thought.

Perhaps it is not simply internalized beliefs or some sort of innate tendencies that keep us in place as men or women, but also our interpersonal and social environments. Because there is considerable variation in what men and women actually do, maintaining gender-role differences may require the weight of social organization and constant reinforcement. Psychoanalysis provided a theory of how gender identity is acquired in early childhood. Theories of sex roles and androgyny help us move beyond strictly psychological analyses of gender. Cognitive development theory explained the mechanisms by which children acquire stable understandings of gender and the processes of self-socialization that accompany gender constancy. Feminist psychoanalysts provide a much-needed corrective to the androcentric theories of Freud and push us to consider the effects of current gender arrangements on gendered development. However, the inability of all of these theories to fully account for difference, power, relationality, cultural variation, and, above all, the institutional dimension of gender means that we will need to build other elements into the discussion. We turn next to anthropological discussions of gender.

Summary

Freud's theories of psychosocial development provide a bridge between anatomical explanations of gender and theories of social construction. Freud believed that, for boys, the Oedipal crisis required rejection of the mother and identification with the father; for girls, the crisis involves the need to identify with the mother and abandon any thought of possessing her. Freud theorized that girls necessarily experienced "penis envy" in this stage. The key insights of Freudian theory, for our purposes, are that Freud (a) dislocates gender and sexuality from biological inevitability; (b) links the acquisition of gender identity and sexual orientation; and (c) reinstates traditional gender stereotypes as the hallmark of healthy gender development. Still, Freud, unlike many of his contemporaries, did not view homosexuality as a moral failing or psychological disorder. Freud's theories have nonetheless been subject to severe criticism, not least because of the small clinical sample on which he based his cases and, perhaps most damningly, his retreat from evidence that his women patients were actually survivors of sexual traumas including incest. Despite these and many other criticisms, Freud's theories have had great impact.

Sex-role theory took part of its impetus from Terman and Miles's studies of masculinity and femininity, published in 1936 as *Sex and Personality*, which relied upon the M-F test. By the 1950s, social psychologists were moving beyond the test to question the social requirements for male and female sex roles. The authors of *The Authoritarian Personality* theorized that males with feminine internal psychological identification overcompensated, consequently yielding highest scores on measures of racism, hypermasculinity, and authoritarianism. Talcott Parsons and other sociologists examined the social utility of sex roles in production and reproduction, highlighting the unintended impact of gender roles on society and social organization. Sandra Bem and other social psychologists challenged the rigidity of sex-role theory in the 1970s, further analyzing the "health" of dichotomized gender roles. Bem found that individuals varied greatly in the rigidity of their gender schemas and that the best-adjusted people were androgynous and did not polarize gender. Though androgyny was extensively critiqued, gender schema theory remains an intriguing explanation of how we learn gender. Joseph Pleck continued a social focus on gender identity and its social function. By testing and falsifying propositions identified with the male sex role, Pleck argued that the role itself was the problem, resulting in male sex role strain (MSRS). Therefore, sex roles were not necessarily adaptive or healthy and might be inherently contradictory, inconsistent, and even psychologically damaging. Sex-role theory consequently developed significantly, but its problems remained. It (a) remains unable to account for varieties of masculinities and femininities and, more broadly, within-sex differences; (b) obscures the power difference between traditional men's "roles" and women's "roles" and cannot account for male domination; and (c) locates gendering in individuals, without giving enough attention to institutions.

Cognitive development theory, developed by Lawrence Kohlberg, argues that gender identity is developed in childhood, though somewhat more slowly than Freudian theory would have it. Kohlberg argued that children learn gender roles and identities according to age-related modes of reasoning. Children proceed by learning their own maleness or femaleness (by age two) and then interpreting gendered information from the outside world. At this age children may have both a fluid and an over-rigid understanding of gender, believing that they might change genders if they performed an action "appropriate" to the opposite sex. By age six, children have acquired a stable and constant sense of gender and are capable of socializing themselves by analyzing behaviour based on its appropriateness for males or females. Cognitive development theory offers insights into how children learn gender, but little information on how gender roles are developed in the first place.

Feminists and other critics have identified significant problems with Freudian and later theories of gender development. Freud's theory of penis envy in particular has been criticized, including by Freud's own women followers, psychoanalysts Melanie Klein and Karen Horney. They argued that girls were probably less envious of male anatomy than conscious of the power difference between men and women. Some advanced the theory of "womb envy," while a later generation used Freud's theories to analyze the phenomenon of male dominance. Kohlberg's stages of moral reasoning have also been criticized, most significantly by Carol Gilligan, who introduced the idea that women tended to reason from an "ethic of care," in contrast to men's more prevalent "ethic of justice." Gilligan's theories, though criticized, continue to be influential in a number of fields.

Finally, the real psychological differences between men and women may be more elusive than once thought. Maccoby and Jacklin's 1974 meta-analysis found only four areas of consistent difference; more recently, Janet Hyde's study also found few significant differences. She therefore advanced the "gender similarity hypothesis," arguing that there are few actual psychological differences between the sexes. Interestingly, however, psychological differences may be emerging in the most gender-egalitarian societies, possibly as a reaction to gender integration or gender equality itself. Though all of the theories examined have contributed to our understanding of gender differences in psychology, they fully fail to account for power, relationality, and institutional dimensions of gender. We therefore turn to sociological and anthropological explanations of gender in Chapter 4.

Questions for Critical Thinking

1. Some people believe that Freud's theories have been totally discredited and serve no further purpose. Would you agree? Which, if any, of his theories do you see as having merit? How have Freud's ideas remained active in popular culture and belief?

2. Why do you think sex-role theory was so much more concerned with boys' successful acquisition of "appropriate" gender identity? What about girls?

3. Looking at the M-F test and its questions decades after the questions were created, what do you think the text shows about the nature of gender identity? Are the features the test codes as "masculine" or "feminine" still seen as such today? How might culture, class, and ethnicity influence one's results on the test?

4. Have you ever seen "overcompensation" in action? Do you agree with Bem's conclusion that the healthiest individuals are least likely to be hypermasculine or hyperfeminine? If so, why do you think this might be so?

5. Do you find cognitive development theory more convincing than Freud's theories of gender development? Where do the theories disagree or complement one another?

6. How would a "care" perspective and a "justice" approach evaluate a particular crime

(choose any one you like). What are the strengths and weaknesses of these modes of moral reasoning? Can you think of Canadian issues that would benefit from analysis using an "ethic of care"?

7. Why do you think men's and women's personalities are diverging in wealthy modern societies? Why are men in these societies becoming more competitive, for example?

Key Terms

androgyny

castration anxiety

cognitive development theory

cult of compulsive masculinity

ego

Electra complex

ethic of care

ethic of justice

expressive roles

external world

gender constancy

gender schemas

gender schema theory

gender similarities hypothesis

id

instrumental roles

male sex role identity (MSRI)

male sex role strain (MSRS)

M-F test

object-relations theory

Oedipal crisis

penis envy

primary feminine phase

psychoanalysis

sex-role theory

social psychologists

super-ego

womb envy

Spanning the World
Culture Constructs Gender Difference

Human nature is potentially aggressive and destructive and potentially orderly and constructive.

—Attributed to Margaret Mead

Biological models assume that sex determines gender: that innate biological differences lead to behavioural differences, which in turn lead to social arrangements. Psychological models of gender identity suggest that gender identity is the result of childhood development, which proceeds in—more or less—universal ways.

The evidence, however, suggests otherwise. How do we account for the dramatic differences in the definitions of masculinity and femininity around the world? Why do some societies have much wider ranges of gender inequality than others do? On these questions, the biological record is mute and psychological theory often less than convincing.

Anthropological research on cultural variations in the development of gender definitions arose, in part, in response to casual biological determinism. The more we found out about other cultures, the more we learned about the diversity of cultural constructions of gender. Yet some themes do remain constant. Virtually all societies manifest a gendered division of labour, differences between women and men, and some form of male domination. So anthropologists have also tried to explore the link between the near-universals of gender difference and gender inequality

The Variations in Gender Definitions

When anthropologists began to explore the cultural landscape, one of the first things they found was far more variability in the definitions of masculinity and femininity than any biologist would have predicted. Men whose anatomy was identical seemed to exhibit dramatically different levels of aggression, violence, and, especially, aggression toward women. Women with similar brains, hormones, and ostensibly similar evolutionary imperatives have widely varying experiences of passivity, PMS, and spatial coordination.

One of the most celebrated anthropologists to explore these differences was Margaret Mead, who conducted research in the South Seas (Samoa, Polynesia, and Indonesia). Mead was clear that sex differences are "not something deeply biological," but rather are learned. Here's how she put it:

> I have suggested that certain human traits have been socially specialized as the appropriate attitudes and behaviour of only one sex, while other human traits have been specialized for the opposite sex. This social specialization is then rationalized into a theory that the socially decreed behaviour is natural for one sex and unnatural for the other, and that the deviant is a deviant because of glandular defect, or developmental accident.[1]

In *Sex and Temperament in Three Primitive Societies* (1935), Mead explored the differences in those definitions, whereas in several other books, such as *Male and Female* (1949) and *Coming of Age in Samoa* (1928), she explored the processes by which males and females become the men and women their cultures prescribe. No matter what she seemed to be writing about, though, Mead always had one eye trained on the United States. In generating implicit comparisons between her own and other cultures, Mead challenged those Americans who believed that their culture's mores must be right and could not be changed. Her works, read throughout the world, provided ample fodder for a critique of modern industrialized societies and rigid traditional gender norms.[2]

In *Sex and Temperament*, Mead directly took on the claims of biological inevitability. By examining three very different cultures in New Guinea, she hoped to show the enormous cultural variation possible in definitions of masculinity and femininity. The first two cultures exhibited remarkable similarities between women and men. Women and men were not "opposite" sexes. For example, all members of the Arapesh culture appeared gentle, passive, and emotionally warm. Males and females were equally "happy, trustful, confident," and individualism was relatively absent. Men and women shared child rearing; both were "maternal," and both discouraged aggressiveness among boys and girls. Although female infanticide and **polygamy** were not unknown, marriage was "even and contented." Indeed, Mead pronounced the political arrangements "utopian." Here's how she summed up Arapesh life:

> quiet and uneventful co-operation, singing in the cold dawn, and singing and laughter in the evening, men who sit happily playing to themselves on hand-drums, women holding suckling children to their breasts, young girls walking easily down the centre of the village, with the walk of those who are cherished by all about them.[3]

By contrast, Mead describes the Mundugamor, a tribe of headhunters and cannibals, who also viewed women and men as similar but expected both sexes to be equally aggressive and violent. Women showed little "maternal instinct"; they detested pregnancy and nursing and could hardly wait to return to the serious business of work and war. "Mundugamor women actively dislike child-bearing, and they dislike children," Mead writes. "Children are carried in harsh opaque baskets that scratch their skins, later, high on their mother's shoulders, well away from the breast." Among the Mundugamor, there was a violent rivalry between fathers and sons (there was more infanticide of boys than of girls), and all people experienced fear that they were being wronged by others. Quite wealthy (partly because of their methods of population control), the Mundugamor were, as Mead concludes, "violent, competitive, aggressively sexual, jealous, ready to see and avenge insult, delighting in display, in action, in fighting."[4]

Here, then, were two tribes who saw gender differences as virtually non-existent. The third culture Mead described was the Tchambuli, where, as in the United States, women and men were seen as extremely different. This was a culture in which **polygyny** was accepted. Here, one sex was composed primarily of nurturing and gossipy consumers who spent their days dressing up and going shopping. They wore curls and lots of jewelry, and Mead describes them as "charming, graceful, [and] coquettish." These, incidentally, were the men. The women were dominant, energetic, economic providers. Completely unadorned, they were efficient, business-like, controlled all the commerce and diplomacy of the culture, and were the initiators of sexual relations. Mead writes that "[w]hat the women will think, what the women will say, what the women will do lies at the back of each man's mind as he weaves his tenuous and uncertain web of insubstantial relations with other men." By contrast, "the women are a solid group, confused by no rivalries, brisk, patronizing, and jovial."[5]

What Mead found, then, were two cultures in which women and men were seen as similar to each other and one culture in which women and men were seen as extremely different from each other—but exactly the opposite of the model familiar to us. Each culture, of course, believed that women and men were the way they were because their biological sex *determined* their personality. None of them believed that women and men were the outcome of economic scarcity, military success, or cultural arrangements.

Mead's findings were attacked almost immediately, first by her ex-husband Reo Fortune, who had shared her fieldwork, and then later by New Zealand anthropologist Derek Freeman. Though Freeman's charges have been convincingly debunked, Mead's popular reputation has suffered significantly. She has been criticized for **cultural determinism**, for allowing herself to be duped by her informants and for misrepresentation of the cultures she studied.[6] The first of these critiques may be valid, but Mead's findings remain valuable. She made outstanding contributions to the field of anthropology, to feminist theories of gender construction. Her ideas, and the question of cultural variability, remain important topics of discussion.

Mead urged her readers to "admit men and women are capable of being molded to a single pattern as easily as a diverse one."[7] While she demonstrated that women and men are *capable* of similar or different temperaments, she did not adequately explain *why* women and men turn out to be different or the same. These questions remain unanswered: What are the determinants of women's and men's experiences? Why should male domination be nearly universal? These issues have been taken up by other anthropologists.

The Centrality of the Gender Division of Labour

In almost every society, labour is divided by gender (as well as age). Certain tasks are reserved for women, others for men. How do we explain this gender division of labour, if not by some biologically based imperatives?

One school of thought, **functionalism**, maintains that a sex-based division of labour arose as groups became larger and their activities more complex. Because human activities such as hunting and gathering required skills that took years to acquire, it was beneficial for society to apportion these activities to different groups, in this case, males and females.[8] Functionalists differ as to whether this division of labour had any *moral* component, whether the work of one sex was more highly valued than the work of the other. Neverthe-less, they agree that the sex-based division of labour was functionally necessary.

The sex-based division of labour is found nearly everywhere, and it may have a long history. Apparent evidence of this division of labour has been found among Neanderthals, for example. While hunter-gatherer societies—at least modern ones—divide labour based on gender, many scholars have focused on the adoption of plough-based agriculture as the origin of the most enduring and rigid gender systems. According to these scholars, using the plough required maximum upper-body strength and was incompatible with child care; therefore, it was allocated to men, with knock-on effects that are still with us.[9]

Still, there is scholarly disagreement on when and why—and whether—various groups adopted gendered divisions of labour. Studying the bones of hominids of the past can test hypotheses about labour divisions by showing us whether male and female individuals focused on particular tasks. Bone stress and lateralization (the development of one side of the body, as might be expected with activities such as spear throwing) indicate whether individuals specialized in tasks. Studies have found great variation from site to site, rais-ing more questions about the division of labour than the studies can answer. Assessing the evidence for gendered division of labour in early agricultural societies, Diane Bolger argues, "the notion of a gendered division of labour . . . seems increasingly untenable and should not be assumed."[10]

Increasingly, the sex-based division of labour is being investigated as a phenomenon that arose in different times and places for different reasons, and not a necessary part of being human. "The sexual division of labour as we know it today probably developed quite recently in human evolution," writes anthropologist Adrienne Zihlman.[11]

Gender-based divisions of labour, though based in history, come to be conflated with biology: "Man can't give birth, woman can't fish," in the words of one Bangladeshi fisher-man.[12] However, precisely because the sex-based division of labour has a history, it is not biologically inevitable. Today, such a division of labour is functionally anachronistic—and its supposed biological bases are eroded. In the place of such foundations, though, lie social customs and traditions that continue to dictate what is appropriate for one sex and not the other. The gender-based division of labour has become a part of our culture, not a part of our physical constitutions.

If a sex-based division of labour has outlived its social usefulness or its physical im-peratives, it must be held in place by something else: the power of one sex over the other. Where did that power come from? How has it developed? How does it vary from culture to culture? What factors exaggerate it; what factors diminish it? These are among the ques-tions that anthropologists have endeavoured to answer.

Theories of Gender Differentiation and Male Domination

Several theorists have tried to explain the sexual division of labour and gender inequal-ity by reference to societies' organizing principles and structures. They've pointed to the impact of private property, the demands of war, and the importance of male bonding as possible explanations.

Private Property and the Materialism of Male Domination

In the late nineteenth century, Friedrich Engels applied ideas that he developed with his collaborator, Karl Marx, and assigned to private property the role of central agent in determining the division of labour by sex. In *The Origins of the Family, Private Property and the State*, Engels suggested that the three chief institutions of modern Western society—a capitalist economy, the nation-state, and the nuclear family—emerged at roughly the same historical moment—and all as a result of the development of private property. (Prior to that, Engels asserts, families were organized on a communal basis, with group marriage, male-female equality, and a sexual division of labour without any moral or political rewards going to males or females.) Private property created the need for clear lines of inheritance.

Out of this need to transmit inheritance across generations of men, the traditional nuclear family emerged, with monogamous marriage and the sexual control of women by men. (Men now became concerned with ensuring that their heirs were legitimately *theirs*.) If inheritance were to be stable, these new patriarchs needed to have clear, binding laws, vigorously enforced, that would enable them to pass their legacies on to their sons without interference from others. This required a centralized political apparatus (the nation-state) to exercise sovereignty over local and regional powers that might challenge them.[13]

Some contemporary anthropologists continue in this tradition. American anthropologist Eleanor Leacock, for example, argues that prior to the rise of private property and social classes, women and men were regarded as autonomous individuals, who held different positions that were held in relatively equal esteem. "Their status was not as literal 'equals' of men . . . but as what they were—female persons, with their own rights, duties and responsibilities, which were complementary to and in no way secondary to those of men." In her ethnographic work with Innu people on the Labrador Peninsula, Leacock shows the dramatic transformation of women's former autonomy by the introduction of the fur trade. The introduction of a commercial economy turned powerful women into homebound wives. Here again, economic shifts resulted in gender inequality.[14]

Karen Sacks (now Karen Brodkin) examined four African cultures and found that the introduction of the market economy shifted egalitarian roles toward male dominance. As long as production focused on the community, men and women were relatively equal. However, the more involved a tribe became in a market exchange economy, the higher the level of gender inequality, and the lower the position of women. Conversely, when women and men shared access to the productive elements of the society, the result was a higher level of sexual egalitarianism.[15]

Warfare, Bonding, and Inequality

Another school of anthropological thought traces the origins of male domination to the imperatives of warfare in primitive society. How does a culture create warriors who are fierce and strong? Anthropologist Marvin Harris has suggested two possibilities. The culture can provide different rewards for the warriors, based on their dexterity or skill. However, this would limit the solidarity of the fighting force and sow seeds of dissent and enmity among the soldiers. More effective would be to reward virtually all men with the services of women, excluding only the most inadequate or cowardly men. Warrior societies tend to practise female infanticide, Harris observes, ensuring that the population of females remains significantly lower than that of males (consequently the males compete for the women). Warrior societies also tend to exclude women from the fighting force, because their presence would reduce the motivation of the soldiers and upset the sexual hierarchy. In this way, warfare leads to female subordination as well as **patrilineality**, because the culture will need a resident core of fathers and sons to carry out its military tasks. Males come to control the society's resources and develop patriarchal religion as an ideology that legitimates their domination over women.[16]

Two other groups of scholars use different variables to explain the origins of society and male domination. **Descent theorists**, like Lionel Tiger and Robin Fox, stress the fixed nature of the mother-child bond. Men, in contrast, lack the tie that mothers have with their children, because for most of human history they could never be certain of biological paternity. How, then, can they achieve that connection to the next generation, the connection to history and society? In all societies, men must somehow be bound socially to the next generation, to which they are not connected in inextricable biological ways. Male solidarity, or what Tiger called "male bonding," and monogamy are the direct results of men's needs to connect with social life. Men form bonds with other men in the hunting group, therefore forming the basis for larger social groupings. Because male bonding is at the heart of the social contract, prestige, resources, and women are allocated to dominant males.[17]

Alliance theorists like Claude Levi-Strauss are less concerned with the need to connect males to the next generation than they are with the ways that relationships among men come to organize social life. Levi-Strauss argues that men turn women into sex objects whose exchange (as wives) cements the alliances among men.[18] Both descent and alliance theorists treat these themes as invariant and natural, rather than as the outcomes of historical relationships that vary dramatically not only over time but also across cultures. Primatological studies seem to confirm some of these arguments; for example, one study found that male chimps hunted and shared meat strategically in order to cement male alliances.[19]

Property, warfare, and male bonding may all play a role in the origins of gender inequality, but anthropologists have identified many other determinants, to which we now turn.

Other Determinants of Gender Inequality

As we have seen, virtually every society claims some differentiation between women and men, and virtually every society exhibits patterns of gendered inequality and male domination. Yet the variety within these universals is still astounding.

What, then, are the factors that seem to determine gender inequality in society? Under what conditions is women's status improved, and under what conditions is it minimized? One of the key determinants of women's status has been the *division of labour around child care*. Women's role in reproduction has historically limited their social and economic participation. Although no society assigns all child care functions to men, the more that men participate in child care and the freer women are from child-rearing responsibility, the higher women's status tends to be. There are many ways to free women from sole responsibility. In non-Western societies, several customs evolved, including employing child nurses who care for several children at once, sharing child care with husbands or with neighbours, and assigning the role of child care to elders whose economic activity has been curtailed by age.[20]

Relationships between children and their parents have also been seen as keys to gender inequality. Sociologist Scott Coltrane found that the closer the relationship between father and son, the higher the status of women is likely to be. Coltrane found that in cultures where fathers are relatively uninvolved, boys define themselves *in opposition* to their mothers and other women and therefore are prone to exhibit traits of **hypermasculinity**, to fear and denigrate women as a way to display masculinity. The more mothers and fathers share child rearing, the less men belittle women. (Elizabeth Zelman, whose work on ritual is discussed below, found the same thing.) Margaret Mead also emphasized the centrality of fatherhood. Most cultures take women's role in child rearing as a given, whereas men must learn to become nurturers. There is much at stake, but nothing is inevitable: "every known human society rests firmly on the learned nurturing behaviour of men."[21]

That men must learn to be nurturers raises the question of masculinity in general. What it means to be a man varies enormously from one culture to another, and these definitions have a great deal to do with how much time and energy fathers spend with their children. Such issues are not simply incidental for women's lives either; it turns out that the more time men spend with their children, the less gender inequality is present in that culture. Conversely, the freer women are from child care—the more that child care is parcelled out elsewhere and the more that women control their fertility—the higher will be their status. Coltrane also found that women's status depends upon their control over property, especially after marriage. A woman's status is invariably higher when she retains control over her property after marriage. These two variables—the *father's involvement in child rearing* and *women's control of property after marriage*—emerge as among the central determinants of women's status and gender inequality.

Also important is *gender segregation*. In one of the most wide-ranging comparative studies of women's status, Peggy Reeves Sanday found that **sex segregation** was highly associated with women's lower status, as if separation were "necessary for the development of sexual inequality and male dominance." (By contrast, a study of a sexually egalitarian society found no ideology of the desirability of sex segregation.) In addition, in cultures that viewed the environment as relatively friendly, women's status was significantly higher; cultures that saw the environment as hostile were more likely to develop patterns of male domination.[22]

Finally, Sanday found that women had the highest levels of equality, and accordingly the least frequency of rape, in societies with *equal contribution to food supplies*. When women contributed equally, men tended also to be more involved in child care. Women's status tended to be lower when they contributed either very little or a great deal to subsistence, and more equal when their contribution was about equal.

Rituals of Gender

One of the ways anthropologists have explored the cultural construction of gender is by examining specific gender rituals. Because questions of reproduction and child rearing loom so large in the determination of gender inequality, it makes sense that many such rituals are concerned with reproduction. Elizabeth Crouch Zelman proposed, in a 1977 cross-cultural study, "the ritual associated with the female reproductive cycle, in particular, is a mechanism for developing and maintaining sex roles."

Zelman argues that rituals around female reproduction are of two kinds: pollution-avoidance, which segregates women and views them as dangerous and polluting to men; and male ritual, which men perform in tandem with (or in imitation of) the female reproductive cycle. **Couvade**, for example, is a term describing a number of rituals that men in some cultures observe when their wives are having babies. Men may restrict their movement, confine themselves as if they were giving birth, or even mimic pregnancy. Through her analysis, Zelman found that pollution-avoidance rituals tended to be associated with more complex societies in which women performed most child care, had little access to resources or institutional power, and had low status. Male rituals relating to female reproduction were found in more simple societies in which women contributed to subsistence and men to child care, and where resources and prestige were more evenly shared between men and women. The rituals didn't *cause* these other societal features, of course; but, Zelman asserts, such rituals instruct on proper roles and reinforce either gender difference or gender similarity.[23]

Jeffrey and Karen Paige studied similar rituals in their book *The Politics of Reproductive Ritual*. Paige and Paige offer a materialist interpretation of these rituals, locating the origins of male circumcision, couvade, and **purdah** in the culture's relationship with its immediate material environment. Paige and Paige see couvade differently from Zelman. They argue that couvade is significant in cultures where there are no legal mechanisms to keep the couple together or to assure paternity. Couvade is a way for men fully to claim paternity, to know that the baby is theirs. It is also a vehicle by which the men can control women's sexuality by appropriating control over paternity.[24]

Paige and Paige also examine the politics of purdah. Ostensibly, this requirement is to protect women's chastity and men's honour; however, it institutes control of women's sexuality and enshrines gender difference. Women are both vulnerable and tempting, while men are both weak and sexually aggressive. In order to protect women from *men's* sexual rapaciousness, men must control women and take away the source of the temptation.[25]

Sociologist and geographer Daphne Spain argues that the same cultures in which men developed the most elaborate sex-segregated rituals were those cultures in which women's status was lowest. Spain mapped a number of cultures spatially and found that the greater the distance the men's hut was from the centre of the village, the more time the men spent at their hut. As well, the more culturally important the men's rituals were the lower women's status. "Societies with men's huts are those in which women have the least power," she writes.[26]

Similarly, anthropologist Thomas Gregor found that spatial and **ritual segregation** between males and females are associated with gender inequality. The Mehinaku of central Brazil, for example, have well-institutionalized men's huts where the tribal secrets are kept and ritual instruments are played and stored. Women are prohibited from entering. As one tribesman told Gregor, "[t]his house is only for men. Women may not see anything in here. If a woman comes in, then all the men take her into the woods and she is raped."[27]

Segregation may arise from pollution-avoidance, or may be spatial; another form of segregation is restriction from religious rituals. In Virginia Fink's study of a representative sample of 93 societies, 50 societies restricted women's participation in religious rituals, which were dominated by men. The strongest predictor of restrictions on women was male inheritance of property, but other predictors were the sex of God and/or mythical ancestors, importance of agriculture, and male control of resources. Religious restrictions cemented a gender inequality that is also entrenched in social relations.[28]

Religions, of course, are not simply statements of gender domination. In Christianity, to take one example, beliefs in both Eve's culpability for the fall and the divinely ordained nature of male domination have coexisted with an assertion of spiritual gender equality (and even rejection of a purely masculine God). Similar ambiguities are found in most religions, as well. Nevertheless, religious ritual and restriction have been strong bulwarks of gender difference and gender inequality. In a recent article, Stephanie Seguino analyzed data from the World Values Survey and found that religiosity of any kind "is consistently negatively correlated with gender attitudes and outcomes."[29] As fundamentalist religious adherence grows, so too may a fervent belief in immutable gender difference and inequality.

Rituals of gender difference sometimes include bodily alteration. **Circumcision**, the excision of the foreskin of a boy's penis, is a ritual incorporating a male into his society. The age at which this ritual is performed varies; one survey of twenty-one cultures that practise circumcision found that four perform it in infancy, ten when the boy is about ten years old (before puberty), six perform it at puberty, and one waits until late adolescence.

Why would so many cultures determine that membership in the world of adult men requires genital alteration? Theories, of course, abound. In the Jewish Bible, circumcision is a visible sign of the bond between God and man, a symbol of man's obedience to God's law. (In Genesis 17:10–11, 14, God commands Abraham to circumcise Isaac as a covenant.) However, circumcision also seems to have been seen as a way of acquiring a trophy. In I Samuel 18:25, King Saul demands that David slay 100 Philistines and bring back their foreskins as a bride-price. David brings back 200.

In other cultures, ethnographers suggest, circumcision creates a visible scar that binds men to one another and serves as a rite of passage to adult masculinity. Whiting, Kluckhohn, and Anthony argue that it symbolically serves to sever a boy's emotional ties to his mother and therefore to ensure appropriate masculine identification. Other writers point out that cultures that emphasize circumcision of young males tend to be those where both gender differentiation and gender inequality are greatest. Circumcision simultaneously cements the bonds between father (and his generation) and son (and his generation), links the males together, and excludes women, visibly and demonstrably. Circumcision, then, tends to be associated with male domination, as do other forms of male genital mutilation. In a very few cultures, for example, the penis is ritually bled by cutting. Such cultures still believe in bleeding as a cure for illness—in this case, illness brought about by sexual contact with women, who are believed to be impure and infectious. We know also of four cultures that practise hemicastration, the removal of one testicle. In one culture, people believe it prevents the birth of twins.[30]

Female "circumcision," more generally known as **female genital mutilation (FGM)/ female genital cutting (FGC)**, is also practised in many cultures, most of them in Africa. The World Health Organization (WHO) recognizes four "types" of FGC/FGM, from the removal of the hood of the clitoris (analogous to male circumcision) all the way to **infibulation,** which involves the removal of most of the external genital tissue and the sewing together of the remaining tissue with only a very small opening left to allow for urination. FGC/FGM is almost always performed by adult women, though almost one-fifth of procedures are now performed by medical personnel. The goals of such genital alteration range from improving the appearance and "cleanness" of the genitals to preventing female promiscuity. In some cultures, the goal is also to produce a recognizably "female" body, because the clitoris is viewed as a masculine body part. It is estimated by UNICEF that more than 200 million girls and women have undergone some form of FGC/FGM in 30 countries in which the ritual is practised, with half of these women living in just 3 countries (Egypt, Ethiopia, and Indonesia). The highest prevalence is in Somalia, where more than 98 per cent of women are cut. Every year, another 3 million girls are at risk of having the procedure performed. Nor is the practice confined to high-prevalence countries: in a six-month period in 2015, more than 2,000 cases of female genital cutting were reported to authorities in the UK. However, the prevalence of the practice is declining in some countries.[31]

Interestingly, both cultures that circumcise men and those that practise FGC/FGM tend to be those where men's status is highest. The purpose of the ritual reveals some of this difference. For men, the ritual is a marking that simultaneously shows that all men are

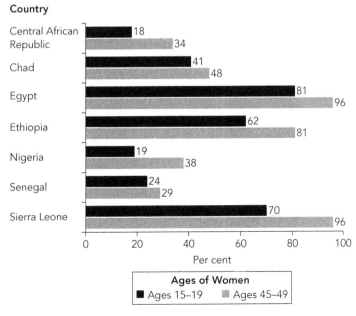

Figure 4.1 Declining prevalence of FGC/FGM among younger women.

Source: Charlotte Feldman-Jacobs and Donna Clifton, *Female Genital Mutilation/Cutting: Data and Trends Update 2014* (Washington, D.C.: Population Reference Bureau, 2014). Copyright © 2016, Population Reference Bureau. All rights reserved.

biologically *and culturally* alike—and different from women. Accordingly, it can be seen as reinforcing male dominance.

However, this cannot explain the prevalence of male circumcision in twentieth-century North America. Historically, male circumcision was viewed as medically beneficial, because it reduced the possibilities of penile and urinary tract infection by removing the foreskin, a place where bacteria could congregate. Circumcision was also viewed as preventing excessive masturbation. Consequently, in twentieth-century North America, infant circumcision became a routine part of hospital birth. Until 35 years ago, most boy babies in Canada were routinely circumcised.

Today, more than 90 per cent of newborn male Canadians are left intact, and only about 31 per cent of males under 20 are circumcised.[32] Among advanced industrial societies, only the United States continues widespread routine infant circumcision. In the US, the practice was in decline but has recently increased, in part because of studies suggesting health benefits such as a reduced risk of (rare) penile cancer, sexually transmitted diseases, and urinary tract infections. Meanwhile, one Saskatoon study found that circumcision status of a baby's father was a very important predictor of parents' desire to circumcise their baby.[33]

Female "Circumcision"

The traditions and practices of FGC/FGM vary greatly from place to place; experiencing the practice as a young woman, for example, may be quite different from experiencing it in childhood. Here is a description of FGC/FGM from one who underwent it as a child, a Sudanese woman working as a teacher in the Middle East at the time of her testimonial:

I will never forget the day of my circumcision, which took place 40 years ago. I was six years old. One morning during my school summer vacation, my mother told me that I had to go with her to her sister's house and then to visit a sick relative in Halfayat El Mulook [in the northern part of Khartoum, Sudan]. We did go to my aunt's house, and from there all of us went straight to [a] red brick house [I had never seen].

While my mother was knocking, I tried to pronounce the name that was on the door. Soon enough I realized that it was Haija Alamin's house. She was the midwife [who performed circumcisions on girls in my neighbourhood]. I was petrified and tried to break loose. But I was captured and subdued by my mother and two aunts. They began to tell me that the midwife was going to purify me.

The midwife was the cruellest person I had seen. . . . [She] ordered her young maid to go buy razors from the Yemeni grocer next door. I still remember her when she came back with the razors, which were enveloped in purple wrappings with a crocodile drawing on it.

> The women ordered me to lie down on a bed [made of ropes] that had a little hole in the middle. They held me tight while the midwife started to cut my flesh without anesthetics. I screamed till I lost my voice. The midwife was saying to me "Do you want me to be taken into police custody?" After the job was done I could not eat, drink, or even pass urine for three days. I remember one of my uncles who discovered what they did to me threatened to press charges against his sisters. They were afraid of him and they decided to bring me back to the midwife. In her sternest voice she ordered me to squat on the floor and urinate. It seemed like the most difficult thing to do at that point, but I did it. I urinated for a long time and was shivering with pain.
>
> It took a very long time [before] I was back to normal. I understand the motives of my mother, that she wanted me to be clean, but I suffered a lot.[34]

For women, genital alteration has never been justified by medical benefits; indeed FGC/FGM is medically dangerous, both at the time of the cutting, when many girls succumb to infections, and, in many cases, during childbirth. Moreover, FGC/FGM is designed to curtail sexual pleasure and directly impedes adequate sexual functioning. FGC/FGM seems to be associated with men's control over women's sexuality.

Currently, political campaigns are being waged to prohibit FGC/FGM as a violation of women's human rights. However, some of these efforts—and much of the discussion of FGC/FGM—have been marred by neglect of the cultural context of the practice. After all, as anthropologist Bettina Shell-Duncan states, "First and foremost, what we need to understand is that people are doing this because they want to assure the future for their girls, like every parent everywhere."[35] Campaigns that urge individuals to "say no" cannot succeed in a context where FGC/FGM ensures girls' social acceptance and marriageability. "We need to tread carefully since female genital mutilation is deeply rooted into the culture," says Masai girls' advocate, Priscilla Nangurai, former headmistress of a church-sponsored girl's boarding school. "We can end it through education, advocacy, and religion."[36]

There have been many criticisms of anti-FGC/FGM campaigns driven by Western organizations and movements. Critics suggest that anti-FGC/FGM rhetoric has positioned Africans in particular as "barbaric" while ignoring issues such as cosmetic surgery and infant male circumcision in Western culture; they have also pointed to the existence of acceptable forms of FGC that are ignored by Western commentators.[37] (So far, there are no widespread political campaigns against male circumcision, though some individuals have recently begun to rethink the ritual as a form of genital mutilation, and a few men are even undergoing a surgical procedure designed to replace the lost foreskin.)[38] Others counter that the right to control one's own body is a fundamental human right and that cultures that practise such behaviours must conform to universal standards. To a great degree, these debates have diminished as African women take leadership roles in the elimination of FGC/FGM.

One particularly influential group is known as the Tostan movement. In 1991, the NGO Tostan ("breakthrough" in Wolof) was formed to spark basic education and community

Beauty Contests

Gender inequality means that women and men have different access to the sorts of resources that would enable them to succeed in the dating and marriage market. Men have greater access to money and material goods; in the absence of such resources, women most often use their physical attractiveness as a currency.

Wodaabe beauty contest.

In the 1970s, an activist used to stage male beauty contests in which men would parade around in bathing suits and formal attire to be judged by a panel of female judges, so they could experience objectification first-hand. One culture, however, does this routinely. Among the Wodaabe of Mali, each year the men dress up in ceremonial garb, paint their faces and lips, and parade in front of the women, who choose which man they will sleep with. As documented in Werner Herzog's fascinating film *Herdsmen of the Sun*, the Wodaabe prize height, white teeth, and white eyes, and so the men try to set off their teeth (by staining their lips black for contrast), stand on tiptoes, and open their eyes as wide as possible. The women cluster together and observe, mock, and judge them, and then each chooses her partner for the evening. The ritual has attracted a great deal of attention for its very rarity, but it is worth contemplating what beauty contests reveal about gender relations in Wodaabe society— and in our own.

development in Senegal. After 1997, women who had been through Tostan's education program began a campaign to end FGC/FGM through village-by-village voluntary abandonment of the practice. Since then, more than 7,200 villages in Senegal and other African countries have pledged to abandon FGC/FGM and child/forced marriage.[39] As this suggests, FGC/FGM exists as part of community and cultural practice; change is therefore driven by communities themselves. Evidence of such community-driven change can be found not only in organizations like Tostan, but also in emigrant communities such as the Somali community in Norway. While Somalia has the highest prevalence of FGC/FGM in the world, Somalis in Norway have largely changed their views of the practice.[40]

We can now summarize the findings of cross-cultural research on female status and male dominance:

1. Gender inequality is lessened when men and women work together, with little sexual division of labour.
2. Gender inequality is more pronounced when one gender (usually men) controls material resources.
3. inequality is lessened when men participate in child care and when both sexes contribute equally to subsistence.
4. Gender inequality is heightened by segregation of the sexes.
5. Gender inequality is strengthened by rituals that highlight gender differences and segregate the genders, and by the exclusion of one gender from religious participation.

As we have seen, pioneering anthropological work focused on diversity in definitions of masculinity and femininity. Scholars have continued to find evidence of gender and sexual diversity in cultures around the world.

How Many Genders Are There?

The discussion of gender difference often assumes that differences are based on fixed biological realities. Consequently, we assume that because there are two biological sexes (male and female—or so we assume—as we'll discuss in Chapter 11), there must only be two genders (men and women). Regardless, some societies recognize more than two genders—sometimes three or four. Research on indigenous and traditional cultures is particularly fascinating and provocative. The Navajo (*Diné*), for example, appear to have had three genders—one for masculine men, one for feminine women, and another, called the **nadle**. *Nadles* might be either clearly male or genitally ambiguous, and performed tasks assigned to both women and men; they were typically treated as women and addressed using feminine kinship terms. However, being treated as a woman was not a demotion in Navajo society. Historically, women were given high status and accorded special rights and privileges—including sexual freedom, control over property, and authority to mediate disputes. *Nadles* were considered lucky or beneficial for a community and were granted high status.[41]

The *nadle* is an example of what anthropologists call a **berdache**, a group also found in Southeast Asia and the South Pacific. (The term is considered offensive by First Nations and other Aboriginal people, who increasingly use the term **Two-Spirited**.) *Berdaches* are members of one biological sex who adopt the gender identity of the other sex, although such a practice is far more common for males than for females. In his path-breaking study *The Spirit and the Flesh*, anthropologist Walter Williams explored the world of the *berdache* in detail. They were men who dressed, worked, and generally acted as women—though everyone knew that they were biologically male. Among the Crow in North America, the *berdaches* were simply males who did not want to become warriors.[42]

© Jill Peters

Albanian sworn virgin.

Among the indigenous cultures of the Great Plains, the *berdaches* were revered as being possessed of special powers, enjoyed high social and economic status, and frequently controlled ritual life. Anthropologist Sabine Lang documented the wide range of cross-gender activities engaged in by *berdaches* in North American indigenous cultures.[43]

Though there are far fewer documented instances of *female* biological sex and third gender, there are examples from around the world.[44] Among the Nahani of northern British Columbia and the Yukon, a husband and wife might decide that they had too many daughters and too few sons to hunt for them when they got old. They would choose one of their daughters to live like a man. When she was about five years old, the dried ovaries of a bear were tied to her belt, and she was treated as if she were a boy from then on. As an adult, she would most likely have lesbian sexual relations.[45] In Albania, a family without sons might designate a daughter as a **sworn virgin**. Such a daughter would adopt a masculine identity and behaviour, for the rest of her life living like a man and enjoying the privileges of maleness—except sexual relations, because sworn virgins promised lifelong chastity—and the dubious honour of being a target for blood feuds. Though most remaining sworn virgins are elderly, they testify to a life of social acceptance and even prestige.[46]

These stories should caution us against regarding third genders as analogous to modern transgender or homosexual people; indeed, the term "Two-Spirited" recognizes the distinct rootedness of this category in indigenous cultures. Third-gender people followed many different paths to their identities. Some were designated at birth, some chose a new identity in adulthood, some responded to family needs for a differently gendered member. However, third-gender people were not "expressing their identity" in the ways characteristic of modern societies. Indeed, the variability of the phenomenon of third genders shows that culture, rather than the expression of individual gender-bending tendencies, is the central actor here.

The Mohave (*Aha macave*) of the western United States seemed to have four genders and permitted both women and men to cross genders to carefully demarcated roles. A boy who showed preferences for feminine clothing or toys would undergo a different initiation at puberty and become an **alyha**. He would then adopt a female name, paint his face as a woman, perform female roles, and marry a man. When they married, the *alyha* would cut his upper thigh every month to signify "her" menstrual period, and he would learn how to simulate pregnancy and childbirth.[47]

If a Mohave female wanted to cross to the other gender, she would undergo an initiation ceremony to become a **hwame**. *Hwame* lived men's lives—hunting, farming, and the

Bestows names on children/adults
Has function in Sun Dance
Is matchmaker
Has special religious functions
Acts upon dream
Participates in war/raids
Ritual to confirm status
Test to confirm status
Imitates female physical aspects
Is undertaker
Sweats in sweat house with men
Is "sacred" person
Is intersex
Does feminine art crafts
Relationships/marriages with women
Does man's work
Is healer, medicine person
Is acting upon a vision
Does women's work better than women
Feminine as a child
Preference for company of women
Sex with men
Feminine body language, language
Relationships/marriages with men
Cross-dressing
Does women's work (specified)

100 90 80 70 60 50 40 30 20 10 0

Number of tribes from which the trait has been reported

Figure 4.2 Components of the woman-man (male-bodied *berdache*) role.

Source: Sabine Lang. *Men as Women, Women as Men: Changing Gender in Native American Cultures*, John L. Vantine, trans. (University of Texas Press, 1998), p. 256. Copyright © 1998 University of Texas Press.

like—and assumed paternal responsibility for children, though they were prohibited from assuming positions of political leadership. Neither *hwame* nor *alyha* was considered deviant.

Biologically male third genders are relatively widespread. In southern Mexico's Zapotec communities, **muxes** are biological males who dress as women and fulfil characteristically female roles—whether traditional ones or "modern" feminine roles as hairdressers or wedding planners.

Many families, and particularly mothers, "consider it a blessing" to have a muxe in the family because muxes assist with the "womanly" domestic, trading, and crafting work. In addition, "while daughters marry and leave home, a *muxe* cares for his parents in their old age."[48]

Melissa Breyer; www.melissabreyer.com/more

Zapotecan *muxe* dressed in traditional clothing.

Bandhu Social Welfare Society.

Hijras at a pride celebration in Bangladesh, November 2014.

In South Asia, **hijras**—who are generally biologically male or intersex—were once seen as members of a caste and continue to form a community. They perform female gender roles and, though often socially marginal, have a religious function.

In 2009, Pakistan recognized them as members of a distinct gender, followed by India in 2014. Recognition as a separate gender entitles hijras to their own quotas of jobs and post-secondary education spaces, where such quotas exist; legal recognition also means that harassment of hijras is now categorized as gender discrimination.[49]

In the Middle East, we find a group of Omani males called **xanith** who are biologically males, but whose social identity is female. Certainly, the key challenge to biological determinism that emerges from study of third (and fourth) genders is many cultures' refusal to see gender and biological sex as inextricably linked.

Sexual Diversity

Studies of gender diversity are complemented by studies of sexual variation. Taken together, they provide powerful arguments about the cultural construction of both gender and sexuality. Anthropologists have explored remarkable sexual diversity and accordingly have suggested that biological arguments about the naturalness of some activities and arrangements may be dramatically overstated. For example, not only is homosexual activity ubiquitous in the animal kingdom, but also it is extraordinarily common in human cultures. What varies is not the presence or absence of same-sex activity—which is pretty much a constant—but the ways in which homosexual activity is treated in those cultures. We've already seen that many cultures honour and respect those who transgress gender definitions and adopt the gender of the other sex. Some of these might be considered "homosexual," if your definition of "homosexual" has to do only with the biological sex of your sex partner.

Even by that definition, though, we find astonishing variation in the ways in which homosexuals are regarded. In 1948, anthropologist Clyde Kluckhohn surveyed North American Aboriginal groups and found homosexuality accepted by 120 of them and rejected by 54. Some cultures (Lango in East Africa, Koniag in Alaska, and Tanala in Madagascar) allow homosexual marriages between men. Some cultures have clearly defined homosexual roles for men and women, with clearly defined expectations.[50]

In a remarkable ethnography, Gilbert Herdt described the sexual rituals of the "Sambia," a pseudonym he gave to mountain people who live in Papua New Guinea. The Sambia practise ritualized homosexual acts as a way to initiate young boys into full adult manhood. Young boys daily fellate the older boys to receive the older boy's vital life fluid (semen) and therefore become (heterosexual) men. "A boy must be initiated and [orally] inseminated, otherwise the girl betrothed to him will outgrow him and run away to another man," was the way one Sambia elder put it. "If a boy doesn't eat semen, he remains small and weak." When they reach puberty, these boys are then fellated by a new crop of younger boys. Throughout this initiation, the boys scrupulously avoid girls and have no knowledge of heterosexuality until they are married. Neither the boys nor the older men think of themselves as engaging in homosexual behaviour: Older men are married to women, and the younger men fully expect to be. There is no adult homosexuality among the Sambia. Nevertheless, these young boys must become, as Herdt puts it, "reluctant warriors." How else are the boys to receive the vital life force that will enable them to be real men and warriors?[51]

Nearby, also in Melanesia, are the Keraki, who engage in a related practice. There, the boys are sodomized by older men, because the Keraki believe that without the older men's semen, the boys will not grow to be men. This ritual practice occurs until the boys enter puberty and secondary sex characteristics appear—facial hair, dropped voice—at which point the ritual has accomplished its task. When an anthropologist asked Keraki men if they had been sodomized, many responded by saying, "Why, yes! Otherwise how should I have grown?" Other ritualized homosexual practices have been reported from other cultures.[52] Interestingly, such ritual practices, as among the Sambia and Keraki, are more evident in cultures in which sex segregation is high and women's status is low. This conforms to other ethnographic evidence that, as we have seen, suggests that elaborate rituals of male bonding have the effect of excluding women from ritual life and accordingly correlate with women's lower status. Sex segregation is almost always associated with lower status for women.[53]

Some cultures take permissiveness regarding homosexuality to a remarkable level. Among the Aranda of Australia, Siwans of northern Africa, and Keraki of New Guinea, every male is homosexual during adolescence and bisexual after marriage. The purpose of this is to divert adolescent sex away from young girls and prevent teenage pregnancy and therefore to keep the birth rate down in cultures that have very scarce resources. The well-studied Yanomamo have an institutionalized form of male homosexuality as well as female infanticide. This warrior culture fears population explosion and the depletion of resources to females.[54]

The Etero and the Marind-anim, both in New Guinea, prefer homosexuality to heterosexuality, even though they maintain heterosexual marriages, in some cases leading to extremely low fertility.[55] Another Melanesian society, called "East Bay" in William Davenport's ethnographic study, practises "institutionalized male bisexuality" in the forms of sexual relations among boys and between boys and men. Nearly every male has extensive homosexual sexual contact at some point in (or even throughout) his life, though all are also heterosexual and married to women. (None is exclusively homosexual.) Women and men are seen as relatively equal in terms of sexual drive, and there are no taboos against contact with women.[56]

As these examples suggest, sexual customs display a dizzying diversity, implying that sexual behaviour is anything but organized around reproduction alone. Where, when, how, and with whom we have sex varies enormously from culture to culture. Ernestine Friedel, for example, observed dramatic differences in sexual customs between two neighbouring tribes in New Guinea. One, a highland tribe, believes that intercourse makes men weaker and that women are naturally prone to tempt men, threatening them with their powerful sexuality. They also find menstrual blood terrifying. These sexual ideologies pit women against men, and many men would rather remain bachelors than risk contact with women. As a result, population remains relatively low, which this culture needs because it has no new land or resources to bring under cultivation. Not far away, however, is a very different culture. Here, both men and women enjoy sex and sex play. Men worry about whether women are sexually satisfied, and they get along relatively well. They have higher birth rates, which is manageable because they live in a relatively abundant and uncultivated region, where they can use all the hands they can get to farm their fields and defend themselves.[57]

Sex researchers have explored the remarkable cultural diversity of sexual behaviours and in so doing have exposed the ethnocentrism of those arguments that stress the inevitability and naturalness of our own behaviours. Though most of these studies might be less than completely reliable, they indicate great cultural variation in what is considered "normal."

For example, some cultures never have sex outside. Others believe that having sex indoors would contaminate the food supply (usually in the same hut). Whereas for us kissing is a virtually universal initiation of sexual contact—"first base," as it were—other cultures find it disgusting because of the possibility of exchanging saliva. "Putting your lips together?" say the Thonga or the Siriono. "But that's where you put food!" Some cultures practise almost no foreplay at all but instead go directly to intercourse; others prescribe several hours of touching and caressing, in which intercourse is a necessary but sad end to the proceedings. Some cultures include oral sex in their lovemaking; others have never even considered it. Alfred Kinsey found that 70 per cent of the American men he surveyed in 1948 had had sex only in the missionary position and that 85 per cent had an orgasm within two minutes of penetration. In his survey of 131 Aboriginal cultures, Clyde Kluckholn found the missionary position preferred in only 17.[58]

These are but a few examples. Such sexual variety suggests that the biological imperative toward reproduction can take many forms but that none is more "natural" than any other.

Anthropology as History

Anthropological research has helped to expose the faulty logic of those who argue that the universality of gender difference or of male domination is somehow natural and inevitable. By exploring the variety of cultural definitions of masculinity and femininity and by examining cultural configurations that either magnify or diminish gender inequality, cross-cultural research has taken us beyond apparent biological imperatives. In another sense, anthropological research on our human ancestors has also provided a historical retort to biological inevitability. Take, for example, the arguments we saw earlier that male domination was a natural development in the shift to hunting-and-gathering societies. Remember the story: Men's superior physical strength led them naturally toward hunting, whereas weaker women stayed home and busied themselves with gardening and child rearing. Tidy and neat—but also, it appears, historically wrong.

It turns out that such stories actually read history backward, from the present to the past, seeking the historical origins of the patterns we find today. Nevertheless, recent research suggests that meat made up a rather small portion of the early human diet, which meant that all that celebrated hunting counted for little. Moreover, those weapons men invented, the great technological breakthrough that enabled cultures to develop—placing cultural development squarely on the backs of men. It turns out that the great technological leap was most likely the sling, a device developed by women that allowed them to gather food while still carrying their babies. It may even be true that the erect posture of human beings derives not from the demands of hunting, but rather from the shift from foraging for food to gathering and storing it. Although celebrants of "masculinist" evolution credited the demands of the hunt for creating the necessity of social (male) bonding to ensure the survival of the community, surely, it is the bond a mother has with an infant that literally and materially ensures survival. Painting a more accurate anthropological picture would require that we acknowledge that females were not simply passive and dependent bearers of children, but rather were active participants in the technological and economic side of life.[59]

Another way to look at this is suggested by Helen Fisher. She notes startling similarities between contemporary American culture and early human cultures. The elements we have inherited as the biologically natural system—nuclear families, marriages with one partner for life, and the dramatic separation of home and workplace—all seem to be relatively recent cultural inventions that accompany settled agricultural societies. On the other hand, divorce and remarriage, institutionalized child care, and women and men working equally both at home and away are more typical of the hunting-and-gathering societies that preceded ours—and lasted for millions of years. It may be, Fisher suggests, that after a brief evolutionary rest stop in settled agricultural domains (during which time male domination, warfare, and monotheism all developed), we are returning to our "true" human evolutionary origins. "As we head back to the future," she suggests, "there's every reason to believe the sexes will enjoy the kind of equality that is a function of our birthright."[60]

Fisher's view of prehistoric equality is contested, to say the least. Most anthropologists agree with Michelle Rosaldo, who concluded that "human cultural and social forms have always been male dominated," or with Bonnie Nardi, who finds "no evidence of truly egalitarian societies. In no societies do women participate on an equal footing with men in activities accorded the highest prestige."[61] However, one school of feminist anthropologists sees such universality as "an ethnological delusion," and this school argues that there have been, and are, societies in which women and men have been, and are, equal. Based on archeological excavations in places like Crete, Marija Gimbutas and Riane Eisler have argued that Neolithic societies were goddess-worshipping and gender-equal—and that women and men may have occupied separate spheres but were equal and mutually respectful. Symbolized, Eisler writes, by the chalice—the symbol of shared plenty—these ancient peoples evidenced a "partnership" model of human interaction.[62]

Then, Eisler claims, the barbarians invaded, instituting male domination, introducing a single omnipotent male God, and unleashing "the lethal power of the blade"—a violent and hierarchical world drenched in the blood of war and murder. In such a world, "having violently deprived the goddess and the female half of humanity of all power, gods, and men of war ruled," Eisler writes, and "peace and harmony would be found only in the myths and legends of a long lost past."

Most likely, it's just another "just-so" story. One should always be skeptical of arguments that point to a dimly lit historical past for our models of future social transformation, because they so often rely on selective evidence and often make for retrogressive politics. After all, the contemporary world, for all its murderous, rapacious, and bloodthirsty domination, is *far* less violent than hunter-gatherer societies. Ethnographic data suggest that only about 10 per cent of such societies rarely engage in war; most cultures are engaged in conflict either continuously or more than once a year. The "!Kung" bushmen celebrated by Eisler as the "harmless people" have a murder rate higher than that of Detroit or Washington, DC. "The sad archeological evidence," writes Frances Fukuyama, "indicates that systematic mass killings of men, women, and children occurred in Neolithic times. There was no age of innocence."[63]

On the other hand, why would we want to believe that male domination is somehow natural and inevitable? Some of Eisler's arguments are on firm evolutionary footing: It is likely, for example, that descent was originally traced through **matrilineality**. This would make descent far more certain in cultures that did not understand the relationship between sexual intercourse and birth nine months later.

Moreover, there is evidence of cultures that, although not fully female-dominated, evince women's power in all public and private arenas. Maria Lepowsky's impressive ethnography of the Vanatinai, a matrilineal, decentralized culture in New Guinea, found no evidence of male domination—no men's huts, no special ceremonial cults. Boys as well as girls care for their younger siblings. Men do child care. Additionally, both women and men exercise sexual freedom. Women have, Lepowsky writes, "equal opportunities of access to the symbolic capital of prestige derived from success in exchange." Though Lepowsky found some evidence that exclusively male activities held more prestige than women's, she argues that both women's and men's economic participation give everyone possibilities of prestige and honour.[64]

Peggy Sanday's fascinating study of the matrilineal Minangkabau of western Sumatra, one of the largest ethnic groups in Indonesia, is a case in point. Instead of looking for a mirror-image world, in which women wield power as men do, Sanday finds instead a culture in which women's ways of governing parallel men's ways and at times even supplant men's ways. Here, women are self-confident and independent of their husbands, and although men hold many of the formal political offices, women "rule without governing." They "facilitate social bonding outside the machinations of political power," which enables "the men's job of adjudicating disputes according to the rules of *adat* [customs] and consensus decision-making."[65]

Today, small-scale matrilineal societies like the Mosuo (Na) people of China or some groups in India's Meghalaya state continue their old traditions. The Mosuo have even become the focus of a burgeoning tourism industry catering to Han Chinese. In Canada, many First Nations continue to practise matrilineality, and the revitalization of traditional matrilineal systems has been identified as critical to implementing gender equity within the framework of decolonization.[66] These examples show us that women's status varies widely from place to place, depending on many cultural and historical factors. That alone makes it clear that male domination is neither natural nor inevitable.

The Values of Cross-Cultural Research

If anthropologists have demonstrated anything, it is the rich diversity in human cultural arrangements and the disparate definitions of gender and sexuality that we have produced within our cultures. Several theories explain the historical origins of these patterns and suggest ways we can modify or abandon some historically coercive or exploitative practises without doing damage to our evolutionary legacy. **Cultural relativism** also suggests

Neolithic Figurines and the Gendered Meanings of Prehistory

Discerning gender roles from archeological evidence is a challenging task that has resulted in much controversy. When the evidence in question is art, the task becomes even more difficult. Figurines and statuary from Bronze-Age Europe have long been analyzed for what they might tell us about social structure and gender roles in the prehistoric past. While the figurines' meaning has been hotly contested, the questions they raise are interesting in themselves.

The so-called "Venus of Willendorf" (now often called "Woman of Willendorf") was discovered in 1908 in Willendorf, Austria. It is a small figurine, certainly capable of being held in a hand. It has obscured facial features, but is unmistakably female, with pendulous breasts and plump hips and belly. Carved 25,000 years ago, the Venus has been interpreted as "Paleolithic pornography," a childbirth talisman, or evidence of goddess-worship. In 2006, a neuroscientist suggested that the exaggerated features of the figurine were related to the harsh Ice-Age environment, which "hard-wired" the artist's brain to isolate and amplify fat and reproductive features.

Some 16,000 years after the Venus of Willendorf was carved, the town of Catal Hüyük flourished in what is now Turkey. Excavated from 1958 to 1965, and again since the 1990s, Catal Hüyük was a well-ordered town of perhaps 10,000 people and boasted a rich symbolic and artistic life. One of the most famous objects recovered from the town is the "Seated Woman," a clay sculpture depicting a corpulent woman seated on a throne with two felines at her side.

The "Venus of Willendorf."

Wellcome Library, London

continued

The find excited much discussion, because unlike many other contemporary figurines, this one clearly depicts a woman in a position of power. Was she a mother goddess or an icon of fertility? What is the meaning of the cats seated beside her (or forming part of her "throne")? In addition, what are we to make of the fact that there are so many "Venus" figurines in prehistoric Europe and that female representations vastly outnumber male ones? Even more importantly, perhaps, how should we interpret the many anthropomorphic sculptures with no sexual characteristics whatsoever?

that, in this enormous cultural variety and historical evolution of custom and culture, we may shed those customs we no longer need, even if once they served some societal purpose. "Assertions of past inferiority for women should therefore be irrelevant to present and future developments," writes Eleanor Leacock.[67] Still, questions linger. Given such diversity of sexuality and gender, why is male dominance so universal? If it's avoidable, how do we explain its persistence? As Cecilia Ridgway argues, the staying power of gender inequality may be a living legacy of cultural constructions that are, as anthropologists have shown, fundamental organizing principles in many societies.

> Cultural meanings associated with gender do not stay within the bounds of contexts associated with sex and reproduction. Instead, the use of gender as a framing device spreads gendered meanings, including assumptions about inequality that are embedded in those meanings, to all spheres of social life that are carried out through social relationships. Through gender's role in organizing social relations . . . gender inequality is rewritten into new economic and social arrangements as they emerge, preserving that inequality in modified form over socioeconomic transformations.[68]

Therefore, our cultural beliefs may lead us constantly to reinvent and retrench gendered inequalities, in the institutions and social relations that constitute the gendered society.

Summary

Anthropological research on gender-related cultural variation arose in part in response to biological determinism. Despite dramatic cultural variations, however, some themes remain constant. Virtually all cultures observe sex differences and exhibit some form of male dominance. Anthropologists therefore try to explore links between gender difference and gender inequality; to examine societies in which women hold power; and to examine rituals, beliefs, and customs that either increase or decrease inequality.

One of the most celebrated anthropologists to explore cross-cultural variation in gender was the twentieth-century American anthropologist Margaret Mead. In several influential works, she examined differences in definitions of masculinity and femininity and the processes by which males and females became "normal" men and women within their cultural contexts. She believed that men and women were capable of being moulded into a variety of different definitions. Though her findings were criticized almost immediately and remain controversial, she stimulated great interest in (and much further research on) the cultural construction of gender.

Other anthropologists have examined the determinants of gender differences and gender inequality. One of the most important topics examined has been the gendered division of labour, which is virtually universal although the tasks assigned to men and women vary from culture to culture. Functionalists view the sex-based division of labour as the result of necessity and tend to believe that it contains elements of inevitability. In modern industrialized societies, however, the division of labour is anachronistic, held in place where it still exists by other factors, particularly the greater power of men. We are therefore thrown back upon gender inequality.

For more than 100 years, theorists have attempted to explain gender inequality by reference to larger societal forces. Engels attempted to link male dominance to the emergence of private property and early capitalist accumulation, which he thought enhanced men's need to control women's sexuality in order to ensure paternity. Contemporary anthropologists have continued to examine the impact of accumulation and other economic factors upon gender relations.

Another group of scholars traces male domination to warfare and hunting. Marvin Harris argues that warrior societies develop patrilineality, male dominance, and, for purposes of legitimation, patriarchal religion. Descent theorists like Lionel Tiger and Robin Fox emphasize that men's uncertain paternity drives them to form bonds with other men in the hunting/warfare group (rather than with women and children). Alliance theorists like Claude Levi-Strauss focus instead on the defining of acceptable marriage partners, which leads to a system in which men exchange women to cement alliances, a practice that diminishes women's status as a prerequisite for social cohesion.

The determinants of women's generally lower status have been examined by a number of scholars. The consensus among them is that there several non-exclusive contributors to male dominance: strong sexual division of labour; men's control of property; men's absence from child care; unequal contribution to subsistence; sex segregation; and rituals that highlight gender difference and separate or exclude on the basis of gender.

Anthropologists have explored cultural constructions of gender through examining specific gender rituals. Though they vary dramatically, some, like genital alteration, are quite widespread. Male circumcision and FGC/FGM are widespread practices in a number of cultures and can have a variety of meanings and purposes. In general, however, both are associated with cultures in which men are dominant. Jeffrey and Karen Paige suggest that many widely differing reproductive rituals have in common their rootedness in anxieties about paternity and female sexuality.

Another avenue for exploring the cultural construction of gender has been research on so-called third and fourth genders, individuals of one biological sex who perform gender roles normally associated with the other sex. Some societies recognize multiple genders and do not view gender as inextricably linked to biological sex. Much research has focused on the *berdache*, a third gender found in many indigenous American cultures.

In general, *berdaches* historically enjoyed high social status. First Nations and other Aboriginal cultures now prefer the term "Two-Spirited" when referring to this phenomenon. Other research has examined third genders in other cultures. There are few commonalities among third genders, except that it seems to be (or to have been in the past) much more common for biologically male individuals to be assigned "female" gender than the opposite. Third genders challenge biological determinism but should not be read as equivalent to modern transgender identities.

Studies of sexual diversity have further complicated our view of what is normal or biologically determined. Same-sex sexuality is present in virtually every human culture, yet viewed very differently. Sexual customs vary dramatically too, indicating that biological imperatives are an unreliable or at least incomplete guide to human sexuality.

Anthropological theory has gone far beyond the man-the-hunter theory in recent years. Most anthropologists now concede that traditional narratives of early human history ignored or underestimated the contributions made by women to survival, success, and technological innovation. While most feminist anthropologists argue that human societies have always privileged men, others have argued for the current, historical, or prehistoric existence of egalitarian (or even matriarchal!) societies. While there is little evidence for any prehistoric or historic **matriarchy**, there is widespread evidence of variability in the degree and nature of male dominance, suggesting that there is nothing inevitable about women's and men's status in any given society.

Anthropological research has demonstrated rich diversity in human cultures and arrangements regarding gender. Many scholars have attempted to account for this diversity and for the variation in women's status throughout the world. No completely compelling theory of male dominance has been suggested; a sociological perspective therefore adds a critical dimension to anthropological, biological, and psychological explanations of the gendered society.

Questions for Critical Thinking

1. Of the critical determinants of women's status, which do you think is most important? Is any one of these explanations unconvincing?
2. What do *you* believe caused male domination in so many human societies?
3. Can you think of any rituals of gender that emphasize reproduction or sexuality in your own society or culture? Do the rituals you can think of have anything to do with the control of women's sexuality or anxiety over paternity?
4. What does the presence of third genders in a given society indicate about that society's views of gender?
5. In your opinion, what would constitute evidence *for* or *against* theories that Neolithic societies were more egalitarian than the historical societies that followed?
6. How do you interpret the Wodaabe beauty contests and the Neolithic figurines as evidence of gender equality or inequality within a given society?

Key Terms

alyha
berdache
alliance theorists
circumcision
couvade
cultural determinism
cultural relativism
descent theorists
female genital cutting (FGC)/female
    genital mutilation (FGM)
functionalism
hijras
hwame
hypermasculinity

infibulation
matriarchy
matrilineality
muxes
nadle
patrilineality
polygamy
polygyny
purdah
ritual segregation
sex segregation
sworn virgin
Two-Spirited
xanith

The Social Construction of Gender Relations
Sociological and Feminist Perspectives

Society is a masked ball, where everyone hides his real character, and reveals it by hiding.

—Ralph Waldo Emerson, "Worship" (1860)

My self . . . is a dramatic ensemble.

—Paul Klee

In one of its most thoughtful definitions, **sociology** was described by C. Wright Mills as the intersection of biography and history, its goal to locate an individual in both time and space and understand the contexts in which a person constructs his or her identity. Sociology's bedrock assumption, upon which its analyses of structures and **institutions** rest, is that individuals shape their lives within both historical and social contexts. We do not do so simply because we are biologically programmed to act in certain ways, nor because we have inevitable human tasks to solve as we age. Rather, we respond to the world we encounter, shaping, modifying, and creating our identities through those encounters with other people and within social institutions.

Accordingly, sociology takes as its starting points many of the themes raised in earlier chapters. Sociological perspectives on gender assume the variability of gendered identities that anthropological research has explored, the biological "imperatives" toward gender identity and differentiation (though sociology locates the source of these imperatives less in our bodies and more in our environments), and the psychological imperatives toward both autonomy and connection that modern society requires of individuals in the modern world. To a sociologist, both our biographies (identities) and histories (evolving social structures) are gendered.

Like other social sciences (and like feminist theory, as we shall see below), sociology begins with a critique of biological determinism. Instead of observing our experiences as the expressions of inborn, interplanetary differences, the social sciences examine the variations *among* men and *among* women, as well as the differences *between* them. The social sciences therefore begin with the explicitly social origin of our patterns of development.

Our lives depend on social interaction. Literally, it seems. In the thirteenth century, Frederick II, emperor of the Holy Roman Empire, decided to perform an experiment to see if he could discover the "natural language of man." What language would we speak if no one taught us language? He selected some newborn babies for what has been called, with good reason, "the forbidden experiment." The babies were given basic care, but speech, songs, and lullabies—the stuff of normal parent–child interaction—were strictly prohibited. All the babies died. Moreover, you've probably heard those stories of "feral children"—babies who were abandoned, raised by animals, and incapable of being socialized to live in society after about age six. In many of the stories, the children died young, as did many of the "isolates," those little children who were locked away in closets and basements by sadistic or insane parents. Those who did manage to survive were profoundly damaged.[1]

Such stories suggest that biology alone—that is, our anatomical composition—doesn't determine our development as we might have thought. Interacting, socializing, and being part of society—not our bodies—are what makes us who we are.

Often, the first time we hear that gender is socially constructed, we take it to mean that we are, as individuals, not responsible for what we do. "'Society' made me like this," we might say. "It's not my fault." We use this rationale to deflect individual accountability

Isolated Children

Some children have been isolated from almost all human contact by abusive caregivers. One of the best-documented cases of an isolated child was "Isabelle," who was born to an unmarried, deaf-mute teenager. The mother's parents were so afraid of scandal that they kept both mother and daughter locked away in a darkened room, where they had no contact with the outside world. In 1938, when she was six years old, Isabelle escaped from her confinement. She was unable to speak except to make croaking sounds, she was extremely fearful of strangers, and she reacted to stimuli with the instinct of a wild animal. Gradually she became used to being around people, but she expressed no curiosity about them; it was as if she did not see herself as one of them. Nevertheless, doctors and social scientists began a long period of systematic training. Within a year, she was able to speak in complete sentences, and soon she was able to attend school with other children. By the age of 14, she was in the sixth grade, happy and well-adjusted. She managed to overcome her lack of early childhood socialization, but only through exceptional effort.

Studies of other isolated children reveal that some can recover, with effort and specialized care, but that others suffer permanent damage. It is unclear exactly why, but no doubt some contributing factors are the duration of the isolation, the child's age when the isolation began, the presence of some human contacts (like Isabelle's mother), other abuse accompanying the isolation, and the child's intelligence. The 1994 film *Nell* starred Jodie Foster as a near-isolate who gradually learns language and social interaction well enough to fall in love with her doctor (played by Liam Neeson).

and responsibility. It is a misreading of the sociological mandate. When we say that gender identity is socially constructed, what we *do* mean is that our identities are a fluid assemblage of the meanings and behaviours that we construct from the values, images, and prescriptions we find in the world around us. Our gendered identities are both voluntary—we choose to become who we are—and coerced—we are pressured, forced, sanctioned, and sometimes physically beaten into submission to some rules. We neither make up the rules as we go along, nor do we fit casually and without struggle into pre-assigned roles.

For some of us, becoming adult men and women in our society is a smooth and almost effortless drifting into behaviours and attitudes that feel as familiar to us as our skin. For others of us, becoming masculine or feminine is an interminable torture, a nightmare in which we must brutally suppress some parts of ourselves to please others—or, simply, to survive. For most of us, though, the experience falls somewhere in between: There are parts we love and wouldn't part with, and other parts where we feel we've been forced to exaggerate one side at the expense of others. It's the task of the sociological perspective to specify the ways in which our own experiences, our interactions with others, and the institutions combine to shape our sense of who we are. Biology provides the raw materials, whereas society and history provide the context, the instruction manual that we follow to construct our identities.

A Social Constructionist Perspective

In the first chapter, we identified four elements of a social constructionist perspective on gender. Definitions of masculinity and femininity vary, first, *from culture to culture*, and second, *in any one culture over historical time*. Accordingly, social constructionists rely on the work of anthropologists and historians to identify the commonalities and the differences in the meanings of masculinity and femininity from one culture to another and to describe how those differences change over time.

Third, gender definitions also vary *over the course of a person's life*. The issues confronting women when they are younger—in both the workplace and intimate relationships, for example—will often be very different from the issues they face at menopause or retirement. In addition, our behaviours and attitudes change too. For example, today men often report a "softening" when they become grandfathers—developing a greater interest in caregiving and nurturing than when they became fathers.

Finally, as discussed previously, definitions of masculinity and femininity will vary *within any one culture at any one time*—by race, class, ethnicity, age, sexuality, education, region of the country, etc.

Social constructionism therefore adds specific dimensions to the exploration of gender. What constructionism contributes are the elements that the social psychology of sex roles cannot explain adequately: difference, power, and the institutional dimensions of gender. To explain difference, social constructionism offers an analysis of the plurality of gender definitions; to explain power, it emphasizes the ways in which some definitions become normative through the struggles of different groups for power—including the power to define. Finally, to explain the institutional dimension, social constructionism moves beyond socialization of gendered individuals who occupy gender-neutral sites to the study of the interplay between gendered individuals and gendered institutions.

What's Wrong with Sex "Roles"?

As we saw in Chapter 3, social psychologists located the process of acquisition of gender identity in the developmental patterns of individuals in their families and in early childhood interaction. Specifically, sex-role theorists explored the ways in which individuals come to be gendered and the ways in which they negotiate their ways toward some sense of internal consistency and coherence, despite contradictory role definitions.

First, *the use of the idea of role has the curious effect of actually minimizing the importance of gender.* Role theory uses drama as a metaphor—we learn our roles through socialization and then perform them for others. However, to speak of a gender role makes it sound easily changeable. Gender, as Helena Lopata and Barrie Thorne write, "is not a role in the same sense that being a teacher, sister, or friend is a role. Gender, like race or age, is deeper, less changeable, and infuses the more specific roles one plays; thus, a female teacher differs from a male teacher in important sociological respects (e.g., she is likely to receive less pay, status, and credibility)." Cecilia Ridgway agrees that "role" obscures the fixity of gender but also adds that gender is less a role than a category:

> Gender is frequently referred to as a role that people play. If gender is a role, however, it is unlike other roles as we commonly use the term. In contrast to other roles such as, say, teacher and student, boss and worker, or leader and follower, gender is not inherently attached to a defined set of positions in specific types of organizations or institutions. Instead, gender is about types or categories of people who are defined in relation to one another.[2]

Gender, then, is not just a role that one adopts or sheds, but also a relatively fixed category of assignment that structures our relations with one another and the world. *To make gender a role like any other role is to diminish its power in structuring our lives.*[3]

Second, *sex-role theory posits singular normative definitions of masculinity and femininity.* If the meanings of masculinity and femininity vary across cultures, over historical time, among men within any one culture, and over the life course, we cannot speak of masculinity or femininity as though each were a constant, singular, universal essence. Is there really only *one* male sex role and only *one* female sex role?

By positing this false universalism, sex-role theory assumes what needs to be explained—how the normative definition is established and reproduced—and explains away all the differences among men and among women. Yet differences—race, class, ethnicity, sexuality, age, region—all inform, shape, and modify our definitions of gender. Therefore, social constructionists speak of *masculinities* and *femininities.*

What's more, social constructionists see the differences among masculinities or femininities in a manner opposite to that of sex-role theorists. The latter, if they can accommodate differences at all, see these differences as aberrations, as failure to conform to the normal sex role. In early studies of sex roles, social psychologists argued that, for example, black men or women, or gay men or lesbians, evidenced either "too much" or "too little" adherence to their appropriate sex role. In that way, homosexuals or people of colour were seen as expressing sex-role problems.

Social constructionists, on the other hand, believe that the differences among definitions of masculinity or femininity are themselves the outcome of the ways in which those groups interact with their environments. As a result, we cannot understand the differences in masculinity or femininity based on race or ethnicity without first looking at the ways in which institutional and interpersonal racial inequality structures the ways in which members of those groups actively construct their identities.

This leads to a third arena in which social constructionism challenges sex-role theory. Gender is not only plural, but relational. Nevertheless, *sex-role theory posits two separate spheres, as if sex-role differentiation were a matter of sorting a herd of cattle into two appropriate pens for branding.* Boys get herded into the masculine corral, girls the feminine. Such a static model also suggests that the two corrals have virtually nothing to do with one another. "The result of using the role framework is an abstract view of the *differences* between the sexes and their situations, not a concrete one of the *relations* between them."[4] However, what surveys indicate is that men construct their ideas of what it means to be men *in constant reference* to definitions of femininity. What it means to be a man is to be "notawoman," as Robert McElvaine claims. Indeed, social psychologists have emphasized that although different groups of men may disagree about other traits and their significance in gender definitions, the "anti-femininity" component of masculinity is perhaps the dominant and universal characteristic.[5]

Fourth, *sex-role theory ignores the fact that because gender is plural and relational, it is also situational.* What it means to be a man or a woman varies in different contexts. Those different institutional contexts demand and produce different forms of masculinity and femininity. "Boys may be boys," comments feminist legal theorist Deborah Rhode, "but they express that identity differently in fraternity parties than in job interviews with a female manager."[6] Gender is therefore not a property of individuals, some "thing" one has, but rather a specific set of behaviours that is produced in specific social situations. Gender changes as the situation changes.

Sex-role theory cannot adequately account for either the differences among women and men or their different definitions of masculinity and femininity in different situations without implicitly assuming some theory of deviance. Nor can it express the relational character of those definitions. In addition, sex-role theory cannot fully account for the power relationships between women and men and among different groups of women and different groups of men. Consequently, the fifth and perhaps most significant problem in sex-role theory is *that it depoliticizes gender, making gender a set of individual attributes and not an aspect of social structure.* "The notion of 'role' focuses attention more on individuals than on social structure, and implies that 'the female role' and 'the male role' are complementary (i.e., separate or different, but equal)," write sociologists Judith Stacey and Barrie Thorne. "The terms are depoliticizing; they strip experience from its historical and political context and neglect questions of power and conflict."[7]

How can one speak of gender without speaking of power? As pointed out in the introduction, a pluralistic and relational theory of gender cannot pretend that all masculinities and femininities are created equal. North American men and women must also contend with a singular vision of both masculinity and femininity, specific definitions that are held up as models against which we all measure ourselves. As we saw, R.W. Connell calls these the "hegemonic" definition of masculinity and the "emphasized" version of femininity. Both are normative constructions, the ones against which others are measured and, almost invariably, found wanting. The hegemonic definition is a "particular variety of masculinity to which others—among them young and effeminate as well as homosexual men—are subordinated."[8] We consequently come to know what it means to be a man or a woman by setting our definitions in opposition to a set of "others"—racial minorities, sexual minorities, etc. One of the most fruitful areas of research in sociology today is trying to specify exactly how these hegemonic versions are established and how different groups negotiate their ways through problematized definitions.

Sex-role theory's inability to explore the relationship between gender and power leads to the sixth and final problem—*sex-role theory is inadequate in comprehending the dynamics of change.* Movements for social change, like feminism or gay liberation, become movements to expand role definitions and to change role expectations. Their goal is to expand role options for individual women and men, whose lives are constrained by stereotypes. However, social and political movements are not about only expanding the opportunities for individuals to break free of the constraints of inhibiting sex roles, to allow their "true" selves to emerge; they are also about the redistribution of power in society. They demand the reallocation of resources and an end to forms of inequality that are embedded in social institutions as well as sex-role stereotypes. Only a perspective that begins with an analysis of power can adequately understand those social movements. A social constructionist approach seeks to be more concrete, specifying tension and conflict not between individuals and expectations, but rather between and among groups of people within social institutions. Consequently, social constructionism is inevitably about power.

What's wrong with sex as a "role" can finally be understood by analogy. No reputable scholars today use the terms "race roles" or "class roles" to describe the observable aggregate differences between members of different races or different classes. Such a term would flatten all the distinctions and differences among members of the same race. It would also ignore the ways in which the behaviours of different races—to the extent that they might be seen as different in the first place—are the products of racial inequality and oppression and not the external expression of some inner essence. The analogy of "class roles" or "race roles" makes clear that gender is not a role, but a category produced within a system of inequality.

The positions of women and ethnic minorities have much in common, as sociologist Helen Hacker pointed out in her groundbreaking article "Women as a Minority Group," which was written more than a half-century ago. Hacker argued that systematic structural inequality produces a "culture of self-hatred" among the target group. Yet we do not speak of "race roles." Such an idea would be absurd because

1. the differences within each race are far greater than the differences between races;
2. what it means to be white or black is always constructed in relationship to the other; and
3. those definitions make no sense outside the context of the racially-based power that white people, as a group, maintain over people of colour, as a group.[9]

Movements for racial equality are about more than expanding role options for people of colour.

Ultimately, to use role theory to explain race or gender is to blame the victim. If our gendered behaviours "stem from fundamental personality differences, socialized early in life," suggests psychologist David Tresemer, then responsibility must lie at our own feet. This is what R. Stephen Warner and his colleagues call the "Sambo theory of oppression." "[T]he victims internalize the maladaptive set of values of the oppressive system. Thus behaviour that appears incompetent, deferential, and self-degrading is assumed to reflect the crippled capabilities of the personality."[10] In this worldview, social change must be left to the future, when a more egalitarian form of childhood socialization can produce children better able to function according to hegemonic standards. Social change comes about when the oppressed learn better the ways of their oppressors. If they refuse, and no progress is made—well, whose fault is that?

A Note about Power

One of the central themes of this book is that gender is about difference as well as about inequality (that is, power). At the level of gender relations, gender is about the power that men as a group have over women as a group as well (or that some men have over other men, and women have over other women). It is impossible to explain gender without adequately understanding power—not because power is the consequence of gender difference, but rather because power is what produces those gender differences in the first place.

To say that gender is a power relation is among the more controversial arguments of the social constructionist perspective. In fact, the question of power is among the most controversial elements in all explanations of gender. Yet it is central; all theories of gender must explain both difference and domination. Whereas other theories explain male domination as the result of sex differences, social constructionism explains differences as the result of domination.

Yet a discussion about power invariably makes those with gender, race, sexual, or class privilege uncomfortable or defensive. When challenged by the idea that the gender order means that men have power over women, men often respond with astonishment. "What do you mean, men have all the power? What are you talking about? I have no power at all. I'm completely powerless. My wife bosses me around, my children boss me around, and my boss bosses me around. I have no power at all!" Other men (and women) might point to undeniably powerful women, such as Margaret Thatcher or Oprah Winfrey, as evidence of female power.

Here, in a sense, is where feminism has failed to resonate for many men. Because, although men as a group may be *in* power, most individual men are not "in power," and they do not feel powerful. Men often feel themselves to be equally constrained by a system of stereotypic conventions that leaves them unable to live the lives to which they believe they are entitled. The feeling of powerlessness is one reason why so many men believe that they are the victims of reverse discrimination.

Like gender, power is not the property of individuals—a possession that one has or does not have—but rather a property of group life, of social life. Power *is*. It can neither be willed away nor ignored. Here is how the philosopher Hannah Arendt put it:

> Power corresponds to the human ability not just to act but to act in concert. Power is never the property of an individual; it belongs to a group and remains in existence only so long as the group keeps together. When we say of somebody that

he is "in power" we actually refer to his being empowered by a certain number of people to act in their name. The moment the group, from which the power originated to begin with . . . disappears, "his power" also vanishes.[11]

To a social constructionist, power is not an attitude or a possession; it's not really a "thing" at all. It cannot be "given up" like an ideology that's been outgrown. Power creates as well as destroys. It is deeply woven into the fabric of our lives—it is the warp of our interactions and the weft of our institutions. Moreover, it is so deeply woven into our lives that it is the most invisible to those who are the most empowered.

In addition to its focus on power, sociology adds three crucial dimensions to the study of gender: the life-course perspective, a macro-level institutional analysis, and a micro-level interactionist approach.

Gender through the Life Course

Sex-role theory overemphasizes the developmental decisiveness of early childhood as the moment that gender socialization happens. Developmental psychologists have provided compelling evidence concerning the acquisition of gender identity in early childhood. Through socialization, especially in families and schools, the basic elements of gender identity are established, the foundation laid for future elaboration and expression.

Some developmental psychology proposes that once one acquires gender identity it is fixed, permanent by age five or six. Sociologists embraced some of that idea, although they often pushed the age limit up to that tumultuous period called "adolescence." Both agreed that gender identity was fixed indelibly by puberty, which is marked, after all, by all the physical changes that mark the full-fledged assumption of adult masculinity and femininity.

This emphasis on socialization as an affair of youth was also evident in sociology's institutional analysis. Sociologists used to think that the three primary institutions of socialization were the family, school, and church; the three primary bearers of their socializing message were parents, teachers, and religious figures (priests, ministers, rabbis, imams, and the like). This model has proved inaccurate for two reasons. First, it assumes that socialization is a smooth process that is accomplished by the end of childhood, when family, school, and church have receded in significance in a person's life. Second, it views the socialization process from the point of view of the socializer, not the socialized. That is, from the point of view of the child, the chief agents of socialization (parents, teachers, and religious figures) translate as grown-ups, grown-ups, and grown-ups.

Kids know better. They also know that a primary agent of their socialization is their peer group—the other boys and girls, and later men and women—with whom they interact. They also know that the images and messages that daily surround them in the media are constantly giving them messages about what men and women are supposed to look and act like. Media and peer groups are, today, part of the pentagram of socializing institutions.

Media and peer groups, however, do not recede after early childhood; indeed, one might say they pick up where family, church, and school leave off. Some of the messages from peer groups and media reinforce what we've learned; other messages directly contradict those earlier messages. It's up to us to sort it out.

Gender socialization continues throughout the life course. The process is neither smooth nor finite—it's bumpy and uneven and continues all our lives. What masculinity or femininity might mean to us in our twenties, will change dramatically by our forties or our sixties. In addition, although a small part of the explanation has to do with biological stages of development—puberty, reproductive years, menopause, and aging—these stages vary so significantly from culture to culture that the meaning of such biological shifts must be sought in the ways in which changing bodies interact with their social context.

Take, for example, a well-known "factoid" about the differences between male and female sexuality. We hear, for example, that males reach their sexual "peak" at around age 18, but that women arrive there somewhat later, perhaps in their early to mid-thirties. This biological mismatch in hitting our sexual stride is often attributed to different maturational trajectories or different evolutionary strategies. A man reaches his sexual peak when he is capable of producing the greatest number of high-quality sperm A woman, however, reaches her sexual peak at the age where her greatest number of fertile ovulatory cycles occur and before age-related risks begin to affect her ability to bear healthy offspring. However, can we explain this divergence solely in terms of different rates of maturation, hormones, and bodies? Probably not. This divergence in sexualities is far more easily and convincingly explained by putting male and female sexuality in context and by questioning some of the assumptions that researchers make. What would increasing evidence of a female sexual peak at 40 (when fertility and hormone levels begin to decline precipitously) do to the idea of the evolutionary function of women's sexual desire? What about evidence that the prevalence of sexual dysfunction in women actually declines with advancing age? Clearly, when dealing with human sexuality, we need to consider not just hormonal and evolutionary factors, but more importantly the social context in which women and men shape and express their sexuality. [12]

Alternatively, consider the **mid-life crisis**. In the 1970s, two bestselling books (*Seasons of a Man's Life* and *Passages*) popularized the belief that middle-aged men (and to a lesser extent, women) go through a developmental "crisis" characterized by a pressure to make wholesale changes in their work, relationships, and leisure.[13] Thirty years later, the mid-life crisis remains a popular concept, the subject of pop psychology books and websites offering advice to people who struggle with the symptoms of the "crisis": depression, angst, irrational behaviour, and strong urges to seek out new partners.

Careful research clearly demonstrates that this so-called crisis is not typical. Disconfirming research became available shortly after the concept was introduced, and recent research finds no empirical support for mid-life crisis as a universal experience for either men or women. People go through challenges and crises in every life stage. The triggers are usually changes in work, health, or relationships rather than a mere accumulation of birthdays. One recent study found that from their twenties to their forties, women's incidence of reported crises went from 49 to 59 per cent, men's from 39 to 46 per cent. While there is no doubt that incidence of crisis increased, one might reasonably conclude from the data that life brings crises at every age. By far the most significant crises reported were divorce and debt accumulation, both of which are more prevalent in the older groups.[14]

Belief in mid-life crisis may partially hinge on what's called **confirmation bias**, whereby a single case or a few cases of the expected behaviour confirm the belief, especially when the behaviour is attention-getting or widely reported. In other words, if we happen to know a man who spent the year after his 45th birthday getting a divorce, dating a 22-year-old, buying a sports car, and taking up skydiving, we might believe in the mid-life crisis, even though we know a dozen other middle-aged men who have done none of these things.

On the other hand, the mid-life crisis may be so compelling because it feels right; in this sense, it may simply ring true to many middle-aged people trying to find **narrative coherence** in their lives and the world around them.[15] After all, there is increasing evidence that human happiness—in North America and globally—follows a "U-shaped" pattern. That is, happiness is high in early life, declines to its lowest levels somewhere around the early forties, and then climbs to high levels again as we age.[16] What's clear, however, is that mid-life changes cannot be simply reduced to the expression of an unchanging gender identity (or a changing biology). These complex changes need an equally complex analysis.

Clearly, gender is a lifelong project, and the life course itself is gendered. The meanings of masculinity and femininity that we take into adulthood and beyond resonate in different ways as we age. For example, men and women face retirement differently. Men in retirement often end up with a more attenuated friendship and support network, fewer friends, and greater sense of isolation, which in turn might lead to earlier death because loneliness and isolation are risk factors for aging people. Women are far more likely to have maintained close contact with children, with workplace colleagues, and with friends and head into retirement with their larger friendship and support network intact. Buttressed by that support, women will be less isolated and lonely and therefore, perhaps, likely to live longer.

As the reference to difference in life expectancy shows, gender is just as salient at the end of our lives as it was during them. Because women live longer than men do, the elderly (particularly the very elderly) are more likely to be female. According to Statistics Canada data, in 2010, 80 per cent of Canadian centenarians were women, as were 56 per cent of those 65 and older.[17]

Why do women live longer? To be sure, some part of the explanation is surely physical: Physicians have long speculated that women have stronger constitutions and more immunity to disease. Testosterone is believed to have something to do with this, as are the "overall metabolic effects of maintaining more skeletal muscle mass than women do."[18] British researcher David Goldspink found that men's hearts weaken much more rapidly as they age: Between the ages of 18 and 70, their hearts lose one quarter of their power, but healthy 70-year-old women have hearts nearly as strong as those of 20-year-olds (but don't worry, regular cardiovascular exercise can slow or stop the decline). The global ubiquity of earlier male mortality and "faster male senescence" suggest that it is at least in part a physiological phenomenon. However, much of the life expectancy gender gap must be cultural, because the gap varies so dramatically from place to place. According to 2014 statistics from the World Health Organization, while women outlive men in every country, the gap is 2 years in Mozambique, 12 in Lithuania.[19]

The lifespan gap is not only variable but also malleable. The gap between Canadian men and women has narrowed from 7.4 years in 1977 to 5.4 years in 1999, 5.2 years in

2000, 4.8 years in 2004, and 4.3 years in 2012. (If nothing else, this is further proof that one cannot attribute this gender difference to biology alone.) What reasons might account for this change? Some have suggested that as gender inequality lessens and more women work outside the home, it's to be expected that the gap will decrease as women's stress levels increase. Others point to more subtle explanations, such as increased survival in the 25–49 age group for men, which apparently contributes greatly to the narrowing expectancy gap. The reduction in violent and accidental deaths among adult men, and more "masculine" patterns of female smoking and drinking, also contribute.[20]

Still, in wealthy countries, better health care and nutrition mean that *both* women and men are living longer. The social effects of an aging population are many and may include important implications for gender. The strength of sociology's life course approach is that it permits us to understand that gender is not simply a role, but a complex interplay among biology, identity, and environment that changes through an individual's lifespan in ways that affect not only the individual but also his or her society.

Gender as an Institution

The earlier argument that power is not the property of individuals is related to the argument that gender is as much a property of institutions as it is part of our individual identities. One of the more significant sociological points of departure from sex-role theory concerns the institutional level of analysis. As we've seen, sex-role theory holds that gender is a property of individuals—that gendered people acquire their gender identity and move outward, into society, to populate gender-neutral institutions. To a social constructionist, however, those institutions are themselves gendered. The gendered identity of individuals shapes those gendered institutions, and the gendered institutions express and reproduce the inequalities that compose gender identity.

This observation is the beginning of a sociological perspective—the recognition that the institutions themselves express a logic—a dynamic—that reproduces gender relations between women and men and the gender order of hierarchy and power. We can see this by looking at politics. Men *and* women have to express certain traits to occupy a political office, and their failure to do so will make the officeholder seem ineffective and incompetent. When then-justice minister Kim Campbell was photographed bare-shouldered behind legal robes, many people believed that somehow she had diminished herself—and her office. Similarly, former MP Belinda Stronach was often subjected to gendered slurs ("dog," "bitch") and sexist media comments about her attractiveness during her time in office. Of course, men are not immune to this sort of criticism. A man too concerned about his appearance may appear weak, duplicitous, or of suspect masculinity, as Reform Party founder Preston Manning found out when he became leader of the opposition in the House of Commons and undertook what came to be called his "Eastern makeover."[21] Nevertheless, women seem—still—to face a stricter scrutiny, as was seen when New Democrat MP Ruth Ellen Brosseau ran for office in 2011. A young single mother and bartender, she earned the nickname "Vegas girl" after traveling to the Nevada city for a birthday vacation during the campaign. However, she won at the polls—something that indicates a degree of change since Kim Campbell's time!

Would politics change, then, if it were dominated by women instead of by men? Perhaps, but to argue that institutions are gendered is *only* the half of the story. It's as simplistic to argue that the individuals who occupy those positions are genderless as it is to argue that the positions they occupy are gender-neutral. Gendered individuals occupy places within gendered institutions. Accordingly, it is possible that if *all* positions were filled with the gender that has been raised to avoid conflict instead of the gender that is accustomed to drawing lines in the sand, the gendered mandates of those institutions would be affected, modified, and moderately transformed.

To say, then, that gender is socially constructed requires that we locate individual identity within a historically and socially specific and equally gendered place and time and that we situate the individual within the complex matrix of our lives, our bodies, and our social and cultural environments. A sociological perspective examines the ways in which gendered individuals interact with other gendered individuals in gendered institutions. As such, sociology examines the interplay of those two forces—identities and structures— through the prisms of socially created difference and domination.

Gender revolves around three themes—identity, interaction, institution—in the production of gender difference and the reproduction of gender inequality. These themes are the processes and experiences that form core elements of our personalities, our interactions with others, and the institutions that shape our lives. Our experiences are shaped by our societies, and we return the favour, helping to reshape our world. We are gendered people living in gendered societies.

A social constructionist perspective, however, goes one step further than even this. Not only do gendered individuals negotiate their identities within gendered institutions, but also those institutions *produce* the very differences we assume are the properties of individuals. Different structured experiences produce the gender differences that we often attribute to people.[22]

Let's illustrate this phenomenon first with an ordinary example and then with a more analytically complex one. At the most mundane level, think about public washrooms. In a clever essay on the "arrangement between the sexes," the late sociologist Erving Goffman playfully suggested the ways in which these public institutions produce the very gender differences they are supposed to reflect. Though men and women are "somewhat similar in the question of waste products and their elimination," Goffman observes, in public, men and women use sex-segregated washrooms, clearly marked "gentlemen" and "ladies." These rooms have very different spatial arrangements, such as urinals for men and more elaborate "vanity tables" and other grooming facilities for women. We think of these as justifiably "separate but equal."

Nevertheless, in the privacy of our own homes, we use the same bathrooms and feel no need for separate space. What is more, virtually no private homes have urinals for men, and few have separate and private vanity tables for women. (Of course, in some cultures, these functions are performed publicly, with no privacy at all.) If these needs are biologically based, Goffman asks, why are they so different in public and in private?

> The *functioning* of sex differentiated organs is involved, but there is nothing in this functioning that biologically recommends segregation; *that* arrangement is a totally cultural matter. . . . Toilet segregation is presented as a natural consequence of the difference between the sex-classes when in fact it is a means of honouring, if not producing, this difference.[23]

In other words, by using separate facilities, we "become" the "gentlemen" and "ladies" who are supposed to use those separate facilities. That means we are not just "gentlemen" who stand up or "ladies" who powder their noses; washrooms imply much more about who the "standard" human being is. Until recently, most washrooms had very few accommodations for the disabled; in North America, almost no washrooms contain accommodations (for example, smaller fixtures) for children, which are commonplace in Sweden. Men's washrooms seldom contain diaper changing tables, as many frustrated fathers can attest; this both reflects and creates an assumption that the "average" man does not need to change diapers. In addition, although gender-neutral washrooms are increasing in number, they remain few and far between. Public washrooms consequently reinforce a whole set of assumptions about gender, size, ability, and social function.

At the less mundane—but certainly no less important—level, take the example of the workplace. In her now-classic work, *Men and Women of the Corporation*, Rosabeth Moss Kanter demonstrated that the men's and women's behaviours in organizations had far less to do with their individual characteristics than with the structure of the organization. Organizational positions "carry characteristic images of the kinds of people that should occupy them," she argued, and those who occupied them, whether women or men, exhibited those necessary behaviours. Though the criteria for evaluation of job performance, promotion, and effectiveness seem to be gender-neutral, they are in fact, deeply gendered. "While organizations were being defined as sex-neutral machines," she writes, "masculine principles were dominating their authority structures." Once again, masculinity—the norm—was invisible.[24]

In a series of insightful essays, sociologist Joan Acker has expanded on Kanter's early insights and specified the interplay of structure and gender. It's through our experiences in the workplace, Acker maintains, that the differences between women and men are reproduced and through which the inequality between women and men is legitimated. Institutions are like factories, and what they produce is gender difference.

Institutions accomplish the creation of gender difference and the reproduction of the gender order, Acker argues, through several "gendered processes." These gendered processes mean that "advantage and disadvantage, exploitation and control, action and emotion, meaning and identity, are patterned through and in terms of a distinction between male and female, masculine and feminine." She observes five of these processes.

The first process is the production of **gender divisions**—the ways in which "ordinary organizational practices produce the gender patterning of jobs, wages, and hierarchies, power and subordination." In the very organization of work, gender divisions are produced and reinforced, and hierarchies are maintained—often despite the intentions of well-meaning managers and supervisors.

The second process is the construction of **gender images**—symbols and images that "explain, express, reinforce, or sometimes oppose those divisions." Advertisements— one such example—reproduce the gendering of positions so that the image of a successful manager or business executive is almost always an image of a well-dressed, powerful man.

The third process is the interactions between individuals—women and men, women and women, and men and men—in all the forms and patterns that express dominance and submission. For example, conversations between supervisors and subordinates typically involve power dynamics, such as interruptions, sentence completion, and setting the topic for conversation, which, given the gendered positions within the organization, will reproduce observable conversational gender differences.

The fourth process is the internal mental work of individuals "as they consciously construct their understandings of the organization's gendered structure of work and opportunity and the demands for gender-appropriate behaviours and attitudes." This might include patterns of dress, speech, and general presentation of self.

The fifth process is the ongoing logic of organizations themselves—how the seemingly gender-neutral theories of organizational dynamics, bureaucracy, and organizational criteria for evaluation and advancement are actually very gendered criteria masquerading as "objective" and gender-neutral.[25]

As we've seen, sex-role theory assumed that gendered individuals enter gender-neutral sites, maintaining the invisibility of gender-as-hierarchy and specifically the invisible masculine organizational logic. On the other hand, many organizational theories assume that genderless "workers" occupy those gender-neutral sites. The problem is that such employees are assumed able to devote themselves single-mindedly to their jobs, have no children or family responsibilities, and may even have familial supports for such single-minded workplace devotion. Consequently, the genderless job-holder turns out to be gendered as a (stereotypical) man. Once again, the invisibility of masculinity as the unexamined norm turns out to reproduce the power differences between women and men, because women are more likely to have the responsibilities that, according to the logic above, make them less committed employees.

One or two more examples should suffice. Many physicians complete college by age 21 or 22, medical school by age 25 to 27, and then endure three more years of internship and residency, during which time they are occasionally on call for long stretches of time, sometimes even two or three days straight. They consequently complete their residencies by their late twenties or early thirties. Such a program is designed for a male doctor—one for whom the birth of children will not disrupt these time demands, and one who may even have someone at home taking care of the children while he sleeps at the hospital. No wonder women—today the majority of Canadian medical students—began to complain that they were not able to balance pregnancy and motherhood with their medical training.

According to *Maclean's* magazine, "soon the entire health care system will be dominated by female physicians," which causes concern, particularly because women "have been shown in the past to work fewer hours than their male counterparts." Another article discussed the plight of a pregnant Toronto woman who had gone through three doctors in the past few years. "[E]very one of them was a woman who'd left for her children."[26] Discussions have often emphasized that women just don't want to work as much or as hard as male physicians traditionally have; some have darkly grumbled about the cost of training physicians who end up leaving the field after a relatively short career.

These discussions have rarely mentioned the fact that the medical profession, like other high-pressure fields, has always relied upon a highly gendered division of labour—not just within hospitals but within the homes of its physicians. Male doctors have traditionally worked more hours than their female counterparts do, but most were still able to have families. Why? Because they had "doctor's wives"—that is, their wives played an essential support role. In the classic model, a young woman supported her partner (often financially) while he attended school, and then stayed home to manage the family and household (and, sometimes, the accounts). Consequently, some semblance of a "normal" life could be combined with the demands of the job. For various reasons, this model of family is not one most women doctors can access. It's not just about women's lack of commitment to the profession or about personal choices; it's about how family and workplace are gendered and how medical practice was designed based on gendered assumptions.

Similarly, lawyers just out of law school who take jobs with large corporate law firms are expected to bill up to 50 to 60 hours per week—a process that probably requires working 80 to 90 hours per week. Assuming at least six hours of sleep per night, a one-hour round-trip commute, and one half-day of rest, these young lawyers are going to have a total of about 17 hours per week to eat, cook, clean their house, talk with and/or make love with their spouse (or date if they're single), and spend time with their children. Without that half-day off on the weekend, they have about one hour per day for everything else. Failure to submit to this regimen could place a lawyer on a "mommy track" or a "daddy track." Being on a parental "track" means that everyone will think well of that lawyer for being such an involved parent, but that she or he is certain never to be promoted to partner, and to join all the rest of the lawyers who made such sacrifices for their careers.

Or, finally, take academic tenure. In a typical academic career, a scholar completes a Ph.D. about five to six years after the MA, or roughly by the early thirties. Then he or she begins a career as an assistant professor and has six more years to earn tenure and promotion. This is usually the most intense academic work period of a scholar's life—he or she works night and day to publish enough scholarly research, prepare and teach courses, and serve on the many committees that govern and manage universities. The thirties are also the most likely child-bearing years for professional women. The academic tenure clock is consequently timed to a *man's* rhythms—and not just any man, but one who has a wife or other family supports to relieve him of family obligations as he works to establish his credentials. Remember the adage "publish or perish"? Often, to academics struggling to make tenure, it feels as though publishing requires that family life perish. Small wonder that according to 2001 Statistics Canada data, academic women were significantly less likely to have children even than women lawyers and women physicians. In the US, 70 per cent of tenured male faculty members have children compared to 44 per cent of women.[27]

Observing the institutional dimension also offers the possibility to observe adjustment and readjustment within institutions as they are challenged. Sometimes, their boundaries prove more permeable than originally expected. For example, what happens when the boundaries between work and home become permeable, when women leave the home and enter the gendered workplace? Judith Gerson and Kathy Peiss suggest that boundaries "*within* the workplace (e.g., occupational segregation) and interactional micro level boundaries assume increased significance in defining the subordinate position of women." Therefore, occupational segregation can reproduce gender difference *and* gender inequality by assigning women to secondary statuses within organizations. For those women who enter non-traditional positions, though, microlevel boundary maintenance would come into play—"the persistence of informal group behaviour among men (e.g., after-work socializing, the uses of male humour, modes of corporate attire)—act to define insiders and outsiders, thus maintaining gender-based distinctions."[28] How women attempted to breach these boundaries can be seen in the heavily padded shoulders of the 1980s "power suit." In its female version, the power suit attempted to mimic a typically masculine torso profile and accordingly make the wearer look more "corporate."

Embedded in organizational structures that are gendered, the differences between women and men appear to be the differences solely between gendered individuals. When women do not meet an organization's criteria (or, perhaps more accurately, when the criteria do not meet women's specific needs), we see a gender-segregated workforce and wage, hiring, and promotional disparities as the "natural" outcomes of already-present differences between women and men. It is in this way that those differences are generated and the inequalities between women and men are legitimated and reproduced.

Of course, one should note that it is through these same processes that the "differences" between various "classes" of people are produced, legitimized, and reproduced. (Such groups include the working class and professionals, disabled and able-bodied, Aboriginals and non-Aboriginals, whites and visible minorities, immigrants and non-immigrants, and heterosexuals and homosexuals.) Making gender visible in these organizational processes ought not to blind us to the complex interactions with other patterns of difference and principles of inequality. Just as a male pattern becomes the unexamined norm, so, too, does a white, able-bodied, heterosexual, and middle-class pattern become the unexamined norm against which others' experiences and performances are evaluated.

The idea of **organizational gender neutrality**, then, is the vehicle by which the gender order is reproduced. "The theory and practice of gender neutrality," writes Acker, "covers up, obscures, the underlying gender structure, allowing practices that perpetuate it to continue even as efforts to reduce gender inequality are also under way."[29] Organizations reflect and produce gender differences; gendered institutions also reproduce the gender order by which men are privileged over women and by which some men are privileged over other men.

"Doing Gender": The Interactionist Approach

There remains one more element in the constructionist explanation of gender. According to sex-role theory, we acquire our gender identity through socialization, and afterward we are socialized to behave in masculine or feminine ways. It is consequently the task of society to make sure that the men act in the masculine manner and that the women act in the feminine manner. Our identity is fixed, permanent, and—now—inherent in our personalities. We can no more cease being men or women than we can cease being human.

In an important contribution to the social constructionist perspective, sociologists Candace West and Don Zimmerman argued that gender is less a component of identity—fixed, static—that we take with us into our interactions, than it is the product *of* those interactions. They argued, "a person's gender is not simply an aspect of what one is, but, more fundamentally, it is something that one *does*, and does recurrently, in interaction with others." We are constantly "doing" gender, performing the activities and exhibiting the traits that are prescribed for us.[30]

If our sex-role identity is inherent, West and Zimmerman might ask, in what does it inhere? What are the criteria by which we sort people into those sex roles to begin with? Typically, our answer returns us to biology and, more specifically, to the primary sex characteristics that we believe determine which gender one will become. Biological sex—externally manifested genitalia—becomes socialized gender role. Those with male genitalia are classified in one way; those with female genitalia are classified in another way. These two sexes become different genders, which are assumed to have different personalities and require different institutional and social arrangements to accommodate their natural—and now socially acquired—differences.

Most of the time we carry around these types of common-sense understandings. We see **primary sex characteristics** (those present at birth) as far more decisive than **secondary sex characteristics** (those that develop at puberty) for the assignment of sex and therefore, gender-role identity. However, how do we know? When we see someone on the street, it is his or her *secondary* sex characteristics that we observe—breast development, facial hair, and musculature. Even more than that, it is the behavioural presentation of self—how someone dresses, moves, or talks—that signals to us whether that someone is a man or a woman. Indeed, it would be a strange world if we had constantly to ask to see people's genitals to make sure they were who they appeared to be!

One method that sociologists developed to interrogate this assumption has been to imagine that primary and secondary sex characteristics did not match. As we have seen, in many cases, intersex infants—whose primary sex characteristics cannot be easily discerned visually—have their genitals surgically reconstructed. Intersexuality pushes us to reconsider the genitals as the defining feature of biological sex. Gender, as William Reiner, a urologist and a psychiatrist who treats intersex children, says, "has far more to do with other important structures than external genitals."[31]

Perhaps, but the genitals remain the common-sense "location" of biological sex. In a brilliantly disconcerting study, *Gender: An Ethnomethodological Approach*, Suzanne Kessler and Wendy McKenna proposed two images in which primary and secondary sex characteristics did not match (see Figures 5.1 and 5.2). Which one is the "man," and which is the "woman"? How can you tell?

Looking at those images, many people might feel lost in their social bearings and threatened by a kind of "gender vertigo"[32] in which the dualistic conceptions that we believe are the foundations of our social reality turn out to be more fluid than we believed or hoped. It's as though our notions of gender are anchored in quicksand. One sociologist reported how she became disturbed by the sexual ambiguity of a computer salesperson:

> The person who answered my questions was truly a salesperson. I could not categorize him/her as a woman or a man. What did I look for? (1) Facial hair: She/he was smooth skinned, but some men have little or no facial hair. (This varies by race, Native Americans and Blacks often have none.) (2) Breasts: She/he was wearing a loose shirt that hung from his/her shoulders. And, as many women who suffered through a 1950s adolescence know to their shame, women are often flat-chested. (3) Shoulders: His/hers were small and round for a man, broad for a woman. (4) Hands: Long and slender fingers, knuckles a bit large for a woman, small for a man. (5) Voice: Middle range, unexpressive for a woman, not at all the

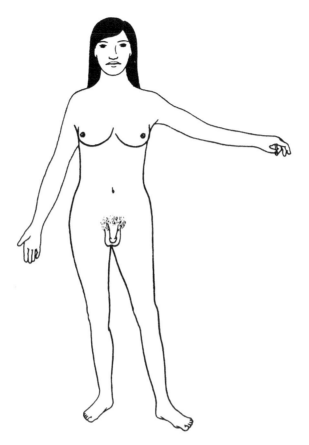

Figure 5.1 Figure with penis, breasts, hips, no body hair, and long hair.

Source: Republished with permission of John Wiley and Sons, from *Gender: An Ethnomethodological Approach* by Kessler and Mckenna. Copyright 1985; permission conveyed by Copyright Clearance Center, Inc.

exaggerated tones some gay males affect. (6) His/her treatment of me: Gave off no signs that would let me know if I were of the same or different sex as this person. There were not even any signs that he/she knew his/her sex would be difficult to categorize and I wondered about this even as I did my best to hide these questions so I would not embarrass him/her while we talked of computer paper. I left still not knowing the sex of my salesperson, and was disturbed by that unanswered question (child of my culture that I am).[33]

As drag queens know, gender is a performance, a form of drag, by which, through the successful manipulation of props, signs, symbols, behaviours, and emotions, we attempt to convince others of our successful acquisition of masculinity or femininity. Just ask RuPaul, who seems to float almost effortlessly between the two, and who says, "We are born naked. The rest is drag."

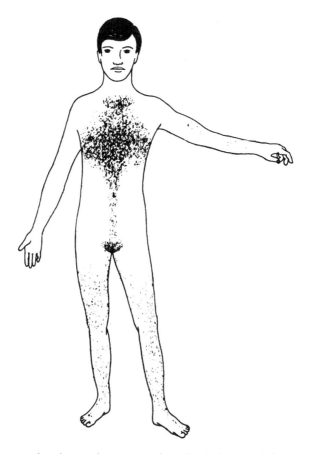

Figure 5.2 Figure with vulva, no breasts, no hips, body hair, and short hair.

Source: Republished with permission of John Wiley and Sons, from *Gender: An Ethnomethodological Approach* by Kessler and Mckenna. Copyright 1985; permission conveyed by Copyright Clearance Center, Inc.

Drag will always live on the fringe, because at its core it mocks the matrix; it mocks identity. It will never be mainstream because most people can't accept the idea that they are not who it says they are on their driver's license or their birth certificate. It's a concept that would force them to deconstruct their whole belief system, and no one's going to do that.[34]

As RuPaul suggests, most of us find gender boxes comforting. We learn gender performance early in childhood, and it remains with us virtually all our lives. When our gender identities are threatened, we will often retreat to displays of exaggerated masculinity or exaggerated femininity. Moreover, when our sense of others' gender identity is disrupted or dislodged, we can become anxious, even violent. "We're so invested in being men or women that if you fall outside that easy definition of what a man or woman is, a lot of people see you as some kind of monster," commented Susan Stryker, who is a male-to-female transsexual (transwoman).[35] Understanding how we do gender, then, requires

Gender as performance: Two genders of RuPaul.

that we make visible the performative elements of identity, as well as the audience for those performances. It also opens up unimaginable possibilities for social change. As Suzanne Kessler points out in her study of intersexuals:

> If authenticity for gender rests not in a discoverable nature but in someone else's proclamation, then the power to proclaim something else is available. If physicians recognized that implicit in their management of gender is the notion that finally, and always, people construct gender as well as the social systems that are grounded in gender-based concepts, the possibilities for real societal transformations would be unlimited.[36]

Kessler's gender utopianism does raise an important issue in the sociological perspective. In saying that we "do" gender, we are saying that gender is not only something that is done to us. We create and re-create our own gendered identities within the contexts of our interactions with others and within the institutions that we inhabit.

Constructing Gender: Feminist Views and Movements

Almost 300 pages into her famous book, *The Second Sex*, Simone de Beauvoir issued a statement that became the cornerstone of **second-wave feminism**'s view of gender: "One is not born, but rather becomes, a woman."[37] Writing from the perspective of a curious philosopher, Beauvoir systematically analyzed the evidence for the biological character of gender before turning to its historical and psychological construction. She argued persuasively that men had defined themselves in opposition to women, creating in woman a mysterious, dangerous, and misunderstood "Other."

These powerful insights made *The Second Sex* one of the key texts of the twentieth-century feminist movement, but they were not wholly original to Beauvoir. Indeed, Mary Wollstonecraft (1759–1797) argued that the "defects" of women were caused not by their nature but by the "deforming" influences of society:

> Women are everywhere, in this deplorable state; for, in order to preserve their innocence, as ignorance is courteously termed, truth is hidden from them, and they are made to assume an artificial character before their faculties have acquired any strength. Taught from their infancy that beauty is woman's scepter, the mind shapes itself to the body, and roaming around its gilt cage, only seeks to adore its prison.[38]

Against the idea of an eternal feminine nature, Wollstonecraft argued that men and women were largely the same, only shaped to different characters and destinies by the norms of their society. Wollstonecraft's radical (for her time) approach to gender was echoed by Olympe de Gouges (1748–1793), a participant in the French Revolution who wrote a "Declaration of the Rights of Woman and the Female Citizen," criticizing the Revolution and claiming for women the rights that it had granted to men only.

The call for women's rights was taken up in the nineteenth century by Harriet Taylor and John Stuart Mill, both of whom advocated education and property rights for British women. Elected to the House of Commons, Mill campaigned for women's rights and against domestic violence. By Mill and Taylor's time, it had become possible to speak of the **woman movement**, which we now call **first-wave feminism**. In twenty-first-century Canada, it's difficult to imagine the gendered world of the 1800s: a world of frank colonial exploitation in which race-based slavery existed; in which women and children (and men) were routinely and viciously exploited in employment; in which women in many countries enjoyed virtually no legal protection from abuse, property rights within marriage, or parental rights. The issues taken on by the woman movement in 1800s Europe and America were many, from the well-known battle for women's suffrage and the abolition of slavery to campaigns involving temperance, marital property, and men's sexual privilege. Even issues no longer popularly associated with feminism, such as prevention of animal cruelty and anti-vivisectionism, were deeply influenced by feminism. Many first-wave feminists advocated vegetarianism, animal welfare, or both.[39]

The multiplicity of issues addressed by the woman movement is related to the diversity of its origins. In fact, first-wave feminism arose within a number of other social movements. In the US, for example, the feminist movement grew alongside and from within evangelical religion and the movement for the abolition of slavery. In continental Europe, utopian socialism and the critique of industrial capitalism nurtured women activists whose commitment to class equality was not less than their passion for rights for women. Moreover, in Britain and Canada, both voluntary social reform movements and the movements already listed fostered the development of feminism.

In the US, the first convention to discuss women's rights was held in Seneca Falls, New York, in 1848, with many others held in the decade following. Few other nations can identify such a starting point for first-wave activism, but the 1850s were a period of intense activity in Britain, too. There, petitions, for married women's property rights were presented forming the basis for organizing women's groups. The Contagious Diseases Acts, commencing in 1865, further galvanized women's activism, this time with regard to prostitution and male sexual privilege.

Between the 1850s and the end of the century, Canada, Australia, New Zealand, Germany, France, Chile, Brazil, Peru, Japan, China, Russia, Turkey, Persia, and other nations saw significant discussion of women's rights, and many developed homegrown feminist movements. These movements were themselves varied and diverse. For example, the woman movement counted among its followers both those who advocated Social Purity—the prohibition of prostitution and pornography—and others like Victoria Woodhull, who scandalized society with her support for "free love."

The woman movement also included women whose concern for women's rights was part of a larger project for class and racial equality. US feminism had its birthplace in abolitionism, of course; and the National Woman Suffrage Association supported the black suffrage amendment. When black men were enfranchised by the Fifteenth Amendment in 1870, and women were denied the vote, Stanton and others were bitter. Still, there were those who continued to locate their gender activism within broader class and racial movements. Emma Goldman's socialist-anarchist activism is one example; the anti-lynching activities of Ida B. Wells are another. Wells, a teacher and the daughter of former slaves, researched lynching across the US, decisively disproving the commonly held belief that African-American men were being lynched for sexual attacks on white women. She exposed lynching for what it was: a racist attack on African-American men, women, and children, and an attempt to exclude and terrorize. Unfortunately, Wells and other African-American women activists of her time were not successful in placing race relations at the heart of the broader feminist movement.

By the 1880s, the term "feminism" had been introduced. It was used first in France (*féminisme*), entering other European countries by the 1890s. In England, it generally appeared as a deprecating term. In North America, the term became widespread between 1910 and the outbreak of the First World War.[40]

The first-wave feminist movement steadily gained momentum from the 1850s until the end of the First World War, eventually coming to focus on the vote as the means to advance the status of women and, more generally, social progress. At the same time, however, the movement was never united on the central importance of suffrage. The Women's Christian Temperance Union, founded in the 1870s, had chapters throughout the US and in Canada and focused on abstention from alcohol, which members saw as the primary driver of domestic violence and other social ills. The organization was divided over the desirability of women's voting, though the WCTU supported suffrage in the 1890s. Indeed, by the turn of the century suffrage galvanized the myriad groups and interests that constituted the woman movement.

Not surprisingly, when this unitary focus was gone, the movement also diminished. In the wake of the First World War, as nation after nation granted women suffrage, the feminist movement began to fragment. By the Second World War, many people believed that feminism was a thing of the past. Indeed, much of what women had fought for had been achieved; married women had property rights, (most) women could vote,[41] and many women had jobs. What was left?

In part, the question resulted from the unresolved tensions within first-wave feminism itself. While most first-wave feminists accepted the "natural" differences between men and women, they turned those distinctions over, arguing, for example, that women's heightened moral sense made them ideal candidates for activities in the public sphere. This same trait qualified women to be mothers, and many first-wave feminists believed that most women, because of their natural interests, would choose a life as wives and mothers.

Still, even feminists who resisted the idea of women's suffrage and accepted innate sex difference believed that many of women's apparent weaknesses were the result not of weak female nature, but of the manner in which women were raised, educated, treated, and excluded from many societal benefits and institutions. Consequently, first-wave feminism tended to argue both the distinctness of women and their sameness at the level of rights—a tension that would bequeath to subsequent movements a "Janus face."[42] The general acceptance of women's "difference" also limited the movement's ability to coalesce around other issues, for example, the 1920s attempt at passing an Equal Rights Amendment to the American Constitution.

As a result, feminism entered the postwar period with a fundamental question unanswered: are women the same as men, or different? Should their rights be ensured through equality, or through special protections? What is a woman's place in society, anyway?

The answer to that question came from several places. Probably the first work to make a significant contribution to the discussion was Beauvoir's *Second Sex*, published in 1949. (During the last several decades, it has been translated into many languages, including English only four years after initial publication.) In North America, another important work that found a massive popular audience was Betty Friedan's *The Feminine Mystique*. First published in 1963, Friedan's book was based on surveys of her college graduating class, which revealed that despite living lives of relative privilege and apparent success, suburban women were deeply uneasy with their lives and identities. Friedan argued that women were provided with a role that required them to define themselves entirely in terms of others (husbands and children), leading to a deep malaise that she called "the problem with no name." Though the work has been criticized in the years since its publication, it struck a chord with readers; by the end of 1964, the book had sold 1.3 million copies, becoming the non-fiction bestseller of the year.[43]

By the late 1960s, driven by the political ferment and critical social movements of the time, women were not only reading Friedan and Beauvoir but meeting with others and organizing meetings and protests. Feminism had once again become a social movement as well as a philosophy. In Canada, women's groups demanded that the government respond to their concerns. As a result, Prime Minister Lester B. Pearson created a Royal Commission on the Status of Women, which conducted hearings throughout the nation in 1968, receiving hundreds of briefs on everything from pensions to the Indian Act and family law. The commission made 167 recommendations, many of which were implemented in the 1970s.

Like first-wave feminists, the feminists of the late 1960s and early 1970s attempted to increase women's legal rights and combat continuing inequalities between the sexes. Nevertheless, the new feminists differed from their predecessors in their willingness and ability to discuss, analyze, and protest power imbalances in personal and intimate relations.

Part of this related to changed social norms; simply put, it was now possible to discuss issues such as sexuality with a frankness that was simply impossible in the nineteenth century. The euphemisms of the first wave gave way to insistent rhetoric. The discourse and even the title of the new feminist movement revealed its focus and urgency; feminism was now called the **Women's Liberation Movement**, a term often shortened to Women's Lib by both supporters and detractors.

The new women's movement also had new tools and approaches. **Consciousness-raising**, which brought women together in small groups to discuss every aspect of their lives, allowed women to perceive that experiences and thoughts they had felt to be theirs alone were indeed the result of gender construction, shared widely with other women.

Proclaiming that "the personal is political," second-wave feminists protested beauty pageants, created shelters for survivors of domestic and sexual abuse, and constantly pushed their society to recognize the interlocking of gender and power in everyday life, including in "universal" language. Though often seen as dangerous radicals in the 1970s, second-wave feminists catalyzed many changes in society, from the overhauling of criminal and family law to the use of the title "Ms" to describe women. They also spearheaded the inclusion of knowledge produced by and about women in the academic curriculum, particularly at the post-secondary level. Beginning in the early to mid-1970s and continuing to the present day, women's studies programs have been developed at many colleges and universities to present knowledge about women and a critical perspective on sex and gender. (Today, most women's studies programs and departments have broadened their mandates to include masculinities and men's studies. Many have renamed themselves "gender studies," and others have adopted names that foreground critical race studies or critical perspectives on social justice.).

The women's movement of the 1970s and 1980s was highly successful—so much so that today, we take much of what the movement achieved for granted, Of course, a movement of such size quickly became both diverse and fractious. As a movement for social justice, moreover, feminism was constantly pushed to criticize its own assumptions, practices, and exclusions. To a great degree, while commenting on the marginalization of women, second-wave feminism struggled with intra-movement issues based on class, ethnicity, and sexual orientation.

In the 1960s, one of the most obvious fault lines emerged in the US between heterosexual and lesbian women. The National Organization for Women was formed in 1966 with a diverse group of 300 charter members. Betty Friedan drafted the statement of purpose and the NOW Bill of Rights for women, a document that called for abortion on demand and the passage of the Equal Rights Amendment. However, Friedan had no intention of including lesbian rights in NOW's platform, and she feared that taking a stand in favour of lesbian rights would make NOW look "anti-male" to the American public. The resulting rift within NOW led many lesbian feminists to leave the organization for more radical groups.[44] The schism also pointed to a fundamental question about the nature of feminism. Was it a movement for employment and political rights, or was it something more fundamental? Was feminism a place where relatively privileged women such as Friedan set the agenda, or would its commitment to women's rights and equality be extended to *all* women? These questions would continue to be the focus of debate—some of it bitter—during the 1970s.

NOW and comparable organizations, both in the US and in other countries, came to represent the most "mainstream" form of second-wave feminism. This form is generally known as **liberal feminism**. Focusing on the reform of society to make it as gender-neutral as possible, liberal feminists emphasized safe legal abortion, an end to legal discrimination, the election of women to public office, shared parenting and housework, and political and workplace equality. In the US, these goals were also promoted by *Ms. Magazine*, founded by Gloria Steinem in 1972. Liberal feminism was (and still is) highly successful in achieving legal reforms and attracting public support; not surprisingly, many of its overt goals related to equal access to the rights enjoyed by men in the public sphere. These goals were easier to achieve in that they could be readily legislated; moreover, the goals of liberal feminism were arguably less threatening to the status quo than some subsequent feminist activism would be.

Despite its success, liberal feminism had many detractors within the feminist movement. The exodus of lesbians from NOW, discussed above, is one example, but there are many others; during the 1970s and 1980s, critique of liberal feminism would fundamentally reshape the women's movement and the goals it set itself.

In the late 1960s, many young women attracted to feminism had participated in New Left and student movements where they found themselves relegated to auxiliary roles because of their sex. Such women came to feminism with a well-developed analysis of gender but also with an economic and class analysis that liberal feminism lacked. Other women who had been involved in leftist politics (Simone de Beauvoir was one of these) also felt that feminism had to be about more than women's access to the existing capitalist system. For such feminists, the system itself had to change, and feminism must include concern for economic justice. **Marxist and socialist feminisms** consequently developed as a significant wing of the second-wave feminist movement, arguing that economy, not merely a lack of legal and customary equality, was at the heart of women's previous oppression as a "sex-class." For socialist feminists, economy, law, and culture all play a role in the subordination of women, as do racial and class discrimination.

Many of the lesbians who left NOW in the late 1960s found a new home within **radical feminism**. Radical feminism was called "radical" because it sought fundamental changes rather than legislative reforms. As Bonnie Kreps stated to the Royal Commission on the Status of Women in Canada in June 1968, "We, in this segment of the movement, do not believe that the oppression of women will be ended by giving them a bigger piece of the pie, as Betty Friedan would have it. We believe that the pie itself is rotten."[45] Radical feminism argues that patriarchy, and particularly its control over women's sexuality, is the root of women's second-class status. While changing women's legal rights and ensuring economic equality is important, women need to have control over their own bodies, and to combat patriarchal violence in the form of rape, domestic abuse, and warfare. **Lesbian feminism** took this one step further, claiming in the 1970s that heterosexuality itself oppressed women, and that lesbianism—or even complete separation from the world of men—could be a liberating political option.

Feminists in a school sometimes known as **difference feminism** or **essentialist feminism** have also tended to focus on separation from men. Like radical and lesbian feminists (though for different reasons), essentialist feminists have found themselves at odds with liberal feminism, which tends to see the differences between the sexes as an unnecessary relic of differential socialization. Basing their theory on psychoanalytic and psychological theories of gender difference, particularly the work of Carol Gilligan (see Chapter 4), they argue for a woman-centred culture that would value women's difference instead of seeing it as evidence of inferiority.

Many difference feminists also believe that valuing women's difference would mean fundamentally altering the world. In the 1970s and 1980s, essentialist feminists argued that war was a masculinist activity and that women, particularly as mothers, were protectors of life. In the Cold-War environment of the early 1980s, the time was particularly ripe for this message. Undoubtedly, the best example of this **maternalist** activism was the women's peace camp at the UK's Royal Air Force base Greenham Common. Established by Women for Life on Earth in 1981, the camp protested the installation of nuclear weapons, maintaining a constant presence for 19 years. Other essentialist feminists drew on a perceived connection between women and nature; though not all ecofeminists are essentialist, difference arguments have been important to the development of **ecofeminism** and its linkage of gender and environmental justice.

Liberal feminism, then, was criticized almost from the moment of its inception by a number of groups who saw its program as incomplete. No critique was more influential, however, than that of non-white feminists who found themselves marginalized within the movement they helped found. Today, many people seem to believe that 1970s feminism was a "white thing": but one 1972 US poll found that two-thirds of African-American women were sympathetic to the women's movement—*twice* the proportion of white women.[46] The issue, then, wasn't that feminism itself alienated non-white women. Indeed, NOW and other liberal feminist organizations attracted **women of colour**, but they often experienced marginalization within the movement. This might be marginalization as individuals (exclusion from leadership positions, for example); but even more often women of colour raised issues related to racism only to find the issue sidelined in favour of other issues seen as more important by white women.

Throughout the 1970s, women of colour (particularly in the US) developed an anti-racist critique and practice that defined a new **multiracial feminism**, in which all forms of domination were seen as feminist issues. The 1981 anthology *This Bridge Called My Back* collected the views of women of colour who responded to the following call:

> We want to express to all women—especially to white middle-class women—the experiences which divide us as feminists; we want to examine incidents of intolerance, prejudice, and denial of differences within the feminist movement. We intend to explore the causes and sources of, and solutions to these divisions. We want to create a definition that expands what "feminist" means to us.[47]

Working-class, Jewish, lesbian, disabled, and other feminists who were not necessarily women of colour responded enthusiastically to the critique developed in *This Bridge* and other similar texts, developing further discussions of how their "hyphenated" identities had shaped their experiences (and often their exclusion). **Identity politics** became central to feminist debates and discussions, and fundamentally reshaped the commitments and philosophy of second-wave feminism.

At the same time, however, troubling questions remained. Many of the identity debates took place within a North American context of relative privilege. As the 1980s began—and with the new aggressive foreign policy of the Thatcher-Reagan years—some feminists began to question their role as beneficiaries of a deeply inequitable division of global power and resources. By the 1980s, second-wave feminism had become a large, international, and diverse movement. This was amply demonstrated by the global conferences on the status of women convened by the United Nations in Mexico City (1975), Copenhagen (1980), Nairobi (1985), and Beijing (1995). At these conferences, it became clear that women's issues differed widely based on location—not just national location, but also ethnic and class status.

The 1980 United Nations World Conference on Women in Copenhagen highlighted tensions between "First-World" and "Third-World" feminists. In many ways, the debates at Nairobi echoed the arguments that had galvanized and divided 1970s feminists in North America. What constituted a "feminist" or "women's" issue? Can gender oppression be separated from other forms, such as class, racial, imperial, or economic domination? At Copenhagen it became clear that—just as the authors of *This Bridge Called My Back* had argued—feminism could not claim to speak for all or even a majority of women until it engaged with all forms of domination and marginalization. By the time of the Nairobi conference, this had become a shared understanding among First- and Third-World feminists, and the meeting of more than 13,000 delegates was much more successful than its predecessors. That said, the progress of women's global human rights has not been as encouraging as might have been hoped at the beginning of the UN's Decade for Women in 1975.[48]

By the end of the 1980s, Third-World women had fundamentally changed feminist activism; their perspectives also changed feminist theorizing. Chandra Mohade Mohanty's essay "Under Western Eyes," published in 1985, is a case in point. Arguing that "Western" feminists have created the "Third-World woman" as a frozen and stereotyped "Other," Mohanty called for a feminism that does not see "women" as a universal category of oppression, and that attends to the complexities of various social and national locations.[49] The essay is undoubtedly one of the most influential and most-cited works in feminist theory.

The critique of universalism continued from within the US. In 1989, Kimberlé Crenshaw published an essay called "Demarginalizing the Intersection of Race and Sex." Working from a black feminist legal studies perspective, Crenshaw sought to understand and theorize the invisibility of black women in the workplace and within "white feminism." Crenshaw coined the term **intersectionality** to describe the multiple axes on which women are located, all of which contribute to their experiences of marginalization. Structural intersectionality, according to Crenshaw, is the way in which women of colour are located at the intersection of race and gender, which makes their experience difference from that of white women. Political intersectionality refers to the membership of women of colour in at least two subordinated groups "that frequently pursue conflicting agendas."[50]

Arguably more influential than any other theoretical tool developed by feminism, intersectionality has become a key commitment of feminist theorizing and has spread well beyond feminism or women's studies. Feminist consensus today recognizes "the relationship among multiple dimensions and modalities of social relations and subject formations," as the best way of understanding gender. Therefore, according to most feminists, one cannot analyze the category "women" without recognizing that it is complicated by issues of ethnicity, class, culture, sexuality, ability, etc. Indeed, these complications may mean that talking about "women" may be meaningless in a given situation. According to Leslie McCall, this may be "the most important theoretical contribution that women's studies, in conjunction with related fields, has made so far."[51]

By the mid-1980s, then, feminism had become a diverse, fractious, and complex global movement with a well-developed theoretical foundation. Feminist activism, at least as measured by the number of feminist events convened, was at its peak. Since then, though its death is sometimes proclaimed in the popular media, feminism has continued to be a vibrant social movement and an important theoretical orientation. Scholars who study gender in many academic disciplines have been profoundly influenced by feminist theories and methodologies, which of course also inform research in women's, gender, and sexuality studies.

Post-colonial feminism and **post-modern feminism**, both of which emerged during the 1990s, share two key ideas: first, they oppose the idea of a "universal female subject" whose fundamental oppression is by virtue of gender; second, they agree that language is an important means by which domination is created and perpetrated. Both strands of feminism continue to be important in academic inquiry and, particularly in the case of post-colonial feminism, within social movements. Post-colonial feminism starts with the recognition of social and historical location presented in Chandra Mohanty's "Under Western Eyes" (discussed on p. 124). This variety of feminism is "post-colonial" because it recognizes the enormous historical impact of Western colonialism, not only on the material conditions of colonized people but also on the production of knowledge. Post-colonial feminisms oppose the idea that women all over the world experience comparable gender oppression and criticize the tendency of privileged Western women to speak for, misunderstand, and stereotype non-Western women.

Post-modern feminism, especially through the work of Judith Butler, has caused us to question fundamentally not only the sisterhood of women but also the existence and usefulness of the category itself. In her classic *Gender Trouble*, published in 1990, Butler argued that gender is essentially performative (in this, agreeing with the sociologists discussed above): that is, we "do" gender in order to be recognized as properly gendered subjects. Her key insight is that this performance actually produces not just gender but sex; there *is* no clear distinction between sex and gender, because the gender system actually produces the "sexed" bodies it demands. This can be seen, according to Butler, not just in intersex and trans surgeries, but also in the very labelling of a baby at birth. The proper work of feminism, then, is not to posit universal categories like "woman," but to question and dissect the category and disrupt its meanings, For this reason, Butler is particularly interested in drag queens and other "queer" enactments of gender. Because they are "imperfect" repetitions of gender, they call our attention to the performance that we all engage in.[52] Butler's work has been highly influential both in feminist theory and in other areas such as **queer theory**.

Key post-modern and post-colonial works were published precisely as some were proclaiming the "death of feminism," or the new **post-feminism**. In response, in the early 1990s, Rebecca Walker published an essay in which she argued that she and others like her were not post-feminist but "third-wave."[53] The **riot grrrl movement** of the early 1990s brought

third-wave feminism to punk and alternative music, combining a "do-it-yourself" ethic with powerful and aggressive lyrics and sounds. The explosion of the Internet in the 1990s contributed to the growth of third-wave feminism within popular culture. Third-wave feminism challenges what it perceives as limitations of second-wave feminism, celebrating ethnic diversity, complex identity, gender fluidity, individual agency, and self-expression (whether in sexuality, in dress, or in art). In keeping with its commitment to gender fluidity, third-wave feminism has been amenable to the inclusion of new perspectives such as queer and **transfeminism**. According to Emi Koyama, transfeminism is:

> primarily a movement by and for transwomen who view their liberation to be intrinsically linked to the liberation of all women and beyond. It is also open to other queers, intersex people, transmen, non-transwomen, non-transmen and others who are sympathetic toward needs of transwomen and consider their alliance with transwomen to be essential for their own liberation. Historically, transmen have made greater contribution to feminism than transwomen. We believe that it is imperative that more transwomen start participating in the feminist movement alongside others for our liberation.[54]

The inclusion of **transwomen** (and **transmen**) in feminism is far from complete and has a long and thorny history; but Koyama's call for a movement based not on "sex" (a concept critiqued by Butler and others) but on commitment to justice and liberation is timely—and hints at a positive and liberatory future for feminism.

Feminism has contributed immeasurably to our understanding of the social construction of gender. Feminism has also embraced the idea that gender cannot be analyzed independently of other modes of domination and determinants of social relations. Aside from this important theoretical contribution, feminist *activism* has also, quite obviously, changed Canadian (and other) societies throughout the past 150 years.

Masculinity, Men's Studies, and the Men's Movement: Extending the Critique of Gender

Feminist movements have always counted a number of male supporters, but many of the changes brought by both first- and second-wave feminism took place with men on the sidelines. Society changed, but men's socially approved roles did not. At the same time, masculinity was tested and challenged by feminism, by gay rights, and by movements for racial equality in the US and elsewhere. In addition, scholarship about men was both everywhere and nowhere. It was *everywhere* because—as women's studies advocates had pointed out in the 1970s—virtually every academic discipline was dominated by knowledge made by and about men. However, it was *nowhere* because virtually no one studied men *as men*. Indeed, as R.W. Connell points out, the "First Sex" has never received the sustained and careful treatment that Simone de Beauvoir gave women in her magisterial work on the topic.[55] Instead, the topic of masculinity was almost completely understudied; only psychology, as we have seen, dedicated significant attention to how masculinity was created.

At the same time as Beauvoir was writing about women, the pioneering attempt "to create a social science of masculinity" was underway within the study of sex roles. As discussed in Chapter 3, sex-role theory initially posited the "adaptive" nature of different sexual roles, but increasingly recognized that individuals might find their gendered roles constricting. As early as the late 1950s, there were signs of masculine discontent with the breadwinner role; according to Barbara Ehrenreich, the extraordinary success of *Playboy* magazine was an early indication of this "male rebellion":

> . . . through its articles, its graphics and its advertisements, *Playboy* presented, by the beginning of the sixties, something approaching a coherent program for the male rebellion. . . . Playboy was not the voice of the sexual revolution, which began, at least overtly, in the sixties, but of the male rebellion, which had begun in the fifties, The real message was not eroticism, but escape—literal escape, from the bondage of breadwinning.[56]

In the 1970s, Joseph Pleck built a sustained critique of the male sex role, proposing the "male sex-role strain model" (see Chapter 3). Nevertheless, the problems identified in role theory earlier in this chapter marred this scholarship, most notably by obscuring the power difference between male and female sex roles. Both roles might be constricting, but their hierarchical relationship was often overlooked in scholarship that focused on male "role strain." (Here we are discussing only scholarship, but role theory also affected the 1970s men's movement and its eventual split, as discussed below.) Furthermore, scholarship that focused on men's breadwinning role was uniformly heterosexual, white, and middle-class in emphasis, at a time when feminism was grappling (however painfully) with diversity.[57]

In the 1970s, feminist scholars investigated women and gender as categories of analysis, developing bodies of scholarship on structures of male domination, the sexual division of labour, and sexuality and power. They also began to engage in the study of men. As historian Natalie Zemon Davis wrote in the 1970s, studying women, without also studying men, seemed like studying peasants without understanding the elite; women were only part of a society, and they existed in a complex web of social relations with men.[58] Increasingly, *gender*, not women, became the category of study. In history, anthropology, and especially sociology, scholars of both sexes began to study men and masculinity; more male scholars, in particular, began to work in this area, usually from a position sympathetic to feminism.

Unlike sex-role theory and the masculinity studies that emerged within it, the new masculinity studies took seriously the insistence of feminism that gender was about power. Studying masculinity and its relationship with power, 1980s masculinity scholars published many important works and developed key theories that have continued to animate the field to the current day. R.W. Connell's *Gender and Power*, published in 1987, is a landmark work, specifically because it identified persistent and global inequalities between men and women, and established the universal subjection of women to men as the basis of (varied) definitions of masculinity and femininity. *Gender and Power* also systematically explained Connell's theories of hegemonic masculinity and emphasized femininity.[59]

As discussed in Chapter 1, hegemonic masculinity is the idea that at any time and place, there is one version of masculinity that is "culturally honoured." That masculinity is defined in relation to women but also in relation to other forms of masculinity that are subordinated. Connell offered this idea in part as a critique of sex-role theory, which failed to deal with the fact that there were *different* forms of masculinity, some of which were oppressed or marginalized; this notion of a "hierarchy of masculinities" was deeply influenced by Connell's observations of homophobia.[60]

What Connell brought to masculinity studies in the form of theory, others contributed to empirical study. Gail Bederman's *Manliness and Civilization* studied four Americans from the late nineteenth and early twentieth centuries, a period when the US was undergoing significant change and when class and race domination were virtually national obsessions. Bederman argued that the period saw the transition from Victorian ideas of "manliness," which emphasized duty, morality, and self-restraint, to "masculinity." In comparison to the manly ideal of the past, the new American masculinity was aggressive, domineering, and sexualized. Bederman demonstrated from an historical perspective how "hegemonic" ideals of masculinity could be altered in a relatively short period, and how those ideals intersected with class and race relations. Michael Kimmel followed, exploring an earlier period in US history. Beginning with the phrase "American men have no history," Kimmel's *Manhood in America* (1998) studies the development of American masculinity since the eighteenth century. Like Connell, Kimmel emphasizes the competition among men, stating, "masculinity is largely a homosocial enactment." For Kimmel, the diverse historical experiences of American men are united by "the quest for manhood—the effort to achieve, to demonstrate, to prove our masculinity."[61]

These themes—hegemonic masculinity, masculinity's intersections with national histories and social relations, and the need for men to struggle for their manhood—thread through much of the masculinity-studies scholarship that has emerged throughout the past three decades. A current database search using the term "hegemonic masculinity" retrieves more than 800 articles. Among them, one finds the concept of hegemonic masculinity used to investigate fatherhood and divorce, violence against women, homophobia, political campaigning, sports, education, and men's health.[62]

Like any foundational theory, Connell's hegemonic masculinity has been subject to critique and revision. Some scholars have criticized the undertheorizing of femininity in Connell's work. One of the great strengths of Connell's theory was the insistence that male domination of women formed the basis of masculinity; Connell also argues that "masculinity" does not exist except in contrast with "femininity."[63] Nevertheless, Connell's attention to femininity goes little further. Jeff Hearn therefore recommends adding three elements to Connell's theoretical foundation: exploration of the distinctions between different groups of men and their attitudes and practices toward women; observation of how women support or subordinate certain forms of masculinity; and examination of how men are formed within a hegemonic order that also forms boys, women, and other genders. Hearn also argues that the theory of hegemonic masculinity presents men as relatively powerless in the face of constructs of masculinity. Instead, he argues, men are both objects and agents of the gender system, "both a social category formed by the gender system and dominant collective and individual agents of social practices."[64]

Demetrakis Demetriou has also emphasized the importance of diversifying the concept of hegemonic masculinity; he sees it not as a "white, heterosexual phenomenon," but as a hybrid built of many forms of masculinity to ensure the continuance of patriarchal practice. Rather than simply being marginalized, non-hegemonic masculinities have a role to play—interacting with and influencing the dominant form. (One might see the "metrosexual" as an example of this type of interplay, as style norms drawn from an "abject" or subordinated homosexual form of masculinity were incorporated into the "hegemonic" version.) Steven Arxer examined how, in a homosocial pub setting, emotional conversation and acceptance of an individual who identified as gay were incorporated into group activities, even as women and masculine minorities were still excluded and subordinated.[65]

Despite these critiques, Connell and James Messerschmidt point out that the concept of hegemonic masculinity has weathered the test of time for more than 20 years. The many studies that have used the concept have confirmed Connell's key finding: that "certain masculinities are more socially central, or more associated with authority and social power than others," therefore indicating that hegemonic masculinity remains a core theory for the study of men and masculinity, both in North America and around the world.[66]

The field of masculinity or **men's studies** built by scholars such as those discussed above has coexisted with (and sometimes within departments of) women's and gender studies. Many of the theoretical and political commitments of masculinity studies are pro-feminist or anti-sexist. Scholars who work within masculinity studies generally accept a social constructionist point of view and critique male domination, for example.

Nevertheless, masculinity studies has also grown alongside the **men's movement**, which has a somewhat uneasy relationship both with feminism and with the direction that masculinity scholarship has taken. The history of the movement is instructive. As second-wave feminism grew in adherents and impact in the late 1960s and early 1970s, many men responded negatively, but some responded with support—and with interest in what feminism could mean for men. In 1970, some feminist events were already hosting workshops for "men's liberation"; five years later, North America boasted a generally pro-feminist **men's liberation movement**, and several books had been published on the topic. Many of the intellectuals initially attracted to the movement's goals came from the field of psychology; Joseph Pleck was one of them. Such scholars, and the movement leaders they influenced, believed that both men and women were oppressed by the sex roles into which they were socialized. Pragmatically, this proved to be an ideal way to attract men to the movement—as Michael Messner wryly notes, the message of **symmetry in oppression** was much more attractive than "a program that positioned men as oppressors whose only morally correct action would be self-flagellation."[67]

In the 1970s, men within the men's liberation movement engaged in practices comparable to feminist consciousness-raising; they gathered to share their experiences and emotions, and to engage in "masculinity therapy." Men would "get in touch with their feelings" and learn to undo the harms of a society that forced them into the rigid boxes of machismo. According to Harold C. Lyon, writing in 1977,

> . . . at long last men are beginning to seek one another out to create a common ground upon which to rebuild their confidence and to express their softer emotions, which have been suppressed and starved during years of dissembling and

self-avoidance. It is not a moment too soon. Men have become isolated inside the barren barricades of machismo, afraid to let anyone in and afraid to let themselves out. They live in constant fear that someone will see, behind the loud posturing, a lonely person locked inside himself. The rage and helpless feelings, which result, are hard to share.[68]

Much of the rhetoric of the late 1970s men's movement was supportive of feminism and its goals. Still, as Messner notes, the discourse of the men's liberation movement "walked a tightrope from the very beginning":

> First, movement leaders acknowledged that sexism had been a problem for women and that feminism was a necessary social movement to address gender inequities. But they also stressed the equal importance of the high costs of the male sex role to men's health, emotional lives, and relationships. In short, they attempted to attract men to feminism by constructing a discourse that stressed how the "male role" was "impoverished," "unhealthy," and even "lethal" for men (Jourard 1971). Thus, from the outset, there were obvious strains and tensions from the movement's attempt to focus simultaneously on men's institutional power and the "costs of masculinity" to men.[69]

As discussed above, the sex-role paradigm through which scholars were studying masculinity in the 1970s contributed to this tension.

By the end of the 1970s, the tension between supporting feminism and seeing men as "equally oppressed" by their sex roles came to a head; the result was a split within the movement. Part of the context was the success of feminism, but other historical processes only partially connected to feminism undoubtedly played a role in producing the men's rights movement too. One important factor was the decline, throughout the Western world, in the well-paid, unionized industrial employment so associated with "men's work" at that time. Rising divorce rates, the flood of women into paid employment, the gay-rights movement, and changing race relations all brought significant change for North American ideals of masculinity. The stereotypical red-blooded heterosexual breadwinner and household head seemed to many men an endangered species.[70]

Through the 1980s, then, the men's movement went in three distinct directions. Some men's groups continued to support feminism, and **pro-feminist** men's groups continue to be a feature of the movement today. However, these groups and individuals have been less prominent than those in the **men's rights movement** (who have criticized what they believed to be a disadvantaging of men in contemporary American law, economy, and culture). A third network, the **mythopoetic/new men's movement**, discussed further below, arose in the 1980s to carry on the consciousness-raising and therapeutic work of 1970s masculinity therapy from a new cultural perspective.

The men's rights movement drew on the 1970s idea of "symmetry in oppression" to develop a critique of both contemporary society and feminism. Remember that in the 1970s, men's groups examined the "costs" of the masculine role, arguing that both men and women were oppressed by the sex-role system. By the mid- to late 1970s, some men were arguing that in fact men were *more* oppressed than women and that male privilege was actually a "myth." Psychologist Herb Goldberg's 1976 book *The Hazards of Being Male: Surviving the Myth of Male Privilege* makes clear in its title the new emphasis of the movement.

> Precisely because the tenor and mood of the male liberation efforts so far have been one of self-accusation, self-hate, and a repetition of feminist assertions, I believe it is doomed to failure in its present form. It is buying the myth that the male is culturally favoured—a notion that is clung to despite the fact that every critical statistic in the area of longevity, disease, suicide, crime, accidents, childhood emotional disorders, alcoholism, and drug addiction shows a disproportionately higher male rate.[71]

Goldberg's work made many claims, including:

- American society is "matriarchal," breeding dependency in men's relationships with women, making them exceptionally vulnerable to relationship breakdown.
- The American man is expected to "perform" sexually in a context of monogamy and unhappy relationships antithetical to true sexual enjoyment.
- The American man is sexually attractive to women only insofar as he is successful and oppressed by his own fears of homosexuality.
- The American man is humiliated by the prostitutes he frequents in search of a moment of authentic sexual connection.

Goldberg steered clear of overt attacks on the women's movement, and in fact assured men that women's liberation was a good thing. However, he made clear that in the absence of a comparable men's movement, the effect of feminism would be damaging to men.

Within a few years, Goldberg's book had become the "Bible" of the new men's rights movement. Men's rights groups formed across the US and to some extent in Canada; and as the 1980s proceeded, overt hostility to feminism and the "matriarchy" (and their male supporters) became characteristic of the movement. Turning the arguments of the women's movement on their ear, the men's rights movement claimed widespread masculine oppression and reverse sexism in every aspect of American life: employment, marriage law, child custody, media representations, rape prosecution, prostitution, pornography, heterosexuality, and domestic violence. For example, an analysis of more than 300 father's rights websites in the US found that three themes were central to the groups' discourse: that domestic violence allegations are false, that joint custody should be presumptive and child support lessened, and that women are the chief perpetrators of domestic abuse.[72]

The changing tone of men's activism in the 1980s can be seen in the path taken by Warren Farrell, who in the 1970s was part of the men's liberation movement but who moved to a more radical men's rights position. His 1993 book *The Myth of Male Power: Why Men Are the Disposable Sex* took Goldberg's argument further, claiming that men were "disposable" in contemporary society and comparing men's oppression to that of African-Americans. As evidence, Farrell cited compulsory military service, applied to men only; he also argued that fathers' rights (and children's welfare) were being trampled by courts captured by feminism. Known among men's rights activists as the "red pill,"

Farrell's book has become the central text of the movement. [73]Along with Farrell's book, the most important catalyst for the men's rights movement was undoubtedly the growth of the Internet. In the "manosphere," men's rights forums thrive along with their own language and acronyms: MGTOW, for example, are "Men Going Their Own Way," who have renounced the expected course of relationships with women; "manginas" are male supporters of feminism. As some of the language used online suggests, men's rights rhetoric has changed since the days of Goldberg. Overtly hostile attacks on feminists, on women in general, and on particular women have characterized the online presence of the movement. The most extreme example of this hostility was manifested in the Elliot Rodgers murders of 2014. Rodgers's 141-page autobiographical manifesto revealed his participation in the online "pickup-artist community," which fuelled his hatred of women and his rage at their "rejection" of him.[74] Despite some disavowal of Rodger's actions, the increasingly hostile and violent rhetoric of the men's rights movement has not abated. Meanwhile, the movement continues to attract at least some followers, both men and women. A Voice for Men, founded by Paul Elam in 2009, has become an umbrella for the US movement, and hosted its first national gathering in Detroit in 2014 amid angry protests.[75]

As we have seen, the men's rights movement was, to a great extent, an elaboration of the 1970s men's liberation movement and its founding idea—that men were disadvantaged by their sex role. This idea, and the "masculinity therapy" of the 1970s, would become the basis of the third strand of the men's movement in the 1980s and 1990s, the mythopoetic/new men's movement. Like the men's rights movement, the new men's movement had its own foundational text: in this case, poet Robert Bly's *Iron John*. Published in 1990, *Iron John* remained on *The New York Times* bestseller list for more than a year. Bly accepted some of the basic tenets of Farrell and Goldberg's critique: in *Iron John*, he identifies Western men as "soft," feminized by culture, in contrast to the "hairy" man. To counteract this feminizing, Bly suggested men needed to return to their hunter-gatherer roots. He called for the gathering of men in homosocial groups to engage in drumming, rituals, and the mentoring of boys into manhood (through rituals of initiation conducted by older men).[76] Enormously successful in the 1990s, the movement has diminished in the new century, though it still has adherents, especially in New Age and religious circles.

From 1970 to the present, then, the feminist movement has been paralleled (and sometimes supported) by a loose movement that investigates and comments on our culture's norms of masculinity. In the scholarly arena, masculinity studies have become one of the most vibrant strands of gender scholarship, with the theory of hegemonic masculinity supplying the lynchpin for a great deal of productive research. Men's gender activism, however, has been split since the late 1970s, with the men's rights movement arguably the most active (and antagonistic) counterpart to the women's movement.

Toward an Explanation of the Social Construction of Gender Relations

We have argued that gender is socially constructed: that it is neither the expression of biology nor simply a role. Then how *shall* we think about gender? The elements of a definition seem clear enough. We'll explore three related levels: identity, interaction, and institution—and, of course, the interactions among them, in order to explain the related phenomena: gender difference and gender inequality.

First, *we understand that gender, as an identity, is not a "thing" that one possesses, but rather a set of activities that one does.* When we do gender, we do it in front of other people; it is validated and legitimated by the evaluations of others. Gender is less a property of the individual than it is a product of our interactions with others. West and Zimmerman call gender a "managed property," which is "contrived with respect to the fact that others will judge and respond to us in particular ways." Women and men are distinct social groups, constituted in "concrete, historically changing—and generally unequal—social relationships." What the great British historian E.P. Thompson once wrote about class applies equally to gender. Gender "is a relationship, not a thing"—and like all relationships, we are active in their construction. We do not simply inherit a male or female sex role, but we actively—interactively—constantly define and redefine what it means to be men or women in our daily encounters with one another. Gender is something one *does*, not something one *has*.[77]

Second, *we understand that we do gender in every interaction, in every situation, in every institution in which we find ourselves.* Gender is a situated accomplishment, as much an aspect of interaction as it is of identity. As James Messerschmidt puts it, "gender is a situated accomplishment in which we produce forms of behaviour seen by others in the same immediate situation as masculine or feminine." Gender is what we bring to these interactions and what is produced in them as well.[78]

Third, *we do gender not in a genderless vacuum but, rather, in a gendered world, in gendered institutions.* Our social world is built on systemic, structural inequality based on gender; social life reproduces both gender difference and gender inequality. We need to think of masculinity and femininity "not as a single object with its own history, but as being constantly constructed within the history of an evolving social structure." As Karen Pyke defines it, gender is:

> an emergent property of situated interaction rather than a role or attribute. Deeply held and typically non-conscious beliefs about men's and women's essential natures shape how gender is accomplished in everyday interactions. Because those beliefs are moulded by existing macrostructural power relations, the culturally appropriate ways of producing gender favour men's interests over those of women. In this manner, gendered power relations are reproduced.[79]

In short, social constructionism is able to explain both what is really different between women and men and what is not really different but only seems to be, as well as the ways in which gender difference is the product of—and not the cause of—gender inequality. We are gendered people living gendered lives in a gendered society—but we do actually live on the same planet. (In fact, it may be that only on this planet would such differences make a difference.)

In the remainder of this book, we'll look at some of the institutions that create gender difference and reproduce gender inequality—families, schools, and workplaces—and observe some of the ways in which those differences and that inequality are expressed through our interactions with one another—in love, sex, friendship, and violence.

Summary

Beginning from a critique of biological determinism, the social sciences (including sociology), along with feminist theory, view human behaviour as largely socially constructed. As the experiences of social isolates suggest, even basic human behaviour is determined by interaction with others. The belief that we are the product of interactions rather than of our biology is referred to as social constructionism.

As discussed in Chapter 1, the four elements of a social constructionist perspective are that gender varies from culture to culture, in any one culture over historical time, over the course of a person's life, and within any one culture at any one time. Social constructionism accordingly offers the ability to explain variations within gender, and therefore adds an analysis of difference, power, and gender's institutional dimensions.

In contrast, sex-role theory is more limited in its ability to explain these phenomena. Social constructionists identify six related problems with sex-role theory, which minimizes the importance of gender; posits singular definitions of masculinity and femininity; ignores the relational dimension of gender; negates the situational quality of gendered interactions; depoliticizes gender by making it an individual, not societal, attribute; and, finally, cannot account for the dynamics of change. Indeed, sex-role theory almost implies that the roles people play are the result of fundamental personality differences socialized early in life *rather* than the result of power-laden social relations themselves. In some senses, then, sex-role theory "blames the victim."

This book, in contrast, argues that gender is fundamentally about differences *and* power. Gender is not just a role, but also a power relationship between men and women that also operates among groups of men and women. This doesn't mean that all men are powerful, or that all women are powerless; it means that men *as a group*, in most places in the world, are more powerful than women are as a group. Power is not just an individual possession, but also a property of group and social life. It is deeply woven into our lives, our interactions, and our institutions. For sociologists and feminists, power is a central part of gender analysis. Sociology also adds three essential components to the study of gender. First is a *life-course approach*, which acknowledges how much gender varies through the course of any individual's life. Childhood, early adulthood, middle age, and senior years bring tremendous transformations in experiences of and perspectives on gender. For social constructionists, these changes are the result not of biological processes of maturation and aging but of the *meanings* societies ascribe to these processes and the changing institutions in which an individual finds him- or herself.

The second critical contribution of sociology to the study of gender is a *macro-level institutional analysis*. Sociologists consider institutions of the utmost importance to the constitution of any society and its individual members. Institutions, like individuals, are gendered. They create normative gendered standards, express gendered logic, and are major factors in the reproduction of gender inequality. Scholars have studied many social institutions—from paid employment to public washrooms—and have uncovered compelling evidence that institutions are not "gender-neutral" sites, but places that reinforce gender difference and reproduce the gendered social order.

Finally, sociology contributes a *micro-level interactionist approach* that sees gender not as a fixed character or set of traits that we acquire through role socialization but as something that emerges and changes through various social interactions. Gender, in this view, is something that we perform differently in various situations in our lives. Gender is not something we "have," but something we "do."

These views are shared not only by sociologists but also by feminist theorists and activists. Feminists have long argued that women were not essentially different from men as had been claimed, but were instead socialized differently. Though first-wave feminists were less likely to advance this claim, second- and third-wave feminists became strong proponents of social constructionism. Feminists of all "waves" contributed a cogent analysis of gendered power, and organized activism to confront male privilege. This activism has had a massive effect on society, to such an extent that many feminist claims of the past are now regarded as "standard operating procedure," from women's voting rights to reformed sexual assault laws. Still, as feminism became a massive social movement in the 1970s, it became increasingly diverse and fractious, with many different "schools" or approaches with diverse perspectives on power and social construction of gender. Despite these differences, in Canada and around the world, feminism has catalyzed dramatic changes and contributed to our knowledge and awareness of the social construction of gender. Among the most important theoretical contributions of recent feminism, intersectionality stands out as a recognition that gender analysis is complicated by other features of social relations (racism, for example).

The theoretical contributions of feminism have been important to the development of masculinity studies, which now constitutes an important domain of gender studies. During the 1970s, masculinity studies focused on sex-role theory and the oppressive effects of the male sex role on men. In keeping with the general limitations of sex-role theory, this approach had the effect of obscuring the fact that male and female "roles" were situated differently with regard to power. During the 1980s, R.W. Connell developed the theory of hegemonic masculinity, which more clearly articulated what masculinity was as well as its relationship to power. Connell argued that masculinity was premised upon male domination, but that in any time and place there might be multiple forms of masculinity, only one of them "hegemonic" or culturally honoured. While scholars have reviewed and commented on elements of Connell's theory, it remains the core theoretical tool of masculinity theory.

Masculinity studies, generally anti-sexist or pro-feminist, have an uneasy relationship with the men's movement. The movement originated in the 1970s in response to feminism and took a generally pro-feminist stance. Over the course of the decade, this changed, and in the 1980s, the movement bifurcated into an antifeminist men's rights wing and a mythopoetic new men's approach that was less hostile to feminism but concerned about the "feminization" of men and culture. Both strains of the men's rights movement have criticized contemporary masculinity, though from a very different perspective from that of masculinity studies scholars.

This chapter has argued that gender is neither an expression of biology nor a role. Instead, we argue, gender difference and gender inequality emerge at three levels: identity, interaction, and institution. At the level of identity, gender is not a possession but a set of activities that one performs for others. At the second level, interaction, we perform gender in accordance with our situations. We bring gender to our interactions and produce gender through those interactions at the same time. Finally, we do gender in gendered institutions, within evolving social structures built on structurally unequal gender relations. Our differences are not just within us, and this book argues that they are smaller than we often think. Nevertheless, we are gendered people, and more importantly, we have gendered interactions within a gendered society.

Questions for Critical Thinking

1. Considering the four elements of a social constructionist perspective—that definitions of gender vary from culture to culture, in any one culture over time, throughout the course of an individual's life, and within any one culture at any one time—can you identify examples of each variation from your own knowledge or experience?
2. Given that power is situational, can you imagine examples of how someone might be powerful in one situation and yet relatively powerless in another?
3. Thinking about a particular social interaction, can you explain how gender is a thing that one *does* and not a thing that one *has*? Do you agree with this assessment of how gender identity works?
4. Consider any particular social institution you can think of—or perhaps one with which you are personally familiar. How does that institution (a) create normative gendered standards; (b) express a gendered logic; and (c) reproduce gender inequality?
5. How do you believe feminist theory or activism has affected your life? Do you believe that feminism has continued relevance in either examining or challenging the construction of gender? How would the concept of intersectionality affect a gendered analysis of your life or your community?
6. Why do you think that the men's movement has split in the way that it has?

Key Terms

confirmation bias
consciousness-raising
difference feminism
ecofeminism
essentialist feminism
first-wave feminism
gender divisions
gender images
identity politics
institutions
intersectionality
lesbian feminism
liberal feminism
maternalist
Marxist and socialist feminisms
men's movement
men's liberation movement
men's rights movement
men's studies
mid-life crisis
multiracial feminism
mythopoetic/new men's movement

narrative coherence
organizational gender
   neutrality
post-colonial feminism
post-feminism
post-modern feminism
primary sex characteristics
pro-feminist
queer theory
radical feminism
riot grrrl movement
secondary sex characteristics
second-wave feminism
sociology
symmetry in oppression
third-wave feminism
transfeminism
transmen
transwomen
woman movement
women of colour
Women's Liberation Movement

Part 2

Gendered Identities, Gendered Institutions

6

The Gendered Family
Gender at the Heart of the Home

*To the family—that dear octopus from whose tentacles we never quite escape, nor,
in our inmost hearts, ever quite want to.*
—Dodie Smith, *Dear Octopus*

In the 1980s and 1990s, some North Americans believed that the family was "in crisis"—
falling apart because of divorce, teen pregnancy, single parenthood, "latchkey children,"
and the gay-rights movement. The so-called "Moral Majority" of the US and REAL Women
of Canada were responses to this "crisis."[1] REAL Women, and other social conservatives
in Canada and the US, uphold what they call the "traditional" nuclear family. According
to one of its defenders, this family form is based on "a legal lifelong sexually exclusive,
heterosexual monogamous marriage, based on affection and companionship, in which
there is a sharp division of labour with the female as full-time housewife and the male
as primary provider and ultimate authority." In the US, punitive policy initiatives have
attempted to shore up this "besieged" institution through laws that restrict divorce and
abortion, reiterate a heterosexual norm in family life, and recast marriage from a legal
contract to a sacred "covenant."[2]

The North American family *has* changed dramatically. Nevertheless, discussions of
the so-called "traditional" family often ignore the many changes in this basic institution
over the course of human history. What we call "traditional" may in fact be a very recent
construction. Canadian families have changed dramatically over the course of our history
and continue to adapt to changing circumstances.

A Brief History of the Canadian (and North American) Family

Though this discussion will focus primarily upon Canada after colonization, any history of the Canadian family must begin with **Aboriginal** peoples. Generalization about
pre-contact history is difficult, given the paucity of sources and the diversity of indigenous cultures, but it's clear that Aboriginal families were different in many ways from the

"ideal" family structures imagined by colonizing Europeans (and imposed upon Aboriginal people with damaging consequences).

Before Europeans colonized Canada, First Nations and Inuit people lived in family structures based on diverse traditions and practices. **Nuclear families** were important everywhere, as they were to Europeans. However, overlapping with nuclear and **extended family** structures were **clan** structures that also provided a concept of "family ties," as can be seen through common prohibitions on marrying someone from one's own clan.[3]

In part because of the importance of clans and extended kin, pre-contact Aboriginal families cannot be described as patriarchal. The "sexual contract" varied widely among Aboriginal groups, and some granted men greater status. However, many Aboriginal groups were relatively egalitarian or, more accurately, practised **gender complementarity**. That is, a division of labour assigned different tasks to men and women, but male privilege either did not exist or was limited by other forms of customary power. Though not all Aboriginal groups were matrilineal or **matrilocal**, matrilineage was common. Among some groups, particularly the Iroquoian nations, the customary power of women as mothers extended to significant control over both material resources and political structures. For this reason, some Aboriginal women today argue that "equality" is a meaningless goal for them, because they once enjoyed a different but celebrated role.[4]

In early colonial Canada, New France's missionaries attempted to inculcate Christian family life, including male domination and female obedience, in First Nations people. Their successes were limited not only by the relatively few Aboriginal groups with whom they worked but also by resistance, particularly on the part of women.[5] However, not all Aboriginal people resisted Christian teachings; some women (and men) adopted the new religion and adapted its "spiritual toolkit."[6]

Other groups of Europeans were much less interested in reforming Aboriginal families than they were in joining them. For European fur traders, the knowledge and kin ties of First Nations wives were critical to success and even survival.[7] The children of fur traders and their wives (whether officially married or "country wives") became the founders of the Métis people, one of Canada's three recognized Aboriginal groups and a distinct culture of great significance to the nation's history.

The Métis family, however, did not become the Canadian norm. As European colonization spread, more European women arrived, and settlers began to create households based on marriages between European men and women. These households were unlike the nuclear families we now think of as traditional. Most were agrarian, and such households, like Aboriginal ones, were productive entities in which everyone worked to ensure family survival. Therefore, settler women often enjoyed customary control over household matters and performed valued and essential tasks. Still, European settler society granted greater prestige and status to men. Men defined manhood through their status as landowners, heads of household, and participants in community and political life. Women owed men respect and deference.

Still, it's worth noting some of the ways in which these settler families differed from what we now think of as the norm. There was far less differentiation between "his" and "her" spheres: Women and men both worked in and around their homes, producing many of the things needed for the family and for sale to others. Everyone worked to a rhythm of family and the seasons, as is captured by a diary entry written in 1891 by Mary Smith of Cape Breton, then 79:

> A very dry high easterly wind. The first tub Butter full 22 lbs. The little mare very sick. The boys hear helping doctor her. Flora washed her weeks washing. I washed breakfast dishes then cleared the kitchen cupboard and washed all the things that was in it and after that the men moved it out of the clothes room into the kitchen. I washed dinner dishes and then had a rest and Sarah moved everything out of the dining room took up the carpet and swept and dusted and I washed the windows. The two girls washed up the floor and Sarah got tea ready and after tea she churned. Flora picked the geese and then put them down in the calf pasture; the children and G.P. finished picking stone a little while after dinner and then the men fixed the fence to keep the geese in. Sarah cleaned up the milk house all ready to wash the shelf and the floor and Flora and the girls finished it up.[8]

Men's work and women's work were separate, but occurred within the same spaces and times, complementing one another, in US historian Laurel Thatcher Ulrich's famous metaphor, like the "warp and weft" of a piece of gingham. Men's work and women's work were distinct and separate, like the contrasting colours within the cloth, but they were woven together.[9] Children worked alongside the men and women, growing into their distinct gendered duties as they grew into adulthood.

In pre-industrial Canada, just as women and men were involved in the worlds of work, fathers and mothers were both involved in child rearing. Mothers undoubtedly did the lion's share, charged by custom with infant care and the rearing of young children. Given the high fertility and infant mortality of the time, the lives of women were disproportionately dedicated to birthing, caring for, and, sadly, burying children. Fathers took over more responsibility as children grew, particularly as sons began to learn the skills and behaviours that would be required of them as men.

This family structure was changed in Canada, as elsewhere, by the linked processes of industrialization and urbanization, which began (however tentatively) in the first decades of the nineteenth century and spread throughout the nation by 1900. By about 1850, throughout the industrializing world, a gap between work and home was growing, both in reality and in ideology, to create the **separation of spheres**. Family life "was wrenched apart from the world of work," and the workplace and the home clearly demarcated as *his* and *hers*. In 1849, Alfred Lord Tennyson expressed this separation of spheres in a poem, "The Princess":

> Man for the field and woman for the hearth: Man for the sword and for the needle she: Man with the head and woman with the heart: Man to command and woman to obey; All else confusion.[10]

Men experienced this separation in two ways. First, for most men, work shifted from home and farm to mill, factory, shop, and office, becoming synonymous with *paid* labour. As farm mechanization spread, the agricultural workforce shrank and men moved to where work was, the day's rhythm shifting to that of industry. Second, men's share of the work around the home was gradually industrialized and eliminated as such tasks as fuel provision, leather working, and grain processing shifted to the external world. This further "liberated" men to exit their homes and leave the rearing of both sons and daughters to their wives.

Women's position was also changed. In popular literature, from pulpits and in high art, women's (unpaid) labour was re-conceptualized, not as "work" at all but rather as a God-given mission. Although some home-based work was gradually eliminated, such as spinning and weaving, much of women's sphere remained intact; women still cleaned, cooked meals, and baked bread, even if their husbands no longer grew and milled the grain or butchered the meat they cooked. "Domestic" labour was now increasingly known as "housework" and associated with women.

As men's and women's spheres separated, the relationship between the sexes remained hierarchical. As Catharine Beecher and Harriet Beecher Stowe wrote in their celebrated book, *The American Woman's Home* (1869):

> When the family is instituted by marriage, it is man who is head and chief magistrate by the force of his physical power and requirement of the chief responsibility; not less is he so according to the Christian law, by which, when differences arise, the husband has the deciding control, and the wife is to obey.[11]

Many historians of Europe and North America argue that this new ideology actually represented a *decline* in women's status. However, men's "liberation" from the home was also partly illusory. As early as the 1820s and 1830s, US critics were complaining that men spent too little time at home. "Paternal neglect at the present time is one of the most abundant sources of domestic sorrow," wrote the Reverend John S.C. Abbott in *Parents Magazine* in 1842. The father, "eager in the pursuit of business, toils early and late, and finds no time to fulfill . . . duties to his children." Theodore Dwight attempted to persuade men to resume their responsibilities at home in *The Father's Book* (1834), one of America's first advice books for men.[12]

The family had now become the "haven in a heartless world" that the great French writer Alexis de Tocqueville observed when he visited the United States in the early 1830s. "Shorn of its productive functions, the family now specialized in child rearing and emotional solace, providing a much needed sanctuary in a world organized around the impersonal principles of the market."[13]

Of course, the ideology and reality of the separate spheres were largely white and middle class, because only relatively high incomes could support a stay-at-home wife. Everywhere, working-class and non-white women "laboured to maintain, sustain, stabilize, and reproduce their families while working in both the public (productive) and private (reproductive) spheres."[14] In Canada, well into the twentieth century, many families were sustained not by a male **breadwinner**, but by the pooled earnings of men, women, and children.

Until the late nineteenth century (and in Quebec, the twentieth century), the earnings of all family members belonged legally to the family's male head. At a time when the average man consumed more alcohol than men do today, the allocation of family income to excessive drinking fuelled the **temperance movement**, which united feminists and religious reformers.[15] Therefore, the picture of family found in separate-spheres ideology—with a sober, hardworking father and a domestic "angel in the house"—was experienced by relatively few.

As the family changed and became associated with women, its economic and social importance also declined—but its *symbolic* importance increased. Events that had been casually organized now became family events; community celebrations became household celebrations. US historian John Gillis writes:

> When men had worked at home, mealtimes had seldom been private, or even very regular. Holidays had revolved around community festivals and visiting rather than home-cooked meals and private family celebrations. Leisurely dinner hours, Sunday family time, and nuclear family togetherness on holidays such as Christmas were invented during the mid-nineteenth century.[16]

By 1900, North American commentators were fretting about the crisis of the family. "In 50 years, there will be no such thing as marriage," predicted esteemed Harvard psychologist John Watson.[17] Canadian Christian commentators, too, worried about the decline of the ideal Christian family and masculine family leadership (as they would 100 years later).[18] As large-scale immigration flooded North America with non-British immigrants, white concerns about **race suicide** and sexual contact between white women and non-white men spread—particularly in provinces, like British Columbia, that experienced significant Asian immigration.

Canadian Aboriginal families also became the target of reformist zeal. From the passage of the Indian Act (1867) to the end of the nineteenth century, reports consistently advocated the education of Aboriginal children, and both residential and day schools were established in various locations across the country. By 1920, amendments to the act had made school attendance mandatory. The goal of schooling was frankly assimilationist. In the words of Duncan Campbell Scott, the "whole object" was "to continue until there is not a single Indian in Canada that has not been absorbed into the body politic, and there is no Indian question, and no Indian department."[19] Because Aboriginal parents were viewed as an obstacle to the acculturation of their offspring, separating children—even extremely young children—from their parents for up to ten months at a time was seen as appropriate and desirable. By 1930, there were 80 church-run **residential schools** in operation throughout Canada.

As the **Truth and Reconciliation Commission** (TRC) process has made painfully clear, the residential school experience and its effects—known now as "residential school syndrome"—were devastating for the entire Aboriginal community. In addition to enduring painful separations from their parents and communities, children in these schools generally received substandard education, were poorly nourished, and were subjected to aggressive forced acculturation and abuse. Students were beaten and tortured for "infractions" including speaking their native languages, and many were sexually abused by the clergy who taught in the schools, by lay staff members, and even by other students. In 2007, the federal government implemented financial compensation for survivors of these traumas. In June 2015, the TRC released its report and a list of 94 actions required to effect reconciliation between Aboriginal and non-Aboriginal Canadians; many of the recommendations relate to ameliorating the harms to the Aboriginal family produced by colonialist policy.[20]

The attack on the Aboriginal family by assimilationist practices was severe indeed; ironically, commentators through the twentieth century were less concerned with this attack than with what they perceived as a general decline of the non-Aboriginal family. Indeed, the separation of spheres provided the foundation for a virtual "perpetual crisis" of the family throughout the twentieth century.

As we have seen, from the 1850s, North American women had been demanding more rights—to property, to education, to employment, and to protection from marital abuse. Over the next seventy-odd years, women won many new rights, culminating in women's suffrage at the end of the First World War. (As noted in Chapter 5, not all women were able to vote; those who were part of a group excluded from suffrage—such as Chinese and Aboriginal Canadians—did not benefit from this new "women's" right.) Women's new ability to vote (and, increasingly, to attend higher education and earn their own money) exemplified the era of the so-called **New Woman**, who did not need to depend upon a man. Not everyone approved.

Between the First and Second World Wars, women's efforts to go to college, enter the labour force, join unions, attend professional schools, and manage their fertility were met with significant resistance. Nonetheless, women continued to enter employment outside the home, even during the Great Depression, when many people felt that employed women were "stealing men's jobs." In Toronto in 1931, one of every four wage-earners was a woman, and many Canadian women found themselves the sole breadwinners for their families.[21] Economic realities drove many women to work, even as the Canadian ideal remained the nuclear family with a male breadwinner head.

The Second World War disrupted this pattern further, as women entered the labour force in dramatic numbers, driven by the wartime shortage of male labour and federal incentives such as the full tax exemption for working wives regardless of income. Post-war, however, the North American nuclear family was stabilized by economic boom (fuelled by massive government expenditures in highway and school construction) and veterans' bills (such as the 1942 Veterans' Land Act) that made land and home ownership more accessible.[22]

The period between 1945 and 1960 brought a dramatic increase in marriage rates and a sharp decline in the ages of first marriage. In 1946, the US marriage rate hit an all-time high of 14.2 per 1000 (compared to 9.6 in 1867). A similar pattern emerged in post-war Canada, where traditionally higher ages at first marriage dropped significantly. By 1950, about half of women aged 20–24 were married. (The comparable rate for 1871 was 38 per cent; in 2002 it was 11 per cent!)[23]

Therefore, despite some distinctions between Canada and the US, we can see that across North America a distinct 1950s pattern of family life emerged. This model—characterized by high rates of marriage (and young age at marriage), high fertility, and low and stable rates of divorce—"was the product of a convergence of an unusual series of historical, demographic and economic circumstances unlikely to return again," in the words of two leading family historians.[24]

Yet as soon as this new family form emerged, it was declared to be natural and "traditional"—that is, both biologically inevitable and morally appropriate. In academia,

Courtesy of The Advertising Archives

The (white, middle-class, suburban) family romance of the 1950s. This advertising image shows Father returning to his well-appointed home, where modern appliances and a well-tended family eagerly await.

the structural-functionalist school of social science gave this new family model legitimacy, arguing that the isolated **suburban** nuclear family, with distinct separation of spheres, served the needs of both children and society.[25]

In the 1950s, a generation of middle-class men tried to toe the line of bland conformity as suburban breadwinners. A generation of women cooked and cleaned, dusted and mopped, washed and ironed, toiling to meet ever-increasing standards of cleanliness and **intensive mothering**.

For many parents and children of the baby boom, this family form worked well. Middle-class North Americans took family vacations and hung out together in family rooms. Some husbands doted on their wife-companions, and together they built lives more stable, comfortable, child-centred, and companionable—divorce being a last resort—than anything their own parents had ever envisioned. Many women found their roles, particularly motherhood, fulfilling.

Still, the veneer of domestic bliss only partially concealed an increasing restlessness on the part of both husbands and wives, many of whom felt frustrated and unhappy with this supposedly "natural" family form. Some fathers felt alienated from their families and especially from their children. Wives, many of whom had attended university and/or been employed before marriage, now laboured under the "senseless tyranny of spotless shirts and immaculate floors," swallowing their growing resentment as the world passed them by. In his 1957 book *America as a Civilization*, historian Max Lerner argued, "the unhappy wife has become a characteristic culture type."[26]

Such unhappiness also fuelled an increasingly politicized anger. Women had won significant and unprecedented rights in the early twentieth century, and yet their lives seemed to run on as they always had. As Doris Anderson wrote in a *Chatelaine* editorial in October 1958, "We have had the vote for a good long 40 years," and yet,

> We seem to be stuck at an awkward halfway point. We're constantly being praised for advances that were made by women almost two generations ago. It's true that we have some of the most elaborate kitchens, the sleekest figures, and the best clothes in the world. But it's incredible that we are not serving our country as effectively as other women do where the right to vote is as new and remarkable as a push-button stove.[27]

North American women's discontent boiled over in 1963, when Betty Friedan's feminist call to arms, *The Feminine Mystique*, hit the bestseller lists. Calling the suburban home a "comfortable concentration camp," Friedan declared that real life lay outside it. Men too chafed at the responsible role of the suburban breadwinner; the launch of *Playboy* magazine in 1953 and the rise of beatnik culture can both be seen as signs of masculine rebellion.[28]

In fact, the so-called "traditional" family was already beginning to crack under its own symbolic weight. The family was now supposed to be the sole source of comfort and pleasure in an increasingly cold, bureaucratic world; the marital union was now the single most important and sustaining bond of intimacy and friendship that a person could have. Gone were the more "traditional" supports of community networks, civic participation, and extended kinship ties—now the family was supposed to provide for all psychological and emotional needs. It was almost too much to bear: The "traditional" family was an anachronism from the moment of its birth.

State of the North American Family

Much of the talk of "crisis" is really about nostalgia for a short-lived family form that was less well-adapted to modern society than its proponents thought it was. However, there is no doubt that the Canadian family is very different today from what it was 50 years ago.

Many families are indeed in crisis, partly because of growing social inequality. Statistics suggest that the average American family is worse off today than 50 years ago. In 1970, 15 per cent of all American children under age 18 were living in families defined as "poor"; today that number is 22 per cent, with 45 per cent of children living in "low-income" families.[29]

Canada follows a different methodology for measuring income. There is no clear threshold for poverty; instead, Statistics Canada establishes a **Low-Income Cut Off** (LICO) line, which represents 50 per cent of the median income (based on family and community size). Because Statistics Canada changed its methodology for the 2012 survey, it is difficult to assess whether trends in poverty are the same as in the US. Certainly, though, the numbers should give us pause: about 14 per cent of Canadians earn less than the LICO. Canada's rate of **child poverty** may look good compared to that of the US, but we have the second-worst rate among industrialized nations. As of 2012, despite admonitions from the United Nations, Canada's child poverty rate remains stuck and even worsening: more than 16 per cent of children live in low-income families, according to Statistics Canada. Campaign 2000, a coalition formed in 1991 to work toward Canada's stated goal of eliminating child poverty by 2000, has even grimmer statistics. According to the group's 2014 report, child poverty has increased from 15.8 per cent in 1989 to 19 per cent in 2013. Children are more likely than any other age category to live in poverty. Poverty rates for children of single mothers and Aboriginal children are even higher.[30]

Indeed, Aboriginal families are worse off, on average, on most indicators. According to the National Collaborating Centre for Aboriginal Health, on-reserve First Nations child mortality rate is up to seven times the general Canadian rate. Aboriginal teens become pregnant at seven times the Canadian rate. Aboriginal children are also at greatly increased risk of tuberculosis, diabetes, suicide, substance abuse, fetal alcohol syndrome, living in poverty and substandard housing, poor nutrition, and being unimmunized.[31]

These poorer prospects for Aboriginal children are a reflection of the generally poorer conditions in which Canada's First Nations, Inuit, and Métis people live. Canada is ranked third in the world on the Human Development Index. However, when the index is applied to Aboriginal people only, the ranking slips to 68. Though the Aboriginal population of Canada is growing dramatically (in part because of changes in reporting, but also because of actual growth), many Aboriginal individuals and communities suffer from endemic poverty and intractable social problems. None of these problems can be divorced from the broader context of colonialism and its interventions into Aboriginal life:

> Aboriginal families are nested in communities and nations, which have seen their lands alienated, their laws dismissed as "customs," and their beliefs ridiculed. Families have been at the centre of a struggle between colonial governments bent on absorbing "Indians" into Euro-Canadian society and parents, Elders, and leaders, who have been equally determined to maintain their identities as peoples with unique and continuing responsibilities in the world. The current challenges that Aboriginal families face are rooted in that history of struggle. The future trajectory of Aboriginal family life will be determined in large part by the success of Aboriginal collectives in establishing their place as peoples and nations within Canada.

While recognizing the challenges faced by the Aboriginal family, we must also recognize the damaging effects of family-related policies. These policies include the residential school system; the **sixties scoop** that saw both the massive child apprehensions by the child welfare system and the redefinition of Aboriginal women as "bad mothers";

and **Section 12(1)b** of the **Indian Act**, which disenfranchised many women and children (as well as many other interventions). However, as, Marlene Brant Castellano writes, there are tremendously hopeful signs of renewal within Aboriginal communities, suggesting an emergence "from the shadow of colonization that has marred perceptions and distorted relationships for generations." Moreover, on some indicators Aboriginal families may do better than non-Aboriginal families because of resilient cultural practices. For example, in British Columbia Aboriginal women are more likely to engage in sustained breastfeeding of their children than are non-Aboriginal women.[32]

Child poverty and the challenges facing Aboriginal families aside, the *shape* of Canadian families is also changing. For example, Canadian families have steadily become smaller since 1971, and more of us live outside a family setting than ever before. The average family in 1971 contained 3.7 persons; by 2011, it contained 2.9. There are now more households comprising couples without children than couples with children—an indication of the aging of the population but also of the increase of childlessness. In 2011, for the first time, households consisting of only one person outnumbered "couple" households with children.

If Canadian households are now less likely to contain children, households *with* children have also changed. The two-parent family remains the norm, but it is slowly declining. Of families raising children, 25 per cent are now headed by a lone adult; and these families tend to have more children than families headed by two adults.

Even two-parent families are changing, in part because we are marrying less. According to 2011 census data, while legally married couples remain the dominant family structure, their share is diminishing. After a small increase in marriages around the year 2000, the Canadian marriage rate has steadily declined to a record low, by 2008, of 4.4 marriages per 1000, less than half the peak 1940s rate of 10.9 and even less than the marriage rate in the Great Depression of the 1930s. In 2006, for the first time (according to Census data), more than half of the adult population of Canada was unmarried. The gap has widened since. Canada's declining marriage rate is echoed in other nations such as the United Kingdom and Australia, which have rates similar to ours. (Notably, Canada's marriage rate is significantly lower than that of the US, where the projected 2015 rate of 6.74 per 1,000 was the lowest on record.)[33]

Those of us who do marry are doing it later and later. The average age at first marriage is 31.1 for men and 29.1 for women versus 24.9 and 22.5 in 1972. While the post-war pattern of young age at marriage was historically unusual, the current ages at marriage are significantly higher than the prewar comparators. (From the 1920s until the post-war period, the age of women at first-marriage tracked between 24 and 25 years, for men around 28.) In 1981, only 32 per cent of men (and a mere 20 per cent of women) in their late twenties had never been married. Today, the corresponding percentages are 78.8 and 67.4 per cent. Particular groups are much more likely to marry. In Canada, the likelihood of marriage increases with wealth, and non-Aboriginals are more likely to marry; in the US, there is also a strong association with ethnicity, with white much more likely to marry than African-Americans and the rich much more likely to wed than the poor.[34]

Despite what some refer to as a "retreat from marriage" across the Western world, a majority of Canadians older than 15 (57.7 per cent) live as part of a couple. Therefore, while marriage may be (slowly) declining, coupling remains the norm. **Common-law**

marriage has increased dramatically since 1981, when the federal government began keeping statistics on the phenomenon. Then, almost 94 per cent of couples were married, with slightly more than 6 per cent living common-law. In 2011, in contrast, common-law couples represented about 20 per cent of all couples. Common-law unions have increased in all age groups, except the 21–24 age group. (Both marriage and common-law union have declined in this group, reflecting a tendency not only to marry later but also to couple later.)

According to the 2011 census, about 16.7 per cent of all families are common-law unions. This number conceals significant regional variations; in Quebec, for example, almost 38 per cent of couples are in common-law unions, while in Nunavut the percentage is almost 46 per cent.[35] By 2011, 13 per cent of all children aged 0 to 14 lived in families headed by common-law couples.

Another major change in the Canadian family since 1981 has been the rise of families headed by same-sex couples. On July 20, 2005, Bill C-38 received royal assent, defining civil marriage in Canada as "the lawful union of two persons to the exclusion of all others" and, making Canada the fourth nation in the world to legalize same-sex marriage. Though there was initial outrage among many Canadians, along with vows to make the issue an election hot potato, Canada adapted very quickly to the new reality; a 2006 Angus Reid poll showed that most Canadians were in favour of keeping the legal change.[36]

Acceptance of same-sex marriage in the US was not as rapid. As in Canada, lobbying for same-sex marriage rights emerged in the 1990s as the logical outcome of gay-rights activism from the 1960s. In response, a number of states enacted legislation enshrining a heterosexual definition of marriage while a few jurisdictions implemented same-sex marriage. By 2008, six states had either legalized gay marriage or made a commitment to do so. In contrast to Canada, by 2009, Americans had become even more opposed to same-sex marriage than they were in 2007; a Gallup poll found that 57 per cent remained opposed, 40 per cent in favour, with much greater support among younger people and self-identified liberals. Over the next six years, however, states continued to alter their same-sex marriage laws. In June 2015, the US Supreme Court made state-level action unnecessary in a 5–4 decision that the US Constitution protects the right of same-sex couples to marry. Comparing this change to previous changes in marriage law, the majority declared, "Changed understandings of marriage are characteristic of a Nation where new dimensions of freedom become apparent to new generations."[37]

As Table 6.1 shows, same-sex couples are still a tiny percentage of Canadian couples but are nonetheless are a growing segment of the population, particularly among the young (about a quarter of those in same-sex couples are under age 35).

Common-law and same-sex relationships have changed the way that Canadians form families, but the way families dissolve has also changed significantly over the past few decades. By 2011, more than 43 per cent of marriages could be expected to end in divorce. Social conservatives such as REAL Women of Canada see the growth of divorce and same-sex marriage in the same light, as diminutions of marriage as an institution: "Gay marriage is only one small stop on a tour that includes rising divorce rates, falling childbirth rates and the abandonment of responsibility by twenty- and even thirty-somethings."[38] Whether or not this negative view is warranted, the growth and acceptance of divorce represent a significant historical change in Canadian society.

Table 6.1 Changing Canadian couples, 2001 to 2011

Couples in census families	2001 Number	%	2006 Number	%	2011 Number	%
All couples	7,059,830	100.0	7,482,775	100.0	7,861,855	100.0
Opposite-sex couples	7,025,630	99.5	7,437,430	99.4	7,797,280	99.2
Married	5,901,425	83.6	6,098,445	81.5	6,293,950	80.1
Common-law	1,124,200	15.9	1,338,980	17.9	1,567,905	19.9
Same-sex couples	34,200	0.5	45,345	0.6	64,575	0.8
Married	0*	0.0	7,465	0.1	21,015	0.3
Male couples					11,540	0.1
Female couples					9,475	0.1
Common-law	34,200	0.5	37,885	0.5	43,560	0.5
Male couples					23,660	0.3
Female couples					19,900	±0.2

* Same-sex married couples were not enumerated in 2001.

Sources: Statistics Canada, censuses of population, 2001, 2006, and 2011. Cat. no. 98-312-X2011002.

Between 1857 and 1968, Canada's divorce laws changed very little, and there were few divorces by modern standards. In 1900, there were only 11 divorces granted in the entire country (although divorces increased dramatically thereafter, especially after the First World War). The greatest increases, however, followed the liberalization of the **Divorce Act** in 1968. Rates more than doubled from 54.8 (per 100,000 people) in that year to 124.2 the year after. Thereafter, throughout the 1970s and well into the 1980s, the divorce rate continued to climb to a peak of 362.3 in 1987. Since then, rates have declined. Our current rate is 211 per 100,000 population, a fairly high rate but still significantly lower than the US rate (about half of US first marriages end in divorce, with higher rates for second and third marriages) and well below the rate of the Russian Federation, where the majority of marriages end in divorce.[39]

From 2006 to 2011, there was an 8 per cent decline in the divorce rate, some of which may be simply the result of the decline of marriage itself. (When common-law spouses split, there is no trace of this in the statistics). A more nuanced view of divorce can be obtained by looking at divorce rates by age group. Rates among those younger than 50 have declined steeply—again, probably because of the decline of marriage in this age group. When we look at those in their late 50s, rates are much higher: 21.6 per cent of women and 18.9 per cent of men in this age group have been divorced. In the US, the divorce rate among older adults has doubled since 1990, while it has stabilized and even declined for younger age groups.[40]

Divorce has been a lightning rod for discussions of the health (or lack thereof) of the family. Still, Canadian attitudes toward families and their formation are changing. In 1975, when Reginald Bibby began the nationwide surveys that have become known as the Project Canada Survey Series, we were quite a conservative lot, and in Bibby's words, "bigotry was alive and well."

> More than a third of us, for instance, believed that a woman shouldn't work outside the home if her husband was capable of supporting her. Half of us believed that black people and white people should not marry. Three-quarters of us believed homosexuality was aberrant—and abhorrent. [41]

By 2009, in contrast, 40 per cent of Canadians believed there was no ideal family model. The vast majority of Canadians—92 per cent—approved of interracial marriage, and more than two-thirds approved of same-sex marriage. These data from 2009 show that our opinions on a vast range of subjects have changed; we now embrace the ideas of multiculturalism, diversity, and relativism, which we increasingly see as part of our national identity. Bibby links our changing views to a number of social changes, in particular official multiculturalism, the baby boomer generation, and the "XX factor," the increasing influence of women in public life. (On most measures in the survey, women are consistently more liberal than men are.) Interestingly, however, while Canadians are accepting of diversity, most still aspire to the "traditional" family model themselves—testament to the enduring power of nostalgia.[42]

The "traditional" family (comprising a breadwinner dad, a stay-at-home mom, and their children) has never been the reality for all families and is even less so today. It represents the last outpost of traditional gender relations. Families have been and remain gendered institutions; they reproduce gender differences and gender inequalities among adults and children alike. Families raise children as gendered actors and remind parents to perform appropriate gender behaviours. It is no wonder, then, that each specific aspect of family life—marriage, child rearing, housework, divorce—continues to express the differences and the inequalities of gender, even as both gender and the family undergo dramatic changes.

The (Gendered?) Benefits of Marriage

For many years, people have seen the family as society's foundation, and marriage as its cornerstone. However, as the changes enumerated above took place, scholars and policymakers began to investigate the utility of marriage. From the early 1970s, researchers found that marriage seemed to be beneficial for those who experienced it. By 1995, Linda Waite could confidently attest that marriage produced "better health, longer life, more and better sex, greater earnings (at least for men), greater wealth, and better outcomes for children." Steven Nock summarized this research a decade later: "The accumulated research shows that married people are typically healthier, live longer, earn more, have better mental health, have better sex lives, and are happier than their unmarried counterparts. They have lower rates of suicide, fatal accidents, acute and chronic illness, alcoholism, and depression."[43]

Many potential causes for this **marriage premium** have been contemplated from a theoretical perspective. Nock summarizes them as institutionalization, specialization, and domestication. First, marriage is a hallowed institution with legal and social support.

This means that married people have a celebrated and meaningful social role; this may bring both intrinsic rewards (knowing and feeling good about one's role as a married person) and extrinsic rewards (being preferred for a job over an unmarried candidate). When two people marry, they also tend to develop efficient divisions of labour and benefit from economies of scale (e.g., requiring only one dwelling—the same as a single person). Finally, married couples are domesticated. The effects of domestication are particularly marked for men; that is, they engage in fewer high-risk behaviours, work more, and generally integrate more into society. If marriage is understood as social integration, Nock suggests, its effects on health are easily understood.

This view of marriage's benefits served as rationale for pro-marriage US public policy into the current century; but the scholars who documented the marriage premium had more questions than answers. First, if, as seemed true, marriage had such enormous benefits, was this a protection effect or a *selection* effect? That is, was it true that marriage made people happier and healthier—or were happier, healthier people just more likely to get married in the first place? In the last decade, many new studies have both confirmed and complicated some of the early findings about the protective effects of marriage. It *does* seem that richer, happier, and healthier people are more likely to get married, which may explain some of the protective effect.

Another complicating factor is that early studies compared currently married people with all categories of singles (never-married, divorced, or widowed). As it turns out, the case may be less that marriage is beneficial than that its end is detrimental. Divorced and widowed people are significantly less healthy and happy than those who never married. The benefits of marriage for health, for example, "appear to reflect the strains of marital dissolution more than they reflect the benefits of marriage."[44]

Moreover, the marriage premium doesn't seem to exist everywhere; globally, married/cohabiting people have better health than those who have been widowed, divorced, or separated, but *worse* health than the never-married.[45] (Indeed, the wisdom of avoiding separation and widowhood may be one of the clearest messages the amassed research offers.)

In North America, the marriage premium seems to be diminishing, in large part because the never-married are experiencing greater health than previously. Finally, though marriage defenders might wish to argue otherwise, most of the benefits of marriage also accrue in cohabiting relationships. Consequently, while the benefits of marriage seem clear on a broad epidemiological level, "once individual differences are taken into account, it is far from a blanket prescription for individual well-being."[46]

From the earliest days of this discussion, it has been suggested that the benefits of marriage are differentially weighted by gender. Indeed, the division of labour within marriage (she gets greater economic protection, he gets emotional support, social integration, and higher wages) was presumed to be part of the premium for both partners. However, some scholars took a more critical view of the workings of gender within marriage. In the early 1970s, sociologist Jessie Bernard identified two distinct marriages, "his" and "hers," arguing that "his" was better. According to Bernard and other confirming studies, indices of happiness and depression suggested that married men were much happier than unmarried men, whereas unmarried women were somewhat happier than married women. (The greatest difference emerged between married and unmarried men.) A greater proportion of men than women eventually married; husbands reported being more satisfied than wives with their marriages; husbands lived longer and enjoyed better health benefits than unmarried men, as well as better health than women (married or unmarried); and fewer men than women initiated divorce. As well, single men were less likely to be employed, tended to have lower incomes than married men, and were more prone to crime and drug use. As *The New York Times* writer Natalie Angier summed up this research, "marriage is pretty good for the goose much of the time, but golden for the gander practically all of the time."[47]

Interestingly, however, both the gap between married and unmarried men and the gap between men and women seems to have narrowed during the past 30 years. On the other hand, there are signs that gender remains an important (if not the only) variable: data from the 2002 Canadian Community Health Survey showed that while unmarried men were more likely to be depressed than married men (especially as they aged), the opposite was true for women (nearly 42 per cent of unhappily married women were depressed!). A recent large-scale Asian study found similar results in China, where single men and unhappily married women were worst off in regard to health; though this was not the case in the other countries studied, the researchers did find that consistently across countries, "the health benefits of marriage could be outstripped by the health losses associated with dissatisfied marriages."[48]

While the scholarly debate about the benefits of marriage (and their gendering) continues, currently married men and women seem largely happy with their marriages. Those who identify their spouses as their best friends are particularly content, but married Canadians are much more likely than singles to report general satisfaction with their lives. (Older married couples and those without children in the home tend to be happiest.)[49]

The gendered effects of marriage may have diminished since the early 1970s, but there is one area that remains highly gendered: the wedding. For women, far more than men, the wedding remains virtually a goal in itself: a day important enough to plan for months, and a day that routinely costs more than a young couple might need for a down payment on a first home. For example, in a 2015 poll of readers of Canada's *Wedding Bells* magazine, brides-to-be reported that they were spending an average of $30,717 (up from $19,274 in 2009) on "the big day." Planning the wedding requires not only money but also time. The average reader surveyed in 2006 spent more than 10 months planning and arranging her wedding.

Even though the wedding expresses a traditional gendered logic that is disharmonious with the rest of our lives, there is no other ritual that we celebrate with the fervour (and dollars) granted to the white wedding. Forty-eight per cent of *Wedding Bells* readers reported that their fiancés had requested permission from their fathers to marry them. The romance of traditional marriage, it would seem, is alive and well—on the wedding day, at least. That romance also undoubtedly influences another gendered difference: the vast majority of North American women (except among the professional and highly educated) still take on their husbands' surnames, while very few men adopt the surnames of their wives.[50]

Both women and men remain interested in getting—and staying—married. For women in particular, but arguably for both sexes, marriage remains an important part of a successful life plan. In recent years, however, the benefits of marriage have become less clear, and the health toll of marital dissolution seems to be worsening.[51] This suggests that the debate about the benefits of marriage is far from over.

Gendered Parents, Gendering Children

Having and raising children are arguably the *raison d-être* of the family. It is in the family that the seeds of gender difference and gender identity are planted, that we first understand the different, and unequal, meanings of being a man or a woman, a boy or a girl.

The most obvious form of gender socialization is direct gender instruction, for example the old admonition that "boys don't cry." However, there are other ways in which parenting socializes gender. First, parents themselves exhibit gendered behaviours, "modelling" gender for their children. They also participate in child rearing differentially by gender, both in how much child rearing they do and in the way they do it; and they treat their children differently (intentionally and unintentionally) based on *the children's* sex. Finally, parents have different "styles" based on gender.

Differential treatment may be both intentional and unintentional. Certainly, most parents possess a set of ideas of what their children need; parents vary in how gender-specific those ideas are and therefore in what their *intentional* practices may be. For example, one set of parents might be united in the belief that gender socialization is detrimental, while another set may view the thought of an "effeminate" son with horror. (Sometimes, a couple may even find that their individual views on these matters are diametrically opposed.) Their views will influence whether, for example, they permit their toddler son to dress up as a princess. However, not only our intentional practices matter; parents were themselves socialized to some belief in what girls and boys of various ages are like, and such training is hard to shake. Even those who wish to be as "gender-neutral" as possible may engage in unconscious gendering practices, particularly those that are not as obviously gender-linked as the example above.

Gender stereotyping and differential treatment begin even before the child is born. Prior to the widespread use of ultrasound and amniocentesis (a medical technique that can be used to detect genetic defects as well as the gender of the fetus), parents spent hours speculating about the sex of the as-yet unborn child, often making guesses based upon the amount of kicking and other intrauterine behaviour. Relatives and friends contributed opinions on whether the baby was "high" or "low" and made such comments as, "With that much activity, it must be a boy!"

Today, everywhere sonography and amniocentesis are in use, the majority of parents choose to learn their baby's sex through routine ultrasound. In some nations where boys are highly preferred, this may lead to sex-selective abortion, which generally targets girls and is particularly widespread in China and parts of India, where sex ratios have become alarmingly skewed in favour of males by the practice. Similarly, in some countries, such as India, there is evidence of significant differential treatment, with boys receiving more child care, longer breastfeeding, and better medical care, resulting in differential child mortality by sex. A 2013 study found that this differential treatment began in the womb, with mothers seeking more prenatal care when they knew themselves to be pregnant with boys (resulting in increased neonatal mortality of girl babies).[52]

In North America, there is little evidence of such dramatically differential treatment or of sex-selective abortion, and the preference for sons has largely disappeared. Learning the sex of a baby before birth, however, has become a normal part of pregnancy. Knowledge of sex may increase mothers' closeness to their unborn babies; certainly, the importance of gender is suggested by parents' desire to know and satisfaction in knowing. As one 25-year-old mother-to-be told a researcher,

> It's more fun to think of the baby as a "him" or a "her" than an "it." You can decorate things better too—but I just really like being able to refer to it as something other than "it," which is something non-human to me.[53]

The connection between being gendered and being human is made clear by the comments above; also noticeable is that knowing the sex of a fetus enables a parent (usually the mother) to start shopping for the baby. Accordingly, researcher Medora Barnes argues, the current generation of middle-class infants is actually experiencing a heightened gendering, at least as regards "gender-appropriate" consumer goods. (The degree to which consumerism increases gender differentiation is a vast topic, but it is worthwhile noting that we didn't always dress babies and young children differently according to their sex. However, the practice does make us spend a lot more!)

Knowing the sex of an unborn baby affects more than simply what parents buy: it seems to affect perceptions of and behaviour toward a fetus. As parents (again, especially mothers) have learned to talk to their babies in utero, their "conversations" with their unborn babies seem to be gendered, for example, in the use of a "little-girl voice" to talk to a girl baby. Very often, knowing the sex of the fetus allows the parents to name it (informally) before birth. While it is hard to know what effect these activities might have on a fetus, their effect on the parents—reinforcing and intensifying their later gender socialization of their infants—is important.[54]

Certainly, there is evidence that parents perceive newborn infant girls differently, as "finer, smaller, less coordinated, quieter, weaker, and more delicate than boys." The rest of the world concurs. Announcing the child's birth announces its gender (often using "gender-appropriate" images and colours). The remarks of visitors during the first days echo the same gendered sentiments. Although some people may feel that gender stereotyping is inappropriate, in a majority of cases boys are still greeted with such comments as "What a brawny little guy," while girls are more likely to elicit such comments as "She's beautiful; she's so petite!" Knowing a baby's sex is so important to us that in 2011, when two Toronto parents decided to keep their third baby's sex to themselves for the time being, a media firestorm was ignited around "Baby Storm" and the possible harms to his or her identity from such gender-neutral parenting. Allegations of "experimentation" and "child abuse" were rampant.[55]

During infancy, gendered perceptions and expectations lead to different behaviours by parents and other adults. One relatively obvious difference in the treatment of infants is their environment. The colours, toys, motifs, and accessories placed in an infant's bedroom are in many cases as gendered as the clothes in which the newborn is dressed. While the effects of this on infant development are difficult to assess, the shaping of the environment makes it clear that the gender of the child is important to the parents—so much so that a parent who has erroneously anticipated a child of one sex will complain of having to repaint the nursery!

Pink and Blue: Colour-Coded Children for a Gendered Society?

Today, it is common for North American parents to dress their newborn children in pink and blue. Many hospitals still use pink and blue blankets to colour-code newborns, and many men wouldn't be caught dead in pink. (Even though three-quarters of American and British men in a 2013 survey agreed, "men and women don't need to conform to traditional roles and behaviours anymore," only 36 per cent thought it was acceptable for men to wear "pink or other traditionally 'girly' colours."[56])

The association of pink and blue with girls and boys seems completely natural to contemporary North Americans, so much so that it is often referred to as "traditional." However, in the nineteenth century, infants were dressed not only in similar colours but in similar garments. Boys and girls alike wore dresses, until boys graduated into short trousers later in childhood. Class was probably a more important determinant of clothing than gender. As the image below of US President Franklin Delano Roosevelt shows, prosperous families dressed young boys almost identically to girls.

As Jo Paoletti documents in her *Pink and Blue: Telling the Boys from the Girls in America*, it was accepted well into the twentieth century that babies were indistinguishable by gender. In the aftermath of the First World War, however, gendering of clothing became more common. Pink and blue (colours associated with infancy since the nineteenth century) now became assigned to girls and boys. There was some confusion, however: "becomingness" of colour was often more important than gender, with mothers advised to consider their infants' blondness or brunetteness in selecting pink or blue. Moreover, where colour was associated with gender, pink was often suggested for boys because it was associated with warmth and robustness! After the 1940s, under the influence of Freudian and sex-role theories, colour-coding of children's clothing settled into the pattern we know today.[57]

However, the women's movement of the 1960s and 1970s brought a great interest in unisex clothing, and many gender-neutral designs characterized children's clothing in these decades. Colours were often gender-neutral too, though girls were kitted in blue clothing, in an obvious parallel to the way adult women were entering hitherto male domains.

In the 1980s, gendered clothing and colours were resurgent, and the rise of pink

Franklin Delano Roosevelt, age two and a half.

Bettmann/Getty Images

continued

began in earnest. Now not only clothing was pink: under the influence of Disney and a burgeoning consumer culture, all aspects of a girl's bedroom and life could reflect the perfect "pink princess" theme. Girls' and boys' toys were readily identifiable by the colour of the aisle: the boys' aisle more variable, the girls' aisle a sea of bubblegum pink. Though many retailers have recently abandoned the explicit labelling of toys as belonging to either girls or boys, the colour-coding does the job. For example, it is hard to imagine that many North American boys go to sleep in the Disney Princess Toddler Bed, with its layers of pink; or that many baby boys receive Fisher-Price's Little Glamour Gift Set, featuring Baby's First Purse and the Diamond Ring Rattle. (However, Fisher-Price does offer the [blue] Hammerin' Rattle for "your little handyman.")[58]

While one doesn't want to overstate the "Princess effect," it is interesting that the more gendered roles have expanded, the more dedicated we are to product-linked gender socialization—and the more we think of it as "traditional." What are the long-term effects of pink and blue clothing, "Princessification," and segregated toy aisles? We don't know, but as Cordelia Fine writes, "the smart money would say the effects won't be trivial, given that children are enveloped in some of the most relentless stereotyping to be found in the twenty-first century."[59]

Studies of differential infant treatment have yielded a large body of research that we can only briefly summarize. Scholars disagree on how differently parents treat their infants and on the nature and cause of the differences that do emerge. Conclusions are made more difficult by the fact that infant and child temperament and behaviour influence parents' behaviour, so some researchers argue that gendered treatment of infants is actually elicited by the infants' own sex-related temperaments. A further complication has arisen because many studies examined how parents engaged with their children (for example, whether they showed warmth and affection to them) rather than looking at what parents did with their children. Despite these arguments, some of the distinctions that do emerge in infancy are interesting. During the first six months of life, several studies have found, mothers tend to look at and talk to girl infants more than to boy infants, and mothers tend to respond to girls' crying more immediately than they do to boys' crying. A recent study found that babies were much more exposed to mothers' speech than to fathers' speech, and that mothers responded more to baby girls' vocalizations than to those of baby boys.[60]

Parents' interest in building autonomy or independence seems in part to explain this difference. As a result of gender stereotypes, parents believe that boys rather than girls should be independent; and parents therefore encourage boys to explore and master their world. Many mothers start to wean their sons from physical contact with themselves at an earlier age. Nonetheless, parents' early treatment of their infant is usually not a deliberate effort to teach the child a "proper" gender role, but rather reflects the fact that the parents themselves accept the general societal roles for men and women. Sons are still often treated as though they are "naturally" sturdy and active; they are played with more roughly and are greeted with smiles and other indications of pleasure when they respond appropriately. Daughters are still thought to be more delicate and gentle, and for them, sweetness and co-operation are likely to elicit parental approval.

Other adults reinforce these different parental behaviours. Researchers have found that people interact with infants based on their gendered assumptions rather than the infants' own characteristics. For example, subjects in one experiment consistently gave gender-specific toys (dolls for girls, hammers for boys) to infants whom they were told were either girls or boys. The subjects described the babies, whose sex they did not know, with highly gendered adjectives—"strong" and "big" for those they thought to be boys and "soft" and "pretty" for those they thought were girls. Another experiment showed a videotape of a nine-month-old's reaction to a jack-in-the-box, a doll, a teddy bear, and a buzzer. Half the observers were told the child was a boy; the other half were told it was a girl. The child's reaction to the jack-in-the-box was agitation and crying. Those who thought the child was a boy thought "he" was angry; those who thought the child was a girl thought "she" was afraid.[61]

As a child moves from the infant to the toddler stage, somewhere around age two, research shows that gender typing increases. Parents exhibit gender-differentiated tolerance for behaviours and emotions. Boys' aggression, competition, and anger are more readily tolerated, and their independence, aggression, and suppression of emotion are rewarded. Failure to suppress fear and other "girly" emotions is discouraged. However, there is some evidence that this is changing, and that fathers (who once typically responded to their sons' fear with disapproval) now seek to reassure boys when they are anxious. However, boys are still encouraged to separate from their mothers and from the world of women. While even a teenager or adult woman may proudly claim to be "daddy's little girl," to be a "mama's boy" is stigmatized. Girls are strongly censured for aggression and anger, but are permitted to show fear more than are boys. One recent study of four-year-olds and their mothers found that mothers use more "emotion talk" with girls than with boys, even though the children of both genders were equally skilled and knowledgeable about emotions.[62] Girls are encouraged to express and discuss emotions—and to be dependent on others. Consequently, the emotional world of children begins to diverge early, with obvious implications for gender differences in adulthood.

Parents' gender matters; both sexes spend more time with their same-sex children, and separated UK fathers see sons more than they see daughters. (The same is true of African-American fathers in the US.) Mothers are more expressive with their daughters than with their sons (though mothers match the expressions of their male infants more than they do those of their female infants). Fathers and mothers seem to have a different type of emotional interaction with infants, with fathers more likely to engage in higher-arousal interactions. Play also seems to be a more important component of fathers' activities. Beginning in toddlerhood, fathers tend to engage in more physical play with their sons. From an early age, the association of masculinity with play, physical competence, and outdoor activities is encouraged. Similarly, fathers engage in more literacy activities with their daughters, again with implications for later gender difference.[63]

In general, parents are more restrictive with their daughters and create more limits on their acceptable behaviour from a very early age. When it comes to explicitly *gendered* behaviours, however, parents tend to be more tolerant of non-conforming behaviour on the part of girls than on the part of boys—and fathers tend to be generally less tolerant of such behaviour, regardless of the sex of the child, than are mothers. These findings are summarized as indicating, "[f]athers tend to police [non-gender conformity] more than mothers, and everyone polices boys more than girls."[64]

As discussed above, the toys children play with generally are designed to be sold as girls' toys or boys' toys. Girls are given dolls and, increasingly and at all ages, "glamour toys" designed to introduce them to the world of fashion and beauty. Boys get trucks and building blocks and face disapproval if they want to play with girls' toys. These labels come originally from adults, because it has been noted that even though many two-and-a-half-year-old boys prefer dolls and doll houses, they are urged away from them. Even at preschool age, boys report that their fathers believe that playing with "girls' toys" is "bad."

Parental responses to play are quickly absorbed by children, who shortly thereafter display quite different toy and game preferences. Advertisements, salespeople, and other agents of socialization all reinforce these cues from parents. Boys prefer male-stereotyped toys more than girls prefer female-stereotyped ones, perhaps because of the strong messages of disapproval they receive for playing with "girly" things. However, girls' toys are also associated with greater complexity of play, no matter whether boys or girls play with them—so boys who are steered away from such toys may lose out.[65]

From a very early age, physical characteristics are tied to social definitions of masculinity and femininity. Girls are rewarded for appearing attractive and neat, whereas boys are more frequently rewarded for physical performance. These differences continue well into adolescence. Girls are taught to capitalize on good looks, cuteness, and coyness and learn to look in mirrors and seek reflections of themselves from others. Boys, in contrast, discover that toughness, athletic ability, and performance are what count for males.

Parents are critical socializers of their children, obviously, but so too are other children, both siblings and peers outside the family. Interacting with their age-group peers, children express and utilize the gender expectations that they have picked up from parents and the world around them. Most experimental research suggests that boys and girls begin very early to exhibit **homophily**, the tendency to cluster in same-sex rather than opposite-sex networks and relationships. Consequently, from a very early age children develop two dramatically different gender cultures. In their sex-segregated play worlds, boys learn the prototypes of behaviours that will be expected of them as men, including those behaviours that characterize the sexual expectations of adult men. At the same time, girls learn prototypes of the behaviours that will be expected of them as women, also including sexual expectations. Boys play in larger, often competitive groups, girls in smaller groups based on "sharing," in the process entrenching boy-cultures of leadership and competition and girl-cultures of co-operation, intimacy, and inclusion (not to mention, sometimes, exclusion). Even where children's toys seem similar, language used to describe those figures delineates gendered expectations. The standard 11-inch human figure made for girls (think Barbie) is a "doll," but one made for boys is called an "action figure" (think G.I. Joe).[66]

Much has changed in the way we socialize children, but the direction of change has largely opened "masculine" pursuits to girls rather than "feminine" one to boys. Generations of girls have worn the label "tomboy" with pride, and from the 1970s, formal organized sports leagues, such as in soccer and softball, have been opened to girls. For boys, opportunities to play at girls' games are rare; the label "sissy" is more negative than is the label "tomboy." Girls have more "boy toys" than boys have "girl toys." There is a series of "boy things" that is all right for girls to do, but, by and large, there is no transfer the other way.

Barbie, Bratz, and Monster High

That toys are gendered is hardly news. A stroll through your neighbourhood Toys 'R' Us would suggest that there is a clearly demarcated gender division of toy land, a pink zone and a blue zone, as clear as the parted Red Sea. Boys' toys have remained remarkably constant—militarized or sports themed toys, games, and action figures (please don't call them "dolls!"). Girls' toys have always anticipated traditional women's roles—dressing up as nurses, choreographing elaborate tea parties, and, of course, playing with dolls. Throughout the early and mid-twentieth century, "dolls" were generally babies, and girls played "mother" from early childhood until prepubescence.

Fifty years ago, Barbie changed all that: Based on the very adult German cartoon and doll Bild Lili, Barbie was a near-grown-up. She was the first doll for children with breasts, and her feet were shaped permanently in a high-heeled pose. Ruth Handler, the doll's designer, was convinced that a doll representing a mature woman rather than a baby would sell to girls.

> Handler believed that girls await the moment when they grow breasts; they dream of it, and this is the reason behind their desire to play with dolls that really do have adult, womanly bodies and features. Whilst playing with Barbie, girls simultaneously play mature femininity *defined through the body*, not through household-related responsibilities and child care, as is the case with newborn baby dolls.[67]

Barbie became one of the most successful toy franchises ever, available in any number of variations and special editions, and with her own glamorous world of sports cars, townhouses, and ball gowns. Whatever women were doing, Barbie did it too—from firefighting to surgery—and always looking fabulous. She was far better dressed than any doll before her, with oodles of new outfits released every year and eventually a whole line of consumer merchandise not only for the doll but for her fans. By the 1990s, Barbie was a billion-dollar-plus juggernaut, with no end in sight.

In 2001, a new girl, or rather several new girls, arrived on the scene: Bratz quickly became the most popular dolls in the world, becoming "the clear No. 1 fashion doll in the US" by the last quarter of 2006. Like Barbie, Bratz were billed as having "a passion for fashion"—and apparently in need of outfits for virtually every occasion. Both were manufactured under dubious labour conditions; both promoted a particular body image that conforms much more to Connell's emphasized femininity than to a desire for health. What caused most consternation among parents, though, was that Bratz seemed more overtly sexualized, "like pole dancers on their way to work at a gentleman's club." "Even at her most Malibu," one mother wrote, "Barbie wasn't nearly as sexualized as these dolls are."[68]

In response to the Bratz phenomenon, Mattel reimagined Barbie as "My Scene" Barbie, in versions like "Juicy Bling." However, in late 2008, Mattel won a massive legal victory against MGA industries (the manufacturer of Bratz). It was found that the designer of the

continued

Bratz doll was working for Mattel when he made the drawings on which they were based; MGA was ordered to stop making the popular dolls.[69] In 2011, however, after much legal wrangling, MGA's rights to the dolls were legally confirmed. Since then, Barbie's sales have slipped (even though another Mattel product, Monster High, has come to the forefront).

Monster High dolls were launched in 2010. (My Scene dolls were phased out soon thereafter.) Quickly labelled "Goth Barbies," the dolls portray relatives of famous monsters, such as Dracula, and have an edgy fashion sense. Spectra Vondergeist, for example, likes silk with "just a touch of metal." According to Mattel, the Monster High message is acceptance of uniqueness and "freakiness," but commentators quickly noticed the dolls' uniformly stereotypical proportions, fashion obsessions, and conventional (white, sexualized) beauty:

> Instead of providing a valuable representation for children of other races and ethnicities, children who fail to conform to our rigid expectations of body-type, LGBT children, and so on, Mattel has populated yet another fantasy universe with superficial, mostly white, wealthy (each of the three main characters is obsessed with shopping—and they all have famous dads), and boy-crazed teens. Monster High is not at all a departure from the norm: it's just more of the same.[70]

Between Monster High's new cachet and Barbie's new life-sized Dream House attractions (one of which opened amidst controversy in Berlin in 2013), the Barbie-style doll is still in expansion mode. The history of Barbie and her competitors shows the intensification of a particular gendered message for girls: femininity and womanhood are about beauty, desirability, and consumption. If G.I. Joe is an action figure, Barbie and her contemporaries are "fashion figures," promoters of the fantasy of feminine beauty. Unfortunately, this fantasy is being conveyed to and consumed by the very young. Manufacturers claim that the dolls are for preteens, but most girls who consume Barbies and Monster High dolls are much younger—from ages three to six.

This asymmetry indicates the greater prestige of masculinity and the degree to which a boy's adoption of "feminine" traits or behaviours is still perceived as shameful and somehow diminishing. Accordingly, masculinity is far more rigid a role construction than is femininity; that rigidity is part of the coercive mechanisms of gender role socialization. Children's play both expresses and anticipates the inequality that informs gender relations in adulthood.[71]

Boys and girls both understand the inequality between women and men and understand, too, that their less-than-equal status gives girls a bit more latitude in the types of cross-sex (gender-inappropriate) behaviour they may exhibit. Though this is changing, girls think they'd be better off as boys, and many of them declare that they would rather be boys than girls. By contrast, boys tend to see being girls as a fate worse than death. "If I were a girl," one third-grader said, "everybody would be better than me, because boys are better than girls."

Statements like this make us wince because they are so frank. This little boy, like millions of other little boys, has come to understand that his status in the world depends upon his ability to distance himself from femininity. By exaggerating gender difference, he both assures and reassures himself of his higher status. It is largely through the routine daily events of family life that children learn what it means to be boys or girls, and it is through those same events that gender inequality is reproduced between grown-up women and men. Children's interactions "are not preparation for life," sociologist Barrie Thorne concludes. "They are life itself."[72]

The Gendered Politics of Housework and Child Care

That women now work outside the home as a matter of course, of economic necessity, and of ambition has dramatically altered the life of the modern family. Some would like to turn back the clock to the rather unusual and short-lived family form that emerged in the 1950s and reassert it as the norm. Such a vision is unlikely to be embraced by most men (almost all men express preference for wives who earn money). Additionally, most women work outside the home both because they want to and because they have to.

Working mothers report higher levels of self-esteem and are happier and less depressed than are full-time housewives. Nonetheless, they may be enjoying life less. Consistently, and in every industrial country, women report higher levels of stress than do men (in the US, ethnic minorities also report more stress than do whites). Perhaps one reason women are so fatigued is that they remain largely responsible for what sociologist Arlie Hochschild labelled the **second shift**, the unpaid housework and child care that every family must do to function properly.[73]

In 1970, a young feminist writer described what she saw as "the politics of housework." In the spirit of the feminist slogan "the personal is political," Pat Mainardi argued that the separation of spheres that defined the traditional family and made housework "women's work" was a reflection of male domination, not the expression of some feminine biological predisposition toward laundry or dishwashing. Women did housework and child care because they *had* to, she argued, not because they *wanted* to or because of some genetic master plan; men didn't do housework, because they could get out of it.[74]

Few people actually *like* doing housework. "A woman's work is never done, and happy she whose strength holds out to the end of the [sun's] rays," wrote Martha Moore Ballard in her diary in 1795. Nearly a century later, Mary Hallock Foote wrote, "I am daily dropped in little pieces and passed around and devoured and expected to be whole again next day and all days and I am never *alone* for a single minute." In 1881, Helen Campbell wrote that spring housecleaning was "a terror to everyone, and above all to gentlemen, who resent it from beginning to end."[75]

Dozens of studies have assessed the changing patterns of housework, child care, and the different amounts of investments in family life. One statistic about family involvement is revealing of a larger pattern. Forty years ago, virtually no fathers were present at the births of their children; today, more than 90 per cent are present in the delivery room. If men *want* to change their involvement in the family, there is evidence that they are capable of doing so quickly and relatively easily—and they have done so in the area of parental involvement, as we discuss below.[76]

When it comes to housework, the evidence reveals slower change. For many years, men's involvement in housework increased very little, despite women's labour-force participation. Recent studies have found men's participation in housework increasing. Overall, between 1965 and 1998, American men more than doubled their housework hours to a high of 11 per week, which fell to 10 hours a week by 2010. Canada's General Social Survey of 2005 found that men had increased their housework hours from an average of 2.1 per day in 1986 to 2.5 in 2001. Women, on the other hand, had decreased theirs from 4.8 in 1986 to 4.2. Overall, less housework is done now than in the 1970s. The convergence in both paid employment and household work has continued since 2005 in all OECD nations, particularly among people born after 1957 and those at the youngest ages. This suggests that on average, when both unpaid and paid labour workers are taken into account, men and women are doing about as much work. In fact, the group that reports the fewest hours of work (even when multitasking is taken into account) is the "subgroup of mothers who were *not* in the labour force"). Newly married couples in first marriages now seem to share housework equitably in most industrialized nations.[77] So then, why do women feel resentful, and why do women report more stress?

First, these data may be complicated by everything that the averages conceal—for example, the existence of smaller groups of women who work full time and then "come home and do the second full-time job," in the words of one woman. In Canada, the "woman's double burden," where a woman does more unpaid work than her partner and at least as much paid work, is estimated to affect 26 to 27 per cent of couples. The reverse of this, the "man's double burden," affects only 8.8 per cent. So clearly, averages can hide wide variations. Moreover, certain types of work, such as eldercare, planning and organizing family life, and **emotion work**, might go unreported.[78]

Furthermore, these data are based solely on reported hours and not on the tasks performed. Thinking of work in terms of hours spent is undoubtedly valuable, allowing interesting comparisons not only between the sexes but also among nations and ethnic groups. However, thinking about housework only in these terms may also obscure some of the gendered character of work in the home. For example, if one person spends two hours mowing the lawn while the other spends two hours preparing dinner, cleaning the living room, and planning a shopping trip while simultaneously getting the children bathed and through their homework, one may feel considerably more stressed (and unfairly burdened) than the other, even though their hours worked are identical. Women's greater tendency to multitask may consequently be a factor in their greater stress. A 2011 study found that American women were spending 10.5 more hours per week multitasking than were men, making multitasking "an important source of gender inequality," according to the study's authors. As Meg Luxton points out, some of the increase in men's domestic labour may reflect taking over aspects of this multitasking, as when, for example, a father "watches the children" while his wife prepares dinner. In this case, his hours of unpaid labour may increase without diminishing hers.[79]

Women also may face the most stressful and least desirable duties, such as getting up in the night (or staying up all night) with infants or sick kids. In the US, women in dual-earner couples with infants are three times more likely than are men in the same situation to report interrupted sleep. Earning status is not as important as gender in determining who gets up in the night, it seems; stay-at-home mothers are six times more likely to be the "one who gets up" than are stay-at-home fathers. Additionally, being the breadwinner for the family does not seem to lift the burden of being the one who cleans. Furthermore, while stay-at-home fathers may be regarded more positively than are stay-at-home mothers, breadwinning mothers do not seem to benefit from the same social approval.[80]

Men may have the ability, conversely, to select the duties they wish to perform in the domestic sphere. For example, many men now participate in cooking, which is an important change from the 1980s. Many men report both cooking and their enjoyment of it. More than half of British men surveyed by market researchers described cooking as a hobby, and some researchers have found that men often cook in a "leisure" capacity (e.g., for entertaining) rather than being the ones responsible for preparing the regular evening meals, as is characteristic of women. In fact, it seems that more men than women may have the *choice* whether or not to cook. As one recent study of Canadian men suggests, many men who cook regard it as "work-leisure," an enjoyable activity that they perform in a different manner than is typical of women (for example, taking their time and focusing on the task, rather than being required to rush while supervising children or doing laundry at the same time). While this is a new area of scholarship, the study of a task such as cooking can point to the many nuances within gendered divisions of housework.[81]

Women may also be held responsible for the home in ways that men are not, and in turn may experience domestic work as linked to their gender identity. Men tend to see their participation in housework *in relation* to their wives' housework; women tend to see their work as necessary for family maintenance. Women and men also perceive women as more competent in (or fussy about) domestic tasks. Though one seldom hears men referring to "babysitting" their own children these days, men still use terms like "pitch in" or "help out" to describe the time they spend in housework—as if the work was their wives' to do. "When men do the dishes it's called helping," Anna Quindlen, op-ed writer for *The New York Times*, observed wryly. "When women do dishes, that's called life." Interestingly, it may not even *be* all that helpful. According to the Center for Work-Life Policy, 40 per cent of professional wives felt that their husbands actually create *more* work around the house than they perform.[82] Bearing responsibility for managing the household, allocating tasks, and planning family life is in itself work, though it may go unrecognized even while it elevates women's stress levels.

Finally, another problem with the "hours" model results from self-reporting. Both women and men over report the amount of housework they do—according to one study, men over report by about 150 per cent, more than double the over reporting by women (68 per cent). Interestingly, more-privileged husbands with egalitarian gender attitudes tend to over report at a higher rate than more traditional husbands do. Less-privileged "stay-at-home moms" are more likely to over report their housework than more-privileged working mothers do because only such inflated hours could justify their staying at home. The over reporting by men was so significant in one study that the researchers became cynical, doubting "that husbands have increased their supply of domestic labour to the household in the past 25 years." Other studies have found that housework is quite equitable among newly married couples without children, but this equality diminishes, as couples become parents, "a transition that solidifies women's responsibility for household work and men's for wage work." Equality does not rebound, either; according to one

German study, men's participation decreases over time and does not significantly recover with the growth of children to adulthood or the re-entry of a spouse into the workforce.[83]

One shouldn't be too cynical, though; believing that one *ought* to be doing housework undoubtedly affects men's participation in it. A recent Australian study found that "traditional" gender attitudes were "the most consistent predictor of housework," a result replicated in other studies. Accordingly, parents with more traditional gender ideologies tend to organize their homes in stereotypical ways that influence their children to develop similar ideologies, at least in childhood.[84]

Gender ideologies often differ by ethnicity, with obvious implications for the division of labour. For example, African-American women and men have less "traditional" attitudes toward women's work than do whites, while some studies show Hispanic Americans as more traditional. Not surprisingly, in every single subcategory (meal preparation, dishes, cleaning, shopping, washing, outdoor work, auto repair and maintenance, and bill paying), for example, African-American men do significantly more housework than their white counterparts.[85]

Regardless, ideology isn't necessarily determinative. Though working-class men are more likely than professional men to espouse traditional gender ideologies, blue-collar fathers, regardless of race—municipal and service workers, policemen, firefighters, and maintenance workers—are twice as likely as those in professional, managerial, or technical jobs to care for their children while their wives work. This difference is enabled by "informal flex time," a split-shift arrangement with one's spouse, which is negotiated by about one-fourth of all workers in the United States and by one-third of all workers with children under age five.[86]

Therefore, when it comes to being fathers, men are evidently willing to do more. As well, they've had support in becoming more active fathers. Dr Benjamin Spock's multi-decade bestselling book *Babies and Child Care* noted (and perhaps even encouraged) the shift in thinking about fathers' involvement. In the first edition (1946), Dr Spock suggested that men could be somewhat involved in child care as an assistance to the mother; by the 1990s, the book presented men's involvement in child care as part of being a parent.[87]

Between 1975 and 2010, married American fathers' child care time rose from 2.4 hours per week to 7.2 hours per week. However, unlike the case of housework, *more* child care overall seems to be being done, and some of the child care tasks fathers take on may be "fun" activities that do not eliminate the need for the everyday tasks more usually performed by mothers. As a result, perhaps, married American mothers almost doubled their time in the same period so that today married mothers are still doing 1.9 hours of child care for every hour done by fathers. Canadian men are ahead of their US and UK counterparts in their participation in child care. One major policy shift that has enabled this shift was the extension of parental benefits to men through the Employment Insurance (EI) program. As the program has grown, so has men's participation. In 2000, only 3 per cent of Canadian men took paid parental leaves. By 2006, that rate had jumped to 20 per cent, about where it has remained since. The majority of fathers now take some time off at or around the births of their children. Fathers also now take significantly more time off work for personal and family reasons; in 1997, the average American man used 1.8 days this way, while fathers in 2006 missed, on average, 6.3 days of work. (This is more than claimed by women, whose time off work has remained relatively stable in the same period.) There is strong evidence that leave-taking by fathers enhances their ability to parent in more than just an auxiliary role to women; however, leave-taking is constrained by culture and by the fact that where leave is split, the mother may wish to take all of the available leave.[88]

The benefits of fathering are clear. Men who have closer relationships with their children report greater marital satisfaction and better health. They feel less stress and less pressure to be successful, powerful, and competitive. They also live longer, causing the normally staid British financial magazine *The Economist* to quip, "Change a nappy, by God, and put years on your life." "When males take full responsibility for child care," sociologist Barbara Risman points out, "they develop intimate and affectionate relationships with their children." Nurturing their children is good for men's health. Of course, while men's child care doesn't necessarily include doing the dishes, increased family involvement by men benefits women. Recall that anthropologists found consistently that women's economic and political status is highest in those cultures in which men do more domestic work.[89]

While the data on housework raise numerous questions, one thing is clear: men and women are still struggling over the distribution of duties, and many women are stressed and resentful. This is true among married couples, and among cohabiting couples too, despite their tendency to espouse greater support for gender egalitarianism than those in married couples. One recent study of young working-class cohabiting couples in the US categorized couples as "conventional" (40 per cent), "contesting" (at least one partner attempting to engage in more gender-equal roles, 37 per cent), or "counter-conventional" (woman as breadwinner, 23 per cent). In each category, women assumed the dominant share of housework. In "conventional" couples, both couples saw the man's work as a priority. In turn, both the women and their male partners tended to downplay women's contributions, whether financial or domestic. Still, both partners expressed relative satisfaction with the arrangement. In "contesting" couples, both couples contributed more or less equally to earnings, and split bills. However, women still performed the bulk of the housework (on average two-thirds), and many of them were dissatisfied. For example, one participant reported that:

> Well, I thought it would be a little bit better than what it is. He doesn't do the deep clean. Oh, it's definitely an 80–20 split. He does [the] dishwasher and takes out the trash. And he'll do laundry. He'll clean it, but he won't fold it, put it away. I'm the organizer. I'm the one that gets the house looking nice. I'm the cleaner, the deep cleaner. I clean the entire house. He's pretty good about helping me though. If I ask him to help, he will.[90]

A quote like this usefully illustrates some of the key fault lines between couples and their perceptions of domestic work. The man's tasks are relatively short-duration ones. Yet he may feel that he "does the laundry," even though folding and putting away the laundry takes considerably longer than putting it into the washing machine and transferring it to the dryer. Similarly, when this woman's partner was asked who cleaned the bathroom, he reported that his partner did the "gritty" work, while he did the stuff that was "easy to do," such as cleaning his hair up after he shaved. As this example shows, a task that many women see as personal care or "cleaning up after oneself" might be evaluated by men as contributing to the overall housework. Finally, the quote demonstrates that in many heterosexual couples, the woman is still viewed as responsible for the management of the house, with her male partner assisting her if required. In this couple, as in so many, the man evaluated the division of labour as much more equal and fair than did the woman. The resultant conflict is everywhere.

Perhaps the most interesting findings from the study arose in the sample of "counter-conventional" couples, in which the woman by default ended up as the primary earner. The men in the sample, despite the fact that their partners were earning the majority or even all of the family income, downplayed their financial contributions. Whereas female partners in "conventional" families saw assuming the bulk of household chores as their attempt to offset and appreciate their male partners' economic contributions, none of the "counter-conventional" men expressed the same attitude. As one female participant stated,

> He doesn't do any labour and I do it all (laughs). I mean like he doesn't wash dishes or I have found that just ask him to wash dishes or doing any type of housework is like pulling teeth. He doesn't like to do that. So I mean, now the division of labour is I clean, sometimes he'll clean if he sees that I'm just really mad or frustrated at him but I basically do all of it to avoid arguments now.

While her partner agreed with her characterization, he traced his inability to perform household labour back to his mother, who did everything for him when he was a child. "It's hard for me now," he explained to the researchers "Every little thing I do I feel like it's a lot! I'll say 'Well I did the dishes! I took out the trash!'" In this study, regardless of family breadwinning status, women did the majority of the household labour. In the majority of the couples, women were dissatisfied with this situation. As more and more women become breadwinners for their families, this is a serious social concern. A 2011 *Forbes* survey of 1,259 women found that 44 per cent of the women brought in the majority of the household income, but also reported that they were responsible for the majority of the household work, child care, and even play. Of working mothers, 63 per cent agreed with the comment "Sometimes I feel like a married single mom"; 47 per cent of them reported never getting a break, but 93 per cent said that their partners do; 92 per cent of working moms say they are overwhelmed; and 70 per cent report feeling resentful toward their partners over shared parenting duties.[91]

Of course, there are increasing numbers of couples who share duties equally. Moreover, it is possible for women to be content with the division of labour even when duties are unequally shared: perceptions of fairness do not require a mathematical equality. Nonetheless, widespread discontent of North American women suggests that further change is needed. Interestingly, literature on same-sex couples suggests that the division of labour in these couples may be less problematic, which makes sense when gender delegation of tasks becomes impossible. One recent American study found that both gay and lesbian couples reported equal distribution of tasks, a marked difference from heterosexual couples. (However, these couples were childless, which may represent the differences in the comparison.) Confirming data came from a large-scale Dutch study that found that same-sex couples divide paid labour more equally and that lesbians did not tend to divide roles after childbirth in the manner characteristic of heterosexual couples. However, some US studies have found that same-sex couples' division of labour after child-bearing mirrored that of heterosexuals, and that biological lesbian mothers took on more care than their partners did. Therefore, same-sex relationships may not be a utopian paradise of gender equality, but the differences (and similarities) they exhibit highlight the relationship between gender and power and the necessity of change.[92]

Whatever the case, the situation is urgent. Balancing work and family pulls working women in different directions, and either way they move, they are bound to feel guilty and frustrated. One high-level executive who quit her job confessed that she "had as much going my way as any working mother could have. And I was absolutely flat-out. All I managed to do were the kids and my job. I could have continued to do this indefinitely, but I would have been a shell of myself."[93]

Family Organization and the Well-Being of Children in the Twenty-First Century

It has become increasingly clear that we are in the midst of sweeping and perhaps unprecedented changes to the structure of the family. Frank Furstenberg summarizes these changes as the breakdown of the link between marriage and sex; the weakening of marriage in most nations and the rise of cohabitation; rising rates of child-bearing outside marriage; later child-bearing; and a growing class divide in family formation that has accompanied growing social inequality.[94]

Since the family's prime purpose has been the raising of children, many of these changes are debated in terms of the effects they will have on children. These debates reveal the continued importance of gender and the nostalgia we retain for the "traditional" family form of the 1950s. However, discussions also reveal the effects of growing social inequality in North America, which affects families in many ways, often differentiated by gender.

Daycare

One of the major challenges in both Canada and the US is that while the relationship of women to work has changed, social policy still views the care of children as a "private matter," leaving it to increasingly exhausted and cash-strapped parents to navigate the necessary care for their children. Despite the lingering feeling among many Canadians that parents (usually mothers) should care for young children in the home, this is no longer practical. In the US, more than half of mothers will return to work before their babies are one year old; 64 per cent of mothers of children under six are in the workforce. Numbers are similar in Canada once children are older than a year. In Canada, most mothers of children under six are employed (the rate went from 31 to 67 per cent between 1976 and 2009, with 69 per cent of mothers of those two and under in the workforce). That means, for most children, the need for some form of daycare. In 2011, almost half of parents of children under 14 and more than half of parents of children under four reported using some form of child care.[95]

That women's entry into the workforce would necessitate more daycare has been recognized since 1970, when the first national child care program was proposed. In 1984, when Brian Mulroney's Conservative government came to power, it promised a program—but never delivered. Liberals were critical, but by the time they took power in 1993, deficits provided the rationale for scrapping the plan. In the 2004 election campaign, the Liberals promised to resuscitate the idea of national daycare, offering $5 billion to fund 250,000 spaces by 2009. Before the proposal was implemented, the Liberal government fell.

Stephen Harper's Conservative government, elected in 2006, brought in a plan called "Choice in Child Care." Designed to placate conservative critics who view daycare funding as unfair to "traditional" families, the plan offered all parents of children under six a monthly $100 payment to be used as each family saw fit. In 2014, income splitting was added to the mix, giving an additional $2,000 (maximum) tax credit to families in which one partner has no or a much lower income than the other—ostensibly to make it more possible for one partner to stay home or work part-time. Thirty years after the Mulroney promise, Canadian children continue to be "served" by a patchwork of care, much of it unregulated and some of it substandard. Only in Quebec has a universal, affordable provincial system been created. According to Jody Dallaire of the Child Care Advocacy Association of Canada, "the federal government has simply failed to meet the child care needs of Canadian families." As a result, our existing child care arrangements, Rianne Mahon writes, "work to reinforce class differences between families while at the same time contributing to the maintenance of unequal gender relations within them."[96]

Throughout the past 30 years, some striking claims have been made for both the benefits and the harms of daycare. In the early 1970s, the first studies found (much to most people's surprise) that daycare wasn't harmful to the mother–child bond and might even have benefits. However, many people weren't reassured by these findings, and some studies reported adverse effects.

In the 1980s, because of concerns both among the public and within the academic community, the American National Institutes of Child Health and Human Development (NICHD) established a long-term, large-scale Study of Early Child Care and Youth Development. Secure attachments to mothers (an early concern) were found to be just as prevalent among children in child care, bearing out the results of other studies. This was true regardless of the quantity or quality of the child care children experienced. The study also found evidence that children who experienced quality daycare (especially in daycare centres) exhibited cognitive and academic benefits that continued into high school; this may be because of the enriched environment in daycares, but may also reflect working mothers' tendency to provide (on average) a more enriched home environment.[97]

Indeed, the most common conclusion from the research on the impact of daycare on children's development has been that there are no negative consequences to being in daycare, and that **quality child care** has positive effects on children, particularly those of low socio-economic status. On the other hand, the NICHD study found links between assertive, disobedient, and aggressive behaviours and children's amount of time in care between the ages of birth and 4.5 years. More recently, a study found that as the number of Quebec children in daycare increased from 1994 to 2002, so did children's anxiety and depression. In fact, the authors claim boldly, "[f]or almost every measure, we find that the increased use of child care was associated with a decrease in their well-being relative to other children." A reason for this might be that many current daycare settings are of relatively low quality. In such settings, stress (as measured by cortisol levels) is a constant companion, perhaps leading to anxiety and depression.[98] Some conservative commentators might feel that such research proves how wrong it is to put children in care. Nonetheless, the preponderance of evidence suggests that there are no damaging effects on children, and many benefits of high-quality care. A more cautious approach to this research suggests that we need to be concerned about the *quality* of care that children are receiving.

In Canada, all provinces allow unregulated home-based daycare, often called "family daycares." (Home-based daycare may also be regulated in a separate category). Most providers of unregulated care are women who are often caring for their own children at home, and only about 10 per cent have a credential in early childhood education. Home daycares (regulated and unregulated) are used by almost one-third of all Canadian families who use care. Of parents who use child care, 98 per cent report being satisfied or very satisfied with their children's care, regardless of type used. However, after the deaths of several children in unlicensed home daycares in Ontario in 2013, the quality of care in Canada has become a much more prominent issue. Unregulated child care operates without any effective oversight, though there are limitations on how many children may be cared for in both regulated and unregulated settings. Still, because there is no inspection or oversight, these limitations may be ignored. This became painfully clear in the case of a toddler's death in 2013 in an unregulated home daycare that contained 29 children and 14 dogs.[99]

Therefore, there really is a "problem" with daycare: There's not enough of it, it's not affordable, and the government and our employers don't seem to care very much about our children. Nevertheless, we keep thinking about it in terms of whether or not women—not parents—should be placing their children in daycare in the first place. The "problem" of daycare turns out to be a debate about whether or not women should be working outside the home. This means we're asking the wrong question. For one thing, it poses a class-based contradiction, because we encourage poor women to leave the home and go to work and ask middle-class women to leave the workplace and return home. Since the late 1990s, most provinces have enacted reforms to social assistance, cutting benefits and making fewer people eligible. The most extensive reforms were in Ontario, where benefits were cut to encourage recipients to enter paid employment. Only seniors and the disabled were exempted. After 1998, single mothers had to demonstrate that they were attempting to find work or retrain in order to continue to receive benefits. Similar efforts to encourage mothers of young children to find employment have been made in British Columbia. "It is difficult to argue that poor mothers should find jobs but that middle-class mothers should stay home," writes family researcher Andrew Cherlin.[100]

Nor is there any reason why they should. In fact, most of the evidence indicates that both direct and indirect benefits accrue to children of working mothers. Such children tend to have expanded role models, more egalitarian gender role attitudes, and more positive attitudes toward women and women's employment. Daughters of employed women are more likely to be employed, and in jobs similar to those of their mothers, than are daughters of non-employed women. Moreover, adolescent children of working mothers assume more responsibility around the home, which increases their self-esteem.[101]

Throughout the European Union, child care is available, affordable, and expedient. Parents still balance career and family, and child care, to some degree, still reflects traditional gender ideologies—but there is far more support for child care than anywhere in North America (except Quebec). In Canada in 2012, there were only enough regulated child care spaces for one out of every five children needing space. In order to create substantial change we need to stop seeing child care as an issue for individual families and start seeing it as a societal issue of importance to all of us. As Joan Peters argues, women can work outside the home successfully "only if men take half the responsibility for child care." Again, the "solution" turns out to be social and political. Both nationally and in each family, the solution turns out to be greater gender equality—not women working less outside the home, but rather men working more inside and for it.[102]

Teenaged Pregnancy, Lone Parenting, and "Fatherlessness"

In the 1950s and 1960s, "unwed mothers" faced a great deal of social stigma, particularly if they were young. Consequently, it wasn't uncommon for teenagers to marry. Concerns about teenaged pregnancy flourished in the 1960s, and as rates continued to grow, teenaged pregnancy remained a hot-button issue from the 1980s into the new century. In the past decade, the movie *Juno* (2007), the so-called "Gloucester Pregnancy Pact," and the pregnancy of Bristol Palin, daughter of the 2008 vice-presidential candidate Sarah Palin, all catalyzed debate in the US. What no one seemed to notice in the media frenzy was that America's rate of teenaged pregnancy has been quietly but steadily declining since 1990—paralleling a pattern seen earlier in Canada. In 2010, US rates of teen pregnancy, teen birth, and teen abortion reached historic lows among all ethnic groups (though rates still differ by ethnicity and class).[103]

Although the stigmatizing of adolescent mothers and pregnant teenagers is damaging and wrongheaded, there are probably reasons to feel good about Canada's declining rate of teenage pregnancy. While pregnancy is not a "problem" for all adolescents, young age at pregnancy is associated with poorer outcomes for mother and child and greater risks of abuse. The effects on mothers' education and economic status are generally deleterious. (Bear in mind that adolescent mothers, more often than not, are single mothers and therefore part of a vulnerable group quite aside from their age.) Adolescent pregnancy rates are accordingly considered an important health and social indicator. Canada's declining rate of teenage pregnancies—a rate that includes abortions, live births, and miscarriages—is a sign that young women have "increasing opportunities and capacity to control their sexual and reproductive health."[104]

Still, concern over children with only one parent, or with unmarried parents, has continued. Throughout the 1980s and well into the current century, many North American commentators lamented the "rise of fatherlessness." A 2005 article lamented the "tsunami" of US-style "radical fatherlessness" striking black families in Toronto, linking it to the wave of shootings then terrorizing that city. David Blankenhorn's *Fatherless America* and David Popenoe's *Life without Father* blamed absent fathers for social problems ranging from juvenile delinquency to crime and violence to unemployment "Boys raised by traditionally masculine fathers generally do not commit crimes," wrote Blankenhorn. "Fatherless boys commit crimes." In a home without a father, Robert Bly (the father of the mythopoetic new men's movement) writes somewhat more poetically, "the demons have full permission to rage."[105]

It is true that more children of both sexes are being raised in lone-parent homes and that the "single parent" doing that child raising is more often than not a woman. Canada's rates of single motherhood, however, lag behind those of the US. Whereas 11 per cent of US children were being raised by unmarried mothers in 1970, 24 per cent were being raised that way as of 1996. Today in the US, about 40 per cent of births are to unmarried mothers, including more than half of births among women under 30. Most of these births do not represent lone parenting, because the mothers are in cohabiting relationships; however, cohabiting relationships break up even more than marital ones. Lone parenting is the present or future reality of many parents, whether married or unmarried, in heterosexual and same-sex relationships.[106]

In Canada, lone-parent families represented about 16.3 per cent of census families in 2011—still a minority, but double the rate of 50 years prior. The rate is much higher (31 per cent) among Aboriginal families. In Canada, lone-father families account for about 20 per cent of all lone-parent families, a ratio that has remained relatively stable over the past 50 years. (In the US, single-father families seem to be growing more rapidly, and currently represent about 23 per cent of all lone-parent families.)[107]

Lone parenting is undoubtedly challenging. Single fathers, however, may at least benefit from being seen as heroic. A 2011 study of 1,351 Americans found that single mothers were viewed more negatively than single fathers were, both in terms of their competence and in terms of personal characteristics. Indeed, one of the surprising findings of a 2011 Pew Research Center Study was how many Americans thought the rise of single-mother families was bad for society: 69 per cent of respondents thought so, the highest disapproval rating found for various forms of family. (The study did not ask about single fathers.)[108]

Not surprisingly, lone-parent families are at greater risk of poverty. According to Statistics Canada data, in 2004, despite the fact that almost 70 per cent of lone mothers worked, 38 per cent of female-headed lone-parent families fell below the Low-Income Cut Off line. Lone-parent families headed by men were slightly better off; only 13 per cent of them fell below the LICO; but compared to two-parent families, of whom only 7 per cent fell below the LICO, lone fathers were also disadvantaged. The same pattern exists in the US, where single fathers make significantly more than single mothers but still far less than the median earnings of two-parent families. Large-scale comparisons of single mothers and fathers yield interesting information. Specifically, lone fathers are more likely to have higher incomes and more stable jobs, to return to education, to receive more social support, to parent fewer children, to be white, to be older, and to survive without social assistance.[109] So, while lone parenting leaves families financially vulnerable, this burden is disproportionately distributed, and a major contributor to making women and children (particularly racialized and Aboriginal ones) the new face of poverty.

Research on single mothers also confirms that their health and happiness suffer—not surprisingly given the economic insecurity and stigma in which they tend to live. Children of single-mother families also seem to be at greater risk for school dropout. Children of lone-parent families, whether headed by mothers or fathers, perform less well academically (on average) than children from two-parent families. None of this is surprising given the economic insecurity of lone-parent families. When researchers control for socio-economic status, single mothers do well compared to single fathers, even in the area most associated with fathers by the public: rule setting and supervision. Children of lone fathers are actually more likely to engage in delinquency and suffer adjustment difficulties. Still, single fathers have been found to be warmer, to score higher on parenting scales, and to do more housework than married heterosexual fathers.[110]

Very few single parents set out to be lone family heads. For most, their status is the result of relationship breakdown, particularly divorce. Although liberalized divorce laws may have reduced gender inequality within marriage, they seem neither to have reduced it entirely nor to have reduced it after the marriage is dissolved. Just as there are "his" and "her" marriages, there are also "his" and "her" divorces, because divorce affects wives and husbands differently. In the mid-1980s, US family researcher Lenore Weitzman calculated that following divorce, the woman's income drops a precipitous 73 per cent, whereas her ex-husband's income increases 42 per cent. In recent years, these data have been revised as overly dramatic, but researchers still agree that women's resources decline more than men's do. As sociologist Paul Amato writes, "the greater the inequality between men and women in a given society, the more detrimental the impact of divorce on women." This trend, observable for the past 40 years, is still with us, according to a study published in 2009 by University of Toronto researcher Tahany Gadalla; the most dramatic effects on women's incomes are observable in the year after divorce, but effects continue for several years thereafter. In a number of nations—including Canada, the US, Germany, Sweden, the United Kingdom, and the Netherlands—the same pattern holds; women experience a sharp short-term drop in income after divorce, while men experience a modest increase in income. Men may take longer to recover emotionally from divorce, but their economic rebound is faster than women's. The causes of this are the continuing wage gap between men and women and the greater likelihood of women's retaining custody of children after divorce.[111]

Aside from effects on income, divorce has other important effects. More than half of all divorces in Canada involve couples with children still at home. When parents cannot agree on arrangements for the care of their children, the courts step in to adjudicate custody. While, historically, men have been advantaged in cases of marital dissolution, by the end of the nineteenth century courts were increasingly influenced by the so-called "tender years" principle. According to this idea, the interests of children (particularly young children) were best served by placing them in their mother's custody, at least until puberty or just before (when they were thought to need their same-sex role model). This model was replaced in the 1980s (i.e., in the Divorce Act of 1985) by the gender-neutral principle of the "best interests of the child," which dictated that only a child's interests should influence a custody decision. The best interests of the child were presumed to include regular visitation by the non-custodial parent, which led to the incorporation of the "friendly parent" principle, which encouraged awarding custody to the parent most likely to permit the other access.[112]

While the principles of Canadian child custody are gender-neutral, in practice both Canadian and American women tend to be more likely to receive custody than are fathers. This has led to a large fathers' rights movement throughout North America and to assertions of **Parental Alienation Syndrome** (PAS), an alleged phenomenon resulting from the attempts of mothers to poison their children's minds against their fathers. While scholars and the American Psychological Association have rejected PAS as a scientific concept, it has been deployed with success to discredit mothers' and children's allegations of abuse.

Despite this, some of the wilder claims of fathers' rights activists have in turn discredited allegations of gender bias in the courts, and women's continued greater responsibility for child rearing surely plays a role in judges' more frequently awarding custody to mothers.[113]

All things being equal, joint physical and legal custody arguably ought to be the norm in custody decisions. Here, of course, "all things being equal" means that there is no discernible danger to the child of sexual or physical abuse; that the parents can manage to contain their own post-divorce conflict and prevent the children from becoming pawns in a parental power struggle; and that the parents agree to support the children financially and emotionally. Such arrangements may be more difficult for parents than for children, who often report "a sense of being loved by both parents," as well as "feeling strongly attached to two psychological parents, in contrast to feeling close to just one primary parent." Contrary to some popular opinion, joint custody "does not create uncertainty or confusion" and seems to benefit children, who say they are more satisfied with the arrangement than those in single-custody homes and that they consider themselves to have two homes.[114]

Joint custody benefits men, relieving the deep sense of loss, disengagement, and depression often experienced by men who are cut loose from continued involvement with their families. Men with joint custody are also more likely to continue to share financial responsibilities. A recent metastudy found that while parents of either sex are more satisfied when they have sole custody, joint custody is associated with a number of positive outcomes including a stronger father–child relationship, less parenting stress, and less parental conflict (interpersonal and legal), and better overall adjustment. Perhaps the most judicious system of child custody will be one that recognizes the difference in "inputs" between parents in the actual experiences of the children—time spent in child care, level of parental involvement in child development—while at the same time presuming that both parents are capable of and interested in (absent any evidence to the contrary) continued committed and involved relationships with their children.[115]

Greater involvement of fathers may also help thwart the tendency of many men to disappear from their children's lives after divorce. Many divorced fathers "lose almost all contact with their children over time," writes David Popenoe. For whatever reason, it appears that many men "see parenting and marriage as part of the same bargain—a package deal," write sociologists Frank Furstenberg and Andrew Cherlin. "It is as if they stop being fathers as soon as the marriage is over." In one US study of 11- to 16-year-old children living with their mothers, almost half had not seen their fathers in the previous 12 months. Father dropout has continued to be documented in recent studies from both the US and Canada.[116]

Ironically, it also appears, that those men who were more involved with their children prior to the divorce who are most likely to disappear after it, whereas those men who were relatively uninvolved prior to divorce tend to become more active with their children afterward. In part, as the University of British Columbia's Edward Kruk observes, this counterintuitive difference stems from the more "traditional" outlooks of the less-involved fathers, which would increase their sense of commitment to family life even after divorce. In contrast, the men who were more "liberal" were more likely to see themselves as "free" from family responsibilities.[117]

Discussion of parenting after divorce leads naturally to one of the most contentious themes in the study of divorce: its effects on children. In a widely publicized study of 61 families in an affluent California suburb, psychologist Judith Wallerstein found that a significant number of children "suffer long-term, perhaps permanent detrimental effects from divorce." A lousy marriage, she concluded, beats a good divorce.[118]

Although such dire warnings as Wallerstein's have fuelled countless magazine covers and public discussion, her research design was flawed.[119] Still, no one doubts that divorce is difficult for children or that all things being equal, being raised by two parents (of whatever sex) is probably better than being raised by one. Single parents are more likely to be tired, stressed, overworked, and poor. If stepparents are present, certain risks increase (e.g., for girls especially, sexual abuse). If we compare educational achievement, sense of well-being, or psychological and emotional adjustment of children in non-divorced two-parent families with those of children in single-parent, post-divorce families, we find that children in two-parent families fare better. Such comparisons are misdirected, however, because they compare two types of families—divorced and intact—as if they were equivalent. Divorce is not a remedy for marriage; it is a remedy for a *bad* marriage, and children in bad marriages suffer.

Andrew Cherlin, a sociologist and demographer at Johns Hopkins University, found that the line of causation ran exactly counter to Wallerstein's clinical assertions. "We found that children whose parents would later divorce *already* showed more emotional problems at age 7 than children from families that would stay together," he writes. The University of Alberta's Lisa Strohschein concurs. Her longitudinal research indicates "the family dynamics that increase the likelihood of later divorce first act to increase the mental health problems of dependent children." Another British study tracking 17,000 families also found that children's problems long antedate divorce and that problems among young children, in fact, can be a good predictor of eventual divorce. Other longitudinal research has found that children in families that eventually divorce manifest problems long before the actual divorce; therefore, many of the consequences attributed to divorce may be caused by the marital conflict and family stress that precede a divorce, rather than from the divorce itself. Blaming the problems of children on their parents' divorce "is a bit like stating that cancer is caused by chemotherapy," argues the president of the Family and Divorce Mediation Council of Greater New York. "Neither divorce nor chemotherapy is a step people hope to have to take in their lives, but each may be the healthiest option in a given situation." Family sociologists Paul Amato and Alan Booth conclude that divorce "is beneficial for children when it removes them from a high-conflict marriage."[120]

Most research on divorce finds that most children recover from the stress of divorce and show few adverse signs a few years later if they have adequate psychological supports and economic resources. One study found that children in divorced families indeed did feel lonely, bored, and rejected more often than those in intact families did—but that children in families led by unhappily married couples felt the highest levels of neglect and humiliation.[121]

The solution that some propose is simple: make divorce harder to obtain. In the US, three states have instituted "covenant marriages," which, unlike the contractual legal marriage, demand that couples take literally and seriously the provision of "until death do us part." In Arizona, Arkansas, and Louisiana, marrying couples have the option of two forms of marriage: regular and covenant. If they choose a covenant marriage, they must undergo premarital counselling, swear a special oath, accept a two-year waiting period for divorce, and in some cases enrol in mandatory marriage counseling. Only a tiny proportion of those marrying (2 per cent in Louisiana, fewer in other covenant states) have chosen covenant marriages. Preliminary results suggest that they break down much less than do "regular" marriages, though this is probably because of self-selection factors among those who choose "covenant." (Premarital counseling may also help.) Such measures have not been taken in Canada; however, Canadian William Gairdner, author of *The Trouble with Canada*—and divorced, himself—has argued that tougher divorce laws are needed to keep people from "taking the easy way out." Yet most family researchers agree that such a triumph of form over content—making divorce harder to get without changing the content of the marriage—would "exacerbate the bitterness and conflict that are associated with the *worst* outcomes of divorce for kids."[122]

Divorce might better be seen as a social indicator that something is wrong not with one-half of all marriages, taken individually, but rather with the institution of marriage, that the foundation upon which marriage rests cannot sustain and support one-half of all the marriages that take place. US Family therapist Betty Carter pointed out that if any other social institution were failing so many of the people who entered it, we would demand that the institution change to fit people's new needs, not the other way around.[123]

Same-Sex Parenting

Discussions of same-sex parenting arose in the 1970s in the context of custody disputes and divorce settlements involving lesbian mothers leaving heterosexual marriages. Almost all decisions radically restricted lesbians' access to their children and portrayed them as "bad mothers." The main assertions were three: children of lesbians would have "abnormal" psychosexual development; they would suffer from bullying and ostracism; and they would suffer psychological problems related to the stress of their family situations. In response, scholars in the US and UK began the first academic studies of children raised by lesbians, comparing outcomes for children in lesbian-mother families with those of children in single-mother families. These studies, and many others that followed them, consistently showed that there were no differences in outcomes for children from these two family types.[124]

Despite the claim of REAL Women of Canada and many other social conservatives that "[s]ame-sex parenting is harmful to children," there is no evidence that gay fathers or lesbian mothers exert any negative influence on child development. A 2003 study commissioned by the Canadian federal government found no evidence that lesbian-led families produced poorer outcomes; indeed, of 100-plus studies reviewed by Concordia University researcher John Hastings, more found superior outcomes for children of lesbian parents than found weaker outcomes. A 2010 metastudy found that lesbian mothers enjoyed numerous advantages in child rearing, including more compatible and satisfying co-parenting, greater parenting awareness skills than heterosexual men, warmer relationships, more play, less discipline and corporal punishment, and less emphasis on conformity. "In other words," wrote the researchers, "two women who chose to become parents together seemed to provide a double dose of a middle-class 'feminine' approach to parenting." However, jealousy and lack of complete parity were issues for lesbian parents, and some of the same factors that produce the strengths of co-mothering may lead the unions of lesbians to be less durable than those of heterosexuals.[125]

Studies of children raised by gay fathers are still very rare, but those that exist suggest that having two gay fathers does not produce the effect of "doubling" typical heterosexual-father interactions. Gay male couples tend to adopt practice more typical of mothers (though they may be more inclined than lesbians are to promote gender conformity). As one gay father stated:

> As a gay dad, I'm not a mom, but sometimes I think I have more in common with moms than I do with straight dads. I mean, these straight dads that I know are essentially weekend dads: they don't parent with the same intensity that I do or that their wives do. In many ways, despite being a man, I am a dad, but I am like a mom too.[126]

In some ways, then, gay fathers challenge gender norms even more than lesbian mothers do.

One clear finding from various studies is that children of gay and lesbian couples exhibit more gender-egalitarian attitudes than do children of heterosexual couples. A recent meta-analysis of social science studies of gay and lesbian parenting suggests that children of these parents are more accepting of homosexuality and may be more likely to indicate a willingness to consider homosexual relationships themselves, although they are no more likely to identify themselves as "gay" than are children of heterosexual parents. More interestingly, however, are the *gender* consequences, as opposed to the sexual ones: Daughters of lesbian and gay parents are more assertive, confident, and ambitious, and sons are less conforming to traditional notions of masculine aggression and domination and more fluid in their gender identities. Such sentiments, as family sociologist Judith Stacey points out, might well "serve as child-rearing ideals for a democracy."[127]

Not everyone agrees, even among scholars. In 2012, Mark Regnerus ignited a controversy with his analysis of data from the New Family Structures Study, a data collection project that surveyed young American adults (18–39). Regnerus found persistent deficits for adult children of people who had engaged in same-sex relationships, relative to children of parents in stable heterosexual marriages. Numerous critiques of the flaws in Regnerus's study and findings ensued, but his work points to areas in the existing literature that require further study and attention to flaws in research design.[128]

Lone parents, cohabiting parents, married parents, heterosexual parents, same-sex parents—in the end, comparisons of which is "better" founder on the complexity of the analysis. Studies show that good parenting can be found in many kinds of families. As Timothy Biblarz and Judith Stacey write in summary:

> Every family form provides distinct advantages and risks for children. . . . At this point, no research supports the widely held conviction that the gender of parents matters for child well-being. To ascertain whether any particular form of family is ideal would demand sorting a formidable array of often inextricable family and social variables. We predict that even "ideal" research designs will find instead that ideal parenting comes in many different genres and genders.[129]

The Family of the Future

As the quote above attests, the *form* of the family (whether intact or divorced, single-parent or multi-parent, lesbian or gay) matters far less for children and adults than its *content* does. One study summarized its findings this way: "processes occurring in all types of families are more important than family structure in predicting well-being and relationship outcomes." A home free from violence and filled with love, respect, and economic and emotional support is the strongest predictor of future physical, emotional, and psychological health of both children and their parents. Family sociologist Arlene Skolnick writes that the most reliable studies "find that . . . what children need most is a warm, concerned relationship with at least one parent."[130]

In the nineteenth century, the ideology of the separation of spheres "imprisoned" women in the home while "exiling" men from it. In the twenty-first century, perhaps we will witness a "reintegration of spheres," in which home and work will become increasingly similar, and men and women will be more active participants in both spheres. We should "insist on a closer integration between people's professional lives and their domestic lives," writes social critic Christopher Lasch. "Instead of acquiescing in the family's subordination to the workplace, [we] should seek to remodel the workplace around the needs of the family." We should also take seriously growing evidence that social inequality is producing two forms or two "tiers" of family formation and question why family forms are diverging so radically on the basis of class.[131]

Our families are places in which we are both constrained by duty and obligation and inspired by love, respect, and honour. Love, we've found, can abide in traditional families, in single-parent families, and in gay and lesbian families. It can sustain children in intact families or after divorce. What matters is the content of the family, not its form. Love can abide, nourish, and sustain—wherever it lives and in whatever form.

Summary

The emergence of the "family values" debate in the 1980s and 1990s highlighted the changing family. Since 1990, family structures and attitudes toward the family have changed more dramatically than could have been anticipated. However, history teaches us that the family has *always* changed and that far from being the "haven in a heartless world," the family has always been linked to other social institutions.

The Canadian family has changed dramatically throughout the past 500 years. With industrialization (circa 1850) came the emergence of the notion of separate spheres for men and women. The new family model claimed that men should be breadwinners and women "homemakers," in a domestic sphere newly construed as non-productive.

Soon thereafter, however, women began to push for rights and possibilities outside their allotted domestic sphere. By the beginning of the twentieth century, women were becoming assimilated into employment (including breadwinning), education, and political rights. As the twentieth century progressed, most people still supported the ideological construct of the male breadwinner and the female homemaker, resisting changes in women's roles.

After the Second World War, both government policy and a wave of nostalgia pushed women back into the home. Men and women embraced this nostalgia, marrying and having children early, and divorcing rarely. The 1950s family model they created was almost immediately enshrined as the most "natural" and healthiest form possible. However, by the late 1950s, women's discontent was evident, and in the 1960s, it boiled over into a bona fide social movement against confinement in domesticity. This change, along with many others, placed strain on the post-war nuclear family model, which had become an anachronism almost as soon as it was created.

The current Canadian family undoubtedly faces stresses. Canada's rate of child poverty continues to be unacceptably high, and Canada's Aboriginal families face tremendous challenges, not least poverty and the continuing legacy of residential schools. Canadian families are also changing in other ways: families are smaller, couples are less likely to be married, and divorce is more common than it was for most of Canadian history. Our ideas about family have also changed. Canadians are highly accepting of diversity in family structures, even while they aspire to a "traditional" family model in their own lives. In this, Canadians are on the vanguard of a global trend.

Despite the fact that marriage is declining and cohabitation growing rapidly, marriage remains important to many of us, and its cultural script remains highly gendered. We still think of it as something women want and men try to avoid. We also think of it as something with demonstrable health benefits. However, recent research is calling this into question, and the "marriage premium" seems to be diminishing. Since the early 1970s, studies have demonstrated that the benefits of marriage are highly gendered; while some of this gendering seems to have disappeared, marriage still seems slightly better for women than for men, as measured by health and happiness indicators. Same-sex marriage was legalized in Canada in 2005 and 2015 in the US, which should bring further changes in the institution of marriage. Still, same-sex couples still represent a tiny percentage of the total number of couples.

Child rearing, like marriage itself, remains highly gendered. We still gender-type infants—arranging their environments and clothing to conform to our expectations for their gender. Most research suggests that we treat them differently, particularly in terms of encouraging autonomy and exploration in males and closeness in females. We also attribute gendered emotions and motivations to infant behaviour.

Gender-typing increases as children enter the toddler stage. Though girlhood, and to some extent boyhood, have changed in the 50 years since Mattel's Barbie made her debut, the gendered cultures of childhood are very much alive. Meanwhile, boys continue to see femininity as lower in status than masculinity.

The gendered cultures of childhood are an anachronism given the major transformations of the past 50 years, and particularly given the large-scale entrance of women into the workplace. On the other hand, there are signs that the transformation of the family is incomplete. Women everywhere report greater stress than do men, in part because of the "double shift," which requires women to both work outside the home and retain responsibility for the domestic sphere. While men have greatly increased their participation in child care, men still do significantly less domestic labour than women do, and this is true in a variety of family constellations. Greater economic contribution does not correlate with less housework for women. For women's second shift to change dramatically, men must learn and be supported to do child care and housework, and to share full responsibility for all aspects of family life. Because this issue is a major contributor to women's stress and satisfaction in marriage, it is an urgent issue.

Like the division of household labour, many of the current challenges in family life arise from the struggle between gender ideologies and a changing society; much of the discussion of these changes has centred on the well-being of children. If children are the reason for the family, how do different family structures and organizations can affect the well-being of children? Instead of being nostalgic for the (imagined) families of the past, what supports can we offer the family we now have?

While more than half of Canadian children regularly access daycare, we continue to argue about whether daycare is harmful to children. The scholarly consensus is that daycare in itself does not harm children but that quality of care matters. Children in high-quality care exhibit outcomes as good as (or even better than) those of children cared for by their parents. Daycare is not a "women's problem," or a luxury, but an increasingly necessary support for the Canadian family.

The question of "fatherlessness" arises regularly with regard to crime and social dislocation. While more children are being reared in lone-parent families, particularly those headed by women, Canada has a lower rate of lone parenthood than does the US. Moreover, poverty, not the simple presence or absence of a father in the home, is the most likely explanation for the participation of lone-parented youth in crime.

The discussion of fatherlessness is clearly related to changes in divorce and child custody throughout the past 30 or 40 years. Since divorce was liberalized in Canada in the late 1960s, the divorce rate has increased dramatically (though it has declined significantly lately, largely as a result of the decline of marriage itself). Like marriage, divorce remains gendered. Since the 1980s, Canadian courts have been encouraged to consider the child's best interests in making child custody decisions; mothers are more likely to receive custody than fathers are. This has led to the growth of a fathers' rights movement that argues against alleged gender bias in the courtroom.

The effects of divorce upon children have been studied, particularly in the US, since the dramatic increase in the divorce rate approximately 40 years ago. One of the major findings to emerge from newer studies is that children in families that will later divorce show mental health problems even before the divorce; marital conflict, not divorce itself, may be responsible for these problems. Ultimately, though, divorce is less a problem in itself than an indicator of strains on the institution of marriage and our expectations of it.

Since the 1970s, scholars have studied same-sex parents to see whether there are differences in outcome for their children. These studies have shown that outcomes for children of these families are at least as good as for children of heterosexual couples; however, studies focused overwhelmingly on lesbians. The few studies of gay male parents have concluded that they, too, parent in a positive manner. Evidence suggests that while outcomes for children may not differ, both the parenting styles of lesbians and gay men and the attitudes of their children show evidence of greater gender egalitarianism and fluidity.

The first decades of the twenty-first century have witnessed tremendous changes in the family, and some of these, particularly how family forms are diverging because of social inequality, are troubling. The overwhelming consensus of research on the family is that we worry a great deal about the form of the family, which matters much less than its content. Much more important than the number or sex of one's parents is a home filled with love, respect, and support; adequately sustained by material resources; and free of violence and abuse.

Questions for Critical Thinking

1. Why do you think the 1950s nuclear family concept became frozen in our minds as the "ideal" and "traditional" family?
2. Why do you think child rearing can lead to such a decline in marital happiness?
3. Why do you think men have been more eager to embrace child care than to take on housework?
4. How "gendered" do you think contemporary child-rearing practices are? In your experience, can you think of examples of differential treatment of girls and boys?
5. Thinking about marriage as a gendered institution, do you think that same-sex marriage will change the nature of that institution?

Key Terms

Aboriginal
breadwinner
child poverty
clan
common-law marriage
Divorce Act
emotion work
extended family
gender complementarity
homophily
Indian Act
intensive mothering
Low-Income Cut Off (LICO)
marriage premium
matrilocal

New Woman
nuclear families
Parental Alienation Syndrome (PAS)
quality child care
race suicide
residential schools
Section 12(1)b
second shift
separation of spheres
sixties scoop
suburban
temperance movement
Truth and Reconciliation
    Commission (TRC)

7

The Gendered Classroom
Formal Education and the Hidden Curriculum

The Higher Education of Women is one of the great world battle-cries for freedom; for right against might. It is the cry of the oppressed slave. It is the assertion of absolute equality.

—Henry Fowle Durant, President, Wellesley College, "The Spirit of the College" (1877)

As we saw in the last chapter, our gendering experiences begin long before we get to school. When we enter our first classroom, we will learn more than our ABCs, more than spelling, math, and science, more than physics and literature. In school, we learn—and teach one another—what it means to be men and women. Just as gender infuses the family, it also structures formal education, such as who teaches us, what they teach us, how they teach us, and how the schools are organized as institutions. Both in the official curriculum (textbooks, etc.) and in the parallel **hidden curriculum** of our informal interactions with both teachers and other students, we become gendered. This is reinforced in the parallel curriculum presented by the mass media.

The message that students get from both the content and the form of education is that women and men are different and unequal. As law professor Deborah Rhode writes, "What schools teach and tolerate reinforces inequalities that persist well beyond childhood."[1]

Traditional Education: Learning to Be a Man

Most of us are aware that formal education was historically limited by sex and class (and in many cases in the modern world, by race). In the eighteenth century, education was largely reserved for upper-class boys and men. Women were viewed as insufficiently rational by "enlightened" thinkers, while those rooted in the Christian tradition used other justifications for the exclusion of female students from anything but rudimentary education. In the eighteenth century as throughout history, some girls and women, particularly religious women and those of elite status, became highly educated; but the idea of being educated was powerfully linked to the idea of being masculine.

This was also true in Canada's colonial history. In New France, education was in the hands of the Catholic Church. Nuns and friars provided education to settler girls and boys in towns and, to some extent, rural areas. However, most children received only a basic education; "learning," for them, meant the less formal process of vocational learning within the home or, in some cases, in apprenticeship. Higher education was confined mainly to those entering the clergy or professions, who were often educated in the colony's Jesuit colleges. After the British takeover, Canada's system imitated that of England. Canada's first university outside Quebec, King's College, was established at Windsor, Nova Scotia, in 1789; from then until Confederation, Canada's universities would be staffed by Britons and would emulate traditions and trends from the mother country.

Throughout the nineteenth century, formal education expanded significantly, particularly because Canada's rulers saw education as the best way to assimilate Canada's diverse society into something resembling a nation. By the 1820s, there was significant support for state education, though there was also resistance, particularly from the Catholic Church in Quebec. After the rebellion of 1837–38, education was seen as even more valuable in moulding "freely obedient subjects"—and in correcting the "gender imbalance" in Québécois society, according to Arthur Buller's report on education in the region:

> The difference in the character of the two sexes is really remarkable. The women are the men of Lower Canada. They are the active, bustling, business portion of the *habitans* [*sic*]; and this results from the much better education which they get gratuitously, or at a very cheap rate, from the nunneries which are dispersed over the province.[2]

By Confederation, governments were giving financial support to Catholic and "public" schools, though this support was small by twenty-first-century standards. By the end of the nineteenth century, most parents were enrolling their children in school, even before almost all of the provinces passed legislation making school attendance mandatory. (Only Quebec held out until 1943, as a result of parental, church, and employer opposition.)

The presence of girls within this system was uncontroversial, but there was disagreement concerning what girls should be learning. Egerton Ryerson, one of the most influential figures in nineteenth-century Canadian schooling, felt that girls should be educated for their "proper sphere" and not for paid employment. Girls were discouraged from pursuing the "difficult" courses required, for example, for university admission. Therefore, while "universal" education was a commonly held goal, some forms of exclusion remained part of the system. As we discussed in the previous chapter, Aboriginal students were to go to separate schools where most received a substandard education; in addition, the treatment received at the school has marred Aboriginal communities' relations with formal education to this day. In addition, black-white segregation within nineteenth-century schools was tolerated even though it was against the law.[3]

Canada's education system, both at the primary and higher levels, expanded dramatically precisely during the phase when education was most linked, throughout the British Empire, to notions of **imperial manhood**. According to these ideas, education played a major role in creating the ideal British subject. Boys all over the empire learned about the triumphs of British civilization, were instructed in manly Christian morality, and developed healthy bodies and character through playing British sports. *Tom Brown's Schooldays* (1857), was the apogee of this "new educational ethos," presenting Rugby School as a microcosm of the well-ordered British society. Sports and education consequently became ever more linked with ideas about what it meant to be masculine—not to mention British. In the form of "muscular Christianity," these ideas spread throughout North America.[4]

We've seen earlier how during this same period, the ideology of the separate spheres saw men and women as fulfilling completely different destinies. Not surprisingly, in the nineteenth century many argued that "manly" education was not suited for women. Much of the debate centred on whether or not women could be educated, especially in colleges and universities. One writer suggested that a woman "of average brain" could attain the same standards as a man with an average brain "only at the cost of her health, of her emotions, or of her morale." Another prophesied that women would grow bigger and heavier brains and that their uteruses would shrink if they went to college. Perhaps the most famous social scientist to join this discussion was Edward C. Clarke, Harvard's eminent professor of education. In his bestselling book, *Sex in Education; or, A Fair Chance for the Girls* (1873), Clarke argued that women should be exempted from higher education because of the tremendous demands made upon their bodies by reproduction.[5]

Opponents of women's equality argued that higher education for women would result in "monstrous brains and puny bodies" with "flowing thought and constipated bowels," because it would violate the "plan" women's bodies held for them. Many of the Victorian opponents of women's education believed that women could not withstand and would not wish to subject themselves to the rigours of higher education, while others deplored the possibility that educated women would seek employment outside the home. The University of Toronto had to be compelled by law to permit women to attend classes, and the male medical students welcomed their female colleagues by filling their seats with filth. Nonetheless, the first degree granted to a woman in the British Empire went to a Canadian, Grace Annie Lockhart, who received her B.Sc. from Mount Allison in 1875.[6]

While some worried about higher education for women, others worried that the presence of women in universities would "emasculate" and "water down" the university curriculum and de-gender both men and women. In his influential treatise on adolescence, the great psychologist G. Stanley Hall warned against co-education because it "harms girls by assimilating them to boys' ways and work and robbing them of their sense of feminine character," whereas it harms boys "by feminizing them when they need to be working off their brute animal element." By making boys and girls more alike, he warned, co-education would "dilute" the mysterious attraction of the opposite sex—that is, co-education would cause homosexuality. (Of course, Hall could not yet have previewed Alfred Kinsey's studies of human sexuality, which found that most homosexual experimentation among males occurred precisely in those single-sex institutions—all-male schools, summer camps, Boy Scouts, the military, and prisons—that Hall believed would be palliatives against homosexuality.)[7]

Of course, there were also strong supporters of women's education in both Canada and the US, such as the founders and first presidents of historically women's colleges, like Henry Durant (Wellesley) and the "Methodist millionaires" who supported the extension of women's education in nineteenth-century Ontario. Many supporters of women's education were essentially conservative in their view of education, but Durant went as far as to argue that the real meaning of women's education was revolt—"against the slavery in which women are held by the customs of society—the broken health, the aimless lives, the subordinate position, the helpless dependence, the dishonesties and shams of so-called education."[8]

By 1900, about 10 per cent of Canadian university undergraduates were women. By 1920, the proportion had increased to about 25 per cent. Women were "stuck" at this rate until the 1960s, when rates began to increase dramatically. By 1980–1981, the majority of students enrolled in university were women, a trend that has continued to the present.[9] An education that 150 years ago was a training in manhood, has accordingly opened to women. The classrooms that women struggled so hard to enter, however, did not completely and willingly accommodate them. Women entered gendered classrooms, and our classrooms continue to be gendered in ways both predictable and surprising.

The Gendered Classroom

Today, Canada's schools enrol more than 5 million students, with close to 2 million students in post-secondary education.[10] (As detailed in the previous chapter, the majority of Canada's preschool-aged children are also in care, but there is no early childhood education system in place as of yet.)

Canada's education system, relative to systems in much of the world, is gender-neutral. Yet the formal educational gendering process begins the moment we enter the classroom and continues throughout our educational lives. Take an environmental example: in preschools and kindergarten classes, we often find the heavy blocks, trucks, airplanes, and carpentry tools in one area and the dolls and homemaking equipment in another area. Although they may be officially "open" to anyone for play, the areas are often sex-segregated by invisible but real boundaries.

In the elementary school years, informal play during out-of-school hours involves different sports, different rules, and different playground activities, but the rule of segregation is the same. Boys and girls learn, and teach each other, the appropriate behaviours and experiences for boys—and girls and make sure that everyone acts according to plan.

What's less visible are the ways the teachers and curriculum overtly and subtly reinforce not only gender difference, but also the inequalities that go along with and even produce that difference. The classroom setting reproduces gender inequality. "From elementary school through higher education, female students receive less active instruction, both in the quantity and in the quality of teacher time and attention," note education professors David Sadker and the late Myra Sadker, summarizing the research in their important book *Failing at Fairness*. (The study was published in 1995, but the 2009 revised edition finds the situation the same.) Many teachers perceive boys as being active, capable of expressing anger, quarrelsome, punitive, alibi-building, and exhibitionistic, and they perceive girls as being affectionate, obedient, responsive, and tenacious. When teachers assign "helper" tasks to girls or boys, they will often ask boys to do physical or technological assistance, while requesting girls' assistance with "softer" tasks such as assisting another student or taking attendance. When boys "put girls down," as they often do at that age, teachers (female usually) often say and do nothing to correct them, therefore encouraging the boys' notion of superiority. Many teachers assume that girls are likely to "love" reading and "hate" mathematics and sciences, and they expect the opposite of boys.[11]

The Sadkers document a number of other differences. Teachers call on boys more often and spend more time with them. They ask boys questions that are more challenging, and wait longer for them to answer. They urge boys to try harder, constantly telling boys that they can "do it." One study found that in all 10 of the college classrooms observed, boys were more active, regardless of the gender of the teacher, though a female teacher increased girls' participation significantly. Another study, from the UK, found that boys received more attention than did girls, including receiving more reprimands (with a small group of boys the focus of most reprimands); boys also were asked and answered more questions. However, girls asked more questions of the teacher and requested more help. A report sponsored by the American Association of University Women (AAUW)—in *How Schools Shortchange Girls*—summarized these studies when it concluded that whether "one is looking at preschool classrooms or university lecture halls . . . research spanning the past 20 years consistently reveals that males receive more teacher attention than do females." Part of the reason for this is that boys demand more attention, and part of the reason is that teachers also treat boys and girls differently. When the Sadkers were re-searching their book, they asked teachers why they paid more attention to the boys. The teachers told them things like "Because boys need it more," and "Boys have trouble read-ing, writing, doing math. They can't even sit still."[12]

Journalist Peggy Orenstein observed another junior high school class, where boys "yelled out or snapped the fingers of their raised hands when they wanted to speak, [while the] girls seemed to recede from class proceedings." As one girl told her, "Boys never care if they're wrong."

As these examples suggest, teachers and others often rely on what Leanne Dalley-Trim calls "common-sense" understandings of masculinity in their work with boys. Instead of seeing abusive behaviours as intolerable and avoidable, for example, teachers dismiss them as what boys do. Based on her research in Australia, Dalley-Trim argues that when teach-ers accept certain behaviours as "just boys being boys," they risk supporting simplistic ideas about masculinity that harm boys and girls alike. Teachers may also stereotype girls while taking the opposite approach to their misbehaviour. Diane Reay's study of girls in a largely working-class London (UK) classroom reported that teachers were far less toler-ant of girls' misbehaviour, describing misbehaving seven-year-olds as "little cows," "real bitches," and "too mature." In the gendered classroom, both sexes are stereotyped.[13]

Interactions with teachers and other students are one important part of the gen-dered classroom, but they are not the only influence upon children. Early in the school years, children learn to read, and to rely upon the textbooks prescribed by their teachers. Canadian research shows that teachers use textbooks for up to 90 per cent of classroom time, and that the structure of these textbooks significantly influences the decisions that teachers make. Therefore, textbooks matter. (As we shall see in Chapter 9, students also observe the content of other media—television, films, and cartoons.) Textbooks can be one way in which the school-based curriculum reinforces gender stereotypes and makes them seem as though they were based on something "natural."

Until recently, studies of children's books and anthologies have consistently reported traditional sex differences and pro-male biases. Females have been vastly underrepresented, and often absent, in pictures, in titles, and as main characters. In addition, female characters have usually been cast in insignificant or secondary roles. Their activities have been limited to loving, watching, or helping, whereas males have engaged in adventuring and solving problems. Women have not been given jobs or professions; motherhood has been presented as a full-time, lifetime job. The son in the family has worn trousers, and the daughter has worn a skirt; he has been active, she has been passive. In biographies, women have often been portrayed as dependent. For example, Marie Curie has been depicted as a helpmate to her husband, rather than as the brilliant scientist and Nobel Prize winner that she was.

In 1972, Lenore Weitzman and her colleagues surveyed winners of the Caldecott Medal for the best children's books published in the US from 1967 to 1971. Since then, the research has been updated twice, most recently in 1987; the researchers now find that although females are more visible in the books, their portrayal still reveals gender biases. In 1975, the US Department of Health, Education, and Welfare surveyed 134 texts and readers from 16 different publishers, looking at the pictures, stories, and language used to describe male and female characters. "Boy-centred" stories outnumbered "girl-centred" stories by a 5:2 ratio; there were three times as many adult male characters as adult female characters; six times as many biographies of men as of women; and four times as many male fairy tales as female. Recalling her American history classes, one scholar recently remembered a strange biological anomaly—"a nation with only founding fathers." A recent study of 5,618 children's books published in the US during the twentieth century found that male characters (human or non-human) were featured in titles and as protagonists nearly twice as often as female characters overall and more during certain periods, a trend the authors described as "symbolic annihilation." (The publisher of Little Golden Books was the worst offender.) Though recent surveys suggest that history texts are improving, children's illustrated books and teacher-training texts continue to demonstrate substantial gender bias. One recent Alberta study shows that teachers are often unaware of the ideological content of children's literature and may therefore adopt books uncritically. In some cases, school boards, such as the one in Surrey, BC, have attempted to ban library books that present same-sex parents as "normal."[14]

One shouldn't underestimate the changes of the past 40 years. In children's books today, girls and women are far more likely than before to be depicted as the main character and far less likely to be depicted as passive, without ambition or career goals. In fact, the major change in all media images—books, television, and movies—has been that women are no longer cast as domestic helpmates or workplace subordinates; but gender stereotypes are still with us.

Gender Divergence in Adolescence: Girls

As we have seen, the separation of girls and boys into segregated play cultures takes place at a tender age; similarly, differential treatment of girls and boys by teachers begins with their earliest entry into school. This divergence continues, culminating in the intensely gendered experience of adolescence. Some scholars have found that in early adolescence, girls and boys enter a period of **gender intensification** in which they view gender roles as more rigid than they did before adolescence.[15] The combination of exclusion from the curriculum, gender stereotypes in the media, and the often-invisible discrimination in the classroom produces and intensifies this divergence.

In elementary school, girls have somewhat higher **self-esteem** and higher achievement levels than boys; in junior high, however, while girls' achievement continues, their self-esteem plummets. (Boys' self-esteem also declines, though less precipitously.) While Dove Canada, Girl Guides, the YWCA, and Big Brothers Big Sisters launch campaigns to increase girls' self-esteem, no single organization can change one tremendous shock to the system. In early adolescence, girls find out that they are valued more for their appearance than for their talents. In this period in their lives, girls begin to understand the nature of emphasized femininity—that their socially valued role is to be attractive to men.

As a result, girls become more focused on their bodies and less on their competence; often, a girl will develop, according to Peggy Orenstein, "a scathingly critical attitude toward her body and a blossoming sense of personal inadequacy." More and more as they proceed through high school, girls view their appearance as the measure of their worth. One Irish study found that physical appearance was "the single best predictor of global self-worth" for adolescent girls in mixed-sex schools. Ashley Reiter, a winner of the US Westinghouse Talent Competition for her project of mathematical modelling, remembered the day she won her first math contest, which coincided with the day she got her first pair of contact lenses. When she showed up at school the next day, triumphant about her victory, "[e]veryone talked about how pretty I looked," she recalled. "Nobody said a word about the math competition." Is it any wonder that, in one survey, adolescent girls were about half as likely as boys were to cite their talents as "the thing I like most about myself," but about twice as likely as the boys were to cite some aspect of their appearance? Alternatively, should we be surprised that, as feminist literary critic Carolyn Heilbrun puts it, girls sacrifice "truth on the altar of niceness"?[16]

Declining self-esteem is not, however, universal or inevitable. One longitudinal study of US girls between 9 and 14 found the typical decline in white girls but not in black girls. Since then, many studies have confirmed that African-American girls experience no decline or a much smaller drop relative to the self-esteem crash experienced by white girls. These findings may seem contradictory, given that African-American girls face multiple and intersecting forms of discrimination. However, both African-American body ideals and black mothering seem to protect black girls. Another study conducted in Manitoba found that sports participation might increase self-esteem (though not necessarily for girls with a very "feminine" gender role orientation). A recent study of African-American girls and sports participation found that it was protective against both victimization and declining self-esteem.[17] In other words, if girls lived in a culture that valued them as more than just decoration—and celebrated strong and capable female bodies rather than thin ones—they might be better off. As it stands, many girls experience their adolescence as a time of self-loathing and insecurity. Eating disorders, such as anorexia and bulimia, are significant problems from junior high school through college, and the evidence is that their incidence is increasing—and at increasingly younger ages.

What about the Boys?

Given the divergent patterns of adolescence, you might think that the systematic demolition of girls' self-esteem, the denigration of their abilities, and the demotion of their status would yield positive effects for boys—that boys would rise as the girls declined. However, that isn't what happens. In fact, from early childhood, boys, on average, seem to learn more slowly and face more risks of learning and behavioural challenges. One recent UK study finds five-year-old girls dramatically outperforming boys on most measures of early learning. In the elementary grades, boys are about four times more likely to be sent to child psychologists and far more likely to be diagnosed with dyslexia and attention deficit disorder (ADD) than are girls. Beginning in elementary school and continuing throughout their schooling, boys receive poorer report cards; they are far more likely to repeat a grade. Nine times more boys than girls are diagnosed as "hyperactive"; boys represent 58 per cent of those in special education classes, 71 per cent of the learning disabled, and 80 per cent of the emotionally disturbed. Nearly three-fourths of all school suspensions are of boys. By adolescence, boys are more likely to drop out, flunk out, and act out in class. Their self-esteem also declines during adolescence—not, admittedly, as much as girls' self-esteem, but it does drop.[18]

These data are often used to suggest that boys, not girls, are the true victims of gender discrimination in schools. After all, what happens to boys in schools? They have to sit quietly, raise their hands, be obedient—all of which does extraordinary violence to their "natural," testosterone-inspired, rambunctious playfulness. "Schools for the most part are run by women for girls. To take a high spirited second or third grade boy and expect him to behave like a girl in school is asking too much," comments Christina Hoff Sommers, author of *The War against Boys*. The effect of education is "pathologizing boyhood." "On average, boys are physically more restless and more impulsive (than girls)," comments school consultant Michael Thompson. "We need to acknowledge boys' physical needs, and meet them." While we've been paying all this attention to girls' experiences—raising their self-esteem, enabling them to take science and math, deploring and preventing harassment and bullying—we've ignored the boys. "What about the boys?" asks the backlash chorus.[19]

Make no mistake: Boys' needs do merit our serious attention, and many parents are clearly concerned not only about national indicators but about their own sons. Leonard Sax's *Boys Adrift* and books like it have therefore received massive popular acclaim. Sax's study promises to decode the "epidemic" of underachievement among boys and young men, and some of Sax's arguments and data are compelling. Sax argues that boys are in trouble, and their trouble is caused by a combination of inappropriate teaching methods, video gaming, the over-prescription of drugs like Ritalin, devaluation of masculinity, and environmental endocrine disruptors.[20]

Sax makes some excellent points about the over diagnosis of ADHD, effects of environmental toxins on children, and the harms of the gaming obsessions now so common among young men. However, his desire to prove that boys' *biological* needs are being neglected by society leads him perilously close to simplistic biological determinism. For example, he claims that boys universally tend to draw action rather than people, using a limited and monochrome palette, and that teachers discourage and diminish boys by asking them to use more colour and draw people. It's difficult to understand how this drawing style is an expression of some inherent sex tendency given the long-term achievements of men in fields like, for example, figure painting. (The tradition of Western painting, as any visit to the Louvre will tell you, has long been dominated by men—and they used colours and drew faces!) Do boys paint black cars because of their biology or because of boy culture? (Moreover, what did they draw before cars came along?)

Some people think that concerns about boys' aggression are all about "controlling" boys' naturally exuberant and physical play because of hysterical fear. However, many boys and girls can testify to the less innocuous practices of boys' aggression. Instead of uncritically celebrating "boy culture," we might inquire instead into the experience when boys cease being themselves and begin to posture and parade an exaggerated masculinity before the evaluative eyes of other boys.[21] Perhaps the central mechanism that maintains gender inequality in schools is the way boys see success in terms of gender conformity. High schools have become far more than academic testing grounds; they're the central terrain on which gender identity is tested and demonstrated.

Gender inequality means that just when girls lose their voice, boys *find* one—but it is the inauthentic voice of hegemonic masculinity: of bravado, of constant posturing, of foolish risk taking and gratuitous violence. According to psychologist William Pollack, boys learn that they are supposed to be in power and accordingly begin to act like it. "Although girls' voices have been disempowered, boys' voices are strident and full of bravado," he observes. "But their voices are disconnected from their genuine feelings." Therefore, he argues, the way we bring boys up leads them to put on a "mask of masculinity," a posture, a front. They "ruffle in a manly pose," as the poet William Butler Yeats put it, "for all their timid heart."[22]

Boys' bravado may dampen their achievements. In one study, sociologist Shelley Correll compared thousands of eighth-graders in similar academic tracks and with identical grades and test scores. Boys were much more likely—remember, their scores and grades were identical—to say, "I have always done well in math" and "Mathematics is one of my best subjects" than were the girls. The boys were no better than the girls were; they just *thought* they were.[23]

This difference, and not some putative discrimination against boys, is the reason why girls' mean test scores in math are now approaching those of boys in many countries and exceeding them in a few. According to 2012 PISA scores, the average difference between male and female math scores globally is about the equivalent of three months of schooling, while the gap in reading scores (favouring girls) is much larger, about the equivalent of a year's schooling. (Moreover, in the US, there is no longer a gap between boys' and girls' scores, though boys are still overrepresented at the high end of math ability.) Girls' mean test scores in English and foreign languages, as noted above, outpace boys' scores. However, this is not because of "reverse discrimination," but likely because the boys bump up against the norms of masculinity. Boys regard English as a "feminine" subject. Shelley Correll found that the same boys who had inflated their abilities in math suddenly rated themselves as worse than their female classmates did in English and languages.[24]

Pioneering research in Australia by Wayne Martino and his colleagues found that boys are uninterested in English because of what an interest might say about their (inauthentic) masculine pose. "Reading is lame, sitting down and looking at words is pathetic," commented one boy. "Most guys who like English are faggots", commented another.

The traditional liberal arts curriculum is seen as feminizing; as Catharine Stimpson put it sarcastically, "real men don't speak French."[25]

It is not the school experience that "feminizes" boys, but rather the ideology of traditional masculinity that keeps boys from wanting to succeed. "The work you do here is girls' work," one boy commented to a researcher. "It's not real work." Added another, "[w]hen I go to my class and they [other boys] bunk off, they will say to me I'm a goody goody." Such comments echo the consistent findings of social scientists since James Coleman's path-breaking 1961 study that identified the "hidden curriculum" among adolescents in which good-looking and athletic boys were consistently more highly rated by their peers than were good students.[26]

What is the hidden curriculum for boys? Simply, hegemonic masculinity. Boys learn that to "succeed" in school is to be a "bad lad," in Leanne Dalley-Trim's phrase. They learn that real men don't value academic achievement, or as one student puts it, "in high school, doing honours chemistry or something is for wusses." They learn that sexual harassment (see below) is a handy way to establish domination. In addition, they learn, above all, to disguise their own vulnerability. To be sure, we should not confuse exuberance with disruptive behaviour; but viewing disruptive behaviour as boys' biological imperative, rather than as their performance of a masculine stereotype, won't help us either.[27]

Bullying

As is suggested above, one key element of the school experience is the enforcement of the "hidden curriculum" by peers. In many cases, this "policing" takes the form of **bullying**. Students can be bullied for any putative "cause," from being overweight to having a "geeky" interest in academics—or for no reason at all. Bullying can comprise many behaviours, but it is generally defined as repeatedly doing or saying hurtful things to a person with an intent to harm him or her. This bullying arises within a context of a power imbalance (real or perceived) between the bully and the victim; this is what distinguishes bullying from "fighting" or interpersonal conflict. As we shall see, both boys and girls can be bullies and victims, but there are important gender differences in bullying.

The prevalence of bullying has become much clearer throughout the past 15 years, as schools and education specialists have recognized it as a problem. According to the Canadian Institute of Health Research, one in three Canadian adolescents has recently experienced bullying, and reported rates for Canada rank ninth among 35 countries. Rates in the US seem comparable. A survey of 15,686 American students in grades six to ten published in the *Journal of the American Medical Association* (JAMA) found that 29.9 per cent reported frequent involvement with bullying—13 per cent as the bully, 10.9 per cent as the victim, and 6 per cent as both. Junior high or middle school is identified as being the period of the most intense bullying, rendering this time of life a "brutalizing" one for many students.[28]

The stereotypical form of bullying is physical aggression (e.g., pushing or hitting another child). Physical bullying is undoubtedly a significant and highly visible form. Nevertheless, bullying can also take the form of verbal aggression, such as name-calling. While many of the older generation were taught that "sticks and stones may break my bones/but names will never hurt me," both physical and verbal bullying have harmful and lasting effects on victimized children. As our understanding of bullying has grown, other forms of bullying have been identified. Relational bullying refers to attempts to damage peer relationships, often to isolate the victim. Indirect bullying, meanwhile, depends on mobilizing a third party to do the victimizing on behalf of the bully.

While both girls and boys can bully and be bullied, important gender differences emerge from studies of bullying. Findings vary from study to study, but a few things are clear. Girls clearly prefer relational and indirect forms of bullying to physical bullying. Based on evolutionary theory and existing gender difference, a few scholars have suggested that this should predict a relatively equal *amount* of bullying by girls and boys, with only the *form* differing. Nevertheless, the growing consensus is that, in general, boys bully more than girls do; as well, they are far more likely to engage in physical forms of bullying and they bully at least as much in relational ways.[29]

The relationship of gender with bully victimization is also interesting—and much less clear. While some scholars find that boys are more often victimized than are girls, others have found the opposite. According to the AAUW study cited above, the *majority* of boys are bullied in school, generally but not exclusively by other boys. The content of bullying is clearly related to gender. Boys are often harassed through the assertion of sexual dominance ("suck my dick!"). Males who manifest "atypical gender-related behaviours" are much more likely to be targeted (see below), while girls who are perceived as either more or less attractive than average are more frequently bullied.[30] The content of bullying sometimes blurs into sexual and gender harassment. The effects of bullying and sexual harassment may be similar, and they are sometimes treated as the same phenomenon. Nevertheless, they are treated differently by law and have different features, so we address them separately here.

Sexual Harassment

In September 2015, a 13-year-old Baltimore boy was charged with assault after kissing a girl, against her will, on a dare made by a group of other boys. Online commenters of both sexes overwhelmingly decried the "Big Brother" mentality that turns an "innocent" kiss into a crime. This is only the most recent in a series of widely reported incidents involving boys "unfairly" disciplined for kissing or touching girls at school. While public opinion appears to support the idea that "boys will be boys" and such incidents are harmless, there is more and more evidence of the prevalence and dangers of **sexual harassment** at school.

Sexual harassment is generally defined as unwelcome conduct of a sexual nature. This broad definition includes many types of behaviour. In Canada, provincial human rights codes define sexual harassment as engaging in actions of a sexual nature, which one knows or ought to know are unwelcome. These actions might include a proposition, a comment about someone's body or mannerisms, or touching—and there are many other possible forms of harassing behaviour. Unlike bullying, sexual harassment does not require an intent to harm. Its key feature, in distinction to bullying, is that *sexual harassment is about gender*—whether it is a "come-on" or the creation of a **hostile environment**, and whether it is directed at girls or boys.

Adolescent girls are sexual targets everywhere in our culture, and schools are no exception. In some cases, students attract the sexual attention of teachers. In BC, for example, of 37 teachers disciplined by the BC College of Teachers between 1998 and 2003, 24 were involved in inappropriate sexual relationships. Between 1989 and 1996, Ontario had more than 100 cases of the same. The vast majority (96 per cent) of perpetrators used to be male, while about 76 per cent of victims are female. However, during the past decade the number of female teachers involved with adolescent students has increased, to the point where female teachers in the US now represent about a third of those involved in sexual misconduct with students. Such inappropriate relationships appear to be growing in number, perhaps enabled by the growth of social media.[31]

Overwhelmingly, however, it is not teachers, but peers, who engage in inappropriate sexual conduct. In 1980, the first survey of sexual harassment in US schools found the problem widespread. Canada has been no different. In the early 1990s, June Larkin and Pat Staton authored a report for the Ontario Ministry of Education that found frequent harassment in the province's schools. Larkin and Staton's report contained shocking verification of what girls already knew: that, for example, the practice of boys' "rating" girls on physical attractiveness using numbers was common, even in elementary schools. In fact, much of the behaviour described as harassment went far beyond this. Later in the 1990s, June Larkin conducted a study of students from four Canadian high schools representing urban, rural, and small-town settings and diverse populations. Many of the students considered the behaviours they experienced as "just guys being guys," reserving the term sexual harassment for physical assaults like rape. Yet students described incidents of sexual harassment, sometimes combined with racism, which in extreme cases spilled over into threats of violence:

> It was in my science class, and we had this teacher who was totally against women and everything about them. . . . He called his own wife a bitch, things that were unbelievable. In that class we learned everything he felt about women and toward women . . . like I learned nothing about science that year. . . . there was one guy in my first class . . . he'll go, "When are you going to sleep with me?". . . . He'll go "I hear black women are good in bed."
>
> I was talking to a guy . . . who sits behind me. . . . He said a sentence and ended up calling me "a bonehead." I then said, "You're the one who's a boner." He said, "You'd better shut up before I stick my dick up your ass so hard you won't be able to breathe."

Larkin concludes, not surprisingly, that because of the hidden curriculum of sexual harassment, "life for many female students is often a grim battle against a hostile and threatening school environment." Both the Toronto District School Board and the Canadian Centre for Addiction and Mental Health have collected statistics showing how common the experience of sexual harassment (and even sexual assault) is within Canadian schools. At the extreme end of this threatening continuum, sexual violence and school shootings (as discussed in Chapter 13) both disproportionately target girls.[32]

Slut-shaming was once simply business as usual in North American schools, but it is now understood as a form of sexual harassment. Often deployed against girls who "mature early" or are considered attractive to boys, the epithet "slut" is also used to police gender in a variety of other ways, from enforcing appropriate dress to shaming those who dare to defy the double standard. However, recent attention to the phenomenon, including the creation of the term "slut-shaming," has emphasized the latter. Many people therefore understand "slut-shaming" as necessarily a response to female promiscuity. In fact, the term "slut" is simply another form of sexual harassment, a powerful slur that damages social relationships and girls' self-esteem. A girl need not be sexually promiscuous, or even sexually active, in order to be deemed a "slut." In fact, precocious puberty and extroversion were some of the key themes identified by Emily White in her study of the phenomenon. Another recent study noted how the label "slut" is used among college girls to enforce class boundaries. So far, there are very limited hints at how the "slut" label may intersect with racialized sexualization and victimization.[33]

For many years, some girls lost their entire adolescence to the nightmare of "slut-shaming," which was (like bullying) seen as just part of the fabric of school life. In recent years, attention has been drawn to the often-tragic consequences of being branded as a "slut," which has led to a number of high-profile suicides. The "UnSlut Project" and numerous other initiatives have arisen to combat the pervasiveness of "slut" discourse; at the UnSlut Project's website, women and girls can share their stories, which are many, traumatic, and often heartbreaking, summarized in one woman's simple statement that "middle school was hell." In addition, **Title IX**, a US law that prohibits discrimination in schools, has given students and their parents a way to battle sexual harassment. In 1991, 19-year-old Katy Lyle was awarded $15,000 to settle a lawsuit she brought against her Duluth, Minnesota, school district, because school officials failed to remove explicit graffiti about her from the walls of the boys' bathrooms, even after her parents complained several times. That same year, the US Supreme Court unanimously sided with a young girl, Christine Franklin, in her case against the Gwinnett County, Georgia, school board, and awarded her $6 million in damages resulting from a violation of Title IX.

Despite some progress in raising awareness, sexual harassment continues in the US as in Canada. In 2011, the AAUW issued a new report on sexual harassment based on a nationwide survey of 1,965 students in grades 7 to 12. Nearly half of students had experienced sexual harassment within the past year, more than half of girls and 40 per cent of boys. Not only were girls more likely to experience almost every form of sexual harassment, but they were also dramatically more likely to experience unwanted touching or being forced to participate in sexual acts. The only areas in which girls and boys experienced the same levels of sexual harassment were in "flashing" and homophobic harassment (discussed further below). When students were asked to identify the risk factors that made a student vulnerable to sexual harassment, the results were equally gendered. Students of both sexes said that girls who were especially "well-developed" or especially attractive were the most likely groups to experience sexual harassment, followed by boys who were "not athletic or not very masculine" and girls who were not very feminine or attractive. Attractive boys were the group least likely to be viewed as at risk of sexual harassment, with only 11 per cent of students believing that this would put boys at peril. Accordingly, as the authors of the report point out, a double bind exists for girls:

> Those who fulfill feminine standards of beauty are at high risk for sexual harassment, yet girls who are viewed as too masculine or not pretty are also at risk. These results reinforce the complexity of predicting who may be the victim of

sexual harassment in middle and high schools, as unwanted sexual attention and the policing of gender norms are both part of sexual harassment.[34]

Boys are usually the perpetrators, but girls play a role in sexual harassment. A frequent comment in the UnSlut Project's submitted stories is some variation on the theme of female complicity. With that said, boys remain the leaders and main agents. In the 2015 AAUW study, 66 per cent of students reported being harassed by either one boy or a group of boys; only 19 per cent reported being harassed by either one girl or a group of girls. (The remaining 15 per cent had been harassed by mixed-sex groups.) In the infamous case of the Spur Posse, a group of relatively affluent young boys in southern California simply took these messages a little further than most. In 1993, a large group of young women and girls—one as young as 10—came forward to claim that members of the Spur Posse had sexually assaulted and raped them. Members of the group of boys apparently competed with one another to see who could have sex with the most girls. "My dad used to brag to his friends," one Posse member confessed on a TV talk show. The Spur Posse incidents resulted in much soul-searching about rape culture in high schools and the impunity of male athletes. However, a decade later, little had changed—except the overwhelming presence of social media. In August 2012, a high school student in Steubenville, Ohio, was sexually assaulted during a period of hours, an assault documented in its various stages by students who shared commentary and photographs over social media.[35]

When parents and other adults minimize the importance of incidents like the one in Baltimore in September 2015, the damage caused by sexual harassment is obvious. Difficulty sleeping, emotional problems, avoiding school, or living in fear are all effects. It is worth asking ourselves: would we tolerate a workplace or church in which someone suddenly approaches us and plants an open-mouthed kiss on our lips while others laugh and jeer? Would we tolerate such behaviour from someone on the street? If those incidents would be experienced—and viewed by the law—as assaults, why do so many people still see the school as a zone in which the normal rules of interaction are suspended? Moreover, if education is a training ground for life, what message is sent by the prevalence of sexual harassment within school walls?

"That's So Gay" to "No Homo": Gender Harassment and Homophobia in Schools

Many people still think of sexual harassment as an unwanted sexual come-on. However, much of sexual harassment relates to gender rather than to sexual desire. One prevalent form of sexual harassment in school is gender harassment, often through the policing of heterosexuality and normative masculinity. Most commonly, this occurs through abusive imputations of homosexuality, particularly to boys ("sissy," or more commonly today, even in elementary schools, "faggot!").

Lesbian, gay, bisexual, transgender, and queer/questioning (LGBTQ) students experience homophobic slurs and acts of violence that dramatically limit feelings of safety. According to a 2008 survey by *Égale* Canada, 75 per cent of LGBTQ students felt unsafe at school, and half of straight students agreed that their schools are unsafe for LGBTQ people. A 2014 study found the highest rates of sexual harassment among trans youth (81 per cent), followed by lesbian/queer girls (72 per cent). Bisexual girls and gay/queer boys also had high rates (61 per cent). Homophobic harassment is used to police the behaviour of all students. In the AAUW's 2011 survey, 18 per cent of boys and girls reported experiencing such slurs. For all students, the daily reiteration of "faggot," "dyke," and "that's so gay" reinforce the messages that abuse and domination are okay, that heterosexuality is the norm, and that non-heterosexuals are fair game.[36]

Accusations of homosexuality provide a way to police heterosexuality, but as every student reading this knows, they are also a way to police gender and punish those, gay or straight, who don't conform to stereotypical gender norms. Here is high school student Dave, explaining how he "knows" if a guy is gay: "if they show any sign of weakness or compassion, then other people jump to conclusions and bring them down. So really, it's a survival of the fittest. It's not very good to be sensitive. If you have no feeling or compassion or anything like that, you will survive." Alternatively, listen to the words of famous American gender theorist Eminem. When asked in 2001 why he was always rapping about "faggots," Eminem replied that in the context of battle-rap, calling someone a "faggot" was not a slur on his sexuality, but rather on his gender. "The lowest degrading thing that you can say to a man . . . is to call him a faggot and try to take away his manhood. Call him a sissy. Call him a punk. 'Faggot' to me doesn't mean gay people. 'Faggot' just means taking away your manhood." (While many have speculated that Eminem may be rapping from the perspective of Slim Shady, his "vile" alter-ego, the rapper has continued to create controversy with virulently anti-gay lyrics.)[37] Whether or not the intent of calling someone a "faggot" is homophobic or "just" emasculating, the effect is victimization.

Small wonder that the phrase "no homo" has emerged as a way to disavow homosexuality before it can be attributed, as in "I love you, man—no homo." Like the phrase "that's so gay," it arises from a negative attitude toward homosexuality. Some believe that these phrases have an evolving meaning that cannot be equated to simple homophobia. Scholar Mark McCormack points out that in his research, older people reacted more strongly to these phrases than did youth (straight and gay), who were more likely to have positive attitudes toward homosexuality *and* more likely to view these phrases as harmless.

There may be something to McCormack's insistence that the power of such words is diminishing among youth. Another study found that as groups become more powerful, they gain resilience from relabelling themselves with previously derogatory labels. Therefore, perhaps gay and straight youth who say "no homo" or "that's gay" are actually participating in that relabelling. For now, the jury is out. Another recent study found that LGBTQ students who heard this phrase were likely to report negative effects on both mental and physical health.[38]

Cyberbullying

School bullying was once largely confined to the school setting, though telephone calls and other techniques could expand the arena of bullying beyond the schoolyard. Today, digital communications technologies have enabled a dramatic expansion of bullying. This has led to the identification of **cyberbullying**—defined as "an aggressive, intentional act carried out by a group or individual, using electronic forms of contact, repeatedly and over time against a victim who cannot easily defend him or herself." Cyberbullying encompasses a vast number of behaviours: spreading rumours about or attacking someone through social media, sending vicious emails or texts, sharing embarrassing photographs of someone, and hacking into someone's accounts and posing as that person in order to post or send materials that will tarnish the person's reputation are just a few examples. Cyberbullying can include both conventional bullying and sexual or gender harassment; so far, most studies of cyberbullying do not distinguish between the two.

Most studies find that cyberbullying is less common than in-person bullying, but its prevalence is increasing dramatically as more and more youth spend more time online. A 2015 study found that, in a sample of 1,001 Canadian children, about one-seventh had experienced cyberbullying, while one-thirteenth had perpetrated it, with rates similar across demographic groups. These rates are lower than those that were reported by a 2006 study, which found that 25 per cent of 264 students had experienced cyberbullying. The difference is probably explained by the fact that the larger study looked at children aged 10 to 17, while the smaller study looked only at children in junior high (the worst time for bullying, as noted above). In Girlguiding UK's 2015 Girls' Attitudes Survey, cyberbullying and online trolling were a concern for 37 per cent of girls, second only to mental health issues. (Interestingly, girls perceived their parents as out of touch with this issue, and much more concerned with issues such as smoking, drinking, and teenaged pregnancy, which were less important to girls themselves.)[39]

While there are many commonalities between bullying and cyberbullying, the latter has distinct characteristics that are not shared with "traditional" bullying, including the bully's potential for anonymity, the extreme aggression sometimes seen in electronic bullying, and the potential for the bully to impersonate others (including the victim).

Because cyberbullying is an indirect form of attack, some scholars have predicted that girls would predominate as cyberbullies. This is also the belief of many students, as is suggested by several recent studies. However, the indication so far is that as with in-person bullying, boys are more likely to perpetrate cyberbullying. While studies' findings vary, gender differences in cyberbullying perpetration seem to be much smaller than in real-life bullying, so it is quite possible that girls will come to equal boys' rates.[40]

Bullying harms children profoundly. While many survive the experience relatively well, there is increasing evidence of the seriousness of bullying. Some victims withdraw, becoming depressed, alienated, or despondent. Some self-medicate with drugs or alcohol. An increasing number commit suicide. (Then there are those boys who explode. There have been more than 100 school shootings in North America since 1980, almost all of them perpetrated by boys and men. Some of the shootings have been linked to bullying.)[41]

Challenging stereotypes, refusing to tolerate school violence, and decreasing bullying enable both boys and girls to feel safer at school. The classroom is not immune to the strong influences emanating from popular culture, which celebrates a particularly limited form of masculinity (as we shall see in Chapter 9). Still, to create a healthier school experience for adolescents of both sexes, what is needed is not a return to simplistic notions of gender difference, but a commitment to addressing the ways in which gender cultures and gender ideologies themselves produce such radical gender divergence in adolescence—to the detriment of both sexes.

Where Are the Men? The Post-Secondary "Crisis"

As recently as 10 years ago, discussions of gender and post-secondary education were most likely to discuss the "chilly classroom climate" for female students or equity among male and female faculty members.[42] Today, a new concern has arisen. Women's participation in post-secondary education continues its upward trajectory, which we can see as a trend that began much more than a century ago when women fought to gain access to university classrooms. Across North America—and in most of the high-income countries belonging to the Organisation for Economic Co-operation and Development—women now constitute the majority of students on college campuses.

Women now outnumber men in the social and behavioural sciences by about three to one, and they've made inroads into such traditionally male bastions as engineering, where they now make up about 20 per cent of all students, and biology and business, where the genders are virtually on par. In 2004, for the first time, most graduating Canadian medical students were women. The growth in female participation in post-secondary education has caused some hysterical comment. One reporter tells us that if present trends continue, "the graduation line in 2068 will be all females."[43]

However, the numbers cited by critics conceal some interesting variations. First, enrolments are in general going up. In 1990, only 28 per cent of young Canadian adults aged 20 to 24 were enrolled in some form of post-secondary education (PSE: for example, university, college, or trades training). By 2006, that rate had increased to 40 per cent. However, in both Canada and the US, women's enrolments have increased much more quickly than have those of men. (This is also true for First Nations men and women; though there is an acknowledged educational gap between non-Aboriginal and Aboriginal Canadians, First Nations women are more likely than First Nations men are to have college and university credentials.) In 2006, 44 per cent of Canadian women were enrolled in PSE, versus 36 per cent of their male counterparts; this translated, by 2010, into a female majority (56 per cent) among university undergraduates in Canada. In the US, the "female majority" means that women now face tougher admission competition in private institutions, which are permitted to discriminate based on sex to maintain gender balance.[44]

Second, the female presence decreases as the level of education rises. In Canada, women now form a majority of master's students (56 per cent), but are a minority (46 per cent) among Ph.D. students. (Women's participation in doctoral programs increased dramatically from 1980 to 2000, but has held steady since.) Finally, men still equal or outnumber women at the eight traditional "Ivy League" universities in the US.[45]

Third, there is still significant segregation according to discipline or field of study, with women a minority in some programs that lead to prestigious and well-paid employment. In Canada, women students are a minority in mathematics and computer and information sciences (26 per cent) and architecture, engineering and related technologies (20 per cent). The situation is reversed in education, where women constitute 77 per cent of the student body. Indeed, large gender disparities continue in university programs in nursing, social work, or education, traditionally far lower-paid occupations than those professions where men still predominate (engineering and computer sciences).[46]

Those who suggest that feminist-inspired reforms have been to the detriment of boys seem to believe that gender relations are a zero-sum game and that if girls and women gain, then boys and men lose. In fact, however, the reasons for the gender gap in post-secondary education may not be as simple as women's gains at the expenses of men. According to economist Michael Hoy, the gender imbalance in university exists because women can expect a higher **educational premium** than can men. That is, because women traditionally have had poor access to well-paid jobs unless they have advanced education, they are more willing to enrol in PSE. Alternatively, as one student puts it, "guys can get good jobs in the bush without it, so why go to school?"[47]

The danger, of course, is that as Canada's economy shifts and resource-extraction-based jobs diminish, many men may find themselves without the qualifications for other kinds of work. Moreover, we probably should pay attention to signs that some young men may be "dropping out": for example, the number of young men who spend more than seven hours a week playing video games. However, women have not "taken" men's places at university. In fact, affordability, accessibility, and class are the real issues, and they're significantly gender-neutral. There are also significant gendered issues, such as sexual harassment and sexual assault on campus. The fact that women are a majority on campus has not prevented them from being targeted for abuse. This was made clear by the scandal that erupted in December 2014 at Dalhousie University's dentistry school. A student revealed the existence of a men-only Facebook page that assessed female dentistry students' attractiveness and speculated on "hate-fucking" them. Further investigations into the dentistry program revealed that the student lounge had long been covered in misogynist, racist, and homophobia graffiti, and that there were "systemic problems" that had contributed to the incident. Despite some attempts to minimize the infractions and the toxicity of the culture in the dental program, universities across the country are recognizing that the incidents at Dalhousie might have happened elsewhere. Efforts to address sexual assault and sexual harassment are therefore underway at a number of Canadian campuses.[48]

Thinking about gender equality in PSE means not only worrying about the "domination" of post-secondary education by a new female majority but also paying careful attention to the inequalities that exist within disciplines, schools, and university cultures. Both women *and* men, girls *and* boys will benefit from real gender equality in education. "Every step in the advancement of woman has benefited our own sex no less than it has elevated her" was how an editorial in the Amherst College (Massachusetts) campus newspaper, *The Amherst Student*, put it when the school first debated co-education at the turn of the twentieth century.[49]

The School as Gendered Workplace

Historically, women and girls were excluded from the classroom not only as students, but also as teachers. In the eighteenth and nineteenth centuries, teaching had been seen as a respectable profession for a man. However, the mid- to late-nineteenth-century gender ideology of the "separation of spheres" meant that women were pushed out of other arenas of work, and they soon began to see elementary education as a way they could fulfil both their career aspirations and their domestic functions of maternal nurturance.

This coincided conveniently with the expansion of public elementary school education. Remember that nineteenth-century budgets for education and social services were minuscule compared to ours. Public education was therefore expanding dramatically at a time when it was woefully underfunded. The solution, according to Alvin Finkel,

> . . . was to hire young women as the teaching force and pay them miserable salaries on the grounds that they would supposedly soon marry and leave teaching to be supported financially by their husbands. In contrast, men were employed at relatively decent wages for the positions of superintendents, inspectors, principals, and headmasters. As in the health field, there was a gender hierarchy for the workforce that left women in a subordinate position to men.[50]

As a result, elementary education became "feminized." This meant that the occupational prestige and salaries of teachers dropped, discouraging men from entering the field and ensuring that it would become even more populated by women. Teaching was "women's work." (More correctly considered, "spinster's work," because women who married were expected to leave the teaching workforce; "marriage bans" were common throughout North America until the 1940s.[51]) Nonetheless, school administration has remained largely a masculine arena.

The frightful consequences of a female teaching force were much debated at the start of the twentieth century. Some warned of the "invasion" of women teachers as if it were the "Invasion of the *Boy* Snatchers." One of the founders of American psychology, J. McKeen Cattell, worried about the "vast horde of female teachers" to whom boys were exposed. In a foreshadowing of Leonard Sax's argument, commentators argued that this had serious consequences. A boy taught by a woman, one admiral believed, would "render violence to nature," causing "a feminized manhood, emotional, illogical, non-combative." Another worried that "the boy in America is not being brought up to punch another boy's head or to stand having his own punched in a healthy and proper manner."[52]

Throughout the twentieth century, women still held most of the primary education positions and virtually all positions in pre-kindergarten and special education. Only during the Depression, when opportunities for men diminished severely, did Canadian men enter normal school (teachers' college) in substantial numbers. In 1994, 72.5 per cent of all US public and private school teachers were women; and 60 per cent of women teachers were in the elementary grades. At about the same time in Canada, the female majority was smaller than in the US, with women accounting for about 60 per cent of teachers. However, that number had increased to 69 per cent by 2005 and to 74 per cent by 2011. The female majority is even larger at the kindergarten and elementary levels, where 84 per cent of teachers are women. (The majority grows as student age lowers: 97 per cent of early childhood educators are women.[53])

As the Canadian statistics indicate, the percentage of teachers who are male is actually *dropping* in North America and Europe, prompting one Ontario report to call for vigorous attempts to attract men to the profession. Ontario is not alone; one Irish article claims that the decline in male teachers is "robbing boys of their role models." Often, according to Wayne Martino and Michael Kehler of the University of Western Ontario, the call for male teachers is driven by a "recuperative masculinity politics." That is, the media have created a **moral panic** based on the idea of rampant fatherlessness and a lack of appropriate role models, which they blame for social ills. The manly male teacher, therefore, needs to ride in and save boyhood from feminization. The idea rests on, and celebrates, the value of traditional hegemonic masculinity and interplanetary gender difference.[54]

Despite these impassioned calls, however, men are not flooding the classrooms of North America (or anywhere else, for that matter). Men are dissuaded from entering teaching by stereotypes about men in female-dominated professions and, some say, because they are afraid of allegations of sexual misconduct. In reality, the major reason why men don't flood into teaching is related to the pay. As we'll see in Chapter 8, sex composition of the labour force is related to its salary structure. It is virtually axiomatic that the greater the proportion of women in the field, the lower the salary.

This has several implications. The first relates to female teachers; within the educational field, women continue to earn less money than men do doing the same jobs. Some of this is explained by qualifications, but one careful study removed that kind of variable and found that "salary discrimination against female teachers exists in all high school sectors." At every level of the educational system, men continue to out-earn their female colleagues.

The second implication of the teaching salary structure relates to men. While they are often better paid than their female colleagues are, it should be noted that salaries in teaching are low compared to salaries in male-dominated professions and trades. This is particularly true in the US, where a study in the 1990s found that median earnings of male teachers were 18 per cent below the median earnings of male professionals, and even below the median earnings of men with bachelor's degrees, though many teachers had master's degrees. (The study yielded inconclusive results for female teachers, because women "still earn substantially less in the marketplace than men.") Moreover, the situation has been getting worse, according to Statistics Canada data and analysis; between 1981 and 2001 real wages declined "in female-dominated disciplines, such as health and education," while real wages in areas such as engineering, mathematics, and computer science increased.[55]

Should we then be surprised that the number of men in these female-dominated fields declined along with wages? Rather than recognizing that both male and female teachers are underpaid relative to other professions—and that teaching, like operating heavy equipment or doing an energy audit, is hard work—too often, media coverage slips into arguing that men aren't attracted to teaching because of their "breadwinner role" (see Chapter 8).

The Heroic Male Teacher, Hollywood Style

For more than 50 years, the movies have been grappling with the role of the teacher in inspiring, mentoring, and saving at-risk students. The first of these films was *Blackboard Jungle* (1955), with its rock-and-roll soundtrack and its edgy tale of a white teacher confronting unruly and cynical black youth.

Twelve years later, the actor who played one of those cynical youths got his chance to be the teacher-hero. The movie *To Sir, With Love* (1967) starred Sidney Poitier as the idealistic black American teacher saddled with a room full of working-class, mainly white, hard-bitten London teenagers. The movie, which also spawned a hit song, was a huge

Moviestore/REX/Shutterstock

Sidney Poitier in *To Sir, With Love*.

success, and put a new kind of hero on the map: the "teacher-saviour," in the words of William Ayers.

According to Ayers, the teacher-saviour is the teacher who recognizes that schools are in the business of saving students. While his colleagues, "the slugs," aren't up to the challenge, the teacher-saviour is marked not necessarily by his overwhelming success but by his refusal to give up on students. This teacher just won't abandon the kids, no matter what, and therefore wins their grudging respect and transforms lives.[56]

Twenty years after *Sir*, Edward James Olmos starred in yet another successful teacher movie, *Stand and Deliver* (1989). In this film, based on a true story (they usually are), Olmos played a high school mathematics teacher confronted with—you guessed it—a hard-bitten, unruly, largely Latino class of underachievers, this time in East Los Angeles. He never gives up on his students, not even when they are accused of cheating on a major exam. In the end, the students perform brilliantly on a repeat math exam, succeeding academically, exonerating themselves, and validating their teacher's pedagogy and courage.

The saviour-teacher is not always found in the inner-city classroom, however. In the same year that *Stand and Deliver* was released, Robin Williams starred in his own teacher movie, *Dead Poets' Society*. In this film, the teacher isn't facing an unruly mob; his showdown is against a pack of prep-school conformists. The result, however, is the

continued

same; Williams teaches these academically solid, privileged boys how to live life consciously and fully.

You may have noticed something about this list of movies. If the male teacher is a minority in the classroom, he's a dominant figure on the big screen. Indeed, it's hard to find a female teacher to place in the company of these icons (and the others we haven't even mentioned). Drew Barrymore's "Ms Pomeroy," from 2001's *Donnie Darko*, is a nuanced character, but she is hardly the focus of the movie (and is counterbalanced by a highly stereotypical portrayal of an uptight, aging female teacher). Female teachers are usually a support to storylines rather than their focus and are often stereotyped as obstacles to the main characters rather than as mentors or role models.

One exception from the 1990s can be found in *Dangerous Minds*, a 1995 release loosely based on the true story of a Marine who became a teacher of—that's right—a group of hard-bitten inner-city children. Though it's hard to imagine a more feminine actor than Michelle Pfeiffer, it's interesting to see how her image transforms through the movie, as she takes on some of the masculine characteristics of the typical saviour-teacher. By the film's end, she is much tougher, right down to her black leather jacket.

The male teacher-hero is often an outsider. If he's white, perhaps he is a loner coming from some failure in the past. He also may be constructed as the white saviour of otherwise helpless people of colour, a tendency seen in the 1974 movie *Conrack* (and, though with a female lead, in *Dangerous Minds* [1995]). If he's from an ethnic minority, he's battling the odds, showing that with moral rectitude, education, and guts, anyone can succeed. Whether he's white or of colour, to succeed in his difficult task, he has to fight: *for* his students (usually against unfeeling administrators) and even *against* his students, as in *Blackboard Jungle* (1955), *To Sir, with Love* (1967), and *Stand and Deliver* (1988). In short, he has to teach his students through example (and through his own brutal trials) what it means to be a man.

Our obsession with teacher-heroes, or antiheroes, isn't all bad. Teachers are important role models to many children, and for children with troubled families, a teacher can be a hero and a lifeline. Nevertheless, we should ask ourselves why these heroic teachers are so often male, and why so many of the ideas associated with hegemonic masculinity are repeated in these films.

Sometimes these pop-culture stereotypes can even colour our views of real teachers. For example, a recent survey of New Zealand school principals found that they wanted more male teachers (only 18 per cent of New Zealand teachers are male); but they didn't want just *any* men. While rugby-playing "real men" were sought as appropriate "role models" and "father figures," effeminate men were distrusted. In one case, a principal described passing over male candidates with "limp handshakes" in favour of "strong" female candidates. (You can probably see where the principal in question was going with this: As Martino and Kehler argue, homophobia is often part of the discussion of the need for male teachers.)

In the wake of this study, one interesting thing happened; one teacher's college put up a billboard recruiting male students with an image of a man knitting and the slogan "Real Men Teach (and Knit)." Rather than trying to prove how macho male teachers could be, perhaps by showing one jumping out of a plane or pumping iron, this particular training institute decided to take on limiting stereotypes of masculinity. Therefore, even if Hollywood and some principals don't always know it, boys and men are changing, and our view of the male teacher should too. So watch the big screen—you may see a knitting teacher-hero there sometime soon.[57]

If the number of male teachers has declined at the elementary and secondary levels, the number of women teaching at the post-secondary level has increased. In 1999, women made up 29.2 per cent of full-time university professors; by 2005, this had increased to 35.5 per cent. The percentage of women teaching full-time at college was even greater. In 2013, women were close to 40 per cent of full-time university professors and almost half (48.6 per cent) of college and vocational institute instructors. The same increase has occurred in the US. The division of labour that saw women dominate primary education, while men shared secondary education and dominated higher education, is now changing. Increasingly, *all* teaching is becoming a women's profession.

Women's greater presence in post-secondary teaching does not necessarily imply that gender equity is even close to having been achieved. As the statistics above indicate, women are less and less represented the higher up the educational ladder one climbs. In the US, more than two-thirds of women teach at two- and four-year colleges; men are equally divided between research universities and all other institutions. Men continue to dominate in sciences, while women dominate in the human services professions (nursing, social work, and education) and those fields that require significant classroom contact, like languages.[58]

Women also dominate the ranks of the most populous arena of post-secondary teaching—untenured lecturers and instructors. Part-time instructors, victims of both an educational glut and covert gender discrimination, currently teach up to one-half of all university classes, yet they are paid by the course or hired on yearly contracts. In Canada, only about 15 per cent of university professors were non-permanent in 1999; by 2005, the proportion had more than doubled, to almost a third. In the US, more than half of such "flexible workers" are women. Only about one-third of untenured women are on the tenure track in the US. In Canada, the situation has improved for women even while casualization continues to be a serious issue. In 2005, while 88 per cent of male faculty members were either tenured or on the tenure track, only 65 per cent of women were either tenured or in positions that could get them tenure. Today, if Ontario is any indication, more than 80 per cent of full-time women faculty members are in tenured or tenure-track positions. Women remain, however, a small percentage of senior-level university administrators.[59]

One reason for this disparity, of course, is that just like in all other workplaces, the efforts to balance work and family fall disproportionately on women's shoulders. At all ranks, and in all types of educational institutions, female professors and teachers with children spend much more time on family life (child care, care for aging parents and relatives, and housework) than do their male counterparts.[60] Balancing work and family remains an obstacle to women's advancement in education—just as it does in every other workplace.

While family plays a role in women's situation within the academic workforce, we should not discount simple discrimination. Administrators, other faculty, and students exhibit gendered attitudes toward professors. For example, a California study found that male students were significantly more likely to nominate a male as their best professor. Students also tended to describe their best professors in highly gendered ways. When women were chosen as best professors, they were most often described as accessible/approachable, passionate, and relating to students, while male professors were most often described as knowledgeable, passionate, and innovative. Both male and female students emphasized the interpersonal skills of their best female professors and the scholarship and knowledge of their male professors. Overall, the study showed a tendency among male students to judge their female faculty more critically than their male counterparts did.

A North Carolina study published in 2015 tested this tendency by having two instructors report their gender differently to different groups within their online classes. Regardless of their real gender, the instructors were evaluated more critically when they told students they were female. In some cases, the difference in scores was dramatic. For example, the "male" instructors were assessed a 4.35/5 on promptness of grading, while the "female" instructors received only 3.55. In many cases, it seems, we have differential expectations of men and women on the basis of gender, and we punish those who do not live up to those expectations. Overall, however, we punish women *more* because we see them as lower in status than men. Given the importance of student evaluation in tenure and promotion decisions at universities, these tendencies may have career effects for women faculty, particularly those marginalized by intersecting discriminations; for example, in the US, studies have found that black professors are rated more harshly than white faculty. One study found that female professors received lower evaluations than male, professors of colour received lower evaluations than white ones, and women of colour received the lowest evaluations; however, while non-native speakers of English received lower evaluations than did native speakers, *male* non-native speakers received harsher evaluations. This suggests the complexity of intersectionality in assessments of teacher competence. Certainly, these intriguing studies of student evaluations suggest how customary and unconscious our discriminatory attitudes might be. (Those interested in exploring this issue through the lens of "Rate My Professor" data might wish to use Ben Smythe's online tool to do their own analysis.[61])

While professors may be stereotyped by students, there is evidence that the same is true in reverse. A widely reported recent study conducted at Yale University demonstrated that when presented with identical resumes of recent graduates, varied only by name ("John" versus "Jennifer"), professors at six major universities were significantly more willing to offer "John" a job. When professors did decide to offer "Jennifer" a job, they offered her on average $4,000 less than was offered to "John"—even though "Jennifer" was rated as more likeable than her (identical) male counterpart was. Both male and female faculty exhibited these tendencies.[62]

The classroom, then, remains gendered. This is true whether it's a kindergarten class or a fourth-year university seminar. Changes have occurred, as we have seen; for example, more and more women professors are making it to the rank of full professor, where they have been greatly underrepresented. Moreover, the dual pay scales that once existed for male and female teachers are no more. Nevertheless, the overall feminization of the profession may have damaging consequences: not the feminization of male students, but declining status and wages for the vocation. Statistics Canada has found that salaries for all educators rose more slowly than the average worker's compensation did during recent years: this may be an indication of what may await as education becomes ever more a "female profession."[63]

The Gender of Education Today

One might think that, after so many years of educational reform, and especially with much attention to the differences between girls and boys, things would be getting better. Simple enumeration of equality may not be the answer. One teacher told journalist Peggy Orenstein that after learning that teachers paid more attention to boys than to girls, she explained to the class that henceforth she was going to call on both sexes exactly equally and that to make sure she did, she would hold the attendance roster in her hand. What happened next surprised her. "After two days the boys blew up," she told Orenstein. "They started complaining and saying that I was calling on the girls more than them. I showed them it wasn't true and they had to back down. I kept on doing it, but for the boys, equality was hard to get used to; they perceived it as a big loss."[64]

Nonetheless, equality is virtually always seen as a loss by the privileged group. If a teacher gives exactly equal time to heterosexuality and to homosexuality, to people of colour and to white people, to women and to men, he or she is invariably going to be criticized as being biased in favour of the "minority" group (even when, as in the case of women, that group is a majority). To some degree, this has happened with education. As girls' achievements have grown, a system originally designed for boys is now seen as "girl-friendly" and "boy-hostile." The nature of the system is invoked to explain increasingly sex-differentiated student achievement. (Interestingly, there wasn't much of a debate about that when girls' achievements lagged.) At the same time, we have surveyed the very real problems faced by students in the gendered classroom, and these problems need addressing.

So what is the answer? Many educators think returning to single-sex schools would make a difference. There are now hundreds of single-sex schools in the US, with a smaller but growing number in Canada. Many school districts are experimenting with single-sex schools or single-sex classrooms. In the US, there have been notable experiments with single-sex schools for black boys and girls. In a sense, such schools propose a "racial" or "gender" remedy for a problem of "class"—because *children*, both boys and girls, would no doubt thrive in schools with a lot of resources, small classes, and fabulously trained teachers. Kenneth Clark, the pioneering African-American educator and long-time advocate of racially integrated education, was unmoved by the call for single-sex classrooms for black kids. "I can't believe that we're actually regressing like this. Why are we still talking about segregating and stigmatizing black males?" he asked.[65]

Some single-sex schools have produced results in academic achievement, pride, school completion, and behavioural change that should be respected. However, the research is inconclusive as to the educational outcomes of single-sex schooling. Much of the earliest research on single-sex schools failed to isolate all of the variables in its quest to prove that single-sex was better. For example, single-sex schools are, for the most part, *private* schools, with all of the advantages that implies. They also tend to offer a more structured and formal environment with rigorous expectations; that structure, rather than the same-sex environment, might produce changes in achievement and behaviour. Still, there are suggestive signs that girls learn better in same-sex classrooms, that they are more willing to enter "non-traditional" subjects, and, interestingly, that they score better on particular self-esteem indicators. Most recently, a study conducted at the University of California found that graduates of girls' schools scored higher on the Standard Admissions Test (SAT) and had greater confidence in math and computing. For boys the results regarding achievement are less consistent. Overall, a 2014 meta-analysis that covered 1.6 million students in 21 countries found no evidence of benefits for single-sex education over co-educational education, though the authors noted that they were unable to assess the value of single-sex education for US ethnic minority boys because of the paucity of available data.[66]

In the 1990s, much of the discussion about single-sex schooling was about overcoming the disabilities of a gendered society. So girls, the argument went, would be served by schools that gave them confidence to explore non-traditional areas and to see their bodies in terms of mastery instead of sexiness. In some ways, those sentiments are still alive. Leonard Sax says that in single-sex schools, boys can overcome gender stereotypes; "the jocks and the geeks can become one and the same." Surely overcoming the boundaries created by normative masculinity is a good thing.[67]

There are two problems with this analysis, however. First, many single-sex schools seem to buy into rigid gender norms. It's difficult not to feel concerned about some of the stereotyping associated with the promotion of one-sex environments. Sax claims that the vast majority of the single-sex schools in the US today are founded on "neuroscience." That is, they subscribe to a particular interpretation of the difference between male and female brains. That produces curricula based on ideas such as: girls are scared of snakes; boys can't hear, smell, or see as well; boys need to be moving to learn; a girl needs to "share something from her own life that relates to the content in class" in order to learn; and so on.[68]

The proposals for single-sex schools seem often to be based on such facile, and incorrect, assessments of some biologically based different educational "needs" or learning styles. To put it as charitably as possible, perhaps such organizations believe they have the best interests of children at heart. They base their claims, though, on the flimsiest of empirical evidence and the wildest of stereotypical assertions. Every day, real boys and girls prove such insulting stereotypes wrong.

Another concern about single-sex schools is that they offer escape from harmful stereotypes and gendered practices rather than confronting them head-on. Isn't it the role of schools, and education in general, to take us *out* of our comfort zones? To expose us to new experiences and expectations, and consequently to make us something more than what we were when we came in? It may well be true, as University of Saskatchewan professor Trevor Gambell suggests, that boys don't want to read books with female protagonists. Nevertheless, shouldn't that be a reason to encourage them to do so rather than a reason to redefine the curriculum so that boys never have to identify with a girl? [69]

John Dewey, perhaps America's greatest theorist of education and a fierce supporter of women's equal rights, was infuriated at the contempt for women suggested by such ideas. Dewey scoffed at "'female botany,' 'female algebra,' and for all I know a 'female multiplication table adapted to the female mind,'" he wrote in 1911. "Upon no subject has there been so much dogmatic assertion based on so little scientific evidence, as upon male and female types of mind."[70]

In coming years, educators may continue to use single-sex schooling to combat the social woes of a society and peer culture that put incredible, and gendered, pressures on both girls and boys. However, as with the family, the form of education is probably much less important than its content. One can only hope that our schools (whether single-sex or co-educational) focus on content; and that they retreat from the kind of thinking that would retrench the most ridiculous (and damaging) of gender stereotypes.

Summary

School is the second primary socializing institution in the traditional sociological schema. We enter education as gendered beings, already exposed to gender difference and gender inequality through families, peers, religions, and media. The classroom reproduces these differences and the inequality that often goes with them.

Education was traditionally limited by sex and class, and in the modern world, has been limited by race. Until the nineteenth century, most Canadian children received very little education, and schooling was conducted under church auspices. By the late nineteenth century, formal education had expanded significantly, and primary school became mandatory in most provinces. Education was conceived of in gendered terms, particularly for boys who were to learn "manliness." In addition to being gendered, education was often segregated by race. At the same time, women were pressing to enter post-secondary studies, from which they had been excluded. By 1900, about 10 per cent of university students were women; not until the 1960s did women's participation rates increase dramatically. By the 1980s, female students had become the majority.

Today, Canada's millions of students are schooled in an officially gender-neutral system. Nevertheless, unofficial gendering is still a large part of the classroom. Environments and play that are considered appropriate for one sex by teachers, parents, and peers may not be allowed to the other sex. The classroom also reproduces inequality in terms of the amount and nature of attention that students receive from teachers. Too often, teachers (like the rest of us) rely on "common-sense" understandings of masculinity and reinforce stereotypes. Textbooks and children's storybooks also may reproduce stereotypical views of gender.

As students enter the secondary-school classroom, they encounter gender intensification both in their own thinking and in the environments around them. For girls, this often takes the form of steeply declining self-esteem. The classroom can be a chilly climate for high school girls, and this is compounded by sexually hostile environments in many schools. Sexual harassment is a common problem for secondary-school girls.

Boys do not escape unscathed. Their self-esteem declines too, though not as precipitously as the self-esteem of girls. Boys are, however, much more prone to a number of problems and demonstrate less academic success on average. While some argue that this is the result of a feminine education system geared to girls, a more plausible explanation sees cultural influences as the cause. Indeed, in adolescence many boys disconnect from their true selves in favour of an exaggerated masculinity that views core human values, and education, as signs of weakness. The problem, then, is not feminization of boys, but an exaggerated masculinization that equips them poorly for the world outside the gendered classroom.

Bullying is a key part of the hidden curriculum. Bullying takes many forms, but it can be defined as using a power imbalance to do hurtful things repeatedly to another person with an intent to harm him or her. Physical, verbal, indirect, and relational bullying are all possible forms this behaviour can take. Bullying is especially common in junior high or middle school. Its main perpetrators are boys, who bully more in all forms. Girls, however, also bully others, particularly other girls. Girls are much more likely to use indirect or relational forms of bullying than physical or verbal attack. Much of the content of bullying relates to gender, and while bullies need no "reason" for their behaviour, especially attractive or early-maturing girls are at risk, as are boys with non-gender-conforming behaviours or less "masculine" appearance.

Sexual and gender harassment are often confused with bullying, and indeed the two categories of abuse share many commonalities. The key distinction is that sexual harassment comprises actions of a sexual nature which one knows or ought to know are unwelcome. There are many forms of sexual harassment, but all are gender-focused. Girls and LGBTQ students of any gender are at high risk for sexual and gender harassment, which at its extreme can include sexual assault. Teachers may perpetrate such abuses, but by far the most common perpetrators are fellow students, usually boys. Sexual harassment is widespread across North America, and its most common forms include "slut-shaming" and homophobia.

At the post-secondary level, the female majority among students has commentators concerned, but men still outnumber women at the doctoral level and in professional degrees. Men are less likely to attend PSE than are women, probably because they perceive greater earning possibilities without advanced training. In the long run, this may be a poor strategy, given the long-term decline in well-paid resource-sector jobs.

Women also outnumber men in the teaching profession. The presence of women in teaching dates to the nineteenth-century expansion of education, when a cheap workforce was needed. In elementary and secondary schools, women became a large and growing majority; this remains true. This has prompted calls for the recruitment of more male teachers. Some have called this a moral panic, as media blame the lack of male teachers for a variety of social ills. Popular movies reinforce the idea that the saviour-teacher is almost always a male who can save his students from the worst social problems that today's youth face. The panic over male teachers also reinforces stereotyped notions of masculinity and gender difference. Men are less and less likely to be present in the classroom, though, largely because of teaching salaries. These salaries are lower than in male-dominated professions, and they have been decreasing, relative to those professions, for more than 20 years.

At the post-secondary level, the number of women instructors has increased dramatically, but women are still much more likely to be found in certain disciplinary areas and in non-permanent positions. The "mommy track" accounts for some of this discrepancy.

As girls' achievements have grown within education, there is increasing concern about a decline in boys' relative performance. Single-sex education has arisen to address these concerns. There are some benefits, particularly social ones, to such education; the research on educational benefits, however, remains inconclusive. A particular concern with the recent explosion of such schools is that most base their curriculum on stereotypical and unsupported ideas about gender difference. In so doing, they may reinforce damaging stereotypes and limit students' growth. In the end, the key to education is not its form but its content; and truly transformative education will mean not retrenching but changing the rules of the gendered classroom.

Questions for Critical Thinking

1. Was there a "hidden curriculum" in your elementary or high school(s)? What was it? Did it change from elementary to high school? Can you remember a point at which gender began to mean more to you and your peers?
2. Are you in favour of single-sex schooling? What are its advantages and disadvantages?
3. Do you think it important for the teaching force to contain both men and women? Why or why not?
4. Who plays a bigger part in the classroom for students: the teacher or peers?
5. Do you believe that relabelling can take the power out of words like "slut" and phrases like "that's so gay"?
6. Comparing the role of the family and the classroom in shaping children's gendered identities and attitudes, which do you think exerts greater influence?

Key Terms

bullying
cyberbullying
educational premium
gender intensification
hidden curriculum
hostile environment
imperial manhood

lesbian, gay, bisexual, transgender, queer/questioning (LGBTQ)
moral panic
self-esteem
sexual harassment
slut-shaming
Title IX

Separate and Unequal
The Gendered World of Work

We must make haste, for when we home are come,
We find again our Work but just begun;
So many things for our Attendance call,
Had we ten Hands, we could employ them all . . .
Yet without fail, soon as Daylight doth spring,
We in the Field again our work begin.

—Mary Collier, *The Woman's Labour* (1739)

In this manner, Mary Collier summarized what would come, 250 years later—to be known today as the "second shift" (see Chapter 6). This poem is a reminder that the world of work has been gendered for as long as we know; and it remains gendered today.

Freud once wrote that the two great tasks for all human beings are "to work and to love." People have always worked—to satisfy their basic material needs for food, clothing, and shelter, to provide for children and loved ones, to participate in community life, and to satisfy more culturally and historically specific desires to leave a mark on the world and to move up the social ladder. It shouldn't surprise us, then, that virtually every society has developed a division of labour, a way of dividing the tasks that must be done in order for the society as a whole to survive.

Additionally, because gender, as we have seen, both classifies us and creates a structure of power relations, it shouldn't surprise us that virtually every society has a *gendered* division of labour. There are very few tasks, in very few societies, that are not allocated by gender. This doesn't necessarily imply that the tasks assigned to one gender are less or more significant to the life of the community than the tasks assigned to the other. Valuing women's work over men's work, or vice versa, is not inevitable; it is an artefact of cultural relationships.

All this hardly comes as a surprise. However, what might surprise contemporary North American readers is that the gendered division of labour that many have called "traditional," the separation of the world into two distinct spheres—the public sphere of work, business, politics, and culture and the private sphere of the home, domestic life, and child care—is a relatively new phenomenon. As we saw in Chapter 6, the doctrine of separate spheres was not firmly established until the nineteenth century, and even then it was often more an ideology than a reality.

What also might surprise us is that the universality of the gendered division of labour tells us virtually nothing about the relative value given to the work done by women and by men. Interestingly, it turns out that in societies where women's work is less valued (i.e., in more traditional societies where women's legal status is lower) women do *more* work than men do, up to 35 per cent more in terms of time. In fact, in most countries, if paid work and unpaid work are both counted, women do more work than men do. According to the 2015 United Nation time-use surveys (see Figure 8.1), women contribute 52 per cent of the work done in the world, while men perform 48 per cent. The gender gap adds up to 21 minutes per day for every woman in the world and is biggest in countries where women's status is lower. In a few countries where women's status is high—Denmark, the Netherlands, New Zealand, Norway, and Sweden—men actually do marginally more work than women (even though women in these countries are much more likely to participate in paid employment than are women in Southern Europe).

Despite the fact that women work more than men, in general, we tend to associate work with the workplace and men with work. In fact, we are still in the midst of a major transformation of work that began in the twentieth century.

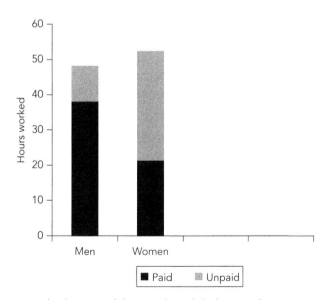

Figure 8.1 Hours worked per week by gender (global): men dominate paid work, though women work more hours overall.

Source: United Nations, Human Development Report 2015, "Work For Human Development" (2015).

The Changing Gender Composition of the Labour Force

In many countries in the twentieth century, the percentage of both women and men entering the labour force increased, but the rate of increase for women far outpaced that of men. The percentage of American women in the labour force rose from about 20 per cent in 1900 to about 57 per cent today. In Canada, women's participation rate in 1900 was 14 per cent—even lower than the US rate. At mid-century, Canada's rate had increased somewhat, to 24 per cent; by 2006 it stood at 62 per cent—higher than the American rate. In addition, where few married women with children worked outside the home until the 1960s, by 2014 about 70 per cent of American women with children under 18 were employed. Indeed, until very recently, women with children at home have been one of the fastest-growing groups in the labour force. This dramatic increase in labour force participation has been true for all races and ethnicities, in both Canada and the US. The effects of this change in the gendered division labour are still being felt.[1]

Since the beginning of the twenty-first century, however, a number of interesting (and sometimes concerning) trends have emerged in **labour force participation**. First, as women's participation in the workforce has grown, men's has begun to shrink—although much more slowly than women's participation has increased. In 1966, for example, 79.8 per cent of Canadian men were in the workforce. By 2003, this number had dropped to 73.6 per cent, and by 2006 to 72.5 per cent. Men's participation rates are now much lower than they were in the mid-1980s. Some of this can be explained by early retirement, particularly among the baby-boom generation. However, male seniors are dramatically more likely than female seniors to be in the workforce, so retirement cannot explain the whole picture. Indeed, a decline of male participation in the workforce can be seen in both Canada and the US, and across many OECD nations.[2]

While women's participation rates are still much *higher* than they were in the mid-1980s, the number of women in the workforce has very recently started to decline. In the US, the percentage of mothers ages 18–69 not employed outside the home started to increase in 1999, after three decades of steady and steep decline. The trend has continued to the present, with nearly 30 per cent of US mothers falling in this category. Analysts suggest that the rising cost of child care in concert with stagnating wages may explain much of this apparent "withdrawal" from the workforce. However, at least one study has traced at least part of the decline in to changing gender-role attitudes.[3]

Whether its source is ideological or practical, a similar trend is underway in Canada, with record numbers of women leaving the workforce in 2014 (the first time since 1977). Because the steepest declines occurred among women aged 40–54, retirement is not a sufficient explanation for the exodus of women from the workforce; neither is it explained by a decline in "women's" jobs, because that number actually increased. In fact, the decline occurred mainly in male-dominated fields. Accordingly, both the employment gap and the wage gap (see below; also discussed in detail on pp. 223–6) grew in 2014 rather than declining.[4]

The employment gap between men and women is a significant and persistent feature of the employment scene in North America and worldwide. While women's participation in paid employment grew significantly in the last third of the twentieth century, women's global employment rates have stagnated since then, with implications that are significant both for developed and for developing nations.

Women in the Workforce and the Fate of Nations

In North America, when we talk about whether women should stay at home or join the workforce, we still think of this as an individual decision driven by personal choice rather than a structural issue. Some commentators have pointed to the lifelong effects on women's earning power of "opting out," while others have linked the wage gap to women's tendency to spend less time in paid employment. In fact, most North American analyses focus on the individual level.

However, there is strong evidence that women's participation in paid employment has effects well beyond individual women and their families. A 2012 report argued that raising female employment to male levels would increase the GDP of nations in significant ways. In the US, for example, the GDP would increase by 5 per cent. In some nations, primarily developing ones, the effects would be much greater. The report's authors corrected for women's potentially lower productivity (primarily because globally, women lack education and skills relative to men). Even after this correction, women's employment would increase Egypt's GDP, for example, by 34 per cent! The OECD, for its part, attributes half of the world's GDP growth in the past 50 years to the growth of education, particularly among the world's women. The organization estimates that if women's participation in employment were to reach the level of men's by 2030, this would result in an overall 12 per cent increase in GDP.

Of course, GDP is not the only way to calculate value. There is no doubt that the unpaid work that women do produces enormous societal value, and feminists such as Marilyn Waring have long been critical of economic analyses that ignore women's unpaid contributions (for example, breastfeeding adds nothing to GDP, while manufacturing weapons certainly does). However, there is evidence that even women's care work is enhanced by economic participation. One often-cited example is children's education. Given that women are more likely to invest household income in children's education than are men, women's employment can have significant knock-on effects in children's educational attainment. As well, of course, greater employment of women can reduce many other areas of female vulnerability, from poverty in old age to domestic violence.

Therefore, there may be reasons to be concerned about the decline in female employment, rather than focusing entirely upon the "choices" individual women make. Writing about the 2014 decline in workforce participation of Canadian women, CUPE economist Toby Sanger writes, "if these trends continue we should all be concerned, not just for this setback on the long march toward greater equality, but for the long-term health of our economy as well." The G20 leaders agree: in November 2014 the organization adopted the goal of "reducing the gap in participation rates between men and women in our countries by 25 per cent by 2025, taking into account national circumstances, to bring more than 100 million women into the labour force, significantly increase global growth and reduce poverty and inequality."[5]

What is driving these changes? Commentators are bemused, to say the least. At the end of the twentieth century, the convergence of men's and women's labour-force participation seemed likely. Instead, confusingly, that convergence has stalled even as other indicators herald the feminization of the workforce.

Women are now 40 per cent of the global workforce, and in Canada and the US, they are about half. Because of the areas in which women cluster, women's employment is also less sensitive to volatile markets. In the Great Recession that began in 2008, American men lost their jobs at almost three times the rate women did. In the aftermath, male unemployment has proved more stubborn than female unemployment.[6]

If these rates are to be understood, it's important to address how and why women are "opting out," as many media outlets have claimed. In part, the trends vary by class. Only 25 per cent of American stay-at-home moms have university degrees; highly educated mothers with family incomes above $75,000 are only 5 per cent of the total number of stay-at-home mothers with working husbands. Single and cohabiting women, who tend to be much poorer, represent a much larger proportion of stay-at-home mothers (one-third). For such mothers, in the absence of affordable quality daycare, the "choice" between continuing to work—only to spend their entire incomes on child care—or staying home is clear, particularly once they have more than one child. One young mother who moved from the UK to the US noted that while none of her friends in the UK had left their jobs after having children, *every* one of her friends in the US had left the workforce. The difference, it seems, is that Britain (like Canada), provides a year of paid maternity leave to mothers. There is no doubt that having sufficient paid maternity leave encourages women to return to work.[7]

While pundits argue, one thing is abundantly clear: recent developments suggest the continued (and even resurgent) importance of gender. Here's how economists from the International Monetary Fund sum up the situation more than a decade into the twenty-first century:

> Women make up a little over half the world's population, but their contribution to measured economic activity, growth, and well-being is far below its potential, with serious macro-economic consequences. Despite significant progress in recent decades, labour markets across the world remain divided along gender lines, and progress toward gender equality seems to have stalled. Female labour force participation (FLFP) has remained lower than male participation, women account for most unpaid work, and when women are employed in paid work, they are overrepresented in the informal sector and among the poor. They also face significant wage differentials vis-à-vis their male colleagues. In many countries, distortions and discrimination in the labour market restrict women's options for paid work, and female representation in senior positions and entrepreneurship remains low.[8]

Still, one should not downplay the dramatic effects of the twentieth century on the world of work. Women's entry into the labour force has taken place at every level, from low-paid clerical and sales work through all the major professions. "The increasing representation of women among the ranks of managers in organizations," writes sociologist

Jerry Jacobs, "is perhaps the most dramatic shift in the sex composition of an occupation since clerical work became a female-dominated field in the late nineteenth century."[9]

We've come a long way, indeed, from the mid-nineteenth century, when a young Mary Taylor wrote to her friend Charlotte Brontë, "there are no means for a woman to live in England, but by teaching, sewing, or washing. The last is the best, the best paid, the least unhealthy and the most free." These changes have rippled through the rest of society, gradually changing the relationship of the family to the workplace and altering forever the notion of the male "breadwinner" who supports a family on his income alone. Today, dual-earner couples are the norm and female breadwinners are increasingly more common.[10]

The Persistence of Gender Ideologies

While the realities of home and workplace have changed, our ideas about them have lagged far behind. Many North Americans still believe in the "traditional" **male bread-winner/female housewife model** even if our own lives no longer reflect it. Our adherence to such gender ideologies has dramatic consequences for women and men, both at work and at home.

Since the early 1800s, the workplace has been seen as a masculine arena where men could test and prove their manhood in the dog-eat-dog marketplace, confirming their manhood as breadwinners and family providers. The workplace was a site of "homosocial reproduction"—a place where men created themselves as men.[11]

As a result, work is often seen as a testing ground of masculinity, and earnings can be its index. Here's one example. Although most married couples are now dual-earner couples, the husband's masculinity may be tied not to being the only worker, but rather to making the most money to support the family. If a husband makes less than his wife does, both partners may engage in **deviance neutralization**, understating her income or exaggerating his to preserve the idea of the male breadwinner. Similarly, both members of a couple may regard her work as more flexible no matter what she does. For example, psychologist Francine Deutsch found that a couple made up of a male physician and a female professor believed that academic work was more flexible, allowing her to make accommodations for the sake of the children. When Deutsch examined the opposite scenario—a couple made up of a female physician and a male professor—surprisingly (or not), both members of this couple regarded medical practice as more flexible than academic work.[12]

Gender ideologies about breadwinning are in flux, but remain resilient. A 2012 American poll found that the vast majority of fathers believed that mothers should work outside the home either part-time or not at all. The biggest gender gap emerged in the "not at all" category, which was selected as ideal by 37 per cent of fathers and only 9 per cent of mothers.[13]

Women's employment also continues to be affected by gender ideologies. As women entered the workforce in the twentieth century, they began in fields that could be considered extensions of women's domestic work or "assistance" to men: nursing, teaching children, secretarial work, and service. Additionally, in many male-dominated workplaces of the twentieth century, many women performed what sociologist Arlie Hochschild calls **emotional labour**, making sure that the masculine workplace was well-oiled and functioning smoothly: Flight attendants, office managers, waitresses and other service workers, and cheerleaders performed work that "ornamented" male–male interactions and made sure they went smoothly (and remained unmistakably heterosexual).[14]

This view of women's work as "auxiliary" to the work of men was widely shared. Many believed that women worked either because they *had* to—because they were single or working class—or because they wanted to earn **pin money** for their trifles. This often made women's work seem somehow illegitimate, even to women themselves. After all, if real men proved themselves in the workplace, real women were supposed to be at home caring for their families.

Of course, many women were unable to access this idealized vision of the breadwinner-homemaker ideal. For black women in the US, for example, paid employment was often not a "choice," but an absolute necessity; wages for black workers were generally low, and black men faced high unemployment rates and workplace discrimination. As a result, however, both black women *and* black men today have much more positive attitudes toward women's work. This plays out in women's labour-force participation, with black mothers more likely than white, Asian, or Hispanic mothers to be in the workforce. What is also clear from these data is that men's work mirrors that of women. Hispanic women are the least likely to remain in the workforce after marriage, while Hispanic men have a much higher labour participation rate than other American men. While black women have the highest participation rates among women, black men have the lowest rates among men.[15]

Canada presents a slightly different pattern from the US. First, women participate in the workforce more overall. Second, there are smaller gaps between the participation of women in different ethnic groups. There is only a small gap between Aboriginal and non-Aboriginal women's participation in the labour force, though Aboriginal women (and men) are much more likely to be unemployed than are non-Aboriginals. Similarly, visible minority women (with the exception of immigrant women) participate in the workforce at virtually the same rate as do non-visible minority women. There is, however, a wide variation *among* visible minority women. Filipina women participate in the labour force at a very high rate relative to non-visible minority women, while Arab women participate at a rate much lower.[16] What do we learn from the variation in participation rates from country to country and culture to culture? Certainly, we can see that decisions about who takes their place in work are both pragmatic (influenced by historic patterns of discrimination and the availability of work) and cultural (influenced by historically situated ideals about marriage, family, and the legitimacy of women's employment).

If women's paid employment has been often seen as "secondary" or illegitimate, women's *unpaid* labour has often been both romanticized and overlooked. All over the world, the tasks that women customarily perform are ignored as labour. It is very difficult to assess the economic impact of this work, but its contribution has been estimated to be equivalent to between 10 and 39 per cent of GDP. Women's ability to dedicate themselves to paid employment is severely hindered by their continuing responsibility for so much unpaid labour. On the other hand, as more and more women have entered the labour force, more and more work—specifically jobs that were traditionally women's unpaid work—has shifted into the labour economy. So today, it is possible to access many things in the marketplace that were once provided in the home by women. Child care, ready-made foods, laundry services, and many other services are all available. Ironically, the provision of such services often becomes the lowest-paid and least valued work available, performed by women. (Immigrants and racialized people are often also overrepresented in this type of work.) Therefore, from a broader social perspective, the devaluation of women's unpaid labour affects both the status of that work in the home *and* the status of that work once it migrates to the marketplace.[17]

As alluded to above, gender ideologies still influence what women and men perceive as the "natural" or legitimate duties of womanhood. Of Canadian women, 90 per cent still say that it is "definitely" or "probably" preferable for a parent to stay home to raise young children. The same number of full-time women workers say that they would like to work part-time to spend more time with their families. Increasing numbers of fathers may also want the same thing. However, North Americans still view child rearing, in particular, as women's work. A 2013 US study found that 51 per cent of Americans surveyed believed that children were better off with a mother who did not work outside the home. When the term "mother" was changed to "father," only 8 per cent agreed.[18]

Stay-at-home fathers were once a tiny percentage of stay-at-home parents, but are rapidly increasing in number. Often, they are at home because of employment circumstances rather than choice; nonetheless, the experience of being a stay-at-home father or a breadwinner can promote greater understanding across genders, with men more aware of and interested in child rearing (and more interested in promoting workplace changes to support families). The experience of being a breadwinner can also change women's attitudes ("Now I know what my dad went through because my mom didn't work"). At the same time, persistent issues related to women's status, such as women's greater tendency to do domestic work even when they are sole income-earners, crop up.[19]

The persistence of traditional gender ideologies makes today's workplace particularly contentious. On one hand, women continue to face gender discrimination: They are paid less, promoted less, and assigned to specific jobs, despite their qualifications and motivations; sometimes they are made to feel unwelcome, like intruders in an all-male preserve. On the other hand, men say they are bewildered and angered by the changes in workplace policy that make them feel like they are "walking on eggshells," fearful of making any kind of remark to a woman lest they be hauled into court for sexual harassment. In addition, both sexes continue to grapple with the relationship between paid and unpaid labour and the stresses of balancing work with family life.

The Persistence of Gender Discrimination in the Workplace

For many years, the chief obstacle facing women in the labour force was sex discrimination. Discrimination occurs when we treat people who are similar in different ways or, sometimes, when we treat people who are different in similar ways. For example, to exclude one race or gender from housing, educational opportunities, or employment would be a form of discrimination. Treating people the same is an important principle: **equality**. But treating people with different needs—disability, for example—"the same" as anyone else—by offering them a staircase by which to climb to a work site—is therefore also a form of discrimination. Treating people fairly according to their needs—**equity**—is, like equality, a key component of non-discrimination.

Employers have historically referred to a variety of "truths" about women in order to exclude them: women don't really want to work, work only until pregnancy, don't need the money, are physically incapable of certain types of work, and have different aptitudes and interests. Such arguments have also provided the rationale for race discrimination in employment and education. Today, discrimination is permissible only under the most exceptional of circumstances. The basis for the discrimination may not rely on any stereotypical ideas about gender (or racial) differences; the discrimination must be based on a **bona fide occupational requirement (BFOR)**.

While few jobs preclude workers of any identifiable group, job requirements may have the effect of discrimination. For instance, up until the 1970s, the RCMP (and many other Canadian police forces) had height and weight requirements that made it very difficult for most women and members of certain ethnic groups to enter the force. What's more, these requirements bore little relation to modern policing. While the six-foot-four, 225-pound Mountie in red serge might have been an awe-inspiring sight, looking imposing is not a BFOR. Accordingly, height and weight requirements have been replaced by the more holistic Physical Abilities Requirement Evaluation (PARE), which measures a candidate's ability to perform a number of tasks related to apprehending a suspect—a bona fide and critical part of the job of policing.[20]

Few people today would uphold traditional exclusionary requirements of height and weight. However, legal decisions also consider whether job-related tests like the PARE might themselves be discriminatory. A landmark decision of this kind was handed down by the Supreme Court of Canada in 1999, in a case brought by Tawney Meiorin, a BC forest firefighter. Meiorin had performed her job satisfactorily for several years when a new fitness test was introduced. She failed one component of the test, so the BC Forest Service fired her. She argued that the test was discriminatory (because of women's generally lower aerobic capacity) and invalid as a measure of a BFOR. The Supreme Court agreed, arguing, "[n]o credible evidence showed that the prescribed aerobic capacity was necessary for either men or women to perform the work of a forest firefighter safely and efficiently." The court implemented a stringent set of guidelines (known as the **Meiorin test**) for employers to consider in establishing job-related requirements.[21]

Most legal cases of workplace discrimination have involved women suing in order to enter formerly all-male workplaces. In one interesting case in the 1990s, however, the Hooters restaurant chain was sued by several US men seeking employment as waiters. Historically, Hooters hired only "voluptuous" women as "scantily clad" bartenders and food servers. The male plaintiffs argued that such a policy violates equal employment statutes. Hooters countered that its restaurants sell sex appeal—and "to have female sex appeal, you have to be female." The US Equal Employment Opportunity Commission (EEOC) quietly dropped its own investigation, and the case was settled out of court, with Hooters paying $3.75 million to the men and adding a few men to its staff as bartenders—but not waiters.[22]

Sex Segregation

Outright gender discrimination is less common than sex segregation, which, writes sociologist Barbara Reskin, "refers to women's and men's concentration in different occupations, industries, jobs, and levels in workplace hierarchies." Segregation can be either "horizontal" or "vertical." **Vertical segregation** refers to segregation associated with differences of education, experience, and skill within the same field. For example, in hierarchically ranked occupations, such as law, the genders are represented differentially as legal secretaries, clerks, paralegal professionals, lawyers, and judges. **Horizontal segregation** refers to segregation within occupations in different fields that are roughly similar in terms of educational and skill requirements, for example, truck driving and secretarial work, or engineering and teaching. Different occupations are seen as more appropriate for one gender or the other, and therefore women and men are guided, pushed, or occasionally shoved into specific positions.[23]

In fact, sex segregation in the workplace is so pervasive that it appears to be the natural order of things. Though almost equal numbers of women and men go off to work every morning, we do not go together to the same place, nor do we have the same jobs even when we work in the same spaces. In 2011, 55 per cent of all Canadian workers in the service sector were women, while 88 per cent of workers in construction were men. The healthcare and social assistance sector was overwhelmingly female at 82 per cent. Men made up 95 per cent of trades workers and 86 per cent of apprentices, with most tradeswomen clustered in a few areas like hairstyling and cooking. The most common occupations for women in 2011 were (in descending order) retail salesperson, administrative assistant, registered nurse, cashier, and kindergarten/elementary teacher. For men, the top spot was also taken by retail salesperson, but from then on, the list diverged: truck driver, retail and wholesale manager, carpenter, and janitor/building superintendent. Additionally, men continue to dominate careers in science, technology, engineering, and mathematics (STEM), as expected.[24]

Though women have been broadening their areas of employment, women's paid work remains less diverse than that of men. In Canada, the top 20 occupations for women account for 45.8 per cent of female workers, while the most common 20 occupations for men account for only 30.1 per cent of male workers. Yet women have colonized men's arenas far more than the reverse, in part because "male" jobs are better. We give more value (and pay) to occupations we associate with stereotypically "masculine" characteristics such as strength, competition, and assertiveness. Because of this, men may be reluctant to enter female-dominated fields that offer poorer pay and may brand men "effeminate." Efforts to recruit men to such fields must work against that stigma.[25]

Rationales for sex segregation often rely on the argument that, because of differential socialization, women and men are likely to seek different kinds of jobs. The girl who plays with dolls grows up to be a nurse, the boy who plays with trucks a construction worker. However, socialization *alone* is not sufficient as an explanation. "Socialization cannot explain why a sex-segregated labour market emerged, why each sex is allocated to particular types of occupations, and why the sex typing of occupations changes in particular ways over time." Instead, we need to think of sex segregation as the outcome of several factors—"the differential socialization of young men and women, sex-typed tracking in the educational system, and sex-linked social control at the workplace, at the hiring stage and beyond."[26]

Socialization is also unable to explain why professions that are male dominated tend to have higher wages, while those dominated by women have lower wages. Although one might be tempted to explain this by the characteristics of the job, it turns out that the

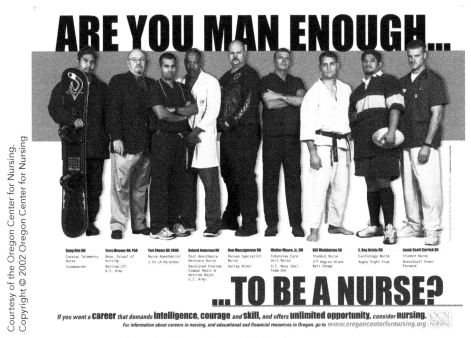

Recruitment poster from the Oregon Center for Nursing.

gender composition of the occupation is actually a better predictor. One of the easiest ways to see the impact of sex segregation on wages is to watch what happens when a particular field begins to change its gender composition. For example, clerical work was once considered a skilled occupation, in which a virtually all-male labour force was paid reasonably well. (One is reminded, of course, of the exception, the innocent and virtuous Bob Cratchit in Charles Dickens's *A Christmas Carol*.) In the early part of the twentieth century, in both Britain and North America, though, the gender distribution began to change, and by the middle of the century, most clerical workers were female. As a result, clerical work was re-evaluated as less demanding of skill and less valuable to an organization; consequently, workers' wages fell. As sociologist Samuel Cohn notes, this is a result, not a cause, of the changing gender composition of the workforce.[27]

Veterinary medicine provides a more recent example. After the 1890s, as veterinary medicine professionalized, it defined itself as steadfastly masculine. As both science and heavy work (in an age when most patients were large animals), veterinary medicine was antithetical to "women's work." This situation lasted into the late 1960s, when only about 5 per cent of American veterinary students were women. Today that number is closer to 80 per cent, and the number of female veterinarians has more than doubled since 1991, whereas the number of male veterinarians has declined by 15 per cent. In North America, women are now the majority of veterinarians (57 per cent in the US and 59 per cent in Canada). Unfortunately, vet incomes have followed the changing gender composition. In the 1970s, when males dominated the field, veterinarians' incomes were right behind those of physicians; today, veterinarians earn approximately half of what physicians do. "Vets are people with medical degrees without the medical income," commented one veterinary epidemiologist. Moreover, female vets earn less than male ones, in part because of unexplained factors and in part because male veterinarians dominate the highest-paid areas of practice, such as food-animal care (caring for the animals that people are going to eat—often at slaughterhouses and large-scale agribusinesses).[28]

The exact opposite process took place with computer programming. In the 1940s, women were hired as keypunch operators, the precursors to programmers, because the job seemed "clerical." In fact, however, programming "demanded complex skills in abstract logic, mathematics, electrical circuitry, and machinery, all of which," sociologist Katharine Donato observed, women provided without difficulty. However, after programming was recognized as "intellectually demanding," it became attractive to men, who began to enter the field, consequently driving wages up considerably (and ultimately squeezing women out).[29]

As William Bielby and James Baron write, "men's jobs are rewarded according to their standing within the hierarchy of men's work, and women's jobs are rewarded according to their standing within the hierarchy of women's work. The legitimacy of this system is easy to sustain in a segregated workplace." Stated simply, "women's occupations pay less at least partly *because* women do them."[30]

In general, legal remedies for sex segregation have yielded mixed results. Perhaps the most studied case was 1980's *EEOC v. Sears*, a case brought by the US Equal Employment Opportunity Commission against the retail giant. Sears had routinely shuttled women and men into different sales positions, resulting in massive wage disparities between the two. Women were pushed into over-the-counter retail positions, with low commissions or straight salary. Men, on the other hand, were concentrated in sales of high-priced goods, such as furniture and appliances, which offered high commissions.

Sears argued that this sex-based division of labour resulted from individual choice. Differential socialization, Sears suggested, led women and men to pursue different career paths; women were interested in flexibility, relationship-centred work, and less competition. The US Supreme Court upheld Sears's acquittal on sex discrimination charges, in part because the court said that no single individual woman had stepped forward and declared that she had sought to enter high-commission sales or had been refused because of these stereotypes.[31]

These choppy legal waters were tested again by a US lawsuit against Wal-Mart, the world's largest retail chain. Plaintiffs argued that although 72 per cent of Wal-Mart's hourly sales employees were women, they represented less than 33 per cent of the company's managers (compared with 56 per cent at competitors). The lawsuit was filed on behalf of nearly 750,000 women. (A lawsuit against Home Depot in the 1990s, alleging similar sex segregation, was settled out of court for $65 million plus $22.5 million in legal fees.) However, in 2011 the US Supreme Court dismissed the case because the plaintiffs had failed to prove the existence of a company policy that produced the sex segregation in question.[32]

Despite the failure of these lawsuits, the Sears and Wal-Mart cases draw attention to the phenomenon of segregation and the ways in which our notions of men's work and women's work contribute to the differential earnings of the sexes.

Precarious Employment

Another way in which the sexes are segregated is in the very *nature* of their employment relationships. We have already seen how women and men cluster in different jobs, but we often overlook the fact that these jobs may differ not only in the work itself, but also in the nature of the employment contract. Typically, female jobs in retail or child care very often can be categorized as **precarious employment**.

When most of us think of "having a job," we think about having a contract with one employer for whom we work on a regular basis through the year. We assume that our job will pay a legally conforming hourly wage, and that we will be entitled to some basic job security (for example, layoff notice). We may expect that we will receive some form of employment benefits, including contribution to Employment Insurance (EI) and the Canada Pension Plan (CPP). When we think of employment in this way, we are thinking about a "standard employment relationship," which some scholars see as linked to the notion of breadwinning and the **family wage**.

The idea of precarious work, in some ways, depends on the notion of the family wage. Regardless of the importance of women's (and sometimes children's) employment to family sustenance, their employment has always been seen as "auxiliary" to male earnings. This has allowed employers to hire women on terms that would be unacceptable to most men, because female work was "just for pin money."

So in contrast to the standard employment relationship, precarious employment is characterized by uncertainty (you might be let go at any time); lack of control over working conditions (absence of a union or collective agreement); lack of regulatory protection (for example, through a Labour Relations Board or similar governmental oversight); and low income (sometimes not even determined on an hourly basis).[33]

Since 1970, precarious employment has been one of the fastest-growing areas of work, to the point where today, some believe that one-third of Canadian jobs fall into this category. Since the economic downturn began in 2008, job loss has come mainly in the area of full-time jobs, while job creation has been overwhelmingly in part-time and temporary positions. Temporary work grew at three times the rate of permanent work between 2009 and 2012. In Canada and globally, precarious work seems to be the wave of the future.[34]

Much of the growth in women's labour-force participation, since 1970, has come from their entry into this kind of work, which can include self-employment, temporary work, the holding of multiple jobs, and part-time or on-call labour. (Controversy about numbers arises over the inclusion of permanent part-time work, which some analysts do not see as precarious.) According to pre-recession data from the Ontario Federation of Labour, 40 per cent of women, compared with about 29 per cent of men, were working in precarious employment. Women were 60 per cent of part-time temporary workers and 75 per cent of part-time permanent employees, for example. Racialized, immigrant, and young women and men are also overrepresented in this form of work, despite the fact that immigrants tend to have higher levels of education than the Canadian-born.[35]

Consider the underpaid retail sales clerk who is forced to scrounge up hours on a weekly basis because there are no full-time jobs available. Or the long-haul truck driver, forced to become an owner–operator (technically self-employed) and then compete with other drivers for work. What about the home-care worker, who is hired as a temporary worker and does not know for certain if work will still be available month after month? Or the warehouse worker, who is working for low pay and faces a perpetual probationary period because they were hired through an employment agency?[36]

One might also add, consider the nanny allowed to enter Canada on a "temporary" visa, unlike other workers who can enter as landed immigrants. She, like agricultural workers and other "contingent" employees, may find herself protected very minimally, if at all, by the labour standards in place to govern standard employment relationships.[37]

Our tolerance of precarious employment relies on gendered (and racialized) ideas, like the idea that women are working not to support families but to earn "extra" money; or the idea that foreign women working as domestic workers may be poorly paid, but are still "better off" than in their own countries and therefore do not merit the protections granted to Canadians doing similar work. The existence of such employment also relies on gender inequality in that women may choose to enter such employment because they find it flexible enough not to conflict with their family responsibilities. However, precarious employment contributes to the vulnerability of women (and other affected groups) to economic downturns or changes in personal circumstances. It makes women more likely, for example, to slip into poverty upon divorce. Additionally, and most obviously, women's overrepresentation in precarious employment contributes to the gender-wage gap.

Income Discrimination: The Wage Gap

At both the aggregate level and the individual level—whether we average all incomes or look at specific individuals' wages for the jobs they do—women earn less than men do. This wage difference is called the **wage gap**.

In both Canada and the US, the wage gap shrank dramatically between 1981 and 1996 and has continued to shrink, albeit more slowly, since then. In the former year, Canadian women's median earnings were 62.5 per cent of those of men; by 1996, that figure had increased to 73.5 per cent. Some argued that these figures overstated the gap, because they measured annual earnings, and men tended to work more hours. Therefore, measurements in Canada increasingly adopted a comparison on the basis of hourly wages. By 2000, female per-hour earnings were somewhere around 80 per cent of those of men. Much of this change was caused by two developments: first, the decline in men's wages caused by the loss of jobs in the high-wage skilled manufacturing sector of the economy; and second, the entry of some women into high-paid male-dominated fields.[38]

These changes lulled some into believing that the wage gap was disappearing. However, since 2000, the wage gap has remained stagnant. Today, on an annual basis, Canadian women continue to earn only about 72 per cent of what men earn; on an hourly basis the gap narrows but remains significant, with women earning on average 87 per cent of men's hourly wages, as is illustrated in Figure 8.2. Looking at young workers aged 20–25 is a good way of assessing the wage gap, since their labour-market experience and job tenure tend to be equal regardless of sex (the gendered effects of child-bearing and child rearing,

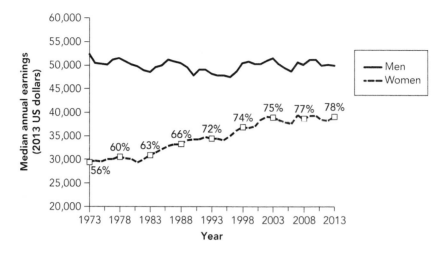

Figure 8.2a Women's Median Annual Earnings as a Percentage of Men's Median Annual Earnings for Full-Time, Year-Round Workers (US), 1973–2013.

Source: United States Department of Labor, www.dol.gov/wb/stats/earnings.htm.

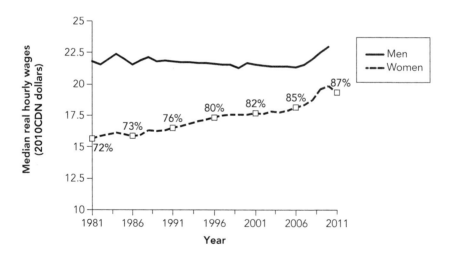

Figure 8.2b Women's Median Hourly Wages as a Percentage of Men's Median Hourly Wages for Full-Time Workers (Canada), 1981–2011.

Source: René Morissette, Garnett Picot, and Yuqian Lu, The Evolution of Canadian Wages over the Last Three Decades (Ottawa: Minister of Industry, 2013).

most notably, tend not to affect this group). Yet in 2005, young women employed full-time earned only 85 per cent of the earnings of their male counterparts. Why? Principally, it seems, because young men's earnings rose sharply after a period of stagnation. The Alberta oil boom gave back what plant closures in the 1980s and 1990s had taken away.

When we talk about a closing wage gap, then, we are often talking about what happens to men's wages rather than real growth in women's.[39]

In recent decades, some have claimed that the wage gap is illusory—that men earn more because they work more hours than women do. In a 2012 article in *The Wall Street Journal*, Kay Hymowitz put it this way: "the famous gender-wage gap is to a considerable degree a gender-hours gap." To be sure, the fact that women work fewer hours (itself related to issues of gender, such as women's greater responsibility for child care) affects women's earnings. For this reason, Statistics Canada looks at *hourly* earnings in assessing the wage gap. This method of assessment shows a persistent wage gap. However, these data also show that the gap is slowly closing, in large part because women have increased their "productivity-enhancing characteristics" (e.g., education, unionization, and longer job tenures) more quickly than have men. So in 1981, the average hourly wage of men (2010 dollars) was $22.55. Women's average wage was $17.38, which is 77 per cent of men's earnings. The average wage for men in 2011 was $25.03, for women $21.85 (87 per cent of men's earnings). This presents a much rosier picture than the 71 per cent figure that results from an analysis that does not correct for hours worked. However, the gap remains. Of course, that gap might partially be the result of other factors, such as industry, age, or education, but even when these factors are considered, women's earnings are still 92 per cent of men's.[40]

Therefore, the wage gap is not a "myth," as some have claimed. A significant, inexplicable wage gap is real and persistent (8 per cent per annum, year after year, adds up to a massive lifetime deficit!); but the wage gap is a complex phenomenon—complicated by age, ethnicity, ability, and level of education. For example, education greatly increases earnings for both men and women. Nonetheless, in 2006, young men employed full-time earned about $10,000 more than their female counterparts did, whether they were university-educated or lacking high-school graduation. The gap increases with age, and the higher up the earnings ladder one goes, the greater the gap gets. In OECD nations, the wage gap averages 16 per cent, but the gap between male and female top earners is 21 per cent.

Therefore, there are three main causes for the wage gap: discrimination, sex segregation, and women's unequal responsibility for child-bearing and child rearing, which leads them to work less. First, during the course of life, women tend to accumulate fewer years of full-time work experience and shorter job tenures, largely because of their family responsibilities. This has a calamitous effect on women's wages and fuels a growing gap. In fact, women who drop out of the labour force have lower real wages when they come back to work than they had when they left. In the 1990s, two sociologists calculated that each child costs a woman 7 per cent in wages. The result is that women aged 50–54 earned only 72 per cent as much as men of the same age did.[41]

Nevertheless, the wage gap is not simply the result of women's disproportionate responsibility for family care. Discrimination and sex segregation are also important. In every field, women tend to be concentrated at the bottom of the pay scale. They face discrimination in hiring, and particularly in promotion (as further discussed on p. 227). Within any occupational category, including female-dominated ones, women are less likely than men to get the promotions that bring higher salaries. In addition, women cluster at the bottom of the pay scale even within high-prestige, highly paid occupations such as medicine. Sociologist Judith Lorber described the reason why female physicians earn less than male physicians did. "The fault may not lie in their psyches or female roles, but in the system of professional patronage and sponsorship which tracked them out of their prestigious specialties and 'inner fraternities' of American medical institutions by not recommending them for the better internships, residencies, and hospital staff positions, and by not referring patients," she writes.[42]

Finally, sex segregation itself explains the wage gap. As already discussed, it seems that "women's work" is simply not valued as highly as the work we assign to men. Simply knowing that work is done by women, or is somehow "feminine" work, still means that it will be seen as meriting less money than so-called "men's work." Is this changing? A 2008 study of 260 Ontario undergraduates suggests not. In that study, though participants rated male- and female-typed jobs similarly in terms of qualification, skills, and working conditions, they still assigned lower salaries to jobs within "female" domains.[43]

How have women coped with this income inequality? In the 1860s, one woman came up with a rather novel solution:

> I was almost at the end of my rope. I had no money and a woman's wages were not enough to keep me alive. I looked around and saw men getting more money, and more work, and more money for the same kind of work. I decided to become a man. It was simple. I just put on men's clothing and applied for a man's job. I got good money for those times, so I stuck to it.[44]

This approach is novel, but not exactly practical for an entire gender. While women have pressed for equal wages—in their unions, professional associations, and in every arena in which they have worked—they face a double bind in their efforts to achieve workplace equality. On the one hand, traditional gender ideologies push them away from those occupations that pay well and toward lower-paying sectors of the economy. On the other hand, while women are protected from discrimination through legislation, when they enter previously male-dominated, higher-paying fields, they face more subtle obstacles as discussed below.

Challenges to Workplace Integration

Glass Ceilings (and Cellars?)

One consequence of sex segregation is discrimination against women in promotion. Women face the twin barriers of the **glass ceiling** and the **sticky floor**, which combine to keep them stuck at the bottom and unable to reach the top. The sticky floor keeps women (and other groups) trapped in low-wage positions, with little opportunity for upward mobility. The glass ceiling consists of "those artificial barriers, based on attitudinal or organizational bias that prevent qualified individuals from advancing upward within their organization into management level positions."[45]

In 1995, the US government's Glass Ceiling Commission found that the glass ceiling continued, "to deny untold numbers of qualified people the opportunity to compete for and hold executive level positions in the private sector."[46] Most significantly, the glass ceiling keeps women from being promoted equally with men, and its effects are multiplied when race, ability, and other intersectional issues are brought into the equation.

The glass ceiling occurs under a variety of circumstances. Corporate management may be either unable or unwilling to establish policies and practices that are effective mechanisms to promote workplace diversity. The company may not have adequate job evaluation criteria that allow for comparable-worth criteria, or may rely on traditional gender stereotypes in evaluation. Limited family-friendly workplace policies will also inhibit women's ability to rise.

Perhaps the most important element that reinforces the glass ceiling is the informal or even unconscious effort by men to restore or retain the all-male atmosphere of the corporate hierarchy. When hiring and promoting, we tend to prefer those like us. If most of those in a position to hire are male, white, and able-bodied, they may—consciously or unconsciously—choose candidates with whom they're comfortable, specifically male, white, and able-bodied. "What's important is comfort, chemistry, relationships, and collaborations," one manager explained. "That's what makes a shop work. When we find minorities and women who think like we do, we snatch them up." One British study of female MBAs, for example, found that by far the "most significant" and "most resistant" barrier to women's advancement was the "'men's club' network."[47]

Sometimes the culture clash between women and the old boys' club is overt. In 2008, the first female senior executives at Bell ExpressVu filed a lawsuit and a human rights complaint alleging gender discrimination based on a "macho corporate culture" at Bell. In 2005, they claimed, they were forced to participate in an "over the top" martial-arts themed retreat. Soon afterward, both women were fired. However, because the glass ceiling is about "culture" rather than overt discrimination, it is difficult to perceive even for those facing it. (It was called glass, after all, because of its invisibility.) In the words of Moya Green, CEO of Canada Post, "I can say I didn't feel the so-called glass ceiling until I got close enough to see it." Sometimes the ceiling is even internal. One American study found that women underestimate their leadership abilities, while men overestimate theirs; however, far more important are the perceptions of others. A recent survey of 501 Canadian women business leaders found that 93 per cent of them believed they were paid less than comparable men were, while 90 per cent of them believed that their image and appearance were considered more important to advancement than they are for men.[48]

Despite broad consensus that the glass ceiling exists, writer Warren Farrell argues that *men* are the true victims of sex discrimination in the workplace. Men, Farrell argues, are the victims of the **glass cellar**—stuck in the most hazardous and dangerous occupations. In fact, Farrell argues, of the 250 occupations ranked by the *Jobs Related Almanac*, the 25 worst jobs (such as truck driver, roofer, boilermaker, construction worker, welder, and football player) were almost all male. In Canada, men are 30 times more likely to die on the job than are women. The most dangerous industries (in ranked order) are logging, fishing, roofing, structural steel and ironworking, electrical power line work, truck driving and traveling sales, farming and ranching, and construction—all heavily male-dominated.[49]

Farrell has a point: Many of the jobs that men take *are* hazardous—and made more so by an ideology of masculinity that demands that men remain stoic and uncomplaining in the face of danger. Consequently, even on dangerous worksites or off-shore oil rigs, men frequently shun safety precautions and equipment as unsuitable for "real" men.

Does this mean that men, not women, are the ones being discriminated against? Such a conclusion flies in the face of both evidence and reason. First, many of the dangerous industries offer relatively high pay—certainly much higher pay than the jobs that are almost exclusively female. These occupations can hardly be regarded as a "cellar" when it comes to compensation. Second, the jobs that are the most exclusively male are also those whose workers have fought most fiercely against the entry of women in the first place. Still, while the clustering of men in dangerous occupations does not necessarily represent discrimination, it represents another way in which work is gendered, often to the detriment of workers.

When the Ceiling Is an Escalator: Differential Experiences with Tokenism

Often, when a few men or women enter workplaces dominated by the other gender, the form integration takes is **tokenism**. Tokens are people who are admitted into an organization but who are recognizably different from the large majority of the members of the organization; the difference might be gender, but it might also be ethnicity, race, or another characteristic that sets the "token" apart from the majority of workers. However, tokens represent more than simply the members of a numerical minority; tokens are accepted not *despite* their minority status but rather *because* of it. They are actively discouraged from recruiting others like themselves. Sometimes, tokens may even become wedded to organizational norms as strongly as members are of the numerical majority.

According to Rosabeth Moss Kanter's, pioneering work *Men and Women of the Corporation*, tokenism widens the contrasts between groups rather than narrowing them. Tokens, Kanter writes, are therefore "often treated as representative of their category, as symbols rather than as individuals."[50] The token is always in the spotlight—everyone notices him or her, but only because he or she is different. Tokens are rarely seen as similar to others in the group. Therefore, tokens have a double experience of visibility—not only are they *hyper*visible as members of their "category," but they are also completely *invisible* as individuals.

Think about a situation where you were virtually the only "something" in a group. (Many readers, sadly, will have had this experience.) It could be that you were the only woman, the only person of colour, the only openly gay or visibly disabled person in a group. How would you feel if someone turned to you and asked, "So, how do Aboriginal people feel about this issue?" or "Give us the disabled point of view." At that moment, you have ceased to be an individual; you are seen only as a representative of the group. That experience of *hyper*visibility and *in*visibility in the workplace is what tokenism feels like.

Simultaneous hypervisibility and invisibility have serious consequences. "The token does not have to work hard to have her presence noticed, but she does have to work hard to have her achievements noticed," Kanter writes. This can take an enormous emotional and psychological toll:

> Tokenism is stressful; the burdens carried by tokens in the management of social relations take a toll in psychological stress, even if the token succeeds in work

performance. Unsatisfactory social relationships, miserable self-imagery, frustrations from contradictory demands, inhibition of self-expression, feelings of inadequacy and self-hatred, all have been suggested as consequences of tokenism.[51]

Kanter argues that her theory of tokenism holds regardless of whether the tokens are male or female. However, men's and women's experiences as tokens are often very different. Subsequent research has suggested different experiences when women are the tokens in a largely male work world and when men are the tokens in a largely female occupation.[52]

One would expect that men entering "female" jobs would face discrimination similar to that faced by women entering male-dominated workplaces. In fact, studies suggest that the opposite is true. Men entering female-dominated occupations don't bump up against a glass ceiling; instead, they ride on what sociologist Christine Williams calls the **glass escalator**. That is, "the effects of sexism can outweigh the effects of tokenism when men enter non-traditional occupations," leading to preferential hiring and promotion. Williams conducted interviews with 76 men and 23 women in 4 fields—nursing, librarianship, elementary education, and social work. She found that men experienced *positive* discrimination when entering those fields and were promoted to managerial positions more rapidly and frequently. Men who do women's work, it appears, may earn less than men who work in predominantly male occupations, but in the same occupation they still earn more and are promoted faster than women are in the same occupation.[53]

Men did experience discrimination and stereotyping, especially in their dealings with the public. For example, male nurses faced a common stereotype that they were gay. Male librarians faced images of themselves as "wimpy" and asexual; male social workers were seen as "feminine" or "passive." One male librarian found that he had difficulty establishing enough credibility so that the public would accept him as the children's "storyteller." Ironically, though, Williams found that these negative stereotypes of men doing "women's work" actually added to the glass escalator effect "by pressuring men to move *out* of the most female-identified areas, and *up* to those regarded as more legitimate and prestigious for men."[54]

Williams concluded that men "take their gender privilege with them when they enter predominantly female occupations: this translates as an advantage in spite of their numerical rarity." When women are tokens, men retain their numerical superiority and are able to maintain their gender privilege by restricting a woman's entry, promotion, and experiences in the workplace. When men are tokens, they are welcomed into the profession and rise quickly in the hierarchy. "Regardless of the problems that might exist," writes Alfred Kadushin, "it is clear and undeniable that there is a considerable advantage in being a member of the male minority in any female profession."[55]

Sexual Harassment

Sexual harassment exists in various arenas (see the discussion on schools in Chapter 7). In the workplace, it has been a common challenge to processes of employment integration. Sexual harassment was first identified as a form of sex discrimination in the mid-1970s.

As women identified the problem, they began to litigate. In Canada, the landmark case, *Bell v. Ladas* (1980), involved two women who alleged that their boss, the owner of the Flaming Steer Steak House in Niagara Falls, Ontario, had sexually harassed them and eventually fired them when they refused his sexual advances. Though both complaints were dismissed, the case provided Canada with a definition of sexual harassment and

Sexual Harassment Hollywood Style

As discussed below, the galvanizing media moment for sexual harassment in North America was surely the 1991 Clarence Thomas hearings in which Anita Hill gave gripping and personal testimony about her harassment at the hands of the would-be US Supreme Court Justice. However, this was not the first time sexual harassment had entered the public eye. The 1980 Hollywood film *9 to 5*, starring Jane Fonda, Lily Tomlin, and Dolly Parton, features a sexist boss who treats his employees abysmally and who sexually harasses Dolly Parton's character. Through an insane set of plot twists, the three women end up kidnapping their boss and holding him captive while they implement a stunning array of workplace reforms that boost company productivity. The top-grossing comedy of 1980, *9 to 5* introduced sexual harassment to audiences unfamiliar with the concept in a comedic manner that nonetheless recognized the seriousness of the issue.

The next major film to deal with sexual harassment, 1994's *Disclosure*, took a dramatic and very different approach. In the film, Michael Douglas plays a software executive who finds out that his new boss is a woman with whom he has previously conducted an affair; she attempts to reinitiate the affair and, when rebuffed, accuses *him* of sexual harassment (a kind of quid pro quo harassment in itself). While the film draws attention to the possibility of men being sexually harassed, the situation depicted in the film is atypical, to say the least. On the other hand, that's precisely what one would expect of a sexual-harassment film that somehow managed to merit the label "hot-button date movie of the year!"

A more realistic portrayal of sexual harassment had to wait for the twenty-first century. The 2005 film *North Country*, starring Charlize Theron, recounted the true story of Lois Jenson, a mineworker in Eveleth, Minnesota, and her battles with a particularly vicious form of **hostile-environment sexual harassment**. Like the few other women mineworkers, Jenson, a single mother and daughter of a mineworker, was repeatedly threatened, humiliated, groped, stalked, and assaulted until she and 20 other women miners went to court in 1984 and eventually won a landmark sexual discrimination lawsuit—the first class-action sexual harassment case in US history. "It really was about getting a better paying job with benefits. I didn't go there to bring up issues. I just wanted to make a decent life for my family," Jenson said in an interview. Unlike *Disclosure*, the film presents sexual harassment unglamorized: not a "hot" thriller-style confrontation between two high-powered executives, but a grinding battle over power in the workplace.[58]

clarified that, as sex discrimination, it was prohibited. (Sexual harassment itself was not prohibited at that time.) In 1989, sexual harassment was defined by the Supreme Court of Canada in *Janzen v. Platy* as "unwelcome conduct of a sexual nature that detrimentally affects the work environment or leads to adverse job-related consequences for the victim of the harassment."[56]

In the US, sexual harassment was defined through litigation in 1976, several years before Canada's first case. Feminist lawyer Catharine MacKinnon argued that sexual harassment is a violation of Title VII of the 1964 Civil Rights Act, which makes employment discrimination unlawful. Sexual harassment, MacKinnon argued, discriminates against women based on their sex and creates a hostile environment for working women.[57]

Despite important litigation during the 1980s, it was not until the 1990s that the extent of the problem and its effects on women in the workplace began to be fully recognized in North America. In October of 1991, Anita Hill declared that she had been sexually harassed by candidate for the US Supreme Court Clarence Thomas when she worked for him at the EEOC, and suddenly millions sat transfixed before their television sets as Thomas's confirmation hearings took a dramatically different turn. Hill alleged that she had been subjected to unwanted sexual advances, vile pornographic attempts at humour, and constant descriptions of Thomas's sexual prowess—even after she had made it clear that she was not interested in dating her boss.

After the hearings, thousands of North American women came forward to describe experiences they had kept secret. An Angus Reid poll of October 1991 found that more than one-third of Canadian women who had worked outside the home reported that they had experienced sexual harassment on the job, while more than 90 per cent of women who responded to a "women in trades" survey reported being harassed. A 1993 Statistics Canada survey on violence against women found that 87 per cent of women reported having experienced some form of sexual harassment. Suddenly women had a name for what had been happening to them for decades in the workplace. By 1997, most North Americans had come to believe that Anita Hill had been telling the truth.[59]

Since that time, sexual harassment has become a major issue in North America. We have learned much, including that women are far more likely to experience sexual harassment in traditionally male-only jobs like mining, construction, transportation, or manufacturing than in professional and white-collar jobs. Clearly, when women try to "cross over" into male-dominated jobs, they are seen as invaders, and sexual harassment is a way to keep them out. In some cases, as in firefighting and emergency services, complaints of sexual harassment have become a virtual epidemic.

Sexual harassment takes many forms, from sexual assault to mocking innuendo. Typically, it takes one of two forms. Canadian law does not distinguish between them (US law does), but the distinctions between the two are useful for thinking about what sexual harassment really is. In the most obvious form, known as **quid pro quo sexual harassment**, a trade is offered: "sleep with me and you'll get promoted" or "don't sleep with me and you'll get fired." (For example, US Senator Robert Packwood's congressional career ended after nearly a dozen former female staffers accused him of unwanted kissing, fondling, attempts at sexual contact, and inappropriate remarks during his otherwise distinguished 27-year career.)

The (arguably more common) second form is more difficult to define. It is generally understood as the creation of a hostile environment, one in which women (or others) feel compromised, threatened, or unsafe. One well-known example involves the Richmond, BC fire department. Between 2000 and 2006, several female firefighters alleged sexual harassment at the hands of male co-workers. For example, one firefighter claimed that she had faced "a culture of systemic discrimination and harassment," including the display of hardcore pornography, the placing of a condom with a sexual slur on it in her locker, human feces in her boots, and tampering with her equipment. The slew of complaints included revelations that police had investigated the BC fire department over allegations of sexual abuse of minors at fire halls in the late 1970s (the allegations supported in sworn affidavits by retired firefighters). Small wonder that Vince Ready—the top arbitrator called in to mediate the complaints—referred in his report to the department's "juvenile and hostile" workplace culture. In 2012, allegations of a similar culture spread to policing. Janet Merlo, a former RCMP officer, alleged that she had endured 20 years of harassment at the hands of colleagues; by early 2015, almost 400 other women had come forward to support her claims.[60]

Whether sexual harassment manifests as quid pro quo or hostile environment, it's rarely about sexual attraction between employees. Of course, co-workers can become sexually attracted to one another; but when unwanted sexual attention becomes persistent or unwanted and one party suffers, the issue is power, not sex. In fact, few cases of sexual harassment have origins in sexual attraction. Sexual harassment is, in fact, more about repulsion. It is about making workers feel unwelcome in the workplace, reminding them that they do not belong because the workplace is men's space. As legal scholar Deborah Rhode writes, it is a "strategy of dominance and exclusion—a way of keeping women in their places and out of men's."[61]

Indeed, as we have seen, sexual harassment need not involve any pretence of sexual attraction whatsoever, nor need it be directed at women. It can also take the form experienced by an "older" Ohio firefighter who sued his department after complaining that mud-soiled adult diapers and pornographic materials depicting older men having gay sex had been placed in his gear. Here, the worker didn't "belong"—not because of sex, but because of age. What's more, one of the alleged harassers was female. Though most harassers remain male, this case shows us that sexual harassment is fundamentally about power, not sex.[62]

In March 1998, the US Supreme Court ruled that men can be the victims of sexual harassment by other men, even if all the men involved are heterosexual (for example, when a straight man persistently attacks another straight man's heterosexuality or masculinity). Between 1990 and 2008, the number of sexual harassment complaints to the EEOC by men doubled from 8 to 16 per cent. In one study, 43 per cent of women and 12 per cent of men said that they had experienced sexual harassment at work. While men—particularly in Canada—are still a minority of complainants, many no longer are willing to put up with being demeaned at work (what used to be considered just "initiation" or "fun"). Still, gender gaps remain: not only in the incidence of sexual harassment, but also in how it's perceived by men and women. For example, men—especially older men—are much more likely than are women—especially younger women—to think it is acceptable to tell a co-worker her outfit is sexy. Much, clearly, remains to be done.[63]

Sexual harassment in the workplace reminds women that they are still, after all their gains, "just women." As proof of this, consider that a US longitudinal study found that female managers are 137 per cent more likely to experience harassment than other female workers are. Such harassment, according to the author of the study, is a way to "strip them of their organizational power." Heather McLaughlin, a sociologist at the University of Minnesota and the study's primary investigator, argues, "Male co-workers, clients, and supervisors seem to be using harassment as an equalizer."[64]

Moreover, it works. Harassed women report increased stress, irritability, eating and sleeping disorders, and absenteeism. An Ontario study found that women lose jobs or quit them to escape harassment but still experienced unsatisfactory resolutions, deterioration of family relationships, loss of self-confidence, and increased substance use. At the societal level, sexual harassment stymies women's equality. Additionally, it is costly. Both private and public sectors lose millions because of absenteeism, reduced productivity, and high turnover of female employees.[65]

It is now virtually impossible for workers to go through their entire working lives without having colleagues, co-workers, or bosses who are different from them. What's more, women are no longer willing to tolerate being victimized because of their gender and many men, who have suffered from the "masculine testing ground" of workplace culture, are no longer willing to tolerate abuse. The integration of women into all-male workplaces may have sparked a great deal of sexual harassment, but in fighting against that harassment, women have improved the workplace for everyone.

Remedies for Workplace Inequality

Despite many positive changes throughout the past few decades, the workplace remains an unequal arena, plagued by persistent sex segregation, wage inequality, sex discrimination, and sexual harassment. How can the workplace become a more equal arena, a place in which women *and* men can earn a living to support themselves and their families and experience the satisfaction of efficacy and competence?

One arena of change is the application of existing law. In 1951, the United Nations' International Labour Organization passed Convention 100, which required signatories to "promote and . . . ensure the application to all workers of the principle of equal remuneration for men and women workers for work of equal value."[66] While most countries have ratified the convention, few have attempted to implement it. There are those who have had to grapple with two concepts under the rubric of **pay equity**: equal pay for equal work and equal pay for work of equal value. While the first is now non-controversial, the second has been far more difficult to grapple with. Yet the second concept is the most important, because, as we have seen, wage inequality emerges not just from paying men and women differently for doing exactly the same tasks but also from sex segregation. Sex segregation takes very similar skills and tasks and hives them off into "his" and "her" versions, allocating them "his" and "her" pay along the way. Therefore, to implement true pay equity, we must wrangle with the messy concept of work's value.

In the US, the 1963 Pay Equity Act prohibits employers from paying different wages to men and women who are doing the same or essentially the same work, while Title VII of the 1964 Civil Rights Act guarantees the absence of discrimination based on race, sex, or national origin. To date, 30 states have undertaken some form of pay equity reform, and about $527 million has been disbursed by 20 state governments to correct wage discrimination, but much more needs to be done. In Canada, pay equity laws have been passed by the federal and some provincial governments. In Quebec and Ontario, some public-sector women workers have received hundreds of millions of dollars in pay equity settlements.[67]

There have been similar developments in the private sector. In the 1990s, workers at Bell Canada launched a request for salary adjustments based on sex segregation. Most female workers were concentrated in areas called "clerical," while most male employees were "skilled craft and trade workers." Because of differential valuation of gendered jobs very similar in function and training requirements, women were heavily overrepresented at the bottom of the pay scale. In 2002, after a decade of wrangling, Bell reached a settlement with workers worth $178 million.[68]

In order to establish pay equity, one has to establish comparable worth. This requires a systematic review of jobs, ordering them on criteria of their complexity and the skills required so that they can be compared and allocating wages accordingly, on a more gender-equal basis. Not surprisingly, this has proved difficult and controversial. Pay equity schemes have therefore taken a very long time and have emphasized responding to complaints. Pay equity remains challenging to institute, despite its importance to wage equality.[69]

Workplace equality also requires interventionist strategies in hiring and promotion. Although in recent years the trend has been for the United States to abandon affirmative action policies, such policies were enormously effective in levelling the playing field. When Barbara Babcock, an assistant attorney general in the Carter administration, was asked how she felt about getting her position because she was a woman, she replied, "It's better than not getting your job because you're a woman." The abandonment of affirmative hiring policies delayed true equality for women and other marginalized groups in the US. Still there are other ways to intervene in hiring and promotion that do not raise the spectres of "affirmative action" or "quotas." Today, most **employment equity** policies emphasize creating attractive workplaces for diverse employees and creating the broadest possible candidate pool from which to draw the most qualified candidate.[70]

In both Canada and the US, discrimination on the grounds of pregnancy is prohibited, and employers may neither fire a woman for becoming pregnant nor fail to accommodate her pregnancy. However, once children are born, the issue becomes murkier. First, breastfeeding, universally recommended by the World Health Organization and pediatricians for healthy infant development, is protected in Canada but not necessarily in the US. In August 2009, the Ohio Supreme Court affirmed the right of Totes/Isotoner to fire an employee for taking breaks to pump breast milk for her five-month-old infant. The court ruled, "Breastfeeding discrimination does not constitute gender discrimination."[71]

If breastfeeding can make a woman a bad employee, the continuing demands of child care can at best put her on the **mommy track**—a subtle way that workplace gender inequality is reproduced. The mommy track refers to discrimination against those workers who happen to take time off to get pregnant, bear children, and raise them. Though as we have seen, it is illegal to discriminate against women because of pregnancy, women are often forced off the "fast track" (focused on career and promotion) onto the mommy track because of what appear to be the demands of the positions they occupy. Young attorneys, for example, must bill a certain number of hours per week; failing to do so will result in their being denied partnerships. Consequently, a woman faces a double bind: To the extent that she is a good mother, she cannot rise in the corporate world; to the extent that she rises in the corporate world, she is seen as a bad mother. Additionally, as we have seen, no matter her choices, being a woman with a family will have a significant effect on her employment and earnings through the lifespan.[72]

This being the case, the most obvious set of remedies to workplace inequality falls under the general heading of **family-friendly workplace policies**—reforms, including on-site child care, flexible working hours, and parental leave, that allow parents flexibility in balancing work and family life. Canada's workplaces are ahead of those of the US in some respects, principally because of the federal government's EI-funded parental benefit plan, which offers substantial parental leaves that can be accessed by parents of either sex. (The US is one of the few nations with no legal requirement for paid maternity leave—or paternity leave.) Still much remains to be done. Nonetheless, even the highest-pressure sectors perceive the importance of family-friendly policies in order to "[retain] the high-performing employees we rely on to serve the needs of our clients," in the words of Karen Wensley of Ernst & Young. The global accounting powerhouse won a 2009 award for its progressive policies on leave and flexible hours and vowed to stay the course despite tough economic times—and apparently, it did. In 2014, the company marked its ninth straight year in the Top Ten of *Working Mother*'s best companies list.[73]

In the end, workplace equality will require significant ideological and structural change—both in the way we work and in the way we live. Structural change is as important as replacing tired clichés. As sociologists Ronnie Steinberg and A. Cook write:

> Equal employment requires more than guaranteeing the right to equal access, the right to equal opportunity for promotion, or the right to equal pay for equal, or even comparable worth. Additionally, it warrants a broader policy orientation encompassing social welfare laws that assume equality within the family; widespread use of alternative work arrangements that accommodate the complexities of family life within two-earner families; and a rejuvenated union movement, with female leadership more active at work sites in defending the rights of women workers. Social welfare laws, family policy, and government services must create incentives toward a more equal division of responsibilities for family and household tasks between men and women. Increasing child care facilities, as well as maintaining programs to care for the elderly, would help alleviate some of the more pressing demands made on adults in families. . . . This also means that tax policy, social security laws, and pension programs must be amended to make government incentives to family life consistent with a family structure in which husbands and wives are equal partners.[74]

Another sociologist, Karen Oppenheim Mason, writes that gender inequality in the workplace is likely to remain "unless major revisions occur in our ideology of gender and the division of labour between the sexes. Ultimately," she concludes, "job segregation is just a part of the generally separate (and unequal) lives that women and men in our society lead, and, unless the overall separateness is ended, the separateness within the occupational system is unlikely to end either."[75]

Despite enormous and persistent gender inequality in the workplace, women are there to stay. Women work for the same reasons that men work—to support themselves and their families, to experience the sense of accomplishment, efficacy, and competence that comes from succeeding in the workplace. Both men and women work because they want to and because they have to. Indeed, women's entry into paid employment is a long-term trend. During the economic downturn, more than two-thirds of Canadian jobs lost were jobs filled by men, while in the US 82 per cent of job losses affected men. This caused writers to speak of a "he-cession" or "man-cession." Many of the jobs lost were in well-paid areas like finance, manufacturing, and construction. Ironically, the poorer-paid, female-dominated occupations have proved much more resilient. Many women have found themselves breadwinners, albeit sometimes badly paid ones![76]

The struggle to balance work and family is even more acute in such situations. "Our jobs don't make room for family obligations," writes Stephanie Coontz. "To correct this imbalance, we need to reorganize work to make it more compatible with family life." That is to say, we will never find that balance if all we do is tinker with our family relationships, better organize our time, outsource family work, juggle, or opt out. It will be possible only when the workplace changes as well. With an overwhelming number of young women workers viewing workplace equality as a "stalled revolution," the time for such changes is now.[77]

Summary

While every society has developed a gendered division of labour, the public–private divide so familiar to North Americans was a creation of the nineteenth (or even more the twentieth) century. Still, the most enduring legacy of that same period is the enormous shift in the composition of the paid labour force; while in 1900 only a minority of women were in the labour force, by 2000 the majority were. Even mothers of young children are now likely to be employed.

However, there is still a persistent gap between male and female employment rates, both in North America and globally. This gap disadvantages women and has broad economic and social effects. Both in North America (in the wake of a recent "withdrawal" of women from the work force) and globally, there have been discussions of the urgency of increasing female workforce participation.

Gender ideologies persist in the area of employment as elsewhere. In particular, the male breadwinner/female housewife model still influences everything from how we evaluate a man's masculinity to the "validity" of a woman's paid employment.

Sex discrimination has been the greatest obstacle to the integration of women into paid employment. While few jobs can actually be said to require one sex or the other, many jobs have had requirements (such as height restrictions) that deliberately or unconsciously have excluded women. As a result, more stringent requirements now require that in order to be legal, discrimination must be the result of a bona fide occupational requirement (BFOR) related to the demands of a job. In the US, Hooters restaurant was able to argue that female sexuality was a BFOR for its servers.

More subtle than sex discrimination, sex segregation concentrates men and women in different occupations. Vertical segregation concentrates women and men in different categories within the same field, while horizontal segregation concentrates them in roughly similar categories within different fields. Sex segregation is so pervasive that we hardly notice it. It matters because we allocate value and pay differentially and preferentially to tasks we associate with men and masculinity. Socialization is not sufficient to explain sex segregation; nor is the explanation of socialization able to explain why segregation produces a wage gap.

While the wage gap has closed considerably throughout the past 25 years, it remains significant. Moreover, since 2000, the gap has remained stable. Its causes are childbearing/child rearing, discrimination, and sex segregation, all of which interact in complicated ways.

Given the importance of discrimination and segregation to the wage gap, workplace integration is surely a key remedy. Yet there are significant challenges to such integration. The first is a form of gender discrimination that emerges within integrated workplaces. Women find their mobility within organizations limited by the sticky floor and glass ceiling. The glass ceiling consists of many practices and biases, usually informal or even unconscious, that limit women's access to promotion. Despite consensus on the existence and damaging effects of the glass ceiling, however, some commentators feel that men are really the ones trapped in a glass cellar of dangerous and dirty work. While there is no doubt that men are disproportionately clustered in the most dangerous occupations, this is not simply the result of discrimination in a way comparable to the glass ceiling effect.

As workplaces are integrated, women (and minorities) within previously male-dominated workplaces are often treated as tokens—representatives of their "group" who are both invisible (as individuals) and hypervisible (as members of a minority group within the organization). Tokenism can be stressful for individuals and fails to produce true workplace integration. Interestingly, men in female-dominated workplaces, it has been argued, do not experience classic tokenism; instead, they are more likely to be placed onto a glass escalator, to be preferred in hiring and promotion.

Another common response to workplace integration has been sexual harassment. Since the 1970s, in both Canada and the US, sexual harassment has been legally defined and prosecuted. In the 1990s, largely because of attention paid to the Anita Hill-Clarence Thomas hearings, many women came forward to share experiences of harassment in their workplaces. Two forms of harassment were legally distinguished in the US: quid pro quo and hostile environment. Neither form is fundamentally about sexual attraction; instead, both aim at asserting power. Not surprisingly, therefore, sexual harassment can involve men as victims, as well as involving perpetrators who are not sexually oriented toward their victims.

Remedies for workplace inequality include pay equity, interventionist hiring and promotion strategies, and family-friendly workplace policies that are the opposite of the mommy track. Today, the emphasis is less upon workplace policies as "women's issues" and more on the creation of better workplaces for men and women. In this way, the long struggle of women for justice within paid employment can be seen to be a benefit to all workers.

Questions for Critical Thinking

1. What do you believe are the causes and implications of the long-term trend to greater workforce participation by women?
2. Do you think that governments should encourage more women to participate in the workforce, or should this be a private decision for women themselves?
3. Can you think of fields or workplaces in your community in which there are examples of horizontal and/or vertical segregation? What about your university or post-secondary institution?
4. Does the glass cellar exist? Why are men overrepresented in dirty, dangerous jobs? Will this always be the case?
5. Does sexual harassment law make it impossible to begin a sexual relationship with a co-worker? Where is the line between sexual attraction and sexual harassment?
6. Which needs to change more to produce work–family balance: work or family?

Key Terms

bona fide occupational requirement (BFOR)
deviance neutralization
emotional labour
employment equity
equality
equity
family wage
family-friendly workplace policies
glass ceiling
glass cellar
glass escalator
horizontal segregation
hostile-environment sexual harassment

labour force participation
male breadwinner/female housewife model
Meiorin test
mommy track
pay equity
pin money
precarious employment
quid pro quo sexual harassment
sticky floor
tokenism
vertical segregation
wage gap

9

The Gendered Media
Difference and Domination, Glamourized and Contested

Mass media schools the young in the values of patriarchal masculinity. On mass media screens today, whether television or movies, mainstream work is usually portrayed as irrelevant, money is God, and the outlaw guy who breaks the rules prevails.

—bell hooks, *We Real Cool: Black Men and Masculinity*

The media are a gendered institution, as bell hooks suggests above. That means, simply, that they, like all other institutions (e.g., schools, churches, families, corporations, or states), *reflect* existing gender differences and gender inequalities, *construct* gender differences, and *reproduce* gender inequality by making those differences seem "natural" and not socially produced in the first place.

Often, media *reflect* existing gender differences and inequalities by targeting different groups of consumers with different messages that assume prior existing differences. Often, women and men don't use or consume the same media—there are women's magazines and men's magazines, chick flicks and action movies, **chick lit** and **lad lit**, pornography and romance novels, guy video games and girl video games, blogs and 'zines—and, of course, advertising intricately connected to each of these different formats. There are also multiple medias based on race, class, ethnicity, and age. Each of these genres *constructs* gender by offering us models of what manhood or womanhood might be.

The gendered media are part of a gigantic cultural apparatus that *reproduces* gender inequality by making it appear that such inequality is the natural result of existing gender differences. First, the media create the differences; then, the media tell us that the inequality is the natural result of those differences.

On the other hand, media are frequently the vehicle for contestation of gender. What's more, we are living through a fundamental transformation of media. New media, discussed below, may be particularly hospitable to changing ideas about gender—while also enabling gender intensification and even gender-based victimization. Therefore, we cannot simply reduce "the media" to a single thing; media may be gendered but in complex ways.

The Media as Socializing Institution

That the media are a primary institution of socialization is an essential starting point in our analysis. However, media are quite unlike other social institutions in some ways. *First*, the media are not based on personal interaction (think of school, religion, and family) and direct communication; as is obvious, they are *mediated* communication. Until recently, their influence seemed to go in one direction only; as a result many of the debates about the effects of the media present the media as the sole actor in the drama—and the consumer, namely us, as passive sponges who uncritically soak up all the messages we're fed.

However, we are not blank slates upon which institutions imprint a uniform cultural code. Were that true, how could we explain the massive diversity we observe around us? We bring ourselves, our identities, and our differences to our encounters with various media; and we can take from them a large variety of messages. We also need to consider the way we act on the media, the way we consume it actively, creatively, and often even rebelliously. Increasingly, as we will see in this chapter, we have the ability to "talk back" to media in ways that complicate the producer–consumer relationship. Increasingly, media consumers may be co-creators.

The media are also not one thing. As the plural title ("media") suggests, this institution comprises many forms of communication, types of ownership, ideological stances, and goals. Therefore, a *second* distinction between the media and other primary socializing institutions is that, in some ways, the media are considerably more complex. While complex and contradictory in their messages, schools have a curriculum, religions have core texts and institutions, and families have their own ideological foundation. The media, in contrast, are comparatively multi-various and lawless.

The type of medium is important. In his classic 1964 study *Understanding Media*, the great Canadian philosopher Marshall McLuhan, father of media studies, famously claimed, "the medium is the message." What he meant is that the medium of communication inevitably affects the user and the nature of the messages received. He urged us to think about not only what we usually think of as the *message* (content) but also how the *medium* (form or technology) affects us.[1] Taking this lesson to heart, we can't talk about a message received from television as though it's the same as information received in a conversation with a friend or from print or from an Internet blog or a text message. In each case, the nature of the medium is a critical part of what we need to consider.

We also need to consider that even each medium contains within it an immense number of variations. So when we talk about the message that "the movies" carry about gender, we are obviously engaged in gross oversimplification. Are we talking about Canadian movies? American movies? American *Indie* movies? Hollywood movies? Movies directed by Steven Spielberg or movies directed by Ingmar Bergman? Good media studies, therefore, are very particular in their analyses and careful in their claims.

The question is never whether or not the media do such and such, but rather *how* the media and their consumers interact to create the varying meanings that derive from our interactions with those media. When we analyze the media in relation to gender, there is much to consider, but there are two key themes that we need to ponder. First is **participation**. How does gender affect the use of media (and employment within them)? The second issue is **representation**. This includes both *whether* groups are represented and *how* they are represented. In what follows, we look at these issues, studying first so-called "old" media, the media in existence before the advent of the Internet; we then look at "new" media and evolving definitions of gender in the digital world.

His and Hers: Television and Film

As the media are saturated with gender, we are saturated with the media. In 1949, Canada had only 3,600 television sets. Today, there are more television sets in Canada than there are people. In Canada, 96.5 per cent of households have television and 92.1 per cent subscribe to television services. Though gradually being supplanted by the Internet (as discussed below), TV remains omnipresent. More Canadian households still subscribe to television services, for example, than have home Internet (89 per cent of households) or gaming consoles (48 per cent). While the death of television has long been predicted, almost half of Canadians report that television is "fundamental to their existence," while more than half feel a sense of loss when their favourite shows end for the season. This is ample testimony to the fundamental reach of the media and the transformation of television (in the second half of the twentieth century) from novelty to necessity.[2]

Canadians adults aged 18–55 average about 28.5 hours per week of television watching, while Americans watch more than 36 hours per week. Teenagers in both countries watch significantly less than adults do. There has been an overall decline in viewing since 1995, but the decline varies by age, gender, income, and education. More educated and wealthier people watch less TV; they are more likely to have used the Internet within the past day than to have watched television. Older Canadians watch significantly more television than younger ones (which is also true in the US). Women watch more television overall than do men. Young men watch the least, while women 60 and older watch the most.

There is, however, evidence of gender convergence in viewing time. In 1995, women watched on average five hours more per week than men did. Today, the gap is closer to two hours. If men's television gaming time (through connected consoles) is factored in, the gap shrinks further. Despite these differences, one is left with the conclusion that television remains pervasive; average viewing remains high, regardless of group variation.[3] Moreover, while restaurants and bars once were a place to socialize away from "screen time," they (and even dentist's offices) now offer TVs mounted on the walls so we can watch, even when we aren't "really" watching.

While the decline of the cinema has often been proclaimed, it should be remembered that some of what Canadians are doing when they watch television or stream content from the Internet is actually movie-watching. At one time, those who wanted to watch movies went to the cinema. From the 1970s on, it became possible to watch movies in one's own home (using now-quaint technologies such as the videocassette). Today, Canadians watch a lot of movies, but 81 per cent of the time they watch at home; only 16 per cent of movie-watching goes on in cinemas. In Canada, more than 60 per cent of domestic movie tickets are purchased by "frequent moviegoers," who are only 16 per cent of the North American population. Frequent moviegoers tend to be young (13–24); and interestingly, women and visible minorities are overrepresented among North American moviegoers.[4] Therefore, we can say that women watch more television *and* attend more movies than do men. It is also safe to say that broadcast/cable television, content streaming, and the movie industry are all in robust good health, and still constitute the most important form of media, at least in terms of the amount of time we dedicate to them.

At one time, there may have been relatively tidy boundaries between "his" and "her" television and film; the stereotypical division would be between sports and news viewing (male) and soap operas (female), and action films and romances. However, that neat division has been muddy for some time and may be gone forever.

At TV's dawn and for decades thereafter, all gender stereotypes were fully in place. Male characters were courageous and active, fighting crime and solving mysteries. Female characters were caring but befuddled housewives who occasionally ventured outside the home only to realize that they really loved baking cookies. These stereotypes are important, especially because much research in the past found that increased exposure to images of inequality often can contribute to more stereotypical ideas; and the more television you watch, the more gender-stereotypic are your gender attitudes likely to be.[5]

The 1950s prototypical female character, Lucy (the inimitable Lucille Ball), spent most of her time devising strategies to get out of the house, but her harebrained adventures always ended with her return to husband Ricky's admonishingly forgiving domestic embrace. Likewise, Alice Cramden of *The Honeymooners* found that by staying home she really was the authority figure.[6] (Though her husband might brandish his fist at her and threaten to send her "to the moon," he never went through with it, unlike some husbands of the time.)

This all changed in 1970, when *The Mary Tyler Moore Show* presented Mary Richards, a go-getter on the job and unwilling to sacrifice career for family life. She wanted it all. It was the first time that a single "career woman" had been the lead character in a TV show—and audiences loved it. Though Mary Richards may appear to modern viewers as a kind of harmless Mary Poppins type, her character opened the door for female characters who were less subservient to men (*Rhoda* and *Cagney and Lacey*); more assertive in the workplace as well as at home (*Roseanne*); not even especially "nice" (*Murphy Brown*); and, finally, gay (*Ellen*).

In fact, television in the 1970s and 1980s transformed itself significantly, largely in response to feminist and visible-minority media critics who began to point out just how separate and unequal the world of the small screen actually was. (The creator of *Cagney and Lacey* got the idea when his girlfriend told him there were no female "buddy" shows.) Critics highlighted:

- how women and men watched (or were presumed to watch) different shows;
- how scheduling "women's" programming during the day presumed that all women were at home ("housewives");
- how news anchors were always white males, while women got stuck in social reporting and/or the role of "weather girl";
- how seldom ethnic minorities were represented;
- how stereotypical the representation of racialized people was when it did occur; and finally
- how, in general, television characters fully reproduced gender and racial stereotypes.

Networks responded, albeit slowly, with the "ensemble" cast, including several female and minority characters, which became a new television norm by the mid-1980s. By the 1990s, ensembles could even be largely non-white; *North of Sixty* was a breakthrough program for Canada, offering the first substantial depiction of Aboriginal people on Canadian television.

The ensemble prime-time drama—like *LA Law* in the 1980s, *ER* and *NYPD Blue* in the 1990s, and in the 2000s, *DaVinci's Inquest, Lost, Grey's Anatomy,* and *Under the Dome*—developed far more racial and gender diversity than any other TV shows in history. (In fact, *Under the Dome*'s casting altered the characterization of Stephen King's all-white Maine story to make it more reflective of a typical American community.)

Recent reviews of Hollywood diversity conclude that while women and ethnic minorities are far from appropriate levels of representation, things are changing. The most careful annual study of diversity in TV and film, UCLA's *Hollywood Diversity Report* tracks changes in TV and film. The latest iteration of the report found that the underrepresentation factor for minorities in lead roles changed from 4:1 to 2:1 in two years—a dramatic rate of change, if it turns out to be sustained. Overall, cast diversity is increasing, but there are interesting variations. For example, women (a bare majority of the US population) are 48.6 per cent of the leads in broadcast TV but only 37.1 per cent of leads on cable TV. For minorities, by contrast, cable is more welcoming than broadcast, though the underrepresentation of visible minorities remains worse than for women. Visible minorities, 37.4 per cent of the US population (and to be the majority by mid-century), receive only 6.5 per cent of lead roles on broadcast TV but 19.3 per cent of lead roles in cable shows.[7]

When the authors of the report coded 536 characters in 16 American TV shows selected for being "diverse," they found that 63.1 per cent of characters were white: a number in keeping with their proportion of the overall population. Black characters were overrepresented on such programs (17.4 per cent of characters versus 13.4 per cent of the population), as were Asian characters (10.3 per cent of characters and about 5 per cent of the population), while Latino characters were greatly underrepresented (5.6 per cent of characters, versus 17.1 per cent of the population). Also underrepresented were Native Americans. Remembering that these programs were selected for their diversity, the continuing issues with representation are noteworthy.[8]

Still, the ethnic diversity of characters is increasing, gender and racial stereotypes are not a feature of "diverse" programs, and, importantly, such programs appear to be highly popular with viewers. *Empire*, for example, has done exceptionally well with all groups, and is "literally the equivalent of a Super Bowl" among African-American women.[9] Moreover, on today's television programs, women appear to be nearly as at home in the workplace as they are at home, and virtually all prime-time dramas include female doctors, lawyers, judges, and cops.

LGBTQ and ability diversity on television and in film has been a longer time coming than ethnic and male/female diversity. People often point to *Ellen*, but it's worth noting that Ellen was a closeted character until the end of the series. Really, not until the late 1990s with NBC's *Will & Grace* was there a program with openly gay main characters. After 2000, however, the number of LGBTQ characters began to increase significantly. GLAAD, an organization that began tracking LGBT representation twenty years ago, issues an annual report on the topic. According to GLAAD, 96 per cent of regular characters on prime-time scripted television are straight, 4 per cent LGBT. This may be close to the representation of LGBT people in the US population; whatever the case, it represents significant change. Increasingly too, gay characters are now often depicted "beyond the coming-out narrative." That is, they are characters who happen to be gay rather than characters whose sexuality is the reason for their presence.[10]

Still, GLAAD identifies persistent stereotypes in relation to some groups. For example, trans characters are becoming more common. Though there are no regular trans characters on traditional prime-time network broadcast programming, there are on cable (4 per cent). Nevertheless, transmen remain underrepresented, and transwomen are still portrayed as sex workers (without a context for why they might be forced into sex work), as tragic victims, and as psychologically disturbed or even psychopathic. Given that 84 per cent of Americans do not know any trans people and therefore get their information about trans people entirely from the media, such stereotypical representations are even more problematic. Bisexual characters, too, are stereotyped as untrustworthy, immoral, manipulative, and self-destructive. Still, the group most underrepresented is people with disabilities. According to GLAAD, people with disabilities make up 12 per cent of the American population, while less than 1 per cent of regular series' characters have disabilities.[11]

Movies are arguably even less representative. If we consider the 10 top-grossing North American films of 2015, seven had male lead characters, while only three had female leads (and two of those—Disney's *Cinderella* and *Inside Out*—were aimed at children). Hollywood actor Geena Davis has long advocated on behalf of greater (and more realistic) representation of women. Her institute, founded in 2006, commissions research reports, the most recent released in 2014. That study moved beyond Hollywood to examine the representation of women in a sample of 120 popular films in the most profitable global markets: Australia, Brazil, China, France, Germany, India, Japan, Russia, South Korea, and the United Kingdom. Only films with the equivalent of PG-13 or lower (age ratings) were examined, because part of the purpose of the study was to examine the kinds of gender representations available to children. About 6,000 speaking characters were identified in these films; only 30.9 per cent were female. The UK, Brazil, and Korea had the highest number of female characters, India and the US the lowest. Across the sample, only 7 per cent of films were directed by women, but Chinese and UK films had much higher representation of female directors.[12]

When the *nature* of the portrayals of women was pondered, the report found that women, unlike men, clustered in certain age categories; fully 60 per cent of all speaking female characters were 21–39. Women were much more likely than men to be depicted as in this age group, and much *less* likely to be depicted as middle-aged (40–64). This has obvious implications, because middle-aged characters are more likely to have "occupations with clout," and younger ones more likely to be sexualized. More than half of the characters (57.2 per cent) were white, 33 per cent Asian. Females were more than twice as likely as males to be depicted in revealing clothing or partially/fully nude; comments about appearance were directed at female characters five times as often as at male characters. While just under 16 per cent of male characters were depicted as thin, more than a third of all female characters were; only about 2 per cent of male characters were referred to as attractive, while more than 16 per cent of female characters were referred to as attractive or beautiful. Women were much less likely than men to be depicted as employed, and when they *were* employed, they were much less likely to be in positions of power, and were depicted most often in stereotypical occupations, particularly nursing and teaching. Interestingly, however, women were 11 per cent of criminal characters, making them more likely to be depicted as criminals than as judges, lawyers, or professors.[13]

When we turn from representation to participation—when we go behind the screen to see who is writing, producing, and directing film and television—diversity lessens. The production end of film and television is exceedingly male and white. Minorities are underrepresented by a factor of 2:1 as film directors and 3:1 as film writers; women are underrepresented by a factor of 8:1 and 4:1 in these same categories. All (100 per cent of them!) film studio heads are male, and 94 per cent are white. Within senior management, 83 per cent are male and 92 per cent are white. So it continues, throughout the whole range of programming. While we may applaud the increasing diversity of representations in television and film, we cannot forget that the production of television and film remains, to a great degree, a white man's game. This is important from an employment equity perspective, of course. In fact, the US Equal Employment Opportunity Commission (EEOC) announced in October 2015 that it was beginning an investigation into discrimination against female film and TV directors. The participation of women, visible minorities, Aboriginal people, the disabled, and LGBTQ individuals in production, writing, and direction is critical. Only by increasing diversity among the storytellers—and the decision makers who decide what to produce and how to produce it—will the stories we watch begin to reflect our communities in all of their variation and colour.[14]

There are still many barriers to full representation and participation in film and television; these media remain deeply gendered. Nevertheless, as we have seen, there are also signs that the screen world is changing. In addition to the increasing diversity of television and film representations, what we watch is increasingly converging. The top regularly scheduled English-language shows in Canada in 2014 were *Game of Thrones*, two iterations of the *Survivor* franchise, *Hockey Night in Canada*, *NCIS*, and *Under the Dome*. Most popular specials were sports events and awards ceremonies. Men and women both watch all of these programs. However, there is still significant variation in viewership by gender for specific programs. In the US, for example, viewership for NFL regular-season games in the 2013 season was 65 per cent male, 35 per cent female. Programs such as *Army Wives*, *The Bachelor*, and *Conveyor Belt of Love* have a viewership at least two-thirds female (and in the case of *Army Wives*, 83 per cent female). In addition, Spike TV, though it claims a large female viewership, offers a highly stereotyped, violent version of "TV for men."[15]

So far we've talked about gender on television and film only in terms of adults, and in Canada, adults indeed do watch more television than children or adolescents. Currently, about 71 per cent of US children and fewer than half of Canadian children have televisions in their bedrooms, despite the stance of the Canadian Paediatric Society, which says no children should have gaming equipment, televisions, or computers in their bedrooms. (A television in a child's bedroom is an independent predictor of obesity and a detriment to school performance.) Canadian children watch an average of 20 hours of television per week (compared to more than 24 in the US); by the time a Canadian child graduates from high school, he or she may have spent more hours watching television than going to school. Television watching peaks in the pre-teen years, but even infant television watching is increasing (again, despite pediatricians' concerns about the effect of television on the very young).[16] For many children, this is one of their largest commitments of waking time; for parents, it often serves as a built-in baby sitter.

Television, films, and other media also habitually portray violence. In the most systematic US investigation, the National Television Violence Study, four teams of researchers found that violence is ubiquitous (61 per cent of all shows contained some violence) and typically perpetrated by a white male, who goes unpunished and shows little remorse. The violence is generally presented as justified; nearly one-half of the shows presented it in a humorous way; and "the serious and long-lasting consequences of violence are frequently ignored." Numerous studies since the 1980s have documented the causal relationship between viewing media violence and increased aggression (verbal and physical) in children. In the 1990s and 2000s, scholars expanded their analysis from television to all forms of electronic media. Today, American children and adolescents spend an average of seven hours per day engaged with such media, and after hundreds of studies, a clear consensus is emerging; media violence has an effect on children and youth. Overall, it appears to desensitize them to violence, increase their aggression, and diminish their empathy.[17]

Canadian programming is often seen as less violent than that of the US. However, this may not matter much to what children see, given that much of our programming is of American origin. Disturbingly, violence on Canadian TV has been steadily increasing since 1993, despite public concern about the issue. Moreover, private networks' programming (much of it, of course, from the US) contains three times the number of violent incidents seen on programs delivered by our public broadcaster.[18]

The presentation of gender roles on children's television shows has been, at least until recently, quite similar to that of children's readers, the playground, and the schools. Boys are the centrepiece of a story; they do things and occupy the valued roles. While iconic Canadian serials *The Friendly Giant* and *Mr Dressup* never presented harmful stereotypes, and offered gentler, slower fare to young viewers, they were still dominated by male characters; it's difficult to imagine female characters becoming as successful or as beloved of both girls and boys. In most American children's shows, girls serve as a backdrop, are helpful and caring, and occupy the less-valued roles. Even *Sesame Street*, hailed as a breakthrough in enjoyable educational programming, presented far more male characters than female.

The CRTC's 1990 study of television representations found that cartoons presented the most gender-imbalanced picture, with fewer than 25 per cent of depicted characters female. In children's live-action shows, slightly more than a third of all characters were female, in line with adult programming. According to the CRTC study, female characters were not only scarcer but younger than males; were more likely to be married; were often seen in a family setting; were shown with children and caring for children; and performed housework. Male characters had paid employment, and both committed and were victims of violence. Although this study is now 25 years old, a 2008 study conducted in 24 countries (including Canada) found much the same pattern:

- There were twice as many male characters as female ones (far more when non-human characters are included).
- There was a dominance of whiteness among all characters.
- There was a gross overrepresentation of blond and redheaded female characters.
- There was a complete absence of overweight girls (not boys, however).
- There was, in general, "a clear under-representation and stereotyped depiction of female characters worldwide."

Despite the strong female characters and ethnic diversity of *Dora the Explorer*, *Rugrats*, and *That's So Raven*, there is much to be done.[19]

Ponies, Bronies, and Gender Fluidity: *My Little Pony* and the Magic of Fandom

As discussed in Chapter 6, children's toys underwent dramatic gender intensification during the twentieth century. After the brief questioning interlude of the 1970s, the "pinkification" of girlhood (and the corresponding "mechanization" of boyhood) resumed with a vengeance. Nowhere was this more visible than in the success of two toy lines, My Little Pony (MLP) and Transformers. Both toys were launched in the first half of the 1980s; both quickly launched corresponding television series (and eventually movie releases); and both were owned by Hasbro, an American toymaker. Throughout the 1990s and the first decade of the twenty-first century, both became highly successful properties for Hasbro. Additionally, both remained clearly gendered. Transformers were dark, hulking, transforming alien robots organized into competing factions; Ponies were, well, *ponies*, except that they came in pastel colours, equipped with flowing, brushable manes and tails, and varied "cutie marks" on their flanks. Unlike real ponies, MLPs were also cooperative, caring, and dedicated to friendship. In short, they were clearly *for girls*, both because they were horses (animals increasingly associated with women and girls rather than with men) and because they were unrelentingly expressive and rooted in "an ethic of care."

Then something happened. In 2010, Hasbro launched a new "generation" of ponies and a new TV series, *Friendship is Magic*. Within days of the pilot, numerous adults, many of them male, had become fans of the series. Image-board website 4chan (where users can post visual content and comments) quickly coined the term **Brony** (a compound of "bro" and "pony"). Enabled by the rapid community-building and anonymity of the Internet, the Brony fandom spread quickly, as can be seen from the user-generated graph shown as Figure 9.1. (While the data should be taken with a grain of salt, of course, the graph is still revealing.)

The Brony phenomenon was predicted to be a "flash in the pan"; but more than five years later, it is going strong. There are Brony conventions, Brony merchandise, and a much-discussed Brony documentary film (2012's *Bronies: The Extremely Unexpected Adult Fans of My Little Pony*). In fact, the web presence of MLP and the Brony fandom has expanded rather than fizzled.

What does it all mean? First, Bronyism is an object lesson in the difference between old and new media (discussed further starting on p. 257). In the "old" days, those who produced television shows targeted them to "appropriate" audiences with relative efficacy. There may always have been adults who watched children's shows, but they kept it quiet. There was no way to unite with like-minded others, no way to form a fandom or "community of believers" as is so common today. The Internet has made possible the coalescing of such fandoms and communities in the face of overall societal disapproval.

Second, and closely related to the foregoing, Bronyism suggests the increased degree of gender fluidity available in the new media environment. The male fandom that erupted in the show's first season surprised everyone, including creator Lauren Faust. Bronies and

continued

POSTS PER DAY IN PONY THREADS

Data compiled by knowyourmeme.com

Growth of the MLP fandom tracked by posts, October 2010 to February 2011. Knowyourmeme.com

scholars alike have made connections between the show and new forms of masculinity that privilege cooperation over competition and friendship over violence. In the documentary *Bronies*, men talk about the values and life lessons they draw from the ponies, applying those values and lessons to issues in their own lives, from military work to thriving with a disability.

Bronies have had their detractors on all sides. First, boys who like ponies have been bullied and victimized, demonstrating that hypervigilant policing of masculinity is hardly a thing of the past. There have been numerous reported incidents of bullying of boys, but one 2014 incident is most notorious: an 11-year-old North Carolina boy attempted suicide after repeatedly enduring homophobic and gendered slurs over his interest in MLP. Fortunately, he survived, though not without injury. When the incident was reported, the Brony community rallied around him and his family. A second aspersion has been cast on Bronies, not surprisingly; as grown and nearly grown men interested in a program and product targeted to young girls, Bronies are "creepy" and sexually deviant. The existence of explicit and "dark" MLP fan fictions and fan art seems to bear this out. Defenders of bronies point to "Rule 34" of the Internet ("if it exists, there is porn of it"), arguing that there is nothing distinct, in this regard, about the MLP fandom.

While the debate about Bronyism (and, often, vicious harassment of bronies) continues on the Internet, one thing is certain. The Brony phenomenon demonstrates both increasing gender fluidity (boys and men can and do like "girl things!") and the persistence and power of boundaries between appropriately "masculine" behaviour and the world of girls and women.[20]

As we have seen, much television programming and many movies offer up a highly gendered vision of the world that, according to many commentators, is out of step with the realities of contemporary North America. Perhaps that's understandable. After all, we look at moving images primarily to be entertained, and not always to receive a crystal-clear reflection of the world around us. Nevertheless, the power of these representations to construct our desires and realities means that depictions of gender on television and in film should be taken seriously. In the 1950s, for example, the *Father Knows Best* family was no more everyone's reality than it is now. Regardless, audiences responded to that representation and made it their own, modelling their own aspirations and realities upon what they saw on screen. Over time, the picture of "family" represented in that show and others became what people saw as the "traditional" family. That doesn't mean, of course, that TV and film imprint themselves on us as if we were blank slates. However, their power is undeniable.

Gender in Advertising

When we discuss gender on TV, we have to remember that television isn't just about programming. On television and in other media, North Americans of all ages see hundreds of advertisements every day. Market research demonstrates that television commercials in particular are highly influential over both adult and child consumers, but advertising is present across various forms of media both new and old.

Consumption is one of the most valued activities in North American society. By linking consumption to success—understood in gendered terms—advertisements make powerful arguments about gender. Advertisements are also one of the key arenas for the circulation of ideas about what kind of male and female bodies are normal, desirable, and beautiful. Not surprisingly, most of these ideas and arguments tend toward gendered stereotype. Perhaps this is the reason that television watching tends to be associated with attitudes that are more rigid toward gender!

Advertising for adults is no less stereotyped. A full discussion of gender in advertising would take at least the entirety of this chapter, but the basic outlines are well documented. (If you want an almost infinite catalogue of examples, see cultural anthropologist Scott Lukas's wonderful website GenderAds.com.) The role of women as decoration in commercials is almost too obvious to mention. Depictions of women's bodies are used to sell a panoply of products. Despite the fact that there are more men (overall) in commercials than there are women, women's bodies, often apparently nude or seminude, appear much more frequently than do men's bodies. Moreover, in all forms of advertising, women are much more frequently objectified by being reduced to specific body parts (especially mouths, buttocks, legs, genitals, or breasts) or compared to animals or inanimate objects. Lukas's GenderAds site contains copious examples of this kind of objectification. Men's *voices*, however, are more frequently present, often heard in voiceovers (except in commercials for feminine hygiene). Accordingly, advertising constructs men and women in relatively distinct ways, with men more likely to be associated with authority and women with beauty. Objectification of men, however, is becoming increasingly prevalent.[21]

Disabled people, people with visible body fat, men and women of colour, and older women are rarely seen in advertising unless it specifically targets "their demographic." For many years, disabled people were either invisible or restricted to "pitiable" representations usually designed to elicit donations to charity. After 1980, this began to change. Additionally, since 2000, disabled people have been much more present (though still not fully represented) in advertising, perhaps as a result of data showing that the disabled constitute a large and relatively untapped consumer market and that the public responds favourably to inclusive advertising. Nevertheless, such advertising may actually, and ironically, exclude disabled consumers, as in Dove ads featuring visually impaired models, which are actually incomprehensible to anyone with a visual impairment. Moreover, such ads often feature only attractive and young disabled people, participating in what is ultimately an "ableist social aesthetic."[22]

Indeed, the Dove Real Beauty campaign is an interesting case study on gender in advertising. Launched in 2004, the campaign was aimed at promoting healthier body attitudes and self-acceptance among women (and selling Dove products, of course). Immediately successful in boosting Dove sales, Real Beauty has become one of the most discussed ad campaigns in history.

Nevertheless, it has not been without controversy. First, numerous media responses, often from men, have taken aim at the "too-real" women and "disturbing" images in the advertising, pointing out that they preferred conventional models and "idealized," retouched images; "the only time I want to see a thigh that big," wrote Chicago journalist Lucio Guerrero, "is in a bucket with breadcrumbs on it." In 2005, an ad for a cellulite "firming creme" was criticized for promoting the body shame Dove purported to reject. In 2007, the American FCC banned Dove's "Pro-age" ad for "showing too much skin." Critics noted that the Unilever brand also owned AXE and Lynx, whose ads were anything but anti-objectification; others criticized Dove for promoting self-acceptance while marketing skin-whitening creams in the Middle East and South Asia, and SlimFast elsewhere (Unilever has since sold the SlimFast brand). In 2010, new controversy surrounded Dove after a Craigslist ad seeking "real women" for the campaign requested "flawless" tattoo- and scar-free skin and "naturally fit" bodies. Dove quickly dissociated itself from the Craigslist ad, saying that it hadn't been approved before posting, but for many the question remained: how "real" was Dove's commitment to "real beauty"?[23]

There is no doubt that Dove's Real Beauty ads have broadened the kinds of images we see on the screen: Dove's ads present more diversity in ethnicity, age, and body than most other advertising campaigns. This may be more a commentary on the general dearth of diversity in advertising than praise for Dove. After more than a decade of the Dove campaign and many scholarly analyses (not to mention excellent sales for the brand!), how much has changed? One recent study by scholars at the University of Toronto notes:

> The Dove campaign, while it contests narrow beauty codes, works within a hegemonic ideology of gendered beauty by refusing to challenge the idea that beauty is an essential part of a woman's identity, personhood, and social success and by legitimizing the notion that every woman should feel beautiful . . . within the Dove campaign more generally, the social imperative for women to be and

feel beautiful is not up for negotiation. Even though the social understanding of beauty is contested, the importance of beauty as a paramount value for women is reproduced and legitimized by the campaign's explicit and unceasing focus on beauty.

Alternatively, as Lindsay Miller recently put it in *Bitch* magazine, "These ads each depend on the assumption that in order to be happy, empowered, or confident, women *need* to feel beautiful. Dove wants us to talk about why women don't feel beautiful. I want to talk about why that's the only question they think is worth asking."[24] The powerful gendering of advertising is harder to escape, it seems, than we may have thought.

His and Hers Print Media

As TV and film are gendered, so too are those older, more established media, like books and magazines. Print media have lost ground to new digital media more quickly than have electronic media such as television and movies. Readership is increasingly defined by age. Canadians older than 65 are 1.4 times more likely than the average Canadian adult to read one book per month, while Canadians 15–24 are only 0.8 times as likely to do the same. Fewer than half of Canadians now read newspapers.[25]

Women and men buy and read different sorts of books and magazines and read them differently. In 2012, American women bought 58 per cent of all books (including electronic books) sold in the US. A 2014 survey by the US National Endowment for the Arts found that fewer than half of Americans had read a novel, play, or poem within the past 12 months; the number rises to 76 per cent if only adults are surveyed, according to the Pew Research Center. Interestingly, however, only 69 per cent of men reported reading a book compared to 82 per cent of women. In the UK, a survey found that women readers were more likely to be "page-turners," unable to put down a book once they began it; twice as many men as women reported not finishing books they started. In the literary world, women outnumber men in the purchase of every single genre (except war and sports stories), and they also buy 80 per cent of all fiction sold in the United States and Europe.[26]

Still, this does not translate into an equivalent domination of the production end of things. Of the ten novels on *The Globe and Mail*'s November 2015 fiction bestseller list, eight bear men's names. (Interestingly, one of those is by *Harry Potter* author J.K. Rowling writing under the name of Robert Galbraith.)[27] A quick browse through the list of Nobel Prize for Literature winners (87.5 per cent men as of 2015), or any list of the top 100 novels of the twentieth century, should convince anyone that the genre is not feminine. Still, one of the most significant developments of the late twentieth century, particularly in Canada, was the emergence of internationally renowned female authors whose works were celebrated and read by both men and women: Alice Munro, Margaret Atwood, Carol Shields, Miriam Toews, and many more. While bestseller lists may still look significantly gendered, Canadian readership is considerably more complex.

When we turn from novels to magazines, we turn from a medium that at least aims for longevity to one that is designed to be read and cast aside. Magazines are also unlike books in that they carry at least as much advertising as content. It has become virtually axiomatic in feminist literature that women's magazines are a prime example of women's

Ahead of Their Time? Doris Anderson and *Chatelaine* Magazine

When Betty Friedan offered her critique of women's magazines in the early 1960s, she clearly wasn't talking about *Chatelaine*. Indeed, as noted above, even the American magazines she criticized serialized her work. Nevertheless, *Chatelaine* did not because the magazine was already "ten years ahead of American feminism," and Friedan's critique was familiar to Canadian readers. The extraordinary character of the magazine is largely attributable to Doris Anderson, its editor from 1957 to 1977. During these years, the lives of Canadian women changed dramatically, and *Chatelaine* never shrank from examining the most important public issues: workforce equality, marriage and divorce law, discrimination under the Indian Act, pay equity, reproductive choice, prostitution, and political representation. These hard-hitting topics were covered in Anderson's editorials and in articles that coexisted with more traditional women's magazine fare: advice, fashion, family-related information, and recipes.

Chatelaine was founded in 1928. From the start, it cultivated a direct relationship with its readers—it was even named through a contest, won by a BC rancher's wife— and combined seriousness with its more frivolous and conventional fare. The September 1929 issue, for example, contained an essay on the **Persons' Case**—accompanied by an ad that advised, "Every man admires lovely, white hands." *Chatelaine* was, then, a typically contradictory and multi-vocal women's magazine right from the start.

Under Anderson, however, the magazine became much more consistently identified with second-wave feminism. Increasingly, *Chatelaine*'s features were substantial and hard-hitting, and Anderson's editorials were the same, "publicizing feminist issues, urging policy changes, and highlighting areas where Canadian society needed revision." Readers didn't always like the magazine's editorial stance, but the magazine's circulation grew, and Anderson published reader opinion whether it favoured the magazine's articles or not. Readers remained faithful even when they were disgruntled, probably because Anderson always remembered that she was making the magazine for her "aunt in Taber"—that is, that the magazine should represent the interests and values of a broad section of Canadian women, not just a regional, ethnic, or class elite.

In fact, the history of *Chatelaine* suggests that our ideas about the relationship between print media and their public need complicating. The magazine was not simply beaming out material to be absorbed by acquiescent readers; rather, it engaged in a long-term relationship with them. Sometimes the magazine seemed to readers to be too far in the political vanguard and received vituperative letters from both women and men—but sometimes it was readers who accused the magazine of being behind the times.

Nowhere was this more clear than in the annual "Mrs Chatelaine" contest, which throughout the 1960s annually selected a "Canadian homemaker" who would receive (in

Keith Beaty/Toronto Star/Getty Images

Doris Anderson

addition to the honour implied by the title) cash and other prizes. While thousands of women vied for the title, submitting lengthy application packages documenting their height and weight along with their housecleaning regimens and other required details, many readers submitted critical letters or mock entries that pointed out how conventional and narrow the "Mrs Chatelaine" contest was. In fact, one reader went so far as to suggest a "Mrs Slob" contest, which she and others like her might have a chance of winning. According to Valerie Korinek, while some readers enjoyed traditional women's magazine fare, others "were resistant, critical, or dismissive and wrote to the magazine to challenge the sometimes narrow definitions of Canadian women." Readers consequently participated in a national conversation that redefined Canadian womanhood. Eventually, in 1969, a working mother won the "Mrs Chatelaine" contest for the first time.

Anderson's tenure as editor came to a close in 1977 when her hoped-for promotion to publisher failed to materialize and she left *Chatelaine*. Thereafter, the magazine's circulation declined until the early 1990s, when, under Rona Maynard's stewardship, the magazine overhauled itself and sought a new generation of readers. Today, *Chatelaine* is the country's top-earning magazine, available across multiple platforms. While the magazine may have lost some of the impact it had in the Anderson years, *Chatelaine* remains a distinctive Canadian voice as well as the top-selling magazine in the country.[29]

oppression. In Betty Friedan's *Feminine Mystique* (1963), she argued that women's magazines constructed "a weak, passive, vacuous woman." "This image," she wrote, " . . . is young and frivolous, fluffy and feminine; passive; gaily content in a world of bedroom and kitchen, sex, babies, and the home." (Never mind that Friedan's book was first serialized in *Mademoiselle* and later in *Ladies' Home Journal* and *McCall's*, where Friedan herself worked as an editor and writer—nor that *Chatelaine* had scooped Friedan by almost a decade!) Others have embraced this critique, from a 1978 volume analyzing the "symbolic annihilation" of women by the media to Jean Kilbourne's trenchant critique of advertising images of women, *Killing Us Softly*, to, finally, Naomi Wolf's debut work, *The Beauty Myth*.[28]

While feminists have criticized women's magazines as oppressive, conservative commentators have often assailed the American women's magazine for having exactly the *opposite* impact: rendering women dissatisfied by instilling ideals of careers, consumerism, and independence, and making them believe that they can "have it all." Christina Hoff Sommers accused such magazines as *Redbook*, *Mademoiselle*, *Good Housekeeping*, and *Parenting* of advancing "Ms information."[30]

Each position is wrong. Women's magazines offer **polyvocality**—multiple voices, differing perspectives. Amy Aronson found that since the first women's magazines appeared, this polyvocality has been one of the hallmarks of women's magazines—which makes them, in a sense, democratic, even as it means that they send confusing messages to women.[31]

Men's magazines in comparison are relatively monotone, as exemplified by *Maxim*, *FHM*, or *Men's Health*. *Men's Health*, now with forty editions in various countries, is the most successful men's magazine in the world. Launched in 1987, and once devoted to organic foods and herbal medicines for various men's illnesses, *Men's Health* reconfigured itself into a "lifestyle" magazine with celebrity covers (from Barack Obama to Hugh Jackman) and appearance-oriented articles. Next to pointers on how to have "abs of steel" flows a steady stream of articles about how to drive her wild in bed, how to be bigger, thicker, harder, and how to have more sexual endurance. *Men's Health* both reflects and creates sexual anxiety by suggesting one can never be potent enough or enough of a sexual athlete. The body obsession signalled by *Men's Health* may reflect—and fuel—the increasing prevalence of body image as a proxy for masculinity.[32]

Still, the bestselling single issue of any men's magazine in America is the "swimsuit" issue of *Sports Illustrated*. Launched in 1964, the swimsuit issue sells 10 to 15 times as many copies as any other issue of *Sports Illustrated*, and has become a "billion-dollar industry" in itself. Consequently, while men's magazines may be becoming more focused on men's bodies, they are still distinct from women's magazines. "What we discovered pretty quickly," UK **lad magazine** publisher Phil Hilton told a journalist, "is that there is not an age any more when men suddenly grow up and start getting interested in IRAs and bathroom tiles. They are never interested in those things. For better or worse, most men stay interested in looking at girls and knowing about cars and talking about football."[33]

While men's and women's magazines still remain distinct, another significant difference between men's and women's reading is that women, in addition to reading more, are still much more likely to read works written by men, works about men, and material identified as "masculine" than the reverse. This can be seen by the vast amount of Internet space given over to the discussion of whether boys and men read (and should read) *Twilight*, and to the shame and embarrassment many male *Twilight* fans experience. There is still a different valuation of "his" and "her" print media, even if many lines have been blurred.[34]

Gender, Race, Rap, and Rock

The gendering of media is arguably even more heightened in popular music. Rock remains by far the top popular music genre in the US, but R&B/hip-hop is second and pop a close third. Rooted in both rhythm and rhyme, hip-hop is a musical form now heard around the world, including among Canadian Aboriginal youth, who are attracted to the genre's ability to tell their stories in an unsanitized form; as a result, hip-hop has become one of the most popular genres among youth both on and off reserve.[35]

Hip-hop's rise to popularity has not been without controversy. Rappers have been accused of vile misogyny, celebration of gangsta thuggery, predatory sexuality, and violence. In its defence, rap's promoters and fans argue that the genre's symbolic assertions of manhood are necessary for an inner-city black youth for whom racism and poverty have been experienced as emasculating. Perhaps so, but gangsta rap was just one form, rooted in the experience of "the black underclass." Yet it became *the* face of rap, in North America and around the world; while more socially conscious rap existed, gangsta *sold*. Rapper David Banner claims that his more positive songs had less impact than his hit "Like a Pimp" because "America is sick. . . . America loves violence and sex." However, being African-American is not the only measure of hip-hop "authenticity," as is proved by Eminem, who burst onto the musical scene in 1999 with *The Slim Shady LP*. Like other rappers, Eminem drew from a deep well of class-based, gendered rage—directed largely at his mother and girlfriend. "Eminem spoke of situations many of his fans shared," according to his biographer, "broken homes, dead-end jobs, drug overindulgence—while exploring taboo emotions many couldn't face—parental hate, gender hate, self-loathing." Eminem's incessant homophobia and misogyny drew equally incessant criticism, and throughout the 2000s debates raged about the misogyny of hip-hop.[36]

Purportedly, about 80 per cent of hip-hop consumers are white (the majority young white men), drawn to the "authenticity" of hip-hop masculinities. "We spend our entire days trying to fit into a perfect little bubble," said one man to author Bakari Kitwana. "The perfect $500 thousand house. The perfect overscheduled kids. . . . We love life, but we hate our lives. And so I think we identify more with hip-hop's passion, anger and frustration than we do this dream world." As cultural critic Kevin Powell wrote, hip-hop may be "just a cultural safari for white people." Nevertheless, the genre, including its more misogynist elements, seems to resonate with disaffected men all over the world.[37]

However, is hip-hop (or rap) truly that misogynist in comparison to other arenas of pop culture? There are numerous historical examples that would suggest otherwise. In 1971, the Rolling Stones released *Sticky Fingers*, an album notable for both its songs and its cover art. On the album was the rock classic "Brown Sugar," which tells the story of (and eroticizes) the beating and sexual abuse of a young female slave. Later in the 1970s, the Stones promoted their *Black and Blue* album with an infamous billboard depicting a bruised and bound model and the caption "I'm Black and Blue from the Rolling Stones and . . . I love it!"

The term "cock rock" arose precisely to describe the attitude toward women that became characteristic of the most popular rock music. The term comes from a 1971 essay by an anonymous feminist who went by the name of "Susan Hiwatt." She wrote about the "devastating" messages rock sends to women: "all that sexual energy that seems to be in the essence of rock is really energy that climaxes in fucking over women . . . attitudes about women like put-downs, domination, threats, pride, mockery, fucking around, and a million different levels of women-hating." Despite this critique, anthologized in 1971, little changed. Van Halen, Foreigner, Def Leppard, Motley Crüe, Bon Jovi, and a host of other successful 1980s bands built their image around macho swagger and its demand for "Girls, Girls, Girls." In live rock performances, as in those of 1970s bands like Led Zeppelin, the guitar functioned, in Steve Waksman's term, as an "electrophallus" that highlighted "the phallic dimensions of the performing male body."[38] The body language might be different from that seen in rap videos, but the message is the same: hegemonic masculinity.

Much of the debate about misogyny and violence in rap music has pretty much ignored the parallel themes in rock, letting white musicians off the same hook used to hang black artists. One UK journalist, while conceding that "some rap lyrics are poisonously sexist," confesses to his irritation as seeing "artists of the breadth and depth of [author John] Updike and [Nick] Cave reduced to nasty little sexists by the M-word."[39] Apparently, a critique of lesser (black) men is all right, but a similar critique of great (white) men just won't do.

However, part of the reason for hip-hop's bad rap is also that rock has been changed. Ever since Suzi Quattro's 1970s performances, female rockers have been proving that they can do cock rock with the best of the boys. Others crafted their own game; from Joni Mitchell, Patti Smith, and Kate Bush to Riot Grrl and Sarah McLachlan's Lilith Fair, there are copious—and successful—examples of powerful, feminist musicians who disprove the sexist cultural script that powered rock for so long. According to Charis Kubrin and Ronald Weitzer, it's not that all hip-hop is misogynist; their survey of 403 rap songs found that only about 20 per cent fell into this category. However, they also found, there's a general *absence* in rap music of "lyrics that describe women as independent, educated, professional, caring, and trustworthy." Feminist and non-sexist hip-hop artists have simply not been as influential or commercially successful enough to impact the genre's message significantly. Indeed, of the 10 highest-earning hip-hop artists of 2014, only one (Nicki Minaj, in ninth place) is female. Minaj is not only a superstar but also an artist who engages explicitly with issues of gender and sexuality. Regardless of her influence, and that of other female artists past and present—such as Queen Latifah, Foxy Brown, Lil' Kim, Missy Elliott, and Lauryn Hill—hip-hop is still associated most with male artists such as Sean Combs (Diddy/Puff Daddy), Dr Dre, Jay Z, and 50 Cent.[40]

Women at Spelman, a venerable African-American women's college in Atlanta, caused a stir in black collegiate circles in 2004 when they protested an appearance by Nelly on their campus. In 2005, *Essence* magazine launched its Take Back the Music Campaign, and a conference was held at the University of Chicago to discuss feminism and hip-hop. The debate has been going for a decade, with increasing attention to the issue. In 2015, two high-profile rappers faced protests over their appearances. First was Big Sean. Before his scheduled performance at Princeton University, a group of students protested his appearance because of his misogynist and homophobic lyrics (which, it must be said, are rather tame by the standards of hip-hop). Next was Action Bronson's summer performance at the North by Northeast (NXNE) outdoor music festival, which was cancelled after thousands signed online petitions protesting his appearance. Many still regard such protests as ill-advised censorship.[41]

Still, as we critique the misogyny so often present in rap and hip-hop, it's important to acknowledge the power of this form to provide a vehicle for change and cultural pride. There *are* contestations of misogyny and male sexual privilege to be found in hip-hop. From Aboriginal Australia to Canada, this musical genre has provided a lexicon for cultural resistance. In the words of Rex Smallboy (Cree), leader of the now-defunct but much celebrated band War Party from Hobbema, Alberta: "It's all about social justice; we're not up there saying anything that isn't true." Speaking truth without entrenching sexist stereotypes is a worthy goal for the many people around the world now translating rap and hip-hop into their own cultures. It may be elusive, however. While the homophobia once present in hip-hop has diminished, and even with female rappers around, sexism and misogyny still animate the form. Perhaps, as Spencer Kornhaber writes, "that sexism persists probably says something about just how deeply ingrained it is, both in rap, and everywhere else."[42]

Gender and New Media

There is no doubt that the twentieth century revolutionized media to an extent not seen since the printing press made it possible to rapidly duplicate and disseminate the printed word. The development of cinema, radio, and television had enormous effects on the world, making it possible for the first time to communicate with vast numbers of people at great distance in real time. Global politics, warfare, and culture were all inexorably changed. Nevertheless, all of the media listed above are "old" media now, made "old" by another transformation: the development of digital or "new" media—most importantly, the Internet.

Old media, for all their undeniable power, lacked some of the most important features of new media. **New media** are distinguished by several characteristics: they are digital; flexible; available on demand; nested (think of hyperlinking and the way content is often "layered" within any digital medium); networkable; and interactive to an extent never seen before. We have already said, in this chapter, that media were never simply "beamed at" us: we absorb, rebuff, and integrate media in ways that are always more complex than the blank-slate model sometimes seen in discussions of the "power of the media." That said, however, there is a difference between a television program that one watches, or a magazine one reads, and the playing of a video game or the reading (and writing) of fanfiction. There is a difference between waiting for the news hour to hear about an event and seeing it unfold (or sharing eyewitness content) on Twitter. The new is simply much more interactive than the old.

In the early days of the Internet, when it was stilled called (in Canada at least), the "information superhighway," there was huge concern about the potential for women and girls to be "left behind" because of their putatively lesser interest in technology. In fact, despite some early gender differences, both women and men are roughly equal users of the Internet.

The average American spends 23 hours per week on social media, texting, and e-mailing, while estimates of the time spent on all electronic platforms (including laptops and smart phones) ranges from 8 (UK) to 11 (US) hours per day. When it comes to browsing online, Canadians lead the world, spending about 36 hours per month browsing websites (compared to 35 and 33 for Americans and Brits).[43]

Studies of gendered differences in Internet use are few but suggestive. For example, although women and men equally use the Internet to buy products and do their banking online, men are more likely to pay bills, participate in auctions, trade stocks, and buy digital content (like Internet pornography). Men search for information more often than women do; women use e-mail to maintain relationships and communicate with friends more than men do. While by some accounts men are more likely to be intensive users, others say women spend more time online per day. Women are more likely to use the Internet to locate information about health, while men are more likely to search for government-related data. Social media provide the most important group contrasts; women are significantly more likely to use social media than are men, particularly Facebook. According to one study of university undergraduates, females are more likely to be "addicted" to Facebook, to feel closer to Facebook friends than to "real-life" friends, to spend more time on Facebook than they would like, to experience negative body-image effects from Facebook photos, and to feel stressed by Facebook. Men, meanwhile, are much more likely to use the Internet at public access points, for example in libraries; and they are much more likely to edit Wikipedia articles—a difference with significant implications for the nature of knowledge on the web. Therefore, though gender differences may be relatively small, the points where differences emerge are not without broader implications.[44]

Age and race, rather than gender, provide some of the starkest contrasts in Internet use. In the US, African-Americans are significantly less likely to use the Internet regularly than are whites. While the oldest people are least likely to use the Internet, the youngest are more likely to see the web as their main source of entertainment and cultural connection. Even among youth 13–24, for example, interesting distinctions emerge. Those 13–17 are significantly more likely to look up to YouTube celebrities, and to feel close to them, while those 18–24 are more oriented toward the celebrities of "old media" (TV and movies). This is an example of how thoroughly new media are changing the cultures of youth.[45]

Assessing the entire world of new media would be an impossible task, but we begin with video games because they create an interesting counterpoint to the "old" visual media (television and film) discussed above. Video games disrupt the position of "watcher" that we adopt with television and movies. Playing video games makes one a participant and even a creator, with increasing availability of opportunities to build content within games themselves. In an interesting twist, video games have even become a spectator sport, with gameplay streamed so that viewers can watch and comment upon competitive game play.

As this makes clear, the world of video games has expanded dramatically since the arcade games of the 1970s and *Pong*, one of the first home video games to make a splash. Today, video games are played on multiple platforms, from seventh-generation consoles to smartphones, tablets, and both Apple computers and PCs. Additionally, massively

multiplayer online role-playing games (MMORPG) are played online, with thousands of people all over the world playing simultaneously. Consequently, to talk about "gender in video games" is about as difficult as talking about "gender in movies," except that the same issues of representation we saw in Hollywood film are also present in games.

One stellar example is the *Grand Theft Auto* franchise, one of the most popular games of all time and a star performer for developer Rockstar Games of the UK. *Grand Theft Auto* is now in its fifth iteration and remains the most successful game series ever invented. A dark, satirical, and canny examination of American society, GTA is also a prime example of some of the stereotypical, misogynist, and violent representations that have created controversy as North Americans become more and more devoted to **gaming**.[46]

More than half of all American homes have at least one console, with numbers only slightly lower in Canada. In addition, computer, mobile device, and online games account for many more passionate users. Canada is a player in the world of video games, not just because of its millions of gamers but because it houses three major production companies, Electronic Arts, UbiSoft, and Activision Blizzard. Quebec, and to some extent British Columbia, are the centres of the industry. Globally, video games made about $50 billion in revenues in 2014, outselling box office receipts for movies ($36.4 billion), not to mention books, CDs, and DVDs. In the United States in 2014, video games earned about $15.4 billion. **First-person shooter** games are among the most popular both in North America and abroad. While sports games also perennially command a large share of the market, action and shooter games, taken together, accounted for almost 50 per cent of units sold in the US in 2014; family, children, and arcade games covered under 5 per cent and strategy games 4.1 per cent. The market share of shooter and action games has increased over time.[47]

In the past, gaming tended to appeal most to adolescent boys and young men. Nina Huntmann, communications professor and avid gamer, is a keen observer who researched games and created the documentary *Game Over* for the Media Education Foundation. "The computer labs in college were completely dominated by guys," she says, "and the fact that I liked games, and liked them for the same reasons that they did, made more than a few somewhat uncomfortable." Jo Bryce and Jason Rutter argue that significant numbers of female gamers have been present since the early 1990s but that male gaming communities, game manufacturers, and academic researchers long ignored their presence. Gareth Schott and Kirsty Horell found that even within individual homes where consoles are owned by girls, male family members may take control of the console and assume the role of "expert." Girl gamers are thereby encouraged to adopt the position of "watcher," allowing male relatives to master games (even when the games and consoles belong to the girl!) before attempting to master them themselves. Within adult couples, women may be less able to use or complete games because of household responsibilities. As one female UK gamer put it, "it's really important for my husband to know how *Spyro* works but it's more important for me to have the dinner cooked! I mean I want to be able to do it, but. . . ." Still, today, women represent 44 per cent of the American game-playing population, and the majority of UK gamers. Twenty-seven per cent of gamers are older than 50 while the most frequent female players are older on average (43) than their male counterparts (35).[48]

Still, the gendered legacy of gaming can be seen in a recent survey finding that while men and women are nearly exactly as likely to say they play video games, women are less than *half* as likely to call themselves "gamers." Women are still more likely to play puzzle and strategy games (such as *Sims* and *Second Life*) than men, who are in turn more likely to prefer shooters. Perhaps more significantly, while participation in game playing has become more gender-balanced, game production is still very much a male realm. In the UK, only 12 per cent of game designers and 4 per cent of programmers are women. A particularly shocking demonstration of how closed the gaming world remains to women arose in 2012 when Anita Sarkeesian, a pop culture blogger, received numerous death and rape threats after speaking out against sexism in video games. In 2014, Sarkeesian and Zoë Quinn, a game developer, were targeted once again in what became known as **Gamergate**, a concerted attack including death and rape threats, harassment, and **doxing** (the practice of researching and posting personal information about an individual on the Internet). "Don't feed the trolls" is an Internet maxim, but these incidents called attention to the gendered character of **trolling**, the targeting of women (or anyone with a female username), and sexism in the gaming community and online.[49]

Video-game use may produce some benefits in computer literacy, entry into high-tech jobs, and comfort with technology, so women's increased gaming may be good news. Research conducted at the University of Toronto found that video-game players were much better at spatial rotation tasks than non-players were. In fact, much of the observed gender difference in this task was actually a player versus non-player difference! Playing action games for only 10 hours produced significant gains in mental rotation and spatial attention abilities (two areas generally perceived as gendered); the gains made by women were more significant than those made by men were.[50]

When we turn from participation in gaming to representation, we see more obvious gendering. Within games, characters are almost always massively exaggerated gender and racial stereotypes. According to a 2009 study, only 10 per cent of playable characters were female in 150 games surveyed. Only black characters appeared in number equivalent to their representation in the population, while Latino and indigenous characters were greatly underrepresented. As to the presence of African-American characters, an earlier study found that 80 per cent appear in one context: as competitors in sports games. Others can be found in highly stereotyped roles. Most male characters, whatever their colour, have biceps that would make G.I. Joe look puny. The bodies of female characters are equally exaggerated, though there is a difference: male characters' physical bulk and power are heightened, while females' slenderness, attractiveness, and sexual characteristics are dramatically increased. Female characters are presented for the uses of male characters, often as "eye candy"; many female characters expose their breasts, which are almost always massive and pneumatic. (Of course, in mature-rated games like *GTA*, female characters often either start out or become unclothed and engage in sexual acts.)[51]

Video games offer an incredibly—and increasingly—immersive experience unlike any other media. In some games, it is possible to share the experience with others, whether they are in the same room or on the other side of the world. Millions of players around the world log on to MMORPGs; about 40 per cent of MMO players are now female. Games like *EverQuest* or *World of Warcraft* (*WoW*) are elaborate fantasy worlds where players battle against each other (PVP) or battle against the game environment (PVE), live, online, in real time. *WoW*, launched in 2004, remains the most successful example of the genre. In the classic model, players all over the world pay (subscribe) for accounts that grant them the right to a number of characters and to log onto the game's servers. *WoW* has managed to maintain this model (and $1 billion annual revenues) despite the growth of free-to-play (F2P) games such as *League of Legends* (*LoL*), launched in 2009, which has tens of millions of players. (*LoL* makes its money not from subscriptions but from in-game transactions.)

In its classic form, exemplified by *WoW*, the MMORPG is both virtual and very real. The boundaries between reality and fantasy are blurred because the environment is so immersive and because the collections of pixels with which one interacts are actual people. Real, too, are the commodities that flow across the borders of cyberspace into the real marketplace. Edward Castronova worried that some players would experience a sort of "toxic immersion," in which their virtual lives become more real, and more pressing, than their real-world lives. Any number of people who identify as current or former MMO addicts would agree. Still, most MMO players, like gamers in general, are capable of managing the relationship between "rl" ("real life") and the game.[52]

Some aspects of MMOs in particular enhance gender stereotyping. Customizable characters in MMOs enable players to create the most intensely stereotypical characters imaginable—fantasies of masculinity and femininity. In fact, the possibilities of customization are often limited by the stereotypes that the game designers themselves brought to the game. A female warrior character, for example, is likely to become less and less clothed the more powerful she becomes. (Many players find it annoying to level up a female character and don a new piece of gear only to find that its power seems to be a result of the amount of skin it reveals.) Moreover, the ethnic variability of most humanoid characters is extremely limited, with few non-white options available. However, the designers are not solely responsible: walking around in any online environment where avatars are customizable, one readily perceives the powerful hold of gender stereotyping on the imaginations of gamers themselves. Nowhere is this more the case than in *Second Life* (*SL*), less a game than an alternative world. Complex, often beautiful, and home to about a million regular users, *SL* is populated by many avatars whose appearance reveals how influenced we are by the dreams of perfect, surgery-enhanced beauty generated by more traditional media. In cases like these, games actually participate in gender intensification, radically exaggerating (because it is possible to do so) the stereotypes of gender and sexuality.

At the same time, games offer some increasing opportunities for diversity. First, games are expanding their representativeness. After years with nary a disabled character in sight, there are now some memorable examples: Lester Quest in *GTA V* and Taimi, a mobility-impaired Asuran engineer in the fabulous *Guild Wars II*. Racial diversity in gaming remains more elusive, with minority characters still stereotyped as criminals or exotics; and where characters of colour are playable, they can become a way for white gamers to "consume the other," as David Leonard argues, by inhabiting stereotypical representations of black athletes or criminals.[53]

As gaming becomes one of the most significant leisure activities around the world, it is worth thinking about the broader implications of this trend, both beneficial and detrimental. Although there is no simplistic causal relationship between playing *GTA V* and, for example, murdering police officers, gaming has effects; indeed, evidence is mounting that playing violent video games even for short periods of time desensitizes players to depictions of real-life violence, diminishes their empathy, and increases aggression. Similarly, the gendered fantasy world of our games deserves our scrutiny. As David Leonard argues, "Video games teach, inform, and control . . . we need to teach about games because games are teaching so much about us . . . and 'them'."[54]

Pornography, New Media, and "Pornification"

The pornography industry is a clear example of the power of new media to effect massive societal changes in the area of gender and sexuality. Worldwide porn revenues approach $100 billion annually. Canadian statistics are hard to come by, but according to one study, Canadians lead the world in the amount of time spent downloading porn from the Internet.[55]

Back before the Internet, porn was available on the newsstand, in adult bookstores, or at special theatres, and only in towns above a certain size. It was made for men, and very few women accessed it. Videocassette rental began to change that in the 1980s, but it was still impossible to consume porn in privacy. When the Internet made it possible to purchase and view pornography in complete anonymity, the industry burgeoned. By 2003, the association between the Internet and pornography was strong enough that a Broadway song, "The Internet Is for Porn," became a widely distributed meme and a generally accepted "rule of the Internet." Around the same time, "Rule 34" of the Internet was invented: "If it exists, there is porn of it." (See the Brony discussion on pp. 247–8.)

As this suggests, the first effect of the Internet was to increase dramatically the availability and scope of pornography—and, therefore, men's consumption of it. Surveys of men confirm that almost all of them have viewed pornography, and many view it regularly. A 2004 poll conducted by MSNBC.com and *Elle* magazine found that 75 per cent of American men said that they had downloaded or viewed erotic films and videos from the Internet. Even groups with supposedly strict sexual mores are not immune to the lure of Internet porn. For example, a 2014 American survey of 388 self-identified Christian men found that of men 18–30, 77 per cent looked at porn at least monthly, 36 per cent daily, and 32 per cent enough to consider themselves addicted. Older men were not much different, nor were men who identified as "born-again" Christians; 95 per cent had looked at porn, with 54 per cent using it at least once per month. Today, the challenge for researchers is finding men who *haven't* used Internet porn.[56]

A second major effect has been the "mainstreaming" of pornography. In the 1960s and 1970s, porn met with significant social disapproval, and most people saw pornography as "obscene." It was a niche market kept largely out of sight. Even then, however, the porn market was growing, particularly after the popularization of VCRs in the 1970s. In response, second-wave feminists made pornography a political issue. Arguing that "porn is the theory, rape is the practice," feminists like Robin Morgan, Andrea Dworkin, and Catherine MacKinnon showed and described pornographic images (which many women had never seen) of women's degradation.

Bonnie Sherr Klein's 1981 National Film Board release *Not a Love Story* galvanized many Canadian women in opposition to the porn industry, fuelling debate and activism throughout the 1980s. In 1992, the Supreme Court of Canada enshrined the idea of pornography's harms in *Regina v. Butler*. In that case, Justice Sopinka decided that restrictions on pornography were a reasonable restriction where sex and violence were explicitly linked, where sex was linked with humiliating treatment, or where explicit sex involved children. Unfortunately, these restrictions were applied in a discriminatory fashion, targeting gay and lesbian pornography and, in particular, Little Sisters bookstore in Vancouver. The resulting outcry put feminists in a difficult position; on one hand, they opposed degrading pornography; on the other hand, the legislation they had considered a victory was used to discriminate against gay people. By the mid-1990s, debates over porn seemed almost as old-fashioned as the temperance movement. When the star of *Not a Love Story* (an exotic dancer) claimed that she had been misrepresented in the film, that seemed to many people to prove that feminists were wrong again, and that opposition to pornography was "anti-sex" and anachronistic.[57]

As the pornography market has grown, so has a general perception of porn "as daily entertainment fare." Our society has become *Pornified*, as journalist Pamela Paul argues in her book of that name. Pornography today, she suggests, "is so seamlessly integrated into popular culture that embarrassment or surreptitiousness is no longer part of the equation." Mainstreaming of pornography has meant greater acceptance in general, accompanied by the growth of women's use of porn. This view is borne out by studies of attitudes toward pornography, particularly among young people. A 2008 study of university students at six American universities found that about two-thirds of men and half of women found porn use acceptable, while almost 90 per cent of men and about a third of women reported using porn themselves. In the same year, a Montreal study hit a barrier when it failed to find male participants who did not use pornography. A 2015 US study found that men's and women's disapproval of pornography had declined significantly between 1975 and 2012 (though the gender gap between the sexes had actually widened).[58]

Indeed, women's use of porn is perhaps the most interesting phenomenon that has accompanied mainstreaming of pornography. For many years, as noted above, consumers of porn were virtually all male. It was assumed by many that this reflected basic sex differences in arousal (women were more interested in relationships and needed less visual stimulation, while men preferred visual stimuli *and* multiple partners). The rapid growth of women's interest in pornography has demonstrated once again that perceived differences between the genders are much more mutable than previously believed. Pornhub, one of the largest Internet porn sites with more than 150 million visitors per month, claims that 25 per cent of its visitors are women. Though Pornhub based this presumption on Google analytics, which determine gender through browsing preferences and are notoriously unreliable, the number accords with those in other, more careful studies. Clearly, attitudes and behaviours have changed.

As a result of women's interest in pornography, there is a "wave" of woman-oriented content being produced. Pornhub's analysis suggests that women prefer lesbian (and gay male) porn to other varieties, but also have more interest in hardcore porn than do men.

Erika Lust's production company—which earns more than $1 million per month and has a female subscriber base of 40 per cent—produces films that are explicit but have strong storylines and lack the more disturbing aspects of mainstream hardcore porn for men, such as choking and abusive behaviour. (According to Lust, such practices "make women want to puke.") Her films are an example of the axiom, now widely accepted by many feminists, that "the answer to bad porn isn't *no* porn; it's better porn." That is the mantra of the Feminist Film Awards, an award ceremony created by the Good for Her sex store of Toronto in 2006 (and on hiatus as of 2016). The awards were intended to recognize those who created **feminist pornography**, defined by criteria including dedication to women's sexuality and pleasure; the presence of women and marginalized groups behind the cameras; and the representation of a broad variety of groups (in terms of ability, ethnicity, age, and sexuality).[59]

As this suggests, the mainstreaming of pornography has broadened (to some extent) the types of porn available. **Ethical porn** or fair-trade porn, though generally distinct from feminist porn, adheres to some of the same principles, most notably the fair and dignified treatment of those who work making porn. However, ethical porn is not as likely as feminist porn to argue the finer points of what sexual practices may be destructive to depict, or which fantasies should be left off-screen, or "quashed" in Julie Bindel's formulation. Young women (and young feminists) involved in pornography are much more likely to take the point of view that sexuality is and should be a realm of freedom, constrained only by the requirement to treat others fairly. Criticizing pornography use in general, or particular fantasies expressed within porn, is viewed by such women as an interference with individual freedom, as Rhiannon Lucy Coslett writes:

> It feels unnatural to be completely against pornography, having grown up in a culture that's so saturated in sex. I remember being a teenager when Christina Aguilera had just done her "Dirrty" video; that to my mother was pornographic, but that to me was normal. I think arguments that are anti-porn do ignore the testimonies of lots of women who are themselves in the sex industry. You're telling women what they can and can't do, you're telling women what they should find arousing and what they shouldn't.

Accordingly, pornography is now broadly accepted and is seen by many, particularly the young, as an indicator and fosterer of sexual liberation.[60]

There are, of course, critics of this position. First, the effects of pornography use remain unclear. It is true that the claims made in the porn debates of the 1980s have proven difficult to verify. For example, much was made of the claim that pornography either makes men more prone to rape or gives men a cathartic release that makes them less prone to rape. Neither hypothesis turns out to be confirmable, nor does porn evidently make men dislike feminism or wish to limit women's rights. Still, recent studies have found that porn increases aggressive attitudes and behaviours toward women for *some* users; in addition, the use of pornography by sexual offenders suggests that there is some connection between visual images and behaviours, even if it is not a simplistic causal link. Moreover, the focus on such causal connections also obscures more interesting questions about how casual pornography exposure affects children and how pornography shapes desire (discussed further in Chapter 12).[61]

Child pornography, as always, is depicted as somewhere beyond the pale. Nevertheless, according to Melinda Reist, "mainstream" Australian pornographer, and Eros Association secretary David Watt, also imports titles depicting "Pigtail Perverts" and "Captive Virgins." At the same time, Watt and the Eros Association promote porn use as the means to sexual liberation.[62] This is a familiar framing: pornography depicts an egalitarian erotic paradise, where people always want sex, get what they want, and have a great time getting it. Still, as in the case of rap, the most commercially viable pornography is neither ethical nor particularly thoughtful, as a cursory Internet search will show. Proponents of ethical porn sometimes sniff at feminist porn critics for trolling the Internet's free sites; yet these are the sites with the most traffic. Most mainstream porn still follows a script in which the so-called equality of desire is a fiction. The typical porn scene finds a woman and a man immediately sexually aroused, penetration occurs immediately, and both are orgasmic within a matter of seconds. The penis, in mainstream heterosexual porn, is sufficient to accomplish all things. Women rapidly achieve orgasm not only from simple penile penetration, but also, apparently, from the act of fellatio itself. (That was the premise of *Deep Throat* [1972], one of the first porn films to go "mainstream.") According to most pornography, the apotheosis of any sexual act is his orgasm—or what is euphemistically referred to as the "money shot." Increasingly, that money shot is a "facial," culminating in some versions in what Antonia Zerbisias describes as "waterboarding by ejaculate."[63]

Even when the fantasy is not too explicitly degrading, the fantasy of mainstream porn is one in which women's sexuality dovetails neatly with men's desires. In the erotic paradise of pornography, both women and men want what men want, or what pornography thinks men want. No wonder anti-pornography activist John Stoltenberg writes that pornography "tells lies about women" even though it "tells the truth about men."[64] Pornography also provides hassle-free vicarious sex. "You don't have to buy them dinner, talk about what they like to talk about," says Seth, a 24-year-old computer programmer in New York. "And even when you do, there's no guarantee that you're gonna get laid. I mean with pornography, no one ever says no." If they do say no, well, they really mean yes. In a sexual marketplace that men feel is completely dominated by women—from women's having the power to decide if men are going to get sex in the first place to all those dispiriting reminders that "no means no"—mainstream heterosexual pornography supplies a world in which no one takes no for an answer.

We need a conversation about pornography that looks at why porn's version of sex works for so many men (and an increasing number of women). As we transmit ever more depictions of explicit sexuality in what Robert Jensen calls "one of the greatest social engineering experiments in history," we need to pay close attention. We need to listen to the voices of those who use pornography but articulate a critical and questioning stance toward its depiction and implications. We need egalitarian depictions of sexuality that exhibit, in Robert Jensen's words, "the possibilities of becoming a human being."[65] Perhaps we need to question the overall sexualization of our culture; sexuality is, for all its excitement and importance, just one aspect of human existence.

Summary

The media are now considered a primary institution of socialization. This wasn't always true; sociologists used to believe that there were only three such institutions: family, school, and church (religion). The recognition that the media play a major role in shaping us came as the media's influence grew in our lives. However, the media are both like and unlike other social institutions. The media are, obviously, mediated communication, and their effect has often been seen as uni-directional. Nevertheless, we are not simply sponges absorbing the media's messages. To analyze effectively how the media socialize us, we need to consider our active negotiation of media; the multiplicity and complexity of media; and how a particular medium (rather than merely its content) affects us. We need to treat the media as a deeply gendered but complex institution saturated with depictions of gender that influence us in complex, powerful ways.

One of the first things to note about the gendered media is that there are "his" and "hers." Though some of the barriers are breaking down, genres still remain gendered. Where crossover occurs, it's much more likely that "she" will cross over into "his" media than the other way around.

Television and film have changed a great deal since their beginnings, but they remain popular. Character depictions were once highly stereotyped, but since the 1970s, stereotyping has been breaking down. The emergence of the ensemble cast in the 1980s provided a means for networks to depict both gender and ethnic diversity. Sexual diversity had to wait for the late 1990s, when the first gay main characters appeared on network television. Still, there's a way to go. Women, the disabled, LGBT people, and visible minorities remain underrepresented. Although children's programming may be changing with the emergence of strong female characters like Dora, here too continued gender stereotyping and increasingly violent depictions are cause for concern. Finally, advertising remains one of the most gender-stereotyped areas of television programming. While there is some convergence in what men and women watch, the emergence of hypermasculine programming like Spike TV suggests that "his" and "hers" remain meaningful categories of TV and film.

Print media have also been highly gender-segregated. Women read more in general, and are more likely to read novels. Women's magazines, however, are quite different from men's magazines in their contradictory and multi-vocal messages. *Chatelaine*, uniquely, is a magazine that promoted second-wave feminism while remaining the "mainstream" magazine for Canadian homemakers through the 1960s and 1970s. Men's magazines are more mono-vocal in nature, particularly when they're the lad magazines that poured onto the market in the 1990s. As in the media in general, gender divisions are breaking down, but that breakdown is coming largely from women's consumption of formerly men's genres.

The popular music world is dominated by rock and rap/hip-hop. Rap has been the biggest new story within pop music for more than a decade. Today, it is the second-biggest genre in the music market and globally is probably number one. Gangsta rap is only one form of the genre, but it's by far the most successful and is noted for its misogyny. Rock too has had its share of machismo and misogyny; but since the 1970s, women have contested rock's stereotypical representations of women. Though race undoubtedly and unfairly plays a role in the demonization of rappers as misogynists, many within the African-American community have become increasingly concerned about the portrayals of women within the genre. As rap becomes "the world's music," translated into cultures around the world, its misogyny should be questioned even as its ability to speak for so many is celebrated.

In the late twentieth century, new media revolutionized the world, enabling long-distance communication in real time and demonstrating distinct characteristics of networkability, flexibility, nestedness, and above all, interactivity. The Internet exemplifies new media. While men and women use it equally, Internet use is the site of important gender differences. Video gaming, which is now overtaking more conventional entertainment media in revenues, also remains gendered. Although there is now near-parity in participation in gaming, women, as well as girls, remain marginalized within the world of game production. Women and men also remain attracted to different genres. Within games, gender and ethnic stereotypes are alive and well; women remain a minority of those depicted, and are often hypersexualized. Men, at the same time, are represented as hypermasculine heroes, most of whom are white. Non-white men play restricted and stereotyped roles within most games. Online games are one of the fastest-growing sectors within gaming, offering a level of complexity and ongoing engagement console games can't supply. As more of us enter into the fantasy worlds of gaming for hours each week, considering the gender implications of that fantasy realm seems particularly important.

Another fantasy world is that offered by pornography, which also remains highly gendered. The growth of the Internet has made porn a massive business that is a key part of the Internet and entertainment economies. While pornography was previously viewed as obscene, and seen as degrading to women by second-wave feminists, it has become increasingly "mainstreamed" within North American society, even while the growth of marginal areas such as overtly violent and child pornography remains "beyond the pale." While mainstream heterosexual porn is not harmful in the clear ways that those kinds of porn are, it nonetheless presents a problematic view of sexuality. It portrays women's desires and pleasures as dovetailing neatly with men's (perceived) needs. Porn also focuses on the penis and male orgasm as the centre of sexual action. Many previous claims about pornography's harms have been disproved or at least criticized, but that doesn't mean that there are no questions to be asked about porn. Porn, no matter how "mainstream," is still "his."

Women and men are more than ever converging. The boundaries between his and hers are becoming more porous, as can be seen by the fact that many women watch Spike TV, while a significant minority of young men enjoy media products such as *My Little Pony* and *Twilight*. Nevertheless, the ubiquity and popularity of representations of hyper- or hegemonic masculinity, and the popularity of pornography, suggest the continuing importance and exaggeration of gender. As the media become more complex in their representations of gender on one hand, they become more simplistic on the other. True gender equality within the media remains elusive.

Questions for Critical Thinking

1. Can you think of three examples of how we "negotiate" our relationship with media? How are we "active" rather than "passive" consumers of media products?
2. Thinking about McLuhan's idea that "the medium is the message," how would you assess the importance of the transition from text-based (books, newspapers, magazines) to visual (television, movies) media? From old media to new media? How do you think these transitions affect the ideas about gender that we take from media?
3. Think about one of your favourite television shows. Does it contain clear messages about gender, or are the messages it contains contradictory? What does this tell you about the nature of gendered messages within the media?
4. Thinking about gaming and pornography, what relationship do these areas of entertainment have with reality? How, if at all, do they influence our views of the world and our behaviour?

Key Terms

Brony
chick lit
doxing
ethical porn
feminist pornography
first-person shooter
Gamergate
gaming
lad lit
lad magazine

massively multiplayer online
      role-playing game (MMORPG)
new media
old media
participation
Persons' Case
polyvocality
representation
trolling

Part 3

Gendered Interactions

10

Gendered Intimacies
Communication, Friendship, and Love

Two are better than one.... For if they fall, the one will lift up his fellow; but woe to him that is alone when he falleth, for he hath not another to help him up. Again, if two lie together, then they have heat; but how can one be warm alone?

—Ecclesiastes 4:9–11

The need for intimacy is fundamentally human; and yet we express it in gendered ways. "Man's love is of man's life a thing apart," wrote the legendary British romantic poet George Gordon, Lord Byron, "'Tis woman's whole existence." A century and a half later, novelist Doris Lessing commented that she'd never met a man who would destroy his work for a love affair—and she'd never met a woman who wouldn't.

However dated they now appear, such sentiments underscore how unconsciously our intimacies have been shaped by gender. Indeed, even today, women and men have different experiences and expectations of intimacy. Part of the "interplanetary theory" of gender emphasizes these differences between women and men. We hear that our celestial or biological natures dictate that women should be emotionally adept at communications while men should be clumsy unemotional clods.

Yet the gender differences in intimate relationships often don't turn out to be the ones we expected; nor are the differences as great as commonsense assumptions predict. Moreover, the differences we observe in contemporary North America did not always exist, and are affected by other differences such as ethnicity, sexual orientation, and class. In this chapter, we explore the gender of **intimacy** by examining communication, friendship, and love. (Love, in this chapter, refers only to the form we emphasize most, romantic love, and not to parental love or other forms.) What we'll see is that the gendering of intimate life is the result of historical and social developments—and the site of continuing change.

The Historical "Gendering" of Intimate Life

Today, women are often considered "emotional experts" relative to men. This was not always the case. From Greek and Roman myths to Renaissance balladry, men's friendships were celebrated as the highest expression of the noblest virtues—bravery, loyalty, heroism, and duty—which only men were thought to possess.[1] Many women agreed. For example, the great eighteenth-century British feminist and writer Mary Wollstonecraft believed that although "the most holy bond of society is friendship," men, not women, were most adept at it. Simone de Beauvoir, whose book *The Second Sex* is one of modern feminism's groundbreaking works, concurred, commenting, "women's feelings rarely rise to genuine friendship." That is, women might gather to gossip and quilt, but their emotions were simply not as profound as those of men. This, it was thought, also affected women's ability to love as truly as did men. Women were fair-weather friends and fickle lovers.[2]

Much of this historical view of gendered intimacies rested on sexist views of women's capacities for "higher" mental and emotional processes. However, even modern scholars have viewed men as more gifted friends. Anthropologist Lionel Tiger, the theorist of male bonding, as discussed in Chapters 2 and 4, argued that the gender division of labour in hunting-and-gathering societies led to deeper and more durable friendships among men. Hunting and warfare, the domains of male activity, required deep and enduring bonds among men for survival, and consequently close male friendships became a biologically based human adaptation.[3]

Whatever the virtue of Tiger's theories for explanation of early hominid societies, contemporary North Americans have reversed the historical notion of intimacy since the early 1970s, fuelled in part by two related developments. On one hand, feminism began to celebrate solidarity among women. Historians like Carroll Smith-Rosenberg found such solidarity in the past, reversing the traditional notion that women could not be friends and uncovering the richness and profundity of Victorian women's lifelong friendship ties.[4] Increasingly, women's emphasis on intimacy and emotional expressiveness were seen not as a liability but rather as an asset. On the other hand, as discussed in Chapter 5, a new generation of male psychologists and advocates of "men's liberation" were critical of the traditional male sex role as a debilitating barrier to emotional intimacy.

Reversing centuries of tradition, *women's* experiences in friendships and *women's* virtues—emotional expressiveness, dependency, the ability to nurture, and intimacy— were now desirable. Psychologist Robert Lewis identified four "barriers" to emotional intimacy among men: competition; the need to be "in control," which forbids self-disclosure and openness; homophobia; and lack of skills and positive role models for male intimacy. In a widely cited study, psychologist Daniel Levinson concluded that real friendship is "rarely experienced by American men." Joseph Pleck, critic of traditional masculinity, lamented the "weak and often absent" nature of men's emotional relationships.[5]

So if men are no longer seen as "better" at friendship and love than women, and are in fact seen as emotionally limited in these areas, what explains this gender difference? Lillian Rubin and Nancy Chodorow, who are both sociologists and psychologists, argue that, as Rubin puts it, "the traditional structure of parenting comes together with the developmental tasks of childhood and the cultural mandates about masculinity and femininity to create differences in the psychological structures of women and men." The young boy must separate from his mother—the source of love, nurturance, and connection—and establish his independence. For girls, by contrast, continued connection with their mothers ensures a continuity of emotionality, love, and nurturance. In fact, it becomes the foundation for women's experience of sexual intimacy, rather than its negation. As a result, separation and individuation are more difficult for women, while connection and intimacy are more difficult for men. This constellation permits women "to be more closely in touch with both their attachment and dependency needs than men are."[6]

Although such explanations "feel" right to many of us, they are neither universal nor essential. In some societies, for example, boys undergo rigorous ritual separation from their mothers; and yet they, and not women, are still seen as having the deeper interior emotional lives and the more intimate and expressive friendships. For example, anthropologist Robert Brain documents several societies in Africa, South America, and Oceania in which men develop very close male friendships, ritually binding themselves together as "lifetime comrades, blood brothers, or even symbolic 'spouses.'"[7]

Psychoanalytic explanations take us part of the way, but even they must be inserted into the larger-scale historical transformation of which they are a part: the social, economic, and cultural transformation of Europe and America in the 1800s and 1900s. Both Rubin and Chodorow recognize this. "Society and personality live in a continuing reciprocal relationship with each other," Rubin writes. "The search for personal change without efforts to change the institutions within which we live and grow will, therefore, be met with only limited reward."[8]

The nineteenth and twentieth centuries witnessed a dramatic transformation in the gendered division of emotional labour. This change began among the upper and middle classes, but eventually affected all groups within Western society. As we saw in Chapter 6, as the separation between the private and public spheres grew, the home became men's refuge from the hurly-burly of the working world. The wife's "job description" now included what Arlie Hochschild calls **emotion work**: in this case, meeting her husband's emotional needs. By the late nineteenth century, the spectre of homosexuality also hung over male friendships, barring the kind of traditional intimacies between men (for example, hugging or sharing a bed) that now seem, to many North Americans, to indicate homosexuality.[9]

These changes did not eliminate male–male friendships, however. Now, as men left their homes and went to work in factories or offices, they socialized in male groups and cultivated new forms of sociability. Men "learned" to be **instrumental**—focusing on tasks or shared activities rather than self-disclosure—in their relationships with other men. In their friendships, men have come to "seek not intimacy but companionship, not disclosure but commitment." The passionate male friendship, so celebrated in myths and legend, became a historical artifact.[10]

Simultaneously, the separation of spheres also positioned women as the intimacy experts: Women became increasingly **expressive**—adept at emotional communication— as men were abandoning that style. The doctrine of separate spheres implied more than the spatial separation of home and workplace; it divided the mental and social world into two complementary halves. Men were to express the traits and emotions associated with the workplace—competitiveness, individual achievement, instrumental rationality— whereas women were to cultivate the softer domestic virtues of love, nurturance, and compassion. Love itself changed meanings, coming to mean tenderness, powerlessness, and emotional expression. Women, said to possess "all the milder virtues of humanity," became the ministers of love.[11]

The cultural equation of femininity with emotional intimacy exaggerated gender differences in friendships and love. These differences, then, were the *result* of the broad social and economic changes, not their cause. Once again, gender inequality produced the very differences that then legitimated the inequalities. This in turn made women seem fundamentally unsuited for the world of work, and particularly for domains like science, thought to be characterized by rationality.

At the same time, the idea of **companionate marriage** became the norm in Western society, replacing earlier and more pragmatic views of the institution. Increasingly, from the eighteenth century on, we viewed "love" as the primary purpose of marriage. It wasn't always this way. Troubadours of the eleventh to thirteenth centuries described undying passion as a hallmark of love for both women and men. However, the **romantic love** they described was generally experienced outside marriage; in fact, the most typical form of courtly love emphasized a young man's service to and love for a married woman. Consequently, this romantic love, though celebrated, was also seen as socially disruptive, a threat to the power of the church, the state, and the family.

"Passionate attachments between young people can and do happen in any society," writes historian Lawrence Stone, "but the social acceptability of the emotion has varied enormously." For example, in many European cultures, parents provided a **dowry** for their daughters to ensure a "good match" (a custom that persists in many places, as does the different but related system of **bride price**). Though good parents attempted to consider their children's feelings, fathers and mothers, not children, were the primary makers of marriage; courtship was generally limited. Accordingly, in the sixteenth and seventeenth centuries, "every advice book, every medical treatise, every sermon and religious homily . . . firmly rejected both romantic passion and lust as suitable bases for marriage." By the 1700s, attitudes had softened, and individuals were advised to make marital choices based on love and affection—provided, of course, that the two families approved and the individuals' social and economic statuses were roughly equal.[12]

It wasn't until the 1800s that it became "normal and indeed praiseworthy for young men and women to fall passionately in love." However, in the nineteenth-century marriage manuals, love is rarely mentioned as a reason to get married. In fact, love "is presented more as a product of marriage than its prerequisite." By 1900, though, "love had won its battle along the whole line in the upper sections of the middle class." Dating developed to allow young people to "fall in love" and select mates, becoming by 1950 the principal mode of courtship. Romantic love "has since been regarded as the most important prerequisite to marriage," though vestiges of the older family-directed model of marriage persist in some Canadian ethnic groups and among the very wealthy.[13]

So romantic love, as we know it—as the basis for marriage and family—is relatively recent. However, it isn't necessarily the foundation of marriage and/or sexual expression among every group everywhere else in the world. Even in our society, love may or may not accompany sexual activity or family life, and it may wax and wane in intensity. In a classic article, sociologist William J. Goode noted that there was little evidence that the ideology of romantic love was believed widely and deeply by all strata of the American population.[14] Still, most North Americans are repelled by the idea of arranged marriage, seeing it as the antithesis of free choice and individualism. This can blind us to the historical novelty of our distinctive view of love and marriage. When we began to marry for love and to distrust all other reasons for marrying, we made the fusion of sexual passion and deep friendship the standard basis of married life.

The emergence of women as "emotional specialists" and the development of companionate marriage had dramatic effects on the gendering of intimacy. So too did new ideas about homosexuality as a fixed sexual orientation. Philosopher Michel Foucault argued, "the disappearance of friendship as a social institution, and the declaration of homosexuality as a social/political/medical problem, are the same process." Prior to the end of the nineteenth century, concern about same-sex acts focused on behaviours (such as **sodomy**), not identity. As is discussed further in Chapter 12, however, late in the 1800s a new word—homosexual—was coined to describe those with a persistent sexual orientation toward the same sex. As sexologists and psychologists developed a picture of "the homosexual," **homophobia** became increasingly significant in men's lives; "the possible imputation of homosexual interest to any bonds between men ensured that men had constantly to be aware of and assert their difference from both women and homosexuals," writes sociologist Lynne Segal.[15]

Industrialization, companionate marriage, the separation of spheres, and the emergence of "the modern homosexual"—these simultaneous forces created the arena in which we have experienced emotional life. Intimacy's division into two complementary gendered domains is part of the story of our gendered society.

Gendered Communications

Intimacy begins with communication, whether it's verbal or non-verbal. Unsurprisingly, studies have found that language and communication are heavily gendered.

Perhaps the most celebrated of studies of gendered communication was by Deborah Tannen, who presented evidence that men and women use language differently and for different *goals*. Indeed, she argued that talk between men and women is "cross-cultural communication." To men, she claimed, conversations "are negotiations in which people try and achieve and maintain the upper hand if they can, and protect themselves from some others' attempts to put them down and push them around." Women, by contrast, use conversations as "negotiations for closeness in which people try and seek and give confirmation and support, and to reach consensus." No matter the good intentions of both parties, their different communication styles get in the way. Therefore, for Tannen, men and women simply do intimacy differently.[16]

The broad brushstrokes of Tannen's discussion of gendered communication have been complemented by more carefully delimited studies. For example, some scholars have examined the content of speech in addition to its goals. They find that in general, men disclose less personal information, use fewer intensifiers, and make direct and declarative statements. Women negotiate in private, ask more questions to maintain the flow of conversation, and use more personal pronouns.

Finally, *styles* of speech are gendered. Style, first of all, can include the actual sounds of a voice. **Sociophonetics**, a field that studies vocal sounds in relation to cultural variation and change, has much to tell us about gender and communication. A particularly interesting case study is provided by pitch. Obviously, pitch or speech register is partly determined by biology; men's voices are typically deeper because of size and structural differences. However, these differences may be exaggerated well beyond what is "natural" to men and women. Almost all cultures have different ideals for male and female speech;

these ideals are highly variable, however, and change over time. For example, cultural value placed on pitch is measurable by asking listeners to evaluate speech. Dutch speakers prefer lower-pitched female voices than do Japanese speakers because of varied cultural ideals. These ideals influence the way we speak but in a complicated manner. For example, there is evidence that Japanese women's speech is significantly higher than that of European and American women, but that lower pitch is becoming increasingly common in Japan. There are also dramatic gender pitch differences from place to place even among speakers of the same language; in California, these differences are much more dramatic than in New Zealand. Intonation also reflects gender. When women speak, they sometimes end a declarative sentence with a slight rise in tone, as if ending it with a question mark. This "High-Rising Terminal" (HRT) is found all over the world among young English-speaking women (except, apparently, in Belfast!) and has been extensively studied. (It seems to be diminishing among today's university students, however.)[17]

Pitch and intonation also help identify speakers as more or less masculine. Some of the most important research on masculinity has focused on identifying what it is to "sound gay." Both higher pitch and varied pitch sound "gay" to many listeners, as do certain consonant sounds. Highly indicative of masculinity to most listeners is **creaky voice**, a very low-pitched, rumbling intonation often associated with male voiceovers in advertising. Such voices are highly regarded, authoritative, and persuasive. Interestingly, while creaky voice is the *sine qua non* of hypermasculinity, it has recently become popular among young American women, and has been found to be more prevalent among gay and trans men than among straight men. (Unfortunately, for any women hoping to sound more authoritative, listeners apparently rate women less positively when they speak in this fashion.) The example of creaky voice suggests, once again, that gender performance and identity are at least as important as biology in determining the way we speak.[18]

Other style differences are informative, though it is important to remember that these differences vary from place to place and are highly malleable. Life stage and relationship status also have an important effect on how we speak and listen. Tannen's work focused on heterosexual adult men and women in relationships, but we cannot assume that her findings hold for youth or for non-heterosexual men and women. Finally, we need to very cautious about deceptive differences—about treating all communication differences as artifacts of gender when they may result from other differences (including differences of power). An intersectional analysis that considers ethnicity, race, age, ability, sexuality, and class is needed to understand fully the differences in communication.

At a general level, women tend to "hedge"—to express tentativeness—and to "backchannel"—using words or making sounds that confirm listening and encourage the speaker to continue speaking. Men, in conversation with women, tend to do more "topic rejection"—deciding what's going to be talked about. As we saw in Chapter 1, men interrupt women far more often than women interrupt men. Crucially, however, all of these differences are differences in *cross-sex* talk. In same-sex conversations, they tend to either disappear, or even more critically, to be replicated on the basis of power differences between the same-sex speakers (for example, employer–employee). This finding led researchers to conclude that it's not the gender of the speaker but rather the gender of the person to whom one is speaking that makes the difference. Therefore, gender matters, but not in the way that interplanetary stereotypes would have it.

The question of *amount* of talk is also an important feature of gendered communication. According to Jennifer Coates and other linguists, in most cultures cultural beliefs about language, or "folk linguistics," devalue women's speech and elevate that of men. Many people believe that women talk more, incessantly "chattering" and "gossiping." While gossip is important to both male and female cultures, data suggest that in fact men talk more than women do, particularly in public. In mixed-sex groups, men dominate, and according to a recent metastudy, "contrary to prediction, men were significantly more talkative than were women."[19]

What then, can be said about the stereotype of the silent, uncommunicative man? Men, it seems, mainly grow silent within intimate relationships. The same man, silent and uncommunicative at home, may be quite talkative at work. Men's silence, therefore, is not an immutable gender trait but a response to a particular situation. Women, similarly, may be much more vocal in the home environment when trying to elicit conversation. In one study of couples within their homes, Victoria Leto DeFrancisco found that women spoke 63 per cent of conversational time to men's 37 per cent. However, having more air time did not translate into being the one dominating the conversation; men either interrupted or gave no response, a delayed response, or minimal responses far more than women did. Women failed to elicit conversations. Women's talk within the home is often viewed by men as "nagging"—persistent attempts to raise a topic or delegate a chore. Nagging, in fact, is not only in the eye of the beholder (very few men have ever been labelled nags) but is also an indication of the relative powerlessness of the "nag" herself. Silence, as psychologist Carol Tavris writes, is power:

> The person who is silent may neither wish to be powerful nor feel powerful, but silence is power nonetheless. The silent partner feels no obligation to speak, no duty to change; he is mysterious, his wishes and feelings unknown. His silence causes those around him either to walk on tiptoe, to avoid the moods they imagine he feels, or to pursue him for connection, communication, and affection. The silent man has a resource that others want: information about what he is thinking, what he desires, how he is reacting, whether he approves of them.[20]

Therefore, what we are seeing, when we observe gendered conversation, may be how "observed sex differences in language mirror the overall difference in power between men and women." In fact, according to one influential study from the 1980s, power differences can *by themselves* produce "the conversational division of labour parallel to the one ordinarily associated with sexual differentiation," while more egalitarian sexual arrangements can overturn conventional gendered communication patterns.[21]

Therefore, some of the classic differences that we attribute to gendered style reflect the fact that women have traditionally been less *powerful* than men have been. In fact, as William O'Barr and Bowman Atkins argued in the 1980s, so-called "women's" communications are largely "a language of powerlessness, a condition that can apply to men as well as to women." This, and not any innate feminine traits, may explain why women's communications are often marked by more "politeness strategies" than those of men—and why the communications strategies of other historically disadvantaged groups may look like "women's language." However, similar social location (status, education, and power) may eliminate these differences. In fact, according to Melanie Ayres and Campbell Leaper, "gender differences appear and disappear, depending on the interaction context." They are not simply the reflection of some fixed gender *difference*, but are the result of cultural preference and gender inequality. This explains why communication patterns are increasingly converging, and reminds us that gendered communication is a reflection of a gendered society.[22]

Gender Differences in Friendship: Real and Imagined

Friends are important to North Americans. In fact, for North American youth, friends are arguably more important than family. One study compared Belgian, Canadian, and Italian youth and found dramatic differences in the importance of family interactions to adolescents. Canadian youths who participated in the study spent more time each day with friends than with their families, in contrast to Italian youths who spent twice as much time with family as with friends. Clearly, we are a friend-oriented culture. Yet friendship is very different from our other important relationships with spouses or family. There we have clear legal ties and obligations. Friendship, in contrast, seems voluntary and somewhat ephemeral. "Being friends" with someone else is a delicate and nuanced matter. There is no clear marker for what constitutes a friend, and yet each of us has a clear idea of "what friends do."[23]

Not surprisingly, such ideas are influenced by gender. Most of the research on gender differences in friendship turns out to reinforce existing stereotypes of women as emotionally expressive and men as inexpressive and either incapable of or uninterested in nurturing. There's even some evidence that brain differences account for friendship differences. A recent study found that whereas men respond to stress with the now-famous "fight-or-flight" response, women look to friends or allies as a source of emotional sustenance in a response labelled "tend and befriend." The researchers believe that this is because men respond to stress by releasing testosterone, which causes the fight-or-flight response, whereas women release oxytocin, which produces a calming effect and a desire for closeness. Past studies have found similarly striking differences. In a revealing portrait of the role of friendship in our lives, Lillian Rubin interviewed more than 300 women and men and found startling differences in both the number and the depth of friendships. "At every life stage between 25 and 55, women have more friendships, as distinct from collegial relationships or workmates, than men," she writes, "and the differences in the content and quality of their friendships are marked and unmistakable." Three-fourths of the women Rubin interviewed could identify a best friend, whereas more than two-thirds of the men could not. While many married men identified their wives as their best friends, wives almost never identified their husbands in this way. Even when a man could identify a best friend, Rubin found that "the two usually shared little about the interior of their lives and feelings." If we understand intimacy to be based on both verbal and non-verbal sharing of thoughts and feelings so that the intimate understands the inner life of the other, then men's friendships are, Rubin concluded, "emotionally impoverished."[24]

Other research corroborates some of her findings. Women seem far more likely to share their feelings with their friends than are men; to engage in face-to-face interactions instead of men's preferred side-to-side style; and to discuss a wider array of issues than men do. Women's friendships seem to be more person-oriented, whereas men's are more activity-oriented. Women's friendships appear to be more "holistic," and men's more "segmented." Even when women seem to have fewer friends, as some studies have found, those they have are more intimate.[25]

In general, these studies of gender differences in friendships confirm the idea that men are more instrumental and women more expressive. However, some of these studies, based on adult heterosexual men and women (and often married ones), may overstate the differences. Age and marital status tend to affect friendship patterns, at least for heterosexuals. For example, unmarried men are more likely to maintain close and intimate friendships with both women and other men than are married men; therefore deriving our information about male friendships from studying married men may be particularly perilous. As a result, scholarship may overlook that, in fact, there is "much more similarity than dissimilarity in the manner in which women and men conduct their friendships," as psychologist Paul Wright writes in a review of the existing literature of gender differences. He notes that women are "somewhat more likely to emphasize personalism, self-disclosure, and supportiveness" and that men are "somewhat more likely to emphasize external interest and mutually involving activities"; but these differences "are not great, and in many cases, they are so obscure that they are hard to demonstrate." What's more, what differences there are tend to diminish markedly and virtually disappear "as the strength and duration of the friendship increases."[26]

Sociologists who explore the impact of race, ethnicity, age, class, or sexuality on social life suggest that factors other than gender may complicate the convenient gendering of friendship. Men and women may be more alike in their emotional lives, but there may be big differences among, say, working-class white women and men, on the one hand, and middle-class immigrant men and women on the other.

Ethnicity, for example, directly affects both men's and women's experiences of friendships, not only because we tend to choose friends of our own ethnic group but because racialized groups may develop their own modes of friendship against the backdrop of a racist society. According to **minority stress theory**, members of marginalized groups experience more rejection and therefore a greater dependence on the support of friends. "For Black men in [US] society," writes journalist Martin Simmons "the world is a hostile, dangerous place—a jungle." Friendship is a survival strategy: "Me and him against the world."[27]

Class also shapes emotional experiences. In the US, for example, working-class black male friendships are often self-disclosing and close. Yet middle-class black men have fewer and less intimate friends than their working-class counterparts. Moreover, some forms of class- and race-based intimacy may be a double-edged sword. Shanette Harris suggests that the very strategies embraced by black men to "promote African American male empowerment and survival" may also lead to such maladaptive behaviours as gang membership.[28]

Another group facing minority stress, LGBTQ people, are similarly likely to rely on friends. As gay communities emerged in the 1960s and 1970s, often formed of individuals who faced not only societal disapproval but also the rejection of their families, friendship became the central glue of community. The **chosen family**, a collection of supportive friends, became essential to the survival of all sexual minorities. "A person has so many close friends," comments a gay male character in Wendy Wasserstein's Pulitzer Prize-winning play *The Heidi Chronicles*. "And in our lives, our friends are our families." As more and more gay people build legally and socially recognized families, this situation has changed, but "the chosen family" remains an institution within gay culture. As a result, there are many studies of LGBTQ friendships, especially among gay men.[29]

In a 1994 survey, Peter Nardi and Drury Sherrod found significant similarities in the same-sex friendship patterns of gay men and lesbians. Both value close, intimate friendships, define intimacy in similar ways, and behave similarly with their friends. Two differences stood out to the researchers—how gay men and lesbians dealt with conflict and the role of sexuality within their friendships. Gay men, for example, were far more likely to sexualize their same-sex friendships than were lesbians. Therefore, like straight men, gay men seemed to experience more sexual tension in friendships with people to whom they might conceivably be attracted. On the other hand, "[l]ike their straight sisters, lesbians can have intensely intimate and satisfying relationships with each other without any sexual involvement," writes Lillian Rubin. Although it may overstate the case to claim, as Rubin does, that asexual gay male friendships are "rare," such gender differences between lesbians and gay men underscore that gender, not sexual orientation, is often the key determinant of our intimate experiences.[30]

Friendship has arguably been more significant to sexual minorities than to heterosexuals; sexual-minority youth have very often "come out" to friends rather than to family members. Moreover, LGBTQ individuals are more likely to have best (and other) friends across genders and sexual orientations; lesbians, however, are as likely as heterosexuals to have same-sex friends. Does this add up to a different valuation or style of friendship, however? Arguably not. A recent study found that despite some differences in homophily, heterosexual and sexual-minority men and women were more alike than different. All rated friends as important to their life satisfaction; there were no effects of sexual orientation on number of friends or importance of friends.[31]

When we sift through the conflicting evidence, two gender differences in friendships do assert themselves with a certain insistence. The first is *sexual tension*, which can emerge in all kinds of friendships, whether same-sex or cross-sex. Virtually all the men and women Rubin interviewed described sexual tension in their cross-sex friendships, which made stability and trust in the relationship more fragile. In the past, homophily in friendship was more common as a result. However, as society has changed, so has our ability to manage the issue of sexual tension. A recent study of American college students found that the vast majority—81.6 per cent—agreed, "men and women can be friends," though women were more likely to be cautious about this statement.[32]

For men, to be emotionally open and vulnerable with another man raises the second significant gender difference in friendship—the impact of *homophobia*. Homophobia is more than simply the irrational fear and hatred of gay people; it is also the fear that one might be misperceived as gay by others. This may explain why gay men are significantly more likely to have best friends who are heterosexual women, or other sexual minorities, rather than straight men—the latter are often unwilling to take the risk of being seen as gay because their best friend is.

"No Homo, Bro": Homophobia, Bromance, and Men's Changing Friendships

Even to raise the question of male friendships has sometimes been seen as raising the "spectre" of homosexuality. In the opening pages of his book on male friendships, Stuart Miller writes that the first person he sought to interview, a philosophy professor, said to him, "Male friendship. You mean you're going to write about homosexuality?" "Everywhere I have gone," Miller reports, "there has been the same misconception. The bizarre necessity to explain, at the beginning, that my subject is not homosexuality." Additionally, Lillian Rubin found the association of friendship with homosexuality "so common among men."[33]

For North American men, homophobia has restricted (and arguably fundamentally distorted) expressions of intimacy among men. One man explained why he would feel weird if he hugged his best friend:

> The guys are more rugged and things, and it wouldn't be rugged to hug another man. That's not a masculine act, where it could be, you know, there's nothing unmasculine about it. But somebody might not see it as masculine and you don't want somebody else to think that you're not, you know—masculine or . . . but you still don't want to be outcast. Nobody I think wants to be outcast.[34]

Seen in this light, the relative lack of intimacy some researchers have found in male friendships is therefore a relic of homophobia rather than of men's personalities or aspirations. In fact, examining boys' friendships suggests precisely this. According to Niobe Way's longitudinal research, boys enter adolescence with passionate attachments to their friends:

> Listening to boys, particularly during early and middle adolescence, speak about their male friendships is like reading an old-fashioned romance novel where the female protagonist is describing her passionate feelings for her man. At the edge of manhood, when pressures to conform to gender expectations intensify, boys speak about their male friends with abandon, referring to them as people whom they love.

These same boys leave adolescence with fewer friends and a more recognizably "masculine" style of friendship, conditioned largely by homophobia.[35]

Now consider the video for Nigahiga's 2012 song *Bromance*. The video begins with one young man's departure from a gathering of friends. He tenderly hugs them all, saying "I love you, man" to each. When one friend rebuffs his hug because it is "weird," he launches into a song whose chorus indicates, "there's nothing really gay about it / Not that there's anything wrong with being gay" and concludes, "I love you in the most heterosexual way." The song plays humorously with the concept of **bromance**, a term

Hartswood Films/REX/Shutterstock

A fine bromance: Benedict Cumberbatch and Martin Freeman as Holmes and Watson.

apparently invented in the 1990s but that made its mainstream media debut around 2005. The term refers to, in Michael Deangelis's words, an "emotionally intense bond between presumably straight males who demonstrate an openness to intimacy that they neither regard, acknowledge, avow, nor express sexually." A bromance, then, is a highly expressive (in line with the traditional view of women's friendships), intimate bond that remains heterosexual. Today, a Google search of the term "bromance" nets more than 10 million results, demonstrating the term's application to areas as disparate as television (*Sherlock* and *Supernatural*, for example) and global politics (Silvio Berlusconi and Vladimir Putin, apparently).[36]

Bromance's ascendancy has been accompanied by several other new terms: the "man crush" is perhaps the most recent. Describing an intense but non-sexual liking or admiration by a heterosexual-identified man for another man, "man crush" has quickly become ubiquitous and has spawned its corollary, the "girl crush" (which is, interestingly, much more sexually ambiguous). It seems that twenty-first-century North America is ready for expressive and passionate attachments among men—as long as they remain strictly heterosexual. Homophobia is therefore still part of the background. "The man-crush is the sincerest form of platonic heterosexual flattery," writes Tom Fordy, while another journalist reassures female readers that "[t]hese crushes do not mean that your man desires his man crush in the way that he desires you." The constant assertions of purely platonic intent indicate the persistent presence of homophobia as the policeman of both bromance and the man crush.[37]

For adolescent and young adult men, a similar policing role is played by the phrase "No homo" (also mentioned in Chapter 7). Arising from 1990s hip-hop and hitting the mainstream around 2008, the term became a way to say sexually suggestive or admiring things about another man while preserving one's heterosexuality. Widespread today

continued

among youth and gamers, "no homo" operates both to permit intimacy and to deny that intimacy any potential sexual content.

Clearly, bromance, the man crush, and "no homo" all partake of homophobia. (NBA Roy Hibbert was fined $75,000 for using the phrase "no homo" because it was regarded as a slur.) However, these phenomena and terms also permit and encourage statements and behaviours that *do* expand the acceptable repertoire of emotional expression for men (for example, saying, "I love you" and hugging). Importantly, "no homo" plays humorously (and often graphically) with the idea of romance and sexual acts between men, and may do so in ambiguous ways. So while some feel that the phrase is inherently homophobic, Joshua Brown cautions against seeing the phrase as "simple homophobia." Others, like Jonah Weiner, note, "there's an appealing sense in which the phrase refuses to function as tidily as some of its boosters might like." Noting Kanye West's consistently anti-homophobic statements and similar changes, Weiner muses that "no homo" may in fact be "helping to make hip-hop a gayer place." A very recent article by Amanda Potts goes further. Studying the use of the phrase in online gaming communities, Potts states that it offers "a unique opportunity to encounter, interpret, and experiment with queer discourse" in a community that is actually largely anti-homophobic and accepting. At the very least, the emergence of these terms in the first decade of this century points to clear transformations in intimacy between men—and perhaps to the troubling of the stranglehold that homophobia exercised over men's friendships in the twentieth century. [38]

As families become smaller, as more of us live alone, and as peers have increasingly become more important, friends are an ever-more-significant part of our lives. All of us want the same things in friends, it seems, but differences affect whom and how we befriend. It's not as simple as "his" friendship and "hers"; indeed, age, sexual orientation, marital status, ethnicity, and class play important roles in our friendships. Where our friendships and friendship styles differ, this is the result not of innate differences, but of the gendered society.

Gendered (Romantic) Love

It seems absurd to feel the need to define something that our culture spends so much time talking about, but when we discuss romantic love, what exactly do we mean? Most scholars would agree that romantic love is characterized by a strong attachment to, physical attraction to, and idealization of another person; in the grips of romantic love, we may feel exhilarated, obsessed with, and absolutely focused on uniting with our love object. As neuroscientists are fond of pointing out, these feelings are accompanied and facilitated by chemical changes, including the elevation of **dopamine** levels.[39]

The nature of such processes across cultures, historically, and in North American gay and non-gender-conforming teens may vary somewhat; but the existence and experience of romantic love is seen as nearly universal. What mainstream North American culture does with the experience of romantic love, however, is not. Commonly beginning in adolescence, our **culturally scripted** experience of romantic love is supposed—perhaps after one or two "heartbreaks" along the way—to lead to marriage, after which we will settle down into a less passionate but still, ideally, deep romantic attachment.[40]

The power of this cultural script has been steadily growing in North American society. The acceptance of love as the basis of marriage grew first among men. This was demonstrated by a series of experiments conducted by William Kephart in the late 1960s. Kephart asked more than 1,000 American college students, "If a boy (girl) had all the other qualities you desired, would you marry this person if you were not in love with him (her)?" In the 1960s, Kephart found dramatic differences between men, who thought that marriage without love was out of the question, and women, who were more likely to admit that the absence of love wouldn't necessarily deter them from marriage. He connected this to women's relative economic dependency.[41]

After the 1960s, sociologists continued to ask this question, and each year fewer women and men said they were willing to marry for any reason but love. By the mid-1980s, 85 per cent of both women and men considered such a marriage out of the question; and by 1991, 86 per cent of the men and 91 per cent of the women responded with an emphatic no. The more dramatic shift among women indicates how much the women's movement has transformed women's lives: Women's economic independence now affords women, too, the luxury of marrying for love alone.[42]

Such studies, however, yield very different results in different countries, suggesting that our definitions of love may have more to do with cultural (and economic!) differences than they do with gender. When students in Japan and Russia were asked the same question in 1992, their answers differed dramatically from those of Americans. More Russian women (41 per cent) and men (30 per cent) answered yes than did either Japanese (20 per cent of the men and 19 per cent of the women) or the Americans (13 per cent of the men and 9 per cent of the women).[43]

Another study compared American men and women with Chinese men and women. The differences between women and men were small—as were the differences between the Chinese and American samples. Culture, not gender, was a far more salient variable in understanding these differences. In both cases, men were more likely to hold romantic and idealized notions about love but were slightly more likely to be willing to marry without love. Note that the difference here is not in the existence of romantic love, as scholars have not yet found a society in which it does not exist; the difference is in the connection between love and marriage. That connection turns out to be malleable and linked to economic and social issues. Interestingly, the societies in which love is most dominant are those in which women's status is highest.[44]

Another interesting thing about the celebration of romantic love, as Eva Illouz points out, is that love hurts. For every story of enduring love or exhilarating passion, there are at least as many stories of abject misery and heartbreak. In the eighteenth century, this truth was immortalized in song in Martini's classic *"Plaisir d'Amour,"* a classic still sung and admired for both its tune and its lyrics, which state that "the pleasure of love lasts only a moment / but the sorrow of love lasts a lifetime." In the twentieth century, while heartbreak was still a feature of love, clinical psychology offered hope; if misery in love was the result of one's individual psychological makeup, it was within human control. Accordingly, the twentieth century brought various novelties to love, not least its growing prestige.

Another change is what Illouz calls "the emergence of marriage markets." As discussed above, until the 1800s, parents, not youth, were the most likely arrangers of marital unions. Rituals and rules that were sometimes flouted, but nonetheless powerful, constrained individual choice. Constraints included not only the "appropriateness" of a potential partner (and therefore whether one had the opportunity to meet at all), but also rules about contact that introduced the potential partners slowly and according to a well-thumbed script. These constraints were successively lifted in favour of the modern "marriage market" described by Illouz, characterized by the "disembedding of individual romantic choices from the moral and social fabric of the group" and "the emergence of a self-regulated market of encounters." That is, selecting a mate was divorced from the rules that had governed it (selecting a mate with regard to family, kin, or economic considerations) and from the social locations that had produced interactions, such as parent-sanctioned or parent-monitored practices such as "calling" or "walking out." In their place emerged "dating," a practice almost entirely regulated by individuals themselves. In this new "market of encounters," emphasis on character, economic prospect, lineage, etc., was supplanted by an emphasis on emotional intimacy and sex appeal: that is, on the experience of falling in love.[45]

The experience of falling in love is governed by rules of attraction that (for heterosexuals at least) draw deeply on gender stereotype. (Most of what follows is based on studies of heterosexuals only. LGBTQ individuals may be more fluid in their attractions, but partner attractions seem to follow very similar rules about attractiveness and social status, with straight and gay men most interested in attractiveness and straight women most interested in social status.) For example, most heterosexual women and girls are attracted "up"; that is, to others who are in some way "above" them, whether that be in terms of wealth, worldly power, age, achievement, or simply body size; men, traditionally, have been attracted "down," to women of lesser achievement, size, and age. (Think about it: Even today, how many women are willing to date a man smaller than they are? Until very recently, how many men were willing to date a woman who earned more than they did?)

French theorist Pierre Bourdieu calls this our culture's (and women's) "spontaneous" acceptance of male domination; it's spontaneous because no one has to force us. In fact, for most of us, this kind of attraction just "feels natural." Before we start blaming ourselves—or as Bourdieu is sometimes accused of doing, blame women for complicity with male domination—let's remember that every fairy tale, from *Cinderella* to *Pretty Woman*, relies on inequality between the partners for its narrative power. However, it's certainly worth considering the implications of our attraction to partners either "above" or "below" us in these ways.[46]

As our attraction to "appropriate" mates is gendered, so too is the experience of falling in love. For example, there is evidence that men are more likely to respond to ephemeral qualities such as physical appearance when they fall in love and are far more likely to say they are easily attracted to members of the opposite sex. Yet most studies have found *men* to be stronger believers in romantic love ideologies than are women. (On the other hand, men also tend to be more cynical about love at the same time.) Men, it seems, are more likely to believe myths about love at first sight, tend to fall in love more quickly than women do, and are more likely to enter relationships out of a desire to fall in love. Romantic love, to men, is an irrational, spontaneous, and compelling emotion that demands action.[47]

Women, on the other hand, show a more "pragmatic orientation" toward falling in and out of love and are more likely to also like the men they love. Once in love, women tend to experience the state more intensely. One experiment found that after only four dates, men were almost twice as likely as women were to define the relationship as love (27 per cent to 15 per cent). By the twenty-first date, however, 43 per cent of the women said that they were in love, whereas only 30 per cent of the men did. The researchers write:

> If by "more romantic" we refer to the speed of involvement and commitment, then the male appears to be more deserving of that label. If, on the other hand, we mean the experiencing of the emotional dimension of romantic love, then the female qualifies as candidate for "more romantic" behaviour in a somewhat more judicious and rational fashion. She chooses and commits herself more slowly than the male but, once in love, she engages more extravagantly in the euphoric and idealizational dimensions of loving.[48]

Despite the fact that men report falling out of love more quickly, it is women who initiate the majority of break-ups. In addition, it seems, women have an easier time accepting their former romantic partners as friends than men do. After a break-up, men report more loneliness, depression, and sleeplessness than women do. This is equally true after divorce: Married men live longer and emotionally healthier lives than divorced or single men; unmarried women live longer and are happier than married women are. So are men the "romantic" sex, women the "pragmatic" one? It's probably not that simple. The separation of spheres "feminized" romantic love so that today love implies "an overemphasis on talking and feeling, a mystification of the material basis of attachment, and a tendency to ignore physical love and the practical aspects of nurturance and mutual assistance." As with friendship, women have come to be seen as the love experts. "Part of the reason that men seem so much less loving than women," argues sociologist Francesca Cancian, "is that men's behaviour is measured with a feminine ruler."[49]

Gendered styles of loving are the products of the large-scale transformations that created the modern system of gender relations. Men's and women's styles of romantic love are the result of gender inequality; these differences, as psychologist Carol Tavris tells us, emerged "because women are expected, allowed, and required to reveal certain emotions, and men are expected and required to deny or suppress them." They are the source of so much miscommunication between women and men that it often feels as though we are from different planets, or at least, in Lillian Rubin's phrase, "intimate strangers."[50]

However, empirical research on the gender of romantic love reveals fewer differences, and of less significance, than we might otherwise expect. One review of the literature, for example, found that women's and men's experiences and attitudes are statistically similar on 49 of the 60 correlates of love. In addition, a recent study found that generally women and men are pretty much equally emotionally expressive—although women are more likely to express those emotions associated with inequality (smoothing things over, unruffling feathers, and the like).[51]

To "read" such differences as revealing something *essential* about women and men would be to miss the structural impact of the modern family arrangement and the way that structural arrangements enhance some relational styles and inhibit others. Our current feminization of love, psychologist Carol Tavris argues, has detrimental effects on women's lives:

> The feminization of love in America, the glorification of women's ways of loving, is not about the love between autonomous individuals. It celebrates a romantic, emotional love that promotes the myth of basic, essential differences between women and men. It supports the opposition of women's love and men's work. In so doing, it derails women from thinking about their own talents and aspirations, rewarding instead a narrowed focus on finding and keeping Mr. Right.[52]

Fortunately, love need not be feminized, as Francesca Cancian argues. Men's way of loving—"the practical help and physical activities"—is, she notes, "as much a part of love as the expression of feelings." Additionally, the feminization of love as the expression of feelings, nurturing, and intimacy also obscures women's capacity for instrumental, activity-centred forms of love and, in effect, freezes men and women into patterns that mask some of their traits, as if right-handedness meant one could never even use one's left hand. Cancian poses an important question: "Who is more loving," she asks, "a couple who confide most of their experiences to each other but rarely cooperate or give each other practical help, or a couple who help each other through many crises and co-operate in running a household but rarely discuss their personal experiences?" Perhaps, Cancian suggests, what we need is a more embracing *universal* definition of love that has as its purpose individual development, mutual support, and intimacy—and that women and men are equally capable of experiencing.[53]

Conclusion

Friendship and love are perhaps the major avenues of self-exploration and the chief routes we take in our society to know ourselves. "Love provides us with identities, virtues, roles through which we define ourselves, as well as partners to share our happiness, reinforce our values, support our best opinions of ourselves, and compensate for the anonymity, impersonality or possibly frustration of public life," writes Robert Solomon. Our friends, Lillian Rubin writes, "are those who seem to us to call up the best parts of ourselves, even while they also accept our darker side."[54]

To sustain our lives, to enable us to experience the full range of our pleasures, to achieve the deep emotional connections with lovers and friends, we must remember the ways that gender does *and does not* construct our emotional lives. Love and friendship are deeply *human* experiences—ones that should unite rather than divide us. As the great British novelist E.M. Forster once wrote of passionate human connection, "men and women are capable of sustained relations, not mere opportunities for an electrical discharge."

Summary

Though we often hear of "interplanetary" differences between the sexes in intimate life, these differences are not as great as we sometimes believe. Moreover, these differences are not inevitable but are the result of historical and social changes, which continue.

Women are now considered the "relationship experts," but this was not always the case. Men's friendships and ways of loving have often been considered superior. However, the nineteenth-century development of industrialization and the so-called separate spheres ideology positioned women as the ministers of love, men as competitors in the strife-filled public arena. As a result, men's and women's styles of intimacy diverged, with men adopting more instrumental styles and women increasingly specializing in the expressive.

The nineteenth century also elevated the idea of companionate marriage and romantic love, which made love, for the first time, the most important basis for marriage. At the same time, homosexuality (as a fixed sexual orientation) was "discovered," leading to new homophobic scrutiny of male friendships. Accordingly, intimacy was divided into two gendered domains, with effects that are still with us.

Communications are one of the most-studied areas of gender difference in intimacy, particularly since the groundbreaking work conducted by Deborah Tannen and others. Indeed, it seems that content, styles, and amount of talk are heavily gendered. Many of these differences are seen across cultures, with "men's talk" generally valued more than characteristically female speech. However, research has found that most differences emerge in cross-sex talk, and that men adopt characteristically "female" modes of talk in situations where they are required to be deferent; the language of gender, therefore, may be less about gender than about power.

Friendship continues to grow in importance in our lives, and scholars have found both similarities and differences in gendered friendship styles. Pioneering research found that women seem to have not only more friends, but also closer ones, with whom they engage in more expressive friendship. Newer research has failed to reliably identify significant differences in these areas, particularly when other factors—such as employment, ethnicity, class, age, and marital status—are considered. Still, there are key areas where gender differences can be seen. Homophobia affects male friendships more than female ones; moreover, men (straight and gay) experience more sexual tension in friendships than do women.

Romantic love exists across cultures; in the modern Western world, however, it is seen as the ideal basis for marriage. Indeed, though women have historically been more pragmatic about marriage, fewer and fewer people of either sex are willing to entertain the idea of marrying without being "in love." Falling in love for most heterosexuals is still governed by rules of attraction that depend heavily on gender stereotypes, particularly the stereotype that a man should be attracted "down," and a woman "up." Once attracted to a partner, heterosexual men and women experience falling in love in gendered ways.

Women remain somewhat more pragmatic about love, tending to fall into love (and out of it) more slowly and accepting the end of relationships with less loneliness and depression than men experience. Women also accept divorce more readily. When marriages remain intact, gender differences emerge, particularly in instrumental versus expressive relationship styles. These differences may reflect not men's incompetence in love, but the feminization of what we think of as appropriate intimacy. Francesca Cancian suggests that we need a universal model of love that brings both expressive and instrumental styles together and that focuses, most importantly, on more meaningful measures (such as individual development and mutual support). In friendship, communications, and love, our society remains gendered.

Questions for Critical Thinking

1. What are the criteria you use to assess whether someone is a "true friend": Do you think that these criteria are influenced by your gender or your membership in another group?
2. What do you think the emergence of bromance, man crushes, and "no homo" means? Are these indications of homophobia?
3. Do you think women have a more "pragmatic" approach to falling in love? If so, why?
4. Can you think of ways in which men and women attracted "down" and "up," respectively? Do you think there are implications for the relationships we enter on this basis?

Key Terms

bride price
bromance
chosen family
companionate marriage
creaky voice
culturally scripted
dopamine
dowry
emotion work

expressive
homophobia
instrumental
intimacy
minority stress theory
romantic love
sociophonetics
sodomy

The Gendered Body
Prescriptions and Inscriptions

"tis in ourselves that we are thus or thus. Our bodies are our gardens, to the which our wills are gardeners; so that if we will plant nettles, or sow lettuce, set hyssop and weed up thyme, supply it with one gender of herbs, or distract it with many, either to have it sterile with idleness, or manured with industry, why, the power and corrigible authority of this lies in our wills.
—William Shakespeare, *Othello* (1.3.677–85)

We think of our bodies either as our own private possessions, over which we exercise control (as Iago argues in the Shakespeare quote above), or as collections of biological impulses over which we have virtually no control at all. For centuries, the body has been shrouded in myth, taboo, and ignorance.

Yet nothing could be more significant—and more interlaced with society—than this most individual, private organism. First, the attributes of our bodies become, whether we like it or not, key elements of our identities. Our skin colour, features, visible sex characteristics, height, weight, visible ability or disability, attractiveness or homeliness—all become who we are in the eyes of the world. However, we also negotiate our bodily identities with the world. We inscribe—dress, pose, style, tattoo, pierce, and shape—our bodies with a wide range of cultural signs and symbols. Our bodies become social texts that we construct to be "read" by others. In fact, significant changes in the past few decades (such as new surgical procedures, birth control, and the Internet) have made us more aware of our bodies than ever before. This has enabled new groups to claim their own embodied agency, a kind of embodied democracy that has also been met, characteristically, with increased backlash.[1] Our bodies, then, are neither private property nor simple biological entities. They are shaped, made meaningful, and scrutinized by our relations with the gendered society.

Gender and Dis/ability

One of the ways in which our bodies are constructed by society relates to ability. If in modern societies the "universal" idea of a person has often been constructed as male, it has also been constructed as able-bodied. Quick: picture a human being. In all likelihood, you pictured someone standing, perhaps nude, probably quite young. (We'll leave aside, for now, any racial and gender attributes of your imagined human.) Did you picture someone with a cane, a wheelchair, or a developmental disability? If not, you are not alone. In our culture, **disability** is often ignored or rendered invisible, seen only when the specific topic of disability is addressed.

This study is not immune to the problem of failing to "see" disability when we talk about gender. Both within broader culture and in the field of gender studies, disability often goes unseen.[2] To the categories of privilege that we have discussed so far—including class, race, gender, and sexual orientation—we must also add *the privilege of ability*. Additionally, to the familiar phenomena of sexism, racism, classism, and homophobia, we need to add **ablism** (or **ableism**), which can be defined both as active discrimination against disabled people[3] and as attitudes that diminish disabled people's competence and focus on disability as their defining characteristic.

Like other forms of discrimination, ablism rests to some extent upon fear. Robert Murphy writes,

> The kind of culture the handicapped American must face is just as much a part of the environs of his disability as his wheelchair. It hardly needs saying that the disabled, individually and as a group, contravene all the values of youth, virility, activity, and physical beauty that Americans cherish, however little most individuals may embody them. Most handicapped people, myself included, sense that others resent them for this reason; we are subverters of an American Ideal, just as the poor betray the American Dream. . . . The disabled serve as constant, visible reminders to the able-bodied that the society they live in is shot through with inequity and suffering, that they live in a counterfeit paradise, and that they too are vulnerable. We represent a fearsome possibility.[4]

While the experience that Murphy describes is probably familiar to almost every disabled person, being feared is not the only thing that disabled people share. People with disabilities are often infantilized or seen as childlike; Murphy describes the way in which many adults with disabilities are dismissed or ignored when shopping or going to a public office. Often, disabled people are ignored while their companions are asked what the disabled person wants—as though the adult with the disability cannot explain it.

As of 2012, approximately 13.7 per cent of the Canadian population reports experiencing a disability that interferes with daily activities. Disability may be visible (for example, requiring the use of a wheelchair or cane) or invisible (such as pain or mental illness). The risk of disability increases dramatically with age. Of working-age Canadians (15–64), 1 in 10 experiences disability; the rate jumps to 1 in 3 for seniors.[5]

These Canadians are at much greater risk of poverty than the non-disabled are. (Of course, the risk is even higher for the 80 per cent of disabled people worldwide who live in low-income countries.) According to Statistics Canada data, the 2006 overall rate of poverty for non-disabled Canadian adults was 9.7 per cent. For adults with disabilities, the rate was 14.4 per cent; and when one factors in the higher cost of living with a disability, the burden of poverty increases. Those with cognitive or psychological disabilities faced an even higher rate of poverty (22.3 per cent). Data collected in 2012 show that the problem persists. Only 47 per cent of disabled adults reported employment, compared with a rate of 74 per cent for the non-disabled. In 2010, the median income of adults with disabilities was only $20,000, compared to $30,000 for non-disabled adults. Disabled adults were half as likely to have university degrees as the non-disabled. As these data suggest, adults with disabilities face significant barriers to employment, particularly discrimination, lack of accommodation, and underestimation of their abilities. When these adults are immigrants, Aboriginal, or from racialized groups, the barriers can be even greater.[6]

If disabled men and women share many aspects of the experience of disability, gender nonetheless interacts with ability in important ways. Women are "overrepresented" among Canadian adults with disabilities, with a rate of disability (14.9 per cent) higher than men's (12.5 per cent). (Women's rate of disability is higher than men's at all ages above 24.) Not only are women's rates generally higher, but women are also significantly more likely to experience visual, pain, mobility, flexibility, dexterity, memory, learning, and mental/psychological disabilities than are men. On the other hand, women are significantly *less* likely to experience hearing and developmental disabilities. Women with disabilities have an even higher rate of poverty than do their male counterparts. Given their greater representation among lone parents, women also face a double whammy with regard to poverty, because lone parents with disabilities are even more likely to live in poverty than able-bodied lone parents (themselves, as we saw in Chapter 6, a vulnerable group). Because employers' ideas of the "ideal worker" may be both sexist and ableist, women with disabilities also face additional barriers to employment. The same is true for racialized people of whatever gender living with disability.[7]

Women living both with disabilities and in poverty are tremendously vulnerable to violence and sexual abuse, even while their sexual agency has often been denied. According to Helen Meekosha, women with disabilities are (and have been) more likely than men to be institutionalized. Eugenics-driven sterilization (see Chapter 2) has also been directed primarily at disabled women (and in North America disproportionately at Indigenous and African-American women). For all of these reasons, women with disabilities may face greater body threat and body scrutiny than do disabled men. Still, some women may feel "liberated" from social expectations as a result of disability—the experience is neither uniform nor monotone, and highlighting the problems disabled women face may end up stereotyping them as victims.[8]

For men, disability may strike at the heart of both physical and sexual performance, which are key elements in hegemonic masculine ideologies. In fact, because masculinity (unlike femininity) is constructed on the basis of strength, damage to self-esteem and a sense of "invalidated masculinity" may be the experience of men with disabilities. As Tom Shakespeare notes, many war films hinge on a veteran's grappling with this issue. Some disabled men may be able to "recover" their masculinity through participation in sport, but for many men this is impossible. However, at least for heterosexual men, damaged masculinity may be more an issue to them than to their female partners; men with disabilities are significantly less likely than disabled women are to experience marital breakup. For all men, however, disability is a complex experience, influenced by issues of sexual orientation, ethnicity, personality, and all of the other attributes that make us unique individuals.[9]

Gender and Sport

Bodily play and sport, which can be enjoyed throughout one's life, provide some of our most enjoyable experiences. Sport and physical activity produce enormous benefits that we are only beginning to understand: not just enhanced bodily health but also improved mood, cognition, and self-esteem. Yet our relationship with play can vary dramatically with sex, race, class, ability, and sexuality. From our earliest days, play is one of the most heavily gendered aspects of our existence. This gendering carries on into adulthood and is perhaps most powerfully expressed in sports, particularly at the highest levels.

As discussed in Chapter 6, children learn quite early on to play in gender-specific ways. In early childhood, boys—whose mastery of sports-related skills is considered important to their development as gendered beings—are encouraged to participate in more physical, rough-and-tumble play than girls are. In modern societies, fighting is no longer a key component of masculine identity, so sport has emerged as perhaps the key area in which masculinity is proved and defined. Indeed, it is in sport that a boy may be first exposed to slurs against his masculinity, such as "sissy" or the dreaded "you throw like a girl." The latter comment, unfortunately still heard today, is not just about the way a boy throws; instead, it serves as a damning indictment of his total gender identity. Interestingly, hearing such comments may actually boost men's athletic performance; for women, however, there is evidence that stereotype threat (discussed earlier in the book) has a detrimental effect on performance. One recent study found that women college athletes performed less well on a difficult sport-related task when they were told that there was a gender difference in performance of the task. The idea of "throwing like a girl" is accordingly a powerful influence on both boys *and* girls, men *and* women.[10]

In fact, throwing is one of the areas of greatest gender difference. According to a metastudy by Janet Hyde, the difference between men's and women's throwing speeds is significantly greater than any other measured gender difference. Throwing is therefore an interesting phenomenon to study, and it sheds light on the gendering of sport. Predictably, many have traced female and male throwing styles (and competence) to biological differences. Such explanations, however, are confounded, first by the existence of women who throw baseballs competently enough to strike out major league players, and second, by the fact that many *men* outside of North America (even skilled athletes) "throw like girls."[11]

So if biology doesn't completely explain this robust difference, what does? The philosopher Iris Young wondered the same thing, given the dramatic differences she saw not just in throwing but also in a variety of other motor skills essential to sport:

> The relatively untrained man . . . engages in sport generally with more free motion and open reach than does his female counterpart. Not only is there a typical style of throwing like a girl, but there is a more or less typical style of running like a girl, climbing like a girl, swinging like a girl, hitting like a girl. They have in common, first, that the whole body is not put into fluid and directed motion, but rather, in swinging and hitting, for example, the motion is concentrated in one body part; and second, that the woman's motion tends not to reach, extend, lean, stretch, and follow through in the direction of her intention.

In various versions of her essay "Throwing like a Girl," Young suggested that girls in modern industrialized societies throw (and use their bodies) awkwardly not because of their anatomy, but because of "basic modalities of feminine body comportment, manner of moving, and relation in space." That is, girls learn to use their bodies in a fundamentally different way than do boys. They learn to hold their bodies modestly, in a "closed" fashion; they become tentative about using their bodies; and they greatly underestimate their physical capabilities. Whether throwing a ball or hitting a tennis backhand, one must "put the body into it"—which opens the stance and chest—and abandon concerns about modesty. Feminine body comportment is consequently the enemy of sporting competence—and, perhaps, overall bodily competence. A 2011 experiment studied motor performance on healthy individuals older than 40 and found that males showed significantly better speed in almost all areas tested.[12]

One barrier to girls' athletic performance is the **self-objectification** that girls learn as inhabitants of female bodies in a gendered society. When we objectify ourselves, we adopt the perspective of an outsider on our bodies and selves. This undermines ability to be comfortable in one's skin, to move the body unselfconsciously in space, and most importantly, to focus completely—another critical skill for sports success. One study of girls 10 to 17 found that "girls who exhibited greater self-objectification also showed poorer throwing performance," regardless of ethnic group. The older girls were more likely to self-objectify (and throw poorly) than were younger girls; this is in line with research that has found the gap between male and female performance widening between the age of three and puberty. If self-objectification can lead to poor sports performance, a more positive influence can flow in the other direction. According to research conducted in Manitoba, grade 11 girls who participated in non-competitive sports reported increased self-esteem.[13]

The gap between girls and boys widens both before and during their time in the school system. School is also the occasion for most children's first exposure to organized sports (though many children begin sports lessons and some even join sports teams before entering school). School experiences consequently have a profound effect on life-long attitudes toward and experiences of sport. The development of school sports (and organized sport in general) can be traced to the nineteenth-century ideals of "imperial manhood" and "muscular Christianity" (discussed in Chapter 7). Sport was conceived of as an inherently masculine pursuit aimed at training boys' bodies and minds to fit them for their roles as men.

Despite the existence of sporting women, and the long-standing participation of women in physical games in both European and Aboriginal societies, it wasn't until the twentieth century that sport was seen as a desirable pursuit for North American girls. In schools, sport entered the girls' curriculum at various Canadian schools in the early twentieth century, but "athleticism never acquired anything like the same hold it had over the equivalent boys' schools." Sport remained associated with masculinity, and was extended to girls only to fit them for greater health "and ultimately motherhood."[14]

This changed gradually through the twentieth century, particularly after the growth of the second-wave feminist movement in the 1960s and 1970s. Abby Hoffman, one of Canada's greatest track athletes of the day, became a fervent spokesperson for the expansion of sports opportunities to girls and women. In 1975, she told *Maclean's* magazine, "most girls . . . haven't the faintest idea how to get any pleasure out of sport." Hoffman, who won many medals for Canada as a middle-distance runner, was familiar with both achievement and exclusion. As a girl, she had disguised her sex in order to play on an Ontario boys' hockey team.[15]

Meanwhile, in the US, the same debates resulted in the 1972 passage of Title IX, an amendment to the Education Act that abolished all forms of sex discrimination in public schools (also see Chapter 7). Title IX has been interpreted as meaning that women's and girls' sports must be funded at the same levels as those played by men and boys. Since then, both girls' and college-age women's participation in sports has soared. Canada has no equivalent to Title IX, though the Canadian Association for the Advancement of Women and Sport and Physical Activity has lobbied for such an amendment. Nonetheless, Canadian human rights cases have established the rights of girls and women to full and equal participation. Since 1996, Canada's Olympic teams have been gender-balanced. Indeed, in the four Winter Olympics leading up to Sochi 2014, women won most of Canada's medals. This was also true of Canada's Paralympic Team at the Athens summer games, when women (though less than half of athletes) won almost two-thirds of Canada's medals.[16]

Nevertheless, girls' and women's relationships with sport continue to be dogged by more subtle forms of discrimination. For example, women who excel in sport are still likely to be perceived as unfeminine or suspected of homosexuality. Since the traits required for success in sport (e.g., competition and physical mastery) are still usually seen as masculine, successful sporting women are often "masculinized" by society. Moreover, because gender nonconformity and sexual orientation are still powerfully linked in the minds of many, this leads to a "slippage": female athlete = lesbian. Sadly, this stereotype sometimes limits athletes' solidarity as heterosexual athletes struggle to distance themselves from lesbianism and establish their "feminine" credentials. Successful female athletes face pressure to be feminine and "sexy," with endorsements more likely to go to traditionally feminine and attractive athletes. Yet studies have found that "sexy" athlete images (of either male of female athletes) actually diminish the athlete's perceived competence in the eyes of viewers. As Janet Fink writes, "the hypersexualization of female athletes serves to (further) erode the public's respect for their athletic abilities. Yet, recent research indicates that younger consumers care about a female athlete's skill, not the sport she plays, her femininity, or her sexual orientation."[17]

As Fink's statement suggest, things are changing—sports fans, especially younger ones, are less and less interested in women athletes as "eye candy." Nevertheless, discrimination persists. Women athletes and coaches earn less; female coaches are often passed over in favour of men, even in women's sport; and women's sport is still fraught with "ladies' rules," such as the three-set rule in tennis, that make women's play seem "lesser." At the level of compensation, the income gap between men and women (see Chapter 8) is dramatically exaggerated in sport. In 2015, the highest paid athlete in the world was boxer Floyd "Money" Mayweather, with earnings of $300 million. The highest paid female athlete in the world in 2015, once again, was tennis star Maria Sharapova, who earned approximately one-tenth of what Mayweather earned. Comparing the earnings of boxers to those of tennis players may seem unfair, but Sharapova's earnings were also only half of those of Roger Federer. More importantly, only two women—both tennis players— appear in *Forbes'* list of the 100 top-earning athletes for 2015. Average salaries are also informative; despite significant fan interest, women's salaries in the WNBA remain a paltry fraction of what male NBA players earn, and many WNBA players must take up other work in the off-season or play overseas to ensure a reasonable income.[18]

Caster Semenya, Sex Testing, and the Gender of Sport

Caster Semenya poses for a portrait at her training facility in fall 2009.

One of the areas in which the gendering of sport becomes clearest is at its boundaries, when an athlete's very ability to participate in sport may be denied. In summer 2009, after South African runner Caster Semenya won a medal at the world championships in Berlin, she found herself at the centre of a sex/gender controversy that threatened her identity and ability to compete in the sport she loves. Her personal-best time in the 800 metre final earned her not only the gold medal (and the record time for a woman in 2009) but an unfortunate comment from an Italian runner: "she is a man." Semenya's time was even more impressive when one considers that she was running under a cloud. The day before the final, the International Association of Athletics Federations (IAAF) had revealed that Caster had been subjected to "gender verification tests." In the days and months that followed, Semenya became a global newsmaker and celebrity. She was the subject of innumerable media reports—a Google search of her name at the time generated more than 7.5 million hits—and unprecedented speculation. Was she a victim of racism? Intersex? A "hermaphrodite"? Did it even matter?

In most sports, biological males enjoy some advantages. This is the rationale for separate competitions for the sexes (though there are at least a few sports in which such separate competition seems to lack reason). In order to prevent men from disguising themselves as women and unfairly winning competitions, female athletes have been subjected to tests to ensure their biological sex. In at least one case, a putatively male

continued

(though perhaps intersex) high jumper competed (for Germany) in "female disguise." (He placed fourth at the 1936 Berlin Olympics.) Also in the Berlin Games, two female sprinters accused each other of being male.

As a result of such concerns, **sex testing** (generally called **gender verification** today) gradually became part of amateur sport. Prior to 1968, for example, female Olympic athletes had to appear nude in front of an examining board who scrutinized their bodies for signs of masculinity. Because of the degrading nature of this exercise, chromosomal tests were substituted, generally relying on a cheek-swab sample of the athlete's cells. After the controversy generated by the sex-testing decision involving Spanish hurdler Maria Martínez-Patiño (discussed in Chapter 2), the IOC revisited sex verification, discontinuing the practice of "blanket" testing in 1999 but reserving the right to insist on testing in specific cases. Sex testing remains common in amateur sport.

As Martínez-Patiño's case made clear, biological sex is not merely a matter of having an XX or XY chromosome. For example, XY people with androgen insensitivity syndrome (see Chapter 2) look female-typical (and even "more feminine" than many XX women do) and have less testosterone in their bodies than average women. Yet chromosomally speaking, AIS people are male. Should they therefore be disqualified from women's sporting events?

The issue of testosterone and its effects on women's bodies has recently become a hot-button issue (again). Dutee Chand was banned for competition in 2014 after she was found to have naturally high levels of testosterone. She and some other female athletes tested for the London Olympics were disqualified, with others subsequently undergoing feminizing surgery. Chand, however, resisted; "I want to remain who I am and compete again," she said. In 2015, she got her wish. Citing evidence that "sex in humans is not simply binary," the Court of Arbitration for Sport upheld Chand's appeal and cleared her for competition—at least until 2017, when the International Association of Athletic Federations will be expected to provide clear evidence if it wishes to prove that women with naturally high testosterone levels have an unfair advantage. Meanwhile, other female runners are concerned about having to compete against women with "rare biologies."

The case raises interesting questions. Philosophically, what is the difference between a natural inheritance of high testosterone and other genetic gifts? Some world-class swimmers have massive feet and other bodily abnormalities; one family of endurance athletes boasts a mutation that enables family members to generate an abnormal number of red blood cells. Some ethnic groups are greatly overrepresented in athletic achievement, perhaps in part because of genetic factors and often because of environmental and societal influences. Success at the highest level of sport relies to a large degree on natural advantages (for example, swimmer Michael Phelps's unusually long arms or a pro basketball player's unusual height); should we therefore consider higher levels of androgens, or a woman's structurally "masculine" body, as another form of natural advantage? Should these advantages be considered "unfair"? If controversy dogs many female athletes, transgender athletes are even more susceptible. The first well-known case involving a transgender athlete's right to compete was that of tennis player Renee Richards. Richards was a prominent player as a junior and young man, making it to the final of the US nationals. At the age of about 40, Richards became a woman and entered professional tennis. Though she had to fight for the right to compete, she triumphed and enjoyed a relatively successful pro career (particularly given her age).

More recently, BC mountain bike racer Michelle Demaresq faced similar barriers. A mountain biker since her boyhood, Demaresq was open about being a transwoman and was welcomed by other women racers. This changed, however, as she began to do better in competition. In July 2006, Demaresq beat a fellow racer by one second to win the national downhill mountain bike championships. On the podium, the second-place winner removed her jersey to reveal a T-shirt that read "100% pure woman." Her racing licence was suspended for three months, and Demaresq's right to compete was accepted. The incident nonetheless revealed persistent issues.

Finally, what about Caster Semenya, who was born female and raised as a woman? She was cleared for return to competition in 2010, and though she has been dogged by injury in the past two years, Semenya is preparing to compete in the Rio Olympics as this book goes to press. Semenya's story shows both the gendered difficulties within sport and the power of sport to enact liberating independence. In a 2015 interview, Caster made this clear: "Running is what I will always do. Even if, maybe, the authorities could have stopped me from running in 2009, they could not have stopped me in the fields. I would have carried on with my running, it doesn't matter. When I run I feel free, my mind is free."[19]

If sport is a ground upon which women often feel like aliens, it is for many boys and men a testing ground and a central site of gender socialization. Sports participation, sports competence, and even sports fandom are the opportunity not only for profound enjoyment and benefit, but also for the demonstration and loss of masculinity.

The proof of masculinity in sport has been, at least since the nineteenth century, tied to the proof of the power and "manliness" (as was then said) of nations. This provides a male athlete an opportunity to become a nation's "hero" (while female athletes are more likely to become, say, "Canada's darling"). For racialized men, this is an opportunity found in few other areas of endeavour. However, it comes at a risk, as the case of Ben Johnson suggests. Johnson was Canada's most successful track athlete in history in the late 1980s; with an astonishing world-record time, he won gold for Canada at the Seoul Olympics in 1988. Unfortunately, he tested positive for anabolic steroids and was stripped of his medal. As Gamal Abdel-Shehid writes, he was also symbolically stripped of his citizenship, transformed in the media from Canadian athlete–hero to disgraced Caribbean immigrant. (Johnson was born in Jamaica.)[20]

If masculine sport is important to nations, it is even more important in individual lives. In earliest childhood, sports serve as an avenue for "disciplining" boys into appropriate gender norms. Boys learn to be tough, to endure pain, and to compete. Boys also learn that aggression is necessary and rewarded. In hockey—Canada's most cherished game—boys from about the age of six participate in a game that tolerates aggression and rule violation.

From an early age, players are taught that competence (a player's ability to contribute to team success) includes certain penalties that are considered good such as hooking (placing the stick around another player's legs or waist and taking them down to the ice) and tripping that prevent goals. Certain penalties are considered bad such as slashing (using one's stick to chop at another player) or elbowing that show a lack of discipline but may not contribute to team success. Bad penalties are those benefitting the opposition. Rule infractions which are expected in certain situations (e.g., to prevent scoring chances) are supplemented by the use of aggressive tactics which are defined as essential for team success.[21]

Willingness to make sacrifices for the team is valorized in hockey, perhaps even more than in other team sports. Sacrificing one's body and safety are also considered characteristic of good (and masculine) players. (This is also true of major-league football, in which players "spend" their bodies so generously that many end up with dementia in their 50s and 60s.) In the 1990s, as skilled European players like Pavel Bure flooded into the National Hockey League, CBC commentator Don Cherry reserved his special contempt for visor-wearing Russians and "Chicken Swedes" who protected themselves and shied away from fights.[22]

Indeed, hockey may be one of the only games in which fighting, though not formally part of the game, is expected, and evaluated as if it were. Fighting is seen as "an essential element of the tradition and culture of hockey" and as something that distinguishes the Canadian game from its effete European counterparts. The team "enforcer," while he may lack the skill and finesse of his teammates, plays a critical role in the game, and is often beloved of hometown fans (though threatened at away games!). Fans, for their part, love a fight. Anyone who has ever attended an NHL game, featuring two well-known opposing-team enforcers will remember the palpable excitement as fans waited to see whether they would "go." Players experience that excitement as both stimulation and pressure:

> [I]t was enough for me to see that they wanted to see that violence thing, and it does promote it—I mean, when the crowd is behind you and cheer when you knock people into the boards—I'm not going to lie, it gets you fired up and wants to make you do more banging of guys into the boards, and lots of times, if it takes that to get the team fired up, then that's what you're going to do.
>
> [F]ans would come up to you and say, that's a great fight you were in . . . and basically, you're getting rewarded for . . . fighting with someone, and people remembered that.[23]

While some spontaneous violence may be an unavoidable consequence of the intense nature of hockey (line) play, the ritualized and important place of fighting in hockey is evidence of its connection with constructs of hegemonic masculinity such as domination and violence. Not surprisingly, that violence sometimes spills off the rink, whether into arena parking-lot team fights or more diffused violent behaviour. The combination of violence, what Don Sabo calls "the myth of the sexual athlete," and sexist sport culture also leads to a great overrepresentation of athletes in sexual assaults. There are no signs that the "sexual athlete" myth has diminished; as one recent study of US football college players put it, they "feel a sense of sexual power over women, which fuels their sense of entitlement to do what they want with women."[24]

Sport, then, is a gendered arena in which the most troubling aspects of the relationship between gender and the body can be seen. However, sport is also where we can establish healthy, transformative relationships with our bodies and where we find some of the most exhilarating role models for gender-role transformation.

Gender and the Beauty Myth

The relationship of beauty with the gendered body has so far provided less food for transformation. Our ideals of beauty and attractiveness themselves remain deeply gendered and, for many of us, the source of personal pain.

Additionally, that pain is unequally distributed between the genders (though this is an area of rapid change). For one thing, we know a lot more about standards of female beauty in other cultures than we know about similar standards for men, in large part because men created those standards in the first place. (Men's valuation in most cultures has been based more on wealth and power, less on beauty.) Specifically sexual standards of beauty often vary. In many tropical cultures, women do not cover their breasts, but this doesn't mean that the men there are in a constant state of sexual frenzy. The breasts are simply not considered a sexual stimulus in those cultures, and attention may be focused elsewhere. Yet in some cultures, women are believed to be so sexually alluring (and men so unable to control themselves when confronted with temptation) that women practice purdah (see Chapter 4), which requires varying degrees of female seclusion and body covering.

Sexual standards of beauty often change and are subject to societal influence. The bound foot, once erotically attractive to Chinese men, would be repellent to almost all today, as would the whale-boned "wasp waist" of nineteenth-century Europe. In Japan, prior to the Second World War, breasts "had a subsidiary role in sexual fantasy and practice," and women's clothing flattened rather than accentuated the breasts. The primary "visible" breast was associated with breastfeeding rather than sexuality. More recently, Japan has been overtaken by "mammary mania" (as any casual viewer of manga or anime can attest). This is an example of how a culture's preference for certain characteristics can alter in a relatively short time. There do appear to be some consistent and "universal" features of feminine beauty among men, such as a preference for symmetry and hips significantly larger than the waist. (Both of these features may reflect a biological tendency to seek mates who are fecund and healthy.) Aside from these characteristics, what constitutes "beauty" varies widely.[25]

The importance placed on beauty also varies. In North America, women's beauty is placed at a high premium and standards of beauty are narrow—even while women enjoy unprecedented legal rights. According to Naomi Wolf, this is the **beauty myth**—a nearly unreachable cultural ideal of feminine beauty that "uses images of female beauty as a political weapon against women's advancement." This beauty myth entraps women in an endless cycle of cosmetics, beauty aids, diets, and exercise fanaticism and makes women's bodies into "prisons their homes no longer were." As Fatima Mernissi writes of her first encounter with North American beauty norms, "Being frozen into the passive position of an object whose very existence depends on the eye of its beholder turns the educated modern Western woman into a harem slave."[26]

Who, then, is the beholder? It would be too simplistic to say "men," but that's part of the answer. More accurately, the beauty myth constantly subjects women not so much to the scrutiny of men as to the **male gaze**. The male gaze is a concept first articulated by Laura Mulvey in the context of film studies, where she noted how, when watching movies, we are often encouraged to take the perspective of a desiring heterosexual male subject. One example of this would be the frequent panning of a woman's body from the ground up when she is first introduced as a character. The camera "forces" us to look at the woman the way a desiring man might. This device is frequently used in slasher films, where the camera not only lingers on women's bodies (often just before they become victims) but also sometimes forces us to view the victims from the perspective of the killer.[27]

The idea of the male gaze has been expanded far beyond film studies to explain how people—regardless of their gender and sexual orientation—look at women in a way that assesses their sexual desirability and positions them as sexual objects. Women even look at themselves in this way; in fact, they must learn to look at themselves in this way if they are to succeed in improving their beauty. As Sandra Bartky writes, "subject to the evaluating eye of the male connoisseur, women learn to evaluate themselves first and best." This is to say, women learn self-objectification in the name of self-improvement (understood as the enhancement of beauty).[28]

Is this emphasis on working to achieve beauty an ironic outcome of women's increased independence—a kind of backlash attempt to keep women in their place just as they are breaking free? It's unlikely that it is any more than a coincidence, but it is worth noting that the first Miss America pageant was held in 1920—the same year US women obtained the right to vote.[29]

North American standards of beauty have been based on celebration of a particular ethnic form of whiteness that we might call Northern European. This has led to a number of trends among white women themselves, most notably the tendency to lighten hair (and, increasingly, to lighten eye colour using contact lenses). Among non-white women, most notably women of Asian heritage, a common operation has been eyelid surgery aimed at producing a rounder-looking eye. Such surgeries obviously reflect, in the words of Eugenia Kaw, "persisting racial prejudice," but it is interesting that white women's attempts to look "whiter" are rarely viewed in such racial terms.[30]

The beauty myth rests not only on the pursuit of beauty but on the avoidance of "ugliness." Despite the popularity of TV's *Ugly Betty* (who wasn't at all ugly) and *Shrek*, ugly is by no means "the new pretty." Attractiveness still rules. It confers social benefits such as higher earning power, greater attractiveness to potential marriage partners, and even imputations of intelligence and moral superiority.[31] For women, whose attractiveness has been seen as more important to their identities than it is for men, being called "ugly" can be devastating.

Because North American standards of beauty celebrate a particular kind of able-bodied fantasy of whiteness, racialized and disabled women are more vulnerable to the "ugly" slur (and self-perception). In North America, the racist stereotype of the "ugly squaw" (as opposed to the "Indian princess") has had a negative effect on generations of Indigenous women. African-American women have also often been slandered as "ugly," an attribution that rests not only on racism but also on **colourism**. Light skin, among African-American women, may operate as a form of "social capital" that enhances their earning power, attractiveness to potential partners, educational attainment, and self-esteem. This remains true despite the 1960s "Black is Beautiful" campaign and subsequent attempts to contest racist ideas of beauty. Today, ironically, "Black is Beautiful" can be one more way of sexualizing women of colour, perpetuating, in bell hooks' phrase, "the pornographic fantasy of the black female as wild sexual savage."[32]

The beauty myth and its corollary, the "ugliness myth," also interact with notions of ability. On one hand, the feminine "beauty myth" may render women with disabilities invisible. On the other hand, as Meekosha writes, disabled women are subject to pressure to "normalize the less than perfect body." While the able female body "is identified as an object for desire," writes Per Solvang, the disabled body is constructed "as an object of disgust," adding to the pressure to disguise or redress "abnormal" characteristics. Additionally, even when the disabled female body is seen as sexually desirable, as among devotees of amputation, all other characteristics of the "standard" beauty myth remain in place, suggesting that disabled women are being **fetishized** rather than valued in their own right.[33]

Perhaps no word is so often heard in combination with "ugly" as "fat." For North American women of all ethnic groups, and particularly perhaps for white women, the fear of fat often forces submission to the tyranny of slenderness.

Fat, Muscle, and the "Obesity Epidemic": Gender and Body Image in Modern North America

The current prevalence of and obsession with fat is a novelty in human history, in which starvation has long been a more present danger than obesity. (This continues to be true in some societies, of course.) In the nineteenth and twentieth centuries, modern societies became increasingly concerned with body norms and healthy eating. Initially, much of this focused on male bodies (though women, as food preparers, were seen as significant in the quest for healthier diets). In the US and the UK, the bodies of new generations of urban men were judged by physicians and military men alike to be generally weak and debilitated. Physical examinations that accompanied the mass mobilizations of the period (especially during and after the First World War) showed compellingly that men's bodies were variable and far from the "ideal."[34]

The masculine ideal was, of course, a body in keeping with the values of hegemonic masculinity: powerful, active, and capable. Increasingly, it was also attractive. The career of Eugene Sandow, the father

Wellcome Library, London

Eugene Sandow in classical pose (and sandals).

of modern bodybuilding, was devoted to the celebration of a muscular male body that was not only useful but beautiful. Sandow (born in Prussia as Friedrich Müller) toured the US and Europe displaying his strength and physique and earning not only significant wealth but the admiration of royalty and commoner alike. In his performances and his publications, Sandow promoted the "Grecian ideal" of the male body, derived from classical Greek sculpture; he was often pictured in classical poses in performances and photographs.[35]

While men were arguably the focus of more body anxiety in the late nineteenth and early twentieth centuries, women were not forgotten. Yet the womanly ideal of the pre-war period remained "maternal" and therefore perhaps more forgiving than it would become later in the century, at least as regards the presence of fat. For example, an article in *Harper's Bazaar* in 1908 declared the normal weight for a healthy woman of 5′8″ to be 155 pounds (70 kg); 133 (60 kg) would have been normal for a woman of 5′3″ (160 cm), and 120 pounds (54 kg) for a woman who stood 5′1″ (155 cm). While these may seem reasonable prescriptions, the trend toward standardization and prescription of body weight was clear.[36]

In the 1920s, as boyish, slender figures became the ideal and corsets were definitively abandoned, "natural" slimness became a new obsession for North American women. It has never gone away. Womanly fat and excessive weight gain during pregnancy were now seen as unhealthy and aberrant. However, men did not escape scrutiny. In the 1920s, Charles Atlas (born Angelo Siciliano) took over where Eugene Sandow had left off, marketing a "dynamic tension" program that would develop skinny men's muscles. In the 1940s, this system was marketed through the famous "97-pound weakling" media campaigns that showed skinny men losing their girlfriends to (and being mocked by) larger, muscular men. The message to both men and women was clear: the body needed to be disciplined into appropriate gender norms. Neither sex was to be "fat," of course, but women were to be slender and shapely while men were to be rugged and muscular.

Though most North Americans encountered these body ideals through the media, the medical world promoted such ideals too, though in the name of health rather than mere beauty. At mid-century, the introduction of "standard" height and weight tables (provided by life insurance companies) made it possible for every North American to see how he or she stacked up to the ideal. The media, however, arguably remained the most important source of information on what constituted acceptable slenderness; over time, advertisers learned that women's fear of fat could be used to sell just about anything.

By the final third of the twentieth century, the fear of fat became ubiquitous in North America—ironically, as North Americans were growing larger and larger. By the late 1990s, an "obesity epidemic" had been identified by the World Health Organization and US health-promotion agencies. While controversy rages over whether this terminology is appropriate, obesity rates continue to increase (although the methodologies behind these rates are themselves controversial). **Fat-shaming** on the Internet and bias against fat people are ubiquitous. The fear and loathing that fat engenders are striking.[37]

The "obesity epidemic" and North America's hate-affair with fat have gendered implications. Women, as mothers and most common providers of food, have been targeted as responsible for childhood obesity, with some even proclaiming that mothers of obese children should be charged with neglect or endangerment. Racialized women in the US have been particularly vulnerable to such accusations. There may be greater bias against fat women than there is against fat men; one study found that African-American women were judged particularly harshly for being overweight. Another interesting gender difference is that men appear to judge overweight people more harshly than women do. Certainly, fat people (regardless of gender and ethnicity) experience significant discrimination resulting in lower earnings, mental health issues, and other negative outcomes.[38]

It is no surprise—given all of this—that many people live in fear of being fat. Women have long been concerned with their weight, and girls are too. "Girls are terrified of being fat," writes Mary Pipher. Simultaneously, childhood obesity has become a major concern in many societies, with approximately one-third of Canadians 5–17 overweight or obese according to Statistics Canada. Given the "fatphobia" of North American culture, it seems odd that North Americans are becoming heavier and heavier. However, it certainly seems understandable, as research suggests, that overweight is associated with a decline in self-esteem both for children and for adults.[39]

Research on adolescents suggests that a large majority consciously trade off health concerns in their efforts to lose weight—and some develop eating disorders. Anorexia involves chronic and dangerous starvation dieting and obsessive exercise; bulimia typically involves "binging and purging" (eating large quantities of food and then either vomiting or taking enemas to excrete the food). Although anorexia and bulimia are extreme and very serious problems that can, if untreated, be life-threatening, they represent only the end of a continuum of preoccupation with the body that begins with such "normal" behaviours as compulsive exercise or dieting.[40]

There is a correlation among body weight, disordered eating, ethnicity, and social class; throughout Europe and the United States, non-white girls are less likely to exhibit eating disorders than are white and middle-class girls. Dramatic increases have, however, been observed among young middle- and upper-class Japanese women,[41] and evidence suggests that fear of fat also affects working-class and black ideals of the feminine body. Largeness "was once accepted—even revered—among black folks," lamented an article in *Essence* magazine in 1994, but it "now carries the same unmistakable stigma as it does among whites." A study the following year found that black adolescent girls demonstrated a significantly higher drive for thinness than did white adolescent girls. Media coverage of Oprah's dramatic weight loss and the depiction of ultra-thin African-American models and actresses may have increased black women's anxieties about their weight.[42]

As described above, men have long been concerned about appearing strong and fit. Ironically, the building of strong muscles seems to increase as a preoccupation and obsession during periods when men are least likely to actually have to use their muscles in their work.[43] Today, successful new men's magazines like *Men's Health* encourage men to see their bodies as women have been taught to see theirs—as ongoing projects to be worked on.

Men's bodily anxieties mirror those of women: that is, both sexes are preoccupied with those aspects of the male and female body that suggest and exaggerate innate biological differences between the sexes. Both sexes are concerned with fat, of course; for men, however, fatness has the added association of effeminacy, while masculinity is associated with lean muscle. It would appear that the more equal women and men become in the public sphere, the more standards of beauty emphasize those aspects that are biologically different—and the more men need to differentiate themselves from women. (On the other hand, both men and women now grapple with the imperative to appear youthful and slender, and to remove virtually all of their body hair, which would suggest convergence rather than emphasis on difference.)[44]

Many men today experience **muscle dysmorphia**, a belief that one is insufficiently muscular. Harrison Pope and his colleagues call it the **Adonis complex**—the belief that men must look like Greek gods, with perfect chins, thick hair, smooth hairless skins, and "six-packs." A recent large-scale study of young men found that many of them were either "lean-concerned" or "muscle-concerned," with sexual-minority men most likely to be concerned with being lean.[45]

Nearly half of all men in one survey reported significant body image disturbance, often related to media images. Increasingly, young men are engaging in the kind of negative "body talk" usually associated with women. A study reported in *Psychology Today* found that 43 per cent of college men were dissatisfied with their appearance, compared with only 15 per cent 25 years earlier. As one college student told a journalist:

> When I look in the mirror, I see two things: what I want to be and what I'm not. I hate my abs. My chest will never be huge. My legs are too thin. My nose is an odd shape. I want what *Men's Health* pushes.[46]

Though men are much less likely to believe they are overweight than are women, increasing numbers of men are exhibiting eating disorders. These problems may be more prevalent among gay men, but increases among young heterosexual men are also pronounced. A survey of Australian college men found that one in five had used restrained eating, vomiting, laxative abuse, or cigarette smoking for weight control. About one in five also reported binge eating and weight control problems. In 2008, "manorexia" got its first public face when actor Dennis Quaid went public with his struggle with disordered eating. Though no one is quite sure how many men are struggling with eating disorders, they now account for 10 per cent of those treated in some clinics.[47]

Just as women have accepted increasingly drastic surgical and medical interventions to create beauty—so, too, are men resorting to increasingly dramatic efforts to get large. The use of anabolic steroids continues to mushroom, especially among college-aged men and adolescents. Steroids enable men to increase muscle mass quickly and dramatically. Prolonged use also leads to dramatic mood changes, increased aggression, risk of HIV infection, and testicular shrinkage.[48]

Eating disorders among women and muscular dysmorphia among men are parallel processes, extreme points on a continuum that begins with almost everyone. There are, for example, very few women who do not have a problematic relationship with food—many, if not most, women mentally count calories, determine whether "indulgence" is worth it, and calculate how much extra time they can spend in the gym to compensate. Men, at the same time, have a problematic relationship with physical power. "Looking strong" is their version of women's "looking slim." If a measure of successful femininity is being slender, and if a measure of masculinity is appearing strong and powerful, then anorexics and obsessive body builders are not psychological misfits or deviants: They are simply dedicated conformists to gender norms to which all of us, to some degree, are subject.

Under the Skin: Permanent Bodily Transformations

Virtually all of us spend some time and energy in some forms of bodily beautification, by wearing fashionable clothes and jewelry, for example. As discussed above, many of us modify our bodies through dieting and exercise. Until recently, however, permanent bodily transformation—piercing body parts other than ears, getting tattoos, having cosmetic surgery, and undergoing sex-change operations—was extremely rare. Today, body piercing can include the tongue, eyebrows, navel, nose, lips, nipples, and even the genitals. Tattoos are ubiquitous. As well, surgical body changes have become widespread and normalized.

Twenty-one per cent of Canadians have at least one tattoo, described by one psychiatrist as a "bumper sticker of the soul." Tattooing has an ancient history and a spiritual connection in many cultures, but in the West, for most of the twentieth century, tattoos were regarded as a sign of criminal involvement (a stigma still present in Japan today). Today, more than one-third of North America's young people are inked. Though men and women are nearly equal consumers of tattooing, the placement of tattoos and the designs themselves are heavily gendered. For example, while 75 per cent of men choose arm tattoos, only 7 per cent of women do. Meanwhile, 27 per cent of women and only 2 per cent of men choose ankle tattoos, while 45 per cent of women and only 15 per cent of men tattoo the lower torso. As this suggests, design and placement are also highly sexually charged; we believe they say something about ourselves and our sexuality. Witness the popularity of the lower-back "tramp stamp," among young women, which has now been usurped by the trendier rib zone—immediately dubbed the "skank flank" by some artists. (As these examples suggest, tattooing is highly susceptible to the whims of fashion; consequently, the new popularity of tattooing has also spawned a new industry—tattoo removal.)[49]

Cosmetic surgery is another growth industry. Developed after the Second World War and initially reserved for the rich and famous, cosmetic surgery spread widely in the last decades of the twentieth century. Among the most common surgeries in North America, not surprisingly, breast augmentation holds pride of place; breasts are "the most visible signs of a woman's femininity," writes Iris Young, "the sign of her sexuality." In 2008, US cosmetic surgeons performed more than 350,000 breast augmentations, a great increase from the 2001 figure (closer to 200,000). While breast augmentation is still by far the most common surgical procedure, the number of augmentations performed has declined in recent years, so that 2014 numbers (showing a 1 per cent decline from 2013) are much closer to the 2001 numbers than to the 2008 statistic. This does not indicate rejection of cosmetic surgery, but rather that the areas targeted seem to be changing while the overall number of procedures continues to increase. While breast augmentation, eyelid surgery, and facelifts all registered modest declines, the fastest-growing surgeries are buttock augmentation and lifts. There have been similarly dramatic increases in surgeries for men, such as pectoral implants and breast reduction, but men remain a tiny minority among surgery-seekers.[50]

Indeed, women are the keenest consumers of cosmetic procedures, in 2014 accounting for 92 per cent of all surgical and minimally invasive procedures (such as Botox injection, fat filling, chemical peels, etc.). Since 2000, men's consumption of all such procedures has risen by 23 per cent. This sounds dramatic until one ponders the comparable figure for women: an increase of 114 per cent.[51] Consequently, while men's obsession with body image has been growing, there is no evidence that they will become a market comparable to the female one; confounding all predictions, women's near-monopoly on cosmetic surgery appears to be growing rather than shrinking.

Still, male patients have increased their numbers. "More men are viewing cosmetic surgery as a viable way of looking and feeling younger," observed ASPRS President Dennis Lynch, MD, "especially to compete in the workplace." It may be, as one writer explains, "the traditional image of women as sexual objects has simply expanded: everyone has become an object to be seen." The question remains: seen by whom? Whom do we imagine seeing us in our newly reconstructed state? For women, the answer is usually men.[52]

For men, though, the answer is also men. Men feel a need to look big, strong, and virile in front of other men. Take one extreme example of this—penile enlargement surgery. This is a dramatic (and expensive) procedure—every year about 15,000 men worldwide undertake it—by which the penis can be lengthened by about two inches. (The average flaccid penis is about 3.5 inches long; erect it's about 5.1 inches long.)[53]

One would think that men engage in this painful procedure to be "better" lovers or to please women more, and indeed many men say that is part of their motivation. However, in many cases it has far less to do with women's potential pleasure than men's visual perception. Men who have this procedure more often experience what one physician called "locker room syndrome"—the fear of being judged as inadequately masculine *by other men*. Take, for example, the testimonial letter from a satisfied customer:

> I was always afraid to get into situations where I would have to shower with other men or be seen by anyone. I can remember avoiding many of the sports and activities I loved dearly, all because I was afraid that I would be seen and made fun of. . . . I even avoided wearing shorts and tight clothes because of my fear that others would notice me.

"The thing I missed most was the changing room camaraderie and male bonding associated with these sports which was always something I enjoyed," writes another. "I felt ashamed to even go to the urinals in a public place and have made sure I never use these whilst other men are there too." Penis enlargement surgery is therefore a surgery undertaken by men for other men; it is also exceedingly rare. Compare the 15,000 annual enlargements worldwide to more than 3 million breast enlargements, lifts, and reductions—and about 115,000 "vaginal rejuvenations"—and the predominance of female body anxiety becomes clear.[54]

As the "vaginal rejuvenation" category makes clear, women, too, undergo genital "reconstruction" surgery, a procedure whose popularity has been increasing dramatically. According to the Toronto Cosmetic Clinic, "within weeks of undergoing the procedure, you, and your partner will be able to see, and feel, the results. Both of you will experience a renewal of sexual pleasure and dramatic increase in sensation from intercourse, achieving a level of sexual gratification that was missing before." The increased availability and acceptability of pornography also have some women requesting "designer vaginas" comparable to the vulvas on display in porn, which are often much "smaller" than those of the average woman. Women increasingly request the trimming of their labia to conform to ideals of beauty on these new frontiers. Finally, hymenoplasty—the surgical reconstruction of the hymen, which is usually broken during first intercourse—once was used by panic-stricken parents of "deflowered" Muslim, Asian, or Latina girls whose value in the marriage market had suddenly plummeted. Now available at some North American clinics, it's increasingly popular among heterosexual women who want to keep their earlier sexual experience a secret, who want their partners to have the "thrill" of being their "first," or who have violated their Christian abstinence pledges.[55]

Nowhere is gender inequality better observed than in the motivations of both women and men in changing their bodies. It is the male gaze—whether of a potential sexual partner, a potential sexual rival, or a competitor in the marketplace or athletic field—that motivates such drastic measures, among both women and men. Additionally, despite many changes in recent years, it is women, far more than men, who endure the pain, risk, and financial burden necessary to achieve surgically created beauty.

Transgender and the Transformation of Bodies

Though there are significant penalties for boys who are effeminate ("sissies") and some, but fewer, penalties for girls who are "tomboys," many adult men and women continue to bend, if not break, gender norms in their bodily presentation. **Transvestite** refers to someone dressing in the clothing of the opposite sex, disrupting the equation of biological sex and social gender by playing with gender (the socially and culturally prescribed adornments and dress). The term *transvestite* is now viewed by many as pejorative. Up until the twentieth century, a woman who wore trousers (in North America and Europe) was "cross-dressing," which was illegal during much of European history. Today, women readily wear masculine (and even men's) clothing without incurring much disapproval or the label of "cross-dresser." A man who wears a skirt, on the other hand, will find himself the object of much more attention. So the continuum is gendered. At one end of our gender-bending continuum, we might have women who wear masculine clothing to work because such clothing gives them the air of confidence as they downplay femininity and exude competence (qualities often seen as antithetical). At the other end are those who wear full cross-gender regalia as a means of self-expression or for sexual pleasure.

For some **transgender** people, though, the bending of gendered norms is insufficient, because their biological sex doesn't match their internal sense of gender identity. Historically, transgender was quite rare, if only because most societies had strict rules regarding appropriate gender norms for the sexes. Third genders, discussed in Chapter 4, are an exception. However, because most third-gender individuals came to their gender status through channels other than free choice, it's difficult to view them as proof of historical transgender identity in the modern sense.[56]

Transgender people offer living proof that the social construction of gender and sexuality is more than simply metaphoric. Typically, transgender is experienced as a general discomfort that becomes increasingly intense during puberty, that is, with the emergence of secondary sex characteristics. As one female-to-male transgender person told an interviewer:

> I hated the changes in my body. . . . I couldn't stand it. . . . It affected my identity.
> I became very upset and depressed. As a matter of fact, by this time in my life, I
> spent most of my time in my room. . . . I thought about suicide. . . .[57]

Transgender remains uncommon (most studies suggest that less than 1 per cent of the population identifies as trans), but almost everyone agrees that trans numbers are growing quickly and that data are unreliable. Surveys have only recently begun to count transgender people. Furthermore, there are many people who may not identify as trans but who also do not feel as if they are completely and comfortably male or female according to their birth assignment—that is, **cisgender**. Therefore, it is difficult to state with any confidence how many people may be transgender,[58] particularly because the breakdown of gender norms has opened the door for many to question their identities and their received genders. Transgender enables us to dissolve what is experienced as an arbitrary privileging of the body-at-birth and to give more weight to who we feel we are, bringing us close to a world in which we can freely choose our gender.

The term **transsexual** came into use in the 1950s, when surgery and endocrinology had made it possible to change not only one's clothing but also one's body. One of the first well-known transsexuals was Christine Jorgenson, a young American who travelled to a Scandinavian clinic for surgery and hormonal treatment, returning to the US to become, for some years, a media darling. Others followed Jorgenson's example, all of them submitting to a variety of tests in order to prove that they were legitimate candidates for what came to be known as **sexual reassignment surgery** (SRS). In 1966, Harry Benjamin published *The Transsexual Phenomenon*, a text that distinguished three categories of transsexuals on the basis of their degree of discomfort with their biological sex. These changes combined to make it possible to change one's sex, particularly after legal challenges established (at least in some cases) the right to be considered as a member of the sex to which one was reassigned.[59]

By 1980, about 4,000 people in the US had undergone these surgical interventions. Almost all of them were biological males seeking to become women through **male to female** (MTF) surgery. Today, though numbers are difficult to come by, it is clear that tens of thousands of North Americans, and more than 100,000 individuals worldwide, have undergone some form of sex reassignment, with hundreds of surgeries taking place in North America annually. The number of biological females seeking **female to male** (FTM) surgery has increased dramatically. For both sexes, the transition from one sex to the other requires two years of radical hormone therapies to mute or reverse secondary sex characteristics (like body hair, voice, breasts); thereafter, some undergo full SRS, by which the original genitalia are surgically excised and new realistic vulvas (vaginoplasty) or penises (phalloplasty) are constructed.

New medical and surgical procedures have continued to facilitate both MTF and FTM transitions. Moreover, the listing of transsexualism as a disorder in *DSM-III* in 1980 allowed for insurance coverage for SRS. In Canada, the province of Ontario funded operations at the Clarke Institute of Psychiatry from 1969 until 1998. Currently, only New Brunswick and PEI do not fund SRS, while all of the other provinces fund at least some components of the procedures.[60]

Because funding for sex reassignment hinges on the idea of mental disorder for which SRS is the "cure," many have been reluctant to challenge the idea that they are mentally ill. Others, though, particularly in the US, have disagreed. In 1994, the *DSM-IV* committee changed the terminology to "gender identity disorder." As trans activism grew, many agitated for the removal of gender identity disorder from the *DSM*, most notably at the

April 2009 meeting of the American Psychiatric Association. The *DSM-V* (2013) steered a middle course, adopting the term **gender dysphoria** while retaining the category.[61]

Transgender identity is often difficult for those who have not experienced it to understand. How, people might ask, could one locate the source of one's unhappiness in having the wrong anatomy? Additionally, and more sociologically, people wonder if sex-reassignment surgery doesn't reinstate the body as the source of gendered knowledge and underscore the biological—indeed, anatomically genital—foundations of gender. Who subscribes more vigorously to biological essentialism than people who change their biological sex to match their internal perceptions of the gender? This has made for some tensions between trans activists and the feminist movement, which critiques biological essentialism and is more likely to call for a breaking down of gender than its realignment with a re-sexed body. The second-wave feminist Gloria Steinem famously commented, "If the shoe doesn't fit, why change the whole foot?" Since then, feminism has become more receptive to transgender, particularly as transwomen have entered the feminist movement. Nonetheless, tensions remain, as is proved by the conflict that erupted in the 1990s when transwoman Kimberly Nixon sought to work for Vancouver Rape Relief. She was expelled from training sessions on the basis of her biological origins as a man. Vancouver Rape Relief held that as someone who had lived much of her life as a man, Nixon could not serve in a position reserved for women. Nixon's contention that she had the right to work as a woman in a woman's shelter was first upheld by the BC Human Rights Tribunal, but ultimately overturned by higher courts.[62]

Increasingly, trans identity is becoming much less rigidly binary than it was in the twentieth century. While many trans people continue to desire and seek medical and surgical interventions to make their bodies match their genders, others may choose to forego either **top surgery** or **bottom surgery**, to eschew surgery totally, and even to reject hormonal intervention (**no-ho**). Trans, non-binary, and non-cisgender identities continue to flourish.

Gender and Health

If transgender highlights the ways in which we gender bodies, health and illness have sometimes appeared to obscure gendering. After all, we all experience health, illness, aging, and eventually death, regardless of our gender. Even the strongest exemplar of hegemonic masculinity must too deal with the body's changes, as has been amply proved by widely circulated images of Arnold Schwarzenegger that make news out of his aging body.

Because health and illness are in some ways "levellers," we have often ignored their gendered nature or seen male bodies as stand-ins for "universal" health studies. For example, studies of heart health long based symptomologies, treatment protocols, and prognoses upon male patients; it is now known that heart disease, heart attacks, and prognoses for recovery vary according to gender. The conflation of masculine bodies with human ones has also meant that "women's diseases" have either received minimal attention or been cloaked in shame. Breast cancer is a stellar example of this. Forty years ago, women diagnosed with breast cancer faced a great deal of shame and stigmatization along with uncertain outcomes. Today, because of women's health activism, breast cancer research is much better funded. Despite what some have criticized as the corporatization of the breast cancer movement, it cannot be denied that survivors are profoundly involved in advocacy, research, and policy-making. Embracing pink as its symbol, the breast cancer movement has foregrounded gender and its relationship to health.[63]

Indeed, careful researchers have long understood gender to be a primary factor in health, particularly as regards health-related social behaviour. As men's health researcher and advocate Will H. Courtenay puts it:

> A man who does gender correctly would be relatively unconcerned about his health and well-being in general. He would see himself as stronger, both physically and emotionally, than most women. He would think of himself as independent, not needing to be nurtured by others. He would be unlikely to ask others for help. He would spend much time out in the world and away from home. . . . He would face danger fearlessly, take risks frequently, and have little concern for his own safety.

Courtenay is quite right. Men take more health-related risks, both by engaging in behaviours like drinking and taking drugs, and by considering it unmasculine to seek health-care treatment. Ignoring health issues, "playing through pain," has been, in fact, a symbol of masculinity. Meanwhile, according to those who study gender and health, "women get sicker, but men die quicker"; men, in general, report less illness, but women outlive men. Canadian life expectancy is now more than 80 years, but a four-year gap remains between the sexes (though that gap is shrinking).[64]

Class and ethnicity complicate the picture. In Canada, Aboriginal people in general experience tuberculosis, HIV/AIDS, heart disease, and diabetes at much higher rates than are characteristic of the general population, Aboriginal life expectancy is significantly lower than the Canadian average, and Aboriginal infant mortality and youth suicide rates are much higher. Throughout the life cycle, Aboriginal people face greater health risks than non-Aboriginals. Clearly, then, gender is only one of many determinants of health. Nevertheless, gender interacts with those determinants in important ways.[65]

Middle-aged black men in the US, for example, have much lower longevity and much higher rates of stress and lifestyle-related diseases (heart attack, stroke, diabetes) than do their white counterparts. Racialization provides much of the answer. Whereas men, "overall, have a particular set of pressures to show strength and not reveal weakness," writes columnist Ellis Cose, "this feeling is intensified in black men." There is, he continues, "an ethic of toughness among black men, built up to protect yourself against racial slights and from the likelihood that society is going to challenge you or humiliate you in some way. This makes it hard to admit that you are in pain or need help." In the US, African-American and Latino men are significantly less likely than white men to see a doctor—even when they are in poor health.[66]

Masculinity also affects one of the most important areas of gender divergence, sexual health. Nowhere is the gendering of health more clear than in the gendering of HIV/AIDS. The onset of the HIV/AIDS epidemic in North America defined the disease as a disease of men—gay men in particular. As a result, major changes occurred in the sexual patterns of gay men, including fewer partners, less anonymous sex, and increases in the practice of safe sex and the number of gay male couples. No matter how important containing the disease was, the emphasis on "safe sex" was seen by many as an effort to "feminize" sexuality and return it to the context of emotional and monogamous relationships, abandoning the earlier gay liberationist ethic of sexual freedom. Many men feared that practising safe sex would mean no longer having "manly" sex and that programs that encourage nonconformity would be doomed to failure. (This is not simply an issue for gay men, of course. Heterosexual women have been trying to get heterosexual men to practice a form of safe sex for decades, finding that their own sexual expressivity is less encumbered when both partners take responsibility for birth control. Fear of pregnancy and fear of HIV transmission both require that one fuse sexual pleasure with sexual responsibility.)[67]

Of course, the epicentre of the HIV epidemic has shifted dramatically since the disease was first diagnosed in 1984. Globally, more than 34 million men, women, and children have died from AIDS, and another 37 million are living with it. More than two-thirds of those infected live in sub-Saharan Africa, with many others resident in South and Southeast Asia, and Latin America.[68]

In the developing world, and particularly in Sub-Saharan Africa, AIDS is emphatically not a masculine disease. The majority of those infected with AIDS have been female, and in some hard-hit areas, girls and women experience an infection rate more than twice that of men. Globally, according to the World Health Organization, AIDS is the leading cause of death among women of child-bearing age. These statistics cannot be separated from social factors. In many regions, women's significantly lower status often renders them powerless to resist sexual advances or refuse sex to their husbands, to insist on safe sex practices, or to have much access to health care; and women's economic vulnerability leads many into sex-trade work where they may face even greater risk of infection. Empowering women is now recognized as the major mechanism to reduce HIV. Dr Pascoal Mocumbi, former prime minister of Mozambique, challenged Africans to "break the silence regarding the sexual behaviour and gender inequalities that drive the epidemic." Unfortunately, years later, young women remain at significantly higher risk of contracting the disease, and account for many of the new infections reported.[69]

In North America and western Europe, the percentage of HIV-positive women is below 25 per cent; in Australia and New Zealand it is under 10 per cent. In these places, AIDS remains a highly "masculine" disease. Although women and men are both able to contract the virus that causes AIDS—and, in fact, women are actually more likely to contract the disease from unprotected heterosexual intercourse than are men—the majority of all AIDS patients in North America are men. Of the approximately 75,000 Canadians living with AIDS, about 78 per cent are male. Class and racialization continue to be important features of the epidemic. In the US, rates of new infections are higher among young black men than among their white counterparts; and in Canada, the rates of infection among Aboriginal people are more than three times the rate of non-Aboriginals; black Canadians are also particularly vulnerable.[70]

Seen in this way, AIDS is arguably the most highly gendered disease in history—a disease that both women and men could get but one that disproportionately affects one gender and not the other. It would be useful to understand masculinity—risk taking, avoidance of responsibility, pursuit of sex—as a risk factor in the spread of the disease, in the same way as we understand masculinity to be a risk factor in drunk driving accidents.

Yet even in areas like drunk driving, there are signs of gender convergence. In fact, more women are disregarding traditional strictures of femininity and taking increased risks. Take drinking, for example. Of course, far more men drink to excess than women do; in the US, drinking is heaviest among young, white, male students attending four-year institutions and often revolves around fraternities and sports events. Nevertheless, an increasing number of women are binge drinking as well. "To be able to drink like a guy is kind of a badge of honour," commented one female student. "For me, it's a feminism thing." Although few feminists would actually suggest that binge drinking is an index of women's liberation, many young women have come to feel that drinking, fighting, smoking, and other typically "masculine" behaviours are a sign of power—and therefore cool. Barbara Ehrenreich disagrees, suggesting that, "Gender equality wouldn't be worth fighting for if all it meant was the opportunity to be as stupid and self-destructive as men can be."[71]

Additionally, there are signs that more men are seeking health professionals and taking better care of their health—a domain traditionally reserved for women. Efforts to develop men's health awareness have been especially successful in the developing world, where campaigns for reproductive health and family planning for women have branched out to include men in health planning. Both women's and men's health needs confront dominant ideas about gender that inhibit men's health-seeking behaviour and often prohibit women's. Gender inequality is bad for both women's and men's health, though in different ways.[72]

As mentioned above, there are also signs of convergence in lifespan, one of the most enduring sites of gender difference. While Canadian women outlived men by 4.7 years in 2005, this is a reduction from 1991, when the gap was more like 6 years; the gap has since fallen to 4 years. Meanwhile, in the global South, gender inequality (e.g., unequal access to health care and nutrition, as well as men's control of reproduction) led the Nobel laureate economist Amartya Sen to estimate that worldwide there are 100 million "missing women." These are women and girls who should be present in national populations based on the number of men in those populations and whose deaths are directly attributable to unequal access to health care, poor prenatal, maternity, and postnatal care, sex-selective abortion, infanticide, and other aspects of gender inequality.[73]

Gender differences persist in our sexual expression and our sexual experiences, in our health experiences and our health seeking, but (in the global North at least) they are far less significant than they used to be, and the signs point to continued convergence.

Summary

Our bodies are not merely "biological realities" but are key elements of our identities. They are shaped, made meaningful, and scrutinized by the gendered society.

First, our bodies are constructed on the basis of a "universal" ideal that is able-bodied. Disability often goes unseen, and ablism affects those who live with disabilities. Canadians with disabilities experience a greater risk of poverty than non-disabled Canadians do, and face significant barriers to employment. There are various ways in which disability is gendered. Women are overrepresented among the disabled, and are even more vulnerable to poverty, violence, and sexual abuse than are disabled men. For men, however, disability may be experienced differently, striking at sexual and physical performance and therefore at the heart of masculine identity. For both men and women, however, disability is experienced in complex ways that interact with other elements of gender and identity.

Sport is also a gendered arena. In early childhood, children are encouraged to adopt different forms of play. As childhood progresses, sport becomes a training (and testing) ground for boys' masculinity. "Throwing like a girl" reveals the need for boys to prove themselves against a denigrated model of femininity; but the way that girls tend to throw and participate in sport also reveals how ideals of feminine bodily comportment can limit women's and girls' achievement. Self-objectification, characteristic of "normal" female development, inhibits athletic performance.

During the course of the twentieth century, girls and women slowly gained access to sporting opportunities that were once reserved for boys. This led, eventually, to second-wave activism that opened greater opportunities, including enforced equality in girls' and boy's sport as exemplified by the US's Title IX legislation. Male and female athletes now have relatively equal opportunities to participate in sport, despite some continuing discrimination.

More subtle forms of discrimination include the ways we see athletes. Female athletes continue to be seen as unfeminine or suspected of homosexuality. In addition, female athletes continue to be compensated less favourably than male athletes are. Finally, the sex-testing of female athletes and controversies over transgender athletes continue the debate over the gendering of sport.

Sport is also gendered, of course, in that it embodies masculinity. For boys, sport is the premier testing ground for masculinity and serves as the terrain on which boys are taught to be men. In sport, boys and men learn masculine ideals of stoicism, aggression, self-sacrifice, and disregard of pain. In hockey, hegemonic masculinity is upheld through these ideals and through the valorization of violence in the service of the team. Nonetheless, for males and females alike, sport provides not only confirmation of the more negative aspects of gender ideology but also models for gender transformation.

If sport is about physical mastery, our bodies are also valued for their beauty. The cultivation of beauty is a heavily gendered aspect of our relationship with our bodies. Around the world, women are more likely to be valued for physical beauty than are men, though standards of beauty vary and are subject to change. In North America, women are particularly vulnerable to the "beauty myth," which emphasizes an unreachable cultural ideal of beauty as the pinnacle of female achievement. This cultural construct makes many women overly concerned with their appearances, enhancing self-objectification under the scrutiny not of men per se, but of the so-called male gaze. Both men and women utilize the male gaze, assessing women's attractiveness, and adopting the stance of a desiring heterosexual male subject.

The beauty myth valorizes Northern European ethnic models of beauty. Because of this implied ethnic model, racialized women are much more vulnerable to cultural slurs of "ugliness." Light skin, "good" hair, and other attributes, based on the value of the dominant ethnic beauty model, may operate as "social capital" for racialized women. Disabled women also may be constructed as "ugly" or may face social pressure to "perfect" the disabled body where possible.

Fear of fat unites many North American women, and this increasingly affects all groups. Men are also concerned about their weight, and body anxieties among men seem to be increasing. Still, the disproportionate concern of women for their appearance remains a key feature of the gendering of bodies. Not surprisingly, then, women remain by far the most willing consumers of cosmetic surgery, even if thousands of men do subject themselves to dubious procedures such as penis enlargements. The male gaze remains critical to both sexes, with disproportionate power over women.

One case in which men have been more likely than women to seek radical bodily transformation is that of transgender. Since about 1950, sexual reassignment has become ever more possible and successful, and there are now more than 100,000 people worldwide who have had such treatment and changed sex. In recent years, the number of FTM trans people has increased dramatically, and the range of options pursued by trans people has expanded beyond SRS.

Health provides both gender similarities and radical gender difference. Health and illness are in some ways levellers, but differences persist. Masculinity and femininity interact with health-related behaviours, and these gender differences interact with class, ethnicity, and sexual orientation. The gendering of the HIV/AIDS epidemic is an excellent example of how gender differences can emerge in strikingly different ways in different contexts.

In health, as in other areas in the gendered society, there are increasing signs of gender convergence. Young women's risk-taking behaviours are starting to replicate those of young men. Men appear to be seeking health care more consistently. Additionally, and for unknown reasons, there are signs of convergence in lifespan in North America. Therefore, we are still parsing the many complexities of embodiment in a gendered society.

Questions for Critical Thinking

1. How would foregrounding disability change your view of the themes dealt with in the previous chapters of this book?
2. Do you believe that sex testing should be eliminated from sport?
3. Do you see the "beauty myth" as important in Canadian society?
4. In your experience, is fatphobia gendered? In which ways?
5. What is the role of *sex* difference and *gender* difference in determining health?

Key Terms

ablism/ableism
Adonis complex
beauty myth
bottom surgery
cisgender
colourism
disability
fat-shaming
fetishized
female to male (FTM)
gender dysphoria
gender verification

male gaze
male to female (MTF)
muscle dysmorphia
no-ho
self-objectification
sex testing
sexual reassignment surgery (SRS)
top surgery
transgender
transsexual
transvestite

Sexualities
Gendered Desires

Sexuality may be about bodies, but it is also about society.

—Jeffrey Weeks, *The Language of Sexuality*

As Jeffrey Weeks, a preeminent investigator of sexuality, suggests above, sexuality lies at the interface of biology and culture. At its most basic, sexuality is about bodies, their functions, and their pleasures. Yet to interpret sexuality this way is grossly simplistic, because sex is above all a social act. Around the world, sexuality has been a longstanding obsession of human societies, which have created rules to shape, manage, and channel human sexual behaviours and desires. Not surprisingly, these rules (and sexuality more generally) have been sites of the most stark and obdurate gender differences. At the same time, however, sexuality has been the site of tremendous change, and as we shall see below, there are signs of gender convergence as well as gender difference.

In Chapter 10, we discussed how friendship and love have become "feminized"—that is, how traditionally "feminine" models of intimacy have come to be seen as normative. If this is true, then one might argue that sexuality has become increasingly "masculinized." The "masculinization of sex"—including the pursuit of pleasure for its own sake, the increased attention to orgasm, the multiplication of sexual partners, the universal interest in sexual experimentation, and the separation of sexual behaviour from love—is partly a result of the technological transformation of sexuality (from birth control to the Internet) and partly a result of the **Sexual Revolution**'s promise of greater sexual freedom with fewer emotional and physical consequences. While there is much debate about the nature of human sexuality and the implications of the Sexual Revolution and its aftermath, there is agreement that we are living through a period of flux in sexual definitions, mores, and behaviours.

A (Brief) History of Sexuality

As stated above, sexuality cannot be analyzed as something distinct from society. This is particularly important when we look at the history of sexuality because it is largely a record of the kind of sexual behaviour demanded and sanctioned by various societies. (Of course, individuals did contravene these guidelines, with varying degrees of tolerance or punishment for such transgressions.) Because of the sheer variety of human societies in the past, with their widely differing structures and mores, generalization is difficult. However, one key similarity across cultures was *patriarchal control over female sexuality*. In many (though not all) cultures, fathers, brothers, and husbands exerted authority over girls and women, attempting to ensure their virginity until marriage and their fidelity afterward. The Laws of Manu, an ancient Indian law code, stated it this way: "Men must make their women dependent day and night, and keep under their own control those who are attached to sensory objects. Her father guards her in childhood, her husband guards her in youth, and her sons guard her in old age." In some cases, as was common in Chinese history, the guarding of women was entrusted to eunuchs.[1]

Men, meanwhile, generally experienced much more sexual freedom, including in marriage. Adultery by a married man has generally been treated much more leniently than the philandering of a married woman; in many cases, "adultery" was itself defined in gendered terms, as sex between a married woman and a man of any marital status. For example, Hammurabi's code (c. 1780 BC) ignored adultery by married men, but prescribed death for married women (and their lovers) caught *in flagrante*. In the twentieth century, numerous law codes still excused a jealous husband who killed a wife caught in adultery, because the insult to his manhood was presumed to be so great that he would "naturally" lose control.

It should not be assumed, however, that the only important sexual rules related to marriage and the control of female sexuality. A second major theme across cultures was the prevalence of *rules governing licit sexual expression*. These rules were not always the same, of course; for example, incest was forbidden across cultures, but the definition of incest might vary. (Rulers were often exempted from the rules: In Hawaiian and Egyptian cultures, among others, royalty commonly married siblings.) Rules governed not only with whom one could have sex, but also what sexual behaviours were permissible. The law of Moses, for example, defined incest and forbade bestiality and same-sex relations between men; but it also proscribed sex with one's own wife during her menstrual period. The Romans, for their part, frowned upon kissing one's wife or showing too much affection in public!

While same-sex relations between men were forbidden by Mosaic law, there was much variation in societies' attitudes. As is well known, in ancient Greece adult male citizens, married and single, engaged in sexual relations with male slaves and tender love affairs with young boys. This was neither frowned upon nor seen as evidence of a distinct "sexual orientation," in the terms that we use now. Similarly, Roman men were free to indulge in both cross- and same-sex relations. In both cases, however, effeminate men, and men who played the "receptive" role in anal intercourse, were denigrated. A man was not judged by the sex of his sexual partners, but rather by his masculinity, seen as synonymous with being active, assertive, and dominant. The Romans had a whole lexicon with which to mock and denigrate freeborn men who permitted themselves (or preferred) to be penetrated or to assume a subordinate (typically feminine) role in relations with other men.[2]

Same-sex relations between women have often been overlooked entirely by law and custom, in part because sexuality has often been defined as penetrative intercourse.

Without the presence of a man, one might therefore say, there was no sex. (Some legal codes, however, forbade sex between women and animals.) Same-sex relations between women therefore leave little historical trace, except in artifacts and the famous poetry of Sappho. While only fragments of Sappho's poems remain, they were compelling enough that both "Sapphist" and "lesbian" (from Sappho's home island, Lesbos) entered the language of female sexuality.

Many ancient religions demanded that spiritual specialists renounce sexuality, in large part because sexuality and reproduction were seen to yoke human beings to the material world. Early Christianity was no exception. However, Christianity also brought new and more rigorous demands of ordinary believers, including men. The Gospel of Matthew brought the shocking revelation that men who looked at women with lust in their hearts were committing adultery—and that marriage after divorce (licit under Mosaic law) was itself a form of adultery. Early Christians were therefore sexual radicals, holding to strict notions of sexual propriety that bound both men and women. Some early Christian communities contained both men and women living chaste lives—this would be a recurring theme in the history of Christianity, whether in officially sanctioned monastic communities or in "heretic" groups such as the Cathars.[3]

The Western view of sexuality was irrevocably marked by Christianity, the hegemonic source of sexual knowledge for centuries. In theory, Christianity demanded complete abstinence before marriage (and for life, for those who became priests or nuns). For married people, Christianity brought a long set of rules of which fidelity (for both men and women) was the most obvious. However, there were also many other rules, all of which derived from the concept that God created sexuality for the procreation of children within Christian marriage. Accordingly, Christians were to be moderate in sexual appetite, to offer sex freely to their spouses, and to avoid abortion and a lengthy list of "sinful" behaviours and positions. In fact, many activities engaged in by today's married couples, from oral and anal sex to intercourse with the woman on top, are illicit from the perspective of historical Christianity. Of course, throughout the history of the Christian West, same-sex relations between men were considered the most sinful sexual act possible: the "nefarious sin," as it was often called, or **sodomy**. In many jurisdictions, sodomy was punishable by death (usually at the hands of secular authorities), and cyclical persecutions occurred with some regularity. On the other hand, too much attention to the rigid rules set down by Christianity obscures the extent to which regulations were regularly flouted, particularly by men. European popular culture was nowhere near as prudish as the rules enumerated above might imply. In fact, until the late 1500s, the Catholic church paid little attention to the sexual behaviour of the faithful (or, for that matter, of its own parish priests).[4]

For hundreds of years, nonetheless, the Christian view of sexuality ruled—not only in Europe, but also in the regions colonized by European kingdoms and nations. The imposition (actual or attempted) of Christian sexual norms was a major component of colonialism in the Americas, Africa, and Asia. Therefore, by the nineteenth century, much of the world lived under at least some semblance of a Christian sexual regime where divorce, although extremely rare, was illegal; sodomy was prohibited; and sex was seen as intended for marriage and procreation. However, the nineteenth century would bring significant changes.

One of the key developments of the nineteenth century was the development of a scientific approach to sexuality. In the second half of the century, as science grew in prestige, sexuality itself became a matter for scholarly study rather than the domain of religious moralists. In the 1840s, Richard Kaan, an Austro-Russian physician, argued that Christian "sins" such as masturbation and homosexuality were actually the result of mental disorders. Later in the century, scholars like Richard von Kraft-Ebbing, Magnus Hirschfeld, and Havelock Ellis took a similar perspective, studying sexual behaviours as an artifact of individual psychology rather than of moral dissolution. By the early twentieth century, sexology was a recognized field of significant influence, with its own regularly published scholarly journal.[5]

The scientific approach ushered in a new concept: stable **sexual orientation** produced by psychological development. Same-sex behaviour (again, mainly by men) was a particular emphasis. The sex scientists, some of them themselves men who engaged in same-sex relations, believed that same-sex attraction was not a sin but a psychological "inversion" of normal sexuality. Around 1870, new terms arose to describe this: not just "inversion" but "Uranism," "contrary sexual feeling," and **homosexuality**. These terms had several key effects. First, they cemented the idea that *same-sex sexual relations were not just a behaviour engaged in by some men but a fixed sexual preference* with its roots in individual development. (Freud, as we saw earlier, would elaborate on the precise mechanism by which this preference came to be.) Second, however unwittingly, the nineteenth-century sex scientists cemented the idea that *homosexuality was abnormal*. Though they generally opposed the persecution of homosexuals, the idea of "inversion" nonetheless upheld the normalcy and naturalness of cross-sex relations. Therefore, the concept of the "inverted" homosexual brought with it another idea, that of **heterosexuality** (though "heterosexual" took much longer to catch on!). The effects on men's behaviour were not immediate, but by the twentieth century, the notion of a strict divide between heterosexual and homosexual men undoubtedly changed sexual mores, particularly among the middle class.[6]

Much of the nineteenth-century study of sex tended to emphasize male sexuality, but the new scientific approach also had a strong impact on views of women. As we have seen, the **double standard** had been in existence for millennia, holding women to a high standard of sexual behaviour while men had more freedom. Often, the need for control of women was explained in terms of women's greater lustfulness—as well as their knack for "overpowering" men with sexual desire. Victorian medical thinkers added a new wrinkle: women were now "naturally" less interested in sex than men, who were at the mercy of powerful sex drives. "The majority of women (happily for them) are not much troubled with sexual feelings of any kind," wrote one physician in the 1890s. According to this view, however, women who *were* sexually active or aggressive were seen as "deviant," "hysterical," or "unnatural." Prostitution, for example, was now explained not in terms of sin (or women's economic condition); instead, some argued, it was a result of individual women's sexual psychology. This view of women's "natural" and "deviant" proclivities would persist well into the twentieth century.[7]

Sigmund Freud, in his 1905 *Three Essays on the Theory of Sexuality*, synthesized, criticized, and commented on the body of nineteenth-century sexual science. As we saw in Chapter 3, his views would become the basis of the twentieth-century view of normal sexual development and behaviour. Freud's view that sexuality (libido) was at the heart of individual psychology was also highly influential. Throughout the twentieth century, sexuality continued to be an object of much study in a variety of fields, principally psychology. Systematic, large-scale studies of sexuality were conducted and published by Alfred Kinsey in the 1940s and 1950s, and by William Masters and Virginia Johnson in the 1960s and 1970s. These studies played an important role in making clear that same-sex behaviours were much more common than had been previously believed. Moreover, these scholarly studies of sexual behaviour found a large popular audience, showing that the public was hungry for information about sexuality and for a new, more open approach to the topic.[8]

Some scholars refer to the late nineteenth century as "the first sexual revolution." The term Sexual Revolution, however, is more commonly associated with the 1960s and 1970s, when youth counterculture, feminism, the gay rights movement, and the birth control pill came together to produce lasting change in virtually every aspect of sexual attitudes and behaviours. While arguably a North American phenomenon, the Sexual Revolution nonetheless had lasting effects all over the world.[9]

One of the key effects—and a controversial one—is the so-called **sexualization of culture**. It could be argued that the sexualization of Western culture began long ago. According to Michel Foucault, it began in the seventeenth century with the proliferation of discussions about sexuality. We might also locate sexualization in the late nineteenth century or in Freud's work of the early twentieth century. However, in general, the term "sexualization of culture" refers to the increased openness and availability of sexual imagery and information, including but not limited to pornography. Therefore, a more accurate timeline would probably begin in the 1970s. (Advertising images from before then, however, clearly "sexualize" women as a means to sell products. Moreover, Kinsey's popular media success may have also been part of sexualization as early as the 1950s!) It is therefore difficult to pinpoint an exact starting point for sexualization; however, it is clearly linked not only to changing attitudes, but also to mass media and to advertising. Sexualization can be seen in many domains: perhaps most prominently, in **pornification**, the proliferation of pornography-derived images and terms outside the realm of pornography itself.[10]

However, sexualization also refers to other processes, not least the increasing importance of sex to satisfying relationships and to a sense of personal fulfillment. In fact, the longer-range historical trend throughout the past several centuries has been to sexualize marriage—to link the emotions of love and nurturing to erotic pleasure within the reproductive relationship. Consequently, sexual compatibility and expression have become increasingly important in our married lives, as the increased amount of time before marriage (prolonged adolescence), the availability of birth control and divorce, and an ethic of individual self-fulfillment have combined to increase the importance of sexual expression throughout the course of our lives.

Finally, sexualization also refers to a process affecting children, who are increasingly likely to be depicted as sexual objects and to be exposed to explicit sexual imagery. The Internet has played its own key role in sexualization, enabling the sharing of sexual knowledge, identities, and intimacies across vast distance. In fact, the Internet itself is a key participant in the history of sexuality, with results yet to be seen.

Beyond Bodies? "Cybersex" and the Horizons of Sex Online

In the critically acclaimed 2013 movie *Her*, set in an imprecise future, a lonely man engages in (bizarre) "phone sex" with an unknown woman before purchasing a new operating system, with which he subsequently falls deeply in love. The film is an excellent exploration of how sexual and romantic intimacy have been irrevocably altered by digital communication. As already discussed, the Internet has changed the availability and ubiquity of pornography and other sexual information. Online communication has also vastly increased our ability to arrange sexual encounters ("discreet" or otherwise) with others. For some groups, such as men who have sex with men (**MSM**), such discretion may be critical to their ability to pursue same-sex relations. Nevertheless, we often see such sexual content as an adjunct to bodily sex. We presume (probably quite accurately) that those who view pornography are using it for masturbation. We assume that those who "hook up" online have, as their goal, some sort of real-life meeting or at the very least a mutual masturbation session, on-camera or off. However, what about the sexual encounters that exist wholly on the Internet itself and involve no real-life masturbation or orgasm?

Since the 1990s, there has been much media discussion of so-called **cybersex**, generally defined as sex enabled by the Internet. The classic examples include pornography viewing, often compulsive. Another common example of cybersex is interactions in chat rooms. These interactions may result in real-life meetings and encounters, or their virtual nature may extend as far as the use of sex toys that can be controlled by the "partner" in the exchange. The category of **teledildonics** includes such toys, as well as the robotic partners and toys that promise sexual release without the "mess" of human interaction. Additionally, when a partner *is* involved, all such interactions may be either "free" (in that no money is exchanged) or commodified. More recently, many have expressed concern about yet another form of cybersex: **sexting**, the transmission of explicit texts and images, principally by youth. Though there is no doubt that adults also "sext," the concern about youth has arisen because of the nonconsensual sharing of sexual images and texts as a form of cyberbullying, with sometimes tragic consequences. Sexting, however, tends to exist within romantic relationships and is dysfunctional or dangerous primarily insofar as it leaves a record that can be used maliciously. It therefore appears less as a "new" form of sexual activity than as an extension of romantic attachment.

In fact, much of what we do sexually online replicates what we do in real life. John Edward Campbell agrees, critiquing the "online disembodiment thesis"—the idea that there is some "radical disjuncture" between sexual experiences in the real world and those in cyberspace.

The history of sexuality is therefore not a narrative of our path from (yesterday's) ignorance to (today's) enlightenment but a much more complicated story. Even as we navigate a world in which sex is increasingly disembodied, many relics of the past are still with us. The double standard persists, as do widespread gender differences in sexual attitudes and behaviours. To be sure, gender is not the only meaningful variable, but it remains a meaningful influence on what we believe about sex and what we do sexually.

What, then, do we make of sex in persistent online worlds such as *Second Life* (SL)? *Second Life* offers users the opportunity to create an entire online presence for themselves—hence the name of the game. Inhabiting avatars and a vast variety of simulated environments ("sims"), users can express and create identities quite distinct from their embodied identities in the real world. This can be beneficial; for example, a group of disabled users who were followed for three months after joining SL showed significant improvement on a variety of psychological measures. SL also allows users the experience of inhabiting bodies of another gender, or intersex/non-gendered bodies. For many people, not least trans people, this can be profoundly liberating. *Second Life's* available avatars also include animalized bodies (realistic or anthropomorphized) that appeal to the large group of users who identify as **furries**. Because of the immersive nature of the virtual world, the experience of operating an avatar can produce a strong sense of "being there," or what some scholars call "telepresence." Not surprisingly, *sexual* telepresence is another large part of many SL users' experience.

Like many online games, *Second Life* is a highly monetized world, with virtually all content available for purchase. Purchasable avatars can be equipped with virtual genitals, sex toys, and sexualized clothing; and adult-oriented sims contain sex-oriented "poseballs," scripted objects that enable avatars to adopt various sexual positions, simulating sex with the avatars of other users. *Second Life* users can purchase furniture equipped with such poseballs for use in their own SL homes. While using the poses, users communicate sexually using instant messaging. Users of other online games, such as *World of Warcraft*, "cyber" using instant messaging (IM), of course; moreover, online role-players often create intense sexual content in their roleplays. However, only SL enables a broader perceptual sexual experience through its realistic avatars, poses, and add-ons.

As can be seen, then, *Second Life* suggests a different horizon for cybersex than the more usual manifestations, pornography, and chat rooms. The "sex" in *Second Life* may have very little connection to real bodies; even real-life masturbation may be absent from the "encounters" of SL users. While research on *Second Life* and similar persistent worlds is still in its infancy, sex in SL raises all kinds of interesting questions. Is sex really sex if it takes place entirely in someone's head, without any kind of genital stimulation or release? What is the role of emotion in mediating sexual encounters online? What is the relationship between online sexuality and sex in real life? The answers to these questions are still unknown, but one thing is clear: the Internet's effects on sexuality go well beyond enabling porn-viewing and hook-ups. Regardless of critiques of the online disembodiment thesis, the Internet must be regarded as opening an entirely new chapter in the history of sexuality—one that is still being written.[11]

Gender, Desire, and Sexual Expression: The Gender Gap

Throughout this book, we have emphasized that gender expression varies across cultures. Sexual behaviour is no exception to this rule. In contemporary North America, several variables other than gender affect sexuality, such as class, age, education, marital status, religion, race, and ethnicity. Take class, for example; Kinsey found that, contrary to the then-prevalent stereotype that working-class people were more sensual because they were closer to their "animal natures" (!), lower-class position does not mean hotter sex. In fact, he found that upper- and middle-class people were more sophisticated in the "arts of love," demonstrating wider variety of activities and greater emphasis on foreplay, whereas lower-class people dispensed with preliminaries and did not even kiss very much.[12]

There is also evidence that race and ethnicity produce variations in sexual behaviour and attitudes, at least according to studies that found less masturbation among Asian-Canadians and African-Americans and more adultery among African-American men. In the US, some studies suggest that blacks hold somewhat more sexually liberal attitudes than whites do and have slightly more sex partners. Black women seem to masturbate more than white women and feel less guilty about it, perhaps because black women also generally have a more positive attitude toward their own sexuality and body image. Hispanics are also apparently more sexually liberal than whites and masturbate more frequently than blacks or whites do. However, they report less oral sex than whites do (yet more than do blacks) and have fewer sex partners, either of the same or opposite sex, than do whites or blacks.[13]

Age also affects sexuality. What turns us on at 50 will probably not be what turned us on at 15. Our attitudes toward sexuality may also change. Sexual attraction, activity, and orientation may be a less important part of our identities. Most intriguingly, we may even find our sexual orientation changing through the life cycle. Ideas of a fixed sexual orientation—cemented in adolescence and with us throughout our lives—are somewhat confounded by research that suggests that for women at least, same-sex desire may ebb and flow, leading some researchers to propose that "variability in the emergence and expression of female same-sex desire during the life course is normative rather than exceptional."[14]

Even when sexual orientation remains constant, other changes occur. Age and other life-course changes may produce a decline in sexual energy and interest, but also change in marital status and family obligations. As Lillian Rubin writes,

> On the most mundane level, the constant negotiation about everyday tasks leaves people harassed, weary, irritated, and feeling more like traffic cops than lovers. Who's going to do the shopping, pay the bills, take care of the laundry, wash the dishes, take out the garbage, clean the bathroom, get the washing machine fixed, decide what to eat for dinner, return the phone calls from friends and parents? When there are children, the demands, complications, and exhaustion increase exponentially.[15]

Therefore, gender is not the only issue that influences sexual attitudes and expression. Culture, class, ethnicity, and age all have their effects. Still, despite a great degree of cross-cultural (and intracultural) variation in sexuality, there are striking commonalities. Additionally, many of these commonalities point to strong gender differences in sexual preferences, attitudes, and behaviours. These differences are robust enough that many researchers see a "gender gap" in the area of sexuality.[16]

In the heterosexual world, men still stand to gain status and women to lose status from sexual experience: as one hoary (and horrid) adage puts it, a key that opens many locks is a master key, but a lock that can be opened by many keys is just a bad lock. The analogy, however ridiculous, is worth exploring for a moment about what it says about male and female sexual roles. A man's job is to "unlock" (conquer the objections of) as many women as possible; a woman, on the other hand, is the gatekeeper of sexuality, whose job is to remain sealed (presumably, to all but one key). These roles are longstanding and well known. "The whole game was to get a girl to give out," one man told sociologist Lillian Rubin. "You expected her to resist; she had to if she wasn't going to ruin her reputation. But you kept pushing. Part of it was the thrill of touching and being touched, but I've got to admit, part of it was the conquest, too, and what you'd tell the guys at school the next day." "I felt as if I should want to get it as often as possible," recalled another. "I guess that's because if you're a guy, you're supposed to want it." The double standard makes sex something men "get" from and do to women, as is recognized by the crude expression, "he *did* her."[17]

The sexual double standard is itself a product of gender inequality, of sexism—the unequal distribution of power in our society based on gender. In an unequal society, sex becomes a contest, not a means of connection; when sexual pleasure happens, it's often seen as his victory over her resistance. Sexuality becomes, in the words of feminist lawyer Catharine MacKinnon, "the linchpin of gender inequality."[18]

Not surprisingly, in a world governed by such powerful sexual scripts, there are clear differences between heterosexual men and heterosexual women on a variety of indicators. For example, most studies find heterosexual women more sexually selective than men and less interested in casual sex. In one survey, women were significantly more likely to believe that one-night stands are degrading (47 per cent of the men agreed and 68 per cent of the women agreed). Additionally, a classic 1989 experiment, in which male and female students were approached (on campus) and propositioned for casual sex, found *no* women willing to have sex (while about 70 per cent of men said yes). For an evolutionary psychologist, these results are perfectly intelligible in terms of men's lower parental investment. However, there are alternative explanations. First, when considering women's willingness to have sex with strangers, the threat of sexual violence or danger must be pondered. Most women would find threatening a scenario in which a random stranger approached them in a public place for sex—no matter how attractive the stranger, and no matter how appealing casual sex might otherwise be to a woman. Similarly, most women know that they are judged more harshly for casual sex, and men know that having more partners enhances their masculinity. A 2014 study confirmed that fear of being stigmatized had a strong effect on women's acceptance of casual sex offers.[19]

Still, men's lack of selectiveness may be supported by surveys in which heterosexual men report many more partners than do women. "Women need a reason to have sex," commented comedian Billy Crystal. "Men just need a place." In the 2007–2008 global Durex survey, Canadian men claimed to have had an average of 23 sexual partners compared to women's 10. However, relying on self-reported sexual history may be dangerous, because men may lie to enhance their reputations (and women to protect theirs!). A recent study addressed this difficulty. One group of participants was interviewed in the standard manner. For the other group, researchers used a fake lie detector to convince study participants that their reports of sexual history would be scrutinized for truthfulness. In the control group, the results were "normal," with men claiming more partners than women.

Under the lie-detector condition, however, the number of partners claimed by men went down significantly, and in fact, *women* ended up reporting slightly more partners (4.4 versus 4.0 for men). So it seems that when men and women tell the truth, evolutionary imperatives are less important than the venerable double standard—which is precisely what some researchers have been saying since the 1950s.[20]

Studies have found strong gender differences in infidelity (not surprisingly, given the harsh penalties historically accorded to women who "stepped out"!). The Ashley Madison hack of 2015 released the e-mail addresses of about 37 million accounts linked to the website. Aside from the surprising news that Canada was the country with the most Ashley Madison accounts per capita, the hack revealed that men vastly outnumbered women on the site, and that the "typical" Ashley Madison user was an "attached male seeking female." When it was revealed that many of the female accounts were actually bots or dummy accounts created by the company itself, the evidence seemed to confirm that adultery is a masculine specialty. Indeed, North American heterosexual men are still more likely to stray than are women (as are gay men, people in cohabiting relationships, people with permissive sexual attitudes, and members of some ethnic groups). According to 2010 statistics, about 15 per cent of American women report affairs compared to 21 per cent of men. However, women's rates of self-reported infidelity have gone up more than 40 per cent throughout the past two decades while men's rates have remained stable. What's driving the catch-up? The likeliest reasons are women's improved economic position and greater opportunities for initiating affairs, including through social media. Interestingly, studies have found that male–female differences in infidelity are amplified among homosexuals, with gay men dramatically more likely than lesbians are (82 per cent versus 28 per cent, in one study) to have sex outside their primary relationships. However, recent studies have questioned whether non-monogamy among sexual minorities should be considered "infidelity" at all. Perhaps framing the issue this way is a form of "mono-normativity" that situates monogamous relationships as the norm—in spite of the fact that many gay men are comfortable with non-exclusive relationships.[21]

Double standards, however, are still with us. Along with those double standards come deeper differences in the understanding of sexual expression. Intercourse and orgasm seem to be more important forms of sexual expression for men than they are for women. Men's orgasmic focus leads to a greater emphasis on the genitals as men's single most important erogenous zone. If men's sexuality is often **phallocentric**—revolving around the glorification and gratification of the penis—then it is not surprising that men often develop elaborate relationships with their genitals. Some men name their penises or give them nicknames like "Hercules" (really). If men do not personify the penis, they objectify it; if it is not a little person, then it is supposed to act like a machine, an instrument, or a "tool." A man projects "the coldness and hardness of metal" onto his flesh, writes the French philosopher Emmanuel Reynaud.[22]

Few women name their genitals; fewer still think of their genitals as machines. In fact, women rarely refer to their genitals by their proper names at all. Most generally describe their external genitalia with the inaccurate "vagina." (We might ask why the term for the part of the female genitalia that envelops the penis has become synonymous with the whole package.) Some even resort to the more euphemistic "down there" or "private parts." It would be rare indeed for a woman to have a conversation with her vulva.[23]

Because North American cultures (post-colonization), like most cultures in the world, have been male-dominant, our view and language of sexuality reflect a male perspective and the **coital imperative**, which defines "real sex" as penetrative intercourse. Most heterosexual men and women, if asked whether they had "had sex" with someone, would immediately reply on the basis of whether or not penile-vaginal intercourse had taken place. This is "real sex," while activities such as cunnilingus (which for most women results in more reliable orgasms than vaginal intercourse) are seen as "foreplay." Calling such activities foreplay means that they are inevitably seen as the prelude to the "real thing"—once again, sex cannot occur without his orgasm, preferably through vaginal penetration. This view affects not only heterosexual sexuality but also the sexuality of non-heterosexuals, whose sexual acts may be seen as "not the real thing" or "abnormal" as a result. The coital imperative also affects heterosexual sexuality in another way; numerous studies have found that within relationships, women frequently participate in heterosexual intercourse to please their partners, whether they desire it or not.[24] (See also discussion of marital rape in Chapter 13.)

The definition of vaginal intercourse as real sex often results in complex rules about what constitutes a **technical virgin**, and permits the fudging of questions about sexual activity. The impeachment trial of US President Bill Clinton in the late 1990s bears this out. Because he and intern Monica Lewinsky did not have vaginal intercourse, Clinton argued that he did not lie when he denied having sex with Lewinsky.[25]

Thinking about sex seems to be a gendered activity, with men reporting far more sexual thoughts than women do. More than 54 per cent of the men surveyed in the most recent large-scale sex survey conducted by the National Opinion Research Center (NORC) at the University of Chicago reported that they think about sex "very frequently," compared with 19 per cent of the women. In addition, 14 per cent of the women said they rarely or never think about sex, compared with only 4 per cent of the men. In a recent study of Canadian adults, almost half of the men (47.1 per cent) reported "having sexual thoughts several times a day," compared to only 10 per cent of the female respondents. However, numerous commentators have correctly criticized the research design of these studies. Another study, by a team led by Terri Fisher, asked university students to track their thoughts during a one-week period. Some were asked to track their thoughts about sleep, others their thoughts about food, and a final group their thoughts about sex. Interestingly, men recorded more thoughts about *all* of these things than did women, but the magnitude of the difference in sexual thoughts was less than had been previously found, and individual variations dwarfed the difference between men and women.[26]

Still, men, straight and gay, seem to want more sex than do women. At virtually every age and relationship stage, heterosexual men tend to want more sex, while women tend to report either satisfaction with the amount of sex they are having or a desire for less frequent sex. Heterosexual men are ready to begin sex earlier in a relationship than are women. In short, "within heterosexual relationships, men want sex more than women at the start of a relationship, in the middle of it, and after many years of it." One scholar has recently surveyed the evidence and claimed that it points to a widespread "male sexual deficit."[27]

There is also a significant difference in the number and nature of sexual fantasies reported by men and women. Women fantasize less frequently and about fewer partners.

The gendered content of sexual fantasies also differs dramatically. Kimmel and a research assistant collected more than one thousand sexual fantasies from students during the 1990s. In those fantasies, definite gender patterns emerged. Men tended to fantasize about strangers, often more than one at a time, doing a variety of well-scripted sexual acts; women tended to fantasize about setting the right mood for lovemaking with their boyfriend or husband but rarely visualized specific behaviours.[28]

Not surprisingly, given their reported greater frequency of sexual fantasy, men also report more interest in masturbation. Indeed, masturbation produces some of the largest gender differences found in the study of sexuality. Most men masturbate; they begin masturbation earlier and masturbate much more frequently than women do.[29]

Men are also more sexually adventurous than are women, expressing interest in a much wider range of sexual practices. While this holds true for practices now (but not always!) considered "normal," such as fellatio, it is also true that men are much more represented among those attracted to abnormal sexual practices, or **paraphilias**.[30]

Where does this sexual gender gap come from? It is quite possible that *some* of the gender differences we have discussed are the result of differential biology or evolution, and that men do, in fact, have a biologically stronger sex drive than women, as many scholars claim.[31] However, even if that were true, a stronger sex drive alone would not account for the numerous sexual differences we have enumerated. Nor would it explain why so many cultures have found it necessary to shame, punish, and even kill women in order to control their sexuality. Nor do biological theories manage to explain why women, when freed from the fear and shame that are part of the double standard, express much more "masculine" attitudes to sex. Fundamentally, it seems, our sexual differences are the result of differential socialization.

Compulsory Heterosexuality and Minority Sexualities

Sexual socialization begins well before adulthood. The first element in the sexual socialization of children is the social institution of **compulsory heterosexuality**, first theorized by feminist Adrienne Rich in an article published in 1980. Focusing on female sexuality, Rich described how heterosexuality is made "compulsory" through a variety of social mechanisms, of which the most important is the cultural assumption—"the lie"—that heterosexuality is "natural" or "innate":

> The lie is many-layered. In Western tradition, one layer—the romantic—asserts that women are inevitably, even if rashly and tragically, drawn to men; that even when that attraction is suicidal (e.g., *Tristan and Isolde*, Kate Chopin's *The Awakening*) it is still an organic imperative. In the tradition of the social sciences it asserts that primary love between the sexes is "normal," that women need men as social and economic protectors, for adult sexuality and for psychological completion; that the heterosexually constituted family is the basic social unit; that women who do not attach their primary intensity to men must be, in functional terms, condemned to an even more devastating outsiderhood than their outsiderhood as women.[32]

Rich's theory of compulsory heterosexuality has been enormously influential, fuelling studies in a wide variety of disciplines. As an instrument of socialization, this institution works through promoting heterosexuality—for example, through stories and films that emphasize heterosexual attraction, courtship, and marriage—while rendering invisible other forms of sexual and intimate partnership. When not strictly invisible, non-heterosexuality becomes abhorrent and unnatural. This form of socialization exists from children's books and films—(e.g., Disney movies and fairy tales) all the way through adulthood.

Compulsory heterosexuality is slowly breaking down, largely because of feminist theory and LGBTQ activism. Nevertheless, its power as an institution remains strong.

Socialization and Sexuality: The Heterosexual Questionnaire

The Heterosexual Questionnaire (of which there are several editions) was developed in the 1970s by Dr Martin Rochlin, an American psychologist. Its intent was to reverse the questions conventionally asked of homosexuals. It remains a potent and humorous reminder of the power of compulsory heterosexuality.

Heterosexual Questionnaire

This questionnaire is for self-avowed heterosexuals only. If you are not openly heterosexual, pass it on to a friend who is. Please try to answer the questions as candidly as possible. Your responses will be held in strict confidence and your anonymity fully protected.

1. What do you think caused your heterosexuality?
2. When and how did you first decide you were a heterosexual?
3. Is it possible your heterosexuality is just a phase you may grow out of?
4. Could it be that your heterosexuality stems from a neurotic fear of others of the same sex?
5. If you've never slept with a person of the same sex, how can you be sure you wouldn't prefer that?
6. To whom have you disclosed your heterosexual tendencies? How did they react?
7. Why do heterosexuals feel compelled to seduce others into their lifestyle?
8. Why do you insist on flaunting your heterosexuality? Can't you just be what you are and keep it quiet?
9. Would you want your children to be heterosexual, knowing the problems they'd face?
10. A disproportionate majority of child molesters are heterosexual men. Do you consider it safe to expose children to heterosexual male teachers, pediatricians, priests, or scoutmasters?
11. With all the societal support for marriage, the divorce rate is spiraling. Why are there so few stable relationships among heterosexuals?
12. Why do heterosexuals place so much emphasis on sex?

continued

13. Considering the menace of overpopulation, how could the human race survive if everyone were heterosexual?
14. Could you trust a heterosexual therapist to be objective? Don't you fear she or he might be inclined to influence you in the direction of her or his own leanings?
15. Heterosexuals are notorious for assigning themselves and one another rigid, stereotyped sex roles. Why must you cling to such unhealthy role-playing?
16. With the sexually segregated living conditions of military life, isn't heterosexuality incompatible with military service?
17. How can you enjoy an emotionally fulfilling experience with a person of the other sex when there are such vast differences between you? How can a man know what pleases a woman sexually or vice-versa?
18. Shouldn't you ask your far-out straight cohorts, like skin-heads and born-agains, to keep quiet? Wouldn't that improve your image?
19. Why are heterosexuals so promiscuous?
20. Why do you attribute heterosexuality to so many famous lesbian and gay people? Is it to justify your own heterosexuality?
21. How can you hope to actualize your God-given homosexual potential if you limit yourself to exclusive, compulsive heterosexuality?
22. There seem to be very few happy heterosexuals. Techniques have been developed that might enable you to change if you really want to. After all, you never deliberately chose to be a heterosexual, did you? Have you considered aversion therapy or Heterosexuals Anonymous?[33]

Homosexuality, Bisexuality, and the Persistence of Gender

Compulsory heterosexuality socializes men and women toward "his" and "her" sexualities. This can be as applicable to homosexuals as it is to heterosexuals. In fact, the gendering of sexuality may be even *more* obvious among gay men and lesbians, because in homosexual encounters there are two gendered men or two gendered women. Gender differences may even be exaggerated by sexual orientation.

This is, of course, contrary to our "commonsense" understandings of homosexuality, as well as those biological studies that suggest that gay men have some biological affinity with women. Gender stereotypes have often dominated the discussion of sexual orientation; we may assume, for example, that gay men are not overly masculine, that they identify with women, and that they even adopt feminine affectations and traits. Similarly, we may assume that lesbians are insufficiently feminine, identify with and imitate men's behaviours, etc. Homosexuality, old stereotypes tell us, is a *gender* "disorder"; reminding us of the "inversion" ideas of the nineteenth century.[34]

As we saw above, we have a century-long legacy upon which we draw such stereotypic ideas. Homosexuality emerged as a distinct identity in the late nineteenth century.

By the turn of the twentieth century, "the homosexual" was characterized by a form of "interior androgyny, a hermaphroditism of the soul," writes Foucault. "The sodomite had been a temporary aberration; the homosexual was now a species." Since Freud's era, we have assumed that male homosexuality, manifested by effeminacy, and lesbianism, manifested by masculine affectations, might not be innate but are, nonetheless, intractable products of early childhood socialization. We also believed that the differences between gays and straights, once established, are the most important influence in their lives' trajectories.[35]

Our old "commonsense" assumption is that gay men and lesbians are gender *non*conformists—lesbians are "masculine" women; gay men are "feminine" men. These commonsense assumptions have completely saturated popular discussions of homosexuality, especially in those advice books designed to help parents make sure that their children do not turn out "wrong." For example, Peter and Barbara Wyden's book *Growing up Straight* argued that "pre-homosexual" boys were identifiable by their lack of early childhood masculinity, which could be thwarted by an overly "masculine" mother, that is, one who had a job outside the home and paid attention to feminist ideas![36]

A few empirical studies have also made such claims. For example, psychiatrist Richard Green tracked a small group of boys (about 55) from preschool to young adulthood. All the boys were chosen for patterns of frequent cross-dressing at home. They liked to play with girls at school, enjoyed playing with dolls, and followed their mothers around the house doing housework. Their parents were supportive of this behaviour. These "sissy boys," as Green called them, were four times more likely to have homosexual experiences than non-feminine boys. However, this research has also been widely criticized; such gender nonconformity is extremely rare (there was great difficulty in finding even 55 boys) and therefore cannot be the source of the great majority of homosexual behaviour. When milder forms of gender nonconformity are examined, most boys who report such behaviour turn out to be heterosexual. Finally, when studies by Green and his colleagues were extended to "tomboys," no difference was found in eventual sexual orientation between girls who reported tomboy behaviour and those who did not. (What Green and his colleagues seem to have found is that being a sissy is a far more serious offence to the gender order than is being a tomboy.)[37]

The evidence points overwhelmingly the other way; that is, gay men and lesbians are, when it comes to sexuality, typical of their genders. To accept such a proposition leads to some unlikely alliances and overenthusiastic gender stereotyping, with the ultraconservative George Gilder writing that lesbianism "has nothing whatever to do with male homosexuality. Just as male homosexuals, with their compulsive lust and promiscuous impulses, offer a kind of caricature of typical male sexuality, lesbians closely resemble other women in their desire for intimate and monogamous coupling."[38]

Since the birth of the gay liberation movement in the **Stonewall** riots of 1969—when gay men fought back against the police who were raiding a New York City gay bar—a gay culture has emerged that militates against the idea of gay men as "feminine." In fact, many gay men are hypermasculine in their acceptance of casual sex and non-monogamy.

Studies of the sexual lives of lesbians have found something quite different and yet similar, since it also amounts to an exaggeration of "typical" female sexual norms. In the lesbian community, there has been more discussion of "the tyranny of the relationship" than of various sexual practices; lesbian couples in therapy complained of **lesbian bed death**, the virtual cessation of sexual activity in committed couples. One woman told an interviewer:

> As women we have not been socialized to be initiators in the sexual act. Another factor is that we don't have to make excuses if we don't want to do it. We don't say we have a headache. We just say no. We also do a lot more cuddling and touching than heterosexuals, and we get fulfilled by that rather than just the act of intercourse. . . . Another thing is that such a sisterly bond develops that the relationship almost seems incestuous after a while. The intimacy is so great. We know each other so well.[39]

Lesbian bed death became a much-discussed phenomenon among scholars and clinicians. However, those who fretted over the "problem" overlooked one central question: how important is sex in a committed relationship? How much is enough? Here, as in the discussion of gay men's "infidelity," is it possible that heteronormative ideals are being imposed upon lesbians? Recent studies suggest that the phenomenon is greatly exaggerated, that most lesbians experience their sexuality positively, and that lesbians engage in a variety of erotic and passionate activities beyond genital sex. Therefore, simply viewing lesbian sexuality as an extension of heterosexual women's "lesser" desire is an imposition of heterosexual norms on lesbian culture—and of masculinist sexual ideals on women.[40]

The debate over "political" versus "intrinsic" forms of lesbianism obscures another gendered difference between male and female sexuality that is now the focus of research: bisexuality and female **sexual fluidity**. Alfred Kinsey, in his pioneering research on male sexuality, discovered that many men had had same-sex sexual encounters. This discovery was key to his development of the **Kinsey scale**, which could be used to rate sexual subjects from 0 (exclusively heterosexual) to 6 (exclusively homosexual). A 3, on the Kinsey scale, was someone attracted equally to either men or women. Nonetheless, the existence of **bisexuality** has always been hotly disputed. For many people, bisexuals are simply people who can't "make up their minds."

More recently, researchers have found intriguing evidence that for women at least, same-sex attraction may be a relatively common phenomenon unassociated with lesbianism or even with bisexual identification. According to one random-sample study, the vast majority of women who report same-sex behaviour or desires identify as heterosexual. Researchers posit that such women represent a characteristically female sexual fluidity, defined as the "capacity for situation dependence in some women's erotic response." One of the key situations capable of eliciting erotic response, for such women, is an intense, passionate relationship so that women may report experiencing same-sex desire only within the context of one deep friendship. What this reveals about women's overall sexuality is unclear; recent suggestions that women are "naturally bisexual" are probably premature. However, it is noteworthy that women's stories of same-sex attraction—whether transitory or a fixed orientation—often emphasize an exclusively emotional (rather than explicitly sexual) basis, unlike similar stories told by men. Sexual fluidity confirms the idea that sexual behaviours and desires remain heavily gendered.[41]

Research on frequency of sexual activity bears this out. In one study, among heterosexual married couples, 45 per cent of those married for 2 years or less reported having sex 3 or more times per week, while only 27 per cent of those married between 2 and 10 years reported that level of frequency. By contrast, of gay couples who had sex 3 or more times per week, 67 per cent of the men had been together up to 2 years, while 32 per cent had been together 2–10 years. One-third of lesbians had sex 3 or more times per week in the first 2 years of their relationship, but only 7 per cent did after 2 years. One interviewer described a lesbian couple:

> She and her roommate were obviously very much in love. Like most people who have a good, stable, five year relationship, they seemed comfortable together, sort of part of one another, able to joke, obviously fulfilled in their relationship. They work together, have the same times off from work, do most of their leisure activities together. They sent me off with a plate of cookies, a good symbolic gesture of the kind of welcome and warmth I felt in their home.[42]

If heterosexuality and homosexuality are so similar, in that men and women express and confirm their gendered identities through sexual behaviour, what then, are the big differences between heterosexuals and homosexuals—aside, of course, from the gender of the partner? One major difference is that gay relationships are more egalitarian, both sexually and otherwise. Accordingly, we can say that in some ways, homosexual relationships model a possible future for heterosexual ones.

Gay men and lesbians have also been more sexually experimental, especially with non-penetrative sex. As one sex therapist writes, "gay men have more ways of sexually relating than do heterosexual men." Masters and Johnson found that gay couples have longer lovemaking sessions than heterosexual couples. Among lesbians, the emergence of the **stone butch**, who focuses on pleasuring her or his partner, but prefers not to be touched her- or himself, is evidence of another kind of sexual experimentalism—the idea that pleasure need not be orgasmically reciprocal to be rewarding. In fact, overall, same-sex couples may have some lessons for heterosexual ones. Whether it be gay men's ability to live contentedly within either monogamous or non-monogamous relationships or lesbians' ability to find sexual satisfaction outside the constraints of prescribed activities and frequency, the lesson is that the relationship, rather than a rigid norm, is what matters. One recent study of sexual frequency among heterosexual couples confirmed this, finding that "a satisfying sex life and a warm interpersonal climate appear to matter more than does a greater frequency of sexual intercourse."[43]

Compulsory Heterosexuality across the Lifespan: Sexual Socialization and Gender

For children, sexual socialization can range from the normal—"nice girls don't play doctor"—to the abhorrent, but unfortunately frequent, experience of sexual abuse at the hands of an adult or older child. For most children, adolescence is the time of the most intense socialization, and peers are the most important "teachers." As one feminist researcher put it, "[a]lthough their sexual interest is focused on the opposite sex, it is primarily to their same-sex peers that adolescents will look for validation of their sexual attitudes and accomplishments."[44]

Consider the contortions of two adolescents trying to negotiate, usually without words, the extent of their sexual contact. It's tremendously complicated for LGTBQ youth, of course; in fact, though almost all non-heterosexual youth report romantic relationships in adolescence, openly courting or dating a same-sex partner is difficult and "faking" heterosexuality is common. Heterosexual relationships, though protected by privilege, are still not simple; both the boy and the girl have goals, though the goals may be very different. "His" goal, of course, is to score—toward that end, he has a variety of maneuvers, arguments, and other strategies that his friends have taught him. "Her" goal may be pleasure, but it is also to preserve and protect her reputation as a "good girl," which requires that she be seen as alluring but not "easy." "Young men come to sex with quite different expectations and desires than do young women," one iteration of the NORC sex survey declared. "Young women often go along with intercourse the first time, finding little physical pleasure in it, and a substantial number report being forced to have intercourse."[45]

This means that significant numbers of young women are raped the first time they have intercourse. Until the 1980s, no one would have called such incidents rape. Rape was something done by strangers in dark alleys. However, in the 1980s, US psychologist Mary Koss conducted a series of surveys of young women that led to her coining the term **date rape** (now often called "acquaintance sexual assault," discussed further in Chapter 13). What she found was that coercion and lack of consent were prevalent in sexual encounters between acquaintances. While her results were controversial at the time, today they are generally accepted by academics and have led to many studies of the complexity of sexual consent.[46]

In fact, for women, the whole idea of consent, or "wanting it," is fraught with difficulties. Because of the double standard, girls and women have traditionally not been permitted to express sexual desire. To do so would be to risk social disapproval and even, up until very recently, rape. Until the 1980s, a standard defence against rape prosecution involved the assertion that "she wanted it," which could be "proved" through evidence of a victim's "wanton" dress, previous sexual activity, or imprudent behaviour—for example, being alone with a boy or man. Racialized or otherwise marginal women were (and remain) particularly vulnerable to such "presumed consent." Small wonder, then, that girls and women have been cautious about overt statements of sexual desire.

However, if saying "yes" to sex has been fraught for women, saying "no" has also been difficult, particularly within the context of an existing relationship. This is a legacy of gender inequality, and of cultural scripts that presumed that, once a woman had sex with a man, she was "his," available for sex as long as the relationship lasted (and sometimes longer). Many studies have found that women acquiesce to unwanted sex, sometimes even painful sex, because they feel that they cannot say no. In addition, a very recent study found that university students still adhere to traditional sexual scripts, accept that men use aggression and deception to get sex, and believe that women are responsible for performing oral sex.[47]

Measuring Sexual Consent: The Sexual Consent Scale (Revised) and the Reasons for Consenting to Unwanted Sex Scale

The Sexual Consent Scale and the Reasons for Consenting to Unwanted Sex Scale (developed at Trent University) measure attitudes and behaviours relating to sexual consent, and assess the reasons why women give in to unwanted sex. The Sexual Consent Scale, developed by Terry Humphreys, measures six different domains relating to consent. The Reasons for Consenting to Unwanted Sex Scale, developed by Humphreys along with Deborah Kennett, surveys 18 reasons why women might consent to unwanted sex, based on findings from previous studies. The two scales, taken together, convey the complexity of consent in heterosexual relationships (and may apply equally in many same-sex relationships).[48]

Subscale 1: (Lack of) perceived behavioral control

— I would have difficulty asking for consent because it would spoil the mood.

— I am worried that my partner might think I'm weird or strange if I asked for sexual consent before starting any sexual activity.

— I would have difficulty asking for consent because it doesn't really fit with how I like to engage in sexual activity.

— I would worry if other people knew I asked for sexual consent before starting sexual activity, that they would think I was weird or strange.

— I think that verbally asking for sexual consent is awkward.

— I have not asked for sexual consent (or given my consent) at times because I felt that it might backfire and I wouldn't end up having sex.

— I believe that verbally asking for sexual consent reduces the pleasure of the encounter.

— I would have a hard time verbalizing my consent in a sexual encounter because I am too shy.

— I feel confident that I could ask for consent from a new sexual partner [R].

— I would not want to ask a partner for consent because it would remind me that I'm sexually active.

— I feel confident that I could ask for consent from my current partner [R].

Subscale 1: Mean

continued

Subscale 2: Positive attitude toward establishing consent

— I feel that sexual consent should always be obtained before the start of any sexual activity.

— I believe that asking for consent is in my best interest because it reduces any misinterpretations that might arise.

— I think it is equally important to obtain sexual consent in all relationships regardless of whether or not they have had sex before.

— I feel that verbally asking for sexual consent should occur before proceeding with any sexual activity.

— When initiating sexual activity, I believe that one should always assume they do not have sexual consent.

— I believe that it is just as necessary to obtain consent for genital fondling as it is for sexual intercourse.

— Most people that I care about feel that asking for sexual consent is something I should do.

— I think that consent should be asked before any kind of sexual behavior, including kissing or petting.

— I feel it is the responsibility of both partners to make sure sexual consent is established before sexual activity begins.

— Before making sexual advances, I think that one should assume "no" until there is clear indication to proceed.

— Not asking for sexual consent some of the time is okay [R].

Subscale 2: Mean

Subscale 3: Indirect behavioral approach to consent

— Typically I communicate sexual consent to my partner using nonverbal signals and body language.

— It is easy to accurately read my current (or most recent) partner's nonverbal signals as indicating consent or non-consent to sexual activity.

— Typically I ask for consent by making a sexual advance and waiting for a reaction, so I know whether or not to continue.

— I don't have to ask or give my partner sexual consent because my partner knows me well enough.

— I don't have to ask or give my partner sexual consent because I have a lot of trust in my partner to "do the right thing."

— I always verbally ask for consent before I initiate a sexual encounter [R].

Subscale 3: Mean

Subscale 4: Sexual consent norms

— I think that obtaining sexual consent is more necessary in a new relationship than in a committed relationship.

— I think that obtaining sexual consent is more necessary in a casual sexual encounter than in a committed relationship.

— I believe that the need for asking for sexual consent decreases as the length of an intimate relationship increases.

— I believe that it is enough to ask for consent at the beginning of a sexual encounter.

— I believe that sexual intercourse is the only sexual activity that requires explicit verbal consent.

— I believe that partners are less likely to ask for sexual consent the longer they are in a relationship.

— If consent for sexual intercourse is established, petting and fondling can be assumed.

Subscale 4: Mean

Subscale 5: Awareness and discussion

— I have discussed sexual consent issues with a friend.

— I have heard sexual consent issues being discussed by other students on campus.

— I have discussed sexual consent issues with my current (or most recent) partner at times other than during sexual encounters.

— I have not given much thought to the topic of sexual consent [R].

Subscale 5: Mean

Figure 12.1a The Sexual Consent Scale (Revised).

The Reasons for Consenting to Unwanted Sex Scale

Instructions: When answering these questions, please think of all the times in which you have consented to unwanted sexual activity. Rate each statement as to how characteristic it is of you as your reason for consenting to unwanted sexual activity using the scale provided.*

0	1	2	3	4	5	6	7	8
Not at all characteristic of me			Somewhat characteristic of me			Very characteristic of me		

continued

1. I felt that I would be jeopardizing the relationship if I did not engage in the unwanted sexual activity.

2. As his girlfriend, I am obligated to engage in the unwanted sexual activity.

3. He verbally pressured me to participate in the unwanted sexual behavior.

4. He begged me to engage in the unwanted sexual activity until I could not argue anymore.

5. I had been drinking or had consumed other types of drugs.

6. I felt guilty for not participating in the unwanted sexual activity.

7. I feared that I would lose my boyfriend if I did not consent to the unwanted sexual activity.

8. I wanted to avoid tension in our relationship.

9. I wanted to prevent my partner from losing interest in our relationship.

10. I consented to the unwanted sexual activity to promote intimacy.

11. I felt it was necessary to satisfy my partner's needs.

12. I felt that I needed to because I consented to the sexual activity before.

13. I didn't want to hurt my partner's feelings.

14. He physically would not let me leave.

15. I didn't want him to feel rejected.

16. I felt that, if I consented to the unwanted sexual activity, he would like/love me.

17. I wanted to feel accepted by my partner.

18. He sweet-talked me into it.

*This scale follows each of the scale statements.

Figure 12.1b The Reasons for Consenting to Unwanted Sex Scale.

Source: Republished with permission of Taylor and Francis Books LLC, from Terry Humphreys, "Sexual Consent Scale, Revised," and Terry Humphreys and Deborah Kennett, "Reasons for Consenting to Unwanted Sex Scale," in Terri D. Fisher, Clive M. Davis, William L. Yarber, Sandra L. Davis, eds., *Handbook of Sexuality-Related Measures* (Routledge, 2013), pp. 173–178; permission conveyed through Copyright Clearance Centre, Inc.

That people have sexual experiences for reasons other than intimacy and pleasure has been a truism in sex research. While coercion and/or force play a strong role in girls' experiences of unwanted intercourse, other factors influence boys and men. Psychologist Charlene Muehlenhard, for example, found that more men (57.4 per cent) than women (38.7 per cent) reported that they had engaged in unwanted sexual intercourse because of being enticed—that is, the other person made an advance that the person had difficulty refusing. More men (33.5 per cent) than women (11.9 per cent) had unwanted sexual intercourse because they wanted to get sexual experience, wanted something to talk about, or wanted to build up their confidence. Additionally, more men (18.4 per cent) than women (4.5 per cent) said they engaged in sexual intercourse because they did not want to appear to be homosexual, shy, afraid, or unmasculine/unfeminine. Peer pressure was a factor for 10.9 per cent of the men but only 0.6 per cent of the women.[49]

Peers provide sexual socialization to adolescents, but so too do the media. Beginning at an increasingly young age, children learn from the media how to perform their appropriate sexual roles. For boys, this means learning heterosexual assertiveness; for girls, it means cultivating self-objectification. While children and teenagers are increasingly finding this information through online pornography (as a 2007 University of Alberta study found), "pornification" of mainstream society makes sexual messages readily available in mainstream media—magazines, video games, and even children's toys.[50]

Peers and the media also shape adult sexuality. For example, when heterosexual men seek therapeutic evaluation for sexual problems, they rarely describe not experiencing enough pleasure. How do they know how much pleasure is enough? Because at least since the launch of *Playboy* in the 1950s, men have been able to access and share information on their sexual experiences, and they have been schooled by media and advertisers on "normal" male sexuality. Therefore, they are now perfectly capable of assessing "how they measure up." One man who experienced premature ejaculation reported that he felt like he "isn't a real man" because he "can't satisfy a woman." Another, with erectile problems, told a therapist that "a real man never has to ask his wife for anything sexually" and that he "should be able to please her whenever he wants." Each of these men expressed a sexual problem in gendered terms; each feared that his sexual problem damaged his masculinity, made him less of a real man. Men with sexual problems are rarely gender nonconformists, unable or unwilling to follow the rules of masculine sexual adequacy. If anything, they are over-conformists to norms that define sexual adequacy by the ability to function like a well-oiled machine (or, increasingly, a porn star).[51]

In this gendered context, we can better understand the enormous popularity of sildenafil citrate (Viagra) and other drugs that minister to men's "sexual problems." The drug company Pfizer marketed Viagra not merely as a product that would assist men with diabetes and spinal cord damage to lead "normal" sexual lives but as a "lifestyle" drug that would enable middle-aged (and older) men to "perform." This entailed "educating" North American men about the prevalence of erectile dysfunction through questionable statements such as "more than half of all men over 40 have difficulties getting or maintaining an erection." Viagra was the most successful new drug ever launched in the United States; more than 35,000 prescriptions were filled within the drug's first two weeks on the market (in late 1998). Many men crowed that they had found the "magic bullet," the fountain of sexual youth. "You just keep going all night," gushed one man. "The performance is unbelievable." The fastest-growing user group for the drug, between 1998 and 2002, was men between the ages of 18 and 45. The Viagra story demonstrates the power of the media—and the fear of judgment—in the sexual socialization of men of all ages.[52]

Pornography as Gender Socialization

One key source of men's sexual socialization is pornography. Despite much growth in women's use of porn (discussed in Chapter 9), men are still more likely than women to use pornography to stimulate sexual fantasy and as a masturbatory aid.[53] Indeed, porn occupies a special place in the development of men's sexuality. Nearly all men have had some exposure to pornography, at least as adolescents; indeed, for many men pornography is their primary sex education. (This is increasingly true for young people of both sexes, with implications discussed below.)

As discussed previously, the 1980s feminist critique of pornography transformed the political debate, arguing that pornography expressed a culture-wide hatred and contempt for women. In contemplating pornography's role in shaping desire, we would be unwise to discount this theory out of hand. Here is one pornographic director and actor, commenting on his "craft":

> My whole reason for being in the [pornography] Industry is to satisfy the desire of the men in the world who basically don't much care for women and want to see the men in my Industry getting even with the women they couldn't have when they were growing up. . . . So when we come on a woman's face or somewhat brutalize her sexually, we're getting even for their lost dreams. I believe this. I've heard audiences cheer me when I do something foul on screen. When I've strangled a person or sodomized a person or brutalized a person, the audience is cheering my action, and then when I've fulfilled my warped desire, the audience applauds.[54]

This may seem extreme and exaggerated. Few porn producers would make the same comment; after all, as we saw in Chapter 9, causal connections between pornography and violent or aberrant sexual behaviour have been difficult to establish. What's more, the 1980s feminist view of porn has been widely rejected by the public and by many scholars. Recent studies have failed to confirm that watching pornography is associated with negative attitudes or behaviours toward women. For example, a 2015 study found that male porn users were more likely to have progressive gender attitudes than non-users, and female porn consumers were just as likely as non-users to have egalitarian attitudes. However, a 2013 study found that men who watched a *lot* of pornography had less egalitarian attitudes and more hostility toward women. Another 2014 study of 373 male university students found that more frequent porn-viewing was associated with lower relationship satisfaction, more gender role conflict, and less sexual satisfaction. It is difficult to know, of course, whether pornography causes such outcomes, or whether men with such attitudes and experiences seek out pornography. Yet whether or not there is *any* empirical evidence that pornography alone causes rape or violence, there remains the shocking fact that on any given day in North America, there are men masturbating to images of women and children enduring torture, genital mutilation, rape, and violence. The fact that such images can be such a routine and casual turn-on for many men should at least give us pause. The increasing availability, in every North American home, of the most shocking images of sexual violence has implications that we are only beginning to contemplate.[55]

Nevertheless, pornography shapes desire in ways that are more mundane. First, pornography exaggerates the masculinization of sex. In typical heterosexual porn video scenes, both women and men want sex, full stop—even when women don't want it, when they are forced or raped, it turns out that they wanted it after all—and what they want is determined by male desire. A 2010 study of a random sample of highly ranked pornographic films found that the most frequent act portrayed was fellatio, followed by vaginal intercourse. Cunnilingus occurred in fewer scenes than did anal sex, and same-sex activities occurred only between women. Almost 60 per cent of ejaculation scenes involved ejaculation in a woman's mouth. "ATM" fellatio (that is, fellatio occurring immediately after anal sex) occurred in 41 per cent of scenes. Mainstream hard-core pornography displays women with surgically enhanced breasts and shaved (and, increasingly, surgically "trimmed" genitals). In porn, women engage willingly and enthusiastically in anal sex, double and triple penetration, and the bathing in and ingestion of semen in the act euphemistically described as a "facial." For some commentators, like Marty Klein, this reflects a "discourse of abundance" that porn viewers recognize as the fantasy it is. What porn offers them, then, is "a narrative of validation—of the viewer's eroticism, of deliberately focusing on (and even enhancing) desire, of the possibility of mutual male–female satisfaction, of the viewer's vision of a world of erotic abundance, playfulness, and self-acceptance."[56]

In fact, mainstream pornography depicts not only a masculine perspective on pleasure but frequent aggression toward women. The 2010 study mentioned above—again, a random sample—found that almost 90 per cent of films depicted choking, gagging, or spanking, with females 95 per cent of the recipients of this treatment. Almost half of the films depicted verbal abuse and name-calling. Fewer than 10 per cent depicted "positive" or loving interactions. While very few scenes of aggression in these films showed men as targets, men were four times as likely to express displeasure when targeted aggressively. Women, by contrast, either were neutral in the face of aggression or expressed pleasure. In the words of the researchers,

> It may be that consumers of pornography are, happily, on the whole uninterested in and unaroused by sexual dominance of unwilling women. However, what has taken its place has been sexual dominance of willing women—many of these same dominating behaviours were evident in these popular films but were met without resistance by women. This consensual depiction of aggression is concerning as we run the risk of rendering true aggression against women invisible.[57]

The aggression commonplace in porn scenes is not concealed. Indeed, aggressive language is used to attract viewers to websites; women are described as "bitches," "whores," and "sluts" who "gag," "swallow," and get "pounded," "hammered," "face fucked," and "split open."

Interracial sexual contact is frequent in pornography; "Blacks" is the most common ethnic search term used in Internet porn searches in the UK and US. Whether in straight or gay pornography, racist stereotypes are often invoked; black men have "huge schlongs" and "gang-bang," black women are insatiable "ghetto skanks," Asian women are servile objects of sex tourism—and Aboriginal people are virtually absent. This may indeed, be a world of abundance—where women and ethnic minorities embrace servitude to phallocentric desire—but it is not the utopian playground Klein describes. As Daniel Bernardi writes,

> This is not intimacy or affection, or mutual desire or sexual expression. It is not, dare I say, love. This is semiotic hate, the history of mediated whiteness, and the

opposite of love. This is not truly open sex. This is sex open to white eyes. This is not multiculturalism. This is colourized hate.[58]

As a result, as anti-pornography activist John Stoltenberg writes, pornography "tells lies about women" (and, one would add, racialized subjects) but it "tells the truth about men." Perhaps more troublingly, pornography *changes* the truth about men (and women), shaping their desire for sexual practices, body characteristics, and sexual partners. For example, the popularity of **bukkake** pornography (when several men ejaculate on a woman [or man]) and so-called "facials" has almost certainly affected the attitudes, desires, and practices of youth. Young women report pressure to participate in anal sex because their partners have seen it in pornographic depictions and want to try it. Additionally, research suggests that at a more mundane level, use of pornography is associated with "permissive sexual scripts" that encourage casual and risky sexual activity.[59]

With the proliferation of pornographic content on the Internet, children's access to explicit sexual content has exploded. Studies suggest that in the 10–16 age group, anywhere from 25 to 40 per cent of children have viewed pornography online, with a much higher rate of viewing among those older than 16. Many very young children have also been exposed, often through accidentally searching for something innocuous—such as cartoon characters—and then finding user-made pornographic versions. Because unsafe sex, sex with strangers, and scenes of domination and violence are normalized within pornography, the "education" children receive from porn is a dubious one. One American mother realized this after her thirteen-year-old son asked her why women liked to be choked. While the effects on youth are unclear, studies have found associations between pornography viewing and sexist attitudes, unsafe sex, and casual sex. The exposure of children to so much pornography, like the proliferation of pornography in itself, constitutes a vast social experiment whose results are only now beginning to be understood.[60]

Closing the Sexual Gender Gap

Despite the persistence of gender differences in sexual attitudes and behaviours, the sexual gender gap has been closing in recent years, as women's and men's sexual experiences come to more closely resemble one another's—or, rather, women's experiences have come to resemble men's experiences. As argued earlier, our experience of love has been feminized, and our sexuality has been increasingly "masculinized." Whereas men's sexual behaviour has changed very little, women's sexual behaviour has changed dramatically, moving increasingly closer to the behaviour of men.

Part of this transformation has been the result of the technological breakthroughs and ideological shifts that were part and parcel of the Sexual Revolution. Since the 1960s, adequate and relatively safe birth control and legal abortion have made it possible to separate sexual activity from reproduction. (Men, of course, always were able to pursue sexual pleasure for its own sake (in this sense, women's sexuality has come to resemble men's sexuality more closely). "I guess sex was originally to produce another body; then I guess it was for love; nowadays it's just for feeling good," was the way one 15-year-old boy summed up the shift. In addition, widespread sex education has made people more sexually aware—but not necessarily more sexually active. In one review of 53 studies that examined the effects of sex education and HIV education on sexual activity, 27 found no changes in rates of sexual activity; 22 observed marked decreases, delayed onset of activity, and reduced number of sexual partners; and only three studies found any increase in sexual activity associated with sex education. Despite the widespread outrage about Ontario's new sex education curriculum, it would appear that sex education enables people to make *better* sexual decisions and encourages more responsibility, not less.[61]

Ideologically, feminism made the pursuit of sexual pleasure, the expression of women's sexual autonomy, a political goal. No longer would women believe that they were sexually uninterested, passive, and virtuous asexual angels. Women were as entitled to pleasure as men were. They knew how to get it, too. After feminists exposed "the myth of the vaginal orgasm," women no longer had reason to feel ashamed of desiring clitoral stimulation. Feminism was therefore, in part, a political resistance to what we might call the "socialized asexuality" of feminine sexuality.[62]

In the past three decades, then, women's sexuality has been transformed as women have sought to express their own sexual agency. Consider, for example, the transformation of the idea of sexual experience. It used to be that men were expected to have some sexual experience prior to marriage, while many North American women and men placed a premium on women's virginity. That is no longer the case. As Lillian Rubin writes, "in the brief span of one generation—from the 1940s to the 1960s—we went from mothers who believed their virginity was their most prized possession to daughters for whom it was a burden." Virginity was no longer "a treasure to be safeguarded"; now, it was "a problem to be solved." North Americans—male and female, heterosexual and non-heterosexual—now come to the marriage bed with at least some sexual experience, while disapproval of premarital sex has reached record lows. (Despite the growth of the **Purity Movement**, with its virginity pledges, rings, and "purity balls," dedication to premarital virginity remains a minority movement, and one with its own problematic issues.)[63]

Rates of and motivations for masturbation have also begun to converge, with men's and women's motivations for masturbation now roughly similar as are sexual attitudes, though women remain less permissive than are men (except on same-sex relationships, where women are more likely to approve than are men). Sexual behaviours, too, have grown increasingly similar. Among teenage boys, age at sexual initiation has remained quite similar since the mid-1940s, with about 70 per cent of all high-school-aged American boys having had sexual intercourse (the rates were about 50 per cent for those who went to high school in the late 1920s). However, the age of sexual initiation for high-school girls has decreased dramatically during the same period both in the US and in Europe; therefore the "experience gap" between teenaged boys and teenaged girls has decreased dramatically. The average age of first intercourse in the US is now 14.3 years, with almost half of high-schoolers reporting that they have experienced sexual intercourse.[64]

One place where one can observe the political ramifications of the gender convergence in sexual behaviour is the university campus. Decades ago, sociologist Willard Waller observed a competitive marketplace, in which students evaluated their marketability in reference to both the opposite sex and the evaluations of their same-sex friends and sought to date appropriately—slightly up, but not too much.[65]

Today, a culture of **hooking up** has virtually erased the older pattern of "rating-dating-mating" observed by Waller. "Hooking up" is a deliberately vague blanket term; one set of researchers defines it as "a sexual encounter which may nor may not in-clude sexual intercourse, usually occurring on only one occasion between two people who are strangers or brief acquaintances."[66] Although that seems to cover most cases, it fails to include those people who hook up more than once or twice, or "sex buddies" (ac-quaintances who meet regularly for sex but rarely, if ever, associate otherwise), or "friends with benefits" (friends who do not care to become romantic partners but may include sex among the activities they enjoy together).

For many young people, the heterosexual marketplace is organized around groups of same-sex peers who go out together and meet an opposite-sex peer group in a casual setting like a bar or a party. Almost all hooking up involves more alcohol than sex. As Melanie Beres's research in Jasper, Alberta, demonstrates, youth hookup culture conveys multiple and conflicting meanings. If on the surface hooking up is understood as casual sex for its own sake, Beres found that many young women saw it as a potential means to begin relationships. As a result, they might avoid intercourse at a first encounter to signal that they were "relationship material," but such efforts were not always successful.[67]

Premarital sex has become the norm for both sexes. In one US survey, 99 per cent of male college graduates and 90 per cent of female college graduates said that they'd had sex before marriage, and about three-quarters of American youth had had sex before their twentieth birthdays. This is a long-term trend. Researchers in one survey of sexual be-haviour from the 1970s found far greater sexual activity and greater variety among mar-ried women in the 1970s than Kinsey had found in the late 1940s.[68]

What turns us on sexually is also growing more similar. In the 1970s, psychologist Julia Heiman developed a way to measure women's sexual arousal. Samples of college women listened to two sorts of tapes—romantic and explicitly sexual—while wearing an intravaginal device that measured blood flow to the vagina. Like men, women were far more sexually aroused—at least according to Heiman's mode of measurement—by explicit sex talk than they were by romance. Women's and men's interest in sexual variety also appears to be converging. Experiences of oral sex have increased dramatically for both women and men—and as we have seen, women are using pornography more.[69]

Conservative groups fret about women's lost modesty, chastity, or even their capitula-tion to male standards of sexual conduct. Such an image is probably insulting to women, who have shown themselves capable of sexual entitlement and agency themselves; and it is certainly insulting to men, because it assumes that men are, equally inevitably, violent, rapacious predators. Perhaps the problem is not the sex, but rather the gender—that is, not the consensual sexual activity between two consenting near-adults, but rather the gender inequality that accompanies it. Mutually—and *soberly*—negotiated sexual contact, with care for the integrity of the partner, can be a pleasurable moment or form the basis of a longer-lasting connection. The question is who gets to decide.

The evidence of gender convergence does not mean that there are no differences be-tween women and men in their sexual expression. However, the old rules are gone, and the new ones contradictory. "It's different from what it used to be when women were supposed to hold out until they got married. There's pressure now on both men and women to lose their virginity," is how one 29-year-old man put it. "But for a man it's a sign of manhood, and for a woman there's still some loss of value." Melanie Beres found much the same thing in her work with youth in Jasper: while there was much general tolerance for the idea of casual sex, young men actually *refrained* from sex with women they considered relationship prospects and demonstrated little interest in pursuing relationships with women with whom they had had casual sex. Whether in the US or Canada, it seems, the double standard lives on.[70]

Women's increase in sexual agency, revolutionary as it is, has not eliminated male sexual entitlement, nor has it sharply increased men's capacity for intimacy and emotional connectedness. Some have suggested that men's "non-relational" sexuality is the problem; psychologists like Ronald Levant seek to replace "irresponsible, detached, compulsive, and alienated sexuality with a type of sexuality that is ethically responsible, compassionate for the well-being of participants, and sexually empowering of men." The notion of **non-relational sex** means that sex is, to men, isolated from other aspects of life and relationships; often coupled with aggression; conceptualized socially within a framework of success and achievement; and pursued despite possible negative emotional and moral consequences. In some cases, non-relational sexuality is enforced by norms of masculinity that see "real men" as those who never refuse any offer of sex.[71]

Although it may be true that non-relational sexuality may be a problem for some men—especially for those who rely on it as their main form of sexual expression—it is not necessarily the only way men express themselves sexually. Many men are capable of both relational and non-relational sexuality. Some men don't ever practise non-relational sexuality because they live in a subculture in which it is not normative. Other men develop values that oppose it.[72] One possibly worthy goal might be to enlarge our sexual repertoires to enable both women and men to experience a wide variety of permutations and combinations of love and lust, without entirely reducing one to the other—as long as all these experiences are mutually negotiated, safe, and equal. It turns out that the more equal women and men are, the more satisfied they are with their sex lives. In a survey of 29 countries, sociologists found that people in countries with higher levels of gender equality—Spain, Canada, Belgium, and Austria—reported being much happier with their sex lives than those people in countries with lower levels of gender equality, like Japan. "Male-centred cultures where sexual behaviour is more oriented toward procreation tend to discount the importance of sexual pleasure for women," said University of Chicago professor, Ed Laumann.[73] A gender-egalitarian culture, by contrast, must recognize the value of sexual pleasure *and* sexual autonomy for both sexes, and for all partners in sexual exchanges regardless of gender and sexual orientation.

Summary

Sexuality is often seen as a matter of bodies but cannot be divorced from society. Throughout human history and across cultures, societies have created rules to shape, manage, and channel sexuality in "appropriate" ways.

The history of sexuality is a diverse one, but there are some commonalities. First, many cultures have been concerned with establishing and maintaining patriarchal control over female sexuality. Men traditionally experienced much more sexual freedom, to the extent that adultery, where the concept existed, was often judged as a "crime" committed only by women. Adulterous women were often punished extremely harshly. A second important commonality is that cultures establish rules governing acceptable sexual behaviour.

These rules might proscribe relationships considered incestuous, prohibit specific be-haviours, limit times when sex was licit, or prescribe solely cross-sex relations. Same-sex relations, however, were far from being uniformly prohibited. However, in ancient Greece and Rome, tolerance of same-sex relations between men was not uniform; men who were effeminate or assumed a "female" role were harshly judged. We know remarkably little about same-sex relations between women.

The idea of sexual renunciation has been important to many spiritual traditions, but was particularly important in early Christianity. In fact, Christianity brought new and rigorous rules to the sexual lives of believers. These rules would decisively shape the nature of sexuality in the West, even though they were not uniformly observed. One of the key features of Christian sexual mores was their abhorrence of homosexuality; but many cross-sex acts, including those between husband and wife, were also prohibited. These and other aspects of Christian sexuality were imported from Europe to the rest of the world through European colonialism.

In the nineteenth century, the scientific study of sexuality replaced a solely religious approach to the topic. Medical and psychological practitioners created this new science, culminating in the creation of sexology. One of the key claims of sexology was that there was something called homosexuality, a stable sexual orientation created through psycho-logical development, which was distinct from the "normal" sexual orientation, hetero-sexuality. This idea would have a profound effect on Sigmund Freud, and in turn, on the entire history of the twentieth century. Ideas of female sexuality were also transformed in the nineteenth century, and the idea that women were "naturally" less sexual than men reinforced the double standard.

Twentieth-century scholars such as Sigmund Freud, Alfred Kinsey, and Masters and Johnson continued to insist on the importance of sexuality to human personality, iden-tity, and fulfillment. The Sexual Revolution of the 1960s and 1970s furthered these ideas and pushed for the liberalization and liberation of sexuality. The effects on attitudes and behaviours were sweeping. Many believe that a steady process of sexualization of culture has been underway since then. The most notable signs of this sexualization are the ever-widening availability and influence of pornography, the greater presence of sexualized im-agery, and the sexualization of children. However, other scholars argue that sexualization is a longer-term process. The Internet, however, has undoubtedly accelerated the pace of sexualization; through new technologies of disembodiment, it may also have altered the very nature of sexuality.

Nevertheless, sexualization has not eliminated the gender gap in sexuality. Despite importance sexual differences produced by class, ethnicity, and age, there are still import-ant differences between men and women, which are present regardless of sexual orienta-tion. In fact, with regard to sexual orientation, women may experience more fluidity than men do. The double standard also persists, undoubtedly influencing other gender differ-ences. Women are more sexually selective than men are; they are less positive about casual sex; and they are less likely than men are to be unfaithful. The double standard has also in-fluenced the way we think about sex. Men are more bound to phallocentric sex, involving the penis and the male orgasm; according to surveys, many men even name their genitals! As a result, heterosexuality has been dominated by the coital imperative, which defines sex as penetrative. Men also think about sex more, masturbate more, fantasize more, and express desire for more sex than do women. Many scholars have claimed that men have a stronger sex drive than women, and that this biological difference is what accounts for the observable gender differences in sexuality. However, this is far from a complete explanation. Most gender differences in sexuality result from differential socialization.

Understanding sexual socialization begins with understanding Adrienne Rich's concept of compulsory heterosexuality. Heterosexuality becomes compulsory primarily through the assumption that it is natural and that alternatives are non-existent or deviant. This assumption is humorously illustrated by the Heterosexual Questionnaire developed by Martin Rochlin in the 1970s.

We often assume that gendered understandings of sexuality might not apply to homosexuals. This assumption is based upon old stereotypes of homosexuality as gender non-conformity rather than simply a sexual orientation. In fact, gay male and lesbian sexuality present typically male and female sexual patterns in heightened form. Gay men tend to be more accepting of casual sex and non-monogamy than women and heterosexual men; the phenomenon of lesbian bed death, meanwhile, has been taken to mean that lesbians are *extreme* versions of women's lesser sex drive. There are, however, differences that arise from sexual orientation. In many ways, gay men and lesbians do seem to be more egalitarian and more sexually adventurous than are heterosexuals.

Heterosexual sexual socialization, constrained by the double standard, is a fraught affair. Consent has emerged as a significant problem. Although both sexes experience unwanted sex, it is women and girls who are at higher risk. For men, peer pressure (rather than direct coercion) is a significant contributor to unwanted sex. Constructions of masculine sexuality as "ever-ready" undoubtedly contribute to such pressure. Pornography, the mainstream media, and even drugs such as Viagra promote the message that "real" men are eager for sex whenever they can get it.

Indeed, pornography has become a significant source of sexual socialization, especially for boys and men (but increasingly for girls and women too). The second-wave feminist critique of pornography has been rejected by many because studies were unable to make clear links between pornography use and violence or aggression toward women. One recent study even claimed that men who used pornography had more progressive attitudes toward women. Others, however, have found signs that porn use, especially when heavy, is associated with relationship difficulties and hostility toward women. Moreover, the nature of much mainstream pornography is troubling. Mainstream pornography features heavily masculinized sexual scripts revolving around the coital imperative, surgically altered female bodies, and women's enthusiastic participation in extreme sexual acts. "Interracial" sex, or sex involving racialized people, is often depicted in stereotypical or even hateful terms. Because children and youth are now often exposed to explicit pornography, they too are being "socialized" by porn, with studies suggesting effects from sexual risk-taking to aggression toward women.

There is some evidence that the sexual gender gap is closing. Female rates of porn use, masturbation, and infidelity have increased significantly, so that the gap between men and women has narrowed (but not disappeared). "Hooking up" and other forms of casual sex have also proliferated, and female agency in seeking hook-ups has increased. At the same time, the double standard is alive and well. It can be seen in the US Purity Movement, which celebrates female virginity while ostensibly requesting continence of both sexes; it can also be seen in the fact that despite all of the convergence, women are still judged more harshly than men are for participating in casual sex.

Ultimately, the solution to the sexual gender gap is not for women to become "just like men"; nor is the solution for all "non-relational" sex to be condemned. Instead, the *real* solution is gender equality, under which both men and women, whatever their sexual orientation, can experience healthy, respectful sexual relations in the circumstances they choose.

Questions for Critical Thinking

1. Do you believe sexual orientation is stable? How do you believe it is formed?
2. Do you agree that the double standard still exists? If so, how is it manifested?
3. Have you seen evidence of "pornification" in your lifetime?
4. What, in your view, is the relationship between online sex and sex in real life? Are they the same?
5. Is "hooking up" among youth a realm of gender equality? Why or why not?

Key Terms

bisexuality
bukkake
coital imperative
compulsory heterosexuality
cybersex
date rape
double standard
furries
heterosexuality
homosexuality
hooking up
Kinsey scale
lesbian bed death
MSM
non-relational sex

paraphilias
phallocentric
pornification
Purity Movement
sexting
sexual fluidity
sexual orientation
Sexual Revolution
sexualization of culture
sodomy
Stonewall
stone butch
technical virgin
teledildonics

The Gender of Violence
Domination's Endgame

All violence consists in some people forcing others, under threat of suffering or death, to do what they do not want to do.

—Leo Tolstoy

Nightly, we watch news reports of brutal sex crimes, racist attacks, school shootings, suicide bombers, homophobic gay-bashing murders, murderous family violence, or drug lords and their legions of gun-toting thugs. Seldom do the news reports note that virtually all of these violent crimes are committed by men—despite the fact that women are more likely to be represented among the poorest and most downtrodden citizens of the globe. All over the world, men constitute 98 per cent of all persons arrested for rape; and the vast majority of those arrested for murder, robbery, assault, family violence, and disorderly conduct. Men are overwhelmingly more violent than women.[1] Imagine, though, if violence were perpetrated largely by women. Would not a gender analysis occupy the centre of every single story? The fact that violent criminals are generally men seems so natural as to raise no questions, generate no media analysis.

From early childhood to old age, violence is the most obdurate, intractable behavioural gender difference; and though age is an important predictor of violence and criminality, gender by far outstrips it in significance. Gender *alone* is a highly significant predictor of violent behaviour. The US National Academy of Sciences puts the case starkly: "The most consistent pattern with respect to gender is the extent to which male criminal participation in serious crimes at any age greatly exceeds that of females, regardless of source of data, crime type, level of involvement, or measure of participation."[2] Yet how do we understand this obvious and nearly universal association, between masculinity and violence? Is it a product of biology, a fact of nature, caused by something inherent in male anatomy, *or* is it yet another result of a gendered society?

Masculinity and Violence

In assessing the relationship between masculinity and violence, we begin by noting that men dominate the field of criminality in general. This is true wherever one looks. In part, male propensity toward violence is thought to be related to men's greater tendency toward risk-taking behaviours and rule-breaking in general.[3]

These male tendencies affect not only criminal behaviour but also the conduct of the police. In the US, some 20 per cent of all high-speed chases end in serious injury or death, most often of innocent bystanders, because police officers—usually young male ones—chase even in the face of risk. In one study in southern Florida, "winning a race" was cited by officers as the objective in a pursuit. This links young male police officers to the young men predominant in risky driving in general and street racing in particular. However, here again, both scholars and media often overlook the operations of gender. Although 90 to 95 per cent of participants in street racing are male, a major US Department of Justice report describes the typical street racer as "18 to 24 years of age, generally living at home and typically having little income" and recommends analyzing the "age, ethnicity, [and] group affiliation" of racers—again, without mentioning gender.[4]

No matter how invisible gender may become in some analyses, men *are* overrepresented among risk-takers and criminals, and this overrepresentation remains particularly acute in the area of violent crime. Criminologist Marvin Wolfgang notes that violent crime rises any time men between the ages of 15 and 24 constitute a high proportion of the population. Psychiatrist James Gilligan observes that the only two innate biological variables that are predictors of violence are youth and maleness.[5] Therefore, gender and age are the two most powerful predictors of violence. Men are far more violent than women, and the likelihood of violence by *either* gender decreases with age.

There has been no shortage of essentialist explanations for male violence based on "the durability, universality, and generality of the relative aggressiveness of males." Some scholars argue that androgens (male hormones), especially testosterone, drive male aggression. The fact that violence is such a significant gender difference suggests at least some validity for this argument.[6]

However, as discussed in Chapter 2, by itself the biological evidence is unconvincing. Testosterone *is* highly correlated with aggressive behaviour; still, it seems that the hormone does not *cause* the aggression, but rather facilitates preexisting aggression. (It does nothing for non-aggressive males, for example.) Nor does the causal arrow always point from hormone to behaviour. Winners in athletic competition experience increased testosterone levels *after* they win, just as prisoners' testosterone levels rise in response to the hierarchical, competitive, and violent nature of prison life. In sum, violence causes increased testosterone levels, and hormonal increases enable violence. Androgens and biological factors in general consequently provide a partial but insufficient explanation for male violence.[7]

Following Freud, some psychoanalysts have looked for the roots of masculine violence in the Oedipal drama: The frustration of the young boy's sexual desires is translated into aggression (the frustration–aggression hypothesis). Stated more neutrally, the young boy must constantly and publicly demonstrate that he has successfully separated from his mother and transferred his identity to his father—that is, that he has become masculine. Male violence is a way to prove successful masculinity. Sex role theorist Talcott Parsons (discussed in Chapter 3) concurred, viewing delinquency and violence as a way for boys to dissociate themselves from their mothers. Some theorists posited violence as a particularly male response to role strain; both men and women experience strain within their roles, but women are socialized to blame themselves, while men blame (and attack) others in self-righteous anger.[8]

Others see male violence as rooted in evolutionary psychology. Sociobiologists and evolutionary psychologists see violence as the result of men's competition for reproductive success—or as an adaptive strategy that enables males to avoid becoming prey themselves. In a fascinating study, Barbara Ehrenreich argues that the origins of society lie in defence—we became social not because we had some deep need for sociability, but rather because only together could we defend ourselves successfully. The near-universal association of masculinity and war, says Ehrenreich, is compensatory and defensive, a "rough male sport" that offers a "substitute occupation for underemployed male hunter-defenders." Some scholars who take an evolutionary perspective may see it differently. One study analyzed population data and conflicts in and among 88 countries, concluding, "the presence of a relatively large number of young men makes coalitional aggression more probable"—not because of self-defence, but rather because collective aggression allows young males "to acquire otherwise unobtainable resources."[9]

Whether one accepts psychological and evolutionary arguments or not, violence *has* long been understood as the best way to ensure that others publicly recognize one's manhood. Fighting was once culturally prescribed for boys. In one of the bestselling early-twentieth-century American advice manuals, parents learned:

> There are times when every boy must defend his own rights if he is not to become a coward and lose the road to independence and true manhood. . . . The strong willed boy needs no inspiration to combat, but often a good deal of guidance and restraint. If he fights more than, let us say, a half dozen times a week—except, of course, during his first week at a new school—he is probably over-quarrelsome and needs to curb. The sensitive, retiring boy, on the other hand, needs encouragement to stand his ground and fight.

In this bestseller, boys were encouraged to fight once a day, except during the first week at a new school, when, presumably, they would fight more often![10]

Lurking beneath such advice was the fear that boys who were not violent would not grow up to be real men. The spectre of the "sissy"—encompassing the fears of emasculation, humiliation, and effeminacy that North American men carry with them—is responsible for a significant amount of masculine violence. Violence is proof of masculinity; one is a "real" man because one is not afraid to be violent. James Gilligan speaks of "the patriarchal code of honour and shame which generates and obligates male violence"—a code that sees violence as the chief demarcating line between women and men.[11]

Listen to one New York gang member describing the reasons that his gang requires random knife slashings as initiation rituals. "Society claims we are notorious thugs and killers but we are not," he says. "We're a family of survivors . . . proud young black men living in the American ghetto. Harlem princes trying to rise up and refusing to be beaten down." Another man recalls his days in a juvenile detention facility where "you fought almost every day because everybody was trying to be tougher than the next person." In Canada—where at least 22 per cent of gang members are Aboriginal—hypermasculine violence offers a way of compensating for "the elimination of traditional means of achieving masculinities (such as supporting families through hunting and trapping)." Being "jumped in" or "doing minutes" (being beaten by other gang members) may also be familiar experiences for youth who have come from abusive, violent backgrounds.[12]

However, even for those who are not gang-involved, the defence of masculinity through violence is a familiar trope. Sociologist Vic Seidler writes, "as boys, we have to be constantly on the alert to either confront or avoid physical violence. We have to be alert to defend ourselves. . . . Masculinity is never something we can feel at ease with. It's always something we have to be ready to prove and defend." Criminologist Hans Toch adds, "in cultures of masculinity, the demonstrated willingness to fight and the capacity for combat are measures of worth and self-worth." As criminologist James Messerschmidt suggests, this element of masculinity may appeal to girls, too, and some adopt masculine violence and masculine identities in part as a response to gender inequality and gendered violence. Masculinity and violence, then, are not synonymous with *maleness* and violence.[13]

From the locker room to the chat room, men and boys of all ages learn that violence is a socially sanctioned form of expression. Male socialization includes being taught the legitimacy of violence—through infant circumcision, arguments with parents and siblings, routine fights with other boys, and socially approved forms of violence in sports, prison, and the military. If any doubt remains that violence is acceptable, epigrams tell them, "don't get mad, get even" and "it's a dog-eat-dog world."

The examples above demonstrate that masculine violence takes different forms, and levels, in different cultures at different times. Such cultural and historical shifts are important if we are adequately to explain violence in the first place.

In the 1980s, social anthropologists Signe Howell and Roy Willis tackled this problem by asking: What can we learn from those societies in which there is very little violence? They found that *definitions of masculinity had a significant impact on propensity toward violence.* In societies in which men were permitted to acknowledge fear, levels of violence were low. However, in societies in which masculine bravado—the posture of strength and the repression and denial of fear—was a defining feature of masculinity, violence was likely to be high. It turns out that those societies in which bravado is prescribed for men are also those in which the definitions of masculinity and femininity are very highly differentiated. For example, Joanna Overing studied two groups living in the Amazon jungle. The extremely violent Shavante define manhood as "sexual bellicosity," a state both superior to and opposed to femininity, whereas their peaceful neighbouring Piaroas define manhood *and womanhood* as the ability to co-operate tranquilly with others in daily life. Overing's findings confirm Howell and Willis's contention that in more violent societies, masculinity and femininity are seen as polar opposites.[14]

In sum, here are a few themes that anthropologists have isolated as leading toward both interpersonal violence and intersocietal violence:

1. The ideal for manhood is the fierce and handsome warrior.
2. Public leadership is associated with male dominance, both of men over other men and of men over women.
3. Women are prohibited from public and political participation.
4. Most public interaction is between men, not between men and women or among women.
5. Boys and girls are systematically separated from an early age.

6. Initiation of boys is focused on lengthy constraint of boys, during which time the boys are separated from women; taught male solidarity, bellicosity, and endurance; and trained to accept the dominance of older groups of men.
7. Emotional displays of male virility, ferocity, and sexuality are highly elaborated.
8. The ritual celebration of fertility focuses on male generative ability, not female ability.
9. Male economic activities and the products of male labour are prized over female.[15]

One of the most significant "causes" of male violence, then, is gender inequality. Additionally, the victims of this are not only women but also men. Taken together, these works provide some insight into what might reduce the amount of gendered violence in society. It seems clear that the less gender differentiation between women and men, the less likely violence will be.[16]

So, in sum, what is the relationship between masculinity and violence? Men's violence is often the result of thwarted entitlement, male domination over women, and competition-driven bravado. To find peaceful societies, we might want to look at societies in which entitlement to power is not present, gender polarity is not entrenched, and bravado is not celebrated as the hallmark of masculinity.

Female Criminality and Violence

The association of masculinity and violence, as we have seen, is so well known as to be virtually invisible to us. We have reviewed some of the ways in which scholars discuss the relationship between violence and masculinity; yet we should not pretend that males' overwhelmingly greater tendency to commit an act of violence or a crime means that women never do so.

Still, women are a minority of offenders. In 2009, about 23 per cent of those accused of committing offences reported to the police in Canada were female, and about 21 per cent of those actually charged with a crime were female. Though this represents a significant increase since 1979, when only about 15 per cent of those charged were female, the rate of crime among females is still only about a quarter of the male rate. What's more, the crimes women commit and their reasons for committing them are often very different from those of men. In cases that make it to court, the highest representation of women is found in fraud, theft, and prostitution—although even there women are only 31 per cent of those processed by the courts. (There are more female prostitutes, but men are frequently charged as pimps and customers.)[17]

The female tendency to cluster in more minor areas of criminality means that women are even less represented among prison populations than among those charged with crimes in general. In Canada, there are now about 600 federal women prisoners in six federal institutions for women (replacing Kingston's infamous Prison for Women, which closed its doors in 2000). One of these institutions, the Okimaw Ohci Healing Lodge, is mandated to provide culturally sensitive and supportive services to Aboriginal women prisoners. While the number of women prisoners may sound large (and has increased significantly throughout the past two decades), it still represents only about 4 per cent of admissions to federal institutions (which generally house those convicted of the most serious crimes). Even if provincial and remand custody are taken into consideration, women still account for less than 10 per cent of inmates. In the US, women (about 200,000 inmates) constitute 8.8 per cent of the prison population. That number represents a vast increase since 1980, indicating growing female tendency to commit serious crimes; but given that two-thirds of women prisoners are incarcerated for non-violent drug-related offences, one should not overstate the new "violence" of female criminals. Women's lower rate of imprisonment also reflects their lesser tendency to reoffend and to "escalate" their criminal involvement. Nonetheless, if women diverge from men in some ways, the female inmate population tends to mirror the male inmate population demographically, including a disproportionate number of non-white, poor, and undereducated and unemployed women. In the US, women of colour and Native American women are greatly overrepresented among the incarcerated; in Canada, Aboriginal women are even more overrepresented among federal prisoners than are Aboriginal men. In 2012–2013, Aboriginal women represented 33 per cent of all federal women prisoners, an increase of 77 per cent over the previous decade. Women prisoners are more likely than men to have multiple rehabilitative needs (such as mental health issues) when admitted to prison; and Aboriginal women are more likely than non-Aboriginal women to have such needs. When these needs are not met, the prisoner is at significant risk for reoffending.[18]

As can be seen from these statistics, despite dramatic changes in women's lives and increases in female criminality, women remain a minority among offenders—particularly those accused of violent crime. (Violent crimes account for about 30 per cent of crimes processed by the courts in Canada.) In the mid-1970s, though, crime rates for women appeared to be increasing significantly precisely as women gained new rights and roles outside their "traditional" spheres. Sociologists Freda Adler and Rita Simon argued that feminism explained women's increasing criminality. "Is it any wonder," asked Adler, "that once women were armed with male opportunities they should strive for status, criminal as well as civil, through established male hierarchical channels?" Simon nuanced her claims a bit more, arguing that feminism actually decreased the rates of female violent crime but increased female property crimes. Others have argued, through curious misreading of data, that female criminality and violence are as significant as men's but are somehow ignored because women commit violent crimes without being charged, or because media ignore supposedly burgeoning rates of female police involvement.[19]

Although both claims may be politically useful to those who want to return women to their "natural" place in the home, they are not supported by empirical evidence. First, the most interesting long-term historical evidence suggests that women's criminality has actually *decreased* since the eighteenth century. Court records reveal a steady decline in women's arrests and prosecutions since that time.[20]

More recently, particularly in the last decade, adult female criminality has declined within Canada. Even in the US, the sex differential in crime has remained roughly the same when seen as a number per 100,000 of population. Consequently, it becomes clear that, as one criminologist put it simply, "relative to males, the profile of the female offender has not changed."[21]

Moreover, what is that profile? First, as already stated, women and girls who engage in crime are less likely to engage in violent crime than their male counterparts are. Females are accused of crimes "against the person" at a rate about one-fifth of the male rate. As the severity of violence increases, female representation decreases: In 2006, according to Canadian government statistics, "[f]emale rates for homicide, attempted murder, and sexual assault were negligible." Still, when girls and women *do* commit violent crimes, they are as likely as male offenders are to inflict injury and to use weapons; women are fully capable of violence even if they deploy it with much less frequency.[22]

Furthermore, we have some evidence that the gender gap in violence is decreasing, though evidence of this is still spotty. It is noteworthy that violent crime appears to be declining in many societies, with Canada no exception. Still, in Canada, while the overall rate at which female youth and adults are charged with crime has been declining steadily since 1992, this is not true for violent crime. Charge rates for those crimes continued to climb dramatically until 2001. Rates of serious violent crime among female adults nearly doubled between 1986 and 2005, while the corresponding rate for men declined. This has brought men's and women's rates of serious violent crime somewhat closer together. In 1986, nine men were charged for every woman charged with a serious violent crime. By 2005, this ratio had shifted to five to one. Will this trend eventually lead to a levelling of gender distinctions within violent crime? There is little evidence to suggest such a trend, but there have been changes in at least *some* women's relationship to serious criminality and, by implication, to violence.[23]

However, most of the increase in female violent crime has come in the area of "Level 1" assaults, those that cause little or no bodily harm; and many of those charged are sex-trade workers, in whose work physical conflict is likely to arise. While no assault is trivial, the data show that in violence, as in crime in general, women cluster at lower levels of seriousness. Moreover, when it comes to the most serious violence, causing death, we see little evidence of gender convergence. Canada's **homicide** rate is relatively low—significantly less than half the US rate, for example—and has been declining since the 1970s. In Canada in 2013, the rate hit its lowest point since 1966, and remained at that rate in 2014. In 2014, 13 per cent of those accused of homicide (and 28 per cent of the victims of homicide) were female. Among both men and women, those 18 to 24 were most likely to be accused of homicide (though the rate for women was one-seventh of the rate for men). Gender is important in homicide perpetration, but so too is ethnicity and the legacy of colonialism. Aboriginal people, both men and women, are much more likely to be accused of homicide than are non-Aboriginal people; but while Aboriginal men are nine times more likely than non-Aboriginal men are to be accused, Aboriginal women are 23 times more likely to be accused than are non-Aboriginal women.[24]

Despite these variations, women kill much less frequently; but they also kill differently. Between 1997 and 2009, Canadian women who committed homicide were most likely to kill a family member, while men were much more likely to murder an acquaintance. For example, almost 24 per cent of homicides perpetrated by women were against a child, while only 6 per cent of those perpetrated by men fell into this category. However, these numbers should not be interpreted to mean that women were more likely than men were to kill their children: even given the high *proportion* of female-perpetrated homicides in which women kill their children, there were twice as many murders by fathers of their children as by mothers in the period in question. In every relationship category, men perpetrated vastly more homicides than did women.[25]

In the US, the trends are similar. There has been an overall large decline in homicide rates, with levels now comparable to those of the early 1960s. Women's rate of offending has fallen dramatically, the result of a precipitous decline in women's spousal homicide rates, at least in part because of the expansion of services for battered women. (In the past, many women charged with spousal homicide were in abusive relationships without access to resources that would allow them to escape.) In the US, as in Canada, women remain much less likely to kill strangers or casual acquaintances than are men, and are much less likely to engage in multiple homicide or **familicide**. Women are also much less likely than men to kill with guns.[26]

Although women convicted of homicide receive, on average, shorter sentences than do men convicted of murder, this sentencing differential seems to have less to do with the gender of the accused than with the circumstances of the homicide, the past criminal history of the accused, and the accused's relationship to the victim. Men who kill an intimate partner tend to receive sentences roughly equal in length to those of women who commit the same crime.[27]

Overall, then, women and girls still represent a minor force in the pattern of criminality. They commit much less crime, are less represented in prison, and tend to cluster in "minor" areas of offending. They are even less represented among perpetrators of violent crime than among offenders in general. Despite somewhat troubling (if slow) growth in female participation in serious crime, violence remains perhaps the most gendered behaviour in our culture.[28]

School Violence, "Active Shooters," and "Mean Girls"

We have considered gendered patterns of violent criminality among men and women. The gendered patterns of violence among children are also revealing, demonstrating the greater tendency of males to commit violence against both other males and females. Among three-year-olds, for example, the most frequent acts of violence are boy-to-boy; girl-to-girl violence, by contrast, is the least frequent, and boy-to-girl violence is far more frequent than girl-to-boy. In one study, two Finnish psychologists contrasted physical, verbal, and "indirect" forms of aggression. They found that girls at all ages (except the youngest) were more likely to engage in indirect aggression (telling lies behind a person's back, trying to be someone's friend as revenge to another, saying to others, "let's not be friends with him or her"). Boys at all ages were more likely to engage in direct aggression (kicking, hitting, tripping, shoving, arguing, swearing, and abusing) and verbal aggression. Does this mean that the sexes were essentially equal in their aggression, but favoured different modes of expression? Not really. Indeed, girls at all ages were also more likely to use peaceful conflict resolution (talking to clarify things, forgetting about it, telling a teacher or parent)—or to withdraw.[29]

As children grow older, peer aggression becomes more threatening; for some, school becomes a dangerous place indeed. Consider the data from a survey of US high school seniors in 1994. Nearly one-fifth of high school boys reported that they hurt someone so badly that he or she needed to be bandaged or to see a doctor. (Only one-twentieth of girls reported that level of violence.) A 2007 US survey of youth in grades 9–12 found little change. Among these students, 16 per cent of boys and 8.5 per cent of girls reported being in a physical fight on school property within the previous year (many more reported crimes against their property). In 2006, about 10 per cent of Canadian youth crimes reported to the police took place on school property; about 27 per cent of those crimes were assaults. So young people face a high risk of violence—even from those they consider friends; Canadian youth who reported physical assaults to police in 2003 were most likely to be assaulted by a close friend, an acquaintance, or an associate.[30]

Youth, it seems, is a violent time, yet we continue to talk about "teen violence," "youth violence," "gang violence," "suburban violence," and "violence in the schools" without considering the role of gender in such violence. When we think about these wrenching events, do we ever consider that, whether white or black, inner city or suburban, bands of marauding "youths" or troubled teenaged shooters are virtually all male?

Until recently, most commentators ignored this glaring fact. According to Patricia Leavy and Kathryn Mahoney, coverage of Columbine (1999) and other school shootings as "kids killing kids" obscured "one of the main issues to flow from these events—the social construction of masculinity in the USA." Instead of looking at gender, a Columbine-obsessed media focused on the alleged bullying of the boys (since called into question) and the deleterious effects of vaguely labelled "goth culture."[31]

Most markedly, of the 160 **active shooter** incidents catalogued by the FBI between 2000 and 2013, virtually all were carried out by a lone boy or man (there were six female shooters). Nearly 25 per cent of these incidents were either "school shootings," carried out at K–12 (16.9 per cent) or higher education (7.5 per cent) institutions. School shootings tended to result in greater numbers of casualties, and high- and middle-school shootings were almost always perpetrated by students at the schools. Again, almost all of them were male—and white. More than three-quarters of school shooters, in fact, have been white, exceeding their representation in the American population. (According to Leavy and Mahoney, class and ethnicity are analyzed in relation to shootings only in those rare cases involving a non-white shooter.)[32]

Not only are shooters generally male but the precipitating factors driving their violent sprees are often related to an assertion of aggrieved masculinity. In some cases, homophobic bullying has been part of the pre-shooting context. In others, the changing status of women and/or "anti-male" state policy played a role. Nowhere was this clearer than in the **Montreal Massacre** of 1989 (discussed on p. 380), in which a lone shooter identified feminism as having ruined his life. Similarly, the perpetrators of the Columbine massacre responded to their own perceived bullying and subordination at the hands of other students. In 2014, a gunman murdered six people and wounded many others at the University of California Santa Barbara before committing suicide. In the remarkably detailed information he left behind, he described his grievances against women (discussed on p. 380) for their apparent "rejection" of his advances. Half-Asian himself, the shooter also detailed his attempts to claim white privilege as a "beautiful Eurasian" and his rage at seeing Asian and black men with beautiful blond women. He then revealed a detailed fantasy of hegemonic masculine power, which he associated with both whiteness and success with women. He, and many other shooters, turned to violence to "reclaim" their masculinity, which they saw as synonymous with competition with other men and domination of or sexual access to women.[33]

There has been little attention to those targeted by shooters, but gender plays a role in victimization as well as in perpetration. In 10 per cent of the FBI's active shooter incidents, for example, men targeted their current or former female partners. In school shootings, similar trends are evident, though they have been often ignored. In a systematic analysis of hundreds of media reports of 12 school shootings between 1997 and 2002, Jessie Klein found that reports mentioned peer abuse (bullying), parents, media, and access to guns, but ignored the mechanisms of targeting and the gender of targets. In fact, according to psychologist Peter Langmann, an expert in school shootings, gender is highly significant in targeting—much more so than bullying:

> In almost no case has a school shooter specifically targeted a kid who has picked on them. When there are specific targets—and in over half the cases I've studied, there are specific people the perpetrators are seeking to kill—the most common targets are school personnel. Teachers who have given them an unacceptable grade, teachers who've failed them for a class, administrators who disciplined them with suspension or expulsion. *And the second most common target of school shooters are girls or women, either specific girls that have broken up with them or targeting females as a general population.*[34] [emphasis added]

As Langmann states, there is growing recognition that girls are targeted as victims in a significant number of cases; and shooters often have exhibited failed relationships with, hostility toward, and abuse of girls. Yet even when adult men enter schools expressly to sexually assault and murder girls—as happened in Pennsylvania and Colorado in 2007—media reports gloss over the relationship between these murders and the larger issues of gendered violence. School violence, then, cannot be divorced from gender and from the kind of gendered entitlement that we saw when discussing male violence in general.[35]

So what about the "mean girls" whom we read about in media reports, and the violent girls we see on widely publicized YouTube videos of "girl fights"? Indeed, mean girls' existence has some basis in fact. First, girls are more likely than women are to engage in criminality. Female youth are three times more likely to be accused of Criminal Code offences than are female adults. During the 1990s, a number of incidents galvanized public panic about the "rising tide" of girl violence. One of the most brutal and tragic of these events was the 1997 murder of Reena Virk, a 14-year-old Indo-Canadian girl from Victoria, BC. In an attack rooted in both "competitive heterosexuality" and racism, Reena endured brutal violence at the hands of a large group of schoolmates before being abandoned to find her way home. Before she could make her way to safety, she was set upon by a girl and a boy from the initial group, who returned and eventually drowned Reena. In the aftermath of the attack, *Maclean's* magazine sounded a nationwide "alarm about rising violence among teenage girls," and numerous media outlets followed the same trend. Despite the fact that ethnicity was a "key factor" in the attack, it was ignored in media coverage in favour of panic over girl violence as a logical outcome of family and social changes including the rise of feminism.[36]

The relationship between feminism and girl violence is difficult to puzzle out. One study from Finland found that girls in the 1990s were much more violent than a decade earlier. The study also found greater acceptance and positive connotation of violence among the girls, who saw it as "something that makes the girl feel powerful, strong, and makes her popular"—in short, doing for girls what violence and aggression have historically done for boys. As James Messerschmidt suggests, this may even lead some girls to adopt masculine identities in the context of gang involvement, consequently gaining the benefit of being "one of the guys." However, such gender-bending seems to be less common among violent girls than is emphasized femininity. According to Sibylle Artz, a University of Victoria researcher who has studied girl violence extensively, violent girls tend to be disconnected from meaningful relationships with their mothers, to see women as second-class citizens, and to focus intensely on heterosexual relationships at the cost of relationships with other girls.[37]

In fact, girls' aggression seems to be quite different from that of boys not only in its nature but also in its motivators. Much violence and aggression among boys arises in the context of competition for dominance and drug and alcohol use. Among girls, jealousy and revenge have proved more common motivators. Girls are more likely to act out aggressively against girls they perceive as competition for male attention because of their appearance or dress. As a result, unlike attractive boys, attractive girls are significantly more likely to be the victims of aggression by their peers. Though evolutionary psychologists may suggest that girls' tactics are the result of deep-rooted genetic imperatives, the forms and motivations of girls' aggression are not the expression of some innately devious feminine wiles, but rather the consequences of gender inequality. In a context in which attractiveness is the most important quality a woman can have—and where male attention is the key to success—it is no surprise that jealousy, competition, and aggression prevail. Therefore, when girls act violently, they are often acting on gendered scripts that may either celebrate emphasized femininity or seek to escape it through alliances with masculinity. There is much to be learned about girls' aggression. Recent studies are questioning the indirect/direct aggression gender binary, but there do seem to be persistent gender differences both in the causes of girls' aggression—for example, girls with depression and girls with ADHD are both more likely than comparable boys to be aggressive—and in the effects.[38]

In sum, girls can be aggressive and violent, but they remain much less likely to transgress criminally than boys. Despite the increases in girls' criminality over previous decades, a substantial majority (72 per cent) of Canadian youth charged with a crime in 2009 were male. Moreover, as in adulthood, female youth offenders tend to cluster in less serious areas of criminality. The introduction of the Youth Criminal Justice Act, which seeks to divert non-violent youth away from the criminal justice system, led to an even greater decline in charges laid against girls than in those laid against boys. This is in large part because girls' crimes tend to be "minor" relative to those of boys. (Nonetheless, in Canada, girls are as likely as boys are to be convicted if charged.) After two decades of increase, in which the rate of increase for girls outstripped that of boys, both the youth crime rate and the severity of these crimes has declined. However, compared to the off-reserve crime rate, the on-reserve youth crime rate remains more than three times higher, and youth crimes on reserve are more likely to be violent. Youth on reserve are accused of homicide at a rate 11 times higher than the off-reserve rate. Gender is therefore arguably a less significant issue in youth offending than are the urgent issues related to the status of Aboriginal people.[39]

As the above statistics demonstrate, youth violence continues to be a serious issue with which Canadians must grapple. However, the media-driven perception of a burgeoning wave of youth crime is far from the truth, as the rates and severity of youth crime have been declining for more than a decade now. So too, the idea of a girl-crime wave is much exaggerated. Youth crime remains gendered, both in the representation of the sexes within it (males far outnumbering females) and in the nature of violence involved. The dominant early childhood pattern is one in which boys aggress both other boys and girls; this pattern holds in youth violence but is complicated by the emergence, in adolescence, of heterosexual abuse that in many ways mirrors that found in adult life. However, rates of victimization, harassment, and abuse among youth far outstrip those found among adults, suggesting that the gendered society serves its youngest members poorly indeed.

Gendered Violence: An Institutional Problem

After the successful test of a nuclear bomb in November 1952, creating a fusion explosion about 1,000 times more powerful than the fission bomb that destroyed Hiroshima seven years earlier, Edward Teller, the Nobel Prize-winning nuclear physicist, wrote the following three-word telegram, to his colleagues: "It's a boy." No one had to point out to Teller the equation of military might—the capacity for untold violence—with masculinity.

It would be easy to catalogue all the phallic images and rhetoric in that vast historic parade of military heroes in decorated uniforms and scientists in white lab coats, suggesting that proving masculinity is a common currency for both warrior and wonk, gladiator and geek. However, this approach turns violence into a screen against which *individuals* project their psychological fears and problems, reducing war and the state's use of institutional violence to a mere aggregation of insecure men desperate to prove their masculinity. To understand institutional violence, we need to explore how "militarism perpetuates the equation between masculinity and violence" and how war "encodes violence into the notion of masculinity generation after generation."[40]

Though masculinity may be associated historically with war, the way we fight today would leave many men without the ability to test and prove their manhood in a conventional military way. After all, most soldiers today are in support services—transport, administration, technical support, maintenance. The increasingly technological sophistication of war has only sped up this process—nuclear weapons, "smart bombs," automatic weaponry, self-propelled military vehicles, and long-distance weapons all reduce the need for Rambo-type primitive warriors and increase the need for cool, rational button-pushers.[41]

Yet there is something powerful in the ways that our political leaders seek to prove an aggressive and assertive masculinity in the political arena. War and its technology confer upon men a "virile prestige," as French philosopher Simone de Beauvoir put it. Military prowess and the willingness to go to war have been tests of manhood. Explaining why US President Lyndon Johnson continued to escalate the war in Vietnam, a biographer writes

> He wanted the respect of men who were tough, real men, and they would turn out to be hawks. He had unconsciously divided people around him between men and boys. Men were activists, doers, who conquered business empires, who acted instead of talked, who made it in the world of other men, and had the respect of other men. Boys were the talkers and the writers and the intellectuals, who sat around thinking and criticizing and doubting instead of doing.

When opponents criticized the war effort, Johnson attacked their masculinity. When informed that one member of his administration was becoming a "dove" on Vietnam, Johnson scoffed, "Hell, he has to squat to piss!" When Johnson celebrated the bombings of North Vietnam, he declared proudly that he "didn't just screw Ho Chi Minh. I cut his pecker off."[42]

Carol Cohn conducted an ethnographic analysis of defence intellectuals in the last days of the Cold War. She recalls,

> lectures were filled with discussion of vertical erector launchers, thrust-to-weight ratios, soft lay-downs, deep penetration, and the comparative advantage of protracted versus spasm attacks—or what one military advisor to the National Security Council has called "releasing 70 to 80 per cent of our mega tonnage in one orgasmic whump." There was serious concern about the need to harden our missiles, and the need to "face it, the Russians are a little harder than we are." Disbelieving glances would occasionally pass between me and my ally—another woman—but no one else seemed to notice.[43]

The relationship of militarism to sexual conquest often becomes painfully clear. While not every conflict is marked by sexual violence, many are; sometimes, sexual violence is used systematically.

- In Darfur (Sudan), the rape of women and children formed part of the strategy of armed militias;
- In the former Yugoslavia, infamous "rape camps" emerged during ethnic war;
- In the "rape of Nanking" in 1937, Japanese soldiers systematically raped and murdered thousands of girls and women;
- In the Second World War, the Japanese army used "comfort women" (sexual slaves, most of them girls);
- In the German concentration camps during the Second World War, camp inmates were forced to perform sexual acts in brothels; and
- In the early years of the Iraq War, US soldiers (including women) sexually tortured and humiliated male and female Iraqi prisoners at Abu Ghraib prison.

The rapes and murders of women and children by the Red Army in the aftermath of the Second World War have only recently been discussed; in 2010, an 80-year-old woman became the first German to speak publicly about the experience. Such violence has long been part and parcel of the domination of the "enemy."

More recently, as women have joined combat forces, sexual violence has been highlighted as a major problem *within* military units. In the fiscal year ending in September 2008, the US army dealt with 2,908 reported cases of sexual abuse involving its members; 10 per cent of victims were men, reminding us that women are not alone in their vulnerability to gendered domination. In the five months after opening its office in September 2015, the Canadian Forces' Sexual Misconduct Response Centre fielded more than 100 complaints. The phenomenon is widespread enough to have generated a new descriptor, **military sexual trauma** (MST), defined by the US Department of Veterans Affairs as "sexual assault or repeated, threatening sexual harassment that occurred while the Veteran was in the military." In 2012, the Secretary of Defense said that the actual annual number of sexual offences in the US military was estimated to be somewhere near 19,000, because most went unreported. Among male and female Iraq and Afghanistan veterans with PTSD, 31 per cent of the women screened positive for military sexual trauma versus only 1 per cent of the men. Another recent study of a smaller group of women veterans found that 41 per cent had experienced MST.[44]

The fact that sexual assault and harassment are so endemic within the history of military action—and in current military forces—demonstrates that gendered violence is far from an individual problem. Rather, the relationships among gender, domination, and violence bleed into every aspect of our society, including relationships and conflicts between societies and states.

Family Violence

For too many people—children and parents alike—the family bears only a passing resemblance to the "haven in a heartless world." For some people, far from shielding their members from the cold and violent world outside its doors, the family *is* that cold and violent world.

Family violence is defined by the Canadian Family Violence Initiative as "any form of abuse, mistreatment or neglect that a child or adult experiences from a family member, or from someone with whom they have an intimate relationship." One way to examine family violence is through police statistics. In 2013, common or "Level 1" assault was the most common family violence reported to police in Canada, representing 58 per cent of incidents. Sexual assaults represented 8 per cent of all incidents, with uttering threats responsible for 12 per cent of all incidents and other intimidation offences accounting for 5 per cent. Though there are many other forms of abuse—such as emotional abuse—that are not police-reported, these statistics still give a good sense of the range of criminal behaviours that constitute family violence.[45]

Like the family in general, family violence is gendered, reproducing and reinforcing gender inequality. This may come as a surprise to anyone who has been victimized by a female family member. Nevertheless, family violence is gendered in two key ways. First, much of the most serious family violence is perpetrated by males—husbands beat wives, fathers hit children, sons hit their parents, boys hit their brothers or their sisters. "The actual or implicit threat of physical coercion is one of many factors underlying male dominance in the family," writes sociologist Murray Straus. Second, the gendered logic of domination infuses family violence, no matter whether its perpetrator is male or female. For this reason, feminist theorist bell hooks describes abuse within the family as **patriarchal violence**, which is "based on the belief that is acceptable for a more powerful individual to control others through various forms of coercive violence." This belief is associated with male domination; but it can be used to describe not just men's violence against women but other forms of violence within the family, such as abuse of children or abuse of a same-sex partner, whether perpetrated by males or females.[46]

For most people, the term "family violence" conjures images of what used to be called "wife battering." For much of our history and until quite recently, a husband enjoyed the right to "discipline" his wife. In 1982, more than 30 years ago, NDP MP Margaret Mitchell raised the issue of violence against women in the House of Commons; male MPs laughed and mocked her, an event, recorded by television cameras, that galvanized women across Canada. Today, things have changed; through concerted efforts at consciousness-raising and legal changes, violence against women is a high-profile concern, not just in Canada but also around the world. The World Health Organization (WHO) estimates that globally, 35 per cent of women have experienced either physical violence from a partner or sexual violence (from a partner or from someone else). About 30 per cent of women worldwide report that they have experienced physical or sexual violence from their partners, while 38 per cent of murders of women worldwide are committed by their intimate partners. That such violence is related to women's status is made clear by the WHO Multi-Country Study on Women's Health and Domestic Violence, which found that across all countries studied, "traditional masculinity" and its associated behaviours were associated with violence against women. The issue remains an urgent one worldwide.[47]

Because of women's historical (and in some cases continuing) lower status relative to men, they have experienced more violence within the family than have men. However, not all of those who experience domestic violence are women. Violence within the family can take many forms, including the victimization of men by their female partners. Therefore, gender-neutral terms have replaced "wife battering." We now speak of **spousal violence** (perpetrated by a former or current married or common-law spouse) and **intimate-partner violence (IPV)** (perpetrated by former or current married or common-law spouses as well as dating partners). As defined in Canada, IPV can include the criminal offences of physical assault, harassment, uttering threats, robbery, sexual assault, homicide, attempted murder, kidnapping and forcible confinement, harassing or obscene telephone calls, and other intimidation offences. It can also include emotional abuse and other forms of abuse that are not criminal and therefore not reportable to the police.

All forms of police-reported family violence have declined throughout the past five years, including homicides of family members. Police-reported spousal violence has declined in Canada since the late 1990s, but it still accounts for nearly half of incidents of family violence reported to police in Canada; it also accounts for almost 60 per cent of family violence incidents causing injury. Interestingly, more than half of police-reported IPV incidents in 2013 were perpetrated by dating partners.[48]

According to police statistics, females are overall more likely than males to be victimized within the family. According to 2013 data, 68 per cent of all police-reported incidents of family violence (of whatever kind) were perpetrated against females. Women were the victims in about 80 per cent of incidents of violence by a current or former spouse; 62 per cent of incidents where the perpetrator was the victim's child; 57 per cent of incidents perpetrated by the victim's parent; and 56 per cent where the perpetrator was the victim's sibling. In every age group, females were most likely to be victimized by family, though the gap is smallest in early childhood and old age. Females were most likely to experience family violence (of whatever kind) between the ages of 30 and 34, while males' rates were highest between 15 and 19. Among Canadians 25–34, women are three times more likely than men are to be victimized by a family member.[49]

Criminal harassment, or **stalking**, is also heavily gendered. Women, especially young and Aboriginal women, are at much higher risk of being stalked than are men; of stalking incidents reported to police in 2006, 76 per cent involved female victims, and many male victims were stalked not by women but by other men. When stalking involved spouses or former partners, women were 90 per cent of victims.[50]

Family violence was largely ignored until the second-wave feminist movement made it a priority in the 1960s and 1970s. The extent of violence against women undoubtedly overshadowed the possibility of violence against men. Since the 1980s and to the current day, however, some have insisted that family violence is perpetrated equally (or even most frequently) by women. This school of thought upholds **gender symmetry** in domestic violence—the idea that rates of domestic violence are roughly equal by gender, but violence against men is underreported or ignored. Gender symmetry holds that women are as likely to hit men as men are to hit women. Indeed, data from Canada's General Social Survey (and US surveys) give support to the notion of symmetry. In contrast to police data (which reflect only incidents reported to the police), the survey asks people whether they have experienced spousal violence in the past five years (whether or not they reported that violence to the police or anyone else). The 2009 survey elicited roughly equal numbers of men and women (about 6 per cent) who report experiencing spousal violence; only 22 per cent of these men and women reported the incident to police. In the US, self-reporting produces the same phenomenon; of those who report having experienced physical violence from a partner, 31.5 per cent are female and 27.5 per cent are male. The most recent statistics have *more* men than women reporting physical violence in the past year.[51] It is difficult to make these data square with those that show women as victims in roughly four times as many cases of IPV. Are police statistics meaningless? Are women "just as violent" as men?

If so, you might ask, why are there no shelters for battered men, no epidemics of male victims turning up in hospital emergency rooms, no legions of battered men coming forward to demand protection? Partly, pundits tell us, men who are victims of domestic violence are so ashamed of the humiliation, of the denial of manhood, they are unlikely to come forward and are more likely to suffer in silence the violence of their wives—a psychological problem that one researcher calls "the battered husband syndrome."[52]

While there may be some truth to the view that men are less likely to report domestic violence to police, the assertion that there are as many "battered men" as "battered women" is not supported by empirical research at all.[53] Surveys, and some gender symmetry studies, ask men and women if they have ever, during the course of their relationship, hit their partner; the results indicate generally equal "yes" responses from both men and women. The problem is that this answer (however alarming) does not tell us who initiated the violence (was it offensive or defensive?); how severe it was (did she push him before or after he'd broken her jaw?); and how often the violence occurred (was it once in a 10-year marriage or much more frequently?). When these three questions are posed, the results look different.

One of the reasons that police data look much different from survey data is that women seem much more likely to experience the most serious *forms and effects* of IPV. In Canada's General Social Survey, women were much more likely to reported having been choked, beaten, or attacked with a weapon than were men. While 44 per cent of women who experienced violence reported being injured, 19 per cent of men did; and while 34 per cent of women reported fearing for their lives, 10 per cent of men did. The fact that in one year (2007–2008) 101,000 women and children were admitted to women's shelters in Canada is testament to the gender imbalance in violence. Clearly, even on the basis of self-reporting, gender has a powerful effect on spousal violence.[54]

Although researchers have found clear and unequivocal evidence that violence against women increases dramatically during and after divorce or separation, the research that found gender symmetry results *excluded* incidents that occurred after separation or divorce. In the US, about 76 per cent of all assaults take place at that time, though—with a male perpetrator more than 93 per cent of the time.[55]

Finally, much of the research that suggests symmetry is based on the **Conflict Tactics Scale** (CTS), a scale that makes it possible to "count" IPV, though at the cost of removing context altogether. The CTS has been criticized for equating a vicious assault with a woman's wrestling or hitting her husband while he is, for instance, assaulting their children. Nor does it take into account the physical differences between women and men, which lead to women's being six times more likely to require medical care for injuries sustained in family violence. Nor does it include the structural factors or non-physical means by which women are compelled to remain in abusive relationships (income disparities, fears about their children, economic dependency). Nor does it include marital rape or sexual aggression.[56]

The point is not to suggest that women's violence is "okay" while men's is "bad." No amount of violence is defensible, and the violence of women against intimate partners should not be excused. As bell hooks recognized when she wrote of patriarchal violence, women are fully capable of deploying it, particularly over those over whom our society has traditionally granted them power, that is, children. Furthermore, there is evidence that there *may* be symmetry in the arena of emotional abuse, and that men's risk of experiencing it may be growing as power relations between the sexes change. We argue here that violence is the result of social arrangements rather than biology, and so it is certainly theoretically possible that women's use of violence will change as society changes. There is need for further research on female-perpetrated IPV and the traits that may predispose a woman to it. We do not deny or seek to minimize the experience of men who suffer at the hands of women. However, according to the US National Institute of Justice, "A review of the research found that violence is instrumental in maintaining control and that more than 90 per cent of 'systematic, persistent, and injurious' violence is perpetrated by men." **Intimate terrorism**, the most serious form of IPV, combines physical abuse with other forms of control and domination, and is almost entirely the province of men, according to Michael Johnson—though this finding has been recently disputed.[57]

In the results of a survey, women and men might appear to be equally violent. However, hospital emergency rooms, women's shelters, and morgues tell a different story. Murray Straus, one of the most cogent and consistent defenders of gender symmetry theory, agrees that intimate terrorism (which he defines more precisely than does Johnson) is overwhelmingly perpetrated by men; he also agrees that the graver effects of male-perpetrated IPV are important: "Attacks by male partners cause more fear, more physical and psychological injury, and more deaths. The greater adverse effect on women is an extremely important difference and it indicates the need to continue to provide more services for female victims of IPV than for male victims."[58]

At the extreme end of spousal violence, its gendering becomes clearer. In the US, there are approximately 2,100 intimate-partner homicides each year, of which about 70 per cent have female victims. In Canada, too, women, particularly young women, are much more likely than men to be killed by their opposite-sex partners. According to 2014 data, Canadian women are four times more likely than men are to be killed by a spouse. Both victims and perpetrators of homicide in Canada are likely to be male (with, however, differential risk for Aboriginal and non-Aboriginal people). Even so, in 2014, only 1 per cent of non-Aboriginal men and 9 per cent of Aboriginal men who were victims of homicide were killed by spouses. Non-spouse intimate partners were responsible for another 3 per cent of the homicides of male victims. In contrast, spouses were responsible for 45 per cent of the homicides of non-Aboriginal women and 33 per cent of the deaths of Aboriginal women. Age difference between partners is also associated with a greater risk of homicide for women. Interestingly, the risk of victimization by family homicide diminishes significantly with age, but gender continues to be important. So while seniors in Canada are very unlikely to be murdered by a family member, senior *female* victims are generally murdered by spouses or adult sons, while senior male victims are more likely to be murdered by their adult sons or stepsons.[59]

The rates for spousal murder are significantly different for women and men; so too are the events leading up to such murders. R. Emerson Dobash, Russell Dobash, and their colleagues argue,

> men often kill wives after lengthy periods of prolonged physical violence accompanied by other forms of abuse and coercion; the roles in such cases are seldom if ever reversed. Men perpetrate familial massacres, killing spouse and children together; women do not. Men commonly hunt down and kill wives who have left them; women hardly ever behave similarly. Men kill wives as part of planned murder-suicides; analogous acts by women are almost unheard of. Men kill in response to revelations of wifely infidelity; women almost never respond similarly, though their mates are more often adulterous.[60]

It is also worth noting that the gender disparity in spousal homicide in Western societies is relatively modest compared with the ratio in developing and more male-dominant societies. Where patriarchal control is relatively unchallenged, assault, rape, and even murder may be seen less as a crime and more as a prerogative.[61]

Intimate-partner violence knows no class, racial, or ethnic bounds. Yet there are some differences. In the US, a few studies have found rates of spousal violence to be much higher in African-American families than in white families. African-American women are three times more likely to experience spousal homicide than are white women. They are often reluctant to turn abusive partners over to a justice system they perceive as racially biased and are therefore more likely than white women are to fight back and to rely on spiritual rather than legal support. In Canada, immigrant women may face a greater risk of spousal violence, though data are inconclusive. What is clear is that "immigrant-specific factors" such as immigration status, isolation, economic dependency, and language barriers make immigrant women much more vulnerable than other Canadians. For example, many women immigrate as **family-class immigrants** and may fear having to leave Canada if they separate from abusive partners.[62]

However, in Canada the most significant differences emerge when Aboriginal and non-Aboriginal people are compared. According to the 2009 General Social Survey,

15 per cent of Aboriginal women had experienced spousal violence in the five years before the study, compared to 6 per cent of non-Aboriginal women. (Interestingly, while the non-Aboriginal rate has remained the same, the Aboriginal rate declined from 21 per cent in the 2004 General Social Survey.) Clearly, domestic violence is significantly more likely within Aboriginal communities, interacting with substance abuse and other legacies of colonization. The violence is also more severe: 60 per cent of Aboriginal women victimized by spousal violence reported being injured, compared to 40 per cent of non-Aboriginal women. Aboriginal women who experienced spousal violence were significantly more likely to fear for their lives than non-Aboriginal women were. Aboriginal women also self-report emotional and financial abuse at a rate twice that of non-Aboriginal women. Poverty and other conditions associated with Aboriginal life in Canada—such as over-crowded on-reserve housing and lack of transportation options—exacerbate the problem and make it more difficult for women and children to escape abusers.[63]

Intimate-partner violence within the LGBTQ community has only been studied systematically in recent years, but there is growing evidence that it is a serious problem. According to Canada's 2009 General Social Survey, those who self-identified as gay or lesbian were twice as likely to report having experienced spousal violence than heterosexuals; bisexuals were four times more likely. In fact, according to a report released in 2013 by the US Centers for Disease Control, LGBTQ people have a higher risk than heterosexuals of being victimized by IPV (defined here as rape, physical violence, and/or stalking). Bisexual women reported the highest rates, at 61 per cent, while 44 per cent of lesbians and 35 per cent of heterosexual women reported experiencing IPV. Among men, bisexuals were also most at risk: their rate of 37 per cent was slightly higher than that of heterosexual women! Of men who reported experiencing IPV, 26 per cent were gay and 29 per cent were heterosexual. According to these statistics, therefore, sexual orientation is a significant risk factor for IPV. However, studies have varied wildly in their findings of prevalence of IPV in the LGBTQ population. What is clear is that LGBTQ people not only experience significant rates of IPV but also face a lack of resources. They are less likely to report to police and highly unlikely to use shelters, in part because they distrust police and shelters may discriminate against them. This is particularly true for trans people, who experience extremely high rates of all forms of violence, including IPV, and suffer frequent discrimination in shelters. MTF trans people appear particularly vulnerable to domestic violence. While few studies have considered trans people, and even fewer have separated transwomen from transmen, one study that did find that transwomen were twice as likely as transmen to experience IPV, a finding in keeping with the higher prevalence among women in general.[64]

Violence within the family varies with the balance of power in a relationship. When all decisions are made by one spouse, rates of spousal abuse—whether committed by the woman or the man—are at their highest levels. Violence against women is accordingly most common in those households in which power is concentrated in the hands of the husband. Interestingly, violence against husbands is *also* more common (though much less likely) in homes in which the power is concentrated in the hands of the husband or, in extremely rare cases, in the hands of the wife. Concentration of power leads to higher rates of violence, period—whether against women or against men. Rates of wife abuse and husband abuse both plummet when relationships are equal.[65]

However, domestic violence is not limited to spousal abuse. Children are often exposed to domestic violence, either as victims or as witnesses. The negative effects of this are well documented. When children who witness IPV grow up, they are at greater risk to use violence in domestic situations (especially if they are male) and may suffer from low self-esteem (especially if female) among various emotional problems. Girls who grow up in homes where their mothers are abused are much more likely than other girls to be abused in their adult relationships. Moreover, children who witness, or experience violence within the home, are much more likely to exhibit aggressive behaviour toward other children. Though boys are much more likely than girls to exhibit aggressive behaviour, both sexes show significantly more aggression if they have witnessed violence.[66]

Violence against children by parents is perhaps the most widespread type of family violence all over the world. Broad support exists for **corporal punishment**—more than two-thirds of Americans and most Canadians believe that it is all right (or even beneficial) for a parent to "spank" a child. Most North Americans have hit their children, and most children have been hit by their parents, often starting in infancy. (Most North American toddlers and preschoolers are physically punished.) In a survey of almost 2,500 Quebec mothers, more than half said they used corporal punishment, and almost half of their children aged zero to two years had already experienced it. While there are more and more parents who do not spank, about half still do. Parents approve of corporal punishment, but it is associated with negative behaviours in children and poorer outcomes in adulthood, including aggression, anti-social behaviour, and mental health problems. The American Academy of Pediatrics has taken an official stand against spanking, as has the Canadian Paediatric Society, which advises, "Physicians should actively counsel parents about discipline and should strongly discourage the use of spanking." Given the preponderance of evidence against the practice, the Canadian Medical Association took a stand against spanking in 2012. It called for the repeal of Section 43 of the Criminal Code (introduced in 1892 and upheld by the Supreme Court in 2004), which permits parents to use reasonable force against their children: "It is time for Canada to remove this anachronistic excuse for poor parenting from the statute book," wrote the editor of the association's journal.[67]

The most evident short-term consequence of parental violence against children is observed in the behaviours of children. Children see that violence is a legitimate way to resolve disputes and learn to use it themselves. Violence against siblings is ubiquitous in North American families. As Straus writes:

> Violence between siblings often reflects what children see their parents doing to each other, as well as what the child experiences in the form of discipline. Children of non-violent parents also tend to use non-violent methods to deal with their siblings and later with their spouses and children. If violence, like charity, begins at home, so does non-violence.[68]

Parents wondering how to discourage violence *among* their children might begin by ending violence *against* them. In ending sibling violence, no message can be more powerful than "in this home, *no one* hits."

The long-term consequences of parental violence against children are also clear. The greater the corporal punishment experienced by the child, the greater the probability that the child will hit a spouse as an adult. The likelihood is also higher that children hit by their parents will strike back. (However, it should be noted that this is a relatively minor risk, even when parents are seniors. Seniors' rate of victimization by adult children is only about one-eighth the rate of physical and sexual assault of children by parents.[69]

North Americans' support for corporal punishment disappears when such violent behaviour by parents against children becomes systematic or extreme, and most who "spank" see themselves as fundamentally different from those who abuse their children physically. Although the most common forms of parental violence against children are spanking or slapping, statistics indicate that 20 per cent of American parents have hit their child with an object, almost 10 per cent have kicked, bit, or hit their child with their fist, and almost 5 per cent of families have experienced a parent beating a child. While spanking does not indicate that one is a child abuser, the most severe psychological and physical abuse is associated with corporal punishment, and some researchers have found correlation between corporal punishment and other societal indicators, such as child and overall homicide rates. Although mothers, as well as fathers, commit violence against children, this is another area where gender symmetry does not exist. In one study, Bergman and his colleagues found that men are more than 10 times more likely to inflict serious harm on their children.[70]

Statistics on family violence against children in Canada reflect only police-reported data because children do not participate in the General Social Survey. According to police data, about two-thirds of children and youth who were victimized in 2013 experienced physical assault, with most of these assaults (81 per cent) relatively minor. Another third experienced sexual assault, discussed further below. Of the physical assaults against children younger than six reported to Canadian police in 2013, 60 per cent were perpetrated by a family member. (Interestingly, police are less likely to lay charges in family violence cases involving child victims than they are when adults are the victims.) Parents are responsible for much of the violence against children, particularly the very young. According to 2008 data, of those accused in family-perpetrated physical assaults of children younger than six, 59 per cent were fathers, while 27 per cent were mothers (other family members accounted for the remaining 14 per cent).

Of family-perpetrated homicides against children and youth in 2003, 60 per cent were perpetrated by fathers, while 32 per cent were committed by mothers (other family members accounted for the remaining 8 per cent). Data from 2008 also reveal that fathers are more likely to be perpetrators. Peter Jaffe, an expert in domestic child homicide, claims that there is a "60/40 split" (fathers/mothers) in perpetration. He also notes that there are disparate gender-related precipitators of such extreme violence. Only about 20 per cent of child homicides arise out of physical abuse; in the other 80 per cent, previous physical abuse is absent. In those cases, women are more likely to kill their children as the result of mental health issues, men to punish a partner who leaves a relationship.[71]

Both women and girls are vulnerable to yet another form of extreme familial violence, the so-called **"honour" killing**. This kind of murder seeks to "cleanse" a family's honour through the murder of a non-conforming female family member who has "stained" the family in some way. In some countries, there is a legal exemption or lesser penalty for such crimes. According to the UN Population Fund, at least 5,000 women are killed (globally) each year in "honour" murders. In recent years, similar killings have occurred in Canada.

In 2009, for example, 23-year-old Hasibullah Sadiqi of Ottawa shot his sister and her fiancé after she moved in with him before the wedding and refused to have her estranged abusive father involved in wedding plans. In another horrific case the same year, a couple and their son were charged with murder after the drowning deaths of their three daughters and the husband's first wife. Between 1999 and 2009, at least a dozen murders in Canada fell into the so-called "honour" category.[72]

Such murders have become controversial within North America and Europe because they tend to be associated with particular immigrant communities. Some feel that singling such murders out obscures the fact that family homicide occurs in all groups; others feel that categorizing these killings as domestic violence obscures their nature and rootedness in religion and culture. Phyllis Chesler notes that "honour" murders are carefully planned, involve multiple perpetrators and the most extreme forms of violence, and suffer little social stigma from extended family and community. Despite these key differences from the more common forms of domestic violence, "honour killings" share with domestic violence the desire to control and dominate. Indeed, in many "honour" murders, victims of such murders had also survived family violence and abuse. Like the other forms of family violence we have examined, these murders reflect the deadly logic of patriarchal violence.[73]

While indicators suggest that the Canadian family is becoming less violent, we are a long way indeed from a society in which the family can be considered a true haven. Broadening our vision so that we refuse to tolerate all violence perpetrated within the family—whether legal or illegal, and no matter who perpetrates it—will allow us to transcend the legacy of patriarchal domination and create true dignity and equality within this most important institution.

Sexual Assault

The logic of patriarchal domination is also reflected in **sexual assault**, and its gendering is even clearer. In Canada, sexual assault has been defined, since 1983, not as penile penetration but more holistically as any non-consensual sexual act. The degree of sexual assault is determined not by penetration, but by level of injury, use of weapon, and danger to life. Our understandings of sexual assault, then, are relatively new and evolving. Indeed, historically it has often been difficult—or irrelevant—to try to understand the difference between consensual and non-consensual sex.

Many disciplines have grappled with understanding sexual assault. While sexual assault may be perpetrated by either gender and against either gender, the primary focus of scholarship has been **rape** of women by men. While studies have shown that both men and women coerce others into sex, evidence suggests that men experience much less of this coercion and perpetrate much more. This may be changing as sexual mores change, particularly among young people. For example, a 2010–2011 study asked young people about perpetration of sexual violence. A small group (4 per cent) reported having attempted or completed rape; of this group, about 20 per cent were female. Predictably, however, much of the discussion of sexual aggression has rooted it in men's biology. Sociobiologist David Barash explains rape as a reproductive adaptation by men who otherwise couldn't get a date. Barash, Thornhill, and other evolutionists argue that men who rape are fulfilling their genetic drive to reproduce in the only way they know how. "Perhaps human rapists, in their own criminally misguided way, are doing the best they can to maximize their fitness," writes Barash. Rape, for men, is simply an "adaptive" reproductive strategy of the less-successful male—sex by other means.[74]

In their book *A Natural History of Rape*, Randy Thornhill and Craig Palmer argue that rape is "a natural, biological phenomenon that is a product of human evolutionary heritage." Males' biological predisposition is to reproduce, and their reproductive success comes from spreading their seed as far and wide as possible; women are actually the ones with the power because they get to choose which males will be successful. "But getting chosen is not the only way to gain sexual access to females," they write. "In rape, the male circumvents the females' choice."[75]

Such arguments ignore the fact that most rapists are not interested in reproduction but rather in humiliation and violence, motivated more by rage than by lust. Most rapists have regular sex partners; quite a few are married. Many children, and women well past reproductive age, are raped. Additionally, why would some rapists hurt, and even murder, their victims, therefore preventing the survival of the very genetic material that they are supposed to be raping in order to pass on? Why would some rapists be homosexual rapists, passing on their genetic material to those who could not possibly reproduce? And what about rape in prison? Using theories of selfish genes or evolutionary imperatives to explain such behaviour cannot take us very far.

Other scholars analyze sexual assault cross-culturally. The research of Peggy Reeves Sanday and others suggests that rape is not the evolutionary reproductive strategy of the less-successful males. Rather, rape is a *cultural* phenomenon. Sexual assault may be a strategy to ensure continued male domination or a vehicle by which men can hope to conceal maternal dependence, according to ethnographers, but it is surely not an alternative dating strategy.

Think, for example, of the way that sexual assault is used in warfare (discussed on p. 359). The mass rape of Bosnian or Sudanese women and children is a direct and systematic effort on the part of one militarized group of males to express and sustain the subordination of a conquered group. Mass rape in warfare is about the final humiliating appropriation of the conquered group.

Moreover, what about rape that is not a crime to be punished but *restitution* for a crime that has been committed? In June 2002, a Pakistani woman, Mukhtar Mai, was gang-raped in a small village in southern Punjab. A local judicial council ordered her to be raped as punishment for non-marital sex. Except she didn't actually have non-marital sex—her brother did, or so they believed. Mukhtar was ordered raped because of a crime her brother was said to have committed. It was later revealed that her brother, age 12, had himself been abducted and sodomized by three elder tribesmen, who fabricated the sex story as a cover-up. While these elder tribesmen were never tried and convicted, the men who sentenced Mukhtar Mai to be gang-raped were eventually brought to justice after a world outcry against such obvious injustice. Although neither of these rapes could even be remotely tied to some evolutionary strategy for reproductive success, together they reveal the way that rape serves to reproduce male domination. Both the dominance hierarchies among men and the hierarchies that place men over women were revealed in this horrific moment.[76]

In her ethnographic study of a gang rape at the University of Pennsylvania, Peggy Reeves Sanday underscores how a campus gang rape looks surprisingly like this Pakistani judicial council. She suggests that gang rape has its origins in both the gender inequality that allows men to see women as pieces of meat and in men's needs to demonstrate their masculinity to one another. Gang rape cements the relations among men. More than that, though, gang rape permits a certain homoerotic contact between men. When one participant reported his pleasure at feeling the semen of his friends inside the woman as he raped her, Sanday sensed a distinct erotic component. The woman was the receptacle, the vehicle by which these men could have sex with one another and still claim heterosexuality. Only in a culture that degrades and devalues women could such behaviours take place. Rape, then, is hardly an evolutionary strategy by which less-successful males get to pass on their reproductive inheritance. Moreover, it is an act that occurs only in those societies where there is gender inequality and by men who may be quite "successful" in other forms of mating but believe themselves entitled to violate women. It is about *gender*, not about *sex*, and it is a way in which gender inequality produces gender difference.[77]

Some psychologists have studied the psychodynamic processes that lead an individual man to such aberrant behaviour. Whether because of childhood trauma, unresolved anger at their mothers, or a sense of inadequate gender identity, psychologists tend to see rapists as characterized by their deviance from the norm. "Rape is always a symptom of some psychological dysfunction, either temporary and transient, or chronic and repetitive." In the popular view, and in some psychological studies, rapists are "sick individuals." However, research has failed to confirm this.[78]

A sociological perspective builds upon these other perspectives, but it also offers a radical departure from them. Sexual assault in general and rape in particular are particularly illustrative because they are something that is performed almost exclusively by one gender—men—although it is done to women, children, and even other men. Therefore, it is particularly useful for teasing out the dynamics of both difference (because only men do it) and dominance. Instead of seeing a collection of sick individuals, sociologists look at how ordinary and normal rapists can be—and then at the culture that legitimates their behaviours. A sociological perspective also assesses the processes and dynamics that force all women to confront the possibility of sexual victimization—a process that reproduces both gender division and gender inequality.

Studies of rapists have found that many are married or have steady, regular partners. Studies of gang rape reveal an even more "typical" guy who sees himself simply as going along with his friends. Rapists see their actions in terms that express power differentials between women and men. They see what they do to women as their "right," a sense of entitlement to women's bodies.

Although rape is an act of aggression by an individual man (or a group of men), it is also a social problem that women, as a group, face. Women may deal with rape as individuals—by changing their outfits, their patterns of walking and talking, their willingness to go to certain places at certain times—but rape affects all women. Rape is a form of "sexual terrorism," writes legal theorist Carol Sheffield, a "system of constant reminders to women that we are vulnerable and targets solely by virtue of our gender. The knowledge that such things can, and do happen, serves to keep all women in the psychological condition of being aware that they are potential victims."[79]

To the sociologist, then, rape expresses both a structure of relations and an individual event. At the individual level, it is the action of a man (or group of men) against a woman. It keeps women in a position of vulnerability as potential targets. In this way, rape reproduces both gender difference (women as vulnerable and dependent upon men for protection, women afraid to dare to enter male spaces such as the street for fear of victimization) and gender inequality.[80]

It doesn't have to be this way, of course. Societies may be located on a continuum from rape-free to rape-prone. Peggy Reeves Sanday found that the best predictors of rape-proneness were levels of militarism, interpersonal violence in general, ideologies of male toughness, and distant father-child relationships. Those societies in which rape was relatively rare valued women's autonomy (women continued to own property in their own name after marriage) and valued children (men were involved in child rearing). Stated most simply, "the lower the status of women relative to men, the higher the rape rate."[81]

North American rates of sexual assault are difficult to calculate, in part because different survey methodologies render vastly different results and measure different intervals and experiences. Some look at all incidents of sexual assault while others measure only rape; some consider only one year's incidence, while others look at lifetime incidence. Some look at police reports, others at survey data. Given the general agreement that most sexual assault is unreported, this distinction is important. According to some surveys, 12–25 per cent of all American women have experienced rape, and another 12–20 per cent have experienced attempted rape. One calculation estimates that 20–30 per cent of all girls will suffer a violent sexual attack during their lives. According to Statistics Canada data, 51 per cent of adult women have experienced sexual or physical assault at least once. In police-reported sexual assaults, 80 per cent of assailants were known to the victim; 28 per cent of victims were assaulted by family members.[82]

What is perhaps more frightening is that many sexual assault victims are children. In Canada and the US, more than half of victims of police-reported sexual assault are children and youth, and their rate of sexual assault is more than twice that of young adults (the next most vulnerable group).[83]

In fact, though we tend to think of sexual assault as a crime most commonly perpetrated against women, sexual assault is in large part a crime against children and youth. According to 2008 statistics, children and youth were the victims of 59 per cent of sexual assaults reported to Canadian police. (Given the fact that children and youth are even less likely than adults are to report such assaults, this number may even be too low.) Assaults of children and youth are gendered, though boy children are much more vulnerable to such assaults than are men. Of the assaulted children and youth in 2009, 82 per cent were female. Girls under 18 have a rate of sexual violence five times higher than boys of their age do; the peak age for girls' victimization was 13–15. A third of sexual assault victims were assaulted by people within their families; 97 per cent of such accused were male, with male extended family members the most commonly accused, followed by fathers and brothers. Children under 12 were more likely to be sexually assaulted within the family and those older than 12 more likely to be assaulted by someone not a family member. Aboriginal children are at particularly high risk. Revelations of pervasive child sexual abuse by Catholic priests (and the Church's subsequent efforts to cover up these crimes) remind us that boys are also vulnerable to such exploitation.[84]

Children are also at risk from exploitation for child pornography, the production of which is itself a form of sexual assault. Between 1998 and 2008, the number of child pornography incidents reported to Canadian police increased by a factor of nine. Roman Catholic bishop Raymond Lahey resigned in late 2009 after charges of child pornography were laid against him. Bill Surkis, a prominent member of Toronto's Jewish community, faced similar charges in May 2009. In February 2010, seven Canadian children were rescued after police received a tip regarding the production and distribution of child pornography by a 36-year-old Surrey (BC) man.[85]

As we saw earlier, different theoretical schools offer different explanations for sexual assault. Arguments that rape is simply the reproductive strategy for losers in the sexual arena are unconvincing. Equally unconvincing are arguments that sexual assault is an isolated, individual act, committed by sick individuals who experience uncontrollable sexual impulses.

Arguments that sexual assaulters are those who were themselves sexually abused are suggestive—many sexual abusers, particularly pedophiliac ones, have been abused—but are obviously quite limited. As a recent metastudy concludes, "A leading candidate for a vulnerability factor is being male: the large majority of sex offenders are male, yet the majority of child victims of sexual abuse are female." If histories of sexual abuse turned one into a victimizer, we would expect to see more *female* than male perpetrators. In Canada, about 97 per cent of those charged with sexual offences are male. Maleness, rather than a history of sexual abuse, remains the most potent predictor of a tendency to abuse; males may abuse at various ages, including in adolescence. Though Internet pundits are fond of muttering about the "hidden epidemic" of female-perpetrated sexual abuse, women remain a tiny minority of abusers; in most cases, women offenders are charged with helping their male partners sexually assault rather than with perpetrating the assault themselves. This is, of course, abhorrent and fully culpable behaviour; however, it suggests that women, for whatever reason, are much less likely to sexually assault than are men (and certainly much less likely to sexually assault than to physically assault).[86]

An adequate explanation of sexual assault has to recognize that it is almost entirely perpetrated by men. We must also ask the more frightening question: Why do so many "otherwise" typical, normal men commit sexual assault? As sociologist Allan Johnson puts it, " . . . the focus of violence against women rests squarely in the middle of what our culture defines as 'normal' interaction between men and women." The reality is that much rape is committed by "regular guys" and "women are at greater risk of being raped or aggressed against by the men they know and date than they are by lunatics in the bushes."[87]

Surveys of young women reveal the prevalence of rape, while surveys of young men indicate how casually rape can be viewed. Mary Koss's 1980s research on acquaintance rape became the subject of vicious backlash attacks, but remains the most impressive and thorough research we have on rape's frequency and scope. She found that 44 per cent of all women surveyed experienced some forms of sexual activity against their will, 15 per cent experienced attempted rape, 12 per cent were coerced by drugs and alcohol, a full 25 per cent had sexual intercourse when they didn't want to because they were "overwhelmed" by a man's unyielding arguments and pressure, and 9 per cent were forcibly raped.[88]

No wonder feminist writer Susan Griffin called rape "the all-American crime," engaged in by normal, all-American guys. Even at the fringes of the phenomenon, where sexual assaults are brutal and even murderous, men may view rape relatively casually. In the early 1980s, Diana Scully and Joseph Marolla interviewed 114 convicted rapists of adult women. These rapists, and their crimes, varied widely, though most were violent and some rapes had resulted in deaths. Nonetheless, a significant number of the rapists denied that the "sex" they had engaged in was non-consensual. These men described their motivations for rape in terms that Scully and Marolla grouped under several themes: revenge and punishment; an "added bonus" (i.e., part of another crime such as burglary); sexual access to women who would otherwise not be available; impersonal sex and power; recreation and adventure; and feeling good. One of the interviewees described the feeling of having raped as "like I had just ridden the bull at Gilley's"; sexual assault provided a sense of achievement and conquest. Scully and Marolla conclude that rape is not merely the act of a twisted, psychotic mind, but an extreme reflection of everyday objectification of women or "the end point in a continuum of sexually aggressive behaviours that reward men and victimize women."[89]

However, can these violent rapists be in any way normal? Scully developed these themes further, finding that rapists are just as likely to be fathers—and to have significant relationships with women, though they have higher levels of *consensual* sexual activity than other men. This finding should effectively demolish evolutionary arguments that men who rape do so out of sexual frustration, desire for relationships with women, or their need to reproduce. Rape was used by Scully's interviewees "to put women in their place," she writes. "Rape is a man's right," one convicted rapist told her. "If a woman doesn't want to give it, a man should take it. Women have no right to say no. Women are made to have sex. It's all they are good for. Some women would rather take a beating, but they always give in; it's what they are for." Men rape, Scully concludes, "not because they are idiosyncratic or irrational but because they have learned that in this culture sexual violence is rewarding" and because "they never thought they would be punished for what they did."[90]

Yet if Scully and Marolla's work suggested that rapists were in many ways "normal," it is also true that most men do not commit rape. Troublingly, in several surveys, many men indicated that they *would* consider rape—provided the conditions were "right" and they knew that they would not get caught. In a survey of American college men (most of these studies have used such samples), 28 per cent indicated that they would be likely to commit rape and use force to get sex; 6 per cent said they would commit rape but not use force, and 30 per cent said they might use force but would not commit rape. Of these men, 40 per cent indicated that they would neither use force nor commit rape—less than half! In another survey, 37 per cent indicated some likelihood of committing rape if they were certain they would not be caught. Some might think things have changed since these studies, but a 2014 survey found much the same thing. While only "hostile" men (about 14 per cent of respondents) indicated their willingness to "rape," 31.7 per cent said that they would act on their intentions "to force a woman to sexual intercourse" if they could get away with it. According to the survey authors, these men were characterized by "callous sexual attitudes" that positioned women as sexual objects and sexual aggression as part of masculinity.[91]

In a sense, what we see is that rapists are *not* nonconformists—psychologically unbalanced perverts who couldn't otherwise get sex. Rather, they are *over* conformists—men who are exceptionally committed to masculine norms, who make every encounter, with every woman, potentially—even inevitably—about sexual conquest. They turn every date into a contest, turning a deaf ear to what a woman might want because, after all, women aren't men's equals to begin with. "The most striking characteristic of sex offenders," writes one researcher "is their apparent normality." Bernard Lefkowitz, author of a chillingly detailed portrait of the gang rape of a developmentally disabled girl by several high-status high school athletes in Glen Ridge, New Jersey, argues, "[f]or a lot of boys, acting abusively toward women is regarded as a rite of passage. It's woven into our culture."[92]

Author Tim Beneke asked "Jay," a 23-year-old stock boy in a San Francisco corporation to think about under what circumstances he might commit rape. Trying to imagine the circumstances, Jay said:

> Let's say I see a woman and she looks really pretty and really clean and sexy and she's giving off very feminine, sexy vibes. I think, wow I would love to make love to her, but I know she's not interested. It's a tease. A lot of times a woman knows that she's looking really good and she'll use that and flaunt it and it makes me feel like she's laughing at me and I feel degraded. . . . If I were actually desperate enough to rape somebody it would be from wanting that person, but also it would be a very spiteful thing, just being able to say "I have power over you and I can do anything I want with you" because really I feel that they have power over me just by their presence. Just the fact that they can come up to me and just melt me makes me feel like a dummy, makes me want revenge. They have power over me so I want power over them.[93]

Jay speaks not from a feeling of power, but rather from a feeling of powerlessness. "They have power over me so I want power over them." In his mind, rape is not the initiation of aggression against a woman, but rather a form of revenge, a retaliation after an injury done to him; but who is injuring him?

Beneke explores this apparent paradox by looking at language. Think of the terms we use in this culture to describe women's beauty and sexuality. We use a language of violence, of aggression. A woman is a "bombshell," a "knockout," and a "femme fatale." She's "stunning," "ravishing," and "dressed to kill." Women's beauty is experienced by men as an act of aggression: It invades men's thoughts, elicits unwelcome feelings of desire and longing, and makes men feel helpless, powerless, and vulnerable. Then, having committed this invasive act of aggression, women reject men, say no to sex, and turn them down. Rape is a way to get even, to exact revenge for rejection, or to retaliate. These feelings of powerlessness, coupled with the sense of entitlement to women's bodies expressed by the rapists Diana Scully interviewed, combine in a potent mix—powerlessness and entitlement, impotence and a right to feel in control.

Consequently, rape is less a problem of a small number of sick individuals and more a problem of social expectations of male behaviour, expectations that stem from gender inequality (disrespect and contempt for women) and may push men toward sexual predation. A completed rape is only the "end point" on a continuum that includes sexual coercion as well as the premeditated use of alcohol or drugs to dissolve a woman's resistance. In the most famous study of college men's behaviours, Mary Koss and her colleagues found that 1 in 13 men admitted to forcing (or attempting to force) a woman to have sex against her will, but 10 per cent had engaged in unwanted sexual contact, and another 7.2 per cent had been sexually coercive. In another study, Scott Boeringer found that more than 55 per cent had engaged in sexual coercion, 8.6 per cent had attempted rape, and 23.7 per cent had provided drugs or alcohol to a woman in order to have sex with her when she became too intoxicated to consent or resist (which is legally considered rape in most jurisdictions). Such numbers belie arguments that rape is simply the crime of sick individuals. Building on these surveys, David Lisak and Paul Miller studied 120 "undetected" rapists (men whose self-reported behaviours meet the definition of rape, but who have never been prosecuted). They found relatively similar proportions of "undetected rapists" as did Koss and Boeringer, but they also found that a relatively small group of repeat rapists perpetrated large numbers of rapes. These rapists avoided prosecution by targeting women within their social networks and avoiding weapons and gratuitous violence, both of which increase the chance of prosecution.[94]

Historically, while prosecution for rape has been rare, prosecution for marital rape has been an impossibility. One of the more dramatic changes in sexual assault laws, therefore, has been the removal of exemptions for husbands. Before the 1983 reforms of Canada's rape law contained in Bill C-127, for example, there was no way to prosecute a husband for raping his wife. Indeed, before 1983 many Canadians believed that rape was a crime one could not commit against one's wife. The case was similar in the US, where as recently as 1985, more than half of states still expressly prohibited prosecution for marital rape, on the grounds that women had no legal right to say no to sex with their husbands. Today, marital rape is illegal, as is any sexual assault by a spouse of either sex.

This legal change was a response to troubling findings. In one study of 644 married American women, 12 per cent reported having been raped by their husbands. One researcher estimates that between 14 per cent and 25 per cent of women are forced by their husbands to have sexual intercourse against their will during the course of their marriage, whereas another claims that about one-third of women report having "unwanted sex" with their partner. In yet another study, David Finklehor and Kirsti Yllo also found that nearly 75 per cent of the women who had been raped by their husbands had successfully resisted at least once, and that 88 per cent reported that they never enjoyed being forced (in case there was any doubt). Despite the fact that sexual assault within marriage has been illegal for many years, however, it continues. A 2010 survey by the US Centers for Disease Control found that 9.4 per cent of women had been raped by an intimate partner within their lifetimes, and an estimated 16.9 per cent of women and 8 per cent of men have experienced sexual violence other than rape by an intimate partner at some point in their lifetime. In 2014, one American woman was dismayed that her ex-husband's repeated rapes—accomplished through drugging her and recorded using his phone's camera—were punished with a suspended sentence and home detention (no jail time). He explained to the jury that he drugged her because she was "snippy." Clearly, then, sexual assault within marriage is still treated differently. Not surprisingly, marital sexual assault is even less likely than other forms of sexual assault to be reported to authorities.[95]

Marital rape is an even more significant problem in countries where husbands remain excluded from prosecution. Sexual assault within marriage often goes hand in hand with other forms of intimate violence. In one study, 80 per cent of rural Egyptian women described beatings as common, particularly when women refused sex with their husbands. According to the WHO's recent multi-country study of violence, from 6 per cent (Japan) to 59 per cent (Ethiopia) of women reported having been sexually assaulted by their intimate partners, with rates in the majority of settings falling between 10 and 50 per cent. In one survey of South African men (randomly selected), 14.3 per cent reported having raped a current or former intimate partner.[96]

Stolen Sisters, the Highway of Tears, and Missing/ Murdered Aboriginal Women in Canada

In 1971, Cree high school student Helen Betty Osborne was abducted by four men on the streets of The Pas, Manitoba. She was taken outside town, beaten, sexually assaulted, and stabbed more than 50 times, then left in the woods by her murderers. Despite the fact that police received information regarding the perpetrators in 1972, and despite physical evidence found in the car of one of the accused, no charges were laid. Not until 1983 was the case reopened, even though rumours circulated in The Pas about the case—and the perpetrators themselves spoke of it. Finally, in 1986, murder charges were laid against two suspects. One man, Dwayne Archie Johnston, was convicted of the crime and sentenced to life in prison with no chance of parole for 10 years.

In the aftermath of the Johnston trial, Aboriginal and non-Aboriginal groups called for inquiry into the causes of the long delay in justice. In the summer of 1989, the Public Inquiry into the Administration of Justice and Aboriginal People heard testimony on "the murder, the investigation, the attitudes prevailing in the community, the situation of Aboriginal students in The Pas, and the relationship between the police and the Aboriginal community." The inquiry also examined the conduct of two lawyers and the Manitoba Attorney General's department. Among other findings of the inquiry, one stands out:

> It is clear that Betty Osborne would not have been killed if she had not been Aboriginal. The four men who took her to her death from the streets of The Pas that night had gone looking for an Aboriginal girl with whom to "party." They found Betty Osborne. When she refused to party she was driven out of town and murdered. Those who abducted her showed a total lack of regard for her person or her rights as an individual. Those who stood by while the physical assault took place, while sexual advances were made, and while she was being beaten to death showed their own racism, sexism, and indifference. Those who knew the story and remained silent must share their guilt.

The Osborne inquiry told Canadians what they might not have wanted to admit but what most of us who grew up in small towns knew: In The Pas, as in cities and towns across the country, non-Aboriginal men harassed Aboriginal women with impunity; they cruised the streets and bars specifically seeking easy sexual access to Aboriginal girls and women. Among many other elements of racism uncovered by the inquiry was the indifference of the RCMP to complaints of Aboriginal girls and women about sexual harassment.

It is now more than 20 years since the inquiry; unfortunately, the problem endures. In 2004, Amnesty International released *Stolen Sisters: A Human Rights Response to Discrimination and Violence against Indigenous Women in Canada*, a report that documented the extreme risk of violence faced by Aboriginal women and the frequent indifference of authorities to even the most egregious cases of violence. In March of that same year, the Native Women's Association of Canada (NWAC) launched its Sisters in Spirit campaign to publicize and investigate the unsolved murders and disappearances of Aboriginal women, and to demand change. In 2005, the Sisters in Spirit campaign, funded by Status of Women Canada, became a five-year initiative involving NWAC, other Aboriginal groups, and the Canadian government. The campaign focused on researching the numbers of missing and murdered Aboriginal women. In 2010, NWAC released *What Their Stories Tell Us*, a summary of findings. The report revealed that NWACs database now contained 582 cases. Analysis revealed that more than two-thirds of the cases came from the western provinces; that Aboriginal women were much more likely to be murdered than non-Aboriginal women (and were more likely to be killed by a stranger); that the perpetrators of violence against Aboriginal women are both Aboriginal and non-Aboriginal; and that many of the missing and murdered were young mothers.

British Columbia provides ample evidence of the tragic costs of ignoring this issue. For more than 10 years, women disappeared from Vancouver's Downtown Eastside. Aboriginal women were overrepresented among such disappearances, though both Aboriginal and non-Aboriginal women were disappearing at an alarming rate. Because many missing women were Aboriginal, drug-involved, and engaged in sex work, police were often reluctant to treat them as missing persons, despite persistent rumours that a serial killer was on the loose. Only in 2001 did the RCMP and Vancouver Police form the Missing Women Task Force to investigate the disappearances of more than 50 women. In 2002, Robert Pickton, a suburban pig farmer, was charged with the first of what would be more than 20 murder charges relating to the disappearances. In December 2007, Pickton was convicted of six murders of women from the Downtown Eastside. He was sentenced to six concurrent life sentences, with no eligibility for parole for 25 years. In 2010, the British Columbia Crown confirmed that the remaining 20 murder charges Pickton faced would be stayed.

In Northern British Columbia, disappearances of women and girls are also well documented, and Aboriginal women and girls are even more overrepresented among the disappeared. Many of these women and girls disappeared along the Yellowhead route (Highway 16) between Prince Rupert and Prince George, a 724-kilometre stretch of lonely highway now known to many as the Highway of Tears. For years, the cases were neglected; for example, teenaged girls who disappeared were seen as runaways who had simply

continued

drifted elsewhere, despite family insistence that this was not the case. Not until a young non-Aboriginal tree planter disappeared while hitchhiking outside Prince George, in the summer of 2002, was the issue given a high profile in the province. In 2005, BC's Unsolved Homicide Unit reviewed the files of three murders of teenaged girls, all of whom disappeared between June and December 1994, and whose bodies were found along the highway. Project E-Pana (named after an Inuit goddess who cares for the souls of the deceased in transit) began in the fall of that year. The project had a staff of about 60 people and involved collaboration among police forces with the goal of studying and solving "cold cases." The task force investigated at least 18 disappearances and murders of girls and women on BC highways, 10 of which are from the Highway of Tears. In 2012, E-Pana was able to decisively link a deceased American convict to several of the murders; in 2014, an Ontario man was charged with two 1970s murders, both of young girls. Despite these successes in solving cold cases, however, E-Pana's budget has been cut significantly, and it now operates with greatly reduced staffing.

The unexplained murders and disappearances of so many Aboriginal women and girls across the country highlight the deadly legacies of colonialism and the intertwining of racism with sexual violence. For years, the federal Liberals have called for a national inquiry into the disappearances and the treatment of such cases by police. In 2014, for the first time, Statistics Canada provided an analysis of its homicide data that focused on Aboriginal people. The analysis revealed that despite a generally declining rate of female homicide since 1991, the rate of Aboriginal female homicide has remained relatively stable since 1980. Aboriginal women therefore make up an increasing proportion of female victims of homicide and are now six times more likely than non-Aboriginal women are to be killed. The Statistics Canada report also confirmed NWAC's finding that the rates of female homicide are particularly high in the western provinces (and territories). Between 1980 and 2014, while 60 per cent of non-Aboriginal women victims of homicide were killed by family members, the corresponding number for Aboriginal women was 53 per cent. However, in contrast to the NWAC study, Statistics Canada did not find that Aboriginal women were more likely to be killed by strangers. The data also revealed that Aboriginal men are at great risk of homicide, and the homicide victimization disparity between Aboriginal and non-Aboriginal people is even starker in the case of men. Despite widespread concern about police handling of high-profile cases, the study found that murders of Aboriginal victims were solved at a slightly higher rate than those involving non-Aboriginal victims were.

In the aftermath of the report, and with an election campaign in the offing, the Liberals continued to call for a national inquiry; meanwhile, a parliamentary report suggested an inquiry would be of little utility and Prime Minister Stephen Harper cautioned against "sociological" interpretations. The controversy continued during the 2015 election campaign, in which the Liberals made a promise to undertake an inquiry. In the immediate aftermath of the Liberal victory in the fall of 2015, the promise was made good; an inquiry has been announced, and planning meetings began in December 2015. It remains to be seen whether the inquiry can help solve the devastating problem of violence against Aboriginal women—and men. As stated above, Aboriginal men are also at extreme risk of homicide, and they represent the bulk of missing and murdered Aboriginal people in Canada. Gender is undoubtedly a critical part of the story of missing and murdered Aboriginal people in this country; but the inquiry will have a unique opportunity to comment on the general victimization and violence faced by Aboriginal people and the remedies required in addition to focusing on the role played by gender. Meanwhile, families of missing and murdered girls and women, deeply traumatized by these murders and disappearances, continue to show tremendous courage and resolve as continuing advocates for their loved ones and the cause of justice.[97]

Gendered Hate Crimes

The murders and disappearances of women in British Columbia link Canada to the phenomenon of **femicide**. Femicide is a term developed by Diana Russell in the 1970s to describe woman-killing as a gendered hate crime; for Russell, femicide is the killing of women or girls because they are women or girls. There is much debate about what constitutes femicide and what does not; some, for example, use the term to describe any killing of a woman or girl. The WHO uses the term to describe any intentional killing of a woman or girl, citing the distinctive characteristics of homicide of females. The region in which the term has been most widely adopted is probably Latin America. There, the term has been widely used to describe serial killings of the type found in Ciudad Juárez, Mexico. There, since 1993, at least 400 girls and women have been murdered, some of them abducted, horribly tortured, and sexually assaulted before being murdered. Though numerous suspects have been identified and arrested, the Mexican state has been derelict in ending the killings, and some have even suggested police complicity. In 2010, Ciudad Juárez earned the title "most violent city in the world" with 3,100 homicides. (Juárez has about 1.5 million people. In Canada in 2010, by comparison, there were 554 homicides. Vancouver, a city comparable to Juárez in size, registered 36 homicides.) However, the use of the term femicide (or *feminicidio* in Spanish) for Juárez has been controversial for two reasons: the vast majority of Juárez's murder victims are male, and the term femicide has been applied to all murders of women in Juárez. In Guatemala, meanwhile, the end of decades of civil conflict has not created a peaceful society. Thousands of women have been murdered in that country since 2001. In 2007 alone, more than 700 women and girls were killed, many of them abducted, tortured, and sexually assaulted before their murders. As in Mexico, the Guatemalan state has permitted a climate of impunity for the perpetrators of such crimes, and families have had to endure not only inaction but also open allegations by police that their loved ones were prostitutes who "deserved" to be victimized. Nonetheless, family members have joined together to advocate for their murdered mothers, sisters, and daughters. Again, however, the majority of those murdered have been men. So why is the concept of femicide useful? While femicide cannot be applied to *every* murder of women or girls, it allows us to identify killings that target women and girls precisely because they are women and girls. Femicide is the most common of gendered hate crimes—so common, in fact, that it remains uncommon to view misogynist sexual attacks as hate crimes or, indeed, as "gendered" attacks.[98]

Occasionally, murders happen that defy any other interpretation. Such a case is the infamous 1989 Montreal Massacre at L'École Polytechnique, in which 14 female engineering students were murdered by a gunman who identified "feminists" as his target. Although, in the aftermath of the incident, many commentators denied that the massacre was anything but the work of a "sick gunman," the killings are now seen as a gendered hate crime precisely because the murderer explicitly identified the victims' sex as the reason for his activities. Similarly, the 2014 Isla Vista shootings perpetrated by Elliott Rodgers were conceived as a punishment for all of the women who "rejected" him: "The Second Phase will represent my War on Women," he wrote in his lengthy manifesto. " . . . I cannot kill every single female on earth, but I can deliver a devastating blow that will shake all of them to the core of their wicked hearts. I will attack the very girls who represent everything I hate in the female gender: The hottest sorority of UCSB." In the event, he killed more men (4) than women (2), largely because he failed to gain admission to the sorority where he had hoped to perpetrate a massacre. While not all of his murders were femicides, femicide is a useful way to describe his intent and the murders of women he perpetrated. However, femicide has not been adopted by North American reporting agencies; therefore, very few crimes that meet the definition of femicide are recorded as hate crimes.[99]

While femicide targets individuals because of their sex, other gendered hate crimes target what Ki Namaste calls "a perceived transgression of normative sex-gender relations." Such crimes tend to victimize **sexual-minority** men, women, and youth (or those perceived as such). Such acts have only recently come to be seen as hate crimes. In fact, until quite recently, men charged with assaulting or murdering a gay man could defend themselves by recourse to **homosexual panic**, a supposed enraged, out-of-control state brought on by being solicited for sex by a homosexual. Until the 1998 "gay-bashing" murder of Wyoming's Matthew Shepard, attacks on gay, lesbian, and trans people were often ignored, minimized, or even applauded. (The infamous Westboro Baptist Church picketed Shepard's funeral carrying signs that said "rot in hell.")

In late 2009, US President Barack Obama signed into law the Matthew Shepard law, which adds sexual orientation, gender identity, and disability as protected categories for the purposes of hate crime prosecution (gender was added to the list in 1994). The hate provisions in the Canadian Criminal Code, sections 318 and 319, have included sexual orientation since 2004; while gender and gender identity are not explicitly protected categories, they can be considered by judges. Such protection is clearly necessary, given the frequent victimization of sexual-minority North Americans. According to a 2005 US study of 719 self-identified lesbian, gay, and bisexual individuals, 13.1 per cent of the sample had experienced violence based on sexual orientation at least once during adult life. Gay men were the group most likely to have experienced this kind of violence, with 24.9 per cent reporting having experienced anti-gay violence. Reports of threatened violence and other forms of aggression and discrimination were also frequent; about half of respondents indicated harassment on the basis of sexual orientation. In sum, according to researcher Gregory Herek, "data indicate that approximately 20 per cent of the US sexual-minority population has experienced a crime against their person or property since age 18 based on their sexual orientation." In the US, the largest motivator of hate crimes is racial hatred (47 per cent), with sexual orientation and religion accounting for 18.6 per cent each; 58 per cent of sexual-orientation hate crimes were directed at gay men. The most recent

Canadian statistics indicate that the overall number of police-reported hate crimes is going down, but this is not the case for those related to sexual orientation. The majority (51 per cent) of hate crimes in Canada are still motivated by racial hatred, with black people most likely to be targeted. Another 28 per cent related to religious hatred, with Jews particularly vulnerable. In 2013, 16 per cent related to sexual orientation. Hate crimes related to sexual orientation were significantly more likely than those in other categories were to be violent. In Canada, violent crimes related to sexual orientation had the highest proportion of male victims (at 81 per cent); more than 80 per cent of those charged with hate crimes were also male. The link to the policing of heteronormative masculinity is clear. Despite increasing acceptance of homosexuality in North America, hate crimes against gay men and lesbians remain a serious concern. The number of hate crimes against sexual-minority North Americans, serious as it is, is dwarfed by the many such crimes perpetrated against sexual minorities throughout the world.[100]

Perhaps the most vulnerable sexual-minority group globally is transgender. Though statistical data on hate crimes against trans people are rare (in part because of constantly evolving definitions of transgender), it is clear that they are frequently victimized both globally and in North America. FBI statistics from 2014 count 69 police-reported hate crimes against trans people, with another 40 against "non-gender-conforming" people. Given the very small transgender population and the rate of underreporting, this statistic is significant. Transgender people report incredibly high rates of sexual violence, ranging from 10–59 per cent in various studies, with sexual assaults beginning at a young age. Many of these cases of sexual violence are hate crimes. One American trans interviewee said in 1999, "in my neighborhood, either they want to beat you up or they want a free blow job"; in another study from Virginia, more than half of trans participants who had experienced forced sex said they thought their gender was the reason for the incident. Some incidents are deadly, as exemplified in a US case from summer 2008. Allen Andrade, 32, met 18-year-old transwoman Angie Zapata on line. The couple met and spent three days together at Zapata's apartment before Andrade viciously attacked and murdered her. The "panic" defence was deployed at Andrade's trial—lawyers argued, "he acted in the heat of passion after discovering that Zapata was biologically male." The jury in the trial was having none of it, however, and Andrade was convicted of first-degree murder and a bias-motivated (hate) crime—the first time in the US that such a conviction was obtained in the murder of a transgender person. In December 2015, a US soldier was convicted of murdering Jennifer Laude in the Philippines in 2014 after discovering she was a transwoman. He was sentenced to 6–12 years in a Philippine prison. These convictions can never return Angie and Jennifer to their families, but send a signal that the sadly commonplace hate crimes against trans people will no longer be treated with impunity.[101]

Conclusion

Violence takes an enormous social toll not just on its victims but also on the very notion of a cohesive and healthy society. It also levies an economic toll, in the massive costs of maintaining legal systems, prisons, and police forces, and in providing care for those harmed by violence. Additionally, it represents an incalculable psychological burden.

Violence has many causes, but we cannot understand it without understanding the role of gender within it. We have to protect women and girls from a culture of violence that so often targets them. Nevertheless, we also have to protect boys "from a culture of violence that exploits their worst tendencies by reinforcing and amplifying the atavistic values of the masculine mystique."[102]

Often, biological explanations are invoked as evasive strategies. "Boys will be boys," we say, throwing up our hands in helpless resignation. However, even if all violence were biologically programmed by testosterone or the evolutionary demands of reproductive success, we still would have to ask: Are we going to organize our society to maximize this propensity for violence or to minimize it? These are political questions, and they demand political answers. "All violent feelings," wrote the great nineteenth-century British social critic John Ruskin, "produce in us a falseness in all our impressions of external things."[103] Until we transform the meaning of gender, we will continue to produce that falseness— with continued tragic consequences.

Summary

Violence remains a key problem in Canada and globally. Violence is also one of the most significant gender differences. Maleness is an important predictor of criminal involvement and violence. While the greater male tendency toward violence may be partially biologically determined, biological evidence is not a sufficient explanation. Similarly, psychoanalytic and sex role analyses offer some insight, but they are not universal. Anthropological explanations suggest that gender inequality, and an emphasis on stark gender difference, produce societies in which violence and male bravado are celebrated. Therefore, masculinity's association with violence is a gender difference associated not with biology but with gender inequality.

Nonetheless, women can and do commit violent acts and engage in criminality, but at a much lower rate. This much lower rate of criminality is matched by an even lower rate of *violent* crime; in fact, women tend to cluster in areas of minor crimes, to reoffend less, and not to escalate their criminal involvement. Still, there is evidence of increasing female violence. While women remain a minority among offenders, increasing female violence is a worrying trend, confirming that propensity to violence is not solely biological.

In youth, the general patterns of adult violence are replicated. Boys tend to be more violent both toward girls and toward other boys. Peer aggression has become a significant problem for youth, even within schools. School shootings, though rare, have attracted much media and scholarly attention; yet little attention has been paid to gender dynamics within them. Virtually every shooter has been male, and females, after school officials, are the most likely targets of shooters. Rising rates of "girl violence," meanwhile, have attracted great media scrutiny. While much of the panic is overblown, it is true that violent crimes make up a larger proportion of youth crimes than was previously the case, and that the increase in girls' violent criminality has outstripped the corresponding rate for boys. The degree of violence among youth is cause for concern and demands a gendered analysis.

The gendering of violence also occurs at the institutional and government levels. This is demonstrated by foreign policy and wartime theorizing that uses the terms of hegemonic masculinity to describe (and criticize) national actions. Sexualization in discussions of military policy is well documented. Equally well known is the tragic tendency, in a variety of conflict situations, toward the sexual assault (and, sometimes, murder) of "enemy" women and children. More recently, this tendency has affected newly sex-integrated armed forces, as suggested by the enormous number of sexual assault complaints laid by US soldiers in Iraq.

The family has been seen as a refuge from such violent tendencies. However, for too many people, the family is also a site of violence. Though women are fully capable of family violence, most family violence is perpetrated by males (husbands, fathers, sons, and brothers). Regardless of the sex of their perpetrators, such acts rest on the logic of patriarchal violence.

Intimate-partner violence still accounts for more than half of all incidents of family violence reported to police. Women far outnumber men in numbers of injuries, and their likelihood of being victimized by their ex-spouses is greater. The idea of gender symmetry recognizes that women use spousal violence too; however, it grossly distorts the nature of spousal violence, and ideas of gender symmetry rest on CTS data that "level" all forms of violence. Nature, severity, and context of spousal violence are gendered. This becomes clear when spousal homicide is considered; women are significantly more likely to be killed by their spouses than are men. Intimate-partner violence also interacts with ethnic and class issues. In addition, immigrant women may face a greater risk of spousal abuse—and are certainly made vulnerable by immigrant-specific factors. The most significant differences in levels of IPV emerge between Aboriginal and non-Aboriginal Canadians.

Violence against children is widespread all over the world and is licit (legal) in most countries. Though most North American parents favour corporal punishment, its negative effects on children have been well documented, and pediatricians warn against the practice. While most parents do not physically abuse their children, most physical abuse is associated with corporal punishment. Men are overrepresented among assaulters of children (relative to other family members). Nonetheless, mothers' presence as a significant group of accused in family-related assaults against children suggests that women are capable of using patriarchal violence against children. An ultimate form of family violence is the "honour killing," which differs from family violence in several significant ways but shares its logic of domination and control.

Domination and control are also hallmarks of sexual assault. Sexual assault has often been seen as synonymous with rape and as such has been analyzed by sociobiologists and evolutionary psychologists, who argue that it reflects a male evolutionary strategy. Cross-cultural studies of rape, however, suggest that it is a cultural phenomenon, varying widely from place to place but associated with male domination. While men and boys clearly perpetrate more assaults, survey data have indicated female perpetration may be growing. While psychologists tend to look at the processes that lead someone to become a rapist, sociologists emphasize the general "normalcy" of rapists and rape.

Sexual assault is widely reported in North America relative to other industrialized regions. Most victims of Canadian police-reported sexual assaults are children and youth. Girls are much more likely to be victimized than boys are, and virtually all perpetrators are men and male youth. Many children and youth are assaulted by male family members. Similarly, many married women report being sexually assaulted by their male partners; though such assaults have been illegal in Canada and much of the US since the 1980s, marital rape remains legal in much of the world. Marital, familial, and acquaintance sexual assault are much more common than assault by strangers. Sexual assault itself is far from strange; it is a problem not of a few sick individuals but of society.

Sexual assault interacts with racialization and other class and ethnic issues. This can be seen in the murders and disappearances of Aboriginal women and girls in Canada, which has exposed patterns of sexual victimization and, sometimes, official indifference. Recent events suggest that such indifference may be changing, thanks to efforts of families and advocates.

Indifference toward other forms of gendered violence is also changing. Horrific woman-killings are increasingly understood as femicide, a kind of killing that targets women because they are women. Other forms of violence target those perceived as gender nonconformists. Gay, lesbian, bisexual, and trans people report high levels of victimization by targeted violence. Canadian and (recently changed) US laws recognize these as hate crimes.

A society without violence may be a utopian dream, but minimizing violence should be a high priority for all of us, both within Canada and globally. A good way to start is through analysis of the ways in which violence is produced and reproduced in a gendered society.

Questions for Critical Thinking

1. What accounts for boys' and men's greater tendency to commit violent acts?
2. Do you believe that girls and women are becoming "more violent"? What factors limit and/or encourage female violence?
3. Are "honour killings" a form of domestic violence, in your opinion?
4. Some argue that the term "sexual assault" has less power than the older term "rape." What do you think of the change in terminology?
5. Is rape a crime of sex or a crime of violence?
6. What kind of killings of women and girls would you consider gendered hate crimes? Of men and boys?

Key Terms

active shooter
Conflict Tactics Scale (CTS)
corporal punishment
familicide
family-class immigrants
femicide
gender symmetry
homicide
homosexual panic
"honour" killing

intimate-partner violence (IPV)
intimate terrorism
military sexual trauma (MST)
Montreal Massacre
patriarchal violence
rape
sexual assault
sexual-minority
spousal violence
stalking

Epilogue
The Future of Gender in a Globalizing World

"A Degendered Society?"

The principle which regulates the existing social relations between the two sexes—the legal subordination of one sex to the other—is wrong in itself, and now one of the chief hindrances to human improvement; and . . . it ought to be replaced by a principle of perfect equality, admitting no power or privilege on the one side, nor disability on the other.

—John Stuart Mill, *The Subjection of Women (1869)*

Early in the twenty-first century, we live in a world that would have astonished John Stuart Mill and his contemporaries; we have transformed gender relations in ways that Mill cannot have even imagined. We now stand upon the brink of pure possibility, looking into an uncharted expanse of the future. Among the many urgent questions we confront as human beings—some of which concern our very future as a species—we now must consider: What kind of society do we want to live in? What will be the gender arrangements of that society?

This book has argued that women and men are more alike than we are different, that we're not at all from different planets. We've argued that it is gender inequality that produces the differences we *do* observe—and that that inequality also produces the cultural impulse to search for such differences, even when there is little or no basis for them in reality. We've also argued that gender is not a property of individuals, which is accomplished by socialization, but rather a set of relationships produced in our social interactions with one another and within gendered institutions.

This book has presented evidence of a significant gender convergence within North America over the past half-century. Whether we look at sexual behaviour, friendship dynamics, efforts to balance work and family life, or women's and men's experiences and aspirations in education or the workplace, we find the gender gap growing ever smaller. (One exception to this process, as we saw in Chapter 13, is violence.)

Many of our ideas about gender have rested on ideas about biology and the body. As we have seen, much of the research on biologically rooted sex difference is problematic to say the least. Moreover, the body has arguably become less significant and more malleable than ever before in human history. Our ability to change sex is one clear example of this. So is the widespread use, in North America and much of the global north, of birth control. Additionally, what about the growth of Internet-mediated communication, which permits the adoption of completely new identities without links to our embodiment? These are all examples of how the relationship between sex and gender is being broken down.

Judith Lorber makes a case for degendering. She suggests that multiplying the number of gender categories we use is one way to do so; a deliberate practice of degendering is another. Lorber's first recommendation is happening, albeit slowly: it is increasingly common for forms to permit a choice other than "M or F." However, why do we need to specify gender at all? Some call for the revision of forms to include gender only when that serves a very particular purpose. More than a decade after Lorber, degendering is accordingly getting underway. However, some scholars point out that because gender continues to matter (for example, in victimization by violence) it is critical that we collect and analyze data with an eye to gender. Many scholars point out that rather than focusing on the elimination of gender itself, we should start by eliminating inequality, allowing difference to recede until the variations among us—by race, age, ethnicity, sexuality, and, yes, biological sex—prove largely epiphenomenal.[1]

This may seem a rarefied debate given the persistent gender issues in Canadian society. The intractability of sexual violence is one example; so too is the irrefutable evidence of continuing bias against women and other marginalized groups, particularly Aboriginal and racialized people. Globally speaking, it is even more absurd to speak of a severing of the relationship between sex and gender, or of degendering processes. Globally, gender inequality remains a massive problem. Poverty, maternal and infant mortality, domestic and sexual violence, abuse and neglect of girl children, differential education rates, exploitation in employment, and an absence of reproductive choices characterize much of the world.

Within Canada, the importance of gender convergence is overshadowed by persistent inequalities between Aboriginal and non-Aboriginal Canadians (and between visible minorities and others), poverty, discrimination, precarious employment of many women (particularly immigrants), as well as a plethora of other gendered issues.

In some cases, gendered transformations in the global North have brought ambivalent changes to the global South. For example, as North American women have entered the workforce, many have delegated responsibility for daily child care to women from lower socio-economic groups and to immigrant women (many admitted as immigrants for precisely this purpose). While many North American families struggle with poverty, many others have experienced a growth in disposable income because of women's earning power. This disposable income has in part fuelled the growth in consumption that brings employment to a new "flexible" global workforce made up, disproportionately, of young women who work in product assembly in countries around the world. Finally, the tremendous growth of tourism in the late twentieth century has not only brought economic growth to many regions but has fuelled the mobility of sexual exploitation, from trafficking to sex tourism. We can therefore no longer divorce our countries from the gendered realities of the rest of the world. While we highlight gender convergence and the many dramatic changes in gender, we must also acknowledge that the gendered society, with its many inequalities, is alive and well in Canada and abroad—and that globalization has in fact produced new constellations of gender inequality.[2]

Yet there are signs of change, growth, and convergence everywhere. Throughout the world, the dawn of the twenty-first century saw increasing demands for women's rights, which have officially become a global priority. Domestic and sexual violence laws have been reformed in many nations, and civil-society groups are demanding not only legal reforms but social ones.

Extremists lament changes to gendered rules as "defeminizing" women. If submission is, as we have seen, one of the traits most associated with femininity globally, then critics are right; women *are* being defeminized. The elimination of gender inequality *will* eliminate many of the differences we observe (or think we see) between the sexes. Is this such a bad thing? Many of the gender differences we identify amount to an arbitrary dividing of human potentialities. Love, tenderness, nurturance, and dependence; competence, ambition, assertion, and autonomy—these are *human* qualities, and all human beings—both women and men—should have equal access to them. What a strange notion, indeed, that such capacities should be labelled as masculine or feminine, when they are so deeply human and when both women and men are capable of a full range of feelings.

Strange and also a little sad. "Perhaps nothing is so depressing an index of the inhumanity of the male supremacist mentality as the fact that the more genial human traits are assigned to the underclass: affection, response to sympathy, kindness, cheerfulness," was the way feminist writer Kate Millett put it in her landmark book, *Sexual Politics*, first published in 1969.[3]

So much has changed since then, including enormous changes that will only accelerate in the next few decades, both in North America and around the world. The society of the third millennium will increasingly degender traits and behaviours.

Such a process may sound naively optimistic, but the signs of change are everywhere around us. In fact, the historical evidence points exactly in that direction. In Canada and elsewhere, the twentieth century witnessed an amazing transformation in the lives, roles, and rights of women—possibly the most significant transformation in gender relations in world history. From the rights to vote and work, asserted early in the century, to the rights to enter every conceivable workplace, educational institution, and the military in the latter half, women shook the foundations of the gendered society. By the end of the twentieth century, Canadian women had accomplished half a revolution—a transformation of their opportunities to be workers and mothers.

The second half of the transformation of gender is just beginning and may be far more difficult to accomplish than the first. That's because the transformation of the twenty-first century involves the transformation of men's lives. Some men (and a few women) express their frustration and confusion by hoping and praying for a return to the old gender regime, the very separation of spheres that made both women *and* men unhappy.

However, the long-term direction of the gendered society, in the new century and the new millennium, is for women and men to become more *equal*, for those traits and behaviours previously labelled as masculine and feminine—competence and compassion, ambition and affection—to be labelled as distinctly human qualities accessible to both women and men who are grown-up enough to claim them. The direction of society is also, increasingly, to question the very significance of labels such as "man" and "woman." Growing numbers of trans people refuse the connection between biological sex and gender; many of them, and an increasing number of people who identify as gender-queer or gender-neutral, refuse the gender binary altogether. Both of these new directions suggest a form of gender proteanism—a temperamental and psychological flexibility, the ability to adapt to one's environment with a full range of emotions and abilities. The protean self, articulated by psychiatrist Robert Jay Lifton, is a self that can embrace difference, contradiction, and complexity, a self that is mutable and flexible in a rapidly changing world.[4] Such a transformation is urgently needed if people all over the world are to embrace the challenges and opportunities of our century. Our top priority can no longer be to uphold the systems of gendered domination that have persisted for so long. Rather, we must focus on our lives and potential as human beings with responsibilities to the earth and one another, and with full rights and dignity. We must focus on building a fully human society, not a gendered one.

Glossary

ablism Prejudice on the basis of ability, with two main features: first, ignoring or rendering invisible of people with disabilities, and second, viewing people with disabilities as fundamentally *defined* and *limited* by disabilities. Ablism has obvious links to overt discrimination against the disabled, but this is not its only form (also **ableism**). (Chapter 11)

Aboriginal A member of one of three indigenous groups (Inuit, First Nations, and Métis) recognized by the Canadian Constitution. Note that many Aboriginal people now use the term "Indigenous" to describe their origins and identity. (Chapter 6)

active shooter An individual actively attempting to shoot people in a confined or populated area. (Chapter 13)

Adonis complex Harrison Pope's term for the increasing body image concerns and poor self-image seen among boys and men, manifesting as eating disorders and muscle dysmorphia. (Chapter 11)

alliance theorists Those who study the constitution of society from the perspective of family formation, in particular emphasizing how women "circulate" as marriage partners in a given society, and how acceptable marriage partners are defined as "not-kin" in varying ways. (Chapter 4)

alyha Among the Mojave people, a boy who underwent a transformation to the social role of a female. (Chapter 4)

androgen insensitivity syndrome (AIS) A defect on the A chromosome that impairs androgen reception, preventing the XY fetus from responding to testosterone. Chromosomally male, AIS children are born resembling girls, and are generally raised as girls. In many cases they are "diagnosed" as intersex only when they fail to menstruate. (Chapter 2)

androgenital syndrome (AGS) The previously used name for **congenital adrenal hyperplasia (CAH)**. (Chapter 2)

androgyny For Sandra Bem, "the combined presence of the socially valued, stereotypic, feminine, and masculine characteristics." Bem originally argued that the most androgynous individuals were psychologically the healthiest. (Chapter 3)

beauty myth According to Naomi Wolf, a system of social control that encourages women to focus on their appearances to the detriment of full development of their humanity. Wolf identifies the development of this myth as a retrenchment of male domination in the face of women's increasing equality in the twentieth century. (Chapter 11)

berdache The term traditionally used by anthropologists to describe third-gender individuals of male sex. The term "female berdache" is also sometimes used in anthropological literature. This term is regarded as offensive by First Nations and other Aboriginal people (see **Two-Spirited**). (Chapter 4)

biological determinism The view that the behaviour and character of an organism, a group, or a system are determined by biological factors. Most careful scientists shun true determinism, but determinist tendencies can be found both among scientists and in popular culture. (Chapters 1 and 2)

biological essentialism Closely related to the idea of biological determinism; an argument that rests on the naturalness of social relations and their rootedness in biology. (Chapter 2)

bisexuality A fixed sexual orientation involving sexual attraction to both men and women. Debates still rage over the existence of the phenomenon and its definition. (Chapter 12)

bona fide occupational requirement (BFOR) A true requirement of a job, meriting a possibly discriminatory effect. For example, to work in a warehouse, one might have to meet height and strength requirements that have the effect of discriminating against many women, some ethnic groups, and disabled people. If the requirement is a BFOR, the discrimination is legal. (Chapter 8)

bottom surgery In the trans community, any of a number of gender-validating surgeries performed on the genitalia. (Chapter 11)

breadwinner An individual whose earnings support dependants. This term arose in the nineteenth century, when most families relied upon multiple sources of income. It has always been gendered; even when women supported families, they have rarely been seen as breadwinners. (Chapter 6)

bride price A sum of money paid by a groom to his wife's family, generally thought to exist in order to compensate the bride's family for the loss of the daughter's productive labour and for her social value; the practice is particularly common in some Asian and African societies. (Chapter 10)

bromance An exceptionally close and intense, but non-sexual, bond between two heterosexual men. (Chapter 10)

Brony A male fan (adult or youth) of *My Little Pony*, a term created by combining the words "bro" and "pony." (Chapter 9)

bukkake A form of pornography (originally Japanese) that emphasizes the use of a woman by many men, with its most important feature being communal ejaculation onto the woman's face. A recent Google search of this term generated more than 30 million hits. (Chapter 12)

bullying Repeatedly doing or saying hurtful things to a person with intent to harm. Unlike fighting, bullying occurs within a context of a power imbalance (real or perceived) between the bully and the victim. (Chapter 7)

castration anxiety For Freud, a deep-seated fear of castration arising when boys see female genitalia and conclude that girls and women have been castrated. Hence, "if it happened to Mom,

it can happen to me!" Castration anxiety is most important during the Oedipal crisis. (Chapter 3)

chick lit A literary genre that came to prominence in the 1990s. Chick lit features the adventures (romantic and otherwise) of young, single, working women. (Chapter 9)

child poverty The phenomenon whereby those under the age of 18 live below the low-income line as established by the **LICO**. (Chapter 6)

chosen family A group of individuals, usually not related through biological or kin ties, who provide emotional commitment, intimacy, and support; chosen families have been particularly important in the LGBTQ community. (Chapter 10)

circumcision The excision of the foreskin of the penis to permanently expose the glans. The term "female circumcision" is sometimes used to describe procedures more analogous to the removal of the penis than to what we call "circumcision" in males (see **FGM/FGC**). Though circumcision exists in many societies, its routine use on infants in North America is being abandoned. (Chapter 4)

cisgender A relatively recent term referring to those whose gender identities match their assigned sex at birth; also used by some to refer to anyone whose presentations and behaviours conform to gender norms. (Chapter 11)

clan A group of people united by kinship, whether actual or symbolic. In First Nations societies before European contact, clans were the basic social unit and often connoted not only kinship but particular social roles and responsibilities. (Chapter 6)

clitoridectomy The excision of the clitoris, sometimes performed on girls with masculinized genitalia. (Chapter 2)

cognitive development theory A theory, originally defined by Jean Piaget, arguing that mental development takes place in a set of relatively orderly and discrete stages involving greater complexity at each level. Lawrence Kohlberg applied this to gender acquisition, arguing that children "learn" gender cognitively, according to their level of reasoning at different stages. (Chapter 3)

coital imperative The idea that "real" heterosexual sexual contact must include penetration and male orgasm, especially through vaginal intercourse. (Chapter 12)

colourism Within racialized communities, a system that privileges and values lighter skin and rewards lighter-skinned people. It may also privilege certain other features, for example, "good" (straighter, non-kinky) hair in African-descent communities. It should be noted, however, that within "white" culture, there is also "good" (blond) hair. (Chapter 11)

common-law marriage A system of customary marriage by which people who present themselves as spouses and fulfil certain criteria (established provincially) are entitled to legal recognition, and increasingly, all of the rights and responsibilities of legally wedded spouses. (Chapter 6)

companionate marriage An ideal of marriage as a loving partnership, which became more common after the late eighteenth century and eventually implied free choice and "marriage for love." Not to be confused with current practices of egalitarian, childless, or dissoluble partnerships sometimes described under the same name. (Chapter 10)

compulsory heterosexuality A theory first articulated by Adrienne Rich, who described heterosexuality as a social institution based on the assumption that heterosexuality was innate and all other forms of sexual expression either deviant or simply invisible. (Chapter 12)

confirmation bias The phenomenon whereby a few cases of the expected behaviour confirm a belief or theory, especially when the behaviour is attention-getting or widely reported. (Chapter 5)

Conflict Tactics Scale (CTS) A survey tool designed by Murray Straus to measure intimate-partner violence. It is both the most widely used and the most controversial measure of IPV. (Chapter 13)

congenital adrenal hyperplasia (CAH) One of a number of conditions producing intersex children. In CAH, chromosomally female fetuses undergo abnormal hormonal development in utero and are born with masculinized genitalia, though they have the potential to bear children. Genetically male fetuses are also affected, though not in ways that create ambiguity of sex (see also **androgenital syndrome** [AGS]). (Chapter 2)

consciousness-raising A technique of analysis, pioneered by North American feminists and Latin American political activists, that emphasized raising awareness of social and political issues through small-group discussion of everyday issues and experiences. (Chapter 5)

corporal punishment Physical punishment inflicted upon the body of someone. Historically, corporal punishment was licit and widely used against a variety of groups, including wives, slaves, employees, soldiers, and servants. Corporal punishment of children remains legal in North America (though not in some European countries). (Chapter 13)

couvade The term used by anthropologists to describe a variety of rituals observed by men whose wives are pregnant in order to "mimic" pregnancy. Men perform the same acts and adhere to the same restrictions as their pregnant wives and may even feign morning sickness or childbirth itself. (Chapter 4)

creaky voice A low and vibrating vocal tone commonly heard among men, particularly on radio and in advertising and recently spreading among young women to the consternation of some. (Chapter 10)

cult of compulsive masculinity Talcott Parsons' theorized result of the long period of contact with femininity characteristic of boys in modern nuclear families. Because boys must rebel against femininity, being a "bad boy" becomes a way of establishing a masculine identity. For Parsons, this "cult" is associated with hypermasculine and/or violent behaviour. (Chapter 3)

cultural determinism The belief that the cultures in which we are raised determine our character, personalities, emotional lives, and behaviours. (Compare with **biological determinism**.) (Chapter 4)

cultural relativism The belief, developed and named by anthropologists, that any individual's beliefs and behaviours should be understood in the context of his or her own culture rather than as the product of innate or universal tendencies and values. (Chapter 4)

culturally scripted Based on a pattern of speech and interaction that is normative within a particular group or culture. (Chapter 10)

cyberbullying Using technology to harass, threaten, or harm another individual (see also **bullying**). (Chapter 7)

cybersex Sexual encounters effected through the Internet, often called "cybering." Such encounters can include the exchange of explicit messages (often accompanied by real-life masturbation); use of webcams; sexual acts between avatars; and even, though very rarely, sexual stimulation of the body through remotely controlled devices (see also **teledildonics**). (Chapter 12)

date rape Non-consensual intercourse forced on someone by an acquaintance, either through physical force or through coercion. (Chapter 12)

deceptive distinctions Differences between men and women that appear to be gender differences but may be the result of different power positions within society. (Chapter 1)

descent theorists In anthropology, those who study kinship; in particular, they examine the ways in which cultures think about and structure consanguineal ("blood") relationships. (Chapter 4)

deviance neutralization Rationalization strategies engaged in to minimize the extent to which one deviates from a real or perceived norm. For example, a woman who worries about how her income affects her husband's self-esteem might claim that his work pays less but is higher-level than hers or might actually minimize her earnings. (Chapter 8)

difference feminism In contrast to **liberal feminism**, which emphasizes the equality or sameness of men and women, this tendency within feminism focuses on the differences between men and women, calling for a valuation of women's distinct traits and abilities and, in some cases, focusing on separation from the world and values of men (see also **essentialist feminism**). (Chapter 5)

differential socialization Associated with the "nurture" side of the nature–nurture debate, this perspective asserts that men and women are different because they are socialized differently from birth, therefore acquiring "masculine" or "feminine" traits, behaviours, and attitudes. (Chapter 1)

disability As defined by the World Health Organization, "an umbrella term, covering impairments, activity limitations, and participation restrictions. An impairment is a problem in body function or structure; an activity limitation is a difficulty encountered by an individual in executing a task or action; while a participation restriction is a problem experienced by an individual in involvement in life situations. Thus disability is a complex phenomenon, reflecting an interaction between features of a person's body and features of the society in which he or she lives." (Chapter 11)

Divorce Act Federal legislation introduced in 1968, and revised in 1985, governing the provision of divorce in Canada. (Chapter 6)

dopamine A brain chemical or neurotransmitter associated with pleasure. (Chapter 10)

double standard A moral code that prescribes different things for different groups; most commonly associated with differential (and conflicting) sexual standards prescribed to men and women. (Chapter 12)

dowry A sum of money settled upon a bride by her family, or transferred to her groom, at marriage. (Chapter 10)

doxing The practice of researching, and publishing on the Internet, an individual's personal or private information. Often, those who dox have malicious intent, though doxing is sometimes a form of vigilantism. (Chapter 9)

ecofeminism Theories and activism linking feminism with environmental concerns. Ecofeminists see male domination and environmental degradation as related phenomena. (Chapter 5)

educational premium The monetary return one receives by pursuing further education. This can be calculated statistically based on average earnings for people with varying degrees of education. (Chapter 7)

ego A component of Freud's concept of the psyche. It is the rational, problem-solving portion of our personality that translates **id** impulses into effective strategies for gratification. (Chapter 3)

Electra complex Carl Jung's name for what Freud called the "feminine Oedipus attitude." The term describes a girl's situation during the Oedipal crisis, when she, like the boy, discovers the anatomical distinction between the sexes and believes that she and her mother have been castrated. Experiencing "penis envy" as a result, she first transfers her desire to her father, competing with her mother, and eventually to the desire for a baby of her own (see **penis envy**). (Chapter 3)

emotional labour As identified by Arlie Hoschild, the performance of workplace tasks primarily aimed at displaying agreeable emotion (pleasantness, friendliness) and producing emotional states (comfort, ease) in others. While emotional labour is required in many workplaces, female-dominated jobs (secretarial work, flight attendance, service) carry the heaviest

emotional-labour burden, and there is evidence that female workers in any workplace are expected to perform more emotional labour than men. (Chapter 8)

emotion work The work performed to maintain emotional ties and harmony, to produce comfort and ease in family members, and generally, to make the family a "haven in a heartless world." The difference between emotional labour and emotion work is that the former is performed as part of an employment relationship, while emotion work (sometimes called emotional work) is performed in the private sphere. (Chapters 6 and 10)

emphasized femininity R.W. Connell's model of female gender ideology, which asserts that femininity is displayed as compliance with gender inequality and is "oriented to accommodating the interests and desires of men." (Chapter 1)

employment equity A term coined in the 1980s by Justice Rosalie Abella to describe a process of planning for full workplace integration of Canada's four equity-seeking groups (women, Aboriginal people, people with disabilities, and visible minorities). Employment equity distinguishes itself from US-style affirmative action. (Chapter 8)

equality For the purposes of this text, sameness of treatment and freedom from discrimination in the form of denial of rights that others enjoy. (Chapter 8)

equity For the purposes of this text, fairness of treatment, which may mean that different individuals are treated differently to ensure that they are able to participate fully in society. (Chapter 8)

essentialist feminism See **difference feminism**. (Chapter 5)

estrus In most female mammals, the reproductive cycle that produces periods of sexual receptivity (often described as "heat") that coincide with ovulation; generally these periods of estrus are accompanied by external signals (visual, olfactory, etc.). (Chapter 2)

ethic of care Carol Gilligan's term for the mode of moral reasoning she found more prevalent in women than in men. This "different voice" makes moral judgments on the basis of the interdependence of human beings and the effects of actions on them (see **ethic of justice**). (Chapter 3)

ethic of justice Carol Gilligan's term for the mode of reasoning she sees as more characteristic of men and of institutions in Western society; ethic of justice describes moral reasoning based on principle and abstract concepts of justice (see **ethic of care**). (Chapter 3)

ethical porn Pornography produced under ethical conditions, meaning that performers are fairly paid and fully consenting, and that their health and safety are protected. (Chapter 9)

eugenics The theory that natural selection can be assisted through conscious efforts to improve human populations, either by preventing the production of the "unfit" or by increasing the health and fitness of reproductive populations. (Chapter 2)

evolutionary psychology The field of study that studies and explains human psychology and mind as the result of evolutionary adaptation. Like sociobiology, evolutionary psychology uses studies of animal behaviour to understand human psychology. (Chapter 2)

expressive A term used to describe traits associated with co-operation, warmth, sensitivity, and communication. (Chapter 10)

expressive roles According to Talcott Parsons, roles, existing to perpetuate the kinship system, that demand tenderness and nurturing (see **instrumental roles**). (Chapter 3)

extended family A term used to refer to kin beyond the nuclear family, whether they share the same household or not. (Chapter 6)

external world The fourth component of Freud's notion of the psyche; the external world is experienced as frequently thwarting the **id**'s desire. (Chapter 3)

familicide The murder of one's spouse and at least one of one's children. (Chapter 13)

family-class immigrants According to Canadian immigration law, those who come to Canada through sponsorship by a spouse, common-law partner, conjugal partner, parent, or other eligible relative. (Chapter 13)

family-friendly workplace policies Policies and workplace cultural changes that reduce conflict between workers' employment and their family responsibilities. Examples include child care, support for breastfeeding mothers, provisions for eldercare, flexible working arrangements such as job sharing or teleworking, leave provisions, and employee assistance programs. (Chapter 8)

family wage A term developed in the nineteenth century to describe a wage sufficient to allow a male breadwinner to support a wife and children. (Chapter 8)

fat-shaming Criticism, harassment, and bullying of overweight and obese people, usually focused on the appearance of their bodies or their eating behaviours. (Chapter 11)

female genital cutting/female genital mutilation (FGC/FGM) A number of practices that involve the alteration of the female genitalia in forms ranging from the removal of the hood of the clitoris (analogous to male circumcision) to infibulation. The term female genital mutilation is preferred by some scholars, while others argue that it places a stigma on women who have undergone the procedure and on cultures that practise it. People of this opinion prefer the term female genital cutting. (Chapter 4)

female to male (FTM) A transgender man (see also **transmen**). (Chapter 11)

femicide Literally, the murder of a woman. Scholars generally use it to refer to a killing that targets someone because she is female, though those who use the term vary in the breadth of their definitions. (Chapter 13)

feminist pornography Pornography produced ethically and from a feminist perspective: that is, respectful to women, made to appeal to women, contesting gender inequality, and sexually empowering for women. (Chapter 9)

fetishized In this context, to be made into an object of habitual erotic fixation. (Chapter 11)

first-person shooter A video-game genre focused on shooting in which one plays "through the eyes" or from the visual perspective of an avatar. (Chapter 9)

first-wave feminism A social movement that lasted from approximately 1850 to the end of the First World War. While first-wave feminism emphasized women's legal status and, eventually, suffrage, first-wave activists took on many social issues. (Chapter 5)

FTM See **female to male** (see also **transmen**). (Chapter 11)

functionalism A school of thought that maintains that the sex-based division of labour arose because it was necessary for the survival of early human societies. Some functionalists also argue that the preservation of the division of labour might be an evolutionary imperative. (Chapter 4)

furries Those who participate in the "furry" subculture, which focuses on adopting the identities of anthropomorphic animal characters. Furries may dress in "fur suits" in real life or inhabit anthropomorphic animal avatars online. Some furries identify as non-human animals. (Chapter 12)

Gamergate A 2014 controversy involving the harassment of high-profile women in the gaming industry, primarily through the use of social media. The controversy called attention to continued conflicts within the gaming community over issues of sexism and racism. (Chapter 9)

gaming The playing of video games on consoles, on PCs, or online. (In Canada, the term "gaming" as used by governments refers to legal gambling, which is not discussed in this text.) (Chapter 9)

gender The meanings attached to the anatomical differences between men and women, or, according to feminist theorist Joan Scott, "a way of referring to the social construction of the relationship between the sexes." (Chapter 1)

gender complementarity The idea that men and women have distinct talents, characters, roles, and spheres of influence that are not ranked hierarchically (that is, in a system of male dominance). (Chapter 6)

gender constancy Lawrence Kohlberg's concept to explain children's realization, at approximately age six, that gender is permanent and fixed. (Chapter 3)

gender divisions According to Joan Acker, the ways in which "ordinary organizational practices produce the gender patterning of jobs, wages, and hierarchies, power and subordination." (Chapter 5)

gender dysphoria A psychiatric category describing persistent discomfort with one's biological sex. (Chapter 11)

gender images According to Joan Acker, symbols and images that "explain, express, reinforce, or sometimes oppose [gender] divisions." For example, symbols and images of workers in a given industry may reinforce the view that only men can perform such work. (Chapter 5)

gender intensification Two linked phenomena of adolescence: (a) increased pressure to conform to gendered expectations; and (b) an increased rigidity regarding gender norms. (Chapter 7)

gender schema An understanding regarding gender and gender roles, allowing one to assess traits, behaviours, personalities, and occupations as "for males" or "for females." This idea is important to both Kohlberg's **cognitive development theory** and Bem's **gender schema theory**. (Chapter 3)

gender schema theory As developed by Sandra Bem through her use of the Bem Sex Role Inventory (BSRI), the idea that though children do develop ideas of gender through gender schemas, adults vary in the rigidity of their schemas. The healthiest individuals, Bem argued, were those with less polarized views of gender. (Chapter 3)

gender similarities hypothesis According to Janet Hyde, the hypothesis that men and women are "similar on most, but not all, psychological variables." This contrasts with generally held prejudices and stereotypes of "interplanetary" difference. Hyde argues that evidence from meta-analyses supports the gender similarities hypothesis. (Chapter 3)

gender symmetry In studies of intimate-partner violence, the concept of relative "balance" in woman-to-man and man-to-woman violence. This theory has been powerfully debunked by Russell Dobash and others. (Chapter 13)

gender verification See **sex testing**. (Chapter 11)

gendered society Any society in which social institutions reproduce and reinforce dominant definitions of gender and "discipline" those who deviate from these definitions. (Chapter 1)

glass ceiling Barriers (often informal, unconscious, or invisible) to the advancement of a qualified person within a given organization, solely on the basis of that person's sex or minority status. (Chapter 8)

glass cellar Warren Farrell's term for the clustering of male workers within hazardous occupations. (Chapter 8)

glass escalator The phenomenon whereby men in female-dominated occupations experience preferential hiring and promotion. (Chapter 8)

hegemonic In this book, something that is upheld as the model for all in a given society; hegemonic ideals may be contested, but cannot be ignored because of their cultural power and ubiquity. (Chapter 1)

hegemonic masculinity A theory developed in the 1980s, most notably by R.W. Connell, to explain male gender ideology. There may be many versions of masculinity operating in a culture, but only one is "culturally honoured" or hegemonic, and other masculinities are organized under it in a hierarchical fashion. This theory emphasizes competition among men for power and dominance within systems of gender inequality or patriarchy. (Chapter 1)

heterosexuality As identified in the late 1800s, a fixed and enduring attraction (emotional, romantic, and sexual) to partners of the other sex. (Compare with **homosexuality**.) (Chapter 12)

hidden curriculum The lessons and rules learned in school that are not part of what is formally transmitted by the teachers and the official curriculum. (Chapter 7)

hijras In India, biological males or intersex people who adopt female social identities. Hijras once formed a distinct caste and now constitute a socially marginalized community that nonetheless has sacred and religious significance (and, as of 2009, legal recognition in India and Pakistan). (Chapter 4)

homicide The killing of a human being by another; both murder and manslaughter are forms of homicide. (Chapter 13)

homophily The tendency to bond with individuals like oneself, particularly, for purposes of this text, in terms of sex, gender, and sexual orientation. (Chapter 6)

homophobia An exaggerated fear and/or hatred of homosexuals and homosexuality. (Chapter 10)

homosexual panic A purported state of psychotic rage brought on by receiving unwanted homosexual advances. Homosexual panic has been successfully used as a defence against criminal charges (including murder) in a variety of nations. (Chapter 13)

homosexuality As identified in the late 1800s, a fixed and enduring attraction (emotional, romantic, and sexual) to partners of the same sex. (Compare with **heterosexuality**.) (Chapter 12)

"honour" killing Family murder, often involving multi-party collusion or multiple perpetrators. These murders target someone, almost always a girl or woman, perceived to have brought shame upon the family. (Chapter 13)

hooking up A sexual encounter between two people who may or may not know one another as friends or acquaintances, and who may or may not engage in sex more than once; whatever its other variations, hooking up implies a casual sexual encounter without commitment to a relationship. (Chapter 12)

horizontal segregation Segregation within occupations in different fields that are roughly similar in terms of education and skill, for example secretarial work and truck driving. (Chapter 8)

hostile environment Originally an American legal category that describes a workplace where workers are subjected to sexual harassment and therefore fear the workplace. The concept is easily transferred to schools. (Chapter 7)

hostile-environment sexual harassment The creation of a threatening and hostile atmosphere aimed at making women (or others) feel unwelcome, unsafe, and compromised. (Chapter 8)

hwame Among the Mojave people, a girl who underwent transformation to a male social role. (Chapter 4)

hypermasculinity The exaggerated display of or adherence to behaviours, traits, and beliefs seen as masculine. (Chapter 4)

id A component of Freud's concept of the psyche. It represents basic animal needs, and "knows" only that it wants gratification. It lacks both morality and the means to get what it wants. (Chapter 3)

identity politics Politics based not on belief systems, party politics, or ideology, but rather on the interests and identities of groups. In contrast to older liberal systems that permitted inclusion on the basis of "universal" concepts (such as citizenship and "mankind"), identity politics focuses on inclusion of groups as distinctive. (Chapter 5)

imperial manhood A concept that linked "manliness" to one's duty to the British Empire and to the success and superiority of British culture; this idea had strong effects on education in the nineteenth century. (Chapter 7)

Indian Act Federal legislation of 1876, revised periodically since then, that governs and defines registered "Indians" (First Nations) and their reserves. (Chapter 6)

infibulation A practice, generally performed on girls, that involves the removal of the clitoris and much of the tissue of the external genitalia, after which the vaginal opening is either stitched or held together with thorns until it heals into a closed structure with only a small opening to permit urination and menstruation. (Chapter 4)

institutional gender neutrality The idea that while people have gender, institutions are gender-neutral (rather than being the product of historical and social constructions in which gender played a great role). The assumption that institutions are gender-neutral can obscure the importance of gender within them. (Chapter 1)

institutions Structures governing the behaviour of individuals and ensuring the society's smooth functioning. Though institutions are everchanging, they nonetheless have a permanence or longevity that exceeds that of the individual. The study and theorizing of institutions is central to the social sciences, and particularly to sociology. Sociologists identify five primary institutions (family, religion, school, media, and peers) and innumerable social ("secondary") institutions. These might be formal—clearly locatable and often governmental or legally constituted (e.g., law or banking). Other institutions are informal—customary and based in behaviour (e.g., politeness or civility). An institution might partake of both of these characteristics, as when we discuss the "institution of marriage." (Chapter 5)

instrumental A term describing traits associated with competition, assertiveness, and action. (Chapter 10)

instrumental roles For Talcott Parsons, roles that exist to perpetuate the occupational system. They demand rationality, autonomy, and competitiveness (see **expressive roles**). (Chapter 3)

intensive mothering According to Sharon Hays, a set of mothering ideals and behaviours that emphasize the mother's primary responsibility for the child; the desirability of full-time mothering; the undesirability of maternal employment and non-maternal care; and the mother's intense and focused attention to her children's needs and well-being. (Chapter 6)

interplanetary theory The idea that men are from Mars and women are from Venus, or that men and women are "opposites" who exhibit complete and universal gender difference. (Chapter 1)

intersectionality The analysis of "intersecting" (multiple) identities and forms of discrimination. Intersectionality theory holds that no one form of discrimination (sexism, for example), can be understood as operating independently from other forms of discrimination such as racism, ablism, homophobia, or ageism (among others). Nor can an identity such as "woman" exist independent from other group categories. (Chapter 5)

intersex/intersexuals People affected by hormonal and chromosomal disorders leading to some degree of ambiguity in biological sex. In the last third of the twentieth century, at least some intersex people were subjected to radical and aggressive interventions to "re-create" them as "properly" sexed individuals. They were also studied for evidence of the biological basis of gendered behaviour. (Chapter 2)

intimacy The feeling of closeness, warmth, and relationship with another person. (Chapter 10)

intimate-partner violence (IPV) Physical, sexual, and emotional abuse and/or threats directed against an intimate partner, whether in a marital, common-law, or dating relationship. IPV may occur within heterosexual or non-heterosexual relationships. (Chapter 13)

intimate terrorism Within a domestic context, coercive power and control that may include sexual, physical, economic, and emotional abuse. In an intimate-terrorism situation, one partner (usually male) controls or attempts to control all aspects of the life of the other partner (usually female). (Chapter 13)

invisibility of privilege The idea that those who are dominant in a society may not be aware of their dominance or special status but can see themselves as "universal" human beings or citizens. Because of the invisibility of privilege, people may not be aware of the extent of discrimination and may become angry when confronted with evidence or assertions of racism or sexism (see **privilege**). (Chapter 1)

IPV See **intimate-partner violence**. (Chapter 13)

Kinsey scale A seven-point scale measuring sexual orientation on which research subjects can be placed by way of a questionnaire. The scale was first published by Alfred Kinsey in his 1948 study of male sexual behaviour. (Chapter 12)

labour force participation The condition of either being employed or being unemployed but seeking work. The labour force participation rate is usually measured as a percentage of the population between 16 and 65. (Chapter 8)

lad lit A literary genre sometimes seen as the less successful "little brother" of **chick lit**. Lad lit highlights the coming to adulthood of young men who are often grappling with self-doubt or confusion about the meaning of manhood. (Chapter 9)

lad magazine One of many magazines launched in the 1990s and after 2000 that focus on "sexy" photos of women (sometimes semi-nude) and typically "masculine" content concerning sports, alcohol, cars and consumer products, and sex. (Chapter 9)

lateralized Describing the relative domination of one brain hemisphere over another or, more commonly, the location of a function (for example, language) in one hemisphere of the brain. In popular culture, this is often grossly oversimplified to describe individuals as "left-brain" or "right-brain" people. (Chapter 2)

lesbian bed death According to Pepper Schwartz, who coined the term, the phenomenon whereby lesbian couples have less sex than any other form of couple, generally because their sexual activity declines precipitously within long-term relationships. (Chapter 12)

lesbian feminism A social movement within 1970s feminism that contributed a critique of heterosexuality as an institution and, in some cases, advocated lesbianism or separatism as a political option. (Chapter 5)

lesbian, gay, bisexual, transgender, queer, questioning (LGBTQ) This is, today, the most commonly used term to encompass all non-heterosexuals. Some people, particularly in Canada, add "2S" to include **Two-Spirited** people. (Chapter 7)

LGBTQ See above. (Chapter 7)

liberal feminism A form of feminism that focuses on legal remedies for inequality between men and women and creating the most gender-neutral society possible. (Chapter 5)

Low-Income cut off (LICO) A boundary established by Statistics Canada that serves as Canada's unofficial measure of poverty. Statistics Canada establishes a number of LICOs based on family size and size of community of residence. (Chapter 6)

male breadwinner/female housewife model A theoretical construct, once supported by legislation and policy, that saw the family as constituted by an earner whose wages supported a dependent non-earner. In this model, "his" role was to provide, "her" role to care. (Chapter 8)

male dominance A system that grants greater power, value, authority, and access to resources to men. Most often, in systems of male dominance, men's authority is reinforced throughout society and its social, political, religious, cultural, and economic institutions. Male dominance is sometimes referred to as "patriarchy," though this term is controversial when used as a synonym for male dominance. (Chapter 1)

male gaze The dominant cultural way of seeing, which adopts the perspective of a desiring heterosexual male subject. Originally theorized by Laura Mulvey. (Chapter 11)

male sex role identity (MSRI) Joseph Pleck's model of the often-contradictory propositions associated with masculine roles. (Chapter 3)

male sex-role strain (MSRS) Joseph Pleck's theory that, given the contradictory and damaging nature of the MSRI, male "problems" were the result not of men's failures to acquire masculine gender identities, but of the sex role itself. (Chapter 3)

male to female (MTF) A transgender woman (see also **transwomen**). (Chapter 11)

marriage premium The additional health, well-being, and economic benefits supposedly enjoyed by married people relative to the unmarried. (Chapter 6)

Marxist and socialist feminisms Forms of feminism united by their emphasis on material conditions as a critical component of gender oppression. Marxist feminisms, however, tend to view the eradication of capitalism as the way to create gender equality, while socialist feminisms have criticized Marxists for their too-rigid focus on economic oppression. Socialist feminism views cultural and economic realities as equally important to the status of women. (Chapter 5)

massively multiplayer online role-playing games (MMORPGs) Role-playing video games distinguished from others by the number of players who participate and by the "persistent worlds" in which the games take place. (Chapter 9)

maternalist Celebrating mothering as a source of prestige and dignity, and as an argument and basis for women's participation in society and politics. (Chapter 5)

matriarchy A woman-centred form of social organization in which women, particularly mothers, are at the centre of prestige and power. (Chapter 4)

matrilineality The practice of reckoning kinship, naming, inheritance, and descent through the mother, rather than the father. (Chapter 4)

matrilocal Determining residence by female kinship rather than by male; therefore, a married couple would reside with the woman's family rather than the man's. (Chapter 6)

mean differences Differences in the *average* scores of men and women (or boys and girls) on standardized tests, which may be taken as representative of *absolute* differences between the sexes (see Figure 1.1). (Chapter 1)

Meiorin test A stringent and multi-part test that employers can apply to ascertain whether a potentially discriminatory requirement is a BFOR (see **bona fide occupational requirement** [BFOR]). (Chapter 8)

men's movement A term that describes movements of men seeking changes, emerging in the 1970s. Initially focused on the **men's liberation movement**, the men's movement split in several directions in the 1990s, and now includes both pro-feminist and anti-feminist groups. (Chapter 5)

men's liberation movement A 1970s movement, sympathetic to feminism, that criticized the restrictions and burdens of the male sex role. (Chapter 5)

men's rights movement A movement that split from the **men's liberation movement** in the late 1970s, becoming focused on alleged discrimination against men in a variety of arenas, most notably child custody and post-divorce financial support. (Chapter 5)

men's studies An interdisciplinary academic field dedicated to the study of masculinities, men's lives, gender, and feminism. (Chapter 5)

M-F Test A multi-component test designed by Lewis Terman and Catherine Miles and used for over 30 years to assess "successful" acquisition of masculine or feminine gender identity. (Chapter 3)

mid-life crisis A developmental "crisis" characterized by a pressure to make wholesale changes in work, relationships, and leisure. (Chapter 5)

military sexual trauma (MST) Trauma resulting from sexual assault or sexual harassment experienced while an individual was serving in the military. (Chapter 13)

minority stress theory A theory that prejudice and discrimination result in chronic and severe stress, and therefore poor health outcomes, among members of marginalized groups. (Chapter 10)

(MMORPGs) See **multi-player online role-playing games**. (Chapter 9)

mommy track The phenomenon whereby mothers might retain paid employment while giving up the possibility of career advancement they might have enjoyed had they not had children and remained on the "fast track." (Chapter 8)

Montreal Massacre The "active-shooter" murder of 14 women on December 6, 1989, at École Polytechnique in Montreal. The shooter separated men from women and described his attack as against feminism. (Chapter 13)

moral panic A popular idea about societal decline; often, moral panics link a real or imagined social problem (e.g., crime) to a particular group of people (e.g., single mothers/fatherlessness). (Chapter 7)

MSM In health-related discussions, men who have sex with men, regardless of whether they identify as **heterosexual**, **homosexual**, **bisexual**, or something else. The term emerged because many men who have sex with men, particularly outside North America and Europe, may not identify as homosexual or bisexual. (Chapter 12)

MST See military sexual trauma. (Chapter 13)

MTF See **male to female** (MTF) (see also **transwomen**). (Chapter 11)

multiracial/ethnic feminism Feminism that emerged in the 1970s as part of a critique of racism and Eurocentrism within the second-wave feminist movement. By the 1980s, important black and Chicana feminist movements had emerged, to be joined later by Asian-American, African, Aboriginal, and other ethnically based feminist movements. Multiracial feminisms have contributed not only a critique of mainstream feminism but insights on racism, social location, and identity as contributors to the status of women. (Chapter 5)

muscle dysphoria A dysmorphic disorder in which, as in anorexia, one sees one's body as thin, puny, or flabby relative to those of other men and to societal ideals (muscle dysphoria is sometimes called bigorexia). (Chapter 11)

muxes In Zapotec communities in Mexico, males who take on feminine modes of dress and social roles. (Chapter 4)

mythopoetic/new men's movement A segment of the **men's movement** that focuses on reclaiming archetypal and mythical forms of masculinity through poetry, literature, and ritual. (Chapter 5)

nadle Among the Navajo, a third gender assigned to either individuals of ambiguous sex or biological males. Individuals might also choose this role. (Chapter 4)

narrative coherence In the simplest terms, narrative coherence is "a story that hangs together." Its application to human life-story telling comes from narrative theory, which argues that the making of stories is fundamental to human cognitive processes. (Chapter 5)

new media Forms of media that emerged in the late twentieth century and are digital, flexible, available on demand, nested, networkable, and highly interactive. (Chapter 9)

New Woman A feminine ideal that emerged at the end of the nineteenth century along with feminist activism and theory. The New Woman would be independent, educated, and assertive. By the early twentieth century, commentators were concerned about the New Woman as a symbol of societal decline. (Chapter 6)

no-ho Referring to trans people who choose not to take sex hormones. (Chapter 11)

non-relational sex Sexuality that is not part of a relationship or a relation to another human being but is rather seen as sport or "just sex." Non-relational sex is generally associated with men. (Chapter 12)

nuclear families A twentieth-century term describing a family structure or household composed of a couple and their children. While it is a common historical form, particularly in Western Europe, it has never been universal. (Chapter 6)

object-relations theory A body of theory identified with Melanie Klein that emphasizes the role of the external world or "others" (both other people and imagined others such as "The Breast") in the development of the personality. (Chapter 3)

Oedipal crisis In Freudian theory, the critical part of the genital stage during which a boy learns to desire sex with women, repudiate femininity, and identify as a man. The boy initially desires his mother, whom he sees as being castrated, and seeks to replace his father. His fear of castration by his father leads him to instead identify with his father and defer his desire for his mother until adulthood, when it is transferred to other women. (Chapter 3)

old media All media in existence prior to the emergence of **new media**, including print media as well as film and broadcast media (television, radio) developed in the twentieth century. (Chapter 9)

organizational gender neutrality The vehicle by which the gender order is reproduced. According to Joan Acker, this "covers up, obscures, the underlying gender structure, allowing practices that perpetuate it to continue even as efforts to reduce gender inequality are also underway." (Chapter 5)

palliative system justification motive A psychological theory that explains why individuals who are disadvantaged by a system justify it. The theory argues that individuals use system justifications to lessen (palliate) their anxiety, guilt, and discomfort, despite the fact that such a justification may be against their own interests. (Chapter 2)

paraphilias Abnormal or deviant sexual desires and behaviours; familiar examples include exhibitionism, fetishism, pedophilia, sexual masochism, sexual sadism, and voyeurism, though new paraphilias are emerging. (Chapter 12)

Parental Alienation Syndrome (PAS) A highly controversial term, originating in the 1980s, to describe a post-divorce situation in which one parent (usually the mother) manipulates a child so that the child unreasonably shuns the other parent (usually the father) or even makes false accusations of maltreatment. (Chapter 6)

parental investment In evolutionary theory, the investment of time, energy, etc., made by a parenting organism that might otherwise be directed toward the fitness of the organism itself. The often-heavier investment by female organisms (particularly mammals) in parenting is thought to lead to greater mating selectivity. (Chapter 2)

participation In media studies, the manner in which groups participate in the consumption and creation of media, as opposed to the ways in which groups are represented within media (see **representation**). (Chapter 9)

patriarchal violence According to bell hooks, family violence "based on the belief that it is acceptable for a more powerful individual to control others through various forms of coercive violence." She links this idea to male domination, but notes that women can and do enact patriarchal violence, particularly against children. (Chapter 13)

patrilineality The practice of reckoning kinship, naming, inheritance, and descent through the father. (Chapter 4)

pay equity A theory and body of legislation and policy comprising two main concepts: the notion of equal pay for the same work and the idea of equal pay for work of equal value. Increasingly, pay equity means simply the latter. (Chapter 8)

penis envy In Freudian theory, a critical part of girls' psychosexual development. The term describes the girl's assumed reaction to her discovery of anatomical sex difference, which she, like the boy, views as the "castration" of the female (see **Electra complex**). (Chapter 3)

Persons' Case The October 1929 legal decision (in response to a petition from five women now known as the "Famous Five") that redefined "persons" under the British North America Act to include women, dramatically expanding the legal rights available to them. (Chapter 9)

phallocentric Focused on male power and privilege, particularly as expressed by the phallus (the erect penis). Phallocentric sexuality centres on the penis and, more broadly, male sexual gratification. (Chapter 12)

pin money Dating back to the seventeenth century, a term still used to describe small amounts of money that can be used by women for discretionary or frivolous spending. (Chapter 8)

polygamy In anthropology and sociology, marriage to more than one partner at the same time. Generally, this takes the form of **polygyny**. (Chapter 4)

polygyny A man's marriage to more than one woman at one time. (Chapter 4)

polyvocality The presence of multiple voices. Within any polyvocal text, multiple meanings and readings are possible. (Chapter 9)

pornification A phenomenon that includes increasing acceptance of explicit sexual imagery; migration of language, themes, and visual motifs from pornography into the mainstream; and celebration of porn stars as celebrities. (Chapter 12)

post-colonial feminism A form of feminism, closely associated with women of the so-called "Third World," that offers a critique of Western feminism's universalizing tendencies and that analyzes colonialism, racism, and global capitalism in relation to the status of women. (Chapter 5)

post-feminism A highly contested and contradictory phenomenon, usually seen as emphasizing one or more of the following: (a) a belief that feminism has achieved its goals; (b) a view that feminism is irrelevant or insufficiently intersectional; (c) a refusal to identify with feminism while accepting many of the movement's beliefs and tenets; and (d) a hostility toward feminism. Many scholars have argued that post-feminism has close links to popular culture and consumer society. (Chapter 5)

post-modern feminism Feminism that draws upon literary and linguistic theory to argue that reality is constructed, primarily through language, and that sex itself has no stable character. Post-modern feminisms have been influential in

scholarship, less so in activism (sometimes referred to as post-structural feminism). (Chapter 5)

precarious employment Work that does not conform with the typical understanding of a stable, full-time job in which one works full-time on the employer's premises with some degree of job security (sometimes called contingent or non-standard employment). (Chapter 8)

primary feminine phase For Klein and other psychoanalysts, the phase in which a child (of either sex) comes to identify with the mother and her desire for the father. (Chapter 3)

primary sex characteristics Sex characteristics present at birth. (Chapter 5)

privilege The advantages that come from being a member of a dominant group (based on gender, race, class, ability, or sexuality), the principal of which may be the presumption of normalcy and universality (see also **invisibility of privilege**). (Chapter 1)

pro-feminist Supporting feminism without considering oneself a feminist or a member of the feminist movement. In general, the term is used of men, in large part because of past controversies over whether men can be or should call themselves "feminists." (Chapter 5)

psychoanalysis An umbrella term for a diverse body of theory and practice based upon the theories of mind and personality developed by Sigmund Freud. Psychoanalysis extends beyond the study and treatment of individual personality to theories of social organization. (Chapter 3)

purdah The (primarily Islamic) practice of the social seclusion of women; a system of segregation aimed at keeping women (particularly married and marriageable ones) completely separated from the world of men. (Chapter 4)

Purity Movement A movement, primarily within US evangelical churches, that emerged in the 1990s, focused on abstinence from sex before marriage and often involving pledges of chastity, "promise" rings, and rituals such as "Purity Balls." (Chapter 12)

quality child care Care that provides trained, skilled, and/or certified staff; warm and healthy interactions between caregivers and children; stimulating environments with toys and materials appropriate for the age of the children being cared for; few children per caregiver; and proper observance of health and safety provisions. (Chapter 6)

queer theory A body of theory, developed in the 1990s, that draws on feminism and LGBTQ activism. Queer theory moves beyond binary notions of gender, sex, and sexuality, focusing on the unstable, multiple ("queer") nature of these and all identity categories. (Chapter 5)

quid pro quo sexual harassment A form of sexual harassment legally recognized in the US; the offer of benefit in exchange for sexual favours, or the threat of retribution if sexual favours are not received. (Chapter 8)

race suicide A late nineteenth-century/early twentieth-century concept that argued, on the basis of evolutionary theory, that the "white race" was in decline; a particular cause, proponents argued, was the declining birth rate among middle- and upper-class white women and the "rampant" fertility of poor whites and racial "others." (Chapter 6)

racialized Seen in terms of and subjected to the application of meaning on the basis of race. Racialization, as a concept, recognizes that the attribution of "race," and the consequences of that attribution, are a process rather than the outcome of an immutable and obvious characteristic. Therefore, race is a *cultural* category and idea rather than a *biological* one. Racialization also recognizes that in terms of experience and identity, one may be made aware of one's "race" in certain contexts or locations but not in others. (Chapter 1)

radical feminism A form of feminism that sees women's unequal status as rooted in patriarchy,

and particularly in its control over the bodies and sexuality of women. (Chapter 5)

rape Penile penetration without consent. (Chapter 13)

representation In media studies, the manner in which groups are represented within media, as opposed to the ways in which they use or create media (see **participation**). (Chapter 9)

residential schools In the Canadian context, boarding schools first founded in the nineteenth century to help "assimilate" Aboriginal children. (Chapter 6)

riot grrrl movement A cultural movement of the 1990s based on punk/alternative music and consciously feminist politics. Ani diFranco, Bikini Kill, and Sleater-Kinney are names sometimes associated with the movement. (Chapter 5)

ritual segregation The segregation of the sexes through rituals that provide a sense of identity and group membership. (Chapter 4)

romantic love A strong attachment to, physical attraction to, and idealization of another human being. While romantic love seems to be universal, it is not always seen as desirable or as the appropriate basis for marriage. (Chapter 10)

sciences, technology, engineering, and mathematics (STEM) See STEM. (Chapter 2)

second shift Housework performed after putting in a workday, or more broadly, the responsibility for the "job" of housework in addition to paid employment. (Chapter 6)

secondary sex characteristics Sex characteristics that develop at puberty, and are less decisive than primary sex characteristics. (Chapter 5)

second-wave feminism A social movement and body of theory that developed after the Second World War, particularly in Western industrialized societies during the 1960s. The movement's greatest impact and vitality can be traced to the 1970s, when many varieties of second-wave feminism emerged. (Chapter 5)

Section 12(1)b A section of Canada's Indian Act that (from 1951 until 1985) removed Indian status from any First Nations woman who married a non-First Nations man. (Chapter 6)

self-esteem A person's sense of worth. It can be measured either by particular indicators, which assess how well one feels about particular aspects of oneself (e.g., "I like my body"), or "globally," in overall terms. (Chapter 7)

self-objectification The process of internalizing an outsider's perspective on one's own body, leading to a preoccupation with one's appearance and comportment as perceived by others. (Chapter 11)

separation of spheres A nineteenth-century ideology that distinguished between private and public in a new way, separating the world of family and love from the world of employment, politics, and competition. Women were to be protected from the latter by their confinement in the private realm, while men could find respite there from the hurly-burly of their activities in the public realm. (Chapter 6)

sex The chromosomal, chemical, and anatomical organization of human bodies that determines biological maleness or femaleness. (Chapter 1)

sex differences Chromosomal, anatomical, and hormonal differences between females and males; to be considered sex differences, these distinctions must be biologically rather than culturally derived. (Chapter 1)

sex-role theory A broad body of theory, drawing from both psychology and sociology, that studies individuals' socialization into gender roles and acquisition of gender identities. (Chapter 3)

sex segregation The concentration of men and women in gender-specific roles and locations within a society. It has been argued that sex segregation is associated with lower status for women. Within employment, the term refers to the concentration of men and women within different occupations, industries, jobs, and fields. This form of sex segregation may be either **vertical** or **horizontal**. (Chapter 4)

sex testing Now called **gender verification**, sex testing has involved a variety of tests conducted on female athletes to be sure that they are biological females. (Chapter 11)

sexting Transmitting sexually explicit real-time messages, usually on mobile phones. Messages may be text-only or may include images. (Chapter 12)

sexual assault Any form of sexual touching without consent. Canada's Criminal Code distinguishes among categories of sexual assault based on degrees parallel to the degrees of common assault. (Chapter 13)

sexual fluidity The ability for one's erotic response to be influenced by situational factors; according to some scholars, particularly prevalent among women. (Chapter 12)

sexual harassment A broad concept that encompasses many behaviours: unwelcomed sexual attention, the offering of benefits for sexual favours, coercion into sexual activity, or bullying and harassment on the ground of one's gender. The standard definition in Canada is "unwelcome conduct of a sexual nature that detrimentally affects the work environment or leads to adverse job-related consequences for the victim of the harassment." In the US, two subtypes are distinguished, **quid pro quo** and **hostile environment**. (Chapter 7)

sexual-minority A descriptor for anyone whose sexual orientation, gender identity, or sexual identity differs from that of the majority culture. (Chapter 13)

sexual orientation A fixed attraction (romantic, emotional, and sexual) toward individuals of one sex. (Chapter 12)

sexual reassignment surgery (SRS) Any or all surgeries aimed at bringing one's body into conformity with one's gender identity (sometimes called gender confirmation or gender-validating surgery). (Chapter 11)

Sexual Revolution The transformation and liberalization, in the 1960s and 1970s, of mores and behaviours relating to sexuality. (Chapter 12)

sexualization of culture A contested phenomenon marked by many changes including preoccupation with and focus on sexuality; the increasing prevalence of sexual imagery; increased commodification of sexuality; and breakdown of sexual categories and mores. Depending on the criteria used, sexualization of culture may be discerned at different points in history. (Chapter 12)

sixties scoop The practice, from the 1960s to 1980s, of removing Aboriginal children from their homes and placing them in (usually non-Aboriginal) foster homes. (Chapter 6)

slut-shaming Discrimination, harassment, bullying, and violence against girls and women who are perceived as violating sexual and gender norms. Slut-shaming can also be a form of bullying deployed to attack particularly attractive girls. (Chapter 7)

social constructionism In this book, the theoretical orientation that sees the expression and organization of gender not as the outcome of biology, but as the result of historical and cultural change, the socialization of individuals, and the continuous interplay between gendered individuals and gendered institutions. Social constructionists view human nature as much more malleable and variable than do biological determinists. (Chapters 1)

social Darwinism Only thinly associated with the theories and work of Charles Darwin, a philosophy that applies the theory of natural selection to differences, competition, and inequality among "races," nations, and families, and between men and women. (Chapter 2)

social psychologists Either sociologists or psychologists, scholars in the field of social psychology, study individual psychology as the result of interactions between individuals and their environments, whether defined as "other people" or as institutions and social structures. (Chapter 3)

sociobiology The study of the biological basis of behaviour in all organisms, including human beings. (Chapter 2)

sociology A discipline within the social sciences that studies social structures and relations, described by C. Wright Mills as "the intersection of biography and history." (Chapter 5)

sociophonetics The study of the relationship among social norms, speech patterns, and changes therein. (Chapter 10)

sodomy Strictly speaking, anal sexual intercourse; historically and in modern "sodomy laws," more broadly applied to any "unnatural" sexuality, particularly if between members of the same sex. (Chapter 10)

spousal violence Violence by one partner in a spousal relationship (including common-law) against the other partner. (Chapter 13)

SRS See **sexual reassignment surgery**. (Chapter 11)

stalking Under Canadian law (Section 264), a form of criminal harassment involving some combination of repeatedly following a person, watching a person, communicating with a person when such communication is not desired, and threatening a person either directly or by proxy. (Chapter 13)

STEM (science, technology, engineering, and mathematics) Fields of study and occupations requiring expertise in one or more of the named areas. (Chapter 2)

stereotype threat A phenomenon in which people performing a certain task feel themselves to be at risk of confirming negative stereotypes about a group to which they belong. The resulting anxiety has been shown to make people perform less well than they would without the condition of stereotype threat. (Chapter 2)

sticky floor The phenomenon, linked to the glass ceiling, that traps women and minorities at the lower levels of organizations regardless of their qualification for advancement. (Chapter 8)

stone butch A masculine or "butch" lesbian who prefers not to be sexually touched and whose sexuality is focused on pleasing her partner. (Chapter 12)

Stonewall a series of 1969 riots against police repression at the Stonewall Inn in New York City. The riots are considered to mark the beginning of the gay rights movement. (Chapter 12)

suburban Relating to the suburbs of a town or city. After 1950, North American suburbs became associated with the white middle class, and with the "traditionally" gendered nuclear family. (Chapter 6)

super-ego A component of Freud's concept of the psyche, the super-ego is an outgrowth of **ego**'s efforts to seek acceptable outlets for **id**'s gratification. Freud saw super-ego as the seat of morality, accepting of the legitimacy of social limitations on gratification. (Chapter 3)

sworn virgin In Albanian society, a daughter who swore perpetual chastity and took on the social role of a man in order to serve as her family's head of household. (Chapter 4)

symmetry in oppression The idea that a system of domination oppresses both the dominant and the dominated group, only in different ways. (Chapter 5)

technical virgin A term used to describe young women who, in a desire to preserve their virginity, engage in "everything but" vaginal intercourse. This seems to have been less a cultural phenomenon than a media one. (Chapter 12)

teledildonics Emergent technologies for remote sex, originally conceived in science fiction. (Chapter 12)

temperance movement A nineteenth- and twentieth-century social movement promoting abstinence from alcohol consumption and various legal reforms to address the social harms of alcoholism. (Chapter 6)

third-wave feminism A form of feminist theory and activism that emerged c. 1990. Third-wave feminism critiques what it sees as the universalizing tendencies of second-wave feminism and incorporates the insights of post-modern, post-colonial, and multiracial feminisms. It also insists on a "positive" view of sexuality. (Chapter 5)

Title IX A US law, enacted in 1972, that states, "No person in the United States shall, on the basis of sex, be excluded from participation in, be denied the benefits of, or be subjected to discrimination under any education program or activity receiving [f]ederal financial assistance." (Chapter 7)

tokenism The phenomenon that makes women and minorities highly visible within previously unintegrated organizations. Because they are always regarded as representing a group, tokens experience a variety of difficulties and frustrations, and their hiring and promotion may not change the workplace significantly for others. (Chapter 8)

top surgery In the trans community, gender-validating surgeries performed on the upper torso. (Chapter 11)

transfeminism The combination of feminism with trans political commitments. (Chapter 5)

transgender Feeling a strong sense of gender identity consistent with inhabiting an other-sex body. (Chapter 11)

transmen Female-to-male trans people (see FTM). (Chapter 5)

transsexual A late-twentieth-century term describing an individual who seeks sex reassignment and consequently changes sex. (Chapter 11).

transvestites Those who dress in the clothing of the opposite sex, for reasons including matters of identity, disruption of social norms, or sexual fetishism. (Chapter 11)

transwomen Male-to-female trans people (see MTF). (Chapter 5)

trolling A variety of Internet behaviours aimed at irritating, harassing, provoking responses, or simply sowing discord. Trolling can range from mischief to much more serious harassment. (Chapter 9)

Truth and Reconciliation Commission (TRC) A commission created as part of the Indian Residential Schools Settlement Agreement. The Commission was created in 2008 and completed its work in 2015. (Chapter 6)

Two-Spirited A term, in use since the 1990s, to describe transgender or gender-variant people in North American Indigenous cultures. The term is sometimes applied to both historical people (e.g., "berdaches") and to contemporary Indigenous people. (Chapter 4)

vertical segregation Segregation associated with differences of education, experience, and skill within the same field, for example, legal

secretarial work and judging, both subsumed within the field of "law." (Chapter 8)

wage gap The difference between the average earnings of male and female full-time workers, either broadly or within a particular field. (Chapter 8)

woman movement A name used to describe the first-wave feminist movement. (Chapter 5)

womb envy A concept, first articulated by Karen Horney, that argues that males envy women's potential to give birth and therefore both disparage and seek to dominate women. (Chapter 3)

women of colour Non-white women; the term is most often associated with black women in the US but is often used to include all women of non-European extraction. (Chapter 5)

Women's Liberation Movement Second-wave feminist activism in the 1960s and 1970s, particularly in the US and UK. (Chapter 5)

xanith Omani biological male whose social and sexual role is female. Xaniths can retain this role throughout life or adopt masculine identities. (Chapter 4)

Notes

Chapter 1

1. John Gray, *Men Are from Mars, Women Are from Venus* (New York, NY: HarperCollins, 1992), p. 5. www.marsvenus.com/john-gray-mars-venus.htm

2. Barbara Risman, *Gender Vertigo* (New Haven, CT: Yale University Press, 1998), p. 25. See also Judith Lorber, *Paradoxes of Gender* (New Haven, CT: Yale University Press, 1994).

3. Catharine Stimpson, *Where the Meanings Are* (New York, NY: Methuen, 1988).

4. For an early work that took the history of masculinity as its topic, see Michael Kimmel, *Manhood in America: A Cultural History* (New York, NY: The Free Press, 1996).

5. Simmel is cited in Lewis Coser, "Georg Simmel's Neglected Contributions to the Sociology of Women," *Signs*, 2 (4), 1977, p. 872.

6. Cited in Coser, "Georg Simmel's Neglected Contributions," p. 872.

7. Cited in James Brooke, "Men Held in Beatings Lived on the Fringes," *The New York Times*, October 16, 1998, p. A16. Valerie Jenness, the sociologist who was quoted in the story, told Michael that she was misquoted and that, of course, she had mentioned gender as well as age—which suggests that the media's myopia matches that of the larger society.

8. Robert McElvaine, *Eve's Seed: Biology, the Sexes, and the Course of History* (New York, NY: McGraw-Hill, 2001), pp. 76–79.

9. R.W. Connell, *Gender and Power* (Stanford, CA: Stanford University Press, 1987), p. 183.

10. Erving Goffman, *Stigma* (Englewood Cliffs, NJ: Prentice-Hall, 1963), p. 128.

11. See Michael E. Starr, "The Marlboro Man: Cigarette Smoking and Masculinity in America," *Journal of Popular Culture*, 17 (4), 1984, pp. 45–57.

12. Connell, *Gender and Power*, pp. 183, 188, 187.

13. Cited in Risman, *Gender Vertigo*, p. 141.

14. Carol Tavris, "The Mismeasure of Woman," *Feminism and Psychology*, 3(2), 1993, p. 153.

15. Cynthia Fuchs Epstein, *Deceptive Distinctions* (New Haven, CT: Yale University Press, 1988).

16. Deborah Tannen, *You Just Don't Understand* (New York, NY: William Morrow, 1991).

17. William O'Barr and Jean F. O'Barr, *Linguistic Evidence: Language, Power and Strategy—The Courtroom* (San Diego, CA: Academic Press, 1995); See also Alfie Kohn, "Girl Talk, Guy Talk," *Psychology Today*, February 1988, p. 66.

18. Alex Witchel, "Our Finances, Ourselves," *The New York Times*, June 4, 1998, p. 13.

19. Ibid.

20. Rosabeth M. Kanter, *Men and Women of the Corporation* (New York, NY: Harper and Row, 1977).

21. Kathleen Gerson, *Hard Choices* (Berkeley, CA: University of California Press, 1985); *No Man's Land* (New York, NY: Basic Books, 1993).

22. Risman, *Gender Vertigo*, p. 70.

23. David Almeida and Ronald Kessler, "Everyday Stressors and Gender Differences in Daily Distress," *Journal of Personality and Social Psychology*, 75 (3), 1998. See also Nancy Stedman, "In a Bad Mood—for a Good Reason," *The New York Times*, October 24, 1998.

24. Risman, *Gender Vertigo*, p. 21.

25. Gayle Rubin, "The Traffic in Women," *Toward an Anthropology of Women*, R.R. Reiter, ed. (New York, NY: Monthly Review Press, 1975), pp. 179–180.

26. Catharine MacKinnon, *Towards a Feminist Theory of the State* (Cambridge, MA: Harvard University Press, 1989), pp. 218–219.

Chapter 2

1. E.O. Wilson, *On Human Nature* (Cambridge, MA: Harvard University Press, 1978), p. 167.

2. Rev. John Todd, *Woman's Rights* (Boston, MA: Lee and Shepard, 1867), p. 26.

3. Londa Schiebinger, "Skeletons in the Closet: The First Illustrations of the Female Skeleton in Eighteenth-Century Anatomy," *Sexuality and Society in the Nineteenth Century*, Catherine Gallagher and Thomas Laqueur, eds. (Berkeley, CA: University of California Press, 1987).

4. Cited in Carl Degler, *In Search of Human Nature: The Decline and Revival of Darwinism in American Social Thought* (New York, NY: Oxford University Press, 1991), p. 107.

5. Todd, *Woman's Rights*, p. 25.

6. California State Historical Society Library, San Francisco, ms. #2334. For a summary of the way biological arguments were used to exclude women from public participation, see Michael Kimmel, "Introduction," *Against the Tide: Pro-Feminist Men in the United States, 1776–1990, a Documentary History*, M. Kimmel and T. Mosmiller, eds. (Boston, MA: Beacon, 1992).

7. Cited in Stephen Jay Gould, *The Mismeasure of Man* (New York, NY: W. W. Norton, 1981), pp. 104–105.

8. Cited in Cynthia Eagle Russet, *Sexual Science: The Victorian Construction of Womanhood* (Cambridge, MA: Harvard University Press, 1989).

9. Jennifer Henderson, *Settler Feminism and Race Making in Canada* (Toronto, ON: University of Toronto Press, 2003), p. 173.

10. See Angus Maclaren, *Our Own Master Race: Eugenics in Canada, 1885–1945* (Toronto, ON: University of Toronto Press, 1990); Jana Grekul, Harvey Krahn, and Dave Odynak, "Sterilizing the 'Feeble-Minded': Eugenics in Alberta, Canada, 1929–1972," *Journal of Historical Sociology*, 17 (4), 2004, pp. 358–384.

11. E.O. Wilson, *Sociobiology: The New Synthesis* (Cambridge, MA: Harvard University Press, 1977). There are several important texts that provide good ripostes to the biological arguments. An excellent recent work is Rebecca Jordan-Young's *Brain Storm: The Flaws in the Science of Sex Differences* (Cambridge, MA: Harvard University Press, 2010). See Ruth Bleir, ed., *Feminist Approaches to Science* (New York, NY: Pergamon, 1986); Lynda Birke, *Women, Feminism and Biology: The Feminist Challenge* (New York, NY: Methuen, 1986); Anne Fausto-Sterling, *Myths of Gender: Biological Theories About Women and Men* (New York, NY: Basic Books, 1985); Deborah Blum, *Sex on the Brain: The Biological Differences between Men and Women* (New York, NY: Viking, 1997; and Robert

Nadeau, *S/He Brain: Science, Sexual Politics and the Myths of Feminism* (New York, NY: Praeger, 1996.).

12. Richard Dawkins, *The Selfish Gene* (New York, NY: Oxford University Press, 1976), p. 152; Wilson, *On Human Nature*, p. 167.

13. Anthony Layng, "Why Don't We Act Like the Opposite Sex?" *USA Today* magazine, January 1993; Donald Symons, "Darwinism and Contemporary Marriage," *Contemporary Marriage: Comparative Perspectives on a Changing Institution*, K. Davis, ed. (New York, NY: Russell Sage Foundation, 1985), cited in Carl Degler, "Darwinians Confront Gender; or, There Is More to It Than History," *Theoretical Perspectives on Sexual Difference*, D. Rhode, ed. (New Haven, CT: Yale University Press, 1990), p. 39.

14. Lionel Tiger, "Male Dominance?" *The New York Times Magazine*, October 25, 1970.

15. Wilson, *Sociobiology: The New Synthesis*.

16. See, for example, Judy Stamps "Sociobiology: Its Evolution and Intellectual Descendants," *Politics and Life Science*, 14 (2), 1995.

17. David Buss, *The Evolution of Desire: Strategies of Human Mating* (New York, NY: Basic Books, 1994), see also Robert Sapolsky, *Monkeyluv* (New York, NY: Scribner, 2006), p. 175.

18. Margo Wilson and Martin Daly, "The Man Who Mistook His Wife for a Chattel," *The Adapted Mind: Evolutionary Psychology and the Generation of Culture*, Jerome Barkow, Leda Cosmides, and John Tooby, eds. (Oxford, UK: Oxford University Press, 1995), pp. 289–324.

19. Christopher Ryan and Cacilda Jethá, *Sex at Dawn: How We Mate, Why We Stray, and What It Means for Modern Relationships* (New York, NY: HarperCollins, 2010). See also Burley, "The Evolution of Concealed Ovulation," *The American Naturalist*, 114, 1979; Mary McDonald Pavelka, "Sexual Nature: What Can We Learn from a Cross-Species Perspective?" *Sexual Nature, Sexual Culture*, P. Abrahamson and S. Pinkerton, eds. (Chicago, IL: University of Chicago Press, 1995), p. 19. See also Sarah Blaffer Hrdy, *The Woman that Never Evolved* (Cambridge, MA: Harvard University Press, 1981).

20. Steven Gangestad, Randy Thornhill, and Christine Garver, "Changes in Women's Sexual Interests and Their Partners' Mate-Retention Tactics across the Menstrual Cycle: Evidence for Shifting Conflicts of Interest," *Proceedings of the Royal Society*, 2002. Not surprisingly, Gangestad repudiated the journalist's interpretation, because it's pretty much the mirror image of his argument that it is more in males' interest to be promiscuous and in females' interest to be monogamous. Personal communication (with M. Kimmel), December 16, 2002.

21. Fausto-Sterling, *Myths of Gender*, pp. 160–163.

22. Lewontin cited in C. Leon Harris, *Evolution: Genesis and Revelations* (Albany, NY: SUNY Press, 1981), p. 250; Gould cited in Daniel Kevles, *In the Name of Eugenics: Genetics and the Uses of Human Heredity* (Berkeley/Los Angeles, CA: University of California Press, 1985); Sapolsky, *Monkeyluv*, p. 30.

23. Pavelka, "Sexual Nature," p. 22.

24. See Jonah Lehrer, "The Effeminate Sheep—and Other Problems with Darwinian Sexual Selection," *Seed*, June 2006; Simon Le Vay, "Survival of the Sluttiest," at Nerve.com, 2000, available at www.nerve.com See also Joan Roughgarden, *Evolution's Rainbow Diversity, Gender, and Sexuality in Nature and People*, Tenth Anniversary Edition (Berkeley, CA: University of California Press, 2013).

25. Richard Bribiescas, *Men: Evolutionary and Life History* (Cambridge, MA: Harvard University Press, 2006), p. 12.

26. Turner is cited in *South Side Observer*, April 29, 1896; C.A. Dwyer, "The Role of Tests and Their Construction in Producing Apparent Sex-Related Differences," *Sex-Related Differences in Cognitive Functioning*, M. Wittig and A. Peterson, eds. (New York, NY: Academic Press, 1979), p. 342.

27. Christina Hoff Sommers, "Why Can't a Woman Be More Like a Man?" *The American* online, March/April 2008, available at www.american.com/archive/2008/march-april-magazine-contents/why-can 2019t-a-woman-be-more-like-a-man (accessed December 3, 2008).

28. Gjisbert Stoet and David C. Geary, "Sex Differences in Mathematics and Reading Achievement Are Inversely Related: Within- and Across-Nation Assessment of 10 Years of PISA Data," *PLOS ONE*, 8 (1), March 2013. Canadian Council of Learning, *Why Boys Don't Like to Read: Gender Differences in Reading Achievement*, February 18, 2009, available at www.ccl-cca.ca/CCL/Reports/Lessons InLearning/LinL20090218Whyboysdont liketoread.htm (accessed April 2, 2009).

29. Ainara González de San Román and Sara de la Rica Goiricelaya, "Gender Gaps in PISA Test Scores: The Impact of Social Norms and the Mother's Transmission of Role Attitudes," IZA (Institute for the Study of Labor) Discussion Paper No. 6338. Bonn, Germany: February 2012.

30. David I. Miller and Diane F. Halpern, "The New Science of Cognitive Sex Differences," *Trends in Cognitive Sciences*, 18 (1), 2014, pp. 37–45.

31. Diane Halpern et al., "The Science of Sex Differences in Science and Mathematics," *Psychological Science in the Public Interest*, 8 (1), 2007, pp. 1–51.

32. Miller and Halpern, "The New Science," p. 38.

33. Jing Feng, Ian Spence, and Jay Pratt, "Playing an Action Video Game Reduces Gender Differences in Spatial Cognition," *Psychological Science*, 18 (10), 2007, pp. 850–855.

34. Darren Lauzon, "Gender Differences in Large-Scale, Quantitative Assessments of Mathematics and Science Achievement." Unpublished conference paper, available at http://qed.econ.queensu.ca/pub/jdi/deutsch/edu_conf/Lauzon2_paper.pdf (accessed April 2, 2009).

35. There are now hundreds of studies of stereotype threat. The classic study is Steven J. Spencer and Diane M. Quinn, "Stereotype Threat and Women's Math Performance," *Journal of Experimental Social Psychology*, 35, 1999, pp. 4–28.

36. Sian L. Beilock et al., "Female Teachers' Math Anxiety Affects Girls' Math Achievement," *PNAS Early Edition* 2009. www.pnas.org/cgi/doi/10.1073/pnas.0910967107

37. Halpern et al., "The Science of Sex Differences," p. 13.

38. Emile Durkheim, *The Division of Labor in Society* [1893] (New York, NY: The Free Press, 1984), p. 21; see also Barbara Ehrenreich and Deirdre English, *For Her Own Good: 150 Years of the Experts' Advice to Women* (Norwell, MA: Anchor Books, 1978); Elizabeth Fee, "Nineteenth Century Craniology: The Study of the Female Skull," *Bulletin of the History of Medicine*, 53, 1979.

39. See, for example, Miguel Burgaleta et al., "Sex Differences in Brain Volume Are Related to Specific Skills, not to General Intelligence," *Intelligence*, 40 (1), 2012, pp. 60–68.

40. See Amber N.V. Ruigrok et al., "A Meta-Analysis of Sex Differences in Human Brain Structure," *Neuroscience and Biobehavioral Reviews*, 39, 2014, pp. 34–50.

41. Doreen Kimura's *Sex and Cognition* (Cambridge, MA: MIT Press, 1999) catalogues brain differences in spatial, verbal, and other forms of reasoning. Because she never tells the reader about the shape of the distribution of these traits, we have no idea whether such differences actually mean anything at all, if they are categorical, or if the distribution is larger among women and among men than it is between women and men—which is the case in virtually every one of these studies. A better source is Lesley Rogers, *Sexing the Brain* (New York, NY: Columbia University Press, 2001).

42. Norman Geschwind as cited in Jo Durden-Smith and Diane deSimone, *Sex and the Brain* (New York, NY: Arbor House, 1983), p. 171. Other influential studies on hormone research include G.W. Harris, "Sex Hormones, Brain Development and Brain Function," *Endocrinology*, 75, 1965.

43. Ruth Bleier, *Science and Gender: A Critique of Biology and Its Theory on Women* (New York, NY: Pantheon, 1984).

44. Dardo Tomasi and Nora D. Volkow, "Laterality Patterns of Brain Functional Connectivity: Gender Effects," *Cerebral Cortex*, 22 (6), 2012, pp. 1455–1462; A.W.H. Buffery and J. Gray, "Sex Differences in the Development of Spatial and Linguistic Skills," *Gender Differences: Their Ontogeny and Significance*, C. Ounsted and D.C. Taylor, eds. (London, UK: Churchill Livingston, 1972); Jerre Levy, "Lateral Specialization of the Human Brain: Behavioral Manifestation and Possible Evolutionary Basis," *The Biology of Behavior*, J.A. Kiger, ed. (Corvallis, Eugene, OR: University of Oregon Press, 1972); Joseph Lurito cited in Robert Lee Hotz, "Women Use More of Brain When Listening, Study Says" *Los Angeles Times*, November 29, 2000; see also Fausto-Sterling, *Myths of Gender*, p. 40.

45. Ruigrok et al., "A Meta-Analysis of Sex Differences."

46. Michael Peters, "The Size of the Corpus Callosum in Males and Females: Implications of a Lack of Allometry," *Canadian Journal of Psychology*, 42 (3), 1988, pp. 313–324; Christine de Lacoste-Utamsing and Ralph Holloway, "Sexual Dimorphism in the Human Corpus Callosum," *Science*, June 25, 1982; but also see William Byne, Ruth Bleier, and Lanning Houston, "Variations in Human Corpus Callosum Do Not Predict Gender: A Study Using Magnetic Resonance Imaging," *Behavioral Neuroscience*, 102 (2), 1988, pp. 222–227.

47. Eileen Luders, Arthur W. Toga, and Paul M. Thompson, "Why Size Matters: Differences in Brain Volume Account for Apparent Sex Differences in Callosal Anatomy: The Sexual Dimorphism of the Corpus Callosum," *NeuroImage*, 84, 2014, pp. 820–824; Anne Fausto-Sterling, *Sexing the Body: Gender Politics and the Construction of Sexuality* (New York, NY: Basic Books, 2000), p. 140.

48. Cordelia Fine, "Will Working Mothers' Brains Explode? The Popular New Genre of Neurosexism," in *Neuroethics*, 1, 2008, pp. 69–72.

49. See, for example, Fiona Macrae, "Sorry, Dear, But Women Really Do Talk More than Men (13,000 Words a Day More to Be Precise)," *Mail Online*, February 20, 2013. www.dailymail.co.uk/sciencetech/article-2281891/Women-really-talk-men-13-000-words-day-precise.html

50. Lise Eliot, "The Trouble with Sex Differences," *Neuron* 72 (6), 2011, pp. 895–98. See also Eliot's *Pink Brain, Blue Brain: How Small Differences Grow into Troublesome Gaps—and*

What We Can Do about It (New York, NY: Houghton Mifflin Harcourt, 2009).

51. Fine, "Will Working Mothers' Brains Explode?"

52. Steven Goldberg, *The Inevitability of Patriarchy* (New York, NY: Simon & Schuster, 1973), p. 93.

53. Kate Melville, "Male Scientists Not So Manly," *ScienceAGogo*, October 22, 2004, available at www.scienceagogo.com/news /20040922054756data_trunc_sys.shtml (accessed April 22, 2009).

54. See James McBride Dabbs (with Mary Godwin Dabbs), *Heroes, Rogues and Lovers: Testosterone and Behavior* (New York, NY: McGraw-Hill, 2000), p. 8; Andrew Sullivan, "The He Hormone," *The New York Times Magazine*, April 2, 2000, p. 48. There is some evidence that AndroGel is dangerous and should not be taken without significant testing. See Jerome Groopman, "Hormones for Men," *The New Yorker*, July 29, 2002, pp. 34–38.

55. Robert Sapolsky, *The Trouble with Testosterone* (New York, NY: Simon & Schuster, 1997), p. 155.

56. Theodore Kemper, *Testosterone and Social Structure* (New Brunswick, NJ: Rutgers University Press, 1990); Arthur Kling, "Testosterone and Aggressive Behavior in Man and Non-Human Primates," *Hormonal Correlates of Behavior*, B. Eleftheriou and R. Sprott, eds. (New York, NY: Plenum, 1975); See also E. Gonzalez-Bono, A. Salvador, J. Ricarte, M.A. Serrano, and M. Arendo, "Testosterone and Attribution of Successful Competition," *Aggressive Behavior*, 26 (3), 2000, pp. 235–240. Anu Aromaki, Ralf Lindman, and C.J. Peter Eriksson, "Testosterone, Aggressiveness, and Antisocial Personality," *Aggressive Behavior*, 25, 1999, pp. 113–123; Peter B. Gray, "Marriage and Fatherhood Are Associated with Lower Testosterone in Males," *Evolution and Human Behavior*, 23, 2002, pp. 193–201; see also the coverage of this study, William Cromie, "Marriage Lowers Testosterone," *The Harvard Gazette*, September 19, 2002; Ellen Barry, "The Ups and Downs of Manhood," *Boston Globe*, July 9, 2002.

57. See, for example, Jed Diamond, *Male Menopause* (Napierville, IL: Sourcebooks, 1998); and Jerome Groopman, "Hormones for Men." For discussion, see Bribiescas, *Men*, pp. 175–191; "Androgel™ Approved in Canada," *Doctors' Guide: Global Edition*, available at www.pslgroup.com/dg/215536.htm (accessed April 22, 2009).

58. See Anne Fausto-Sterling's summary of William Young's classic 1940s experiments in *Sexing the Body*, pp. 212–216; see Bribiescas, *Men*, p. 187, for a summary of studies on the association of testosterone and libido.

59. Winifred Gallagher, "Some Differences between Men and Women II: Sex and Hormones," *The Atlantic Monthly*, March 1998, pp. 77–82. Jane Brody, "Personal Health: A Tad of Testosterone Adds Zest to Menopause," *The New York Times*, February 24, 1998, available at www.nytimes.com /specials/women/warchive/980224_1133 .html (accessed April 22, 2009).

60. Gallagher, "Some Differences."

61. Natalie Angier, *Woman: An Intimate Geography* (New York, NY: Houghton Mifflin, 1999), p. 183.

62. Angier, *Woman*, p. 207.

63. Health Canada, "Benefits and Risks of Hormone Replacement Therapy," (January 2003/March 2004), available at www.hc -sc.gc.ca/hl-vs/iyh-vsv/med/estrogen-eng.php (accessed April 23, 2009).

64. Sarah Romans et al., "Mood and the Menstrual Cycle: A Review of Prospective Data Studies," *Gender Medicine*, 9 (5), 2012, pp. 361–384.

65. Shari Roan, "The Basis of Sexual Identity," *Los Angeles Times*, March 14, 1997, p. E1.

66. See John Colapinto, As *Nature Made Him: The Boy Who Was Raised as a Girl* (New York, NY: HarperCollins, 2000), and John Colapinto, "Gender Gap: What Were the Real Reasons Behind David Reimer's Suicide?" *Slate*, June 3, 2004, available at www .slate.com/id/2101678 Several insightful reviews of the book were gathered in Volume 31 of the *Archives of Sexual Behavior*, 31 (3), 2002, pp. 301–308. Scholarly papers include M. Diamond, "Sexual Identity, Monozygotic

Twins Reared in Discordant Sex Roles and a BBC Follow-Up," *Archives of Sexual Behavior*, 11 (2), 1982, pp. 181–185; M. Diamond and H.K. Sigmundson, "Sex Reassignment at Birth: Long Term Review and Clinical Implications," *Archives of Pediatrics and Adolescent Medicine*, 151, March 1997, pp. 298–304.

67. Gunter Dorner, W. Rohde, F. Stahl, L. Krell, and W. Masius, "A Neuroendocrine Predisposition for Homosexuality in Men," *Archives of Sexual Behavior*, 4 (1), 1975, p. 6. Several books offer useful summaries of "gay biology" research, including Dean Hamer and Peter Copeland, *The Science of Desire* (New York, NY: Simon & Schuster, 1994); Simon LeVay, *Queer Science: The Use and Abuse of Research into Homosexuality* (Cambridge, MA: MIT Press, 1996); Lee Ellis and Linda Ebertz, eds., *Sexual Orientation: Toward Biological Understanding* (New York, NY: Praeger, 1997). Several other works provide valuable rejoinders to the scientific research; see, for example, Vernon Rosario, ed., *Science and Homosexualities* (New York, NY: Routledge, 1997); Timothy Murphy, *Gay Science: The Ethics of Sexual Orientation Research* (New York, NY: Columbia University Press, 1997); John Corvino, ed., *Same Sex: Debating the Ethics, Science and Culture of Homosexuality* (Lanham, MD: Rowman and Littlefield, 1997). A double issue of *Journal of Homosexuality*, 28 (1–2), 1995, was devoted to this theme. For a strong dissenting opinion, see William Byne, "Why We Cannot Conclude That Sexual Orientation Is Primarily a Biological Phenomenon," *Journal of Homosexuality*, 34 (1), 1997; William Byne, "Science and Belief: Psychobiological Research on Sexual Orientation," *Journal of Homosexuality*, 28 (2), 1995.

68. The men were judged "gay or bisexual" because they had died of AIDS. Simon LeVay, "The 'Gay Brain' Revisited," www.Nerve.com (2000); LeVay, "A Difference in Hypothalamic Structure Between Homosexual and Heterosexual Men," *Science*, 253, August 30, 1991; Simon LeVay, *The Sexual Brain* (Cambridge, MA: MIT Press, 1994); Simon LeVay and Dean Hamer, "Evidence for a Biological Influence in Male Homosexuality," *Scientific*

American, 270, 1994. See also "Born or Bred?" *Newsweek*, February 24, 1992.

69. P. Yahr, "Sexually Dimorphic Hypothalamic Cell Groups and a Related Pathway That Are Essential for Masculine Copulatory Behavior," *The Development of Sex Differences and Similarities in Behavior*, M. Haug, R. Whalen, C. Aron, and K. Olsen, eds. (Dordrecht, Netherlands: Kluwer Academic Publishers, 1993), p. 416.

70. Ivanka Savic and Stefan Arver, "Sex Dimorphism of the Brain in Male-to-Female Transsexuals," *Cerebral Cortex*, 21, 2011, pp. 2525–2533. For a summary of the 1990s Dutch study, see Natalie Angier, "Study Links Brain to Transsexuality," *The New York Times*, November 2, 1995. www.nytimes.com/1995/11/02/us/study-links-brain-to-transsexuality.html See also *Chronicle of Higher Education*, November 10, 1995. See also Eileen Luders et al., "Regional Gray Matter Variation in Male-to-Female Transsexualism," *NeuroImage*, 46 (4), July 2009, pp. 904–907.

71. Ivanka Savic, Hans Berglund, and Per Lindstrom, "Brain Response to Putative Pheromones in Homosexual Men," *PNAS*, 102 (20), May 17, 2005, pp. 7356–7361.

72. Savic cited in Nicholas Wade, "For Gay Men, an Attraction to a Different Kind of Scent," *The New York Times*, May 10, 2005, available at www.nytimes.com/2005/05/10/science/10smell.html (accessed May 10, 2005). "PET and MRI Show Differences in Cerebral Asymmetry and Functional Connectivity between Homo- and Heterosexual Subjects," *Proceedings of the National Academy of Sciences*, 105 (27), pp. 9403–9408; "What the Gay Brain Looks Like," *Time*, June 17, 2008, available at www.time.com/time/health/article/0,8599,1815538,00.html (accessed 22 April 2009).

73. Marc Breedlove in Pat McBroom, "Sexual Experience May Affect Brain Structure," available at www.berkeley.edu/news/berkeleyan/1997/1119/sexexp.html See also Jim McKnight, "Editorial: The Origins of Male Homosexuality," *Psychology, Evolution and Gender*, 2 (3), December 2000, p. 226.

74. See F. Kallmann, "Comparative Twin Study on the Genetic Aspects of Male Homosexuality,"

Journal of Nervous Mental Disorders, 115, 1952, pp. 283–298. Kallmann's findings may have been an artifact of his sample, which was drawn entirely from institutionalized mentally ill patients—some of whom had been institutionalized because they were gay. See also Richard Lewontin, Steven Rose, and Leon Kamin, *Not in Our Genes: Biology, Ideology and Human Nature* (New York, NY: Pantheon), 1984. E.D. Eckert et al., "Homosexuality in Monozygotic Twins Reared Apart," *The British Journal of Psychiatry*, 148, 1986, pp. 421–425. J. Michael Bailey and Richard Pillard, "A Genetic Study of Male Sexual Orientation," *Archives of General Psychiatry*, 48, December 1991; J. Michael Bailey and Richard Pillard, "Heritable Factors Influence Sexual Orientation in Women," *Archives of General Psychiatry*, 50, March 1993; Richard Pillard and James Weinrich, "Evidence of a Familial Nature of Male Homosexuality," *Archives of General Psychiatry*, 43, 1986.

75. See Peter Bearman and Hannah Bruckner, "Opposite Sex Twins and Adolescent Same-Sex Attraction," *American Journal of Sociology*, 107 (5), March 2002, pp. 1179–1205.

76. Niklas Langstrom et al., "Genetic and Environmental Effects on Same-Sex Behavior: A Population Study of Twins in Sweden," *Archives of Sexual Behavior*, 39 (1), 2010, pp. 75–80.

77. Durden-Smith and deSimone, *Sex and the Brain*, p. 92.

78. Gunter Dorner et al., "Stressful Events in Prenatal Life of Bisexual and Homosexual Men," *Explorations in Clinical Endocrinology*, 81, 1983, p. 87. See also Dorner et al., "Prenatal Stress as a Possible Paetiogenic Factor of Homosexuality in Human Males," *Endokrinologie*, 75, 1983; and Dorner et al., "Prenatal Stress and Sexual Brain Differentiation in Animal and Human Beings," Abstracts, International Academy of Sex Research, Thirteenth Annual Meeting, Tutzing, June 21–25, 1987. The other side is presented in a clever article by Gunter Schmidt and Ulrich Clement, "Does Peace Prevent Homosexuality?" *Journal of Homosexuality*, 28 (3–4), 1995, 269–75.

79. Marc Breedlove et al., "Finger Length Ratios and Sexual Orientation," *Nature*, 404, March 30, 2000, p. 455; see also S.J. Robinson, "The Ratio of 2nd to 4th Digit Length and Male Homosexuality," *Evolution and Human Behavior*, 21, 2000, pp. 333–345. Also see Tim Beneke, "Sex on the Brain," *East Bay Express*, September 22, 2000, for a superb profile of Breedlove and his research; and Susan Rubinowitz, "Report: Index Finger Size May Indicate Homosexuality," *New York Post*, March 30, 2000. A recent metastudy confirms Breedlove's findings: see Teresa Grimbos et al., "Sexual Orientation and the Second to Fourth Finger Length Ratio: A Meta-Analysis in Men and Women," *Behavioral Neuroscience*, 124 (2), 2010, pp. 278–287.

80. Marc Breedlove, personal communication with M. Kimmel, February 13, 2001; see also David Puts, Cynthia Jordan, and S. Marc Breedlove, "O Brother, Where Are Thou? The Fraternal Birth-Order Effect on Male Sexual Orientation," *Proceedings of the National Academy of Science*, 103 (28), July 11, 2006, pp. 10531–10532. For penis size, see Anthony Bogaert and Scott Hershberger, "The Relation between Sexual Orientation and Penile Size," *Archives of Sexual Behavior*, 28 (3), 1999, pp. 213–221.

81. Anthony Bogaert, "Biological Versus Nonbiological Older Brothers and Men's Sexual Orientation," *Proceedings of the National Academy of Science*, 103 (28), July 11, 2006, pp. 10771–10774.

82. See Alice Domurat Dreger, *Hermaphrodites and the Medical Invention of Sex* (Cambridge, MA: Harvard University Press, 1998); Gert Hekma, "'A Female Soul in a Male Body': Sexual Inversion as Gender Inversion in Nineteenth Century Sexology," *Third Sex, Third Gender*, Gilbert Herdt, ed. (Cambridge, MA: MIT Press, 1993). The term "intersexed" was preferred by the Intersex Society of North America, an advocacy group active from 1993 to 2008. Largely as a result of the success of its advocacy work, it has been replaced by the Accord Alliance, which works on behalf of people with "disorders of sex development," including but not limited

to intersexuality. See www.accordalliance .org/ The 1.7% figure (higher than the generally accepted, though unclearly derived, estimate of 1%) is from Anne Fausto-Sterling's research. See *Sexing the Body*, p. 51.

83. John Money and Anke Ehrhardt, *Man and Woman, Boy and Girl* (Baltimore, MD: Johns Hopkins University Press, 1972).

84. Fausto-Sterling, *Myths of Gender*, pp. 136–137.

85. Ibid.

86. John Stossel, "Just Too Taboo to Talk About," *Orange County Register*, January 30, 2005.

87. See Meyer-Behlberg et al., "Prenatal Androgenization Affects Gender-Related Behavior But Not Gender Identity in 5–12-Year-Old Girls with Congenital Adrenal Hyperplasia," *Archives of Sexual Behavior*, 33 (2), 2004, pp. 97–104.

88. María José Martínez-Patiño, "A Woman Tried and Tested," *The Lancet*, 366 (Special Issue S 38), 2005.

89. See Julianne Imperato-McGinley et al., "Steroid 5-Alpha Reductase Deficiency in Man: An Inherited Form of Pseudohermaphroditism," *Science*, 186 (4170), 1974, pp. 1213–1215; Julianne Imperato-McGinley et al., "Androgens and the Evolution of Male-Gender Identity Among Male Pseudohermaphrodites with 5-Alpha Reductase Deficiency," *New England Journal of Medicine*, 300 (22), 1979, pp. 1235–1237. For an excellent summary of the research, see Gilbert Herdt, "Mistaken Sex: Culture, Biology and the Third Sex in New Guinea," Herdt, *Third Sex, Third Gender*.

90. Herdt, "Mistaken Sex."

91. Goldberg, *The Inevitability of Patriarchy*, pp. 233–234; see also Fausto-Sterling, *Myths of Gender*, p. 124.

92. For an effort to use hormone research and evolutionary imperatives to defend gender norms, see J. Richard Udry, "Biological Limits of Gender Construction," *American Sociological Review*, 65, June 2000, pp. 443–457. Udry's thesis is elegantly demolished by Eleanor Miller and Carrie Yang Costello, "Comment on Udry," *American Sociological Review*, 65, June 2000, pp. 592–598.

93. This is according to a feminist cited in Lewontin et al., *Not in Our Genes*, p. 147.

94. Darrell Yates Rist, "Are Homosexuals Born That Way?" *The Nation*, October 19, 1992, p. 427 and "Born or Bred?" *Newsweek*, February 24, 1992; Michael Bailey and Richard Pillard, "Are Some People Born Gay?" *The New York Times*, December 17, 1991.

95. "Born or Bred?"

96. Karen De Witt, "Quayle Contends Homosexuality Is a Matter of Choice, Not Biology," *The New York Times*, September 14, 1992; Ashcroft cited in Eric Alterman, "Sorry, Wrong President," *The Nation*, February 26, 2001, p. 10. See John Leland and Mark Miller, "Can Gays Convert?" *Newsweek*, August 17, 1998.

97. LeVay, *The Sexual Brain*, p. 6.

98. Ruth Hubbard, "The Political Nature of Human Nature," *Theoretical Perspectives on Sexual Difference*, Deborah Rhode, ed. (New Haven, CT: Yale University Press, 1990), p. 69.

99. Robert A. Padgug, "On Conceptualizing Sexuality in History," *Radical History Review*, 20, 1979, pp. 3–23; p. 9.

100. Anne Fausto-Sterling, *Sexing the Body: Gender Politics and the Construction of Sexuality*, (New York: Basic Books, 2000), p. 253–255. Copyright © 2000 Anne Fausto-Sterling. Reprinted by permission of Basic Books, a member of the Perseus Books Group.

101. Ibid.

Chapter 3

1. Sigmund Freud, "The Dissection of the Psychical Personality," *New Introductory Lectures on Psychoanalysis* [1933] (New York, NY: W.W. Norton, 1965), p. 74.

2. Sigmund Freud, "The Dissolution of the Oedipus Complex," The Standard Edition of the *Complete Psychological Works*, 19, 1924, p. 179.

3. Sigmund Freud, *Letters of Sigmund Freud, 1873–1939*, Ernst Freud, ed. (London, UK: Hogarth Press, 1961), pp. 419–420.

4. See, for example, Jeffrey Masson, *The Assault on Truth* (New York, NY: Farrar, Straus and Giroux, 1984); Alice Miller, *Thou Shalt Not Be Aware: Society's Betrayal of the Child* (New York, NY: Farrar, Straus and Giroux, 1984); and Alice Miller, *For Your Own Good:*

Hidden Cruelty in Child-Rearing and the Roots of Violence (New York, NY: Farrar, Straus and Giroux, 1983).

5. See Carol Glover, "Her Body, Himself: Gender in the Slasher Film," *The Dread of Difference*: *Gender and the Horror Film*, Barry Keith Grant, ed. (Austin, TX: University of Texas Press, 1996), pp. 66–114; Barbara Creed, "Dark Desires: Male Masochism in the Horror Film," *Screening the Male*: *Exploring Masculinities in Hollywood Cinema*, Steven Cohan and Ina Rae Hark, eds. (New Brunswick, NJ: Routledge, 1992), pp. 118–133; Joelle Ruby Ryan, "Reel Gender: Examining the Politics of Trans Images in Media and Film," (Ph.D. dissertation, Bowling Green State University, 2009), pp. 178–192; p. 8.

6. Lewis Terman and Catherine Cox Miles, *Sex and Personality* (New York, NY: McGraw-Hill, 1936); see also Henry Minton, "Femininity in Men and Masculinity in Women: American Psychiatry and Psychology Portray Homosexuality in the 1930s," *Journal of Homosexuality*, 13 (1), 1986.

7. Ronald LaTorre and William Piper, "The Terman-Miles M-F Test: An Examination of Exercises 1, 2, and 3 Forty Years Later," *Sex Roles*, 4 (1), 1978, pp. 141–154.

8. George W. Henry, "Psychogenic Factors in Overt Homosexuality," *American Journal of Psychiatry*, 93, 1937; cited in Minton, "Femininity in Men . . . ," p. 2. Note, however, that Henry's secondary claim is not that these tendencies will simply emerge, but rather that the social response to these traits will exaggerate and sustain them (i.e., that overt responses of homophobia will actually encourage the tendency toward homosexuality).

9. Joseph Pleck offered a superb summary of these studies in "The Theory of Male Sex Role Identity: Its Rise and Fall, 1936 to the Present," *In the Shadow of the Past*: *Psychology Views the Sexes*, M. Lewin, ed. (New York, NY: Columbia University Press, 1984). Much of this summary draws from his essay.

10. Teodor Adorno et al., *The Authoritarian Personality* (New York, NY: Harper and Row, 1950).

11. Robb Willer, "Overdoing Gender: A Test of the Masculine Overcompensation Thesis," *American Journal of Sociology*, 118 (4), 2013, pp. 980–1022. The study was widely reported. See Mary Beckman, "How to Sell Humvees to Men," *Science*, August 4, 2005, available at www.science-now.sciencemag.org/cgi/content/full/2005/804/1 (accessed August 20, 2009); for a confirming study, see Peter Glick et al., "Defensive Reactions to Masculinity Threat: More Negative Affect toward Effeminate (but Not Masculine) Gay Men," *Sex Roles*, 57, 2007, pp. 55–59.

12. Talcott Parsons, "Certain Primary Sources and Patterns of Aggression in the Social Structure of the Western World," *Psychiatry*, 10, 1947, p. 309.

13. Sandra Bem, "The Measurement of Psychological Androgyny," *Journal of Consulting and Clinical Psychology*, 42, 1974; Sandra Bem, "Androgyny vs. the Tight Little Lives of Fluffy Women and Chesty Men," *Psychology Today*, September 1975; Sandra Bem, "Beyond Androgyny: Some Presumptuous Prescriptions for a Liberated Sexual Identity," *The Future of Women*: *Issues in Psychology*, J. Sherman and F. Denmark, eds. (New York, NY: Psychological Dimensions, 1978). See also Alexandra Kaplan and Mary Anne Sedney, *Psychology and Sex Roles*: *An Androgynous Perspective* (Boston, MA: Little Brown, 1980), quote on p. 6; Janet Spence, Robert Helmreich, and Joy Stapp, "The Personal Attributes Questionnaire: A Measure of Sex-Role Stereotypes and Masculinity-Femininity," *JSAS Catalog of Selected Documents in Psychology*, 4, 1974; Sandra Bem, *Lenses of Gender* (New Haven, CT: Yale University Press, 1993), p. 124.

14. Joseph Pleck, *The Myth of Masculinity* (Cambridge: MIT Press, 1981).

15. See, for example, James M. O'Neil, "Assessing Men's Gender Role Conflict," *Problem Solving Strategies and Interventions for Men in Conflict*, D. Moorer and F. Leafgren, eds. (Alexandria, VA: American Association for Counseling and Development, 1990); J.M. O'Neil, B. Helms, R. Gable, L. David, and L. Wrightsman, "Gender Role Conflict Scale: College Men's Fear of Femininity," *Sex Roles*, 14, 1986, pp. 335–350; Joseph Pleck, "The Gender Role Strain Paradigm: An Update," *A New Psychology of Men*, R.

Levant and W. Pollack, eds. (New York, NY: Basic Books, 1995); James Mihalik, Benjamin Locke, Harry Theodore, Robert Cournoyer, and Brendan Lloyd, "A Cross-National and Cross-Sectional Comparison of Men's Gender Role Conflict and Its Relationship to Social Intimacy and Self-Esteem," *Sex Roles*, 45 (1/2), 2001, pp. 1–14.

16. Warren Farrell, *The Myth of Male Power* (New York, NY: Simon & Schuster, 1993), p. 40.

17. That's not to say that Pleck doesn't try valiantly to do so in his "Men's Power over Women, Other Men and in Society," *Women and Men: The Consequences of Power*, D. Hiller and R. Sheets, eds. (Cincinnati, OH: University of Cincinnati Women's Studies, 1977). But the theory is still unable to theorize both difference and institutionalized gender relations adequately.

18. Jean-Paul Sartre, *Anti-Semite and Jew* (New York, NY: Schocken Press, 1965), p. 60.

19. See Jean Piaget, *Plays, Dreams and Imitation in Children* (New York, NY: Norton, 1951); *The Language and Thought of the Child* (London, UK: Routledge, 1952); and *The Moral Judgment of the Child* (New York, NY: Free Press, 1965).

20. Lawrence Kohlberg, "A Cognitive-Developmental Analysis of Children's Sex Role Concepts and Attitudes," *The Development of Sex Differences*, E. Maccoby, ed. (Stanford, CT: Stanford University Press, 1966); and Lawrence Kohlberg and Edward Zigler, "The Impact of Cognitive Maturity on the Development of Sex Role Attitudes in the Years 4 to 8," *Genetic Psychology Monographs*, 75, 1967.

21. Albert Bandura and Althea Huston, "Identification as a Process of Incidental Learning," *Journal of Abnormal and Social Psychology*, 63 (2), 1961, pp. 311–318; Albert Bandura, Dorothea Ross, and Sheila Ross, "A Comparative Test of the Status Envy, Social Power, and Secondary Reinforcement Theories of Identificatory Learning," *Journal of Abnormal and Social Psychology*, 67 (6), 1963, pp. 527–534; Walter Mischel, "A Social-Learning View of Sex Differences," *The Development of Sex Differences*,

E. Maccoby, ed. (Stanford, CT: Stanford University Press, 1966).

22. Julia Kristeva, *Melanie Klein*, trans. Ross Guberman (New York, NY: Columbia University Press, 2001), 118; Karen Horney, "On the Genesis of the Castration Complex in Women," *Psychoanalysis and Women*, J.B. Miller, ed. (New York, NY: Bruner/Mazel, 1973); Melanie Klein, *A Study of Envy and Gratitude* (New York, NY: Routledge, 2003 [1957]).

23. Bruno Bettelheim, *Symbolic Wounds* (New York, NY: Collier, 1962); Wolfgang Lederer, *The Fear of Women* (New York, NY: Harcourt Brace Jovanovich, 1968).

24. Nancy Chodorow, *The Reproduction of Mothering* (Berkeley: University of California Press, 1978); Jessica Benjamin, *The Bonds of Love* (New York, NY: Pantheon, 1984); Dorothy Dinnerstein, *The Mermaid and the Minotaur* (New York, NY: Harper and Row, 1977); Lillian Rubin, *Intimate Strangers* (New York, NY: Harper and Row, 1983); see also Chodorow, "Family Structure and Feminine Personality," *Women, Culture and Society*, M. Rosaldo and L. Lamphere, eds. (Stanford, CA: Stanford University Press, 1974).

25. Chodorow, "Family Structure . . . ," p. 50.

26. Carol Gilligan, *In a Different Voice* (Cambridge, MA: Harvard University Press, 1982), p. 173.

27. Belenky et al., *Women's Ways of Knowing* (New York, NY: Basic Books, 1987); Deborah Tannen, *You Just Don't Understand*; Robert Bly, *Iron John* (Reading, PA: Addison-Wesley, 1991).

28. See H. Crothers, *Meditations on Votes for Women* (Boston, MA: Houghton, Mifflin, 1914), p. 74; *Selected Essays of Schopenhauer*, Ernest Belfort Bax, ed. (London, UK: G. Bell and Sons, Ltd., 1926), available at https://archive.org/stream/selectedessaysof033377mbp/selectedessaysof033377mbp_djvu.txt (accessed February 11, 2016).

29. Carol Gilligan, "Reply," "On In a Different Voice: An Interdisciplinary Forum," *Signs*, 11 (2), 1986, p. 327; affidavit of Carol Gilligan in Johnson v Jones, D Ct, S.C., filed January 7, 1993, p. 3.

30. See Madam Justice Bertha Wilson, "Will Women Judges Really Make a Difference? The Fourth Annual Barbara Betcherman Memorial Lecture," *Family and Conciliation Courts Review*, 30 (1), January 1992, pp. 13–25; p. 24.

31. Tavris, "The Mismeasure of Woman," *Feminism and Psychology*, p. 153.

32. Eleanor Maccoby and Carol Jacklin, *The Psychology of Sex Differences* (Stanford, CA: Stanford University Press, 1974), p. 355.

33. Janet Hyde, "The Gender Similarities Hypothesis," *The American Psychologist*, 60, 2005, pp. 581–559.

34. David P. Schmitt et al., "Why Can't a Man Be More Like a Woman? Sex Differences in Big Five Personality Traits across 55 Cultures," *Journal of Personality and Social Psychology*, 94 (1), 2008, pp. 168–182.

Chapter 4

1. Margaret Mead, *Sex and Temperament in Three Primitive Societies* (New York, NY: William Morrow, 1935).

2. For an example of how broadly Mead's theories were applied, see Doris Chang, "Reading *Sex and Temperament* in Taiwan: Margaret Mead and Postwar Taiwanese Feminism," *NWSA Journal*, 21 (1), Spring 2009, pp. 51–75.

3. Mead, *Sex and Temperament*, pp. 29, 35, 57–58, 84, 101, 128.

4. Margaret Mead, *Male and Female* (New York, NY: William Morrow, 1949), p. 69; Mead, *Sex and Temperament*, p. 171.

5. Mead, *Sex and Temperament*, pp. 189, 190, 197; Mead, *Male and Female*, p. 98.

6. Paul Shankman's 2013 article offered a devastating critique of Derek Freeman's scholarship and his attack on Mead. See Shankman, "The 'Fateful Hoaxing' of Margaret Mead: A Cautionary Tale," *Current Anthropology*, 54 (1), February 2013, pp. 51–70. For the debate, see, among many other sources, Derek Freeman, *Margaret Mead and Samoa: The Making and Unmaking of an Anthropological Myth* (Cambridge, MA: Harvard University Press, 1983) and *The Fateful Hoaxing of Margaret Mead: A Historical Analysis of Her Samoan Research* (New York, NY: Basic Books, 1999); Paul Roscoe, "Margaret Mead, Reo Fortune, and Mountain Arapesh Warfare," *American Anthropologist*, 105 (3), January 2008, pp. 581–591; Micaela di Leonardo, "Margaret Mead and the Culture of Forgetting in Anthropology: A Response to Paul Roscoe," *American Anthropologist*, 105 (3), 2003, pp. 592–595; and David Lipset, "Rereading *Sex and Temperament*: Margaret Mead's Sepik Triptych and Its Ethnographic Critics," *Anthropological Quarterly*, 76 (4), Fall 2003, pp. 693–713.

7. Mead, *Sex and Temperament*, p. 228.

8. For analysis of the calculus involved in adopting a sexual division of labour, see Wataru Nakahashi and Marcus W. Feldman, "Evolution of Division of Labor: Emergence of Different Activities among Group Members," *Journal of Theoretical Biology*, 348, 2014, pp. 65–79.

9. For an engaging and careful discussion, see Gerda Lerner, *The Creation of Patriarchy* (Oxford, UK: Oxford University Press, 1987).

10. Diane Bolger, "The Dynamics of Gender in Early Agricultural Societies of the Near East," *Signs*, 35 (2), Winter 2010, pp. 503–531; p. 521.

11. Adrienne Zihlman, "Woman the Gatherer: The Role of Women in Early Hominid Evolution," *Gender and Anthropology*, S. Morgen, ed. (Washington, DC: American Anthropological Association, 1989), p. 31.

12. Apurba Krishna Deb, C. Emdad Haque, and Shirley Thompson, "'Man Can't Give Birth, Woman Can't Fish': Gender Dynamics in the Small-Scale Fisheries of Bangladesh," *Gender, Place, and Culture: A Journal of Feminist Geography*, 22 (3), 2015, pp. 305–324.

13. Friedrich Engels, *On the Origin of the Family, Private Property and the State* (New York, NY: International Publishers, 1970).

14. Eleanor Leacock, "Women's Status in Egalitarian Society: Implications for Social Evolution," *Current Anthropology*, 19 (2), 1978, p. 252; see also Eleanor Leacock, "Montagnais Women and the Jesuit Program for Colonization," *Women and Colonization*, M. Etienne and E. Leacock, eds. (New York, NY: Praeger, 1980).

15. Karen Sacks, "Engels Revisited: Women, Organization of Production, and Private Property," *Women, Culture, and Society*, M. Rosaldo and L. Lamphere, eds.

16. Marvin Harris, *Cows, Pigs, Wars and Witches*: *The Riddle of Culture* (New York, NY: Random House, 1974); and *Cannibals and Kings* (New York, NY: Random House, 1977).

17. Lionel Tiger and Robin Fox, *The Imperial Animal* (New York, NY: Holt, 1971).

18. Claude Levi-Strauss, *The Elementary Structures of Kinship* (London, UK: Tavistock, 1969); see also Collier and Rosaldo, "Politics and Gender in Simple Societies," *Sexual Meanings: The Cultural Construction of Gender and Sexuality*, S.B. Ortner and H. Whitehead, eds. (Cambridge, MA: Cambridge University Press, 1981).

19. Allan Barnard, *Social Anthropology and Human Origins* (Cambridge, MA: Cambridge University Press, 2011), pp. 25–26.

20. Judith Brown, "A Note on the Division of Labor by Sex," *American Anthropologist*, 72 (5), 1970.

21. Scott Coltrane; *Family Man: Fatherhood, Housework, and Gender Equity* (Oxford, UK: Oxford University Press, 1996), p. 191 passim; Margaret Mead, *Male and Female*, pp. 189, 190.

22. Peggy Reeves Sanday, *Female Power and Male Dominance* (New York, NY: Cambridge University Press, 1981), pp. 75, 128. See also Maria Lepowsky, "Gender in an Egalitarian Society: A Case Study from the Coral Sea," *Beyond the Second Sex: New Directions in the Anthropology of Gender*, P. R. Sanday and R. G. Goodenough, eds. (Philadelphia, PA: University of Pennsylvania Press, 1990). See Carol Tavris and Carole Wade, *The Longest War* (New York, NY: Harcourt, Brace, 1984), pp. 330–331.

23. Elizabeth Crouch Zelman, "Reproduction, Ritual, and Power," *American Ethnologist*, 4 (4), November 1977, pp. 714–733.

24. Karen Paige and Jeffrey Paige, *The Politics of Reproductive Ritual* (Berkeley, CA: University of California Press, 1981).

25. Tavris and Wade, *The Longest War*, p. 314; see also Paige and Paige, *The Politics of Reproductive Ritual*; and Fatima Mernissi, *Beyond the Veil: Male-Female Dynamics in a Modern Muslim Society* (New York, NY: Wiley, 1975).

26. Daphne Spain, *Gendered Spaces* (Chapel Hill, NC: University of North Carolina Press, 1992); "The Spatial Foundations of Men's Friendships and Men's Power," *Men's Friendships*, Peter Nardi, ed. (Newbury Park, CA: Sage Publications, 1992), p. 76.

27. Thomas Gregor, *Mehinaku: The Drama of Daily Life in a Brazilian Indian Village* (Chicago, IL: University of Chicago Press, 1977), p. 255, 305–306. In another passage, Gregor recounts a child's game in which a girl pretends to invade the men's house and the boys pretend to gang-rape her (p. 114). See also Thomas Gregor, "No Girls Allowed," *Science*, 82, December 1982.

28. Virginia S. Fink, "A Cross-Cultural Test of Nancy Jay's Theory about Women, Sacrificial Blood, and Religious Participation," *Journal of International Women's Studies*, 6 (1), November 2004, pp. 54–72.

29. Stephanie Seguino, "Help or Hindrance? Religion's Impact on Gender Inequality in Attitudes and Outcomes," *World Development*, 39 (8), 2011, pp. 1308–1321.

30. John W. Whiting, Richard Kluckhohn, and Albert Anthony, "The Function of Male Initiation Ceremonies at Puberty," *Readings in Social Psychology*, E. Maccoby, T.M. Newcomb, and E.L. Hatley, eds. (New York, NY: Henry Holt, 1958); Edgar Gregersen, *Sexual Practices* (New York, NY: Franklin Watts, 1983), p. 104.

31. World Health Organization, *Female Genital Mutilation* (Fact Sheet), February 2014, available at www.who.int/mediacentre/factsheets /fs241/en/# See also Jessica Algot, "FGM: Number of Victims Found to Be 70 Million Higher than Thought," *The Guardian* online, February 5, 2016, available at www.theguardian.com/society/2016/feb/05 /research-finds-200m-victims-female-genital -mutilation-alive-today (accessed February 6, 2016).

32. "Canada Circumcision Statistics," Circumcision Reference Library, available at www. cirp.org/library/statistics/Canada/

33. Chris Rediger and Andries J. Muller, "Parents' Rationale for Male Circumcision,"

Canadian Family Physician, 59 (2), February 2013, pp. 110–115.

34. Rogaia Mustafa, "Unmasking Tradition," *The Sciences*, March/April 1998, p. 23.

35. Olga Khazan, "Why Some Women Choose to Get Circumcised," *Atlantic Monthly*, April 8, 2015.

36. Frederick Nzwili, "New Ritual Replaces Female Genital Mutilation," *Women's ENews*, April 10, 2003, available at www.womense-news.org/article.cfm/dyn/ aid/1284

37. L. Amede Obiora, "Bridges and Barricades: Rethinking Polemics and Intransigence in the Campaign against Female Circumcision," *Global Critical Race Feminism: An International Reader,* A.K. Wing, eds. (New York, NY: New York University Press, 2000).

38. See, for example, Joseph Zoske, "Male Circumcision: A Gender Perspective," *Journal of Men's Studies*, 6 (2), Winter, 1998; see also Michael Kimmel, "The Kindest Uncut," *Tikkun*, 16 (3), May 2001.

39. See www.tostan.org/female-genital-cutting

40. Abdi A. Gele, Bernadette Kumar, Karin Harsløf Hjele, and Johane Sundby, "Attitudes toward Female Circumcision among Somali Immigrants in Oslo: A Qualitative Study," *International Journal of Women's Health*, 4, 2012, pp. 7–17.

41. Michael Olien, *The Human Myth* (New York, NY: Harper and Row, 1978); M.K. Martin and B. Voorhies, *Female of the Species* (New York, NY: Columbia University Press, 1975).

42. Walter Williams, *The Spirit and the Flesh* (Boston, MA: Beacon Press, 1986).

43. Sabine Lang, *Men as Women, Women as Men* (Austin, TX: University of Texas Press, 1998).

44. For discussion, see Will Roscoe, "How to Become a Berdache," *Third Sex, Third Gender: Beyond Sexual Dimorphism in Culture and History*, Gilbert Herdt, ed., (New York, NY: Zone Books, 1996), pp. 329–372; p. 339.

45. Edgar Gregersen, *Sexual Practices*, p. 270.

46. Antonia Young, *Women Who Become Men: Albanian Sworn Virgins* (New York, NY: Berg, 2000); Rene Gremaux, "Woman Becomes Man in the Balkans," Herdt ed., *Third Sex, Third Gender*, pp. 241–281; Mike Lanchin, "Last of Albania's 'Sworn Virgins,'" BBC News, October 22, 2008, available at http://news.bbc.co.uk/2/hi/europe/7682240.stm (accessed May 5, 2009); Nicola Smith, "Sworn Virgins Dying out as Albanian Girls Reject Manly Role," *Times* online, January 6, 2008, available at www.timesonline.co.uk/tol/news/world/europe/article3137518.ece

47. Martin and Voorhies, *Female of the Species*, p. 97.

48. Carolina Moreno, "Muxes in Mexico: A Third Gender Embraced by the Zapotec People," *Huffington Post*, October 9, 2012, available at www.huffingtonpost.com/2012/10/09/third-gender-muxes_n_1949638.html Also Marc Lacey, "A Lifestyle Distinct: The Muxe of Mexico," *The New York Times*, December 6, 2008, available at www.nytimes.com/2008/12/07/weekinreview/07lacey.html (accessed May 10, 2009).

49. Serena Nanda, "Hijras: An Alternative Sex and Gender Role in India," Herdt, ed., *Third Sex, Third Gender*, pp. 373–417; RIA Misra, "Pakistan Recognizes Third Gender," *Politics Daily*, December 25, 2009, available at www.politicsdaily.com/2009/12/25/pakistan-recognizes-third-gender/ Also Homa Khaleeli, "Hijra: India's Third Gender Claims Its Place in Law," *The Guardian*, April 16, 2014, available at www.theguardian.com/society/2014/apr/16/india-third-gender-claims-place-in-law

50. Cited in Clyde Kluckholn, *Mirror for Man* (Greenwich, CT: Greenword, 1970).

51. Gilbert Herdt, *Guardians of the Flutes* (Chicago, IL: University of Chicago Press, 1981), pp. 1, 165, 282.

52. F.E. Williams, *Papuans of the Trans-Fly* (Oxford, UK: Oxford University Press, 1936), p. 159; see also E.L. Schiefflin, *The Sorrow of the Lonely and the Burning of the Dancers* (New York, NY: St. Martin's Press, 1976); R. Kelly, *Etero Social Structure* (Ann Arbor, MI: University of Michigan Press, 1977); J. Carrier, "Sex Role Preference as an Explanatory Variable in Homosexual Behavior," *Archives of Sexual Behavior*, 6, 1977; Stephen O. Murray, *Homosexualities* (Chicago, IL: University of Chicago Press, 2000).

53. William Davenport, "Sex in Cross-Cultural Perspective," *Human Sexuality in Four Perspectives*, F. Beach and M. Diamond, eds.

(Baltimore, MD: Johns Hopkins University Press, 1977); see also Gilbert Herdt, ed., *Ritualized Homosexuality in Melanesia* (Berkeley, CA: University of California Press, 1984), p. 66.

54. Gregersen, *Sexual Practices*, p. 257.

55. Ibid.

56. Davenport, "Sex in Cross-Cultural Perspective."

57. Ernestine Friedel, *Women and Men: An Anthropologist's View* (New York, NY: Holt, Rinehart, 1975).

58. Clyde Kluckholn, "As an Anthropologist Views It," *Sex Habits of American Men*, Albert Deutsch, ed. (New York, NY: Prentice-Hall, 1948), pp. 88–104; see also Gregersen, *Sexual Practices*.

59. Nancy Tanner and Adrienne Zihlman, "Women in Evolution," *Signs*, 1 (3), Spring, 1976. Nancy Tanner, *Becoming Human* (New York, NY: Cambridge University Press, 1981); Adrienne Zihlman, "Motherhood in Transition: From Ape to Human," *The First Child and Family Formation*, W. Miller and L. Newman, eds. (Chapel Hill, NC: Carolina Population Center, 1978).

60. Helen Fisher, *The Anatomy of Love* (New York, NY: Norton, 1992), p. 57.

61. Michelle Rosaldo, "The Use and Abuse of Anthropology: Reflections on Feminism and Cross-Cultural Understanding," *Signs*, 5 (3), Spring, 1980, p. 393; Bonnie Nardi, review of Peggy Reeves Sanday's *Female Power and Male Dominance* in *Sex Roles*, 8 (11), 1982, p. 1159.

62. Marija Gimbutas, *The Goddesses and Gods of Old Europe, 7000–3500 BC* (Berkeley, CA: University of California Press, 1982), and Marija Gimbutas, *The Living Goddesses* (Berkeley, CA: University of California Press, 1999). See also Riane Eisler, *The Chalice and the Blade* (New York, NY: HarperCollins, 1987), pp. 45, 58.

63. Frances Fukuyama, "Women and the Evolution of World Politics," *Foreign Affairs*, September 1998, p. 27; see also Lawrence Keely, *War Before Civilization*.

64. Maria Lepowsky, *Fruit of the Motherland: Gender in an Egalitarian Society* (New York, NY: Columbia University Press, 1993), p. 219.

65. Peggy Reeves Sanday, *Women Center: Life in a Modern Matriarchy* (Boston, MA: Beacon, 2002), p. 116.

66. See Native Women's Association of Canada, *Revitalization of Matrilineal/Matriarchal/ Egalitarian Systems: An Issue Paper.* 2007, available at www.laa.gov.nl.ca/laa/naws/pdf /nwac-matrilineal.pdf

67. Eleanor Leacock, "Montagnais Women," p. 200.

68. Cecilia Ridgway, *Framed by Gender: How Gender Inequality Persists in the Modern World* (New York, NY: Oxford University Press, 2011), p. 7.

Chapter 5

1. M. Pines, "Civilizing of Genes," *Psychology Today*, September 1981.

2. Ridgway, *Framed by Gender*, pp. 8–9.

3. Helen Z. Lopata and Barrie Thorne, "On the Term 'Sex Roles,'" *Signs*, 3, 1978, p. 719.

4. Tim Carrigan, Bob Connell, and John Lee, "Toward a New Sociology of Masculinity," *Theory and Society*, 14, 1985, pp. 551–604. See also R.W. Connell, *Gender and Power*; R.W. Connell, *Masculinities* (Berkeley, CA: University of California Press, 1995); Judith Stacey and Barrie Thorne, "The Missing Feminist Revolution in Sociology," *Social Problems*, 32 (4), 1985 (for elaboration and summaries of the sociological critique of sex role theory).

5. McElvaine, *Eve's Seed*, pp. 73–78.

6. Deborah Rhode, *Speaking of Sex* (Cambridge, MA: Harvard University Press, 1997), p. 42.

7. Stacey and Thorne, "The Missing Feminist Revolution," p. 307.

8. Carrigan, Connell, and Lee, "Toward a New Sociology," p. 587; see also Connell, *Gender and Power.*

9. Helen Hacker, "Women as a Minority Group," *Social Forces*, 30 (1), October 1951, pp. 60–69.

10. David Tresemer, "Assumptions Made about Gender Roles," *Another Voice: Feminist Perspectives on Social Life and Social Science*, M. Millman and R.M. Kanter, eds. (New York, NY: Anchor Books, 1975), p. 323; R. Stephen Warner, David Wellman, and Leonore

Weitzman, "The Hero, the Sambo, and the Operator: Three Characterizations of the Oppressed," *Urban Life and Culture*, 2 (1), 1973, p. 53.

11. Hannah Arendt, *On Revolution* (New York, NY: Viking, 1976).

12. David P. Schmitt et al., "Is There an Early-30s Peak in Female Sexual Desire? Cross-Sectional Evidence from the United States and Canada," *The Canadian Journal of Human Sexuality*, 11 (1), Spring 2002, pp. 1–18; p. 3.

13. Daniel J. Levinson with Charlotte N. Darrow, Edward B. Klein, Maria H. Levinson, and Braxton McKee, *The Seasons of a Man's Life* (New York, NY: Ballantine Books, 1978); Gail Sheehy, *Passages: Predictable Crises of Adult Life* (New York, NY: Bantam Books, 1984 [1976]).

14. Oliver C. Robinson and Gordon R.T. Wright, "The Prevalence, Types and Perceived Outcomes of Crisis Episodes in Early Adulthood and Midlife: A Structured Retrospective-Autobiographical Study," *International Journal of Behavioral Development*, 37 (5), September 2013, pp. 407–416. See also T. Costa and R.R. McCrae, "Age Difference in Personality Structure: A Cluster Analytic Approach," *Journal of Gerontology*, 31 (1978), pp. 564–570; and G.E. Valliant, *Adaptations to Life* (Boston, MA: Little Brown, 1978).

15. Stanley Rosenberg, Harriet Rosenberg, and Michael Farrell, "The Midlife Crisis Revisited," *Life in the Middle: Psychological and Social Development in Middle Age*, Sherry Willis and James Reid, eds. (Toronto, ON: Academic Press, 1998), pp. 47–76.

16. David Blanchflower and Andrew Oswald, "Is Well-Being U-Shaped over the Life Cycle?" *Social Science & Medicine*, 11 (8), April 2008, pp. 1733–1749.

17. Covadonga Robles Urquijo and Anne Milan, "Female Population," *Women in Canada: A Gender-based Statistical Report* (Ottawa, ON: Minister of Industry, 2011), available at www.statcan.gc.ca/pub/89-503-x/2010001/article/11475-eng.pdf

18. Bribiescas, *Men*, p. 202.

19. D.F. Goldspink, "Aging and Activity: The Effects on the Functional Reserve Capacities of the Heart and Vascular, Smooth, and Skeletal Muscles," *Ergonomics*, 48 (11–14), September–November 2005, pp. 1334–1351; WHO, *World Health Statistics 2014* (Geneva, Switzerland: WHO, 2014).

20. Yves Decady and Lawson Greenberg, "Ninety Years of Change in Life Expectancy," *Health at a Glance* (Statistics Canada). Available at www.statcan.gc.ca/pub/82-624-x/2014001/article/14009-eng.pdf "Gender Gap in Life Expectancy Narrows to 5.2 Years," *Canadian Medical Association Journal*, 168 (11), May 27, 2003; "Canadian Babies Can Expect to See Their 80s: StatsCan," CBC News.ca December 20, 2006. Available at www.cbc.ca/health/story/2006/12/20/life-span.html?ref=rss (accessed June 24, 2009); Frank Trovato and N.M. Lalu, "Narrowing Sex Differentials in Life Expectancy in the Industrialized World, Early 1970s to Early 1990s," *Social Biology*, 43 (1–2), 1996, pp. 20–37.

21. Ahifa Kassam, "Turf War: Bullying of Belinda Stronach Tells Women 'Stay Out,'" *Herizons: Women's News and Feminist Views*, 21 (2), Fall 2007, pp. 16–19; for Preston Manning, see *The Globe and Mail*, June 4, 1997.

22. Janet Saltzman Chafetz, "Toward a Macro-Level Theory of Sexual Stratification," *Current Perspectives in Social Theory*, 1, Scott McNall and G. Howe, eds. (Greenwich, CT: JAI Publications, 1980).

23. Erving Goffman, "The Arrangement Between the Sexes," *Theory and Society*, 4 (3), 1977, p. 316.

24. Kanter, *Men and Women of the Corporation*. See also Rosabeth Moss Kanter, "Women and the Structure of Organizations: Explorations in Theory and Behavior," *Another Voice*, M. Millman and R.M. Kanter, eds.

25. Joan Acker, "Hierarchies, Jobs, Bodies: A Theory of Gendered Organizations," *Gender & Society*, 4 (2), 1990, p. 146; see also Joan Acker, "Sex Bias in Job Evaluation: A Comparable Worth Issue," *Ingredients for Women's Employment Policy*, C. Bose and G. Spitze, eds. (Albany, NY: SUNY Press, 1987); "Class, Gender and the Relations of Distribution," *Signs: Journal of Women in Culture and Society*, 13, 1988; *Doing Comparable*

Worth: Gender, Class and Pay Equity (Philadelphia, PA: Temple University Press, 1989), and Joan Acker and Donald R. Van Houten, "Differential Recruitment and Control: The Sex Structuring of Organizations," *Administrative Science Quarterly*, 19 (2), 1974.

26. Cathy Gulli and Kate Lunau, "Adding Fuel to the Doctor Crisis," *Maclean's*, January 2, 2008, available at www.macleans.ca/scinece/health/article.jsp?conetnt=20080102_122329_6200 (accessed on November 18, 2009); Cathy Gulli, "Where Have All the Men Gone?" *Maclean's*, September 17, 2007, available at www.macleans.ca/education/postsecondary/article.jsp?content1120090924_109282_1 (accessed November 14, 2009).

27. Wendy Robbins, "Tenure Track and Reproductive Track on Collision Course," Canadian Association of University Teachers, available at www.academicwork.ca/en_career_articles_details.asp?cID=7[#] Mary Ann Mason, "In the Ivory Tower, Men Only," *Slate*, June 17, 2013, available at www.slate.com/articles/double_x/doublex/2013/06/female_academics_pay_a_heavy_baby_penalty.html

28. Judith Gerson and Kathy Peiss, "Boundaries, Negotiation, Consciousness: Reconceptualizing Gender Relations," *Social Problems*, 32 (4), 1985, p. 320.

29. Acker, "Hierarchies, Jobs, Bodies," p. 258.

30. Candace West and Don Zimmerman, "Doing Gender," *Gender & Society*, 1 (2), 1987, pp. 140.

31. Cited in Claudia Dreifus, "Declaring with Clarity When Gender Is Ambiguous," *The New York Times*, May 31, 2005, p. F2; see also Suzanne J. Kessler, "The Medical Construction of Gender: Case Management of Intersexed Infants," *Signs* 16 (1), 1990, pp. 12, 13.

32. The phrase comes from R.W. Connell; we take it from the title of Barbara Risman, *Gender Vertigo*.

33. Cited in West and Zimmerman, "Doing Gender," pp. 133–134.

34. Steve Chagollan, "RuPaul on Marriage Equality: We Live in an Age of Openness, but that Window Could Close," *Variety*, June 3, 2015, www.variety.com/2015/voices/news/rupaul-marriage-equality-1201531114/

35. Cited in West and Zimmerman, "Doing Gender," pp. 133–134.

36. Suzanne Kessler, "The Medical Construction of Gender," p. 25.

37. Simone de Beauvoir, *The Second Sex*, trans. H.M. Parshley (New York, NY: Vintage Books, 1989 [1952]), p. 267.

38. Mary Wollstonecraft, *A Vindication of the Rights of Woman* (New York, NY: The Modern Library, 2001).

39. Josephine Donovan, "Animal Rights and Feminist Theory," *The Feminist Care Tradition in Animal Ethics: A Reader*, ed. Josephine Donovan (New York, NY: Columbia University Press, 2007), p. 65.

40. Nancy Cott, *The Grounding of Modern Feminism* (New Haven, CT: Yale University Press, 1987), pp. 14–15; Estelle B. Freedman, *No Turning Back: The History of Feminism and the Future of Women* (New York, NY: Ballantine Books, 2002), p. 3.

41. In Canada, some women were not enfranchised when women received the right to vote in federal elections in 1918. Chinese-Canadian women got the vote in 1947, Inuit women in 1948, and First Nations women in 1960.

42. Cott, *Grounding*, p. 20.

43. Susan Oliver, *Betty Friedan: The Personal is Political* (New York, NY/Toronto, ON: Pearson Longman, 2008), 71. See also Betty Friedan, *The Feminine Mystique* (New York, NY: W.W. Norton and Co.), 1963 and de Beauvoir, *The Second Sex*.

44. Oliver, *Betty Friedan*, pp. 106–110.

45. See Bonnie Kreps, "Radical Feminism 1," *Feminist Theory Reader: Local and Global Perspectives*, Carole Ruth McCann and Seung-Kyung Kim, eds. (New York, NY/London, UK: Routledge, 2003), pp. 48–49.

46. Freedman, *No Turning Back*, p. 89.

47. Cherríe Moraga and Gloria Anzaldúa, "Introduction," *This Bridge Called My Back: Writings by Radical Women of Color*, ed. Cherríe Moraga and Gloria Anzaldúa (Waterton, MA: Persephone Press, 1981), p. xxiii.

48. Judith P. Zinsser, "From Mexico to Copenhagen to Nairobi: The United Nations Decade for Women, 975–1985," *Journal of World*

History, 13 (1), Spring 2002, pp. 139–168. See also Nilüfer Çagatay, Caren Grown, and Aida Santiago, "The Nairobi Women's Conference: Toward a Global Feminism?" *Feminist Studies*, 12 (2), Summer 1986, pp. 401–412.

49. Chandra Talpade Mohanty, "Under Western Eyes: Feminist Scholarship and Colonial Discourses," *boundary 2*, 12/13 (3/1), Spring–Autumn 1984, pp. 333–358.

50. Kimberlé Crenshaw, "Demarginalizing the Intersection of Race and Sex," *The University of Chicago Legal Forum*, 140, 1989, pp. 139–167.

51. Leslie McCall, "The Complexity of Intersectionality," *Signs*, 30 (3), 2005, pp. 1771–1800.

52. Judith Butler, *Gender Trouble: Feminism and the Subversion of Identity* (New York, NY/London, UK: Routledge, 1990).

53. Rebecca Walker, "Becoming the Third Wave," *Ms. Magazine*, 12, January/February 2002.

54. Emi Koyama, "The Transfeminist Manifesto," *Catching A Wave: Reclaiming Feminism for the Twenty-First Century*, Rory Dicker and Alison Piepmeier, eds. (Boston, MA: Northeastern University Press, 2003), pp. 244–260. For the history of feminism and trans inclusion, see Laurie Penny, "Moving Towards Solidarity," *The F Word: Contemporary UK Feminism*, December 2009, www.thefword.org.uk/2009/12/cis_feminists_s/

55. R.W. Connell, *Masculinities*, Second Edition (Berkeley, CA: University of California Press, 2005), p. 19.

56. Barbara Ehrenreich, *The Hearts of Men: American Dreams and the Flight from Commitment* (New York, NY: Anchor Books, 1983), pp. 50–51.

57. Connell, *Masculinities*, Second Edition, pp. 21–27.

58. Natalie Zemon Davis, "European Women's History in Transition: The European Case," *Feminist Studies*, 3 (3/4), Spring/Summer 1976.

59. R.W. Connell, *Gender and Power*.

60. R.W. Connell and James W. Messerschmidt, "Hegemonic Masculinity: Rethinking the Concept," *Gender & Society*, 19, 2005, pp. 829–859.

61. Gail Bederman, *Manliness and Civilization: A Cultural History of Gender and Race in the United States, 1880–1917* (Chicago, IL: University of Chicago Press, 1996); Michael Kimmel, *Manhood in America*, p. 3.

62. See, for example, Beth Skilken Catlett and Patrick C. McKentry, "Class-Based Masculinities: Divorce, Fatherhood, and the Hegemonic Ideal," *Fathering: A Journal of Theory, Research, and Practice about Men as Fathers*, 2 (2), 2004, pp. 165–190; Jeff Hearn and Antony Whitehead, "Collateral Damage: Men's 'Domestic' Violence to Women Seen through Men's Relations with Men," *The Journal of Community and Criminal Justice*, 53 (1), 2006, pp. 38–56; Sheryl Cunningham et al., "Accruing Masculinity Capital: Dominant and Hegemonic Masculinities in the 2004 Political Conventions," *Men & Masculinities*, 16 (5), 2013, pp. 499–516; James Joseph Dean, "Heterosexual Masculinities, Anti-Homophobias, and Shifts in Hegemonic Masculinity: The Identity Practices of Black and White Heterosexual Men," *Sociological Quarterly*, 54 (4), 2013, pp. 534–560; Laura Grindstaff and Emily West, "Hegemonic Masculinity on the Sidelines of Sport," *Sociology Compass*, 5 (10), 2011, pp. 859–881; Clare Bartholomaeus, "I'm Not Allowed Wrestling Stuff": Hegemonic Masculinity and Primary School Boys," *Journal of Sociology*, 48 (3), 2012, pp. 227–247; and Kate Reed, "Beyond Hegemonic Masculinity: The Role of Family Genetic History in Men's Accounts of Health," *Sociology*, 47 (5), 2013, pp. 906–920.

63. Connell, *Masculinities*, Second Edition, p. 68.

64. Jeff Hearn, "From Hegemonic Masculinity to the Hegemony of Men," *Feminist Theory*, 5 (1), 2004, pp. 59–72.

65. Demetrakis Z. Demetriou, "Connell's Concept of Hegemonic Masculinity: A Critique," *Theory & Society*, 30 (3), 2001, pp. 337–362; Margaret C. Ervin, "The Might of the Metrosexual: How a Mere Marketing Tool Challenges Hegemonic Masculinity," *Performing American Masculinities: The Twenty-First-Century Man in Popular Culture*, Elwood Watson and Marc E. Shaw, eds.

(Bloomington, IN: Indian University Press, 2011), pp. 58–75; Steven L. Arxer, "Hybrid Masculine Power: Reconceptualizing the Relationship between Homosociality and Hegemonic Masculinity," *Humanity & Society*, 35 (4), 2011, pp. 390–422.

66. Connell and Messerschmidt, "Rethinking the Concept," p. 846.

67. Michael Messner, "The Limits of 'The Male Sex Role': An Analysis of the Men's Liberation and Men's Rights Movements Discourse," *Gender & Society*, 12 (3), June 1998, pp. 255–276; p. 256.

68. Harold C. Lyon, *Tenderness Is Strength: From Machismo to Manhood* (New York, NY: Harper & Row, 1977), p. 9.

69. Messner, "Limits," p. 256.

70. Judith Newton, *From Panthers to Promise Keepers: Rethinking the Men's Movement* (Lanham, MD: Rowman & Littlefield, 1994), p. 8.

71. Herb Goldberg, *The Hazards of Being Male: Surviving the Myth of Masculine Privilege* (Gretna, LA: Wellness Institute, Inc., 2000 [1976]), p. 17.

72. Leora N. Rose, Molly Draghiewicz, and Jennifer C. Gibbs, "Father's Rights Groups: Demographic Correlates and Impact on Custody Policy," *Violence against Women*, 15 (5), May 2009, pp. 515–531.

73. Farrell, *The Myth of Male Power*.

74. Eliot Rodger, "The Manifesto of Eliot Rodger," *The New York Times*, May 25, 2014, pp. 117–118. Available online at www.nytimes.com/interactive/2014/05/25/us/shooting-document.html

75. Mariah Blake, "Mad Men: Inside the Men's Rights Movement and the Army of Misogynists and Trolls It Spawned," *Mother Jones*, January 28, 2015. Available at www.motherjones.com/politics/2015/01/warren-farrell-mens-rights-movement-feminism-misogyny-trolls See also Jeff Sharlet, "Are You Man Enough for the Men's Rights Movement?" *Gentlemen's Quarterly*, 2014. Available online at www.gq.com/story/mens-rights-activism-the-red-pill

76. See Michael Kimmel and M. Kaufman, "Weekend Warriors: The New Men's Movements," *Theorizing Masculinities*, H. Broad and M. Kaufman, eds. (Thousand Oaks, CA: Sage Press, 1994), pp. 259–288; Alastair Bonnett, "The New Primitives: Identity, Landscape, and Cultural Appropriation in the Mythopoetic Men's Movement," *Antipode*, 28 (3), 1996, pp. 273–291.

77. West and Zimmerman, "Doing Gender," p. 140; Barrie Thorne, 1980, p. 11; E.P. Thompson, *The Making of the English Working Class* (New York, NY: Pantheon, 1963), p. 11.

78. James Messerschmidt, *Masculinities and Crime* (Lanham, MD: Rowman and Littlefield, 1993), p. 121.

79. Carrigan, Connell, and Lee, "Toward a New Sociology of Masculinity," p. 589; Karen D. Pyke, "Class-Based Masculinities: The Interdependence of Gender, Class and Interpersonal Power," *Gender & Society*, 10 (5), 1996, p. 530.

Chapter 6

1. REAL Women of Canada, "Ongoing Discrimination by the Status of Women," *REALity* XXV, (3), May/June 2006, available at www.realwomenca.com/page/newslmj0607 (accessed June 2, 2009).

2. The American debate over family values is too extensive to be summarized here. See, for a few examples, Barbara Dafoe Whitehead, "Dan Quayle Was Right," *The Atlantic*, April 1993, which became the touchstone for her book, *The Divorce Culture* (New York, NY: Random House, 1996); David Popenoe, *Life without Father: Compelling New Evidence that Fatherhood and Marriage Are Indispensable for the Good of Children and Society* (New York, NY: The Free Press, 1996) and his "Modern Marriage: Revising the Cultural Script," *Promises to Keep: Decline and Renewal of Marriage in America*, D. Popenoe, J.B. Elshtain, and D. Blankenhorn, eds. (Lanham, MD: Rowman and Littlefield, 1996). On the other side, see Judith Stacey, *Brave New Families* (New York, NY: Basic Books, 1990); *In the Name of the Family: Rethinking Family Values in a Postmodern Age* (Boston, MA: Beacon 1997); as well as Stephanie Coontz, *The Way We Never Were:*

American Families and the Nostalgia Trap (New York, NY: Basic Books, 1995) and *The Way We Really Are: Coming to Terms with America's Changing Families* (New York, NY: Basic Books, 1998).

3. For a discussion of kinship (and the effects of colonialism upon it) in one group, see Laura Peers and Jennifer Brown, "'There Is No End to Relationship among the Indians': Ojibwa Kinship and Family in Historical Perspective," *The History of the Family*, 4(4), 1999, pp. 529–555.

4. See, for example, Mary-Ellen Turpel-Lafond, "Patriarchy and Paternalism: The Legacy of the Canadian State for First Nations Women," *Women and the Canadian State/ Les femmes et l'état Canadien* Caroline Andrew and Sanda Rodgers, eds., (Montreal, QC: McGill-Queen's Press, 1997), pp. 64–79.

5. For discussion of this process among the Huron and Montagnais, see Karen Anderson, *Chain Her by One Foot: The Subjugation of Native Women in Seventeenth-Century New France* (London/New York, NY: Routledge, 1993). For insight into marriage norms within New France's settler society, see Sylvie Savoie, "Women's Marital Difficulties: Requests of Separation in New France," *The History of the Family*, 4 (4), 1999, pp. 473–485.

6. This is Nancy Shoemaker's argument in "Kateri Tekakwitha's Tortuous Path to Sainthood," *Rethinking Canada: The Promise of Women's History,* Mona Gleason and Adele Perry, eds. (Toronto, ON: Oxford, 2006), pp. 10–25.

7. The classic treatments of fur-trade families, though in a later period than discussed here, are Jennifer Brown, *Strangers in Blood: Fur Trade Families in Indian Country* (Vancouver, BC: University of British Columbia Press, 1980); and Sylvia Van Kirk, *Many Tender Ties: Women in Fur-Trade Society, 1670–1870* (Norman, OK: University of Oklahoma Press, 1983).

8. Quoted in Margaret Conrad, "'Sundays Always Make Me Think of Home': Time & Place in Canadian Women's History," *Not Just Pin Money: Selected Essays on the History of Women's Work in British Columbia,* Barbara K. Latham and Roberta J. Pazdro, eds. (Victoria, BC: Camosun College, 1984), pp. 1–16; p. 7.

9. Laurel Thatcher Ulrich, *A Midwife's Tale: The Life of Martha Ballard, Based on Her Diary, 1785–1812* (New York, NY: Vintage Books, 1991), p. 76.

10. John Demos, *Past, Present, and Personal: The Family and Life Course in American History* (New York, NY: Oxford University Press, 1986), p. 32; see also Tamara Hareven, *Family Time and Industrial Time* (New York, NY: Cambridge University Press, 1982). Tennyson, "The Princess," as cited in Skolnick, *Embattled Paradise: The American Family in an Age of Uncertainty* (New York, NY: Basic Books, 1993), p. 35.

11. Cited in David Popenoe, *Life without Father,* p. 95.

12. Gerda Lerner, "The Lady and the Mill Girl: Changes in the Status of Women in the Age of Jackson," *American Studies Journal*, 10 (1), Spring 1969, pp. 7, 9. Theodore Dwight, *The Father's Book* (Springfield, MA: G. and C. Merriam, 1834). See, generally, Kimmel, *Manhood in America*, Chapters 1 and 2.

13. Christopher Lasch, *Women and the Common Life: Love, Marriage, and Feminism* (New York, NY: Norton, 1997), p. 162.

14. Bonnie Thornton Dill, "Our Mothers' Grief: Racial-Ethnic Women and the Maintenance of Families," *Journal of Family History*, 13 (4), 1988, p. 428.

15. For statistics on Canadian alcohol consumption in the nineteenth century, see "Alcohol, Consumption of, Per Capita (Canada)," Jack Blocker, David Fahey, and Ian Tyrrell, *Alcohol and Temperance in Modern History: A Global Encyclopedia* (Oxford, UK: ABC-Clio, 2003), pp. 20–21.

16. John Gillis, "Making Time for Family: The Invention of Family Time(s) and the Reinvention of Family History," *Journal of Family History*, 21, 1996; John Gillis, *A World of Their Own Making: Myth, Ritual, and the Quest for Family Values* (New York, NY: Basic Books, 1996).

17. Skolnick, *Embattled Paradise*, p. 41; Steven Mintz and Susan Kellogg, *Domestic*

Revolutions: A Social History of the American Family (New York, NY: The Free Press, 1991), p. 110.

18. See Lynne Marks, "'A Fragment of Heaven on Earth?' Religion, Gender, and Family in Turn of the Century Canadian Church Periodicals," Gleason and Perry, eds., *Rethinking Canada*, pp. 124–143.

19. Quoted in Celia Haig-Brown, *Resistance and Renewal: Surviving the Indian Residential School* (Vancouver, BC: Arsenal Pulp Press, 1988), p. 31. The literature on the residential school experience is vast. For a powerful recent publication, see *Response, Responsibility, and Renewal: Canada's Truth and Reconciliation Journey*, Gregory Younging, Jonathan Dewar, and Mike De Gagne, eds. (Ottawa, ON: Aboriginal Healing Foundation, 2009).

20. Truth and Reconciliation Commission of Canada, *Honouring the Truth, Reconciling for the Future: Summary of the Final Report of the Truth and Reconciliation Commission of Canada*, available at www.trc.ca/websites /trcinstitution/File/2015/Findings/Exec_ Summary_2015_05_31_web_o.pdf Truth and Reconciliation Commission of Canada, *Truth and Reconciliation: Calls to Action* (Winnipeg, MB: Truth and Reconciliation Commission, 2015), available at www.trc.ca /websites/trcinstitution/File/2015/Findings /Calls_to_Action_English2.pdf

21. Katrina Srigley, "'In Case You Hadn't Noticed': Race, Ethnicity, and Women's Wage-Earning in a Depression-Era City," *Labour/Le Travail*, 55, Spring 2005, pp. 69–105. See also Joy Parr's classic study *The Gender of Breadwinners: Women, Men, and Change in Two Industrial Towns, 1880–1950* (Toronto, ON: University of Toronto Press, 1998).

22. E.D. Nelson and Barrie Robinson, *Gender in Canada* (Scarborough, ON: Prentice-Hall, 1998), p. 88.

23. Ralph LaRossa, *The Modernization of Fatherhood: A Social and Political History* (Chicago, IL: University of Chicago Press, 1997). Statistics Canada, *Canada E-Book*, available at www43.statcan.ca/02/02d_001a _e.htm (accessed June 2, 2009). For the

nineteenth-century data and comparisons between Canada and the US, see Lisa Dillon, "Women and the Dynamics of Marriage, Household Status, and Aging in Victorian Canada and the United States," *The History of the Family*, 4 (4), pp. 447–483.

24. Mintz and Kellogg, *Domestic Revolutions*, p. 179, 237; Coontz, *The Way We Really Are*, p. 30.

25. William Chafe, *The Unfinished Journey: America since World War II* (New York, NY: Oxford University Press, 1986), p. 125; Morris Zelditch, "Role Differentiation in the Nuclear Family: A Comparative Study," *Family, Socialization and Interaction Process*, T. Parsons and R.F. Bales, eds. (New York, NY: The Free Press, 1955), p. 339.

26. Robert Griswold, *Fatherhood in America: A History* (New York, NY: Basic Books, 1993), p. 204; Lasch, *Women and the Common Life*, p. 94; Ruth Schwartz Cowan, *More Work for Mother: The Ironies of Household Technology from the Open Hearth to the Microwave* (New York, NY: Basic Books, 1983), p. 216; Lerner, cited in Skolnick, *Embattled Paradise*, p. 115.

27 Doris Anderson, "We've Been Emerging Long Enough," reprinted in Mary Eberts, "'Write It for the Women': Doris Anderson, the Changemaker," *Canadian Woman Studies/Les cahiers de la femme*, 26 (2), Summer/Fall 2007, pp. 6–13.

28. See, for example, Ehrenreich, *The Hearts of Men*, on the "male revolt" against breadwinner responsibilities. Also see Kimmel, *Manhood in America*, especially Chapter 7.

29. For the 1970s data, see Nancy A. Crowell and Ethel M. Leeper, eds., *America's Fathers and Public Policy* (Washington, DC: National Academy Press, 1994), p. 1. For 2011 data, see Sophia Addy, Will Engelhardt, and Curtis Skinner, "Basic Facts about Low-Income Children: Children under 18 Years, 2011," National Center for Children in Poverty, January 2013, available at www.nccp.org/publications /pub_1074.html (accessed August 7, 2015).

30. "B.C. Has Highest Child Poverty Rate in Canada: Report," CBC, November 26, 2013, available at www.cbc.ca/news/canada/british -columbia/b-c-has-highest-child-poverty-rate -in-canada-report-1.24409 (accessed August

15, 2015). Campaign 2000, *Let's Do This: Let's End Child Poverty For Good. 2015 Report Card on Child and Family Poverty in Canada* (Toronto, ON: Campaign 2000, 2015); "2008 Report Card on Child and Family Poverty in Canada" (Toronto, ON: Campaign 2000, 2008); Community Foundations of Canada, *Canada's Vital Signs 2008*; summary available at www.vitalsignscanada.ca /pdf/2008-national-news-release-and-back grounder.pdf (accessed July 12, 2009).

31. UNICEF/NCCAH, *Aboriginal Children's Health: Leaving No Child Behind* (Toronto, ON: UNICEF Canada, 2009); Human Resources and Skills Development Canada, "Canadians in Context: Households and Families," available at www4.hrsdc.gc.ca /.3ndic.1t.4r@eng.jsp?iid=37 (accessed June 24, 2009).

32. There is an ample literature on the topic of the Aboriginal family and its relations with Canadian governments and society. See, inter alia, Ernie Crey and Suzanne Fournier, *Stolen from Our Embrace: The Abduction of First Nations Children and the Restoration of Aboriginal Communities* (Vancouver, BC: Douglas & McIntyre, 1997); Marlee Kline, "Complicating the Ideology of Motherhood: Child Welfare Law and First Nations Women," *Mothers in Law: Feminist Theory and the Legal Regulation of Motherhood,* Martha Fineman and Isabel Karpin, eds. (New York, NY: Columbia University Press, 1995), pp. 118–141; Cindy Blackstock, Nico Trocme, and Marlyn Bennett, "Child Maltreatment Investigations among Aboriginal and Non-Aboriginal Families in Canada," *Violence against Women,* 10 (8), August 2004, pp. 901–916; Marlene Brant Castellano, *Aboriginal Family Trends: Extended Families, Nuclear Families, Families of the Heart* (Toronto, ON: Vanier Institute of the Family, 2002); For Aboriginal breastfeeding in BC, see Janet Smylie, *Strong Women, Strong Nations: Aboriginal Maternal Health in British Columbia* (Prince George, BC: National Collaborating Centre for Aboriginal Health, 2014).

33. Statistics Canada, *Portrait of Families and Living Arrangements in Canada: Families,* *Households, and Marital Status* (Ottawa, ON: Minister of Industry, 2012); Statistics Canada, *Fifty Years of Families in Canada: 1961 to 2011* (Ottawa, ON: Minster of Industry, 2015); Statistics Canada, *Canada E-book,* available at www43.statcan.ca/02/02d_001a_e.htm (accessed June 6, 2009); Statistics Canada, *The Daily,* Wednesday, January 17, 2007, available at www.statcan.gc.ca/daily-quotidien /070117/dq070117a-eng.htm (accessed June 6, 2009); Statistics Canada, *The Daily,* Wednesday, March 9, 2005, available at www.statcan .gc.ca/daily-quotidien/050309/dq050309b -eng.htm (accessed June 6, 2009).

34. Employment and Social Development Canada, "Family Life: Marriage," available at http://well-being.esdc.gc.ca/misme-iowb /.3ndic.1t.4r@-eng.jsp?iid=78 Anne Milan, *Marital Status: Overview, 2011* (Ottawa, ON: Ministry of Industry, 2013), p. 1; for wealth-associated marriage in Canada, see Philip Cross and Peter Jon Mitchell, *The Marriage Gap between Rich and Poor Canadians,* Institute of Marriage and Family Canada, February 2014; for ethnic differences in the USA, see Jonathan Vespa, Jamie M. Lewis, and Rose M. Kreider, *America's Families and Living Arrangements, 2012: Population Characteristics,* available at www.census.gov /prod/2013pubs/p20-570.pdf

35. Milan, *Marital Status,* p. 3; Statistics Canada, *Fifty Years of Families in Canada.*

36. "Canadians Would Keep Same-Sex Marriage Legal," *Angus Reid Global Monitor,* December 6, 2006, available at www.angus-reid .com/polls/view/14013 (accessed July 11, 2009).

37. For the Defense of Marriage Act, see Anne Marie Smith, "The Politicization of Marriage in Contemporary American Public Policy: The Defense of Marriage Act and the Personal Responsibility Act," *Citizenship Studies,* 5 (3), 2001, pp. 303–320; Barry D. Adam, "The Defense of Marriage Act and American Exceptionalism: The 'Gay Marriage' Panic in the United States," *Journal of the History of Sexuality,* 12 (2), April 2003, pp. 259–276; Michael J. Kanotz, "For Better or for Worse: A Critical Analysis of Florida's Defense of

Marriage Act," *Florida State University Law Review*, 25 (2), 1998; Jeffrey M. Jones, "Majority of Americans Continue to Oppose Same-Sex Marriage: No Change in Support from Last Year," available at www.gallup.com/poll/118378/Majority-Americans-Continue-Oppose-Gay-Marriage.aspx (accessed July 13, 2009); the text of the US Supreme Court decision is freely available online; see Andrew Soergel, "Supreme Court Affirms Constitutionality of Gay Marriage," *US News*, June 26, 2015, available at www.usnews.com/news/articles/2015/06/26/supreme-court-affirms-constitutionality-of-gay-marriage (accessed July 25, 2015).

38. Daniel Greenfield, "The Deconstruction of Marriage," April 16, 2015, available at www.realwomenofcanada.ca/the-deconstruction-of-marriage/ (accessed August 25, 2015). See also REAL Women of Canada, "Families in the Western World Enduring Perilous Times," Newsletter July/August 2008, available at www.realwomenca.com/index.cfm?page=149&string=families%20in%20the%20western%20world (accessed June 8, 2009).

39. James Snell, *In the Shadow of the Law: Divorce in Canada 1900–1939* (Toronto, ON: University of Toronto Press, 1991), p. 9. Employment and Social Development Canada, "Family Life: Divorce," available at http://well-being.esdc.gc.ca/misme-iowb/.3ndic.1t.4r@-eng.jsp?iid=76[#] Casey E. Copen, Kimberly Daniels, Jonathan Vespa, and William D. Mosher, "First Marriages in the United States: Data from the 2006–2010 National Survey of Family Growth," *National Health Statistics Reports,* 49, March 22, 2012; Sheela Kennedy and Steven Ruggles, "Breaking Up Is Hard to Count: The Rise of Divorce in the United States, 1980–2010," *Demography*, 51, 2014, pp. 587–598.

40. Zosia Bielski, "Divorce Rates Drop across Canada," *The Globe and Mail*, March 29, 2012, available at www.theglobeandmail.com/life/the-hot-button/divorce-rates-drop-across-canada/article4096512/ (accessed June 7, 2015); Susan L. Brown and I-Fen Lin, "The Gray Divorce Revolution: Rising Divorce among Middle-Aged and Older Adults, 1990–2010," *Journals of Gerontology Series B: Psychological Sciences and Social Sciences*, 67 (6), 2012, pp. 731–741. Milan, *Marital Status*; Brigid Schulte, "Till Death Do Us Part? No Way. 'Gray Divorce' on the Rise," *The Washington Post*, October 8, 2014, available at www.washingtonpost.com/blogs/she-the-people/wp/2014/10/08/till-death-do-us-part-no-way-gray-divorce-on-the-rise/ (accessed June 7, 2015).

41. Lianne George, "Maclean's Poll 2006: What We Believe," *Maclean's*, July 4, 2006, available at www.macleans.ca/article.jsp?content=20060701_130104_130104&-source=srch (accessed July 4, 2009).

42. Ibid. Also see Coltrane, *Family Man*, p. 203; Andrew Cherlin, "By the Numbers," *The New York Times Magazine*, April 5, 1998, p. 39.

43. Linda J. Waite, "Does Marriage Matter?" *Demography*, 32 (4), November 1995, pp. 483–507; p. 499. Steven Nock, "Marriage as a Public Issue," *The Future of Children*, 15 (2), Fall 2005, pp. 13–32; p. 17. For a full discussion, see also see Linda J. Waite and Maggie Gallagher, *The Case for Marriage: Why Married People Are Happier, Healthier and Better Off Financially* (New York, NY: Doubleday, 2000).

44. Kristi Williams and Debra Umberson, "Marital Status, Marital Transitions, and Health: A Gendered Life Course Perspective," *Journal of Health and Social Behavior*, 45 (1), March 2005, pp. 81–98; p. 93.

45. Ahmad Reza Hosseinpoor et al., "Social Determinants of Self-Reported Health in Men and Women: Understanding the Role of Gender in Population Health," *PLOS ONE*, 7 (4), April 2012, pp. 1–9; p. 3. See also Woojin Chung and Roeul Kim, "Are Married Men Healthier than Single Women? A Gender Comparison of the Health Effects of Marriage and Marital Satisfaction in East Asia," *PLOS ONE*, 10 (7), July 2015.

46. For further examination, see Williams and Umberson, "Marital Status, Marital Transitions, and Health"; Hosseinpoor et al., "Social Determinants of Self-Reported Health"; Mary Elizabeth Hughes and Linda J. Waite,

"Marital Biography and Health at Mid-Life," *Journal of Health and Social Behavior*, 50, September 2009, pp. 344–358; Kelly Musick and Larry Bumpass, "Reexamining the Case for Marriage: Union Formation and Changes in Well-Being," *Journal of Marriage and the Family*, 74, February 2012, pp. 1–18; Hui Liu and Debra J. Umberson, "The Times They Are a Changin': Marital Status and Health Differentials from 1972 to 2003," *Journal of Health and Social Behavior*, 49, September 2008, pp. 239–253; Shawn Grover and John F. Helliwell, *How's Life at Home? New Evidence on Marriage and the Set Point for Happiness*, Working Paper 20794 (Cambridge, MA: National Bureau of Economic Research, December 2014); Alois Stutzer and Bruno S. Frey, "Does Marriage Make People Happy, or Do Happy People Get Married?" *Journal of Socio-Economics*, 35, 2006, pp. 326–247.

47. Jessie Bernard, *The Future of Marriage* (New York, NY: World, 1972); Walter R. Gove, "The Relationship between Sex Roles, Marital Status and Mental Illness," *Social Forces*, 51, 1972; Walter Gove and M. Hughes, "Possible Causes of the Apparent Sex Differences in Physical Health: An Empirical Investigation," *American Sociological Review*, 44, 1979; Walter Gove and Jeanette Tudor, "Adult Sex Roles and Mental Illness," *American Journal of Sociology*, 73, 1973; "The Decline of Marriage," *Scientific American*, December 1999. See also, for example, Hynubae Chun and Injae Lee, "Why Do Married Men Earn More: Productivity or Marriage Selection?" *Economic Inquiry*, 39 (2), April 2001, pp. 307–319; and Leslie Stratton, "Examining the Wage Differential for Married and Cohabiting Men," *Economic Inquiry*, 40 (2), April 2002, pp. 199–212. See also Paula England's review of *The Case for Marriage in Contemporary Sociology*, 30 (6), 2001; Natalie Angier, "Men. Are Women Better Off with Them or without Them?" *The New York Times*, June 21, 1998, p. 10.

48. Musick and Bumpass, "Reexamining the Case for Marriage," p. 250; P.D. St John and P.R. Montgomery, "Marital Status, Partner Satisfaction, and Depressive Symptoms in Older Men and Women," *Canadian Journal of Psychiatry*, 54, 2009, pp. 487–492; W. Chung and R. Kim, "Are Married Men Healthier than Single Women?" S.B. Patten et al., "Descriptive Epidemiology of Major Depression in Canada," *Canadian Journal of Psychiatry*, 51 (2), February 2006, pp. 84–90.

49. Jamie Brownlee, "Satisfaction," *Recent Social Trends in Canada, 1960–2000*, Lance Roberts, Rodney Clifton, and Barry Ferguson, eds. (Montreal, QC: McGill-Queen's, 2005), pp. 627–633; Bebin and statistics cited in Elaine Carey, "Kids Put a Damper on Marital Bliss: Study," *The Star*, August 15, 1997, pp. A1, A14; Lee Chalmers and Anne Milan, "Marital Satisfaction during the Retirement Years," *Canadian Social Trends*, Spring 2005 (Statistics Canada Catalogue 11-008), pp. 14–17.

50. For the 2015 survey, see www.wedding bells.ca/planning/wedding-trends-in-canada-2015/ (accessed December 15, 2015). For the most complete study of the wedding phenomenon, see Chrys Ingraham, *White Weddings: Romancing Heterosexuality in Popular Culture*, Second Edition (New York, NY: Routledge, 2008). For surnames, see Diana Boxer and Elena Gritsenko, "Women and Surnames across Cultures: Reconstituting Identity in Marriage," *Women & Language*, 28 (2), Fall 2005, pp. 1–11; Alexandra Sifferlin, "How American Women Fought to Keep Their Maiden Names After Marriage," *Time*, December 17, 2015, available at www.time.com/4153417/how-american-women-fought-to-keep-their-maiden-names-after-marriage/ (accessed February 12, 2016); Rajini Vaidyanathan, "A New Wedding Trend? The Men Taking Their Wives' Names," *BBC News*, June 11, 2015, available at www.bbc.com/news/magazine-33085652 (accessed February 12, 2016).

51. Liu and Umberson, "The Times They Are a Changin'," p. 250; Debra Umberson et al., "You Make Me Sick: Marital Quality and Health over the Life Course," *Journal of Health and Social Behavior*, 47 (1), March 2006, pp. 1–16.

52. For a recent survey of the literature, see Rob Palkovitz, "Gendered Parenting's

Implications for Children's Well-Being: Theory and Research in Applied Perspective," *Gender and Parenthood: Biological and Social Scientific Perspectives*, W. Bradford Wilcox and Kathleen Kovner Kline eds. (New York, NY: Columbia University Press, 2013), pp. 215; For differential treatment in India, see Silvia H. Barcellos, Leandro Cavalho, and Adriana Lleras-Muney, "Child Gender and Parental Investments in India: Are Boys and Girls Treated Differently?" National Bureau of Economic Research Working Paper No. 17781, January 2012, available at www.nber.org/papers/w17781 Prashant Bharadwaj and Leah K. Lakdawala, "Discrimination Begins in the Womb: Evidence of Sex-Selective Prenatal Investments," *Journal of Human Resources*, 48 (1), Winter 2013, pp. 71–113; for sex-selective abortion (including evidence for North America), see Sneha Barot, "A Problem-and-Solution Mismatch: Son Preference and Sex-Selective Abortion Ban," *Guttmacher Policy Review*, 15 (2), Spring 2012, pp. 19–22.

53. Quoted in Medora W. Barnes, "Fetal Sex Determination and Gendered Prenatal Consumption," *Journal of Consumer Culture* 15 (3), November 2015, pp. 371–390.

54. Medora W. Barnes, "Anticipatory Socialization of Pregnant Women: Learning Fetal Sex and Gendered Interactions," *Sociological Perspectives*, 58 (2), 2015, pp. 187–203.

55. See Joanne Sweeney and Marilyn R. Bradbard, "Mothers' and Fathers' Changing Perceptions of Their Male and Female Infants over the Course of Pregnancy," *Journal of Genetic Psychology*, 149 (3), 1988, pp. 393–404. For Baby Storm, see Jayme Poisson, "Remember Storm? We Check in on the Baby Being Raised Gender-Neutral," *The Star* online, November 15, 2013, available at www .thestar.com/life/parent/2013/11/15/remember_storm_we_check_in_on_the_baby_being_raised_genderneutral.html (accessed August 20, 2015). For a British case that ignited similar "gender rage" and allegations of abuse, see also Wency Leung, "Parents Finally Reveal 5-Year-Old's Gender," *The Globe and Mail*, January 26, 2012, available at www.theglobeandmail.com/life/the-hot-button/parents-finally-reveal-5-year-olds-gender/article621081/ (accessed July 29, 2015).

56. J. Walter Thompson Intelligence, *The State of Men*, June 2013, available at jwtintelligence .com

57. Jo B. Paoletti, *Pink and Blue: Telling the Boys from the Girls in America* (Bloomington, IN: Indiana University Press, 2012).

58. www.fisher-price.com/en_US/brands/baby toys/products/Brilliant-Basics-Hammerin -Rattle

59. Cornelia Fine, "Biology or Balderdash?" *New Scientist*, 222 (2963), April 5, 2014; B. Lott, *Women's Lives: Themes and Variations in Gender Learning* (Monterey, CA: Brooks/ Cole, 1987). See also L.A. Schwartz and W.T. Markham, "Sex Stereotyping in Children's Toy Advertisements," *Sex Roles*, 12, 1985; and S.B. Ungar, "The Sex Typing of Adult and Child Behavior in Toy Sales," *Sex Roles*, 8, 1982.

60. Betty Vohr et al., "Gender Differences in Adult–Infant Communication in the First Months of Life," *Pediatrics*, 134 (6), December 2014, pp. e1603-e1610.

61. J. Condry and S. Condry, "Sex Differences: A Study in the Eye of the Beholder," *Child Development*, 47, 1976.

62. Amy Kennedy Root and Kenneth H. Rubin, "Gender and Parents' Reactions to Children's Emotion during the Preschool Years," *New Directions for Child and Adolescent Development,* 128, Summer 2010, pp. 51–64; pp. 59–60; Ana Aznar and Harriet R. Tenenbaum, "Gender and Age Differences in Parent–Child Emotion Talk," *British Journal of Developmental Psychology*, 33 (1), March 2015, pp. 148–155.

63. Tracey McVeigh, "Men See Sons More than Daughters after Breakup," *The Guardian* online, June 14, 2015, available at www .theguardian.com/lifeandstyle/2015/jun/14 /fathers-sons-daughters-marriage-split Also see Root and Rubin, "Gender and Parents' Reactions," p. 54; Ashely Smith Leavell et al., "African American, White and Latino Fathers' Activities with Their Sons and Daughters in Early Childhood," *Sex Roles*, 66, 2012, pp. 53–65.

64. For the quote, and a succinct discussion of various studies' findings, see Richard Lippa, *Gender, Nature, and Nurture* (Hillsdale, NJ: Lawrence Erlbaum Associates, 2001), pp. 132–137.

65. Isabelle D. Cherney et al., "The Effects of Stereotyped Toys and Gender on Play Assessment in Children Aged 18–47 Months," *Educational Psychology: An International Journal of Experimental Educational Psychology*, 23 (1), 2003, pp. 95–106.

66. Michael J. Carter, "Gender Socialization and Identity Theory," *Social Sciences*, 3, 2014, pp. 242–263; B. Lott, *Women's Lives*. See also Schwartz and Markham, "Sex Stereotyping in Children's Toy Advertisements"; and Ungar, "The Sex Typing of Adult and Child Behavior."

67. Alina Lisak, "Barbie Dolls," trans. Karol Maslany, in *Cultural Encyclopedia of the Breast*, Merril D. Smith, ed. (London, UK: Rowman & Littlefield, 2014), pp. 25–27.

68. See "Bratz Beat Barbie in Q4," *Playthings*, February 6, 2007, available at www.playthings.com/article/CA6413828.html (accessed July 6, 2009); Margaret Talbot, "Little Hotties," *The New Yorker*, December 4, 2006; Abby West, "Bratz Dolls: Worse than Barbie?" *Sirens Magazine*, August 22, 2007, available at www.alternet.org/story/60387/(accessed July 6, 2009).

69. "Barbie Beats Bratz in US Court," CBC News, December 4, 2008, available at www.cbc.ca/consumer/story/2008/12/04/bratz-mga.html (accessed July 6, 2009).

70. Callie Beusman, "Goth Barbie Celebrates 'Freaky Flaws' by Looking Like Regular Barbie," *Jezebel* online, July 7, 2013, available at www.jezebel.com/goth-barbie-celebrates-freaky-flaws-by-looking-like-re-812447918 (accessed August 18, 2015).

71. See, for example, Barrie Thorne, "Boys and Girls Together . . . But Mostly Apart: Gender Arrangements in Elementary Schools" in *Relationships and Development*, W. Hartup and Z. Rubin, eds. (Hillsdale, NJ: Lawrence Erlbaum, 1986).

72. See, for example, Barrie Thorne and Zella Luria, "Sexuality and Gender in Children's Daily Worlds," *Social Problems*, 33, 1986; Barrie Thorne, *Gender Play* (New Brunswick, NJ: Rutgers University Press, 1993), p. 3; Richard Lippa, *Gender, Nature, and Nurture* (Hillsdale, NJ: Lawrence Erlbaum Associates, 2001), pp. 132–137.

73. Arlie Hochschild, *The Second Shift* (New York, NY: Viking, 1989); Paul Amato and Alan Booth, "Changes in Gender Role Attitudes and Perceived Marital Quality," *American Sociological Review*, 60, 1995; "Stress: Relevations sur un mal francais," *le Figaro*, April 15, 2006, p. 46; Sheldon Cohen and Denise Janicki-Deverts, "Who's Stressed? Distributions of Psychological Stress in the United States in Probability Samples from 1983, 2006, and 2009," *Journal of Applied Social Psychology*, 42 (6), 2012, pp. 1320–1334; Shashi Kala Singh, "Life Satisfaction and Stress Level among Working and Non-Working Women," *The International Journal of Indian Psychology*, 1 (4), 2014, pp. 121–128.

74. Pat Mainardi, "The Politics of Housework," *Sisterhood Is Powerful*, R. Morgan, ed. (New York, NY: Vintage, 1970).

75. Ballard and Foote are cited in Ruth Schwartz Cowan, *More Work for Mother*, p. 43; Campbell is cited in Susan Strasser, *Never Done: A History of American Housework* (New York, NY: Pantheon, 1982), p. 62.

76. For a review of more than 200 articles on the topic published between 1989 and 1999, see Scott Coltrane, "Research on Household Labor: Modeling and Measuring the Social Embeddedness of Routine Family Work," *Journal of Marriage and the Family*, 62, November 2000, pp. 1208–1233; see also Amy Kroska, "Exploring the Consequences of Gender Ideology–Work Discrepancies," *Sex Roles*, 60, 2009, pp. 313–328; Lisa Belkin, "When Mom and Dad Share It All," *The New York Times*, June 15, 2008, available at www.nytimes.com/2008/06/15/15parenting-t.html (accessed October 12, 2009); Scott Coltrane, *Family Man*, p. 46; Dana Vannoy-Hiller and William W. Philliber, *Equal Partners: Successful Women in Marriage* (Newbury Park, CA: Sage Publications, 1989), p. 115; Phyllis Moen and Patricia

Roehling, *Career Mystique: Cracks in the American Dream* (Lanham, MD: Rowman and Littlefield, 2004); Arlie Hochschild, *The Second Shift.*

77. For the US numbers, see Suzanne M. Bianchi, Liana C. Sayer, Melissa A. Milkie, and John P. Robinson, "Housework: Who Did, Does or Will Do It, and How Much Does It Matter?" *Social Forces,* 91 (1), September 2012, pp. 55–63. For Canada see John Conway, *The Canadian Family in Crisis,* Fifth Edition (Halifax, NB; Lorimer, 2003), pp. 213–215; Statistics Canada, "General Social Survey: Paid and Unpaid Work," *The Daily,* Wednesday, July 19, 2006, available at www.statcan.gc.ca/daily-quotidien/060719/dq060719b-eng.htm (accessed July 6, 2009). Also see Scott Coltrane, *Family Man,* p. 46; Vannoy-Hiller and Philliber, *Equal Partners,* p. 115. For the hours of women not in the workforce, see Bianchi, p. 59; see also Sheryl Ubelacker, "Men Inch Forward in Housework, Childcare" (Canadian Press). *The Star* online, March 4, 2008, available at www.thestar.com (accessed July 9, 2009).

78. For a discussion of emotion work, see Daphne Stevens, Gary Kiger, and Pamela Riley, "Working Hard and Hardly Working: Domestic Labor and Marital Satisfaction among Dual-Earner Couples," *Journal of Marriage and the Family,* 63 (2), May 2001, pp. 514–526. For the "double-burden" statistics, see Beaujot Roderic, Jianye Liu, and Zenaida R. Ravanera, "The Converging Gender Trends in Earning and Caring in Canada," Population Change and Lifecourse Strategic Knowledge Cluster Discussion Paper Series/*Un Réseau stratégique de connaissances Changements de population et parcours de vie Document de travail,* 3 (3), Article 2, 2015, available at: http://ir.lib.uwo.ca/pclc/vol3/iss3/2

79. Shira Offer and Barbara Schneider, "Revisiting the Gender Gap in Time-Use Patterns: Multitasking and Well-Being among Mothers and Fathers in Dual-Earner Families," *American Sociological Review,* 76 (6), 2011, pp. 809–883; Meg Luxton, "Two Hands for the Clock: Changing Patterns in the Gendered Division of Labour in the Home," *Through the Kitchen Window: The Politics of Home and Family,* Meg Luxton, Harriet Rosenberg, and Sedef Arat-Koc, eds. (Toronto, ON: Garamond Press, 1990), pp. 39–55; Joel Hektner, Jennifer Schmidt, and Mihály Csikszentmihályi, *Experience Sampling Method: Measuring the Quality of Everyday Life* (Thousand Oaks, CA: Sage Publications, 2007), p. 151.

80. For night duty, see Jennifer Senior, "Why Mom's Time Is Different from Dad's Time," *The Wall Street Journal,* January 24, 2014, available at www.wsj.com/articles/SB10001424052702304757004579335053525792432 (accessed July 22, 2015); see also Jenny H. Van Hooff, "Rationalising Inequality: Heterosexual Couples' Explanations and Justifications for the Division of Housework along Traditionally Gendered Lines," *Journal of Gender Studies,* 20 (1), 2011, pp. 19–30; Jessica Fischer and Veanne N. Anderson, "Gender Role Attitudes and Characteristics of Stay-at-Home and Employed Fathers," *Psychology of Men & Masculinity,* 13 (1), January 2012, pp. 16–31; Ruth Gaunt, "Breadwinning Moms, Caregiving Dads: Double Standard in Social Judgments of Gender Norm Violators," *Journal of Family Issues,* 34 (1), January 2013 , pp. 3–24.

81. Angela Meah, "Reconceptualizing Power and Gendered Subjectivities in Domestic Cooking Spaces," *Progress in Human Geography,* 38 (5), 2013, pp. 671–690; Michelle Szabo, "Foodwork or Foodplay? Men's Domestic Cooking, Privilege and Leisure," *Sociology,* 47 (4), 2012, pp. 623–638.

82. Anna Quindlen, cited in Deborah Rhode, *Speaking of Sex,* p. 8; Moen and Roehling, *Career Mystique;* Shannon N. Davis and Theodore N. Greenstein, "Gender Ideology: Components, Predictors, and Consequences," *Annual Review of Sociology,* 35, June 2009, pp. 87–105; Julie Press and Eleanor Townsley, "Wives' and Husbands' Housework Reporting: Gender, Class and Social Desirability," *Gender & Society,* 12 (2), 1998, p. 214. On men's involvement in family work, see Joseph Pleck, "Men's Family Work: Three Perspectives and Some New Data," *The Family Coordinator,* 28, 1979; "American Fathering in Historical Perspective,"

Changing Men: New Directions in Research on Men and Masculinity, M.S. Kimmel, ed. (Beverly Hills, CA: Sage Publications, 1987); *Working Wives/Working Husbands* (Newbury Park, CA: Sage Publications, 1985); "Families and Work: Small Changes with Big Implications," *Qualitative Sociology*, 15, 1992; "Father Involvement: Levels, Origins and Consequences," *The Father's Role*, Third Edition, M. Lamb, ed. (New York, NY: John Wiley, 1997).

83. Jenny Chesters, "Gender Convergence in Core Housework Hours: Assessing the Relevance of Earlier Approaches for Explaining Current Trends," *Journal of Sociology,* 49 (1), 2011, pp. 78–96; Bianchi et al., "Housework," p. 59; Daneila Grunow, Florian Schulz, and Hans-Peter Blossfeld, "What Determines Change in the Division of Housework over the Course of Marriage?" *International Sociology*, 27 (3), 2012, pp. 289–307.

84. Chesters, "Gender Convergence."

85. Vanessa Wight, Suzanne M. Bianchi, and Bijou R. Hunt, "Explaining Racial/Ethnic Variation in Partnered Women's and Men's Housework: Does One Size Fit All?" *Journal of Family Issues*, 34 (3), 2013, pp. 394–427; Bart Landry, *Black Working Wives: Pioneers of the American Family Revolution* (Berkeley, CA: University of California Press, 2001); Margaret Usdansky, "White Men Don't Jump into Chores," *USA Today*, August 20, 1994.

86. Julia Lawlor, "Blue Collar Dads Leading Trend in Caring for Kids, Author Says," *The New York Times*, April 15, 1998.

87. Benjamin Spock and Steven J. Parker, *Dr. Spock's Baby and Child Care*, Seventh Edition (New York, NY: Pocket Books, 1998), p. 10.

88. Bianchi et al., "Housework," p. 58. Offer and Schneider, "Revisiting the Gender Gap in Time-Use Patterns." For paternal leave, see Katherine Marshall, "Fathers' Use of Paid Parental Leave," *Perspectives*, June 2008 (Statistics Canada Catalogue Number 75-001-X), pp. 5–14; Pat Schroeder, cited in Deborah Rhode, *Speaking of Sex*, p. 7; Erin Rahel, "When Dad Stays Home Too: Paternity Leave, Gender, and Parenting," *Gender & Society*, 28

(1), 2014, pp. 110–132; Jerry Adler, "Building a Better Dad," *Newsweek*, June 17, 1996; Tamar Lewin, "Workers of Both Sexes Make Trade-Offs for Family, Study Shows," *The New York Times*, October 29, 1995, p. 25; Jeremy Adam Smith, *The Daddy Shift: How Stay-at-Home Dads, Breadwinning Moms, and Shared Parenting Are Transforming the American Family* (Boston, MA: Beacon Press, 2009).

89. "Sex, Death, and Football," *The Economist*, June 13, 1998, p. 18; Robert D. Mintz and James Mahalik, "Gender Role Orientation and Conflict as Predictors of Family Roles for Men," *Sex Roles*, 34 (1–2), 1996, pp. 805–821; Barbara Risman, "Can Men 'Mother'? Life as a Single Father," *Family Relations*, 35, 1986; see also Caryl Rivers and Rosalind Barnett, "Fathers Do Best," *The Washington Post*, June 20, 1993, p. C5.

90. Amanda Jayne Miller and Sharon Sassler, "The Construction of Gender among Working-Class Cohabiting Couples," *Qualitative Sociology*, 35, 2012, pp. 427–446.

91. Miller and Sassler, "The Construction of Gender"; Meghan Casserly, "Forbes Woman and The Bump.com Survey Results," *Forbes* online, June 15, 2011, available at www.forbes.com Caroline Cakebread, "Do You Resent Father's Day?" *Chatelaine*, June 17, 2011, available at www.chatelaine.com See also Peggy Orenstein, *Flux: Women on Sex, Love, Kids, and Life in a Half-Changed World* (New York, NY: Knopf, 2012).

92. Lawrence Kurdek, "The Allocation of Household Labor by Partners in Gay and Lesbian Couples," *Journal of Family Issues*, 28 (1), January 2007, pp. 132–148; Eva Jaspers and Ellen Verbakel, "The Division of Paid Labor in Same-Sex Couples in the Netherlands," *Sex Roles*, 68 (5–6), March 2013, pp. 335–348.

93. Jane R. Eisner, "Leaving the Office for Family Life," *Des Moines Register*, March 27, 1998, p. 7A.

94. Frank Furstenberg, "Can Marriage Be Saved?" *Dissent*, 52 (3), Summer 2005, pp. 76–80.

95. Maire Sinha, "Child Care in Canada," *Spotlight on Canadians: Results from the General Social Survey* (Ottawa, ON: Minister

of Industry, 2014); "Daycare: The Debate over Space," CBC News, February 11, 2009, available at www.cbc.ca/consumer/story /2009/02/06/f-daycare.html (accessed January 12, 2010); Statistics Canada, "Child Care: An Eight-Year Profile," *The Daily*, April 5, 2006, available at www.statcan.gc.ca/daily -quotidien/060405/dq060405a-eng.htm (accessed July 6, 2009).

96. Quoted in "Daycare: The Debate over Space"; Rianne Mahon, "Child Care in Canada and Sweden: Policy and Politics," *Social Politics,* 4 (3), 1997, pp. 382–418.

97. National Institute of Child Health and Human Develpment, *The NICHD Study of Early Child Care and Youth Development*: *Findings for Children up to Age 4 1/2 Years* (National Institutes of Health, c. 2012), available at www.nichd.nih.gov/publications/ pubs/documents/seccyd_06.pdf See also the recent analysis in Marion O'Brien et al., "Women's Work and Child Care: Perspectives and Prospects," *Societal Contexts of Child Development*: *Pathways of Influence and Implications for Practice and Policy,* Elizabeth T. Gershoff, Rashmita S. Mistry, and Danielle A. Crosby, eds. (New York, NY: Oxford University Press, 2013), pp. 37–50; See also Jay Belsky, "A Reassessment of Infant Day Care," and Thomas Gamble and Edward Zigler, "Effects of Infant Day Care: Another Look at the Evidence," both in *The Parental Leave Crisis: Toward a National Policy,* E. Zigler and M. Frank, eds. (New Haven, CT: Yale University Press, 1988); J. Douglas Willms and Elizabeth A. Sloat, "Literacy for Life," Atlantic Centre for Policy Research Policy Brief, No. 4 (December 1998); Susan Chira, "Study Says Babies in Child Care Keep Secure Bonds to Mother," *The New York Times,* April 21, 1996.

98. "Child Care Linked to Assertive, Noncompliant, and Aggressive Behaviors: Vast Majority of Children within Normal Range." NIH News Release, July 16, 2003, available at www.nichd.nih.gov/news/releases/child_ care.cfm (accessed July 5, 2009); Michael Baker, Jonathan Gruber, and Kevin Milligan, "What Can We Learn from Quebec's

Universal Childcare Program?" C.D. Howe Institute E-brief, February 1, 2006; Canadian Research Institute for Social Policy, "Daycare Attendance, Stress, and Mental Health," *CRISPfacts* July 2007.

99. Sinha, "Child Care in Canada"; Carolyn Ferns and Martha Friendly, Background paper on unregulated child care, *Home Child Care: More than a Home Project*, Childcare Resource and Research Unit Occasional Paper 28 (Toronto, ON: CRRU, 2015); Allison Jones, "Vaughan Daycare Where Toddler Eva Ravikovich Died Had Host of Health Violations," *Huffington Post*, September 20, 2013, available at www.huffing tonpost.ca/2013/09/20/vaughan-daycare -eva-ravikovich_n_3962247.html

100. For a theoretical/historical analysis, see Shelley Gavigan and Dorothy Chunn, "From Mothers' Allowance to Mothers Need Not Apply: Canadian Welfare Law and Liberal and Neo-Liberal Reforms," *Osgoode Hall Law Journal,* 45 (4), 2007, pp. 733–771; for a discussion of short-term and long-term effects, see Matthew Brzozowski, "Welfare Reforms and Consumption among Single Mother Households: Evidence from Canadian Provinces," Working Paper #2005-10 (RBC Financial Group Economic Policy Institute EPRI Working Paper Series), December 2005; Cherlin, "By the Numbers," p. 40.

101. See O'Brien et al., "Women's Work"; S. M. Bianchi and Daphne Spain, *American Women in Transition* (New York, NY: Russell Sage Foundation, 1986); E.G. Menaghan and Toby Parcel, "Parental Employment and Family Life: Research in the 1980s," *Journal of Marriage and the Family,* 52, 1990; Glenna Spitze, "Women's Employment and Family Relations: A Review," *Journal of Marriage and the Family,* 50, 1988.

102. For Europe, see Rossella Ciccia and Inge Bleijenbergh, "After the Male Breadwinner Model? Childcare Services and the Division of Labor in European Countries," *Social Politics,* 21 (1), 2014, pp. 50–79; Campaign 2000, *2008 Report Card on Child and Family Poverty in Canada,* (Toronto, ON: Campaign 2000, 2008); Joan K. Peters, *When*

Mothers Work: *Loving Our Children without Sacrificing Ourselves* (Reading, MA: Addison-Wesley, 1997).

103. Kathryn Kost and Stanley Henshaw, *US Teenage Pregnancies, Births, and Abortions, 2010*: *National and State Trends by Age, Race, and Ethnicity* (New York, NY: Guttmacher Institute, 2014); Anita Shaw, "Media Representations of Adolescent Pregnancy," *Atlantis: A Women's Studies Journal*, 34 (2), 2010, pp. 55–65; Gail Collins, "Bristol Palin's New Gig," *The New York Times*, May 7, 2009, available at www.nytimes.com/2009/05/07/opinion/07collins.html (accessed May 7, 2009); Heather Dryburgh, "Teenage Pregnancy," *Health Reports*, 12 (1), October 2000, pp. 9–19; Nicholas Bakalar, "Trends Shift, with Births on the Rise," *The New York Times*, January 20, 2009, available at www.nytimes.com/2009/01/20/health/research/20stat.html (accessed May 7, 2009); Vanessa Richmond, "Why Canada's on Top in Teen Pregnancy," *The Huffington Post*, April 26, 2009, available at www.huffingtonpost.com/vanessa-richmond/why-canadas-on-top-in-tee_b_178734.html (accessed July 11, 2009).

104. M.A. Males, *The Scapegoat Generation*: *America's War on Adolescents* (Monroe, ME: Common Courage Press, 1996) and "Adult Liaison in the 'Epidemic' of 'Teenage' Birth, Pregnancy, and Venereal Disease," *The Journal of Sex Research*, 29 (4), pp. 525–545. Thanks to Anita Shaw for these references. Alexander McKay, "Trends in Teen Pregnancy in Canada with Comparisons to USA and England/Wales," *The Canadian Journal of Human Sexuality*, 15 (3/4), 2006, pp. 157–161.

105. "The Many Fatherless Boys in Black Families," *The Globe and Mail*, November 26, 2005. Available at www.theglobeandmail.com/news/national/the-many-fatherless-boys-in-black-families/article921794/ (accessed July 11, 2009); Pittman, cited in Olga Silverstein, "Is a Bad Dad Better Than No Dad?" *On the Issues*, Winter, 1997, p. 15; David Blankenhorn, *Fatherless America*: *Confronting Our Most Urgent Social Problem* (New York, NY: Basic Books, 1993), p. 30; Robert Bly, *Iron John*, p. 96; David Popenoe, *Life without Father*, p. 12.

106. Jason De Parle and Sabrina Tavernise, "For Women under 30, Most Births Occur outside Marriage," *The New York Times*, February 17, 2012, available at www.nytimes.com/2012/02/18/us/for-women-under-30-most-births-occur-outside-marriage.html?_r=0 Gertrude Schaffner Goldberg, "Canada: Bordering on the Feminization of Poverty," *The Feminization of Poverty*: *Only in America?*, Gertrude Schaffner Goldberg and Eleanor Kremen, eds. (Westport, CT; Praeger Publishers, 1990), pp. 59–90; Statistics Canada, "Families, Households, and Housing," *Canada Yearbook Overview 2008*, available at www41.statcan.ca/2008/40000/ceb40000_000-eng.htm (accessed July 10, 2009).

107. Statistics Canada, *Fifty Years of Families in Canada*; Gretchen Livingston, "The Rise of Single Fathers: A Ninefold Increase since 1960," Pew Research Center, July 2, 2013, available at www.pewsocialtrends.org/2013/07/02/the-rise-of-single-fathers/ (accessed July 15, 2015).

108. Carey Goldberg, "Single Dads Wage Revolution One Bedtime Story at a Time," *The New York Times*, June 17, 2001, pp. A1, 16; Sarah L. DeJean, Christi R. McGeorge, and Thomas Stone Carlson, "Attitudes toward Never-Married Single Mothers and Fathers: Does Gender Matter?" *Journal of Feminist Family Therapy*, 24 (2), 2012, pp. 121–138; Paul Taylor, Rich Morin, and Wendy Wang, *The Public Renders a Split Verdict on Changes in Family Structure*, (Washington, DC: Pew Research Center, 2011). See also Ross D. Parke, *Future Families Diverse Forms, Rich Possibilities* (New York, NY: John Wiley & Sons, 2013).

109. Karen Kramer et al., "Comparison of Poverty and Income Disparity of Single Mothers and Fathers across Three Decades: 1990–2010," *Gender Issues*, 33 (1), March 2016, pp. 22–41; Livingston, "The Rise of Single Fathers."

110. Livingston, "The Rise of Single Fathers"; John Ifcher and Homa Zarghamee, "The

Happiness of Single Mothers: Evidence from the General Social Survey," *Journal of Happiness Studies*, 15, 2014, pp. 1219–1238.

111. Demie Kurz, *For Richer, For Poorer: Mothers Confront Divorce* (New York, NY: Routledge, 1995); Leonore Weitzman, *The Divorce Revolution: The Unexpected Social and Economic Consequences for Women and Children in America* (New York, NY: The Free Press, 1985); Patricia A. McManus and Thomas A. DiPrete, "Losers and Winners: The Financial Consequences of Separation and Divorce for Men," *American Sociological Review*, 66, April 2001, pp. 246–268; Paul Amato, "The Impact of Divorce on Men and Women in India and the United States," *Journal of Comparative Family Studies*, 25 (2), 1994; Tahany Ladalla, "Impact of Marital Dissolution on Men's and Women's Incomes: A Longitudinal Study," *Journal of Divorce and Remarriage,* 50 (1), 2009, pp. 55–65; Dorien Manting and Anne Marthe Bouman, "Short- and Long-Term Economic Consequences of the Dissolution of Marital and Consensual Unions: The Example of the Netherlands," *European Sociological Review,* 22 (4), 2006, pp. 413–429.

112. Andrew Schepard, *Children, Courts, and Custody: Interdisciplinary Models for Divorcing Families* (Cambridge, MA: Cambridge University Press, 2004), pp. 15–22; Susan Boyd, "Investigating Gender Bias in Canadian Child Custody Law: Reflections on Questions and Methods," *Investigating Gender Bias in Law: Socio-Legal Perspectives*, Joan Brockman and Dorothy Chunn, eds. (Toronto, ON: Thompson, 1993), pp. 169–190; Mary Jane Mossman, *Families and the Law in Canada: Cases and Commentary* (Toronto, ON: Captus Press, 2004), pp. 635–638, 645.

113. For a critical ethnographic view of the fathers' rights movement, see the article by University of Windsor researchers Carl Bertoia and Janice Drakich, "The Fathers' Rights Movement: Contradictions in Rhetoric and Practice," *Journal of Family Issues,* 14 (4), December 2003, pp. 592–615; for more about the US fatherhood movement, see Anna Gavanas, *Fatherhood Politics in the United States* (Urbana, IL: University of Illinois Press, 2004).

114. See, for example, Joan Kelly, "Longer-Term Adjustments of Children of Divorce," *Journal of Family Psychology*, 2 (2), 1988, p. 131; D. Leupnitz, *Child Custody: A Study of Families After Divorce* (Lanham, MD: Lexington Books, Rowman & Littlefield, 1982); D. Luepnitz, "A Comparison of Maternal, Paternal and Joint Custody: Understanding the Varieties of Post-Divorce Family Life," *Journal of Divorce*, 9, 1986; V. Shiller, "Loyalty Conflicts and Family Relationships in Latency Age Boys: A Comparison of Joint and Maternal Custody," *Journal of Divorce*, 9, 1986.

115. Robert Bauserman, "A Meta-analysis of Parental Satisfaction, Adjustment, and Conflict in Joint Custody and Sole Custody Following Divorce," *Journal of Divorce & Remarriage,* 53 (6), 2012, pp. 464–488; Joan Kelly, "Longer-Term Adjustments," p. 136; Nancy Crowell and Ethel Leeper, eds, *America's Fathers and Public Policy*, p. 27.

116. Popenoe, *Life without Father*, p. 27; Frank Furstenberg and Andrew Cherlin, *Divided Families: What Happens to Children When Parents Part?* (Cambridge, MA: Harvard University Press, 1991); Frank Furstenberg, "Good Dads–Bad Dads: Two Faces of Fatherhood," *The Changing American Family and Public Policy*, A. Cherlin, ed. (Lanham, MD: Urban Institute Press, 1988); William J. Goode, "Why Men Resist," *Rethinking the Family: Some Feminist Questions*, B. Thorne and M. Yalom, eds. (New York, NY: Longman, 1982).

117. Valerie King, "Nonresident Father Involvement and Child Well-Being," *Journal of Family Issues*, 15 (1), 1994; Edward Kruk, "The Disengaged Noncustodial Father: Implications for Social Work Practice with the Divorced Family," *Social Work*, 39 (1), 1994; see also Debra Umberson and Christine Williams, "Divorced Fathers: Parental Role Strain and Psychological Distress," *Journal of Family Issues*, 14 (3), 1993.

118. Judith Wallerstein and J. Kelly, *Surviving the Breakup: How Children and Parents Cope with Divorce* (New York, NY: Basic Books, 1980); Judith Wallerstein and Susan Blakeslee. *Second Chances: Men, Women, and Children a Decade after Divorce* (New York, NY: Ticknor and Fields, 1989), p. 11; Judith Wallerstein, Julia Lewis, and Sandra Blakeslee, *The Unexpected Legacy of Divorce: A 25 Year Landmark Study* (New York, NY: Hyperion, 2000); Judith Wallerstein, Julia Lewis, and Sherrin Packer Rosenthal, "Mothers and Their Children after Divorce: Report from the 25-Year Longitudinal Study," *Psychoanalytic Psychology*, 30 (2), 2013, pp. 167–187.

119. For criticism of Wallerstein's study, see, for example, Andrew Cherlin, "Generation Ex-," *The Nation*, December 11, 2000; Katha Pollitt, "Social Pseudoscience," *The Nation*, October 23, 2000, p. 10 (and subsequent exchange, December 4, 2000); Thomas Davey, "Considering Divorce," *The American Prospect*, January 1–15, 2001; Walter Kirn, "Should You Stay Together for the Kids?" *Time*, September 25, 2000; and Elisabeth Lasch-Quinn, "Loving and Leaving," *The New Republic*, May 6, 2002. For a recent summary, see Judith Cashmore and Patrick Parkinson, "The Use and Abuse of Social Science Research Evidence in Children's Cases," *Psychology, Public Policy, and Law*, 20 (3), August 2014, pp. 239–250.

120. Andrew Cherlin, "Going to Extremes: Family Structure, Children's Well-Being and Social Science," *Demography*, 36 (4), November 1999, p. 425; Lisa Strohschein, "Parental Divorce and Child Mental Health Trajectories," *Journal of Marriage and the Family*, 67, December 2005, pp. 1286–1300; For the British study, see Jane Brody, "Problems of Children: A New Look at Divorce," *The New York Times*, June 7, 1991; Jeanne Block, J. Block, and P.F. Gjerde, "The Personality of Children," president of council cited in Stephanie Coontz, *The Way We Really Are*, p. 108; Amato and Booth, *A Generation at Risk*, pp. 201, 230, 234; Paul Amato and Alan Booth, "The Legacy of Parents' Marital Discord: Consequences for Children's Marital Quality," *Journal of Personality and Social Psychology*, 81 (4), 2001, pp. 627–638; see also Paul Amato, "The Impact of Divorce"; "The Implications of Research Findings on Children in Stepfamilies," *Stepfamilies: Who Benefits? Who Does Not?* and "Single-Parent Households as Settings for Children's Development, Well-Being and Attainment: A Social Networks/Resources Perspective," *Sociological Studies of Children*, 7, 1995; Paul Amato and Alan Booth, "Changes in Gender Role Attitudes and Perceived Marital Quality," *American Sociological Review*, 60, 1995; Paul Amato, Laura Spencer Loomis, and Alan Booth, "Parental Divorce, Marital Conflict, and Offspring Well-Being During Early Adulthood," *Social Forces*, 73 (3), 1995. "Low conflict," by the way, is unhappy but not physically violent.

121. Joan B. Kelly, "Mediated and Adversarial Divorce: Respondents' Perceptions of Their Processes and Outcomes," *Mediation Quarterly*, 24, Summer, 1989, p. 125. See also J. Block, J. Block, and P.F. Gjerde, "The Personality of Children Prior to Divorce: A Prospective Study," *Child Development*, 57, 1986; Skolnick, *Embattled Paradise*, pp. 98–99; p. 212. B. Berg and R. Kelly, "The Measured Self-Esteem of Children from Broken, Rejected and Accepted Families," *Journal of Divorce*, 2, 1979; R.E. Emery, "Interparental Conflict and Children of Discord and Divorce," *Psychological Bulletin*, 92, 1982; p. 100; H.J. Raschke and V.J. Raschke, "Family Conflict and the Children's Self-Concepts," *Journal of Marriage and the Family*, 41, 1979; J.M. Gottman and L.F. Katz, "Effects of Marital Discord on Young Children's Peer Interaction and Health," *Developmental Psychology*, 25, 1989; D. Mechanic and S. Hansell, "Divorce, Family Conflict and Adolescents' Well-Being," *Journal of Health and Social Behavior*, 30, 1989; Paul Amato and Juliana Sobolewski, "The Effects of Divorce and Marital Discord on Adult Children's Psychological Well-Being," *American Sociological Review*, 66, December 2001, pp. 900–921.

122. For covenant marriage see Steven Nock, Laura Sanchez, and James Wright, *Covenant Marriage: The Movement to Reclaim Tradition in America* (New Brunswick, NJ: Rutgers University Press, 2008); A. DeMaris, L.A. Sanchez, and K. Krivickas, "Developmental Patterns in Marital Satisfaction: Another Look at Covenant Marriage," *Journal of Marriage and Family*, 74, 2012, pp. 989–1004; W.D. Manning and J.A. Cohen, "Premarital Cohabitation and Marital Dissolution: An Examination of Recent Marriages," *Journal of Marriage and Family*, 74, 2012, pp. 377–387; Gairdner is quoted in Leah McLaren, "The Kids (of Divorce) Are All Right," *The Globe and Mail*, September 11, 1999; Stephanie Coontz, *The Way We Really Are*, p. 83.

123. Paul Amato and Alan Booth, *A Generation at Risk* (Cambridge, MA: Harvard University Press, 1997) p. 207; see also Susan Jekielek, "The Relative and Interactive Impacts of Parental Conflict and Marital Disruption on Children's Emotional Well-Being," paper presented at the annual meeting of the American University Press, 1980); Terry Arendell, "Divorce American Style," *Contemporary Sociology*, 27, 1996; Carl Degler, *At Odds: Women and the Family in America from the Revolution to the Present* (New York, NY: Oxford University Press, 1998), p. 226. See also Terry Arendall, *Mothers and Divorce: Legal, Economic and Social Dilemmas* (Berkeley, CA: University of California Press, 1986); "After Divorce: Investigations into Father Absence," *Gender & Society*, December 1992; *Fathers and Divorce* (Newbury Park, CA: Sage Publications, 1995).

124. See Jenni Millbank, "Lesbians, Child Custody, and the Long Lingering Gaze of the Law," *Challenging the Public/Private Divide: Feminism, Law, and Public Policy, Susan Boyd, ed.* (Toronto, ON: University of Toronto Press, 1997), pp. 280–303; see also Phyllis Chesler, *Mothers on Trial: The Battle for Children and Custody* (New York, NY: McGraw-Hill, 1986), pp. 48–49 passim.

125. REAL Women of Canada, "Same-Sex Parenting is Harmful to Children," *REALity*, 23 (2), March/April 2004; Mary Ann Mason, Arlene Skolnick, and Stephen D. Sugarman, *All Our Families: New Policies for a New Century* (New York, NY: Oxford University Press, 1998), p. 8; "Study: Same-Sex Couples Just as Good, If Not Better, at Parenting," *The Ottawa Citizen*, May 6, 2007, available at www.canada.com/theprovince/news/story .html?id=38cc20ce-7f14-44ea-b4d9-d4cd 16d7a269&k=9378 (accessed July 9, 2009); William Beezon and Jonathan Rauch, "Gay Marriage, Same-Sex Parenting, and America's Children," *The Future of Children*, 15 (2), 2005, pp. 97–113; J. Schulenberg, *Gay Parenting* (New York, NY: Doubleday, 1985); F.W. Bozett, ed., *Gay and Lesbian Parents* (New York, NY: Praeger, 1987); Katherine Allen and David H. Demo, "The Families of Lesbians and Gay Men: A New Frontier in Family Research," *Journal of Marriage and the Family*, 57, 1995; Ann Sullivan, ed., *Issues in Gay and Lesbian Adoption: Proceedings of the Fourth Annual Peirce-Warwick Adoption Symposium* (Washington, DC: Child Welfare League of America, 1995), p. 5; Judith Stacey and Timothy J. Biblarz, "(How) Does the Sexual Orientation of Parents Matter?" *American Sociological Review*, 66, April 2001, pp. 159–183.

126. Gerald P. Mallon, *Gay Men Choosing Parenthood* (New York, NY: Columbia University Press, 2004); Ross Parke. *Future Families*.

127. Stacey and Biblarz, "(How) Does the Sexual Orientation of Parents Matter?"; see also Michael Bronski, "Queer as Your Folks," *Boston Phoenix*, August 3, 2001, and Erica Goode, "A Rainbow of Differences in Gays' Children," *The New York Times*, July 17, 2001; Belkin, "When Mom and Dad Share It All"; Judith Stacey, "Gay and Lesbian Families: Queer Like Us," *All Our Families: New Policies for a New Century*, M. Mason, A. Skolnick, and S. Sugarman, eds. (New York, NY: Oxford University Press, 1998), p. 135.

128. Mark Regnerus, "How Different are the Adult Children of Parents Who Have Same-Sex Relationships? Findings from the New

Family Structures Study," *Social Science Research,* 41, 2012, pp. 752–770.

129. Stacey and Biblarz, "(How) Does the Sexual Orientation of Parents Matter?"

130. Skolnick, *The Intimate Environment: Exploring Marriage and the Family* (New York, NY: Little, Brown & Co., 1983), p. 426.

131. Lasch, *Women and the Common Life,* p. 119; Paul Amato et al., eds., *Families in an Era of Increasing Inequality* (Gewerbestrasse, Switzerland, Springer International Publishing, 2015).

Chapter 7

1. Deborah Rhode, *Speaking of Sex,* p. 56.

2. Alvin Finkel, *Social Policy and Practice in Canada: A History* (Waterloo, ON: Wilfrid Laurier University Press, 2006), pp. 55, 59, 133; Buller quoted in Bruce Curtis, "The State of Tutelage in Lower Canada, 1835–1851, *History of Education Quarterly,* 37 (1), Spring 1997, pp. 25–43: 26.

3. Neil Guppy, Doug Balson, and Susan Vellutini, "Women and Higher Education in Canadian Society," *Women and Education: A Canadian Perspective,* Jane Gaskell and Arlene McLaren, eds. (Calgary, AB: Detselig Enterprises, 1987), pp. 171–192; Kristin McLaren, "'We Had No Desire to Be Set Apart': Forced Segregation of Black Students in Canada West Public Schools and Myths of British Egalitarianism," *The History of Immigration and Racism in Canada,* Barrington Walker, ed. (Toronto, ON: Canadian Scholars Press, 2008), pp. 69–80.

4. There is a vast and accessible literature on imperial manhood, sport, and the colonial educative mission that carried British notions of manhood around the world. For the purposes of the argument made here, see, inter alia, Myra Rutherdale, *Women and the White Man's God: Gender and Race in the Canadian Mission Field* (Vancouver, BC: University of British Columbia Press, 2002); Rhonda Semple, "Missionary Manhood: Professionalism, Belief, and Masculinity in the Nineteenth-Century British Imperial Field," *The Journal of Imperial and Commonwealth History,* 36 (3), September 2008, pp. 397–415;

Satadru Sen, *Migrant Races: Empire, Identity, and K.S. Ranjitsinhji* (Manchester, UK: Manchester United Press, 2004); Patrick McDevitt, *May the Best Man Win: Sport, Masculinity, and Nationalism in Great Britain and the Empire, 1880–1935* (New York, NY/Houndmills, UK: Palgrave Macmillan, 2004); Axel Bundgaard, *Muscle and Manliness: The Rise of Sport in American Boarding Schools* (Syracuse, NY: Syracuse University Press, 2005); Clifford Putney, *Muscular Christianity: Manhood and Sports in Protestant America, 1880–1920* (Cambridge, MA: Harvard University Press, 2001).

5. Edward C. Clarke, *Sex in Education, or, A Fair Chance for the Girls* (Boston, MA: Osgood and Co., 1873), p. 152; Guppy et al., "Women and Higher Education," pp. 173–175.

6. Clarke, *Sex in Education,* pp. 128, 137; W.W. Ferrier, *Origin and Development of the University of California* (Berkeley, CA: University of California Press, 1930); see also Myra Sadker and David Sadker, *Failing at Fairness: How Schools Shortchange Girls* (New York, NY: Simon & Schuster, 1994), p. 22; Carlotta Hacker, *The Indomitable Lady Doctors* (Halifax, NB: Formac, 2001), p. 22.

7. G. Stanley Hall, cited in Rosalind Rosenberg, *Beyond Separate Spheres: Intellectual Roots of Modern Feminism* (New Haven, CT: Yale University Press, 1983), p. 42; Alfred Kinsey, Ward Pomeroy, and Clyde Martin, *Sexual Behavior in the Human Male* (Philadelphia, PA: W.B. Saunders Co., 1948).

8. Johanna Maria Selles, *Methodists and Women's Education in Ontario, 1851–1925* (Montreal, QC: McGill-Queens University Press, 2003); Henry Fowle Durant, "The Spirit of the College" [1977], reprinted in Michael S. Kimmel and Thomas Mosmiller, *Against the Tide,* p. 132.

9. Martin Turcotte, *Women and Education* (Ottawa, ON: Statistics Canada, 2010), available at www.statcan.gc.ca/pub/89-503-x/2010001/article/11542-eng.htm

10. Statistics Canada, "Back to School … By the Numbers," *The Daily,* July 30, 2014, available at www.statcan.gc.ca/eng/dai/smr08/2014/smr08_190_2014 See also Council of Ministers

of Education, Canada, "Education in Canada," July 2005.

11. Myra Sadker and David Sadker, *Failing at Fairness*, p. 14. These stereotypes are complicated by other, racially based, stereotypes; for example, Asian-American girls are expected to like math and science more than are white girls. For an update, see David Sadker and Karen Zittleman, *Still Failing at Fairness: How Gender Bias Cheats Girls and Boys in School and What We Can Do about It* (New York, NY: Scribner, 2009).

12. David Karp and William C. Yoels, "The College Classroom: Some Observations on the Meanings of Student Participation," *Sociology and Social Research*, 60 (4), 1976: American Association of University Women, *How Schools Shortchange Girls: A Study of Major Findings on Girls and Education* (Washington, DC: American Association of University Women, 1992), p 68; Myra Sadker and David Sadker, *Failing at Fairness*, p. 5; Michael Younger, Molly Warrington, and Jacquetta Williams, "The Gender Gap and Classroom Interactions: Reality and Rhetoric?" *British Journal of Sociology of Education,* 20 (3), September 1999, pp. 325–341.

13. Peggy Orenstein, *Schoolgirls: Young Women, Self-Esteem, and the Confidence Gap* (New York, NY: Doubleday, 1994), pp. 11, 12; Leanne Dalley-Trim, "The Call to Critique 'Common-Sense' Understandings about Boys and Masculinity(ies)," *Australian Journal of Teacher Education* 34(1), February 2009, pp. 54–67; Diane Reay, "'Spice Girls,' 'Nice Girls,' 'Girlies,' and 'Tomboys': Gender Discourses, Girls' Cultures, and Femininities in the Primary Classroom," *Gender Relations in Global Perspective: Essential Readings*, Nancy Cook, ed. (Toronto, ON: Canadian Scholar's Press, 2007), pp. 213–22.

14. See Lenore Weitzman and Diane Russo, *Biased Textbooks: A Research Perspective* (Washington, DC: Research Center on Sex Roles and Education, 1974); Lenore Weitzman et al., "Sex Role Socialization in Picture Books for Preschool Children," *American Journal of Sociology*, 77 (6), 1972; Deborah Rhode, *Speaking of Sex*, p. 56; Angela M. Gooden and Mark A. Gooden, "Gender Representation in Notable Children's Picture Books: 1995–1999," *Sex Roles*, 45(1/2), July 2001, pp. 89–101; Rae Lesser Blumberg, "The Invisible Obstacle to Educational Equality: Gender Bias in Textbooks," *Prospects: Quarterly Review of Comparative Education* online, April 7, 2009, available at www.springerlink.com/content/8372103568644370/fulltext.pdf (accessed July 17, 2009); Janice McCabe et al., "Gender in Twentieth-Century Children's Books: Patterns of Disparity in Titles and Central Characters," *Gender & Society*, 25(2), April 2011, pp. 197–226. For the Alberta study, see Joyce Bainbridge, Dianne Oberg, and Mike Carbonaro, "'No Text Is Innocent': Canadian Children's Books in the Classroom," *Journal of Teaching and Learning,* 3 (2), 2005, pp. 1–14; In 2002, the Surrey School Board was ordered to desist from banning books involving same-sex couples as parents. "Supreme Court Says B.C. School Board Wrong to Ban Same-Sex Books," CBC News, December 20, 2002, available at www.cbc.ca/canada/story/2002/12/20/sex_books021220.html (accessed July 17, 2009).

15. On gender intensification, see J. Hill and M. Lynch, "The Intensification of Gender-Related Role Expectations during Early Adolescence," *Girls at Puberty; Biological and Psychological Perspectives,* J. Brooks-Gunn and A. Peterson, eds. (New York, NY: Plenum Books, 1982); Lisa Pettit, "Gender Intensification of Peer Socialization during Puberty," *New Directions for Child and Adolescent Development*, 106, Winter 2004, pp. 23–34; Jacqueline Granleese and Stephen Joseph, "Self-Perception of Adolescent Girls at a Single-Sex and a Mixed-Sex School," *Journal of Genetic Psychology,* 154(4), December 1993, pp. 525–561.

16. See Orenstein. On girls' being valued for appearance and not achievement, see Myra Sadker and David Sadker, *Failing at Fairness*, pp. 55, 134. On girls' downplaying their talents, see American Association of University Women, *Shortchanging Girls, Shortchanging America* (Washington, DC: American Association of University Women, 1991),

p. 48; Carolyn Heilbrun cited in Peggy Orenstein, *Schoolgirls*, p. 37.

17. K.M. Brown et al., "Changes in Self-Esteem in Black and White Girls between the Ages of 9 and 14 Years: The NHLBI Growth and Health Study," *Journal of Adolescent Health,* 23(1), July 1998, pp. 7–19; Heather Ridolfo, Valerie Chepp, and Melanie Milkie, "Race and Girls' Self-Evaluations: How Mothering Matters," *Sex Roles*, 68, 2013, pp. 496–509; Anne Bowker, Shannon Gadbois, and Becki Cornock, "Sports Participation and Self-Esteem; Variations as a Function of Gender and Gender Role Orientation," *Sex Roles,* 49 (1/2), July 2003, pp. 47–58; Matthew J. Taylor et al., "Sports Participation and Victimization: A Study of African-American Girls," *Violence and Victims*, 27 (3), 2012, pp. 434–452.

18. Anthea Lipsett, "Huge Gender Gap in Young Children's Abilities Revealed in Government Figures," *The Guardian*, July 30, 2009, available at www.guardian.co.uk/education/2009 /jul/29/early-learning-gender-gap (accessed July 30, 2009); also see William Pollack, *Real Boys: Rescuing Our Sons from the Myths of Boyhood* (New York, NY: Random House, 1998).

19. Christina Hoff Sommers, *The War against Boys* (New York, NY: Scribner's, 1999). Sommers cited in Debra Viadero, "Behind the 'Mask' of Masculinity," *Education Week*, May 13, 1998; Thompson, cited in Margaret Combs, "What about the Boys?" *Boston Globe*, June 26, 1998. For more of this backlash argument, see Michael Gurian, *The Wonder of Boys* (New York, NY: Jeremy Tarcher/Putnam, 1997), and Judith Kleinfeld, "Student Performance: Male Versus Female," *The Public Interest*, Winter, 1999. For dissenting opinions, see Michael's review of Gurian, "Boys to Men," San *Francisco Chronicle*, January 12, 1997; Martin Mills, "What About the Boys?" and R.W. Connell, "Teaching the Boys," *Teachers College Record*.

20. Leonard Sax, *Boys Adrift: The Five Factors Driving the Growing Epidemic of Unmotivated Boys and Underachieving Young Men* (New York, NY: Basic Books, 2007).

21. Sax, *Boys Adrift*, pp. 51–2; Kate Fillion, "How to Fix Boys: Let Them Start School Later and, Yes, Let Them Fight and Play with Toy Guns" (interview with Leonard Sax), *Maclean's*, January 9, 2008, available at www.macleans.ca/article .jsp?content=20080109_70985_70985&-source=srch (accessed July 19, 2009).

22. Pollack, cited in Debra Viadero, "Behind the Mask"; see also William Pollack, *Real Boys*.

23. Shelley Correll, "Gender and the Career Choice Process: The Role of Biased Self-Assessments," *American Journal of Sociology*, 106 (6), pp. 1691–1730.

24. Ibid.

25. Wayne Martino, "Masculinity and Learning: Exploring Boys' Underachievement and Under Representation in Subject English," *Interpretation*, 27 (2), 1994; "Boys and Literacy: Exploring the Construction of Hegemonic Masculinities and the Formation of Literate Capacities for Boys in the English Classroom," *English in Australia*, 112, 1995; "Gendered Learning Experiences: Exploring the Costs of Hegemonic Masculinity for Girls and Boys in Schools," *Gender Equity: A Framework for Australian Schools* (Canberra, Australia: Publications and Public Communications, Department of Urban Services, ACT Government, 1997). Catharine Stimpson, quoted in Tamar Lewin, "American Colleges Begin to Ask, Where Have All the Men Gone?" *The New York Times*, December 6, 1998.

26. Wayne Martino, "Gendered Learning Experiences," pp. 133, 134. Martain Mac an Ghaill, *The Making of Men: Masculinities, Sexualities and Schooling* (Buckingham, UK: Open University Press, 1994), p. 59; David Gillborne, *Race, Ethnicity and Education* (London, UK: Unwin Hyman, 1990), p. 63; James Coleman, *The Adolescent Society* (New York, NY: Harper and Row, 1961).

27. The "Honours chemistry is for wusses" comment was made by a forthcoming student in one of Jacqueline's classes, commenting not on his own view, but on the hidden curriculum at his school. See also Dalley-Trim, "Call to Critique," p. 59.

28. T.R. Nansel et al., "Bullying Behaviors among US Youth: Prevalence and Association with Psychosocial Adjustment," *Journal of the*

American Medical Association, 285 (16), 2001, pp. 2094–2100; S.P. Limber et al., "Bullying among School Children: Preliminary Findings from a School-Based Intervention Program," paper presented at the Fifth International Family Violence Research Conference, Durham, NH, June 1997; Juvonen Jaana, Sandra Graham, and Mark Schuster, "Bullying among Young Adolescents: The Strong, the Weak and the Troubled," *Pediatrics*, 112 (6), December 2003, pp. 1231–1237.

29. See Jaana Juvonen and Sandra Graham, "Bullying in Schools: The Power of Bullies and the Plight of Victims," *Annual Review of Psychology*, 65, 2014, pp. 159–185; Ann Marie Popp et al., "Gender, Bullying Victimization, and Education," *Violence and Victims*, 29 (5), 2014, pp. 843–856; Noam Lapidot-Lefler and Michal Dolev-Cohen, "Comparing Cyberbullying and School Bullying among School Students: Prevalence, Gender, and Grade Level Differences," *Social Psychology of Education*, 18 (1), March 2015, pp. 1–16; Özgür Erdur-Baker, "Cyberbullying and Its Correlation to Traditional Bullying, Gender and Frequent and Risky Usage of Internet-Mediated Communication Tools," *New Media & Society*, 12 (1), February 2010, pp. 109–125; Robert Slonje and Peter Smith, "Cyberbullying: Another Main Type of Bullying?" *Scandinavian Journal of Psychology*, 49 (2), 2008, pp. 147–154; Qing Li, "Cyberbullying in Schools: A Research of Gender Differences," *School Psychology International*, 27 (2), 2006, pp. 157–170.

30. Qing Li, "Cyberbullying," p. 160.

31. American Association of University Women, *Hostile Hallways: The AAUW Survey on Sexual Harassment in America's Schools* (Washington, DC: American Association of University Women, 1993); Sandler cited in Myra Sadker and David Sadker, *Failing at Fairness*, p. 111; Jason Winters, Robert Clift, and Anne Maloney, "Adult-Student Sexual Harassment in British Columbia High Schools," *Aggression in Organizations: Violence, Abuse, and Harassment at Work and in Schools*, Robert Geffner et al., eds. (New Brunswick, NJ: Routledge, 2005),

pp. 177–196; Terry Abbott, "More Teachers Are Having Sex with Their Students: Here's How Schools Can Stop Them," *The Washington Post*, Post Everything, January 20, 2015, available at www.washingtonpost.com/posteverything/wp/2015/01/20/more-teachers-are-having-sex-with-their-students-heres-how-schools-can-stop-them/

32. Pat Staton and June Larkin, *Sexual Harassment: The Intimidation Factor*, A Report to the Ontario Ministry of Education (Toronto, ON: Green Dragon Press, 1992); June Larkin, "Walking through Walls: The Sexual Harassment of High School Girls," *Gender & Education*, 6 (3), 1994, pp. 263–280; Rosalyn Shute, Larry Owens, and Phillip Slee, "Everyday Victimization of Adolescent Girls by Boys: Sexual Harassment, Bullying, or Aggression?" *Sex Roles*, 58, 2008, pp. 477–489; "Girls Accepting Sexual Assault at School as Fact of Life: Reports," CityNews.ca, available at www.citynews.ca/news/news_19880.aspx (accessed July 20, 2009); Christopher Bagley et al., "Sexual Assault in School, Mental Health, and Suicidal Behaviors in Adolescent Women in Canada," *Adolescence*, 32 (126), Summer 1997, pp. 361–366; Pat Staton and June A. Larkin, "'If We Can't Get Equal, We'll Get Even': A Transformative Model of Gender Equity," *Canadian Woman Studies*, 17 (4), 1998, pp. 16–22.

33. Adam Milani, "Harassing Speech in the Public Schools: The Validity of Schools' Regulation of Fighting Words and the Consequences If They Do Not," *Akron Law Review*, 28 (2), Fall/Winter 1995, pp. 187–235; Emily White, *Fast Girls: Teenage Tribes and the Myth of the Slut* (New York, NY: Scribner, 2002).

34. Catherine Hill and Holly Kearl, *Crossing the Line: Sexual Harassment at School* (Washington, DC: AAUW, 2011), p. 16.

35. Hill and Kearl, *Crossing the Line*; Jill Smolowe, "Sex with a Scorecard," *Time*, April 5, 1993, p. 41; Jane Gross, "Where 'Boys Will Be Boys' and Adults Are Bewildered," *The New York Times*, March 29, 1993, p. A1; White, *Fast Girls*; Richard Oppel, Jr., "Ohio Teenagers Guilty in Rape that Social Media Brought to Light," *The New York Times*, March 17, 2013; Carrie Rentschler, "Rape Culture and

the Feminist Politics of Social Media," *Girlhood Studies*, 7 (1), Summer 2014, pp. 65–82.

36. On harassment and homophobia in high schools, see Dalley-Trim, "Call to Critique," pp. 60–1; C.J. Pascoe, *Dude, You're a Fag: Masculinity and Sexuality in High School* (Berkeley/Los Angeles, CA: University of California Press, 2007); Tommi Avicolli, "He Defies You Still: The Memoirs of a Sissy," *Reconstructing Gender: A Multicultural Anthology*, Estelle Disch, ed. (New York, NY: McGraw-Hill, 2006), pp. 108–154; Égale Canada, *Youth Speak up about Homophobia and Transphobia: The First National Climate Survey on Homophobia in Canadian Schools, Phase One Report March 2009*, available at www.egale.ca/index.asp?lang=&menu=1&item=1401 Also Hill and Kearl, *Crossing the Line*, p. 16.

37. Richard Kim, "Eminem: Bad Rap?" *The Nation*, March 13, 2001, p. 4. In his film, *8 Mile*, and in subsequent albums, Eminem attempts to repudiate his earlier homophobia. However, as of 2015 he is still mired in controversy about homophobic, misogynist, and transphobic lyrics.

38. Kimberly Mitchell, Michele Ybarra, and Josephine Korchmaros, "Sexual Harassment among Adolescents of Different Sexual Orientations and Gender Identities," *Child Abuse and Neglect*, 38 (2), February 2014, pp. 280–295; Mark McCormack, "The Complexity of 'That's So Gay,'" *Psychology Today*, May 18, 2012, available at www.psychologytoday.com/blog/men-20/201205/the-complexity-thats-so-gay Adam Galinsky at al., "The Reappropriation of Stigmatizing Labels: The Reciprocal Relationship between Power and Self-Labeling," *Psychological Science*, 24 (10), October 2013, pp. 2020–2029; Michael Woodford et al., "'That's So Gay!' Examining the Covariates of Hearing This Expression among Gay, Lesbian, and Bisexual Students," *Journal of American College Health*, 60 (6), 2012, pp. 429–434.

39. Tanya Beran et al., "Children's Experiences of Cyberbullying: A Canadian National Study," *Children and Schools*, 37 (4), 2015, pp. 207–214; Tanya Beran and Qing Li, "The Relationship between Cyberbullying and School Bullying," *Journal of Student Wellbeing*, 1 (2), December 2007, pp. 15–33; Li, "Cyberbullying in Schools"; Erdur-Baker, "Cyberbullying and Its Correlation"; Jeremy Doucette, "Gender and Grade Differences in How High School Students Experience and Perceive Cyberbullying," M.Ed thesis (London, ON: University of Western Ontario, 2013). *Electronic Thesis and Dissertation Repository*. Paper 1250, available at http://ir.lib.uwo.ca/etd/1250 Also see Girlguiding UK, *Girls' Attitudes Survey 2015* (London, UK: Girlguiding, 2015).

40. Erdur-Baker, "Cyberbullying and Its Correlation," pp. 121–122; Rebecca Ang and Dion Goh, "Cyberbullying among Adolescents: The Role of Affective and Cognitive Empathy, and Gender," *Child Psychiatry and Human Development*, 41, 2010, pp. 387–397; p. 396; Lapidot-Lefler and Dolev-Cohen, "Comparing Cyberbullying and School Bullying." For a study in which girls and boys were equal perpetrators of cyberbullying, see Peter Smith et al., "Cyberbullying: Its Nature and Impact in Secondary School Pupils," *Journal of Child Psychology and Psychiatry*, 49 (4), 2008, pp. 376–385.

41. "Fear of Classmates," *USA Today*, April 22, 1999, p. A1; "Half of Teens Have Heard of a Gun Threat at School," *USA Today*, November 27, 2001, p. 6D. Also see Michael Kimmel and Matthew Mahler, "Adolescent Masculinity, Homophobia, and Violence: Random School Shootings, 1982–2001," *American Behavioral Scientist*, 46(10), June 2003.

42. See, for example, the essays in Rodney Clifton, Lance Roberts, and Raymond Perrys, eds., *Gender Equity in Canadian Postsecondary Educational Institutions* (Winnipeg, MB: Centre for Educational Research and Development, University of Manitoba, 1998); see also Joanne Cooper and Pamela Eddy et al., "Improving Gender Equity in Post-Secondary Education," *Achieving Gender Equity through Education*, Second Edition, Susan Klein, ed. (New Jersey: Lawrence Erlbaum Associates, 2007), pp. 631–654.

43. Levin, "Where Have All the Men Gone?" Michael Fletcher, "Degrees of Separation,"

The Washington Post, June 25, 2002; Jamilah Evelyn, "Community Colleges Start to Ask, Where Are the Men?" *The Chronicle of Higher Education*, June 28, 2002; Ridger Doyle, "Men, Women and College," *Scientific American*, October 1999; Kirsteen Burton and Ian Wong, "A Force to Contend With: The Gender Gap Closes in Canadian Medical Schools," *CMA Journal*, 170 (9), April 27, 2004, available at www.cmaj.ca/cgi/content/full/170/9/1385 (accessed July 21, 2009); Brendan Koerner, "Where the Boys Aren't," *US News & World Report*, February 8, 1999.

44. Association of Universities and Colleges of Canada, *Trends in Higher Education in Canada: Volume 1—Enrolment* (Ottawa, ON: AUCC, 2011); Shelly Milligan and Evelyne Bougie, *First Nations Women and Post-Secondary Education in Canada: Snapshots from the Census* (Ottawa, ON: Minister of Industry, 2009).

45. AUCC, *Trends*.

46. Ibid; Daniel Drolet, "Minding the Gender Gap," *University Affairs*, September 10, 2007, available at www.universityaffairs.ca/minding-the-gender-gap.aspx (accessed July 17, 2009).

47. Louis N. Christofides, Michael Hoy, and Ling Yang, "The Determinants of University Participation in Canada (1977–2003)," *Canadian Journal of Higher Education/Revue Canadienne d'Enseignement Supérieur*, 39 (2), 2009, pp. 1–24.

48. Christofides, Hoy, and Yang, "Determinants"; for the importance of class-related expectations in BC youths' post-secondary education decisions, see Lesley Andres et al., "Educational Expectations, Parental Social Class, Gender, and Postsecondary Attainment: A 10-Year Perspective," *Youth & Society*, 39 (2), December 2007, pp. 135–163. For a careful investigation of the Dalhousie events and sexual assault policies at Canadian campuses, see Constance Backhouse, Donald McRae, and Nitya Iyer, *Report of the Task Force on Misogyny, Sexism and Homophobia in Dalhousie University Faculty of Dentistry*, available at www.dal.ca/content/dam/dalhousie/pdf/cultureofrespect/DalhousieDentistry-TaskForceReport-June2015.pdf

49. Cited in James Orton, ed., *The Liberal Education of Women: The Demand and the Method: Current Thoughts in America and England* (New York, NY/Chicago, IL: A.S. Barnes & Co., 1873), p. 208.

50. Finkel, *Social Policy and Practice in Canada*, 56; for a US comparison, and excellent examples of relative nineteenth-century salaries for male and female teachers, see David Tyack and Elizabeth Hansot, *Learning Together: A History of Coeducation in American Public Schools* (Ottawa, ON: Russell Sage Foundation, 1992), pp. 83–89.

51. Sheila Cavanaugh, "Female-Teacher Gender and Sexuality in Twentieth-Century Ontario, Canada," *History of Education Quarterly*, 45(2), Summer 2005, pp. 247–273.

52. Catell, cited in William O'Neil, *Divorce in the Progressive Era* (New Haven, CT: Yale University Press, 1967), p. 81; Admiral F.E. Chadwick, "The Woman Peril," *Educational Review*, February 1914, p. 47; last cited in Myra Sadker and David Sadker, *Failing at Fairness*, p. 214.

53. United States Department of Education, 1996; Patrick Harrigan, "The Schooling of Girls and Boys in Canada," *Journal of Social History*, 23 (4), June 1990; Laverne Smith, "The Gender Composition of the Pool of Prospective School Principals," *Canadian Journal of Education*, 16 (2), 1991, pp. 198–205; Jane Lin, "The Teaching Profession: Trends from 1999 to 2005," available at www.statcan.gc.ca/pub/81-004-x/2006004/9540-eng.htm#a (accessed July 10, 2009).

54. Cooper and Eddy et al., "Improving Gender Equity," 636; "Ontario Urged to Counter Drop in Male Teachers," CBC News, November 13, 2004, available at www.cbc.ca/canada/story/2004/11/12/male_teacher_041112.html (accessed July 12, 2009); Niall Murray, "Decline in Male Teachers 'Robbing Young Boys of Role Models,'" *Irish Examiner*, Thursday, April 1, 2004, available at http://archives.tcm.ie/irishexaminer/2004/04/01/story715017167.asp (accessed July 6, 2009); Wayne Martino and Michael Kehler, "Male Teachers

and the 'Boy Problem': An Issue of Recuperative Masculinity Politics," *McGill Journal of Education*, 41 (2), Spring 2006, pp. 113–131; Brian Jamieson, "Male Presence in Teaching Continues to Decline," *Professionally Speaking: The Magazine of the Ontario College of Teachers*, June 2007.

55. Valerie Lee and Julia Smith, "Gender Equity in Teachers' Salaries: A Multilevel Approach," *Educational Evaluation and Policy Analysis*, 12 (1), 1990, pp. 57–81; Cooper and Eddy et al., "Improving Gender Equity," 636; David Levinson, Peter Cookson, and Alan Sadnovik, *Education and Sociology: An Encyclopedia* (New Brunswick, NJ: Routledge, 2001), 671; "Study: Rising Education of Women and the Gender Earnings Gap," *The Daily*, June 12, 2007, available at www.statcan.gc.ca/daily-quotidien/070612/dq070612b-eng.htm

56. See Ayers, "A Teacher Ain't Nothin' But a Hero: Teachers and Teaching in Film," *Images of Schoolteachers in America*, Pamela Joseph and Gail Burneford, eds. (Mahwah, NJ: Lawrence Erlbaum Associates, 2001), pp. 201–210. See also Robert Lowe's essay in the same volume, "Teachers as Saviors, Teachers Who Care."

57. Martino and Kehler, "Male Teachers," 118; Alanah May Erickson and Martha McKenzie Minifie, "Primary Principals Seek More Real Men," *New Zealand Herald*, February 5, 2008, available at www.nzherald.co.nz/nz/news/article.cfm?c_id=1&objectid=10490687 (accessed July 21, 2009); Alanah May Erickson, "Knitting Trend Used to Attract Male Teachers," *New Zealand Herald*, January 31, 2009, available at www.nzherald.co.nz/alanah-may-eriksen/news/article.cfm?a_id=344&objectid=10554414 (accessed July 21, 2009).

58. AUCC, *Trends*.

59. Canadian Association of University Teachers, *CAUT Almanac of Post-Secondary Education in Canada 2014—2015* (Ottawa, ON: CAUT, 2015); Lin, "The Teaching Profession."

60. Eileen Pollack, "Why Are There Still So Few Women in Science?" *The New York Times*, October 3, 2013, available at www.nytimes.com/2013/10/06/magazine/why-are-there-still-so-few-women-in-science.html?_r=0 (accessed October 7, 2013); Barry Chiswick, Nicholas Larsen, and Paul Pieper, *The Production of PhDs in the United States and Canada*, IZA Discussion Paper No. 5367 (Bonn, Switzerland: Institute for the Study of Labor (IZA), 2010); National Science Foundation, "Characteristics of Doctoral Students," cited in Londa Schiebinger, *Has Feminism Changed Science?* (Cambridge, MA: Harvard University Press, 1999), p. 34.

61. *CAUT Almanac.*

62. See "Disparate Burden," www.insidehighered.com/news/2005/03/21/care (accessed March 31, 2005).

63. Susan A. Basow, Julie E. Phelan, and Laura Capotosto, "Gender Patterns in College Students' Choices of Their Best and Worst Professors," *Psychology of Women Quarterly*, 30, 2006, pp. 25–35; Lillian MacNell, Adam Driscoll, and Andrea N. Hunt, "What's in a Name: Exposing Gender Bias in Student Ratings of Teaching," *Innovative Higher Education*, 40 (4), August 2015, pp. 291–303; for black faculty, see Bettye P. Smith and Billie Hawkins, "Examining Student Evaluations of Black Faculty: Does Race Matter?" *The Journal of Negro Education*, 80 (2), Spring 2011, pp. 149–162; Ben Schmidt, "Gender and Teacher Reviews," available at www.benschmidt.org

64. Corinne A. Moss Racusin et al., "Science Faculty's Subtle Gender Biases Favor Male Students," *PNAS*, 109 (41), 2012, pp. 16474–16479; also see Pollack, "Why Are There Still So Few Women in Science?"

65. Orenstein, *Schoolgirls*, p. 27.

66. See Kim Gandy, "Segregation Won't Help," *USA Today*, May 10, 2002, "Harlem Girls School vs. the Three Stooges," *New York Observer*, March 30, 1998, p. 4; Mike Bowler, "All-Male, All-Black, All Learning," *Baltimore Sun*, October 15, 1995; Susan Estrich, "For Girls' Schools and Women's College, Separate Is Better," *The New York Times*, May 22, 1994.

67. The claims of benefits were challenged empirically by a study by the American Association of University Women (AAUW), which found that although many girls report

that they feel single-sex classrooms are more conducive to learning, they also show no significant gains in achievement in math and science. Another researcher found some significant differences between co-educational and single-sex classes—but only in Catholic schools, not in private single-sex schools, and only for girls. A third researcher found no advantages of one or the other type of school for middle-class and otherwise advantaged students but found some positive outcomes for black or Hispanic girls from low socioeconomic homes. See Pamela Haag, "Single-Sex Education in Grades K–12: What Does the Research Tell Us?" *Separated by Sex: A Critical Look at Single-Sex Education for Girls* (Washington, DC: American Association of University Women Educational Foundation, 1998), p. 34; Valerie Lee, "Is Single-Sex Secondary Schooling a Solution to the Problem of Gender Inequity?" *Separated by Sex: A Critical Look at Single-Sex Education for Girls*, p. 43; Cornelius Riordan, "The Future of Single-Sex Schools," p. 53; Connie Leslie, "Separate and Unequal?" *Newsweek*, March 23,1998, p. 55; Clark, cited in Charles Whitaker, "Do Black Males Need Special Schools?" *Ebony*, March 1991, p. 18; Maria Jimenez, "All Girls—Better Grades," *The Globe and Mail*, April 21, 2009, available at www.theglobeandmail.com/servlet/story /RTGAM.20090421.wlsamesex21art1831/E (accessed April 24, 2009); Pamela Haag, "What Does the Research Say?" *Eric Digest* September 2000, EDO-PS-00-9; Linda Sax et al., *Women Graduates of Single-Sex and Co-educational High Schools; Differences in Their Characteristics and the Transition to* College (Los Angeles, CA: The Sudikoff Family Institute for Education and New Media/ UCLA Graduate School of Education and Information Studies, 2009); Jacqueline Granleese and Stephen Joseph, "Self-Perception of Adolescent Girls at a Single-Sex and a Mixed-Sex School"; Heather Blair and Kathy Sanford, "Single-Sex Classrooms: A Place for Transformation of Policy and Practice," Conference paper presented at the Annual MeetingoftheAmericanEducationalResearch

Association, Montreal, April 1999; Erin Pahlke, Janet Shibley Hyde, and Carlie M. Allison, "The Effects of Single-Sex Compared With Coeducational Schooling on Students' Performance and Attitudes: A Meta-Analysis," *Psychological Bulletin*, 140 (4), 2014, pp. 1042–1072.

68. Sax, quoted in Jimenez, "All Girls," see also Amanda Datnow, Lea Hubbard, and Elisabeth Woody, "Is Single Gender Schooling Viable in the Public Sector? Lessons from California's Pilot Program" (Toronto, ON: Ontario Institute for Studies in Education, 2001).

69. Gambell is quoted in Jimenez, "All Girls."

70. John Dewey, "Is Coeducation Injurious to Girls?" *Ladies Home Journal*, June 11, 1911, p. 60.

Chapter 8

1. Parks Canada, *Canadian Workers in History: An Interpretation*, available at www.pc.gc .ca/eng/culture/proj/tch-cwh/index.aspx (accessed July 29, 2009); Lance Roberts, Robert Clifton, and Barry Ferguson, *Recent Social Trends in Canada, 1960–2000* (Montreal, QC: McGill-Queen's University Press, 2005), pp. 158–159; Irene Padavic and Barbara Reskin, *Women and Men at Work*, Second Edition (Thousand Oaks, CA: Pine Forge, 2002), pp. 26–27; "Labour Force Rates," Canadian Council for Social Development Fact Sheet, available at www.ccsd.ca/factsheets/ labour_market/rates/index.htm

2. Toby Sanger, "Why Are Canadian Women Leaving the Labour Force in Record Numbers?" *Huffington Post*, March 11, 2015, available at www.huffingtonpost .ca/toby-sanger/canadian-women-work force_b_6818522.html Roberts, Clifton, and Ferguson, *Recent Social Trends*; "Labour Force Rates"; OECD, "Achieving Stronger Growth by Promoting a More Gender-Balanced Economy: Report Prepared for the G20 Labour and Employment Ministerial Meeting Melbourne, Australia, September 10–11, 2014," available at www.oecd.org/g20/topics /employment-and-social-policy/ILO-IMF -OECD-WBG-Achieving-stronger-growth

-by-promoting-a-more-gender-balanced
-economy-G20.pdf

3. For pre- and post-recession male and female employment in the US, see *State of the States: The Poverty and Inequality Report*, a special issue of Pathways (Stanford, CT: Stanford Center of Poverty & Inequality, 2015); D'Vera Cohn, Gretchen Livingston, and Wendy Wang, "After Decades of Decline, A Rise in Stay-at-Home Mothers," Pew Research Center Social and Demographic Trends, April 8, 2014, available at www.pewsocial trends.org/2014/04/08/after-decades-of-decline-a-rise-in-stay-at-home-mothers/ Nicole M. Fortin, "Gender Role Attitudes and Women's Labor Market Participation: Opting Out, AIDS, and the Persistent Appeal of House-wifery," *Annals of Economics and Statistics*, 117/118, June 2015, pp. 379–401; "The Return of the Stay-at-Home Mother," *The Economist*, April 19, 2014, available at www.economist .com/news/united-states/21600998-after -falling-years-proportion-mums-who-stay -home-rising-return Claire Cain Miller and Liz Alderman, "Why US Women Are Leaving Jobs behind," *The New York Times*, December 12, 2014, available at www.nytimes .com/2014/12/14/upshot/us-employment -women-not-working.html?_r=0

4. Sanger, "Why Are Canadian Women Leaving."

5. Sanger, "Why Are Canadian Women Leaving"; OECD, *Closing the Gender Gap: Act Now*; DeAnne Aguirre et al., *Empowering the Third Billion: Women and the World of Work in 2012* (Houston, TX: Booz and Co., 2012); Marilyn Waring, *As If Women Counted: A New Feminist Economics* (New York, NY: HarperCollins, 1990); G20 Leaders' Communiqué, Brisbane, November 16, 2014, available at www.g20.utoronto .ca/2014/2014-1116-communique.html

6. *State of the States*; Cohn, Livingston, and Wang, "After Decades of Decline."

7. Cohn, Livingston, and Wang, "After Decades of Decline"; Fortin, "Gender Role Attitudes and Women's Labor Market Participation"; "The Return of the Stay-at-Home Mother"; Miller and Alderman, "Why US Women Are Leaving Jobs Behind."

8. Katrin Elborgh-Woytek et al., *Women, Work, and the Economy: Macroeconomic Gains from Gender Equity* (International Monetary Fund Strategy, Policy, and Review Department and Fiscal Affairs Department, SDN 13/10, September 2013), available at www.imf.org /external/pubs/ft/sdn/2013/sdn1310.pdf

9. Jerry Jacobs, "Women's Entry into Management: Trends in Earnings, Authority, and Values among Salaried Managers," *Administrative Science Quarterly*, 37 (2), 1992, pp. 282–301; p. 282; also see Felice Schwartz, "Management Women and the New Facts of Life," *Harvard Business Review*, January–February 1989.

10. Taylor, cited in Ashley Montagu, *The Natural Superiority of Women* (New York, NY: Anchor, 1952), p. 28.

11. Kimmel, *Manhood in America*; Willard Gaylin, *The Male Ego* (New York, NY: Viking, 1992), cited also in Michael Kimmel, "What Do Men Want?" *Harvard Business Review*, November–December 1993; Marc Feigen-Fasteau, *The Male Machine* (New York, NY: Dell, 1974), p. 120; Patricia Yancey Martin, "'Mobilizing Masculinities': Women's Experiences of Men at Work," *Organization*, 8 (4), 2001, pp. 587–618.

12. Amy Kroska, "Examining Husband–Wife Differences in the Meaning of Family Financial Support," *Sociological Perspectives*, 51 (1), 2008, pp. 63–90; Deutsch, cited in Belkin, "When Mom and Dad Share It All."

13. Cohn, Livingston, and Wang, "After Decades of Decline."

14. See Arlie Hochschild, *The Managed Heart* (Berkeley, CA: University of California Press, 1982); see also Patricia Yancey Martin, "'Mobilizing Masculinities': Women's Experiences of Men at Work," *Organization*, 8 (4), 2001, pp. 587–618.

15. Kathleen Blee and Ann Tickamyer, "Racial Differences in Men's Attitudes about Women's Gender Roles," *Journal of Marriage and the Family*, 57, February 1995, pp. 21–30; "Latest Annual Data," United States Department of Labor Women's Bureau, 2014, available at www.dol.gov/wb/stats/latest_annual_data .htm#labor

16. Tina Chiu and Hélène Maheux, *Women in Canada: A Gender-Based Statistical Report* (Ottawa, ON: Minister of Industry, 2011), available at www.statcan.gc.ca/pub/89-503 -x/89-503-x2010001-eng.pdf

17. Aguirre et al., *Empowering the Third Billion*, p. 22.

18. Reginald Bibby, "Childcare Aspirations" (Press Release), Vanier Institute for the Family, February 10, 2005, available at www .vifamily.ca/newsroom/press_feb_10_05_c .html (accessed August 3, 2009); Pew Research Center, "Growing Number of Dads Home with the Kids," June 5, 2014, available at www .pewsocialtrends.org/2014/06/05/growing -number-of-dads-home-with-the-kids/ Zosia Bielski, "Stay-at-Home Dads on the Rise: Increasingly Because They Want to Be," *The Globe and Mail*, June 5, 2014, available at www.theglobeandmail.com/life/parenting /stay-at-home-dads-on-the-rise-increasingly -because-they-want-to-be/article19014624/

19. Noelle Chesley. "Stay-at-Home Fathers and Breadwinning Mothers: Gender, Couple Dynamics, and Social Change," *Gender & Society*, 25 (5), October 2011, pp. 642–664.

20. For a description of the rationale for and contents of the PARE, see RCMP Recruiting, "PARE," available at www.rcmp-grc.gc.ca /recruiting-recrutement/rec/pare-tape-eng .htm (accessed August 1, 2015).

21. Supreme Court Reports, *Judgments of the Supreme Court of Canada*, available at http:// scc.lexum.umontreal-.ca/en/1999/1999rcs 3-3/1999rcs3-3.html (accessed August 13, 2009); see also Coriaan de Villiers, "Addressing Systemic Sex Discrimination: Employer Defences to Discrimination in Canada and South Africa," *Acta Juridica* (2001), p. 175; The Honourable Claire L'Heureux-Dube, "A Conversation about Equality," *Denver Journal of International Law and Policy*, 29, 2000, p. 65; Dianne Pothier, "Connecting Grounds of Discrimination to Real People's Real Experiences," *Canadian Journal of Women and the Law*, 13, 2001, p. 37; Rachel Cox and Karen Messing, "Legal and Biological Perspectives on Employment Testing for Physical Abilities: A Post-Meiorin Review,"

Windsor Yearbook of Access to Justice, 24, 2006, p. 23.

22. John Baden, "Perverse Consequences (P.C.) of the Nanny State," *Seattle Times*, January 17, 1996; Del Jones, "Hooters to Pay $3.75 Million in Sex Suit," *USA Today*, October 1, 1997, p. 1A.

23. Barbara Reskin, "Sex Segregation in the Workplace," *Women and Work: A Handbook*, P. Dubeck and K. Borman, eds. (New York, NY: Garland, 1996), p. 94; see also *Sex-Segregation in the Workplace: Trends, Explanations, Remedies*, Barbara Reskin, ed. (Washington, DC: National Academy Press, 1984); Barbara Reskin, "Bringing the Men Back In: Sex Differentiation and the Devaluation of Women's Work," *Gender and Society*, 2 (1), 1988, and *Job Queues, Gender Queues: Explaining Women's Inroads into Male Occupations*, Barbara Reskin and Patricia Roos, eds. (Philadelphia, PA: Temple University Press, 1990).

24. Statistics Canada, *Portrait of Canada's Labour Force* (Ottawa, ON: Minister of Industry, 2013), available at www12.statcan .gc.ca/nhs-enm/2011/as-sa/99-012-x/99-012- x2011002-eng.pdf Status of Women Canada, "Fact Sheet: Economic Security," available at www.swc-cfc.gc.ca/initiatives/wesp-sepf /fs-fi/es-se-eng.html Padavic and Reskin, *Women and Men at Work*, pp. 65, 67; see also Andrea Beller and Kee-Ok Kim Han, "Occupational Sex Segregation: Prospects for the 1980s," in Reskin, ed., *Sex-Segregation in the Workplace*, p. 91; Mary Cornish and Fay Faraday, "Redressing Gender Discrimination in Employment: The Canadian Experience," paper presented to Seminar on Workplace Discrimination and the Law in North America, Washington, DC, November 18–19, 2004.

25. Roberts et al., *Recent Social Trends in Canada*, p. 161; Stats Canada data cited and analyzed in "Men/Women and the 10 Highest/Lowest Paid Occupations in Canada," Women and the Economy: A Project of UNPAC, available at www.unpac.ca/economy/wagegap3.html (accessed April 9, 2009); Margaret Mooney Marini and Mary C. Brinton, "Sex Typing

in Occupational Socialization," in Reskin, *Sex-Segregation in the Workplace*, p. 224; Christine Alksnis, Serge Desmarais, and James Curtis, "Workforce Segregation and the Gender Wage Gap: Is 'Women's' Work Valued as Highly as 'Men's'?" *Journal of Applied Social Psychology*, 38 (6), 2008, pp. 1416–1441.

26. Dana Dunn, "Gender-Segregated Occupations," *Women and Work*, P. Dubeck and K. Borman, eds., p. 92; Jerry A. Jacobs, *Revolving Doors: Sex Segregation and Women's Careers* (Stanford, CA: Stanford University Press, 1989), p. 48.

27. Samuel Cohn, *The Process of Occupational Sex-Typing: The Feminization of Clerical Labor in Great Britain* (Philadelphia, PA: Temple University Press, 1985).

28. Service Canada, "Veterinarians," available at www.servicecanada.gc.ca/eng/qc/job_futures /statistics/3114.shtml "Market Research Statistics: US Veterinarians, 2014," available at www.avma.org/KB/Resources/Statistics/Pages /Market-research-statistics-US-veterinarians .aspx Leslie Irvine and Jenny Vermilya, "Gender Work in a Feminized Profession: The Case of Veterinary Medicine," *Gender & Society*, 24 (1), February 2010, pp. 56–82; Yilu Zhao, "Women Soon to Be Majority of Veterinarians," *The New York Times*, June 9, 2002, p. 24; Jeanne Lofstedt, "Gender and Veterinary Medicine," *The Canadian Veterinary Journal*, 44 (7), 2003, pp. 533–535.

29. Kate Boyer and Kim England, "Gender, Work, and Technology in the Information Workplace: From Typewriters to ATMs," *Social & Cultural Geography*, 9 (3), May 2008, pp. 241–256; Denise Gürer, "Pioneering Women in Computer Science," *SIGCSE Bulletin*, 34 (2), 2002, pp. 175–183; Katharine Donato, "Programming for Change? The Growing Demand among Computer Specialists," *Job Queues, Gender Queues: Explaining Women's Inroads into Male Occupations*, B. Reskin and P. Roos, eds. (Philadelphia, PA: Temple University Press, 1990), p. 170.

30. William Bielby and James Baron, "Undoing Discrimination: Job Integration and Comparable Worth," *Ingredients for Women's Employment Policy*, C. Bose and G. Spitze,

eds. (Albany, NY: SUNY Press, 1987), p. 226; Barbara Reskin, "Bringing the Men Back In," p. 64.

31. EEOC v. Sears, Roebuck and Co., 628 F Sup. 1264 (N.D. Ill 1986); 839 F 2d 302 (7th Circuit, 1988).

32. Reed Abelson, "6 Women Sue Wal-Mart, Charging Job and Promotion Bias," *The New York Times*, June 20, 2001, pp. C1, 17; "Court: Wal-Mart Gender Pay Lawsuit Can Go to Trial," CNN, May 2, 2010, available at www.wibw.com/nationalnews/headlines /92640459 (accessed May 3, 2010); Greg Stohr, "Wal-Mart Million-Worker Bias Suit Thrown out by High Court," *Bloomberg* online, June 20, 2011, available at www.bloomberg.com /news/articles/2011-06-20/wal-mart-wins-u-s-supreme-court-gender-discrimination-class-action-case

33. Cynthia Cranford, Leah Vosko, and Nancy Lukewich, "The Gender of Precarious Employment in Canada," *Relations Industrielles/Industrial Relations*, 58 (3), 2003, pp. 454–482.

34. Tavia Grant, "Canada's Shift to a Nation of Temporary Workers," *The Globe and Mail*, May 5, 2013, available at www.theglobe andmail.com/report-on-business/economy /jobs/canadas-shift-to-a-nation-of-temporary -workers/article11721139/

35. Leah Vosko, Nancy Zukewich, and Cynthia Cranford, "Precarious Jobs: A New Typology of Employment," *Perspectives on Labour and Income*, 4 (10), 2003; also see Ontario Federation of Labour, "Contingent Work Fact Sheet: Global Action against Precarious Work," *Metal World*, 1, 2007, pp. 18–21; Stephanie Premji et al., "Precarious Work Experiences of Racialized Immigrant Women in Toronto: A Community-Based Study," *Just Labour: A Canadian Journal of Work and Society*, 22, Autumn 2014, pp. 122–143.

36. Deena Ladd and Len Lewenza, "The Precarious Economy," *The Mark*, October 6, 2009. Available at www.themarknews.com /articles/542-the-precarious-economy (accessed January 10, 2010).

37. See Abigail Bess Dakan and Daiva Stasiulas, *Not One of the Family: Foreign Domestic*

Workers in Canada (Toronto, ON: University of Toronto Press, 1997).

38. Statistics Canada, *Earnings and Income of Canadians over the Past Quarter Century, 2006 Census* (Ottawa, ON: Ministry of Industry, 2008), pp. 18–19; Statistics Canada, *Earnings and Income of Canadians over the Past Quarter Century, 2006*; M. Drolet, "The Male–Female Wage Gap," *Perspectives on Labour and Income*, 2(12), 2001, pp. 5–13; A.D. Bernhardt, M. Morris, and M.S. Handcock, "Women's Gains or Men's Losses? A Closer Look at the Shrinking Gender Gap in Earnings," *American Journal of Sociology*, 101, 1995, pp. 302–328; see also Rhode, *Speaking of Sex*, p. 175; Tamar Lewin, "Women Losing Ground to Men in Widening Income Difference," *The New York Times*, September 15, 1997, pp. 1, 12. See also David Cay Johnston, "As Salary Grows, So Does a Gender Gap," *The New York Times*, May 12, 2002.

39. Nicole Fortin and Michael Huberman, "Occupational Gender Segregation and Women's Wages in Canada: An Historical Perspective" (report), CIRANO Scientific Series 2002s-22 (Montreal: CIRANO, 2002); Bradley Brooks, Jennifer Jarman, and Robert Blackburn, "Occupational Gender Segregation in Canada 1981–1996: Overall, Vertical, and Horizontal Segregation," *Canadian Review of Sociology and Anthropology*, 40 (2), 2003, pp. 197–213.

40. Kay Hymowitz, "Why Women Make Less than Men," *The Wall Street Journal*, April 23, 2012, available at www.wsj.com/articles/SB10001424052702303592404577361883019414296[#] René Morissette, Garnett Picot and Yuqian Lu, *The Evolution of Canadian Wages over the Last Three Decades* (Ottawa, ON: Minister of Industry, 2013), available at www.statcan.gc.ca/pub/11f0019m/11f0019m2013347-eng.pdf Status of Women Canada, "Fact Sheet"; Martin Turcotte, *Women and Education*; see also Carole Vincent, "Why Do Women Earn Less Than Men? A Synthesis of Findings from Canadian Microdata," CRDCN Synthesis Series, September 2013.

41. Alksnis, Desmarais, and Curtis, "Workforce Segregation and the Gender Wage Gap,"
p. 1435; [US] Census 2000, www.census.gov/Press-Release/www/2002/demoprofiles.html See also Ronnie Steinberg, "How Sex Gets into Your Paycheck," *Women's VU*, 20 (2), 1997, p. 1.

42. Elizabeth Becker, "Study Finds a Growing Gap between Managerial Salaries for Men and Women," *The New York Times*, January 24, 2002, p. 18; Shannon Henry, "Wage Gap Widens," *The Washington Post*, January 23, 2002; Statistics Canada, "Occupational Skill Groups by Sex, Canada, 1991, 1996, and 2001," available at www12.statca.ca/english/census01/-Products/Analtyic/companion/paid/tables (accessed August 14, 2009); Judith Lorber, "Women and Medical Sociology: Invisible Professionals and Ubiquitous Patients," *Another Voice*, M. Millman and R. M. Kanter, eds., p. 82.

43. Alksnis, Desmarais, and Curtis, "Workforce Segregation and the Gender Wage Gap," p. 1435.

44. Cited in Julie Mathaei, *An Economic History of Women in America* (New York, NY: Schocken, 1982), p. 192.

45. Lynn Martin, *A Report on the Glass Ceiling Initiative* (Washington, DC: US Department of Labor, 1991), p. 1.

46. "The Conundrum of the Glass Ceiling," *The Economist*, July 21, 2005.

47. *Good for Business: Making Full Use of the Nation's Human Capital* (Washington, DC: US Government Printing Office, 1995); Ruth Simpson, "Does an MBA Help Women?– Career Benefits of the MBA," *Gender, Work and Organization*, 3 (2), April 1996, p. 119.

48. Tonda MacCharles, "Ex-Bell Execs Allege Sexism," *The Star* online, January 14, 2008, available at www.thestar.com/293750 (accessed October 12, 2009). Moya Greene, "Remarks for the HSBC Women of Influence Luncheon Series," September 28, 2007, available at www.canadapost.ca/cpo/mc/about us/corporate/management/moyagreene/women.isf (accessed September 10, 2009); "Study: Women Create 'Their Own Glass Ceiling': Female Managers More likely to Underestimate How Their Work is Valued," Associated Press, August 10, 2009, available

at www.msnbc.msn.com/id/32364451/ns
/business-careers (accessed August 24,
2009), "Canadian Women Business Leaders
Feel Underpaid," CBC News, October 15,
2013, available at www.cbc.ca/news/business
/canadian-women-business-leaders-feel
-underpaid-1.2054440

49. Adriana Barton, "And the 10 Most Dangerous Jobs Are," *The Globe and Mail*, January
15, 2014, available at www.theglobeandmail
.com/life/the-hot-button/and-the-top-10-
most-dangerous-jobs-are/article16352517/
Farrell, *The Myth of Male Power*, pp. 105–106.

50. Kanter, *Men and Women of the Corporation*,
p. 209.

51. Ibid., pp. 216, 221, 230.

52. Lynn Zimmer, "Tokenism and Women in the
Workplace: The Limits of Gender-Neutral
Theory," *Social Problems*, 35 (1), 1988, p. 64;
Nina Toren and Vered Kraus, "The Effects of
Minority Size on Women's Position in Aca-
demia," *Social Forces*, 65, 1987, p. 1092.

53. Christine Williams, "The Glass Escalator:
Hidden Advantages for Men in the 'Female'
Professions," *Social Problems*, 39 (3), 1992;
Still a Man's World: *Men Who Do "Women's
Work"* (Berkeley, CA: University of Califor-
nia Press, 1995); see also Marie Nordberg,
"Constructing Masculinity in Women's
Worlds: Men Working as Pre-School Teach-
ers and Hairdressers," *NORA: Nordic Journal
of Women's Studies*, 10 (1), 2002, pp. 26–37.

54. Christine Williams, "The Glass Escalator,"
p. 296.

55. Ibid.; Alfred Kadushin, "Men in a Woman's
Profession," *Social Work*, 21, 1976, p. 441.

56. Constance Backhouse, "*Bell v. The Flaming
Steer Steak House Tavern*: Canada's First
Sexual Harassment Decision," *University of
Western Ontario Law Review*, 19 (1), 1981,
pp. 141–151; Margaret Crouch, *Thinking
about Sexual Harassment*: *A Guide for the
Perplexed* (Oxford, UK: Oxford University
Press, 2000), pp. 92–93.

57. See Catharine MacKinnon, *Sexual Harassment of Working Women* (Cambridge, MA:
Harvard University Press, 1977).

58. Suzanne Goldenberg, "'It Was Like They'd
Never Seen a Woman Before'," *The Guardian*,

February 3, 2006, available at www.the
guardian.com/film/2006/feb/03/gender.world

59. Canadian Advisory Council on the Status
of Women, *CACSW Fact Sheet: Sexual Harassment* (Ottawa, ON: CASCW, n.d.); Susan
Crawford, "Sexual Harassment at Work Cuts
Profits, Poisons Morale," *The Wall Street Journal*, April 19, 1993, p. 11F; Elizabeth Stanko,
Intimate Intrusions (London, UK: Routledge, 1985); E.Couric, "An NJL/West Survey,
Women in the Law: Awaiting Their Turn,"
National Law Journal, December 11, 1989;
1997 study by Klein Associates; Ellen Neu-
borne, "Complaints High from Women in
Blue Collar Jobs," *USA Today*, May 3–6, 1996.

60. "Harassment Scandal Grows in BC Fire Department," CBC News, March 30, 2006, available at www.cbc.ca/canada/story/2006/03
/30/richmond-firefighters.html (accessed
October 12, 2009); "Female Firefighters All
off the Job," *Vancouver Province*, March 22,
2006; "Fire Department's Sexual Harassment Slammed by Mediator," CBC News,
September 22, 2006, available at www.cbc.ca
/canada/british-columbia/story/2006/09/22
/bc-firefighters-ready.html (accessed October 12, 2009); "RCMP Face Sexual Harassment Class-Action Suit," CBC News, March
27, 2012, available at www.cbc.ca/news
/canada/british-columbia/rcmp-face-sexual
-harassment-class-action-suit-1.1153130 Natalie Clancy, "More Women Alleging Harassment Want to Join Class-Action Suit against
RCMP," CBC News, May 31, 2015, available at
www.cbc.ca/news/canada/british-columbia
/more-women-alleging-harassment-want-to
-join-lawsuit-against-rcmp-1.3089534

61. Deborah Rhode, *Speaking of Sex*, p. 28.

62. W. Ann Maggiore, "Sexual Harassment: It's
Not about Women," *EMS Insider*, 34, No. 12,
2007.

63. *USA Today* "Snapshot," April 5, 2006; Dave
McGinn, "The New Harassment? Same-Sex
Abuse," *The Globe and Mail*, October 5, 2009;
Murad Hammadi, "What Canadians Say
about Sexual Harassment," *Canadian Business*
online, December 4, 2014, available at www
.canadianbusiness.com/blogs-and-comment
/sexual-harassment-in-canada-statistics/

64. Eve Tahmincioglu, "Your Career: Female Bosses and Harassment," *MSNBC* online, August 24, 2009, available at www.msnbc .com/id/32476564/business-careers(accessed August 24, 2009); "Female Supervisors More Susceptible to Workplace Sexual Harassment" (American Sociological Association media release), available at www.eurekalcrt .org/pub_releases/2009-08/asa-fsm073009 .php (accessed October 12, 2009).

65. Wallace Immen, "The Plague that Haunts Us Still," *The Globe and Mail*, September 8, 2004; Susan Crawford, "Sexual Harassment at Work Cuts Profits," p. 11F.

66. The text of ILO Convention 100, available at www.ilocarib.org.tt/projects/cariblex/pdfs /ILO_Convention_100.pdf

67. Mary Cornish, "Closing the Global Gender Pay Gap: Securing Justice for Women's Work," *Comparative Labor Law & Policy Journal*, 28 (2), Winter 2007, pp. 219–250; Fortin and Huberman, "Occupational Gender Segregation and Women's Wages in Canada," p. 21.

68. "Bell Canada Settles Pay Equity Case for $178 Million," CBC News, September 4, 2002, available at www.cbc.ca/money /story/2002/09/04/bell020904.html (accessed August 12, 2009); Ronnie Steinberg, "How Sex Gets Into Your Paycheck," p. 2.

69. Aaron Wherry, "Is This the Quiet End to Pay Equity?" *Maclean's* online, February 21, 2009, available at www2.macleans.ca /2009/02/21/is-this-the-quiet-end-to-pay -equity (accessed October 2, 2009).

70. Cited in Rhode, *Speaking of Sex*, pp. 165, 169.

71. Kate Harding, "Lactate on Your Own Time, Lady," *Salon* online August 28, 2009, available at www.salon.com/mwt/broadsheet /feature/2009/08/28/fired_for_pumping /print.html (accessed September 1, 2009).

72. See, for example, Felice Schwartz and Gigi Anders, "The Mami Track," *Hispanic*, July 1993.

73. "Stay the Course on Creating a Family-Friendly Workplace, Says Ernst & Young" (media release), June 8, 2009, available at www.ey.com/CA/en/Newsroom/News -releases/2009-Progressive-Employer (accessed October 10, 2009); "Ernst & Young LLP Marks Ninth Straight Year among the Top 10 on Working Mother Best Companies List," September 16, 2014, available at www .ey.com/US/en/Newsroom/News-releases /news-ey-marks-ninth-straight-year-among -top-10-on-working-mother-best-companies -list

74. Ronnie Steinberg and Alice Cook, "Policies Affecting Women's Employment in Industrial Countries," *Women Working*, A. Stromberg and S. Harkess, eds. (Mountain View, CA: Mayfield, 1988), p. 326.

75. Karen Oppenheim Mason, "Commentary: Strober's Theory of Occupational Sex Segregation," in Reskin, ed., *Sex-Segregation in the Workplace*, p. 169.

76. Catherine Rampell, "As Layoffs Surge, Women May Pass Men in Job Force," *The New York Times*, February 6, 2009, available at www.nytimes.com/2009/02/06/business /06women.html (accessed February 6, 2009); Raveena Aulakh, "In Shrinking Workforce, Women May Surpass Men," *The Star* online, February 7, 2009, available at www .thestar.com/583904 (accessed August 14, 2009).

77. Coontz, *The Way We Never Were*, p. 52; "Millenial Women Pessimistic about Gender Equality in the Workplace," *The Guardian* online, December 11, 2013, available at www.theguardian.com/world/2013/dec/11 /millenial-women-pessimistic-workplace -equality (accessed January 5, 2015).

Chapter 9

1. Marshall McLuhan, *Understanding Media: The Extensions of Man* (Cambridge, MA: MIT Press, 1994 [1964]).

2. Television Bureau of Canada, *TV Basics 2014–2015*, p. 13, available at www.tvb.ca /page_files/pdf/infocentre/tvbasics.pdf (accessed November 10, 2015); Bart Beaty and Rebecca Sullivan, *Canadian Television Today* (Calgary, AB: University of Calgary Press, 2006), p. 113; Donald Roberts, Ulla Foehr, Victoria Rideout, and Mollyann Brodie, *Kids and Media @ the New Millennium: A Comprehensive Analysis of Children's Media Use*

(Menlo Park, CA: Henry J. Kaiser Foundation, 1999).

3. *TV Basics*; Ingrid Lundgren, "Nielsen: Women Watch More TV than Men, but Connected Consoles Are Changing That," *Techcrunch* online, available at http://techcrunch .com/2012/10/05/nielsen-gaming-tv-console/ (accessed October 28, 2015); Roberts et al., *Kids and Media*, "Television Viewing: Fall 2004," *The Daily*, March 31, 2006, available at www.statcan.gc.ca/daily-quotidien/060331 /dq060331b-eng.htm (accessed July 20, 2009).

4. Telefilm Canada, "Telefilm Canada Releases Report on Audience Trends in Canada," October 20, 2015, available at www.telefilm.ca /en/news/releases/2015/10/29/telefilm-canada -releases-report-audience-trends-canada (accessed October 25, 2015); "Theatrical Market Statistics 2013," www.mpaa.org/wp -content/uploads/2014/03/MPAA-Theatrical -Market-Statistics-2013_032514-v2.pdf (accessed October 25, 2015); Mary K. Allen, *Consumption of Culture by Older Canadians on the Internet* (Ottawa, ON: Minister of Industry, 2013) available at www.statcan.gc.ca /pub/75-006-x/2013001/article/11768-eng.pdf

5. P. McGhee and T. Frueh, "Television Viewing and the Learning of Sex-Role Stereotypes," *Sex Roles*, 6, 1980, pp. 179–188.

6. See, for example, Kay Bussey and Albert Bandura, "Social Cognitive Theory of Gender Development and Differentiation," *Psychological Review,* 106, 1999, pp. 676–713.

7. *Hollywood Diversity Report*: *Flipping the Script*, Ralph J. Bunche Center for African American Studies at UCLA, February 2015, available at www.bunchecenter.ucla.edu/wp -content/uploads/2015/02/2015-Hollywood -Diversity-Report-2-25-15.pdf (accessed October 22, 2015).

8. Ibid.

9. Rick Kissell, "'Minority Report,' 'Quantico' among New TV Shows Drawing Diverse Audiences," *Variety*, October 2, 2015, available at www.variety.com/2015/tv/news/tv-shows -minority-report-quantico-diverse-120160 7557/ (accessed October 22, 2015); Josef Adalian, "*Empire* Is a Massive Hit. Here's What Its Success Could Mean for the TV Business,"

Vulture online, January 28, 2015, available at www.vulture.com/2015/01/what-empires- huge-success-means-for-the-tv-biz.html# (accessed October 22, 2015).

10. GLAAD, *Where We Are on TV, 2015–2016*, available at www.glaad.org/files/GLAAD- 2015-WWAT.pdf (accessed October 23, 2015).

11. Ibid.

12. Stacy Smith, Marc Choueiti, and Katherine Pieper, with assistance from Yu-Ting Liu & Christine Song, *Gender Bias without Borders*: *An Investigation of Female Characters in Popular Films Across 11 Countries* (Geena Davis Institute on Gender in Media, 2014), available at http://seejane.org/wp-content /uploads/gender-bias-without-borders-full -report.pdf

13. Ibid.

14. *Hollywood Diversity Report*; Ted Johnson, "Employment Commission to Interview Women Directors In Gender Discrimination Probe," *Variety*, October 6, 2015, available at www.variety.com/2015/biz/news/eeoc -women-directors-gender-discrimination -aclu-1201611731/

15. Stefanie Kratter, "Gender Equality? Women Are Already Tops in Tennis," *CNBC* online, February 26, 2015, available at www.cnbc .com/2015/02/26/in-tennis-women-are -on-top-kratter-150226-ec.html John Rash, "Gender Equity (Until America Watches TV, That Is)," AdAge.com, January 5, 2010, available at http://adage.com/article/media /tv-ratings-gender-equity-america-watches -tv/141311/ (accessed September 10, 2015); G. Walton and L. Potvin, "Boobs, Boxing, and Bombs: Problematizing the Entertainment of Spike TV," *Spaces for Difference*: *An Interdisciplinary Journal*, 2 (1), 2009, pp. 3–14.

16. Victoria Rideout, Ulla Foehr, and Donald F. Roberts, *Media in the Lives of 8–18-Year-Olds: A Kaiser Family Foundation Study* (Kaiser Family Foundation, 2010), available at https://kaiserfamilyfoundation.files.word-press.com/2013/01/8010.pdf (accessed October 25, 2015); Jean-Philippe Chaput et al., "Electronic Screens in Children's Bedrooms and Adiposity, Physical Activity and Sleep:

Do the Number and Type of Electronic Devices Matter?" *Canadian Journal of Public Health*, 105 (4), 2014, pp. 273–279; see also the results of a study done at the University of Guelph, which found links between television use and physical inactivity that were not found when other sedentary activities (video game use, computer use, reading) were examined. "TV Watching Linked to Increased Physical Inactivity" (news release, December 11, 2006), available at www.uoguelph.ca/ news/2006/12/post_25.html (accessed May 12, 2009).

17. National Television Violence Study (2 vols.) (Thousand Oaks, CA: Sage Publication, 1998), Vol. 2, p. 97; Wendy Josephson, "Television Violence: A Review of the Effects on Children of Different Ages" (report) (Ottawa, ON: Health Canada, n.d.).; Douglas A. Gentile, Sarah Coyne, and David A. Walsh, "Media Violence, Physical Aggression, and Relational Aggression in School-Age Children: A Short-Term Longitudinal Study," *Aggressive Behavior*, 37 (2), March/April 2011, pp. 193–206; Craig A. Anderson et al., "SPSSI Research Summary on Media Violence," *Analyses of Social Issues and Public Policy*, online first, November 4, 2015, DOI: 10.1111/asap.12093; Rachel Naud, "Caution Needed When Allowing Children to Watch TV," *Canada* online, available at www.canada.com/entertainment/Caution1needed1when1allowing1kids1watch/1331738/story.html (accessed July 23, 2009); Jane Ledingham, C. Anne Ledingham, and John Richardson, "The Effects of Media Violence on Children" (report) (Ottawa, ON: Health Canada, n.d.), available at www.phac-aspc.gc.ca/ncfvcnivf/ publications/nfntseffemediarech-eng.php (accessed July 21, 2009).

18. Guy Paquette, "Violence on Canadian Television Networks," *Journal of the Canadian Academy of Child and Adolescent Psychiatry*, 13 (1), February 2004, pp. 13–15.

19. George Spears and Casia Seydegart, "Gender and Violence in the Mass Media" (report prepared for the Family Violence Prevention Unit, Health Canada) (Ottawa, ON: Health Canada, 1993), available at www.phac-aspc.gc.ca/ncfv-cnivf/publications/femviomedia-eng.php#Children's (accessed July 19, 2009); Maya Götz et al., "Gender in Children's Television Worldwide: Results from a Media Analysis in 24 Countries," *Television*, 21, 2009, pp. 4–9; see also Isabelle Cherney and Kaila London, "Gender-Linked Differences in the Toys, Television Shows, and Outdoor Activities of 5- to 13-Year-Old Children," *Sex Roles*, 54, May 2006.

20. Venetia Laura Delano Robertson, "Of Ponies and Men: *My Little Pony: Friendship is Magic* and the Brony Fandom," *International Journal of Cultural Studies*, 17 (1), January 2014 , pp. 21–37; Bethan Jones, "My Little Pony, Tolerance is Magic: Gender Policing and Brony Anti-Fandom," *The Journal of Popular Television*, 3 (1), April 2015, pp. 119–125.

21. *The GenderAds Project: Advertising, Education, Activism*, available at www.genderads.com; Deana Rohlinger, "Eroticizing Men: Cultural Influences on Advertising and Male Objectification," *Sex Roles*, 46 (3/4), February 2002, pp. 61–74; Brett Martin and Juergen Gnoth, "Is the Marlboro Man the Only Alternative? The Role of Gender Identity and Self-Construal Salience in Evaluations of Male Models," *Marketing Letters*, 20, 2009, pp. 353–367. Despite the focus on female beauty and male authority, female sexual agency and male "loserdom" are also features of current advertising. See Rosalind Gill, "Empowerment/Sexism: Figuring Female Sexual Agency in Contemporary Advertising," *Feminist and Psychology*, 18 (1), 2008, pp. 35–60; Michael Messner and Jeffrey Montez de Oca, "The Male Consumer as Loser: Beer and Liquor Ads in Mega Sports Media Events," *Signs*, 30 (3), Spring 2005, pp. 1879–1909.

22. David Bolt, *Changing Social Attitudes Toward Disability: Perspectives from Historical, Cultural, and Educational Studies* (New York, NY: Routledge, 2014); David Bolt, "An Advertising Aesthetic: Real Beauty and Visual Impairment," *British Journal of Visual Impairment*, 32 (1), 2014, pp. 25–32.

23. Josée Johnston and Judith Taylor, "Feminist Consumerism and Fat Activists: A

Comparative Study of Grassroots Activism and the Dove Real Beauty Campaign," *Signs*, 33 (4), Summer 2008, pp. 941–966; Jack Neff, "Dove's 'Real Beauty' Pics Could Be Big Phonies," *Advertising Age*, May 7, 2008, available at www.adage.com/article/news/dove-s-real-beauty-pics-big-phonies/126914/ (accessed September 30, 2015); www.campaignforreal beauty.com/ Rebecca Traister, "'Real Beauty' or Really Smart Marketing?" *Salon* online, July 22, 2005, available at http://dir.salon.com/story/mwt/ feature/2005/07/22/dove /index1.html; Rikki Arundel, "Is America's FCC Stupid? Or Is Dove Just Very Clever?" *The Gendershift Blog*, available at http://gendershift.blogspot.com/2007/04/is-americas-fcc-stupid-or-is-dove-just.html (accessed July 21, 2009).

24. Johnston and Taylor, "Feminist Consumerism and Fat Activists"; Lindsay King-Miller, "Here's What Bothers Me about the New Dove Ad," Bitch Media, April 15, 2015, available at https://bitchmedia.org/post/heres-what-bothers-me-about-the-new-dove-ad (accessed November 15, 2015).

25. Allen, *Consumption of Culture*.

26. Jason Boog, "Women Led 58% of Book Spending in 2012," GalleyCat, August 6, 2013, available at www.adweek.com/galleycat /women-accounted-for-58-of-book-spending -in-2012/76517 (accessed June 2, 2014); Quentin Fottrell, "The Huge Difference between What Men and Women Read," *MarketWatch* online, January 20, 2015, available at www.marketwatch.com/story/fiction-readers-an -endangered-species-2013-10-11 (accessed September 29, 2015); Kathryn Zickuhr and Lee Rainie, "A Snapshot of Reading in America in 2013," Pew Research Center, January 26, 2014, available at www.pewinternet.org/2014/01/16/a-snapshot-of-reading-in -america-in-2013/ (accessed November 15, 2015); Vanessa Thorpe, "Why Women Read More Than Men," *The Guardian* online, March 22, 2009, available at www.theguardian.com/books/2009/mar/22/women-reading -books-study (accessed November 15, 2015); Susan Jeffris and Brandon Robshaw, "Shaking Hands across the Great Divide," *The*

Independent, June 17, 2000, available at www.independent.co.uk/arts-entertainment/books /reviews/shaking-hands-across-the-great -divide-625595.html (accessed July 21, 2009). Denise Winterman, "Jane Austen: Why the Fuss?" *BBC Newsmagazine*, March 9, 2007, available at http://news.bbc.co.uk/2/hi /uk_news/magazine/6426195.stm (accessed July 12, 2009).

27. Michael Schaub, "J.K. Rowling Reveals Why She Created Alter Ego Robert Galbraith," *Los Angeles Times*, November 2, 2015, available at www.latimes.com/books/jacketcopy/la-et-jc -jk-rowling-robert-galbraith-20151102-story .html (accessed December 2, 2015).

28. See Amy Beth Aronson, *Taking Liberties: Early American Women's Magazines and Their Readers* (Westport, CT: Praeger, 2002), p. 3; Betty Friedan, *The Feminine Mystique* (New York, NY: Dell Publishing, 1983), pp. 15–79; Marjorie Ferguson, *Forever Feminine: Women's Magazines and the Cult of Femininity* (London, UK: Gower, 1983), p. 3. *Hearth and Home: Images of Women in the Mass Media*, Gayle Tuchman, Arlene Daniels, and James Benit, eds. (New York, NY: Oxford University Press, 1978); Jean Kilbourne, "Killing Us Softly," available from the Media Education Foundation (www.mef .org); Naomi Wolf, *The Beauty Myth* (New York, NY: William Morrow, 1991).

29. Wendy Robbins, "The Celebration of Her Life," *Canadian Woman Studies*, 26 (2), December 2007, pp. 126–128; "We're Celebrating Eighty Years," *Chatelaine* online, available at http://en.chatelaine.com/english /celebration/article.jsp?content=20080225 _154938_6272 (accessed July 23, 2009); Valerie Korinek, "The *Chatelaine* Legacy," *Canadian Woman Studies*, 26 (2), December 2007, pp. 14–21; p. 21; Katherine Govier, "Rebel Daughter," *Canadian Woman Studies*, 26 (2), December 2007, pp. 114–116; Mary Eberts, "'Write It for the Women': Doris Anderson, Changemaker," *Canadian Woman Studies*, 26 (2), December 2007, pp. 6–13; Valerie Korinek, "'Mrs Chatelaine' vs. 'Mrs Slob': Contestants, Correspondents and the Chatelaine Community in Action, 1961–1969,"

Journal of the Canadian Historical Association, 7 (1) 1996, pp. 251–285; Marco Ursi, "The Top 50," *Masthead Special Report*, June 25, 2009; Lisa Rundle, "What Women Want," *This Magazine*, January-February 2005, available at www.thismagazine.ca/issues/2005/01/whatwomenwant.php (accessed July 23, 2009).

30. Media Research Center, *Landmark Study Reveals Women's Magazines Are Left-Wing Political Weapon* (Alexandria, VA). Christina Hoff Sommers, "The Democrats' Secret Woman Weapon: In the Pages of Glossy Women's Magazines, the Party's Line Is in Fashion," *The Washington Post*, January 13, 1997, p. 22. See also Danielle Crittenden, *What Our Mothers Didn't Tell Us: Why Happiness Eludes the Modern Woman* (New York, NY: Simon & Schuster, 1999), pp. 20–21.

31. Aronson, *Taking Liberties*.

32. Belinda Wheaton, "Lifestyle Sport Magazines and the Discourses of Sporting Masculinity," *Masculinity and Men's Lifestyle Magazines*, Bethan Benwell, ed. (Oxford, UK: Blackwell, 2003); Susan Alexander, "Stylish Hard Bodies: Branded Masculinity in *Men's Health* Magazine," *Sociological Perspectives*, 46 (4), 2003, pp. 535–554; Laramie Taylor, "All for Him: Articles About Sex in American Lad Magazines," *Sex Roles*, 52 (3/4), 2005, p. 155; Tim Adams, "New Kid on the Newsstand," *Observer*, January 23, 2005.

33. Dina Spector, "The Sports Illustrated Swimsuit Issue: A $1 Billion Empire," *Business Insider*, February 12, 2013, available at www.businessinsider.com/business-facts-about-the-sports-illustrated-swimsuit-issue-2013-2; Henry Blodget, "Boobs: 5x as Profitable as Footballs (TWX)," *Business Insider*, February 7, 2009, available at www.businessinsider.com/2009/2/11-of-sports-illustrateds-yearly-ad-revenue-comes-from-swimsuit-issue-twx; Tim Adams, "New Kid on the Newsstand." In fact, however, Hilton left *Nuts* in 2007 to focus on developing a new magazine that would appeal to men who found lad magazines "smutty and adolescent." See "Launch Diary: Former 'Nuts' editor Phil Hilton Reveals How a New Magazine All Comes Together," *The Independent*, September 17, 2007, available at www.independent.co.uk/news/media/launch-diary-former-nuts-editor-phil-hilton-reveals-how-a-new-magazine-all-comes-together-402561.html (accessed July 20, 2009).

34. Melissa Click et al., "Twi-Dudes and Twi-Guys: How *Twilight*'s Male Fans Interpret and Engage with a Feminized Text," *Men and Masculinities*, online first, March 9, 2015; Natalie Wilson, *Seduced by Twilight: The Allure and Contradictory Messages of the Popular Saga* (Jefferson, NC: McFarland and Co., 2011), pp. 100–105.

35. Brett Lashua and Karen Fox, "Rec Needs a New Rhythm Cuz Rap Is Where We're Livin'," *Leisure Sciences* 28 (3), 2006, pp. 267–283; for one example of rap on a (Mohawk) reserve, see Robert Hollands, "Rappin' on the Reservation: Canadian Mohawk Youth's Hybrid Cultural Identities," *Sociological Research Online*, 9 (3), 2004, available at www.socresonline.org.uk/cgi-bin/perlfect/search/search.pl?q=multiculturalism&showurl=%2F9%2F3%2Fhollands.html (accessed July 22, 2009); Ta-Nehisi Coates, "Hip-Hop's Down Beat," *Time*, August 12, 2007, available at www.time.com/time/magazine/article/0,9171,1653639,00 (accessed July 30, 2009).

36. Nelson George, *Hip Hop America* (New York, NY: Penguin, 1998), p. xi; This is also the argument Byron Hurt makes in his film *Beyond Beats and Rhymes*; see also Patricia Hill Collins, *From Black Power to Hip-Hop: Racism, Feminism, and Nationalism* (Philadephia, PA: Temple University Press, 2006), pp. 3–5; Edward Armstrong, "Eminem's Construction of Authenticity," *Popular Music and Society*, 27 (3), 2004, pp. 335–355; p. 343–344; Charis Kubrin, "Gangstas, Thugs, and Hustlas: Identity and the Code of the Street in Rap Music," *Social Problems*, 52 (3), 2005, pp. 36–378; Banner quoted in "Sales of Rap Take Stunning Nosedive."

37. Julie Watson, "Rapper's Delight: A Billion Dollar Industry," *Forbes*, February 18, 2004, available at: www.forbes.com/2004/02/18/cx_jw_0218hiphop.html (accessed December 24, 2005); see also figures cited

in Bill Yousman, "Blackophilia and Blacko-phobia: White Youth, the Consumption of Rap Music, and White Supremacy," *Communication Theory*, 13 (4), November 2003, p. 367. See also Mary Bucholtz, "You da Man: Narrating the Racial Other in the Pro-duction of White Masculinity," *Journal of Sociolinguistics*, 3/4, 1999, pp. 443–460; Ce-celia Cutler, "'Keeping It Real': White Hip Hoppers' Discourses of Language, Race, and Authenticity," *Journal of Linguistic Anthro-pology*, 13 (2), 2003, pp. 1–23; Cecelia Cutler, "Yorkville Crossing: White Teens, Hip Hop and African American English," *Journal of Sociolinguistics*, 3/4, 1999, pp. 428–442; Mary Bucholtz, "Borrowed Blackness: African American Vernacular English and European American Youth Identities," Ph.D. disser-tation, University of California at Berkeley, 1997. The white suburban youth and Powell are cited in Bakari Kitwana, *Wankstas, Wig-gers, Wannabes and the New Reality of Race in America* (New York, NY: Basic Books, 2005), p. 41, p. 53. Kitwana argues that white suburban consumption of hip-hop heralds the arrival of new racial politics in America, a new inclusiveness and opposition to racism on the part of white music consumers.

38. Susan Hiwatt, "Cock Rock: Men Always Seem to End up on Top," *The Rock History Reader,* Theo Calefono, ed. (New York, NY: Routledge, 2006), pp. 125–130; p. 126; Steve Waksman, *Instruments of Desire*: *The Electric Guitar and the Shaping of Musical Experience* (Cambridge, MA: Harvard University Press, 2001), pp. 237–276; p. 244.

39. Adam Wolstenholme, "The Misogyny Police Get the Wrong Men," *Batley & Birstall News*, April 17, 2009, available at www.batleynews .co.uk/adam-wolstenholme/The-misogyny -police-get-the.5181247.jp (accessed July 30, 2009).

40. See Philip Auslander, "I Wanna Be Your Man: Suzi Quatro's Musical Androgyny," *Popular Music*, 23 (1), 2004, pp. 1–16; Ronald Weitzer and Charis Kubrin, "Misogyny in Rap Music: A Content Analysis of Preva-lence and Meanings," *Men and Masculinities Online First*, February 19, 2009, pp. 1–27;

p. 23, available at http://jmm.sagepub.com /cgi/rapidpdf/1097184X08327696v1.pdf (ac-cessed July 20, 2009).

41. Mark Anthony Neal, "Spelman Women Take a Stand," at http://archive.blackvoices .com/articles/daily/mu20040414tipdrill .asp (accessed on March 2, 2005); Jennifer McClune, "'You Told Harpo to Beat Me?' How Hip-Hop Music Defines and Divides Black Women," 2008, available at http:// hiphopnews.yuku.com/topic/997 (accessed July 30, 2009); Deborah Finding, "Why Do We Tolerate Misogyny in Music?" *The Guardian*, March 31, 2009, available at www .theguardian.co.uk/comment   isfree/2009 /mar/31/music-orelsan-rap-misogyny   (ac-cessed July 30, 2009); Jennifer McLune, "Hip-Hop's Betrayal of Black Women," April 26, 2006, *Davey D's Hip-Hop Corner*, available at http://hiphopandpolitics.word press.com/2006/04/26/hip-hops-betrayal -of-black-women-by-jennifer-mclune/ (ac-cessed July 28, 2009); Camille Jackson, "Mi-sogyny and Rap: 'Chickenhead' Means You," *Teaching Tolerance*, April 11, 2005, available at www.tolerance.org/news/article_print.jsp? id=1196 (accessed July 30, 2009); Thomas DeFrantz, "Wait . . Hip-Hop Sexualities," *Introducing the New Sexuality Studies*: *Original Essays and Interviews*, Steven Seid-man, Nancy Fischer, and Chet Meeks, eds. (London, UK/New York, NY: Routledge, 2006), pp. 303–308.

42. Spencer   Kornhaber,   "Action   Bronson and Hip-Hop's Never-Ending Misogyny Debate," *The Atlantic*, May 28, 2015, avail-able at www.theatlantic.com/entertainment /archive/2015/05/action-bronson-nxne -petition-consensual-rape-lyrics/394286/ (ac-cessed October 3, 2015).

43. David Mielach, "Americans Spend 23 Hours Per Week Online, Texting," July 2, 2013, avail-able at www.businessnewsdaily.com/4718- weekly-online-social-media-time.html (accessed September 2015); Madlen Davies, "Average Person Now Spends More Time on Their Phone and Laptop than SLEEP-ING, Study Claims," *MailOnline*, March 11, 2015, available at www.dailymail.co.uk

/health/article-2989952/How-technology-taking-lives-spend-time-phones-laptops-SLEEPING.html#ixzz40GVnhc3H (accessed September 30, 2015); Matt Petronzio, "US Adults Spend 11 Hours Per Day With Digital Media," *Mashable.com*, March 5, 2014, available at www.mashable.com/2014/03/05/american-digital-media-hours/#Rl.ImoC0nSqU (accessed September 30, 2015); Julia Alexander, "Canadians Spend the Most Time Online: Study," *Toronto Sun*, March 27, 2015, available at www.torontosun.com/2015/03/27/canadians-spend-the-most-time-online-study (accessed September 30, 2015).

44. Deborah Fallows, *How Women and Men Use the Internet* (Washington, DC: Pew Internet and American Life Project, 2005); Catherine Middleton, Ben Veenhof, and Jordan Leith, *Intensity of Internet Use in Canada: Understanding Different Types of Users* (Business Special Surveys and Technology Statistics Division Working Papers) (Ottawa, ON: Minister of Industry, 2010); Statistics Canada, "Canadian Internet Use Survey," *The Daily*, August 15, 2006, available at www.statcan.gc.ca/daily-quotidien/060815/dq060815b-eng.htm (accessed July 30, 2009); Sharad Goel, Jake Hofman, and M. Irmak Sirer, "Who Does What on the Web: A Large-Scale Study of Browsing Behavior," *Proceedings of the Sixth International AAAI Conference on Weblogs and Social Media* (ICWSM, 2012); Sharon Thompson and Eric Lougheed, "Frazzled by Facebook: An Exploratory Study of Gender Differences in Social Network Communication among Undergraduate Men and Women," *College Student Journal*, 46 (1), March 2012, pp. 88–98; Laura Dixon et al., "Gendered Space: The Digital Divide between Male and Female Users in Internet Public Access Sites," *Journal of Computer-Mediated Communication*, 19, 2014, pp. 991–1009; Tim Schwanen, Mei-Po Kwan, and Fang Ren, "The Internet and the Gender Division of Household Labour," *The Geographical Journal*, 180 (1), March 2014, pp. 52–64; Eszter Hargittai and Aaron Shaw, "Mind the Skills Gap:

The Role of Internet Know-How in Gender-Differentiated Contribution to Wikipedia," *Information, Communication, & Society*, 18 (4), 2015, pp. 424–442; Sady Doyle, "Wikipedia: It's a Man's World," *Salon* online, September 4, 2009.

45. Goel, Hofman, and Sirer, "Who Does What on the Web"; Defy Media, "Millennials Ages 13–24 Declare It's Not Just the Cord, TV Content Doesn't Cut It: Digital Delivers More Relatable and Entertaining Programming" (press release), March 3, 2015, available at www.defymedia.com/2015/03/03/millennials-ages-13-24-declare-just-cord-tv-content-doesn't-cut/ (accessed July 17, 2015).

46. While *GTA* has been the focus of lawsuits and much media controversy, some scholars see it as a sophisticated cultural critique or satire that has both worth and cultural influence. See the essays in *The Meaning and Culture of "Grand Theft Auto": Critical Essays*, Nate Garrelts, ed. (Jefferson, NC: McFarland & Co., 2006).

47. Entertainment Software Association, *Essential Facts about the Computer and Video Game Industry 2015*, available at www.theesa.com/wp-content/uploads/2015/04/ESA-Essential-Facts-2015.pdf (accessed October 8, 2015); "Banner Year for Canadian Video-Game Sales," *CBC News*, January 16, 2009, available at www.cbc.ca/technology/story/2009/01/16/videogames.html (accessed July 27, 2009); Leonard J. Paul, "Canadian Content in Video Games," *Changing Views-World in Play* (Proceedings of the 2005 DiGRA Conference).

48. Interview with Nina Huntemann, November 1, 2005. *Game Over* is available from the Media Education Foundation; Jo Bryce and Jason Rutter, "Killing Like a Girl: Gendered Gaming and Girl Gamers' Invisibility," *CGDC Proceedings* (Tampere, Finland: University of Tampere Press, 2002), pp. 243–255; Gareth Scott and Kirsty Horrel, "Girl Gamers and Their Relationship with the Gaming Culture," *Convergence: The International Journal of Research into New Media Technologies*, 6 (4), 2000, pp. 36–53; see also Kristen Lucas and John Sherry, "Sex Differences in

Video Game Play: A Communication-Based Explanation," *Communication Research*, 31 (5), November 2004, pp. 499–523; Entertainment Software Association, *Essential Facts about the Computer and Video Game Industry 2015*; Meg Jayanth, "52% of Gamers Are Women: But the Industry Doesn't Know It," *The Guardian* online, September 18, 2014, available at www.theguardian.com/comment isfree/2014/sep/18/52-percent-people-playing -games-women-industry-doesnt-know (accessed September 30, 2015).

49. Maeve Duggan, "Who Plays Video Games and Identifies as a 'Gamer'?" Pew Research Center, December 15, 2015, available at www.pewinternet.org/2015/12/15/who-plays -video-games-and-identifies-as-a-gamer/ (accessed February 8, 2016); Jayanth, "52% of Gamers Are Women"; Antonia Zerbisias, "Internet Trolls an Online Nightmare for Young Women," *The Star* online, January 18, 2013, available at www.thestar.com/news /insight/2013/01/18/internet_trolls_an_online _nightmare_for_young_women.html (accessed January 20, 2013).

50. Jing Feng, Ian Spence, and Jay Pratt, "Playing an Action Video Game Reduces Gender Differences in Spatial Cognition," *Psychological Science*, 18 (10), 2007, pp. 850–855.

51. Jeremy Hsu, "Video Games Lack Female and Minority Characters," *LiveScience* online August 3, 2009, available at www .livescience.com/9696-video-games -lack-female-minority-characters.html (accessed February 1, 2016); Michelle Starr, "The Risk of the Female Game Protagonist," *CNet* online, August 6, 2014, available at www.cnet.com/news/the-risk-of-the -female-protagonist/ (accessed Februay 1, 2016); Derek Burrill, "Watch Your Ass: The Structure of Masculinity in Video Games," unpublished manuscript, University of California at Riverside, 2005; David Leonard, "Not a Hater, Just Keepin' It Real: The Importance of Race and Gender-Based Game Studies," *Games and Culture*, 1 (1), January 2006, pp. 83–88.

52. Edward Castronova, *Synthetic Worlds* (Chicago, IL: University of Chicago Press, 2005).

53. David Leonard, "'Live in Your World, Play in Ours': Race, Video Games, and Consuming the Other," *Studies in Media and Information Literacy Education*, 3 (4), November 2003, pp. 1–9; See also Cathleena Martin, "Children's Video Games as Interactive Racialization," *CLCWeb: Comparative Literature and Culture*, 10 (2), 2008.

54. Christopher Engelhardt et al., "This Is Your Brain on Violent Video Games: Neural Desensitization to Violence Predicts Increased Aggression Following Violent Video Game Exposure," *Journal of Experimental Social Psychology*, 47, 2011, pp. 1033–1036; Tracy Dietz, "An Examination of Violence and Gender Role Portrayals in Video Games: Implications for Gender Socialization and Aggressive Behavior," *Sex Roles*, 38 (5/6), 1998, pp. 425–442; Leonard, "Not a Hater," pp. 85–86; Jeanne Funk et al., "Violence Exposure in Real-Life, Video Games, Television, Movies, and the Internet: Is There Desensitization?" *Journal of Adolescence*, 27, 2004, pp. 23–39.

55. Jessica Williams, "Facts That Should Change the World: America Spends $10 Billion Each Year on Porn," *New Statesman*, June 7, 2004; Melinda Tankard Reist, "Incensed about Censorship," *Online Opinion: Australia's E-Journal of Social and Political Debate*, December 5, 2008, available at www.onlineopinion .com.au/print.asp?article=8176; Ian Gillespie, "Nowadays It's Brutal, Accessible: Pornography," *London Free Press*, June 11, 2008, p. A3; Chris Gudgeon, *The Naked Truth: The Untold Story of Sex in Canada* (Vancouver, BC: Douglas & McIntrye, 2003), p. 184; Pamela Paul, *Pornified: How Pornography Is Transforming Our Lives, Our Relationships and Our Families* (New York, NY: Times Books, 2005).

56. Julie Ruvolo, "How Much of the Internet is Actually for Porn," *Forbes Woman* online, September 7, 2011 (accessed on March 27, 2013); "Christian Porn Stats," *Proven Men Ministries* online, available at www .provenmen.org/2014pornsurvey/christian -porn-stats/ (accessed December 7, 2015); Jonathan Liew, "All Men Watch Porn, Scientists

Find," *The Telegraph*, December 2, 2009, available at www.telegraph.co.uk/women /sex/6709646/All-men-watch-porn-scientists -find.html (accessed December 7, 2015).

57. Alexandra Bennett, "From Theory to Practice: Catharine MacKinnon, Pornography, and Canadian Law," *Modern Language Studies*, 27 (3/4), 1997, pp. 213–230; Susan R. Taylor, "Gay and Lesbian Pornography and the Obscenity Laws in Canada," *Dalhousie Journal of Legal Studies*, 8, 1994, pp. 94–129; Susan Barrowclough, "Not a Love Story," *Screen*, 23 (5), 1982, pp. 26–36; Catherine Dunphy, "Lindalee Tracey, 49: Filmmaker Eyed Naked Truth," *The Star* online, Nov. 3, 2006, available at www.thestar.com/article /127032 (accessed July 30, 2009).

58. Pamela Paul, *Pornified*; Jason Carroll et al., "Generation XXX: Pornography Acceptance and Use Among Emerging Adults," *Journal of Adolescent Research*, 23 (1), January 2008, pp. 6–30; David McCormack, "Porn Study Had to Be Scrapped after Researchers Failed to Find ANY 20-Something Males Who Hadn't Watched it," *MailOnline*, 12 January 2013, available at www.dailymail.co.uk /news/article-2261377/Porn-study-scrapped-researchers-failed-ANY-20-males-hadn-t-watched-it.html (accessed May 19, 2015); Lucia Lykke and Philip Cohen, "The Widening Gender Gap in Opposition to Pornography, 1975–2012," *Social Currents* (online first), September 21, 2015.

59. Taylor Kubota, "How Many Women Watch Porn?" *Men's Journal*, n.d., available at www .mensjournal.com/health-fitness/health /how-many-women-watch-porn-20151124 (accessed December 15, 2015); Nisha Lilia Diu, "What a Girl Wants: The Rise of Porn for Women," *The Telegraph*, August 17, 2015, available at http://s.telegraph.co.uk/graphics /projects/porn-for-women/index.html (accessed September 30, 2015); www.feminist pornawards.com

60. Julie Bindel, "Without Porn, the World Would Be a Better Place," *The Guardian* online, October 24, 2014, available at www .theguardian.com/commentisfree/2014/oct/24 /pornography-world-anti-porn-feminist -censorship-misogyny (accessed October 18, 2015); Coslett quoted in Zoe Williams, "Is There Such a Thing as Ethical Porn?" *The Guardian* online November 1, 2014, available at www.theguardian.com/culture/2014 /nov/01/ethical-porn-fair-trade-sex (accessed September 30, 2015); Rhiannon Lucy Coslett, "Porn's Influence Is Real. Sex Education Is the Answer," *The Guardian* online, January 27, 2014, available at www.theguardian.com /commentisfree/2014/jan/27/porn-influence -real-sex-education-online-fantasies (accessed September 30, 2015).

61. Andrew Brown, "The Relationship among Male Pornography Use, Attachment, and Aggression in Romantic Relationships" (Ph.D. diss, Brigham Young University, 2015); Gert Martin Hald and Neil Malamuth, "Experimental Effects of Exposure to Pornography: The Moderating Effect of Personality and Mediating Effect of Sexual Arousal," *Archives of Sexual Behavior*, 44 (1), January 2015, pp. 99–109; Gert M. Hald, Neil Malamuth, and Theis Lange, "Pornography and Sexist Attitudes among Heterosexuals," *Journal of Communication*, 63 (4), August 2013, pp. 638–660; Kimberly Davies, "Voluntary Exposure to Pornography and Men's Attitudes toward Feminism and Rape," *The Journal of Sex Research*, 34 (2), 1997, pp. 131–137; Feona Attwood, "What Do People Do with Porn? Qualitative Research into the Consumption, Use, and Experience of Pornography and Other Sexually Explicit Media," *Sexuality & Culture*, 9 (2), Spring 2005, pp. 65–86; W.L. Marshall, "Revisiting the Use of Pornography by Sexual Offenders: Implications for Theory and Practice," *Journal of Sexual Aggression*, 6 (1/2), January 2000, pp. 67–77; Stacy L. Smith and Ed Donnerstein, "The Problem of Exposure: Violence, Sex, Drugs and Alcohol," *Kid Stuff: Marketing Sex and Violence to America's Children*, Diane Ravitch and Joseph Viteritti, eds. (Baltimore, MD: Johns Hopkins University Press, 2003), p. 83; Pamela Paul, *Pornified*, p.4.

62. Reist, "Incensed about Censorship."

63. Antonia Zerbisias, "Packaging Abuse of Women as Entertainment for Adults," *The*

Star online, January 26, 2008, available at http://pqasb.pqarchiver.com/thestar/access /1418827751.html?dids=1418827751:141882 7751&FMT=ABS&FMTS=ABS:FT&type =current&date=Jan126%2C12008&author =Antonia1Zerbisias&pub=Toronto1Star& edition=&startpage=L.4&desc=Packaging 1abuse1of1women1as1entertainment1for 1adults%3B1Cruel%2C1degrading1scenes1% 27normalized%271for1generation1brought 1up1in1dot-com1world (accessed July 28, 2009).

64. John Stoltenberg, "Pornography and Freedom," *Men Confront Pornography*, M. Kimmel, ed. (New York, NY: Crown, 1990), p. 64.

65. Jensen quoted in Ian Gillespie, "Now It's Brutal, Accessible: Pornography," Robert Jensen, "Just a John? Pornography and Men's Choices," *Men Speak Out: Views on Gender, Sex, and Power*, Shira Tarrant, ed. (New York, NY: Routledge, 2008), pp. 64–69.

Chapter 10

1. Cited in Drury Sherrod, "The Bonds of Men: Problems and Possibilities in Close Male Relationships," *The Making of Masculinities: The New Men's Studies*, H. Brod, ed. (Boston: Allen and Unwin, 1987), p. 230; cited in Lillian Rubin, *Intimate Strangers* (New York: Harper and Row, 1983), p. 59.

2. Wollstonecraft, *A Vindication of the Rights of Women*, p. 56; de Beauvoir, *The Second Sex*, p. 142.

3. Tiger, *Men in Groups* (New York: Vintage, 1969).

4. Carroll Smith-Rosenberg, "The Female World of Love and Ritual: Relations between Women in Nineteenth-Century America," *Signs*, 1 (1), Autumn 1975, pp. 1–29; also see a special journal volume dedicated to the article and its impact, *Women's History in the New Millennium: Carroll Smith-Rosenberg's "The Female World of Love and Ritual" after Twenty-Five Years*, Journal of Women's History, 12 (3), Autumn 2000.

5. Joseph Pleck, "The Male Sex Role: Definitions, Problems and Sources of Change," *Journal of Social Issues*, 32 (3), 1976, p. 273; Jack

Balswick, "The Inexpressive Male: A Tragedy of American Society," *The Forty-Nine Percent Majority*, D. David and R. Brannon, eds. (Reading, MA: Addison-Wesley, 1976); Mirra Komorovsky, *Blue Collar Marriage* (New York: Vintage, 1964); Robert Lewis, "Emotional Intimacy among Men," *Journal of Social Issues*, 34, 1978.

6. Rubin, *Intimate Strangers*, pp. 58, 159, 205.

7. Sherrod, "The Bonds of Men," p. 231.

8. Rubin, *Intimate Strangers*, p. 206.

9. See the recent furor over claims that Abraham Lincoln was gay. Richard Brookhiser, "Was Lincoln Gay?" *The New York Times*, January 9, 2005, www.nytimes.com/2005/01/09/books/review/was-lincoln-gay.html (accessed October 11, 2009)

10. Sherrod, "The Bonds of Men," p. 221; E. Anthony Rotundo, "Romantic Friendships: Male Intimacy and Middle-Class Youth in the Northern United States, 1800–1900," *Journal of Social History*, 23 (1), 1989, p. 21.

11. Francesca Cancian, *Love in America: Gender and Self-Development* (Cambridge, UK: Cambridge University Press, 1987), pp. 19, 21, 23; see also Mary Ryan, *The Cradle of the Middle Class: The Family in Oneida County, N.Y., 1790–1865* (New York: Cambridge University Press, 1981).

12. Lawrence Stone, "Passionate Attachments in the West in Historical Perspective," *Passionate Attachments: Thinking About Love*, W. Gaylin and E. Person, eds. (New York: The Free Press, 1988), p. 33; Francesca Cancian, *Love in America*, p. 70.

13. Lawrence Stone, "Passionate Attachments," p. 32; Michael Gordon and M. Charles Bernstein, "Mate Choice and Domestic Life in the Nineteenth-Century Marriage Manual," *Journal of Marriage and the Family*, November 1970, pp. 668, 669.

14. William J. Goode, "The Theoretical Importance of Love," *American Sociological Review*, 24 (1), 1959.

15. Foucault cited in Peter Nardi, *Men's Friendships*, p. 184; Lynne Segal, *Slow Motion: Changing Masculinities, Changing Men* (New Brunswick, NJ: Rutgers University Press, 1990), p. 139.

16. Tannen, *You Just Don't Understand*, pp. 42, 181, passim; see also Tannen, *Gender and Discourse* (New York: Oxford University Press, 1994).

17. Robert Podesva and Sakiko Kajino, "Sociophonetics, Gender, and Sexuality," *The Handbook of Language, Gender, and Sexuality*, Second Edition, Susan Ehrlich, Miriam Meyerhoff, and Janet Holmes, eds. (Chichester, UK: John Wiley & Sons, 2014), p. 104; Nicholas Kristof, "Japan's Feminine Falsetto Falls Right out of Favor," *New York Times*, December 13, 1995; Laura Miller, "You Are Doing *Burikko*! Censoring/Scrutinising Artificers of Cute Femininity in Japanese," *Japanese Language, Gender, and Ideology: Cultural Models and Real People*, Shikego Okamoto and Janet Shibamoto Smith, eds. (Oxford/New York: Oxford University Press, 2004), pp. 148–165, 151–153.

18. Podesva and Kajino, "Sociophonetics," p. 115; Gail Sullivan, "Study: Women with Creaky Voices—Also Known as 'Vocal Fry'—Deemed Less Hireable," *Washington Post*, June 2, 2014, www.washingtonpost.com/news/morning-mix/wp/2014/06/02/study-women-with-creaky-voices-also-known-as-vocal-fry-deemed-less-hireable/ (accessed December 1, 2015).

19. Jennifer Coates, ed., *Language and Gender: A Reader* (Oxford: Blackwell, 1998), pp. 2–3; Campbell Leaper and Melanie Ayres, "A Meta-Analytic Review of Gender Variations in Adults' Language Use: Talkativeness, Affiliative Speech, and Assertive Speech," *Personality and Social Psychology Review* 11, 2007, pp. 328–363.

20. Victoria Leto DeFrancisco, "The Sounds of Silence: How Men Silence Women in Marital Relations," *Language and Gender: A Reader*, Second Edition, Jennifer Coates and Pia Pichler, eds. (Chichester, UK: John Wiley & Sons, 2011), pp. 153–160; Carol Tavris, *The Mismeasure of Woman* (New York: Simon & Schuster, 1992), pp. 271–272.

21. Peter Kollock, Philip Blumstein, and Pepper Schwartz, "Sex and Power in Interaction: Conversational Privileges and Duties," *American Sociological Review*, 50, February 1985, pp. 34–46; William O'Barr and Bowman Atkins, "'Women's Language' or 'Powerless Language'?" *Language and Gender*, pp. 432–460; Pamela Hobbs, "The Medium Is the Message: Politeness Strategies in Men's and Women's Voice Mail Messages," *Journal of Pragmatics*, 35, 2003, pp. 243–262; Penelope Brown, "How and Why Women Are More Polite: Some Evidence from a Mayan Community," and Janet Holmes, "Complimenting: A Positive Politeness Strategy," *Language and Gender*, pp. 81–120.

22. O'Barr and Atkins, "'Women's Language' or 'Powerless Language'?"; Leaper and Ayres, "A Meta-Analytic Review of Gender Variations in Adults' Language Use."

23. Michael Claes, "Adolescents' Closeness with Parents, Siblings, and Friends in Three Countries: Canada, Belgium, and Italy," *Journal of Youth and Adolescence*, 27 (2), 1998, pp. 165–184.

24. See S.E. Taylor, L.C. Klein, B.P. Lewis, T.L. Gruenwald, R.A.R. Gurung, and J.A. Updegraff, "Biobehavioral Female Responses to Stress: Tend and Befriend, Not Fight or Flight," *Psychological Review*, 107 (3), 2000, pp. 411–429; Lillian Rubin, *Just Friends* (New York: Harper and Row, 1985), pp. 60–61, 62–63; Lillian Rubin, *Intimate Strangers*, pp. 130, 135.

25. Mayta Caldwell and Letita Peplau, "Sex Differences in Same-Sex Friendships," *Sex Roles*, 8 (7), 1982; Beth Hess, "Friendship," *Aging and Society*, M. Riley, M. Johnson, and A. Foner, eds. (New York: Russell Sage, 1972); Erina MacGeorge, Angela Graves, Bo Feng, Seth Gillihan, and Brant Burleson, "The Myth of Gender Cultures: Similarities Outweigh Differences in Men's and Women's Provision of and Responses to Supportive Communication," *Sex Roles*, 50 (3/4), February 2004, pp. 143–175.

26. Helen M. Reid and Gary Alan Fine, "Self-Disclosure in Men's Friendships: Variations Associated with Intimate Relations," *Men's Friendships*; Jeanne Tschann, "Self-Disclosure in Adult Friendship: Gender and Marital Status Differences," *Journal of Social and Personal Relationships*, 5, 1988;

Paul Wright, "Men's Friendships, Women's Friendships and the Alleged Inferiority of the Latter," *Sex Roles*, 8 (1), 1982. See also Sandra Brehm, *Intimate Relationships* (New York: Random House, 1985), p. 346; Lynne Davidson and Lucille Duberman, "Friendship: Communication and Interactional Patterns in Same-Sex Dyads," *Sex Roles*, 8 (8), 1982, p. 817; N.L. Ashton, "Exploratory Investigation of Perceptions of Influences on Best-Friend Relationships," *Perception and Motor Skills*, 50, 1980; Shavaun Wall, Sarah M. Pickert, and Louis V. Paradise, "American Men's Friendships: Self-Reports on Meaning and Changes," *The Journal of Psychology*, 116, 1984; Helen Hacker, "Blabbermouths and Clams: Sex Differences in Self-Disclosure in Same-Sex and Cross-Sex Friendship Dyads," *Psychology of Women Quarterly*, 5 (3), Spring, 1981; Barbara Bank, "Friendships in Australia and the United States: From Feminization to a More Heroic Image," *Gender & Society*, 9 (1), 1995, p. 96.

27. Shanette Harris, "Black Male Masculinity and Same Sex Friendships," *The Western Journal of Black Studies*, 16 (2), 1992, p. 77.

28. Shanette Harris, "Black Male Masculinity . . . ," pp. 78, 81; see also Clyde W. Franklin II, "'Hey Home'—'Yo, Bro': Friendship among Black Men," *Men's Friendships*, P. Nardi, ed. (Newbury Park: Sage Publications, 1992).

29. Brian Gillespie et al., "Homophily, Close Friendship, and Life Satisfaction among Gay, Lesbian, Heterosexual, and Bisexual Men and Women," *plos one*, June 18, 2015, http://journals.plos.org/plosone/article?id=10.1371/journal.pone.0128900 (accessed June 24, 2016); Robert Baiocco et al., "Beyond Similarities: Cross-Gender and Cross-Orientation Best Friendship in a Sample of Sexual Minority and Heterosexual Young Adults," *Sex Roles*, 70 (3/4), February 2014, pp. 110–121.

30. Peter Nardi and Drury Sherrod, "Friendship in the Lives of Gay Men and Lesbians," *Journal of Social and Personal Relationships*, 11, 1994; Lillian Rubin, *Intimate Strangers*, p. 105; Peter Nardi, "The Politics of Gay Men's Friendships," *Men's Lives*, Fourth Edition, M. Kimmel and M. Messner, eds. (Boston: Allyn and Bacon, 1998), p. 250.

31. Gillespie et al., "Homophily, Close Friendship, and Life Satisfaction"; Baiocco et al., "Beyond Similarities."

32. Diane Felmlee, Elizabeth Sweet, and H. Colleen Sinclair, "Gender Rules: Same and Cross-Gender Friendship Norms," *Sex Roles*, 66, 2012, pp. 518–529.

33. Stuart Miller, *Men and Friendship* (Boston: Houghton, Mifflin, 1983), pp. 2–3; Lillian Rubin, *Intimate Strangers*, p. 103.

34. Scott Swain, "Covert Intimacy: Closeness in Men's Friendships," *Gender in Intimate Relationships*, Barbara Risman and Pepper Schwartz, eds. (Belmont, CA: Wadsworth, 1988), pp. 83–84.

35. Niobe Way, "Boys' Friendships during Adolescence: Intimacy, Desire, and Loss," *Journal of Research on Adolescence*, 23 (2), June 2013, pp. 201–213.

36. Michael Deangelis, ed., *Reading the Bromance: Homosocial Relationships in Film and Television* (Detroit: Wayne State University Press, 2014).

37. Stephen Petite, "What Exactly Is a Man Crush?" *Huffington Post*, May 19, 2014, www.huffingtonpost.com/steven-petite/what-exactly-is-a-man-cru_b_5344282.html (accessed December 15, 2015); Tom Fordy, "Why Do Straight Men Fancy Michael Fassbender?" *The Telegraph*, October 28, 2015, www.telegraph.co.uk/men/thinking-man/11957564/My-Michael-Fassbender-man-crush-is-not-sexual.-Honest.html (accessed December 15, 2015).

38. Carmen Cruz, "Straight Men Now Feel the Need to Say 'No Homo' When Discussing Emotions," *The Guardian*, February 23, 2014, www.theguardian.com/commentisfree/2014/feb/23/gay-rights-homophobia-michael-sam (accessed June 24, 2016); Jonah Weiner, "Does This Purple Mink Make Me Look Gay?" *The Slate*, August 6, 2009, www.slate.com/articles/arts/music_box/2009/08/does_this_purple_mink_make_me_look_gay.html (accessed June 24, 2016); Connor Adams Sheets, "What Does 'No Homo' Even Mean? Roy Hibbert was Unfairly Punished for Using Slur,"

International Business Times, June 3, 2013, www.ibtimes.com/fighting-words/what-does-no-homo-even-mean-roy-hibbert-was-unfairly-punished-using-slur-1288945 (accessed June 24, 2016); Joshua Brown, "'No Homo'," *Journal of Homosexuality*, 58 (3), 2011, pp. 299–314; Amanda Potts, "'Love You Guys (No Homo)'," *Critical Discourse Studies*, 12 (2), 2015, pp. 163–186.

39. See, inter alia, Helen E. Fisher et al., "Defining the Brain Systems of Lust, Romantic Attraction, and Attachment," *Archives of Sexual Behavior*, 31 (5), October 2002, pp. 413–419.

40. Brent Miller and Brad Benson, "Romantic and Sexual Relationship Development during Adolescence," *The Development of Romantic Relationships in Adolescence*, Wyndol Furman, Benson Brown, and Candace Feiring, eds. (Cambridge: Cambridge University Press, 1999), pp. 100–101.

41. William Kephart, "Some Correlates of Romantic Love," *Journal of Marriage and the Family*, 29, 1967.

42. Jeffry Simpson, Bruce Campbell, and Ellen Berscheid, "The Association between Romantic Love and Marriage," *Personality and Social Psychology Bulletin*, 42 (3), 1986, pp. 363–372.

43. Susan Sprecher, E. Aron, E. Hatfield, A. Cortese, E. Potapava, and A. Levitskaya, "Love: American Style, Russian Style, and Japanese Style," paper presented at the Sixth Annual Conference on Personal Relationships, Orono, Maine, 1992.

44. Susan Sprecher and Maura Toro-Morn, "A Study of Men and Women from Different Sides of Earth to Determine If Men Are from Mars and Women Are from Venus in Their Beliefs About Love and Romantic Relationships," *Sex Roles*, 46 (5/6), March 2002, pp. 131–147.

45. Eva Illousz, *Why Love Hurts: A Sociological Explanation* (Cambridge, UK: Polity Press, 2012).

46. Pierre Bourdieu, *Masculine Domination*, Richard Nice, trans. (Stanford: Stanford University Press, 2001).

47. William Kephart, "Some Correlates of Romantic Love"; Kenneth Dion and Karen Dion, "Correlates of Romantic Love," *Journal of Consulting and Clinical Psychology*, 41, 1973; Charles Hill, Zick Rubin, and Letitia Anne Peplau, "Breakups before Marriage: The End of 103 Affairs," *Divorce and Separation: Context, Causes and Consequences*, G. Levinger and O.C. Moles, eds. (New York: Basic Books, 1979); Charles Hobart, "Disillusionment in Marriage and Romanticism," *Marriage and Family Living*, 20, 1958; Charles Hobart, "The Incidence of Romanticism During Courtship," *Social Forces*, 36, 1958; David Knox and John Spoakowski, "Attitudes of College Students toward Love," *Journal of Marriage and the Family*, 30, 1968; George Theodorson, "Romanticism and Motivation to Marry in the United States, Singapore, Burma and India," *Social Forces*, 44, 1965.

48. Hill, Rubin, and Peplau, "Breakups before Marriage."

49. Cancian, *Love in America*, pp. 70, 121

50. Tavris, *The Mismeasure of Woman*, p. 263; Rubin, *Intimate Strangers*.

51. Robin Simon and Leda Nath, "Gender and Emotion in the United States: Do Men and Women Differ in Self-Reports of Feelings and Expressive Behavior?" *American Journal of Sociology*, 109 (5), pp. 1137–1176.

52. Carol Tavris, *The Mismeasure of Woman*, p. 284.

53. Cancian, "The Feminization of Love," pp. 705, 709.

54. Lillian Rubin, *Just Friends*, p. 41.

Chapter 11

1. It is ironic, perhaps, that some of these developments that have made us more aware of our bodies have also enabled us to change (surgery) or conceal (Internet) them.

2. Helen Meekosha, "Body Battles: Bodies, Gender, and Disability," *The Disability Reader: Social Science Perspectives*, Tom Shakespeare, ed. (London, UK/New York, NY: Continuum Books, 1998), p. 164.

3. Some people with disabilities argue for the use of "people-first" language: for example, "person with disabilities" instead of "disabled person." People who take this point

of view consider the use of terms like "disabled people" offensive. While people-first language has done an admirable job of reframing views of people with disabilities, language use is always evolving, and the growth of disability activism has engendered debates about labels. Today, some people with disabilities prefer to be called "disabled people." In this study, both terms are used. For an interesting discussion, see Lisa Egan, "I'm Not a 'Person with a Disability': I'm a Disabled Person," *XOJane*, November 9, 2012, available at www.xojane.com/issues /i-am-not-a-person-with-a-disability-i-am -a-disabled-person

4. Robert Murphy, "Encounters: The Body Silent in America," *Disability and Culture*, Benedicte Ingstad and Susan Reynolds Whyte, eds. (Berkeley, CA: University of California Press, 1995), p. 143.

5. Statistics Canada, *Canadian Survey on Disability: Data Tables* (Ottawa, ON: Minister of Industry, 2013), available at www.statcan .gc.ca/pub/89-654-x/89-654-x2013001-eng .pdf Also Rubab Arim, *A Profile of Disability among Canadians 15 Years of Age and Older, 2012* (Ottawa, ON: Minister of Industry, 2015), available at www.statcan.gc.ca /pub/89-654-x/89-654-x2015001-eng.pdf

6. Council of Canadians with Disabilities, "As a Matter of Fact: Poverty and Disability in Canada," available at www.ccdonline.ca /em/socialpolicy/poverty-citizenship/poverty -disability-canada[#] Also Cara Williams, "Disability in the Workplace," *Perspectives*, 7 (2), February 2006; Arim, *A Profile of Disability.*

7. Fiona Sampson, "Globalization and the Inequality of Women with Disabilities," *Gender Relations in Global Perspective: Essential Readings*, Nancy Cook, ed. (Toronto, ON: Canadian Scholars' Press, 2007), pp. 153–163; Arim, *A Profile of Disability*; Statistics Canada, *Canadian Survey on Disability.*

8. Meekosha, "Body Battles"; Adrienne Asch and Michelle Fine, "Beyond Pedestals: Revisiting the Lives of Women with Disabilities," *Disruptive Voices: The Possibilities of Feminist Research*, Michelle Fine, ed. (Ann Arbor,

MI: University of Michigan Press, 1992), pp. 139–170.

9. Tom Shakespeare, "The Sexual Politics of Disabled Masculinity," *Sexuality and Disability*, 17 (1), 1999, pp. 53–64; Slawomir Rapala and Lenore Manderson, "Recovering Invalidated Adulthood, Masculinity, and Sexuality," *Sexuality and Disability*, 23 (3), Fall 2005, pp. 161–180.

10. Kimberly Hively and Amani El-Alayli , "'You Throw like a Girl": The Effect of Stereotype Threat on Women's Athletic Performance and Gender Stereotypes," *Psychology of Sport and Exercise*, 15 (1), January 2014, pp. 48–55; Aïna Chalabaev et al., "The Influence of Sex Stereotypes and Gender Roles on Participation and Performance in Sport and Exercise: Review and Future Directions," *Psychology of Sport and Exercise*, 14 (2), March 2013, pp. 136–144.

11. Janet Shibley Hyde, "New Directions in the Study of Gender Similarities and Differences," *Current Directions in Psychological Science*, 16 (5), 2007, pp. 259–263; for a discussion of competent throwing in some women and less-competent throwing in many non-North American men, see Greg Downey's post (based on a forthcoming book chapter), "Throwing like a Girl('s Brain)," February 1, 2009, Neuroanthropology.net, available at http://neuroanthropology.net/2009/02/01 /throwing-like-a-girls-brain (accessed December 21, 2009.

12. Iris Marion Young, "Throwing like a Girl: A Phenomenology of Feminine Body Comportment Motility and Spatiality," *Human Studies*, 3, 1980, pp. 137–156; Félix Javier Jiménez-Jiménezat et al., "Influence of Age and Gender in Motor Performance in Healthy Subjects," *Journal of the Neurological Sciences*, 302, 2011, pp. 72–80.

13. Barbara Fredrickson and Kristen Harrison, "Throwing like a Girl: Self-Objectification Predicts Adolescent Girls' Motor Performance," *Journal of Sport and Social Issues*, 29 (1), 2005, pp. 79–101; Thomas and French's 1985 study of motor performance, which demonstrated the widening gap over time, is referenced in Downey's post (see above);

Anne Bowker, Shannon Gadbois, and Becki Cornock, "Sports Participation and Self-Esteem: Variations as a Function of Gender and Gender Role Orientation," *Sex Roles*, 49 (1/2), July 2003, pp. 47–58; Don Sabo et al., "High School Athletic Participation and Adolescent Suicide: A Nationwide Study," *International Review for the Sociology of Sport*, 40 (1), 2005, pp. 5–23; Don Sabo et al., *Her Life Depends on It*: *Sport, Physical Activity and the Health and Well-Being of American Girls* (East Meadow, NY: Women's Sports Foundation, 2004); Don Sabo et al., "High School Athletic Participation, Sexual Behavior and Adolescent Pregnancy: A Regional Study," *Journal of Adolescent Health*, 25 (3), 1999, pp. 207–216.

14. Margaret Ann Hall, *The Girl and the Game*: *A History of Women's Sport in Canada* (Toronto, ON: University of Toronto Press, 2002), p. 29.

15. Hoffman quoted in Hall, *The Girl and the Game*, p. 161; see Abby Hoffman's profile at the Canada's Sports Hall of Fame, available at www.sportshall.ca/hm_profile.php?i=461 (accessed January 3, 2010).

16. Myra Sadker and David Sadker, *Failing at Fairness*, pp. 125–126; "The Attack on Women's Sports," *The New York Times*, February 17, 2003, p. A22; Christine Stolba, "We've Come the Wrong Way Baby," *The Women's Quarterly*, Spring, 2002. On the other side, see the "Title IX FAQ Packet," published by the Women's Equity Resource Center at www.edc.org/womensequity "CAAWS Tells Committee to Add Gender Clause," *The Ottawa Citizen*, May 22, 2002, available www.caaws.ca/e/about/article.cfm?id=195 (accessed January 11, 2010); Sport Canada, *Actively Engaged*: *A Policy on Sport for Women and Girls*, January 1, 2009, available at www.pch.gc.ca/pgm/sc/pol/fewom/101-eng.cfm (accessed January 1, 2010).

17. Nancy Theberge and Susan Birrell, "Structural Constraints Facing Women in Sport," *Women and Sports in the United States*: *A Documentary Reader*, Jean O'Reilly and Susan Cahn, eds. (Lebanon, NH: Northeastern University Press, 2007), pp. 173–174;

Janet Fink, "Homophobia and the Marketing of Female Athletes and Women's Sport," *Sexual Orientation and Gender Identity in Sport*: *Essays from Activists, Coaches, and Scholars*, G.B. Cunningham, ed. (College Station, TX: Center for Sport Management Research and Education, 2012), pp. 49–66.

18. Maurice Garland, "Top WNBA Salaries vs NBA Salaries: Who Gets Paid More?" *Black Enterprise*, December 17, 2015, available at www.blackenterprise.com/lifestyle/wnba-player-salaries-vs-nba-salaries/ (accessed December 17, 2015); Ann Travers, "The Sports Nexus and Gender Injustice," *Studies in Social Justice*, 2 (1), 2008, pp. 79–101.

19. Donald McRae, "Caster Semenya," *The Guardian*, November 14, 2009, available at www.guardian.co.uk/sport/2009/nov/14/caster-semenya-donald-mcrae-training-camp (accessed January 21, 2010); Fausto-Sterling, *Sexing the Body*, pp. 1–5; Alice Dreger, "Where's the Rulebook for Sex Verification?" *The New York Times*, August 22, 2009, available at www.nytimes.com/2009/08/22/sports/22runner.html (accessed September 21, 2009); Robert Ritchie, John Reynard, and Tom Lewis, "Intersex and the Olympic Games," *Journal of the Royal Society of Medicine*, 101, 2008, pp. 395–399; Ross Tucker and Malcolm Collins, "The Science and Management of Sex Verification in Sport," *South African Journal of Sports Medicine*, 21 (4), 2009; Jon Billman, "Michelle Raises Hell," *Outside*, April 2004, available at Outside online (accessed January 21, 2010); "Banned for Mocking Transgender Winner," *The Vancouver Sun*, August 3, 2006, available at www.canada.com/vancouversun/news/story.html?id=b49de62b-e7dc-4699-83ab-ada11000f500 (accessed January 21, 2010); "Doubts Raised over Semenya's return," BBC Sport, January 15, 2010, available at http://newsvote.bbc.co.uk (accessed January 21, 2010); J. Michael Bostwick and Michael Joyner, "The Limits of Acceptable Biological Variation in Elite Athletes: Should Sex Ambiguity Be Treated Differently from Other Advantageous Genetic Traits?" *Mayo Clinic Proceedings*, 87 (6), June 2012, pp. 508–513;

John Branch, "Dutee Chand, Female Sprinter With High Testosterone Level, Wins Right to Compete," *The New York Times*, July 27, 2015, available at www.nytimes.com/2015/07/28/sports/international/dutee-chand-female-sprinter-with-high-male-hormone-level-wins-right-to-compete.html (accessed December 15, 2015); Vivienne Perry, "Body of Evidence," *The Guardian*, August 5, 2004, available at www.theguardian.com/science/2004/aug/05/1 (accessed December 15, 2015); Ben Smith, "Caster Semenya: What I Dream of Is to Become Olympic Champion," BBC Sport, May 20, 2015, available at www.bbc.com/sport/athletics/32805695 (accessed December 15, 2015).

20. Gamal Abdel-Shahid, *Who Da Man? Black Masculinities and Sporting Cultures* (Toronto, ON: Canadian Scholars' Press, 2005), p. 73.

21. Marc Weinstein, Michael Smith, and David Wiesenthal, "Masculinity and Hockey Violence," *Sex Roles*, 33 (11/12), 1995, pp. 831–847.

22. Alan Schwarz, "Wives United by Husbands' Post-NFL Trauma," *The New York Times*, March 14, 2007; Michael Russo, "Clutterbuck Rejects Cherry's Critique of His Fighting Stance," *Star Tribune*, February 2, 2009, available at www.startribune.com/sports/wild/38783922.html (accessed January 21, 2010).

23. Nick Pappas, Patrick McKenry, and Beth Skilken Catlett, "Athlete Aggression on the Rink and off the Ice: Athlete Violence and Aggression in Hockey and Interpersonal Relationships," *Men and Masculinities*, 6 (3), 2004, pp. 291–312.

24. Don Sabo, "The Myth of the Sexual Athlete," Disch, ed., *Reconstructing Gender*, pp. 274–278; Marni Finkelstein, Timothy Baghurst, and Tommy Shavers, "'Cleat Chasers': College Football Players Talk about Women and Sex," *Issues in Social Science*, 3 (1), 2015, pp. 120–137.

25. Laura Miller, "Mammary Mania in Japan," *Positions*, 11 (2), 2003, pp. 271–300; for an example of the fertile literature on cross-culture preferences for a certain hip-waist ratio, see Frank Marlowe, Coren Apicella, and Dorian Reed, "Men's Preferences for Women's Profile Waist-to-Hip Ratios in Two Societies," *Evolution and Human Behavior*, 26, 2005, pp. 458–468.

26. Naomi Wolf, *The Beauty Myth* (New York, NY: William Morrow, 1991), pp. 10, 184; Fatima Mernissi, "Size 6: The Western Woman's Harem," Cook, ed., *Gender Relations in Global Perspective*, pp. 147–151; p. 151.

27. Laura Mulvey, "Visual Pleasure and Narrative Cinema," *Screen*, 16 (3), 1975, pp. 6–18.

28. Sandra Bartky, *Femininity and Domination: Studies in the Phenomenology of Oppression* (New York, NY/London, UK: Routledge, 1990), p. 28.

29. Susan Faludi, *Backlash: The Undeclared War against American Women*, Fifteenth Anniversary Edition (New York, NY: Three Rivers Press, 2006 [1991]), p. 65. Also see Cressida Hayes and Meredith Jones, "Cosmetic Surgery in the Age of Gender," *Cosmetic Surgery: A Feminist Primer*, Cressida Heyes and Meredith Jones, eds. (Farnham, UK: Ashgate, 2009).

30. See Eugenia Kaw, "Medicalization of Racial Features: Asian-American Women and Cosmetic Surgery," *Medical Anthropological Quarterly*, 7 (1), 1993; see also Cressida Heyes, "All Cosmetic Surgery Is 'Ethnic': Asian Eyelids, Feminist Indignation, and the Politics of Whiteness," Heyes and Jones, eds., *Cosmetic Surgery*.

31. Sarah Kershaw, "Move Over, My Pretty, Ugly Is Here," *The New York Times*, October 30, 2008, available at www.nytimes.com/2008/10/30/fashion/30ugly.html (accessed October 30, 2008); Anthony Synnott, "What Is Ugly? Part 2," *Psychology Today* blogs, July 7, 2009, available at www.psychologytoday.com/blog/rethinking-men/200907/what-is-ugly-part-2

32. Daniel Francis, *The Imaginary Indian: The Image of the Indian in Canadian Culture* (Vancouver, BC: Arsenal Pulp Press, 2012 [1992]); Nancy J. Parezo and Angelina R. Jones, "What's in a Name: The 1940s–1950s Squaw Dress," *The American Indian Quarterly*, 33 (3), 2009, pp. 373–379; Margaret L. Hunter, "'If You're Light You're Alright': Light Skin Color as Social Capital for Women of Color," *Gender & Society*, 16 (2), April 2002,

pp. 175–193; Kathy Davis, "Black Is Beautiful, European Perspective," *European Journal of Women's Studies*, 16 (2), 2009, pp. 99–101; bell hooks, "Selling Hot Pussy: Representations of Black Female Sexuality in the Cultural Marketplace," *The Politics of Women's Bodies: Sexuality, Appearance, and Behavior*, Rose Weitz, ed. (Oxford, UK: Oxford University Press, 2003), pp. 122–134.

33. Meekosha, "Body Battles"; Per Solvang, "The Amputee Body Desired: Beauty Destabilized? Disability Re-Valued?" *Sexuality and Disability*, 25 (2), June 2007, pp. 51–64.

34. Joanna Bourke, *Dismembering the Male: Men's Bodies, Britain, and the Great War* (Chicago, IL: University of Chicago Press, 1996).

35. For a sustained treatment of Sandow, see John F. Kasson, *Houdini, Tarzan, and the Perfect Man: The White Male Body and the Challenge of Modernity in America* (New York, NY: Hill and Wang, 2001).

36. See Debra Gimlin, *Body Work: Beauty and Self-Image in American Culture* (Berkeley, CA: University of California Press, 2002), p. 5; "How to Get Plump," *Harper's Bazaar*, August 1908, p. 787.

37. Gordon R. Mitchell and Kathleen M. McTigue, "The US Obesity 'Epidemic': Metaphor, Method, or Madness?" *Social Epistemology*, 21 (4), October–December 2007, pp. 391–423; Natalie Boero, "All the News that's Fat to Print: The American 'Obesity Epidemic' and the Media," *Qualitative Sociology*, 30, 2007, pp. 41–60.

38. May Friedman, "Mother Blame, Fat Shame, and Moral Panic: 'Obesity' and Child Welfare," *Fat Studies: An Interdisciplinary Journal of Body Weight and Society*, 4 (1), 2015, pp. 14–27; Natalie C. Boero. "Fat Kids, Working Moms, and the Epidemic of Obesity, Race, Class, and Mother-Blame," *The Fat Studies Reader*, E. Rothblum and S. Solovay, eds. (New York, NY: New York University Press, 2010); Boero, "All the News That's Fat to Print."

39. Karen C. Roberts, Margot Shields, Margaret de Groh, Alfred Aziz and Jo-Anne Gilbert, *Overweight and Obesity in Children and Adolescents: Results from the 2009 to 2011 Canadian Health Measures Survey* (Ottawa, ON: Minister of Industry, 2012), available at www.statcan.gc.ca/pub/82-003-x/2012003 /article/11706-eng.htm Mary Pipher, *Reviving Ophelia* (New York, NY: Ballantine, 1996); Sharon Kirkey, "Childhood Obesity Underpins Low Self-Esteem: Study," *The Gazette*, June 17, 2009, available at www. montrealgazette.com/health/familychild/ Childhood1obesity1underpins1self1esteem1 Study/1706007/story.html (accessed July 21, 2009); M.E. Collins, "Body Figure Perceptions and Preferences Among Preadolescent Children," *International Journal of Eating Disorders*, 10, 1991, pp. 199–208; A. Gustafson-Larson and R. Terry, "Weight-Related Behaviors and Concerns of Fourth Grade Children," *Journal of the American Dietetic Association*, 92 (7), 1992, pp. 818–822; see also www.healthywithin.com /STATS.htm

40. See L. Smolak and R. Striegel-Moore, "The Implications of Developmental Research for Eating Disorders," *The Developmental Psychopathology of Eating Disorders: Implications for Research, Prevention and Treatment*, M. Smolak, P. Levine, and R. Striegel-Moore, eds. (Mahwah, NJ: Erlbaum, 1996), pp. 235–257. For statistics on eating disorders in Canada, see www.nedic.ca/knowthefacts/statistics .shtml For the UK, Europe, and the US, see www.disordered-eating.co.uk Also "Europe Targets Eating Disorders" at news.bbc.uk/1 /hi/health/197334.stm and "Eating Disorders Factfile" at news.bbc.co.uk/1/hi/health /medical_notes/ 187517.stm

41. See A. Furnham and N. Alibhai, "Cross-Cultural Differences in the Perception of Female Body Shapes," *Psychological Medicine*, 13 (4), 1983, pp. 829–837; D.B. Mumford, "Eating Disorders in Different Cultures," *International Review of Psychiatry*, 5 (1), 1993, pp. 109–113; N. Shuriquie, "Eating Disorders: A Transcultural Perspective," *Eastern Mediterranean Health Journal*, 5 (2), 1999, pp. 354–360, also at www.emro.who.int /Publications/EMHJ/0502/20.htm Sonni Efron, "Eating Disorders on the Increase in Asia" at www.dimensionsmagazine.com/news /asia/html

42. Deborah Gregory, "Heavy Judgment," *Essence*, August 1994, pp. 57–58; G.B. Schreiber, K.M. Pike, D.E. Wilfley, and J. Rodin, "Drive for Thinness in Black and White Preadolescent Girls," *International Journal of Eating Disorders*, 18 (1), 1995, pp. 59–69.

43. For the growth of white men's obsession with body image in the late nineteenth and early twentieth centuries, see Kasson, *Houdini, Tarzan, and the Perfect Man*.

44. For discussion, see Matthew Immergut, "Manscaping: The Tangle of Nature, Culture, and Male Bodily Hair," *The Body Reader: Essential Social and Cultural Readings*, Lisa Moore and Mary Kosut, eds. (New York, NY: New York University Press, 2010); Deni Kirkova, "Men in Their Thirties Spend Most on Beauty," *Mail Online*, December 10, 2013, available at www.dailymail.co.uk/femail/article-2521270/Men-thirties-spend-beauty-Boys-splashing-100-month-anti-ageing-creams-guyliner-spa-trips-according-Debenhams-research.html (accessed March 7, 2014); Dale Hrabi, "Do Men Need Beauty Regimens?" Wall Street Journal, February 28, 2014, available at www.wsj.com/articles/SB10001424052702303880604579404943694260418 (accessed March 7, 2014).

45. Harrison Pope, Katharine Phillips, and Roberto Olivardia, *The Adonis Complex: The Secret Crisis of Male Body Obsession* (New York, NY: The Free Press, 2000); Jerel Calzo et al., "Patterns of Body Image Concerns and Disordered Weight- and Shape-Related Behaviors in Heterosexual and Sexual Minority Adolescent Males," *Developmental Psychology*, 51 (9), September 2015, pp. 1216–1225. For a study that reviews the effects of homosexuality on body satisfaction among a group of gym-active men, see Jac Brown and Doug Graham, "Body Satisfaction in Gym-Active Males: An Exploration of Sexuality, Gender, and Narcissism," *Sex Roles*, 59, 2008.

46. Renee Engelm, Michael Sladek, and Heather Waldron, "Body Talk among College Men: Content, Correlates, and Effects," *Body Image*, 10, 2013, pp. 300–308; quote from Richard Morgan, "The Men in the Mirror," *Chronicle of Higher Education*, September 27, 2002, p. A53.

47. D.B. Woodside et al., "Men with Full and Partial Syndrome Eating Disorders: Community Comparisons with Non-Eating Disordered Men and Eating Disordered Women," *American Journal of Psychiatry*, 158, 2001, pp. 570–574; Edisol Wayne Dotson, *Behold the Man: The Hype and Selling of Male Beauty in Media and Culture* (New York, NY: Routledge, 1999); P.A. McNulty, "Prevalence and Contributing Factors of Eating Disorder Behaviors in Active Duty Navy Men," *Military Medicine*, 162 (11), 1997, pp. 753–758; Pope et al., *The Adonis Complex*; "Anorexic Men Begin to Share Their Hellish Secrets," *The Edmonton Journal*, April 18, 2008, available at www.canada.com/topics/bodyandhealth/story.html?id=a49a2706-ae4c-4573-8882-7cc0ca5471f7 (accessed January 19, 2010).

48. Shawn Radcliffe, "Troubling Trend: Steroid Use on the Rise," available at www.mensfitness.com/training/build-muscle/steroid-use-on-the-rise Peter Walker, "Spiralling Anabolic Steroid Use Leaves UK Facing Health Timebomb, Experts Warn," *The Guardian*, June 19, 2015, available at www.theguardian.com/society/2015/jun/19/anabolic-steroid-use-leaves-britain-facing-health-timebomb Gina Kolata, "With No Answers on Risks, Steroid Users Still Say 'Yes,'" *The New York Times*, December 2, 2002, pp. A1, 19.

49. Mike Faille and Jake Edmiston, "Graphic: The Tattoo Industry," *The National Post*, August 16, 2013, available at http://news.nationalpost.com/news/graphics/graphic-the-tattoo-industry (accessed July 2, 2015); Matt Kwong, "Tattoo Culture Making Its Mark on Millennials," CBC News, September 19, 2012, available at www.cbc.ca/news/canada/tattoo-culture-making-its-mark-on-millennials-1.1149528 (accessed July 2, 2015); Canadian Press/Leger Marketing, "How Canadians Feel about Tattoos and Body Piercing" (Montreal, QC: Leger Marketing, n.d.); See "Motivation for Tattoo Removal," *Archives of Dermatology*, December 1996; See also the website of the American Society of Plastic Surgeons at www.plasticsurgery.org/mediactr/92sexdis.html

50. Hayes and Jones, "Cosmetic Surgery"; American Society of Plastic Surgeons, "American Society of Plastic Surgeons Reports Cosmetic Procedures Increased 3 Percent in 2014," February 26, 2015, available at www .plasticsurgery.org/news/2015/plastic-surgery -statistics-show-new-consumer-trends.html (accessed December 15, 2015).

51. ASPS, "American Society of Plastic Surgeons Reports."

52. Gimlin, *Body Work*, p. 102.

53. George Arnett, "Germany: The World's Capital of Penis Enlargement," *The Guardian*, July 31, 2014, available at www.theguardian .com/news/datablog/2014/jul/31/germany -the-worlds-capital-of-penis-enlargment -country (accessed December 15, 2015); Sam Fields, "Penis Enlargement Surgery," at www .4-men.org/penisenlargementsurgery.html Also, Randy Klein, "Penile Augmentation Surgery," *Electronic Journal of Human Sexuality*, 2, March 1999, pp. 1, 8–9.

54. Letters testimonial to Dr E. Douglas Whitehead at www.penile-enlargementsurgeon .com/diary.html

55. Melanie Berliet, "Designer Parts: Inside the Strange, Fascinating World of Vaginoplasty," *The Atlantic*, April 2, 2012, available at www.theatlantic.com/health/archive /2012/04/designer-parts-inside-the-strange -fascinating-world-of-vaginoplasty/255188/ (accessed December 15, 2015); www.tcclinic .com/vaginal-tightening-surgery.php#ix-zz0eQ86YVEm Also Lisa Rapaport and Elizabeth Lopatko, "'Designer Vagina' Surgery Growing Because of Porn," *Bloomberg* online, May 25, 2007, available at www.bloomberg.com /apps/news?pid=20601102&sid=abrbOGF fldl0&refer=ukl (accessed December 12, 2009); also see David L. Matlock, MD, *Sex by Design* (Los Angeles, CA: Demiurgus Press, 2004); and www.drmatlock.com (accessed June 2, 2006).

56. See Vern Bullough, "Transsexualism in History," *Archives of Sexual Behavior*, 4 (5), 1975, pp. 561–571.

57. Cited in Aaron Devor, *FTM: Female-to-Male Transsexuals in Society* (Bloomington, IN: Indiana University Press, 1997).

58. Mona Chalabi, "Why We Don't Know the Size of the Transgender Population," *FiveThirtyEight*, July 29, 2014, available at http://fivethirtyeight.com/features/why-we-dont-know-the-size-of-the-transgender -population/#fn-5 (accessed November 27, 2015).

59. See Joanne Mayerowitz, *How Sex Changed: A History of Transsexuality in the United States* (Cambridge, MA: Harvard University Press, 2002), pp. 1–9; Harry Benjamin, *The Transsexual Phenomenon* (New York, NY: The Julian Press, 1966).

60. Égale Canada, "Sex Reassignment Surgery Backgrounder," October 1, 2004, available at www.egale.ca/index.asp?lang=E&item=1086 (accessed February 2, 2010); Kaj Hasselriis, "Manitoba Rejects Funding for Trans Surgeries," Xtra.ca, May 8, 2009, available at www .xtra.ca/public/National/Manitoba_rejects_ funding_for_trans_surgeries-6745.aspx (accessed February 2, 2010); Noreen Fagan, "Sex Reassignment Surgery in Canada: What's Covered and Where," *Xtra* online, October 26, 2009, available at www.xtra.ca/public /Montreal/Sex_reassignment_surgery_in_ Canada_whats_covered_and_where-7706. aspx (accessed February 2, 2010).

61. L. Wingerson, "Gender Identity Disorder: Has Accepted Practice Caused Harm?" *Psychiatric Times*, May 19, 2009, available at www.psychiatrictimes.com/display/article /10168/1415037?verify=0 (accessed August 18, 2009); see also Arlene Istar Lev, "Disordering Gender Identity: Gender Identity Disorder in the *DSM-IV-TR*," *Journal of Psychology & Human Sexuality*, 17 (3/4), 2005, pp. 35–69.

62. Lori Chambers, "Unprincipled Exclusions: Feminist Theory, Transgender Jurisprudence, and Kimberly Nixon," *Canadian Journal of Women and Law*, 19 (2), 2009, pp. 305–333. See also Judith Shapiro, "Transsexualism: Reflections on the Persistence of Gender and the Mutability of Sex," *Same-Sex Cultures and Sexualities: An Anthropological Reader*, Jennifer Ellen Robertson, ed. (Malden, MA/ Oxford, UK: Blackwell Publishing, 2005), pp. 141–146. See also Douglas Schrock, Lori

Reid, and Emily Boyd, "Transsexuals' Embodiment of Womanhood," *Gender & Society*, 19 (3), June 2005, pp. 317–335.

63. Samantha King, "Pink Ribbons, Inc.: The Emergence of Cause-Related Marketing and the Corporatization of the Breast Cancer Movement," *Governing the Female Body*: *Gender, Health, and Networks of Power*, Lori Reed and Paula Saukko, eds. (Albany, NY: SUNY Press, 2010), pp. 85–111.

64. See Will Courtenay, "Engendering Health: A Social Constructionist Examination of Men's Health Beliefs and Behaviors," *Psychology of Men and Masculinity*, 1 (1), 2000, pp. 4–15; "Men's Health," editorial in *British Medical Journal*, January 13, 1996, pp. 69–70. For more about men's health specifically, see *Men's Health on the Internet*, M. Sandra Wood and Janet M. Coggan, eds. (Binghamton, NY: Haworth Information Press, 2002); Will H. Courtenay, "College Men's Health: An Overview and a Call to Action," *Journal of American College Health*, 46 (6), 1998; see also Lesley Doyal, "Sex, Gender and Health: The Need for a New Approach," *British Medical Journal*, November 3, 2001, pp. 1061–1063; CBC News, "Life Expectancy Hits 80.4 Years: Statistics Canada," available at www.cbc.ca/canada /story/ 2008/01/14/death-stats.html (accessed February 10, 2010).

65. J. Reading, *The Crisis of Chronic Disease among Aboriginal Peoples*: *A Challenge for Public Health, Population Health and Social Policy* (Victoria, BC: University of Victoria Centre for Aboriginal Health Research, n.d.).

66. Linda Villarosa, "As Black Men Move into Middle Age, Dangers Rise," *The New York Times*, September 23, 2002, pp. F1, 8.

67. On these changes generally, see Martin Levine, *Gay Macho*: *The Life and Death of the Homosexual Clone*, M.S. Kimmel, ed. (New York, NY: New York University Press, 1998).

68. Facts and Figures: Women and HIV/AIDS. UN Women.org, available at www.unwomen .org/en/what-we-do/hiv-and-aids/facts-and -figures (accessed January 5, 2015); and World Health Organization at www.who.int /hiv/facts/plwha_m.jpg

69. Michele Landsberg, "UN Recognizes Women Double Victims of AIDS," Toronto Star, July 1, 2001.See also Judith Lorber, *Gender and the Social Construction of Illness* (Newbury Park, CA: Pine Forge Press, 1997); Amartya Sen, "The Many Faces of Gender Inequality," *The New Republic*, September 17, 2001, pp. 35–40.

70. CATIE, "The Epidemiology of HIV in Canada" (Fact Sheet), available at www.catie.ca/en /fact-sheets/epidemiology/epidemiology -hiv-canada (accessed January 15, 2016); Barbara Clow, "An Invisible Epidemic: The Implications of Gender Neutrality for Managing HIV/AIDS in Low-Incidence Countries" (Ottawa: Centres of Excellence for Women's Health Research Bulletins (CEWHRB), 2006).

71. See Diana Jean Schemo, "Study Calculates the Effects of College Drinking in the US," *The New York Times*, April 10, 2002, p. A21; Jodie Morse, "Women on a Binge," *Time*, April 1, 2002, pp. 57–61; Barbara Ehrenreich, "Libation as Liberation?," *Time*, April 1, 2002, p. 62.

72. Lorber, *Gender and the Social Construction of Illness*.

73. Sen, "The Many Faces of Gender Inequality"; Sen, "More Than 100 Million Women Are Missing," *The New York Review of Books*, 37 (20), December 20, 1990; Elizabeth Croll, "Amartya Sen's 100 Million Missing Women," *Oxford Development Studies*, 29 (3), October 2001, pp. 225–244; Bob Herbert, "Zimbabwe is Dying," *The New York Times*, January 16, 2009, available at www.nytimes .com/2009/01/17/opinion/17herbert.html (accessed January 3, 2010).

Chapter 12

1. "The Laws of Manu," *The History of Sexuality Sourcebook*, Matthew Kuefler, ed. (Peterborough, ON: Broadview Press, 2007), p. 34.

2. See Eva Keuls, *The Reign of the Phallus*: *Sexual Politics in Ancient Athens* (Berkeley, CA: University of California, 1993); Craig Williams, *Roman Homosexuality* (Oxford, UK: Oxford University Press, 1999).

3. The definitive study of early Christian sexual mores remains Peter Brown's *Body and*

Society: *Men, Women, and Sexual Renunciation in Early Christianity* (New York, NY: Columbia University Press, 1988).

4. Though Florence was atypical, the institutionalization of sodomy there is an interesting case study. See Michael Rocke, *Forbidden Friendships: Homosexuality and Male Culture in Renaissance Florence* (*Studies in the History of Sexuality*) (Oxford, UK: Oxford University Press, 1996 [1976]).

5. For the nineteenth century, see Kevin Amidon, "Sex on the Brain: The Rise and Fall of German Sexual Science," *Endeavour*, 32 (2), 2008, pp. 64–69; Robert Beachy, "The German Invention of Homosexuality," *The Journal of Modern History*, 82 (4), 2010, pp. 801–838; Havelock Ellis, *Psychology of Sex*, Fifth Edition (London, UK: William Heinemann [Medical Books] Ltd., 1939); Havelock Ellis, *Man and Woman: A Study of Human Secondary Sexual Characters* (London /Felling-on-Tyne, UK; Walter Scott Publishing Company, 1916).

6. George Chauncey, *Gay New York, NY: Gender, Urban Culture and the Making of the Gay Male World, 1890–1940* (New York, NY: Basic Books, 1994).

7. Cited in Barbara Ehrenreich and Deirdre English, *For Her Own Good: 150 Years of Medical Advice to Women* (New York, NY: Anchor, 1974).

8. Helen Block Lewis, "Three Essays on the Theory of Sexuality: The Problem of Sex as Instinct," *Freud and Modern Psychology* (New York, NY: Plenum Press, 1983), pp. 67–93; Kinsey, Pomeroy, and Martin, *Sexual Behavior in the Human Male*; Alfred Kinsey et al., *Sexual Behavior in the Human Female* (Philadelphia, PA: W.B. Saunders Co., 1953); William Masters and Virginia Johnson, *Human Sexual Response* (New York, NY: Little, Brown, & Co., 1976).

9. The timing and nature of the "first" Sexual Revolution are matters of scholarly controversy. See, for example, Faramerz Dabhoiwala, *The Origins of Sex: A History of the First Sexual Revolution* (Oxford, UK/ New York, NY: Oxford University Press, 2012); and Kevin F. White, *The First Sexual Revolution: The Emergence of Male Heterosexuality in Modern America* (New York, NY: NYU Press, 1992).

10. Michel Foucault, *The History of Sexuality, Vol. 1: An Introduction*, trans. Robert Hurley (New York, NY: Vintage [Reissue Edition], 1990); Jeffrey Weeks, *The Languages of Sexuality* (New Brunswick, NJ: Routledge, 2011), p. 200.

11. Martin J. Downing, Jr., "Using the Internet in Pursuit of Public Sexual Encounters: Is Frequency of Use Associated With Risk Behavior Among MSM?" *American Journal of Men's Health*, 6 (1), January 2012, pp. 18–27; Michelle Drouin et al., "Let's Talk about Sexting, Baby: Computer-Mediated Sexual Behaviours among Young Adults," *Computers in Human Behavior*, 29 (5), September 2013, pp. A25–A30; Deborah Gordon-Messer et al., "Sexting among Young Adults," *Journal of Adolescent Health*, 52 (3), March 2013, pp. 301–306; John Edward Campbell, *Getting It on Online: Cyberspace, Gay Male Sexuality, and Embodied Identity* (New Brunswick, NJ: Routledge, 2004); Richard Gilbert et al., "Psychological Benefits of Participation in Three-Dimensional Virtual Worlds for Individuals with Real-World Disabilities," *International Journal of Disability, Development, and Education*, 60 (3), 2013, pp. 208–224; M. Lombard and M.T Jones, "Telepresence and Sexuality: A Review and a Call to Scholars," *Human Technology*, 9 (1), 2013, pp. 22–55.

12. For discussion, see Lee Rainwater, "Some Aspects of Lower Class Sexual Behavior," *Journal of Social Issues*, 22, 1966, pp. 96–108.

13. On rates of masturbation, see Edward Laumann et al., *The Social Organization of Sexuality* (Chicago, IL: University of Chicago Press, 1994), p. 86; John Bancroft, *Human Sexuality and Its Problems* (Toronto, ON: Churchill Livingstone Elsevier, 2009), pp. 183–185. See also Brian Zamboni and Isaiah Crawford, "Using Masturbation in Sex Therapy," *Masturbation as a Means of Achieving Sexual Health*, Walter Bockling and Eli Coleman, eds. (New York, NY: The Haworth Press, 2002), p. 127; Judith Treas and Deirdre Giesen, "Sexual Infidelity among Married

and Cohabiting Americans," *Journal of Marriage and the Family,* 62 (1), February 2000, pp. 48–60. Pauline Bart, "Male Views of Female Sexuality: From Freud's Phallacies to Fisher's Inexact Test," paper presented at the Second National Meeting of the Special Section of Psychosomatic Obstetrics and Gynecology, Key Biscayne, FL, 1974, pp. 6–7.

14. Lisa Diamond and Ritch Savin-Williams, "Explaining Diversity in the Development of Same-Sex Sexuality among Young Women," *Journal of Social Issues,* 56 (2), 2000, pp. 297–313; p. 298.

15. Lilian Rubin, *Erotic Wars* (New York, NY: Farrar, Straus, and Giroux, 1991), p. 165. For the significance of sexual orientation to identity see Robert Kertzner, "The Adult Life Course and Homosexual Identity in Midlife Gay Men," *Annual Review of Sex Research,* 12, 2001, pp. 75–92; Diamond and Savin-Williams, "Explaining Diversity."

16. David Schmitt et al., "A Reexamination of Sex Differences in Sexuality: New Studies Reveal Old Truths," *Current Directions in Psychological Science,* 21 (2), April 2012, pp. 135–139.

17. John Sakaluk et al., "Dominant Heterosexual Sexual Scripts in Emerging Adulthood: Conceptualization and Measurement," *Journal of Sex Research,* 51 (5), 2014, pp. 516–531; Rubin, *Erotic Wars,* pp. 28, 42.

18. Catharine MacKinnon, *Only Words* (Cambridge, UK: Harvard University Press, 1996).

19. Terri D. Conley, Ali Ziegler, and Amy C. Moors, "Backlash From the Bedroom: Stigma Mediates Gender Differences in Acceptance of Casual Sex Offers," *Psychology of Women Quarterly,* 37 (3), September 2013, pp. 392–407; Andreas M. Baranowski and Heiko Hecht, "Gender Differences and Similarities in Receptivity to Sexual Invitations: Effects of Location and Risk Perception," *Archives of Sexual Behavior,* 44 (8), November 2015, pp. 2257–2265.

20. Kate Lunau, "Are We Blushing Yet?" *Maclean's,* June 29, 2009, available at www.macleans.ca/2009/06/29/are-we-blushing-yet (accessed July 9, 2009) Billy Crystal, quoted in *The Week,* May 10, 2002, p. 17; Terri Fisher, "Gender Roles and Pressure to Be Truthful: The Bogus Pipeline Modifies Gender Differences in Sexual but Not Nonsexual Behavior," *Sex Roles,* 68, 2013, pp. 401–414.

21. Zachary Davies Boren, "Ashley Madison Hack: 6 Charts That Show Who Uses the Infidelity Website," *The Independent,* August 21, 2015, available at www.independent.co.uk/life-style/gadgets-and-tech/news/ashley-madison-hack-6-charts-that-show-who-uses-the-infidelity-website-10465498.html (accessed August 23, 2015); Alex Hern, "Ashley Madison Denies Allegations of 'Fembot Army,'" *The Guardian,* September 2, 2015, available at www.theguardian.com/technology/2015/sep/02/ashley-madison-denies-allegations-of-fembot-army (accessed September 3, 2015); Frank Bass, "Cheating Wives Narrowed Infidelity Gap Over Two Decades," *Bloomberg* online, July 1, 2013, available at www.bloomberg.com/news/articles/2013-07-02/cheating-wives-narrowed-infidelity-gap-over-two-decades (accessed August 25, 2015); Christopher Ron Shillington, "An Examination of Monogamy Values among Gay Men and the Influence of Masculine Gender Conformity" (MA Thesis, University of Toronto, ON: 2013); Jeffrey Parsons et al., "Non-Monogamy and Sexual Relationship Quality among Same-Sex Male Couples," *Journal of Family Psychology,* 26 (5), October 2012, pp. 669–677; Alan Bell and Martin Weinberg, *Homosexualities* (New York, NY: Simon & Schuster, 1978); William Masters, Virginia Johnson, and Richard Kolodny, *Human Sexuality* (New York, NY: Harper and Row, 1978); Philip Blumstein and Pepper Schwartz, *American Couples* (New York, NY: William Morrow, 1983), p. 317.

22. Rupert Myers, "Men! If You Name Your Penis, You're a Tool," *The Guardian,* July 3, 2015, available at www.theguardian.com/commentisfree/2015/jul/03/name-your-penis-men (accessed August 25, 2015); Emmanuel Reynaud, *Holy Virility,* R. Schwartz, trans. (London, UK: Pluto Press, 1983), p. 41.

23. See, for example, Tavris, *The Mismeasure of Woman;* Harriet Lerner, *Women in Therapy* (New York, NY: Harper and Row, 1989), Chapter 2.

24. Kathryn McPhillips, Virginia Braun, and Nicola Gavey, "Defining (Hetero) Sex: How Imperative Is the 'Coital Imperative?'" *Women's Studies International Forum*, 24 (2), March–April 2001, pp. 229–240; Nikki Hayfield and Victoria Clarke, "'I'd Be Just as Happy with a Cup of Tea': Women's Accounts of Sex and Affection in Long-Term Heterosexual Relationships," *Women's Studies International Forum*, 35 (2), March–April 2012, pp. 67–74.

25. Stephanie Sanders and June Machover Reinisch, "Would you say 'Had Sex' If," *JAMA*, 281, January 20, 1999.

26. Dayna Fischstein, Edward Herold, and Serge Desmarais, "How Much Does Gender Explain in Sexual Attitudes and Behaviors? A Survey of Canadian Adults," *Archives of Sexual Behavior*, 36, 2007, pp. 451–461; Terri Fisher, "How Often Do Men and Women Think about Sex?" *Psychology Today*, December 6, 2011, available at www.psychologytoday.com/blog/the-sexual-continuum/201112/how-often-do-men-and-women-think-about-sex (accessed December 20, 2015); Terri Fisher et al., "Sex on the Brain? An Examination of Frequency of Sexual Cognitions as a Function of Gender, Erotophilia, and Social Desirability," *Journal of Sex Research*, 29, 2012, pp. 69–77.

27. Laumann et al., *The Social Organization of Sexuality*, p. 86; Pepper Schwartz and Virginia Rutter, *The Gender of Sexuality* (Thousand Oaks, CA: Pine Forge Press, 1998), p. 39. Also Roy F. Baumeister, Kathleen R. Catanese, and Kathleen D. Vohs, "Is There a Gender Difference in Strength of Sex Drive? Theoretical Views, Conceptual Distinctions, and a Review of Relevant Evidence," *Personality and Social Psychology Review*, 5 (3), 2001, pp. 242–273; p. 251; Catherine Hakim, "The Male Sexual Deficit: A Social Fact of the 21st Century," *International Sociology*, 30 (3), May 2015, pp. 314–335.

28. Michael Kimmel and Rebecca Plante, "Sexual Fantasies and Gender Scripts: Heterosexual Men and Women Construct Their Ideal Sexual Encounters," *Gendered Sexualities*, Vol. 6 of *Advances in Gender Research*, Patricia Gagné and Richard Tewksbury, eds. (Greenwich, CT: JAI Press, 2002), pp. 55–78. See also E. Barbara Hariton and Jerome Singer, "Women's Fantasies During Sexual Intercourse: Normative and Theoretical Implications," *Journal of Consulting and Clinical Psychology*, 42 (3), 1974; Daniel Goleman, "Sexual Fantasies: What Are Their Hidden Meanings?" *The New York Times*, February 28, 1983; Daniel Goleman, "New View of Fantasy: Much Is Found Perverse?" *The New York Times*, May 7, 1991; Robert May, *Sex and Fantasy: Patterns of Male and Female Development* (New York, NY: W.W. Norton, 1980); David Chick and Steven Gold, "A Review of Influences on Sexual Fantasy: Attitudes, Experience, Guilt and Gender," *Imagination, Cognition and Personality*, 7 (1), 1987–1988; Robert A. Mednick, "Gender Specific Variances in Sexual Fantasy," *Journal of Personality Assessment*, 41 (3), 1977; Diane Follingstad and C. Dawne Kimbrell, "Sexual Fantasies Revisited: An Expansion and Further Clarification of Variables Affecting Sex Fantasy Production," *Archives of Sexual Behavior*, 15 (6), 1986; Danielle Knafo and Yoram Jaffe, "Sexual Fantasizing in Males and Females," *Journal of Research in Personality*, 18, 1984.

29. Baumeister, Catanese, and Vohs, "Is There a Gender Difference in Strength of Sex Drive?"

30. Ibid.

31. Ibid.

32. Adrienne Rich, "Compulsory Heterosexuality and Lesbian Existence," *Signs*, 5 (4), Summer, 1980, pp. 631–660; p. 657.

33. The heterosexual questionnaire is widely available in many versions. See for example, www.whosoever.org/v3i2/hetquest.html (accessed March 24, 2016).

34. See, for example, Peter Wyden and Barbara Wyden, *Growing up Straight: What Every Thoughtful Parent Should Know About Homosexuality* (New York, NY: Trident Press, 1968); Richard Green has provided a more thoughtful discussion of gender and homosexuality in *The "Sissy Boy" Syndrome* (New Haven, CT: Yale University Press, 1986).

35. Foucault, *The History of Sexuality*. See also Jonathan Ned Katz, *The Invention of*

Heterosexuality (New York, NY: E.P. Dutton, 1993).

36. Wyden and Wyden, *Growing up Straight*.

37. Green, *The "Sissy Boy" Syndrome*.

38. George Gilder, *Men and Marriage* (Gretna, LA: Pelican Publishers, 1985).

39. Cited in Steve Chapple and David Talbot, *Burning Desires: Sex in America* (New York, NY: Doubleday, 1989), p. 356.

40. Susanne Iasenza, "Beyond Lesbian Bed Death: The Passion and Play in Lesbian Relationships," *Journal of Lesbian Studies*, 1, 2002, pp. 111–120; K.A.W.L. van Rosmalen-Nooijens et al., "Bed Death and Other Lesbian Sexual Problems Unraveled: A Qualitative Study of the Sexual Health of Lesbian Women Involved in a Relationship," *Women & Health*, 48 (3), 2008, pp. 339–362; Margaret Nichols, "Lesbian Sexuality/Female Sexuality: Rethinking 'Lesbian Bed Death,'" *Sexual and Relationship Therapy*, 19 (4), 2004, pp. 363–371.

41. Lisa Diamond, *Sexual Fluidity: Understanding Women's Love and Desire* (Boston, MA: Harvard University Press, 2008).

42. Data from Blumstein and Schwartz, *American Couples*. The quoted "interviewer" is from Bell and Weinberg, *Homosexualities*, p. 220.

43. Masters and Johnson, of course, had views on homosexuality that have become highly controversial. See Masters and Johnson, *Homosexuality in Perspective* (Boston, MA: Little, Brown & Co., 1978); Leslie Feinberg, *Stone Butch Blues* (Ithaca, NY: Firebrand Books, 1993); Elizabeth A. Schoenfeld et al., "Does Sex Really Matter? Examining the Connections between Spouses' Nonsexual Behaviors, Sexual Frequency, Sexual Satisfaction, and Marital Satisfaction," *Archives of Sexual Behavior*, January 5, 2016, online first, pp. 1–13.

44. Stevi Jackson, "The Social Construction of Female Sexuality," *Feminism and Sexuality: A Reader*, S. Jackson and S. Scott, eds. (New York, NY: Columbia University Press, 1996), p. 71.

45. Laumann et al., *The Social Organization of Sexuality*, p. 347.

46. Mary Koss has published prolifically and been widely cited. See, inter alia, "Sexual Experiences Survey: A Research Instrument Investigating Sexual Aggression and Victimization," *Journal of Consulting and Clinical Psychology*, 50 (3), 1982, pp. 455–457; "Hidden Rape: Sexual Aggression and Victimization in a National Sample of Students in Higher Education," *Rape and Sexual Assault II*, Ann Wolbert Burgess, ed. (New York, NY: Garland Publishing, 1988), pp. 3–25.

47. Eva Elmerstig, Barbro Wijma, and Carina Berterö, "Why Do Young Women Continue to Have Sexual Intercourse Despite Pain?" *Journal of Adolescent Health*, 43 (4), October 2008, pp. 357–363; Sorcha Pollack, "When Sex Is Painful: A Lot of Women Think It's Their Fault," *Irish Times* online, January 5, 2016, available at www.irishtimes.com /life-and-style/health-family/when-sex-is-painful-a-lot-of-women-think-it-s-their-fault-1.2484422 (accessed January 5, 2016). See also Grace Reynolds, Dennis Fisher, and Bridget Rogala, "Why Women Engage in Anal Intercourse: Results from a Qualitative Study," *Archives of Sexual Behavior*, 44 (4), 2014, pp. 983–995; Kristen N. Jozkowski and Zoë D. Peterson, "College Students and Sexual Consent: Unique Insights," *Journal of Sex Research*, 50 (6), 2013, pp. 517–23.

48. Terry Humphreys, "Sexual Consent Scale, Revised," and Terry Humphreys and Deborah Kennett, "Reasons for Consenting to Unwanted Sex Scale," *Handbook of Sexuality-Related Measures*, Terri D. Fisher et al., eds. (New Brunswick, NJ: Routledge, 2013), pp. 173–178.

49. Charlene Muehlenhard, "'Nice Women' Don't Say Yes and 'Real Men' Don't Say No: How Miscommunication and the Double Standard Can Cause Sexual Problems," *Women and Therapy*, 7, 1988, pp. 100–101.

50. The study is cited in Bennett, "The Pornification of a Generation."

51. See Jeffrey Fracher and Michael Kimmel, "Hard Issues and Soft Spots: Counseling Men About Sexuality," *Handbook of Counseling and Psychotherapy with Men*, M. Scher et al., eds. (Newbury Park, CA: Sage Publications, 1987).

52. Joel Lexchin, "Bigger and Better: How Pfizer Redefined Erectile Dysfunction," *PLOS Medicine,* 3 (4), April 2006, pp. 429–432, available at www.plosmedicine.org See also Bruce Handy, "The Viagra Craze," *Time,* May 4, 1998, pp. 50–57; Christopher Hitchens, "Viagra Falls," *The Nation,* May 25, 1998, p. 8.

53. Laumann et al., *The Social Organization of Sexuality,* p. 347.

54. Robert Stoller, *Porn* (New Haven, CT: Yale University Press, 1991), p. 31.

55. Scott R. Braithwaite et al., "The Influence of Pornography on Sexual Scripts and Hooking Up among Emerging Adults in College," *Archives of Sexual Behavior,* 44 (1), January 2015, pp. 111–123; Eric Spitznagel, "How Internet Porn is Changing Teen Sex," *Details,* September 2009, available at www.details .com/sex-relationships/porn-and-perversions /200907/how-internet-porn-is-changing-teen-sex (accessed August 18, 2009). See also Tracy Clark-Fiory, "Generation XXX: Having Sex like Porn Stars," *Salon* online, August 18, 2009, available at www.salon.com/mwt /broadsheet/feature/2009/08/18/gen_porn .html (accessed August 18, 2009). For an older review of the empirical literature on pornography, see Michael Kimmel and An-nulla Linders, "Does Censorship Make a Difference? An Aggregate Empirical Analysis of Pornography and Rape," *Journal of Psychology and Human Sexuality,* 8 (3), 1996. See also T. Kohut, J.L. Baer, and B. Watts, "Is Pornography Really about 'Making Hate to Women?' Pornography Users Hold More Gender Egalitarian Attitudes Than Nonusers in a Representative American Sample," *The Journal of Sex Research,* 2015; Hald, Malamuth, and Lange, "Pornography and Sexist Attitudes among Heterosexuals"; D.M. Symanski and D.N. Stewart-Richardson, "Psychological, Relational, and Sexual Correlates of Pornography Use on Young Adult Heterosexual Men in Romantic Relationships," *The Journal of Men's Studies,* 22 (1), 2014, pp. 64–82.

56. Ana J. Bridges et al., "Aggression and Sexual Behavior in Bestselling Pornography Videos: A Content Analysis Update," *Violence against Women,* 16 (10), 2010, pp. 1065–1085; John Stoltenberg, "Pornography and Freedom," *Men Confront Pornography,* M. Kimmel, ed. (New York, NY: Crown, 1990). Marty Klein, "Pornography: What Men See When They Watch," *Pornography: Film and Culture,* Peter Lehman, ed. (New Brunswick, NJ: Rutgers University Press, 2006), pp. 244–257; pp. 248–249.

57. Bridges et al., "Aggression and Sexual Behavior," p. 1080.

58. Ruvolo, "How Much of the Internet is Actually for Porn"; Daniel Bernardi, "Interracial Joysticks: Pornography's Web of Racist Attractions," Lehman, ed., *Pornography,* pp. 220–243.

59. Braithwaite et al., "The Influence of Pornography on Sexual Scripts"; Breanne Fahs and Jax Gonzalez, "The Front Lines of the 'Back Door': Navigating (Dis)engagement, Coercion, and Pleasure in Women's Anal Sex Experiences," *Feminism & Psychology,* 24 (4), 2014, pp. 500–520; C. Marston and R. Lewis, "Anal Heterosex among Young People and Implications for Health Promotion: A Qualitative Study in the UK," *BMJ Open,* 2014. DOI: 10.1136/bmjopen-2014-004996 (accessed December 3, 2015).

60. Paul Wright, "Pornography and the Sexual Socialization of Children: Current Knowledge and a Theoretical Future," *Journal of Children and Media,* 8 (3), 2014, pp. 305–312; Amy O'Leary, "So How Do We Talk About This? When Children See Internet Pornography," *The New York Times,* May 9, 2012, available at www.nytimes.com/2012/05/10 /garden/when-children-see-internet-porno graphy.html (accessed November 15, 2015).

61. Lillian Rubin, *Erotic Wars,* p. 13; A.C. Grunseit et al., "Sexuality, Education, and Young People's Sexual Behavior: A Review of Studies" manuscript from UNAID, 1997. Allison Jones, "Half of One Toronto School's Students Kept Home to Protest New Sex-Ed," *The Globe and Mail,* September 8, 2015, available at www.theglobeandmail.com/news/national /education/parents-opposed-to-ontarios-sex -ed-curriculum-can-pull-kids-from-class /article26255639/ (accessed September 9, 2015).

62. Amber Hollibaugh, "Desire for the Future: Radical Hope in Passion and Pleasure,"

Feminism and Sexuality: A Reader; Lillian Rubin, *Erotic Wars*, pp. 5, 46.

63. See Laumann et al., *The Social Organization of Sexuality*; on attitudes, see Schwartz and Rutter, *The Gender of Sexuality*, p. 39; Tom W. Smith and Jaesok Son, *Trends in Public Attitudes about Sexual Morality* (Chicago, IL: NORC, 2013); Andreea Nica, "How I Left the Purity Movement," *Salon* online, November 1, 2014, available at www.salon.com/2014/11/02/how_i_left_the_purity_movement/ (accessed November 25, 2015).

64. Lillian Rubin, *Erotic Wars*, p. 13; on rates of change in sexual activity, see Grunseit et al., "Sexuality, Education and Young People's Sexual Behavior"; Smith and Son, *Trends*; Michael Bozon and Osma Kontula, "Sexual Initiation and Gender in Europe: A Cross-Cultural Analysis of Trends in the Twentieth Century," *Sexual Behaviour and HIV/AIDS in Europe: Comparisons of National Surveys*, Nathalie Bajos, Michel Hubert, and Theo Sandfort, eds. (New Brunswick, NJ: Routledge, 2014); L.B. Finer and J.M. Philbin, "Sexual Initiation, Contraceptive Use, and Pregnancy among Young Adolescents," *Pediatrics*, 131 (5), 2013, pp. 886–891; Patrick Baldwin et al., "The Age of Initiation of Drug Use and Sexual Behavior May Influence Subsequent HIV Risk Behavior: A Systematic Review," *ISRN AIDS*, vol. 2013.

65. Willard Waller, "The Rating and Dating Complex," *American Sociological Review*, 2, October 1937, pp. 727–734.

66. "'Hookups': Characteristics and Correlates of College Students' Spontaneous and Anonymous Sexual Experiences," *Journal of Sex Research*, 37 (1), February 2000, pp. 76–88.

67. Melanie Beres, "'It Just Happens': Negotiating Casual Heterosexual Sex," Kimmel et al., *The Gendered Society Reader*, CANADIAN EDITION, pp. 370–380.

68. Finer and Philbin, "Sexual Initiation"; Kinsey, Pomeroy, and Martin, *Sexual Behavior in the Human Female*; Laumann et al., *The Social Organization of Sexuality*; see also Schwartz and Rutter, *The Gender of Sexuality*, pp. 102–103; Sam Janus, *The Janus Report on Sexual Behavior* (New York,

NY: John Wiley, 1993), pp. 315–316; Blumstein and Schwartz, *American Couples*; see also *New Sexual Agendas*, Lynne Segal, ed. (New York, NY: New York University Press, 1997), p. 67.

69. Heiman is cited in Gina Kolata, "Women and Sex: On This Topic, Science Blushes," *The New York Times*, June 21, 1998, p. 3; Lillian Rubin, *Erotic Wars*, p.14.

70. Laura Sessions Stepp, "Study: Half of All Teens Have Had Oral Sex," *The Washington Post*, September 15, 2005; Sharon Jayson, "Teens Define Sex in New Ways," *USA Today*, October 18, 2005. Beres, "It Just Happens."

71. Neill Korobov, "The Management of 'Nonrelational Sexuality': Positioning Strategies in Adolescent Male Talk about (Hetero) Sexual Attraction," *Men and Masculinities*, 8 (4), April 2006, pp. 493–517; Ronald F. Levant, "Nonrelational Sexuality in Men," *Men and Sex: New Psychological Perspectives*, R. Levant and G. Brooks, eds. (New York, NY: John Wiley, 1997), 26; J.O. Billy et al., "The Sexual Behavior of Men in the United States," *Family Planning Perspectives*, 25 (2), 1993; Lisa Bowleg et al., "What Does it Take to be a Man? What is a Real Man?" Ideologies of Masculinity and HIV Sexual Risk among Black Heterosexual Men," *Culture, Health & Sexuality: An International Journal for Research, Intervention and Care*, 13 (5), 2011, pp. 545–559; Laumann et al., *The Social Organization of Sexuality*.

72. *The Centerfold Syndrome* (San Francisco, CA: Jossey-Bass, 1995), and Gary Brooks, "The Centerfold Syndrome," *Men and Sex*. See also Ron Levant, "Nonrelational Sexuality," p. 19; Joni Johnston, "Appearance Obsession: Women's Reactions to Men's Objectification of Their Bodies," *Men and Sex*, pp. 79, 101; Glenn Good and Nancy B. Sherrod, "Men's Resolution of Nonrelational Sex across the Lifespan," *Men and Sex*, pp. 186, 189, 190.

73. "Does Equality Produce a Better Sex Life?" *Newsday*, April 19, 2006; see Edward O. Laumann et al., "A Cross-National Study of Subjective Sexual Well-Being among Older Women and Men: Findings from the Global Study of Sexual Attitudes and Behaviors,"

Archives of Sexual Behavior, 35 (2), April 2006, pp. 145–161; but see Laura Agustin's dissenting opinion on this, "The Other Swedish Model: Gender, Sex, and Culture," at www.thelocal.se/blogs/theotherswedish model/2010/01/11/good-sex-equal-sex-who -has-the-best-sex/ (accessed January 10, 2010).

Chapter 13

1. United States Department of Justice, Uniform Crime Reports, 1991, p. 17; Diane Craven, *Sex Differences in Violent Victimization*, 1994 (NCJ-164508) (Washington, DC: US Department of Justice, 1994); see also Martin Daly and Margo Wilson, *Homicide* (Chicago, IL: Aldine, 1988).

2. Cited in Michael Gottfredson and Travis Hisrchi, *A General Theory of Crime* (Stanford, CA: Stanford University Press, 1990), p. 145. See also Steven Barkan, "Why Do Men Commit Almost All Homicides and Assault?" *Criminology: A Sociological Understanding* (Englewood Cliffs, NJ: Prentice-Hall, 1997); *Masculinities and Violence*, Lee Bowker, ed. (Thousand Oaks, CA: Sage Publications, 1998); Fox Butterfield, *All God's Children: The Bosket Family and the American Tradition of Violence* (New York, NY: Avon, 1995), p.325; Wray Herbert, "Behind Bars," *US News & World Report*, March 23, 1998, p. 33; Jay Livingston, "Crime and Sex: It's a Man's World," *Crime and Criminology*, Second Edition (Englewood Cliffs, NJ: Prentice-Hall, 1996).

3. See James Q. Wilson and Richard Herrnstein, *Crime and Human Nature* (New York, NY: Simon & Schuster, 1985), p. 121.

4. Joe Sharkey, "Slamming the Brakes on Hot Pursuit," *The New York Times*, December 14, 1997, p. 3; Kenneth J. Peak and Ronald W. Glensor, "Street Racing," Problem Oriented Guides for Police No. 28. US Department of Justice, 2004, p. 13. The 90 to 95 percent figure comes from Andrew Leigh, "Youth and Street Racing," *Current Issues in Criminal Justice*, 388, 1995–1996.

5. Marvin Wolfgang, *Youth and Violence* (Washington, DC: US Department of Health, Education, and Welfare, 1970); James Gilligan, *Violence: Our Deadly Epidemic and Its Causes* (New York, NY: G.P. Putnam's Sons, 1996).

6. Wilson and Herrnstein, *Crime and Human Nature*.

7. See the discussion of androgens in Chapter 2.

8. James Messerschmidt, "Masculinities and Crime: Beyond a Dualist Criminology," *Gender, Crime, and Criminal Justice: Original Feminist Readings*, C. Renzetti, L. Goodstein, and S. Miller, eds. (Los Angeles, CA: Roxbury, 2006), pp. 29–43.

9. Barbara Ehrenreich, *Blood Rites: Origins and History of the Passions of War* (New York, NY: Metropolitan Books, 1997), pp. 45, 127; Christian Mesquida and Neil Wiener, "Human Collective Aggression: A Behavioral Ecology Perspective," *Ethology and Sociobiology*, 17, 1996, pp. 247–262. On the sociology of men's violence, see, especially, Michael Kaufman, *Cracking the Armour: Power, Pain and the Lives of Men* (Toronto, ON: Viking, 1993), and Michael Kaufman, "The Construction of Masculinity and the Triad of Men's Violence," *Men's Lives*, Fourth Edition, M. Kimmel and M. Messner, eds.; see also Jackson Toby, "Violence and the Masculine Ideal: Some Qualitative Data," *The Annals of the American Academy of Political and Social Science*, 364, March 1966.

10. J. Adams Puffer, *The Boy and His Gang* (Boston, MA: Houghton, Mifflin, 1912), p. 91.

11. Gilligan, *Violence*.

12. Fox Butterfield, *All God's Children*, pp. 206–207; Kit Roane, "New York Gangs Mimic California Original," *The New York Times*, September 14, 1997, p. A37; others cited in Jack Katz, *Seductions of Crime*, pp. 88, 107; Vic Seidler, "Raging Bull," *Achilles Heel*, 5, 1980, p. 9; Hans Toch, "Hypermasculinity and Prison Violence," *Masculinities and Violence*, L. Bowker, ed. (Newbury Park, CA: Sage Publications, 1998), p. 170; Mark Totten, "Preventing Aboriginal Youth Gang Violence in Canada: A Gendered Approach," paper prepared for Aboriginal Policy Research Conference, March 2009.

13. Seidler cited in Barbara Whitmer, *The Violence Mythos* (New York, NY: SUNY Press,

1997), p. 150; Hans Toch, *Corrections: A Humanistic Approach* (Guilderland, NY: Harrow and Heston, 1997); James Messerschmidt, *Masculinities and Crime*; Messerschmidt, "Masculinities and Crime: Beyond a Dualist Criminology."

14. Signe Howell and Roy Willis, eds., *Societies at Peace* (New York, NY: Routledge, 1983); Joanna Overing, "Styles of Manhood: An Amazonian Contrast in Tranquility and Violence," Howell and Willis, eds., *Societies at Peace*, p. 79–99.

15. Howell and Willis, eds., *Societies at Peace*, p. 38.

16. See, for example, D. Stanistreet, C. Bambra, and A. Scott-Samuel, "Is Patriarchy the Source of Men's Higher Mortality?" *Journal of Epidemiology and Community Health*, 59, 2005, pp. 873–876; Elizabeth Stanko, *Everyday Violence* (London, UK: Pandora, 1990), p. 71.

17. Tina Hotton Mahony, *Women and the Criminal Justice System* (Ottawa, ON: Minister of Industry, 2011), available at www .statcan.gc.ca/pub/89-503-x/2010001/article /11416-eng.pdf Also Rebecca Kong and Kathy AuCoin, "Female Offenders in Canada," *Juristat* 28, No. 1 (2008). Statistics Canada Catalogue No. 85-002-XIE.

18. Correctional Service of Canada, "Research Results: Women Offenders" (fact sheet), November 2014, available at www.csc-scc .gc.ca/publications/092/005007-3014-eng .pdf Also Mahony, *Women and the Criminal Justice System*, p. 38; Nina Bahadur, "The US Is Home To Nearly One-Third Of The World's Female Prisoners," *Huffington Post*, October 1, 2014, available at www.huffingtonpost .com/2014/10/01/women-in-prison-prisoner -population-us-incarceration_n_5900364 .html Also Kong and AuCoin, "Female Offenders."

19. Mia Dauvergne, *Adult Criminal Court Statistics in Canada 2010–2011* (Ottawa, ON: Minister of Industry, 2012), available at www.statcan.gc.ca/pub/85-002-x/2012001 /article/11646-eng.htm Freda Adler, *Sisters in Crime* (New York, NY: McGraw-Hill, 1975), p. 10; Rita Simon, *Women and Crime*

(Washington, DC: US Government Printing Office, 1975), p. 40. Also see Patricia Pearson, *When She Was Bad*: *Violent Women and the Myth of Innocence* (New York, NY: Viking, 1998); see also Larissa MacFarquhar, "Femmes Fatales," *The New Yorker*, March 9, 1998, pp. 88–91.

20. Malcolm Feely and Deborah L. Little, "The Vanishing Female: The Decline of Women in the Criminal Process," *Law and Society Review*, 25 (4), 1991, p. 739.

21. Darrell J. Steffensmeier, "Trends in Female Crime: It's Still a Man's World," *The Criminal Justice System and Women*, B.R. Price and N.J. Sokoloff, eds. (New York, NY: Clark, Boardman, 1982), p. 121.

22. Kong and AuCoin, "Female Offenders in Canada," p. 4.

23. Ibid.

24. Zoran Miladinovic and Leah Mulligan, *Homicide in Canada 2014* (Ottawa, ON: Minister of Industry, 2015), available at www .statcan.gc.ca/pub/85-002-x/2015001/article /14244-eng.pdf Also see Mahony, *Women and the Criminal Justice System*.

25. Mahony, *Women and the Criminal Justice System*, p. 2.

26. Alexia Cooper and Erica L. Smith, *Homicide Trends in the United States, 1980–2008* (US Department of Justice, November 2011), available at http://bjs.gov/content/pub/pdf/ htus8008.pdf (accessed January 10, 2015); Laura Dugan, Daniel Nagin, and Richard Rosenfeld, "Explaining the Decline in Intimate Partner Homicide: The Effects of Changing Domesticity, Women's Status and Domestic Violence Resources," *Homicide Studies*, 3 (3), 1999, pp. 187–214, and Richard Rosenfeld, "Changing Relationships between Men and Women: A Note on the Decline in Intimate Partner Homicide," *Homicide Studies*, 1 (1), 1997, pp. 72–83.

27. Erich Goode, personal communication with M. Kimmel, December 5, 2002; Jerome Skolnick, personal communication with M. Kimmel, December 5, 2002; see also Erich Goode, *Deviant Behavior*, Fifth Edition (Englewood Cliffs, NJ: Prentice-Hall), p. 127, and Kathleen Daly, *Gender Crime and*

Punishment (New Haven, CT: Yale University Press, 1994).

28. See, for example, Ann Donahue, "Population of Female Inmates Reaches Record," *USA Today*, July 21, 1997; Darrell Steefensmeier and Ellie Allen, "Criminal Behavior," p. 85; Correctional Service Canada, *Ten-Year Status Report on Women's Corrections 1996–2006* (Ottawa, ON: Correctional Service of Canada, 2006).

29. Adam Fraczek, "Patterns of Aggressive–Hostile Behavior Orientation among Adolescent Boys and Girls," *Of Mice and Women: Aspects of Female Aggression*, K. Bjorkvist and P. Niemela, eds. (San Diego, CA: Academic Press, 1992); Kirsti M.J. Lagerspetz and Kaj Bjorqvist, "Indirect Aggression in Boys and Girls," *Aggressive Behavior: Current Perspectives*, L.R. Huesmann, ed. (New York, NY: Plenum, 1994).

30. Centers for Disease Control, "Youth Violence: Facts at a Glance" available at www.cdc.gov/violenceprevention Also Andrea Taylor-Butts and Angela Bressan, "Youth Crime in Canada, 2006," *Juristat* 28 (3) Statistics Canada Catalogue No. 85-002-XIE; Kathy AuCoin, "Children and Youth as Victims of Violent Crime," *Juristat* 25 (1) Statistics Canada Catalogue No. 85-002-XIE.

31. Glenn W. Muschert, "Research in School Shootings," *Sociology Compass*, 1 (1), 2007, 60–80; Patricia Leavy and Kathryn Mahoney, "American Reporting of School Violence and 'People Like Us': A Comparison of Newspaper Coverage of the Columbine and Red Lake School Shootings," *Critical Sociology*, 35 (2), 2002, pp. 273–292; see also Dave Cullen, *Columbine* (New York, NY: Twelve Publishers, 2009), which debunks long-held media-fuelled understandings of the massacre and its causes.

32. J. Pete Blair and Katherine W. Schweit, *A Study of Active Shooter Incidents, 2000–2013* (Texas State University and Federal Bureau of Investigation, US Department of Justice, Washington DC, 2014).

33. Michael S. Kimmel and Matthew Mahler, "Adolescent Masculinity, Homophobia, and Violence: Random School Shootings, 1982–2001," *American Behavioral Scientist*, 46 (10), June 2003, pp. 1439–1458; Karen L. Tonso, "Violent Masculinities as Tropes for School Shooters: The Montréal Massacre, the Columbine Attack, and Rethinking Schools," *American Behavioral Scientist*, 52 (9), May 2009, pp. 1266 1285; Johanna Kantola, Ov Cristian Norocel, and Jemima Repo, "Gendering Violence in the School Shootings in Finland," *European Journal of Women's Studies*, 18 (2), May 2011, pp. 183–197; Alyssa Rosenberg, "Elliot Rodger's UCSB Massacre, Sexual Assaults and Campus Speech Codes," *The Washington Post*, May 27, 2014, available at www.washingtonpost.com/news/act-four/wp/2014/05/27/elliot-rodgers-ucsb-massacre-sexual-assaults-and-campus-speech-codes/ (accessed July 15, 2015).

34. Stav Viv, "Author Q&A: School Shooters: Understanding High School, College and Adult Perpetrators," *Newsweek*, January 18, 2015, available at www.newsweek.com/author-qa-school-shooters-understanding-high-school-college-and-adult-300278 (accessed January 10, 2016).

35. See Jessie Klein, "Teaching Her a Lesson: Media Misses Boys' Rage Relating to Girls in School Shootings," *Crime, Media, Culture*, 1 (1), 2005, pp. 90–97; Kim Gandy, "School Shooters Target Girls, Point to Larger Problem of Violence against Women," *National NOW Times*, Winter, 2007.

36. "Teen-on-Teen Girl Fights Sweeping Internet," CBS News, February 3, 2010, available at www.cbstv.com/national/girl.fights.youtube.2.146559.html (accessed February 3, 2010); Taylor-Butts and Bressan, "Youth Crime in Canada, 2006"; Sheila Batacharya, "Racism, 'Girl Violence,' and the Murder of Reena Virk," *Girls' Violence: Myths and Realities*, Christine Alder and Anne Worrall, eds. (Albany, NY: SUNY Press, 2004), pp. 61–80; Margaret Jackson, "Race, Gender, and Aggression: The Perceptions of Girls about the Violence in Their Lives," *Humanities* [Simon Fraser University], Spring 2003.

37. Vappu Viemero, "Changes in Female Aggression over a Decade," Bjorkvist and Niemela,

Of Mice and Women, p. 105; Messerschmidt, "Masculinities and Crime: Beyond a Dualist Criminology"; Sibylle Artz, *Sex, Power, and the Violent Schoolgirl* (New York, NY: Teachers' College Press, 1992); Sibylle Artz and Diana Nicholson, "Aggressive Girls: Female Violence" (report). Ottawa, ON: National Clearinghouse on Family Violence, 2002.

38. Tracy Vaillancourt, "Do Human Females Use Indirect Aggression as an Intrasexual Competition Strategy?" *Philosophical Transactions of the Royal Society,* 368 (1631), 2013; John Tierney, "A Cold War Fought by Women," *The New York Times*, November 18, 2013, available at www.nytimes .com/2013/11/19/science/a-cold-war-fought -by-women.html?pagewanted=all (accessed January 10, 2016); Alan W. Leschied et al., *Female Adolescent Aggression: A Review of the Literature and the Correlates of Aggression 2000-04* (Ottawa, ON: Solicitor-General of Canada, n.d.); Xavier Benarous et al., "Do Girls with Depressive Symptoms Exhibit More Physical Aggression than Boys? A Cross Sectional Study in a National Adolescent Sample," *Child and Adolescent Psychiatry and Mental Health*, 9, 41, November 2015. See also Rachel Simmons, *Odd Girl Out: The Hidden Culture of Aggression in Girls* (New York, NY: Harcourt, 2002); Rosalind Wiseman, *Queen Bees and Wannabes: A Parents' Guide to Helping Your Daughter Survive Cliques, Gossip, Boyfriends, and Other Realities of Adolescence* (New York, NY: Crown, 2002); Sharon Lamb, *The Secret Lives of Girls: Sex, Play, Aggression and Their Guilt* (New York, NY: The Free Press, 2002); Margaret Talbot, "Mean Girls," *The New York Times Magazine*, February 24, 2002, pp. 24–29, 40, 58, 64–65; and Carol Tavris, "Are Girls Really as Mean as Books Say They Are?" *Chronicle of Higher Education*, July 5, 2002, pp. B7–9.

39. *A Statistical Snapshot of Youth at Risk and Youth Offending in Canada* (Ottawa, ON: National Crime Prevention Centre, 2012), pp. 8–9.

40. Paul Higate and John Hopton, "War, Militarism, and Masculinities," *Handbook of Studies on Men and Masculinities*, Michael Kimmel and Jeff Hearn, eds. (Thousand Oaks, CA: Sage, 2005), pp. 432–446; Helen Caldicott, *Missile Envy* (New York, NY: William Morrow, 1984); Barbara Ehrenreich, "The Violence Debate Since Adam and Eve," *Test the West: Gender Democracy and Violence* (Vienna, Austria: Federal Minister of Women's Affairs, 1994), p. 34.

41. R.W. Connell, "Masculinity, Violence and War," *Men's Lives*, Third Edition, p. 129.

42. David Halberstam, *The Best and the Brightest* (New York, NY: Random House, 1972), p. 531. See also Brian Easlea, *Fathering the Unthinkable: Masculinity, Scientists and the Nuclear Arms Race* (London, UK: Pluto Press, 1983), p. 117; see also his "Patriarchy, Scientists, and Nuclear Warriors," *Beyond Patriarchy: Essays by Men on Pleasure, Power and Change*, M. Kaufman, ed. (Toronto, ON: Oxford University Press, 1987); I.F. Stone, "Machismo in Washington," *Men and Masculinity*, J. Pleck and J. Sawyer, eds. (Englewood Cliffs, NJ: Prentice-Hall, 1974).

43. Carol Cohn, "'Clean Bombs' and Clean Language," *Women, Militarism and War: Essays in History, Politics, and Social Theory*, J. B. Elshtain, ed. (Savage, MD: Rowman and Littlefield, 1990), p. 137.

44. Elisabeth Jean Wood, "Variation in Sexual Violence during War," *Politics & Society*, 34 (3), 2006, pp. 307–341; Steven Lee Myers, "A Peril in War Zones: Sexual Abuse by Fellow GIs," *The New York Times*, December 28, 2009; Allan Hall, "German Victim is First to Break Silence on Red Army Rapists after 65 Years," *Mail Online*, March 1, 2010, available at www.dailymail.co.uk/news /article-1254521 (accessed March 1, 2010); M.E. Baaz, and M. Stern, "Why Do Soldiers Rape? Masculinity, Violence, and Sexuality in the Armed Forces in the Congo (DRC)," *International Studies Quarterly*, 53, 2009, pp. 495–518; Department of Veterans Affairs, "Military Sexual Trauma," available at www.mentalhealth.va.gov/msthome.asp (accessed January 5, 2016); Shira Maguen et al., "Gender Differences in Military Sexual Trauma and Mental Health Diagnoses among Iraq and Afghanistan Veterans with

Posttraumatic Stress Disorder," *Women's Health Issues*, 22 (1), January–February 2012, pp. e61–e66; D. Yaeger et al., "DSM-IV Diagnosed Posttraumatic Stress Disorder in Women Veterans with and without Military Sexual Trauma." *Journal of General Internal Medicine*, 21 (3), 2006, pp. S65–S69.

45. Statistics Canada, *Family Violence in Canada: A Statistical Profile, 2013* (Ottawa, ON: Minister of Industry, 2015).

46. Cited in Richard Gelles, *The Violent Home* (Beverly Hills, CA: Sage Publications, 1972), p. 14; bell hooks, *Feminism Is for Everybody: Passionate Politics* (Cambridge, MA: South End Press, 2000), p. 61.

47. World Health Organization, "Violence against Women: Intimate Partner and Sexual Violence against Women" (Fact Sheet 229), January 2016; Tanya Abramsky et al., "What Factors Are Associated with Recent Intimate Partner Violence? Findings from the WHO Multi-Country Study on Women's Health and Domestic Violence," *BMC Public Health*, 11, 2011, pp. 109–125; *Family Violence in Canada: A Statistical Profile, 2013.*

48. *Family Violence in Canada: A Statistical Profile, 2013.*

49. Data from *The New York Times*, August 25, 1997; United States Department of Justice, Family Violence, 1997; Reva Siegel, "The 'Rule of Love': Wife Beating as Prerogative and Privacy," *Yale Law Journal*, 105 (8), June 1996; Deborah Rhode, *Speaking of Sex: The Denial of Gender Inequality* (Cambridge, MA: Harvard University Press, 1997), p. 108; June Stephenson, *Men Are Not Cost Effective*, p. 285; see also Neil Websdale and Meda Chesney-Lind, "Doing Violence to Women: Research Synthesis on the Victimization of Women," *Masculinities and Violence*, L. Bowker, ed.; *Family Violence in Canada: A Statistical Profile, 2013.*

50. Statistics Canada (Canadian Centre for Justice Statistics), *Family Violence in Canada: A Statistical Profile* (Ottawa, ON: Minister of Industry, 2011); Matthew J. Breiding et al., "Prevalence and Characteristics of Sexual Violence, Stalking, and Intimate Partner Violence Victimization: National Intimate Partner and Sexual Violence Survey, United States, 2011," *Surveillance Summaries*, 63 (SS08), September 2014, pp. 1–18; Armin Brott, "The Battered Statistic Syndrome," *The Washington Post*, July 1994; Jodi-Anne Brzozowski and Robyn Brazeau, "What Are the Trends in Self-Reported Spousal Violence in Canada?" *Matter of Fact*, No. 6, 2008, Statistics Canada Catalogue No. 89-630-X.

51. R.L. McNeely and G. Robinson-Simpson, "The Truth About Domestic Violence: A Falsely Framed Issue," *Social Work*, 32 (6), 1987; Breiding et al., "Prevalence and Characteristics."

52. Susan Steinmetz, "The Battered Husband Syndrome," *Victimology*, 2, 1978.

53. M.D. Pagelow, "The 'Battered Husband Syndrome': Social Problem or Much Ado About Little?" *Marital Violence*, N. Johnson, ed. (London, UK: Routledge and Kegan Paul, 1985); Elizabeth Pleck et al., "The Battered Data Syndrome: A Comment on Steinmetz's Article," *Victimology*, 2, 1978; G. Storch, "Claim of 12 Million Battered Husbands Takes a Beating," *Miami Herald*, August 7, 1978; Jack C. Straton, "The Myth of the 'Battered Husband Syndrome'," *Masculinities*, 2 (4), 1994; Kerrie James, "Truth or Fiction: Men as Victims of Domestic Violence?" *The Australian and New Zealand Journal of Family Therapy*, 17 (3), 1996; Betsy Lucal, "The Problem with 'Battered Husbands'," *Deviant Behavior*, 16, 1995, pp. 95–112; Michael Kimmel, "Gender Symmetry in Domestic Violence: A Substantive and Methodological Research Review," *Violence against Women*, 8 (11), November 2002, pp. 1332–1363. Useful data can be found in Callie Marie Rennison, "Intimate Partner Violence and Age of Victim, 1993–1999," US Department of Justice, Bureau of Justice Statistics, October 2001; Kerrie James, "Truth or Fiction," who found the same results in a sample of Australian and New Zealand couples; J.E. Stets and Murray Straus, "The Marriage License as a Hitting License: A Comparison of Assaults in Dating, Cohabiting and Married Couples," *Journal of Family Violence*, 4 (2), 1989; J.E. Stets and Murray Straus, "Gender Differences in Reporting Marital Violence and Its

Medical and Psychological Consequences," *Physical Violence in American Families*, M. Straus and R. Gelles, eds. (New Brunswick, NJ: Transaction Publishers, 1990); Julie Sauvé and Mike Burns, "Residents of Canada's Shelters for Abused Women, 2008," *Juristat* 29 (2), May 2009, Statistics Canada Catalogue No. 85-002-X.

54. Maire Sinha, ed., *Measuring Violence against Women: Statistical Trends* (Ottawa: Minister of Industry, 2013); Brzozowski and Brazeau, "What Are the Trends"; Sauvé and Burns, "Residents of Canada's Shelters"; United States Department of Justice, Bureau of Justice Statistics, *Family Violence*, 1984.

55. Glanda Kaufman Kantor, Jana Janinski, and E. Aldorondo, "Sociocultural Status and Incidence of Marital Violence in Hispanic Families," *Violence and Victims*, 9 (3), 1994; Jana Janinski, "Dynamics of Partner Violence and Types of Abuse and Abusers," available at www.nnfr.org/nnfr/research/pv_ch1.html Also Kersti Yllo, personal communication.

56. See, for example, Jocalyn Clark and Janice Du Mont, "Intimate Partner Violence and Health: A Critique of Canadian Prevalence Studies," *Canadian Journal of Public Health/Revue Canadienne De Santé Publique*, 94 (1), 2003, pp. 52–58; Walter DeKeseredy and Martin D. Schwartz, "Backlash and Whiplash: A Critique of Statistics Canada's 1999 General Social Survey on Victimization," *Online Journal of Justice Studies*, 1 (1), 2003, pp. 1–14.

57. Ryan Shorey et al., "The Association between Impulsivity, Trait Anger, and the Perpetration of Intimate Partner and General Violence among Women Arrested for Domestic Violence," *Journal of Interpersonal Violence*, 26 (13), 2011, pp. 2681–2697; National Institute of Justice, "Measuring Intimate Partner (Domestic) Violence," 2010, available at www.nij.gov/topics/crime/intimate-partner-violence/pages/measuring.aspx (accessed December 15, 2015); Günnur Karakurt and Kristin E. Silver, "Emotional Abuse in Intimate Relationships: The Role of Gender and Age," *Violence and Victims*, 28 (5), 2013, pp. 804–821; Michael Johnson and Janel

Leone, "The Differential Effects of Intimate Terrorism and Situational Couple Violence: Findings from the National Violence against Women Survey," *Journal of Family Issues*, 26 (3), April 2005, pp. 322–349; R. Bachman and L.E. Saltzman, "Violence against Women," p. 6; Murray Straus and Richard Gelles, *Physical Violence in American Families*; Canadian Centre for Justice Statistics, "Family Violence in Canada," p. 13.

58. Murray A. Straus, "Gender Symmetry and Mutuality in Perpetration of Clinical-Level Partner Violence: Empirical Evidence and Implications for Prevention and Treatment," *Aggression and Violent Behavior*, 16, 2011, pp. 279–288.

59. Todd K. Shackelford, "Cohabitation, Marriage, and Murder: Woman-Killing by Male Romantic Partners," *Aggressive Behavior* 27, 2001, pp. 284–291; Noelia Breitman, Todd K. Shackelford, and Carolyn Rebecca Black, "Is Age Discrepancy a Risk Factor for Intimate Partner Homicide?" *Illinois Criminal Justice Information Authority Research Bulletin* 1 (3), 2003; Miladinovic and Mulligan, *Homicide in Canada*, 2014.

60. R. Emerson Dobash et al., "The Myth of Sexual Symmetry in Marital Violence," *Social Problems*, 39, 1992, p. 81; see also R. Emerson Dobash, and Russell Dobash, *Violence against Wives* (New York, NY: The Free Press, 1979); "The Case of Wife Beating," *Journal of Family Issues*, 2, 1981.

61. Ehrenreich, "The Violence Debate."

62. Feminista Jones, "Why Black Women Struggle More with Domestic Violence," *Time*, September 10, 2014, available at www.time.com/3313343/ray-rice-black-women-domestic-violence/ (accessed December 11, 2015); "Immigrant Women and Domestic Violence," CLEO Immigration and Refugee Factsheet; for US data and perspectives, see Noel Cazenave and Murray Straus, "Race, Class, Network Embeddedness and Family Violence: A Search for Potent Support Systems," *Physical Violence in American Families*, M. Straus and R. Gelles, eds. (New Brunswick, NJ: Transaction, 1990); Pam Belluck, "Women's Killers and Very Often Their

Partners," *The New York Times*, March 31, 1997, p. B1; C. Saline, "Bleeding in the Suburbs," *Philadelphia Magazine*, March 1984, p. 82; Murray Straus et al., *Behind Closed Doors*; R.L. Hampton, "Family Violence and Homicides in the Black Community: Are They Linked?" *Violence in the Black Family: Correlates and Consequences* (Lexington, MA; Lexington Books, 1987); R.L. Hampton and Richard Gelles, "Violence towards Black Women in a Nationally Representative Sample of Black Families," *Journal of Comparative Family Studies*, 25 (1), 1994.

63. Shannon Brennan, *Violent Victimization of Aboriginal Women in the Canadian Provinces, 2009* (Ottawa, ON: Minister of Industry, 2011; Native Women's Association of Canada, "Aboriginal Women's Health" (Background paper). NWAC, 2004; Jodi-Anne Brzozowski, Andrea Taylor-Butts, and Sarah Johnson, "Victimization and Offending among the Aboriginal Population in Canada," *Juristat*, 26 (3), June 2006.

64. Statistics Canada, *Family Violence in Canada: A Statistical Profile* (2011); Centers for Disease Control, "NISVS: An Overview of 2010 Findings on Victimization by Sexual Orientation," available at www.cdc.gov/violenceprevention /pdf/cdc_nisvs_victimization_final-a.pdf Also National Coalition of Anti-Violence Programs, *Lesbian, Gay, Bisexual, Transgender, Queer, and HIV-Affected Intimate Partner Violence in 2014*, 2015 Release Edition (New York, NY: National Coalition of Anti-Violence Programs, 2015), available at www.avp.org Also the varying statistics on p. 10 of Taylor N.T. Brown and Jody L. Herman, *Intimate Partner Violence and Sexual Abuse among LGBT People: A Review of Existing Research* (UCLA, Williams Law Institute, 2015); Rebecca Stotzer, "Violence against Transgender People: A Review of United States Data," *Aggression and Violent Behavior*, 14, 2009, pp. 170–179; Vicki Haddock, "Survey Tracks Gay Domestic Violence," *San Francisco Examiner*, October 22, 1996; Janice Ristock, *No More Secrets: Violence in Lesbian Relationships* (New York, NY/ London, UK: Routledge, 2002).

65. See, for example, Kersti Yllo, "Through a Feminist Lens: Gender, Power, and Violence," *Current Controversies on Family Violence*, R.J. Gelles and D. Loseke, eds. (Thousand Oaks, CA: Sage Publications, 1993).

66. Tina Hotton, "Childhood and Exposure to Violence in the Home" (research paper). Ottawa, ON: Statistics Canada/Ministry of Industry, 2003; Richard Gelles, *Family Violence* (Newbury Park, CA: Sage Publications, 1987), p. 165; Canadian Centre for Justice Statistics, *Family Violence in Canada: A Statistical Profile, 2008* (Ottawa, ON: Ministry of Industry/Statistics Canada, 2008), 6–7.

67. Elizabeth Thompson Gershoff, "Corporal Punishment by Parents and Associated Child Behaviors and Experiences: A Meta-Analytic and Theoretical Review," *Psychological Bulletin*, 128 (4), 2002, pp. 539–579. Gershoff's critics suggest that the negative effects are the result of "inept harsh parenting" and not specifically "spanking." See Diana Baumrind, Robert Larzelere, and Philip A. Cowan, "Ordinary Physical Punishment: Is It Harmful?" *Psychological Bulletin*, 128 (4), 2002, pp. 580–589; Marie-Hélène Gagné, Marc Tourigny, Jacques Joly, and Joëlle Pouliot-Lapointe, "Predictors of Adult Attitudes toward Corporal Punishment of Children," *Journal of Interpersonal Violence*, 22 (10), 2007, pp. 1285–1304. Canadian Paediatric Society, "Effective Discipline for Children," *Paediatric Child Health*, 9 (1), 2004, pp. 37–41; Tristin Hopper, "Canada's 120-Year-Old Spanking Law Unlikely to Change despite Doctors' Protest: Justice Department," *National Post*, September 4, 2012, available at http://news .nationalpost.com/news/canada/canadas-120 -year-old-spanking-law-unlikely-to-change -despite-doctors-protest-justice-department (accessed December 11, 2015).

68. Murray Straus, Richard Gelles, and Suzanne Steinmetz, *Behind Closed Doors: Violence in the American Family* (New York, NY: Anchor, 1981), p. 94; see also Murray Straus, *Beating the Devil out of Them* (New York, NY: Jossey-Bass, 1994).

69. Gelles, *Family Violence*, p. 165.

70. Abraham Bergman, Roseanne Larsen, and Beth Mueller, "Changing Spectrum of Child Abuse," *Pediatrics*, 77, 1986; Joan Durrant et al., "Punitive Violence against Children in Canada," CECW Information Sheet No. 41E (Toronto, ON: University of Toronto Faculty of Social Work, 2006).

71. "30 Children Killed by Their Parents in Canada Each Year, Expert Says," CBC News, October 26, 2015, available at www.cbc.ca /news/canada/windsor/30-children-killed -by-their-parents-in-canada-each-year-expert -says-1.3289322 (accessed December 11, 2015); P.G. Jaffe et al., "Children in Danger of Domestic Homicide," *Child Abuse & Neglect*, 36, 2012, pp. 71–74; Kathy AuCoin, "Children and Youth as Victims of Violent Crime," *Juristat*, 25 (1), 2005, Statistics Canada Catalogue No. 85-002-XIE.

72. Amin Muhammad, "Preliminary Examination of So-called 'Honour Killings' in Canada" (Ottawa, ON: Minister of Justice, 2013), available at www.justice.gc.ca/eng /rp-pr/cj-jp/fv-vf/hk-ch/hk_eng.pdf Also Chris Cobb, "Brother Gets Life in Honour Killing," *The Ottawa Citizen*, May 31, 2009, available at www.ottawacitizen.com/news /Brother1gets1life1honour1killing/1647215 /story.html (accessed February 20, 2010); Jill Colvin, "Family Members Charged with Murder in Submerged Car Case," *The Globe and Mail*, July 23, 2009.

73. Phyllis Chesler, "Are Honor Killings Simply Domestic Violence?" *Middle East Quarterly*, 16 (2), Spring, 2009, pp. 61–69; Amber Hildebrandt, "Honour Killings: Domestic Abuse by Another Name?" CBC News, July 24, 2009; Regina Leader-Post, "Cultural 'Honour Killing' Brought to Canada," *Canada* online, June 11, 2007, available at www.canada .com/ vancouversun/story.html?id=d05e437f -4661-4965-9455-ff30c6b9d4a5&k=20265 (accessed February 2, 2010).

74. Cindy Struckman-Johnson, David Struckman-Johnson & Peter B. Anderson, "Tactics of Sexual Coercion: When Men and Women Won't Take No for an Answer," *The Journal of Sex Research*, 40 (1), 2003, pp. 76–86; M.L. Ybarra and K.J. Mitchell, "Prevalence Rates of Male and Female Sexual Violence Perpetrators in a National Sample of Adolescents," *JAMA Pediatrics*, 167 (12), 2013, pp. 1125–1134; David Barash, *The Whisperings Within* (New York, NY: Harper and Row, 1979), p. 54; see also W.M. Shields and L.M. Shields, "Forcible Rape: An Evolutionary Perspective," *Ethology and Sociobiology*, 4, 1983, p. 119.

75. Randy Thornhill and Craig T. Palmer, "Why Men Rape," *The Sciences*, January 2000, p. 30; Randy Thornhill and Craig T. Palmer, *A Natural History of Rape* (Cambridge, MA: MIT Press, 2000), p. 53. See also Richard Alexander and K.M. Noonan, "Concealment of Ovulation, Parental Care and Human Social Evolution," *Evolutionary Biology and Human Social Behavior*, N. Chagnon and W. Irons, eds. (North Scituate, MA: Duxbury, 1979), p. 449.

76. See Salman Masood, "Pakistan's High Court Reviewing Officially Ordered Gang Rape," *The New York Times*, June 28, 2005, p. 3.

77. See Peggy Reeves Sanday, *Fraternity Gang Rape* (New York, NY: NYU Press, 1996).

78. See Robb Willer et al., *Sexual Assault of Children and Adolescents* (San Francisco, CA: Jossey-Bass, 1978).

79. Carol Sheffield, *Feminist Jurisprudence* (New York, NY: Routledge, 1997), p. 203.

80. In this way, rape may itself be understandable as a social institution.

81. Peggy Reeves Sanday, *Female Power and Male Dominance*; quote from Larry Baron and Murray Straus, "Four Theories of Rape: A Macrosociological Analysis," *Social Problems*, 34 (5), 1987, p. 481.

82. See, for example, Diana Scully, *Understanding Sexual Violence: A Study of Convicted Rapists* (New York, NY: HarperCollins, 1990); Diana Russell, *Rape in Marriage* (New York, NY: Macmillan, 1982), and *Sexual Exploitation* (Beverly Hills, CA: Sage Publications, 1984); Deborah Rhode, *Speaking of Sex*, pp. 119–120; Allan Johnson, "On the Prevalence of Rape in the United States," *Signs*, 6 (1), 1980, p. 145. For more on this, see also Diana Scully and J. Marolla, "'Riding the Bull at Gilley's': Convicted Rapists Describe the Rewards of Rape," *Social Problems*, 32, 1985; Jennifer

Truman and Lynn Langton, *Criminal Victimization 2014 Bulletin*) (Washington, DC: US Department of Justice Bureau of Justice Statistics, August 2015), available at www.bjs.gov/content/pub/pdf/cv14.pdf

83. United States Department of Justice, "Child Rape Victims, 1992" (NCJ-147001), June 1994; Eugene Kanin, "False Rape Allegations," *Archives of Sexual Behavior*, 23 (1), 1994.

84. Lucie Ogrodnik, *Child and Youth Victims of Police-Reported Violent Crime, 2008* (Ottawa, ON: Minister of Industry, 2010); AuCoin, "Children and Youth as Victims of Violent Crime."

85. Ogrodnik, *Child and Youth Victims*; AuCoin, "Children and Youth as Victims of Violent Crime"; "Bishop Surrenders on Child Porn Charges," *Toronto Sun*, October 1, 2009, available at www.torontosun.com/news/canada/2009/10/01/11230971.html (accessed October 10, 2009); "Former Jewish Community Activist Facing Child-Porn Charges," May 29, 2009. CTV.ca, available at http://montreal.ctv.ca/servlet/an/local/CTV News/20090529/mtl_surkis_child_porn _charges_090529?hub=MontrealHome (accessed January 20, 2010); "Seven Children 'Rescued' as Surrey Child Porn Charges Laid," *The Vancouver Sun*, February 5, 2010, available at www.vancouversun.com/life/relationships /Seven1children1rescued1Surrey1child1porn1 charges1laid/2527908/story.html

86. Dauvergne, *Adult Criminal Court Statistics in Canada 2010–2011*; Ashley Jespersen, Martin Lalumiere, and Michael Seto, "Sexual Abuse History among Adult Sex Offenders and Non-Sex Offenders: A Meta-Analysis," *Child Abuse and Neglect*, 33 (3), 2009, pp. 179–182; David Finkelhor, "The Prevention of Childhood Sexual Abuse," *The Future of Children*, 19 (2), 2009, pp. 170–194.

87. Johnson, "On the Prevalence of Rape," p. 145; Scully, *Understanding Sexual Violence*, p. 53.

88. Mary Koss, Christine A. Gidycz, and Nadine Misniewski, "The Scope of Rape: Incidence and Prevalence of Sexual Aggression and Victimization in a National Sample of Higher Education Students," *Journal of Consulting and Clinical Psychology*, 55 (2), 1987.

89. Susan Griffin, "Rape: The All-American Crime," *Ramparts Magazine*, September 1971, pp. 26–35; Scully and Marolla, "'Riding the Bull at Gilley's'"; also Scully, "Convicted Rapists' Perceptions of Self and Victim: Role Taking and Emotions," *Gender and Society*, 2 (2), June 1988, pp. 200–213.

90. Scully, *Understanding Sexual Violence*, pp. 74, 140, 159, 166.

91. John Briere and Neil Malamuth, "Self-Reported Likelihood of Sexually Aggressive Behavior: Attitudinal versus Sexual Explanations," *Journal of Research in Personality*, 17, 1983; Todd Tieger, "Self-Rated Likelihood of Raping and Social Perception of Rape," *Journal of Research in Personality*, 15, 1991; Sarah Edwards, Kathryn Bradshaw, and B. Hinsz Verlin, "Denying Rape but Endorsing Forceful Intercourse: Exploring Differences Among Responders," *Violence and Gender*, 1 (4), December 2014, pp. 188–193.

92. J.L. Herman, "Considering Sex Offenders: A Model of Addiction," *Signs*, 13, 1988; Bernard Lefkowitz, *Our Guys* (Berkeley, CA: University of California Press, 1997); Don Terry, "Gang Rape of Three Girls Leaves Fresno Shaken and Questioning," *The New York Times*, April 28, 1998; see also Jane Hood, "'Let's Get a Girl': Male Bonding Rituals in America," *Men's Lives*, Fourth Edition, M. Kimmel and M. Messner, eds.

93. Tim Beneke, *Men on Rape* (New York, NY: St. Martin's Press, 1982), p. 81.

94. See Mary P. Koss, Christine Gidycz, and Nadine Misniewski, "The Scope of Rape," and Scott Boeringer, "Pornography and Sexual Aggression: Associations of Violence and Nonviolent Depictions with Rape and Rape Proclivity," *Deviant Behavior*, 15, 1994, pp. 289–304; David Lisak and Paul Miller, "Repeat Rape and Multiple Offending among Undetected Rapists," *Violence and Victims*, 17 (1), 2002, pp. 73–84.

95. Diana Russell, *Rape in Marriage*; David Finklehor and Kirsti Yllo, *License to Rape: Sexual Abuse of Wives* (Newbury Park, CA: Sage Publications, 1985), pp. 217, 208. On marital rape generally, see also Raquel Kennedy Bergen, "Surviving Wife Rape: How Women

Define and Cope with the Violence," *Violence against Women*, 1 (2), 1995, pp. 117–138 and the special issue of *Violence against Women*, 5 (9), September 1999, Bergen edited; Raquel Kennedy Bergen, *Wife Rape: Understanding the Response of Survivors and Service Providers* (Thousand Oaks, CA: Sage Publications, 1996); Anne L. Buckborough, "Family Law: Recent Developments in the Law of Marital Rape," *Annual Survey of American Law*, 1989; "To Have and to Hold: The Marital Rape Exemption and the Fourteenth Amendment," *Harvard Law Review*, 99, 1986; M.C. Black et al., *The National Intimate Partner and Sexual Violence Survey (NISVS): 2010 Summary Report* (Atlanta, GA: National Center for Injury Prevention and Control, Centers for Disease Control and Prevention, 2011); Matt Pearce, "No Prison Time for Indiana Man Convicted of Drugging, Raping Wife," *Los Angeles Times*, May 19, 2014, available at www .latimes.com/nation/nationnow/la-na-nn -indianapolis-rape-sentence-20140519-story .html#page=1 (accessed December 12, 2015).

96. See, inter alia, John Simister and Parnika S. Mehta, "Gender-Based Violence in India: Long-term Trends," *Journal of Interpersonal Violence*, 25 (9), 2010, pp. 1594–1611; Faridah Ali et al., "Association of Various Reproductive Rights, Domestic Violence, and Marital Rape with Depression among Pakistani Women," *BMC Psychiatry*, 9 (77), 2009; David Frank, Tara Hardinge, and Kassia Woswick-Correa, "The Global Dimensions of Rape-Law Reform: A Cross-National Study of Policy Outcomes," *American Sociological Review*, 74, April 2009, pp. 272–290; Kwong-Leung Tang, "Rape Law Reform in Canada: The Success and Limits of Legislation," *International Journal of Offender Therapy and Comparative Criminology*, 42 (23), 1998, pp. 258–270; Indira Jaising, "Bringing Rights Home: Review of the Campaign for a Law on Domestic Violence," *Economic and Political Weekly*, 44 (44), October 31, 2009, pp. 50–57; World Health Organization, "Sexual Violence" (fact sheet), 2012, available at http:// apps.who.int/iris/bitstream/10665/77434/1 /WHO_RHR_12.37_eng.pdf

97. *The Death of Helen Betty Osborne*, Volume II of the Report of the Aboriginal Justice Inquiry of Manitoba (Aboriginal Justice Implementation Commission, 1999), available at http://ajic.mb.ca/volume.html (accessed April 15, 2016); Amnesty International, *Stolen Sisters: A Human Rights Response to Discrimination and Violence against Indigenous Women in Canada* (report) (Ottawa, ON: Amnesty International, 2004); Native Women's Association of Canada, "Sisters in Spirit–Background," available at www.nwac.hq.org/en/ background .html Also Shelagh Day, Dani Bryant, and Christian Morey, "Nothing to Report" (submission of the BC CEDAW Group to the United Nations Committee on the Elimination of All Forms of Discrimination against Women), 2009; Yasmin Jiwani and Mary Lynn Young, "Missing and Murdered Women: Reproducing Marginality in News Discourse," *Canadian Journal of Communication*, 31, 2006, pp. 895–917; "Federal Liberals Call for Highway of Tears National Investigation," *Vanderhoof Omineca Express*, February 9, 2010, available at www.bclocalnews .com/bc_north/ominecaexpress/community /83847667.html (accessed February 9, 2010); "List of Women on 'Highway of Tears' Doubles," CTV.ca, October 12, 2007, available at www.ctv.ca Also Lori Cuthbert and Neal Hall, "Highway of Tears Probe Points to 2,000 'Persons of Interest,'" Canwest News Service, December 13, 2009, available at www .calgaryherald.com "Police Reveal Details of E-Pana Investigation into 18 female unsolved Cases in Northern BC," Canwest News Service, December 12, 2009, available at www.kelowna .com Also Native Women's Association of Canada, *What Their Stories Tell Us: Research Findings from the Sisters In Spirit Initiative* (Akwesasne, Ontario: NWAC, 2010); Miladinovic and Mulligan, *Homicide in Canada, 2014*; Gloria Galloway, "Report Rejects Call for Inquiry into Violence against Aboriginal Women," *The Globe and Mail*, March 07, 2014, available at www.theglobeandmail.com /news/politics/study-into-violence-against -indigenous-women-rejects-call-for-inquiry

/article17368559/ Also Adam Jones, "Aborigi-nal Men are Murdered and Missing Far More than Aboriginal Women. A Proper Inquiry Would Explore Both," *National Post*, April 27, 2015, available at http://news.nationalpost.com /full-comment/adam-jones-aboriginal-men -are-murdered-and-missing-far-more-than -aboriginal-women-a-proper-inquiry-would -explore-both; Eric Andrew-Gee, "Aborig-inal Men Murdered at Higher Rate than Aboriginal Women," August 22, 2014, avail-ableatwww.thestar.com/news/gta/2014/08/22 /aboriginal_men_murdered_at_higher_rate _than_aboriginal_women.html

98. Diana Russell and N. Van de Ven, *Crimes against Women: The Proceedings of the International Tribunal* (Millbrae, CA: Les Femmes Publishing, 1976); WHO, "Femicide," available at http://apps.who .int/iris/bitstream/10665/77421/1/WHO _RHR_12.38_eng.pdf (accessed April 10, 2016); "What Is a Hate Crime?" CBC News online, June 2011, available at www.cbc.ca /news/canada/what-is-a-hate-crime-1.1011 612 (accessed April 10, 2016); Nadera Shalhoub-Kevorkian, "Reexamining Fe-micide: Breaking the Silence and Crossing 'Scientific' Borders," *Signs*, 28 (2), 2003, pp. 581–608; Mark Ensalaco, "Murder in Ciudad Juarez: A Parable of Women's Struggle for Human Rights," *Violence against Women*, 12 (5), 2006, pp. 417–440; Heather Robin Agnew, "Reframing 'Femi-cide': Making Room for the Balloon Effect of Drug War Violence in Studying Female Homicides in Mexico and Central America," *Territory, Politics, Governance*, 3 (4), 2015, pp. 428–445; Teresa Bo, "Guatemala's Fe-micide Crisis," Al-Jazeera.net, August 5, 2009, available at http://english.aljazeera. net/focus/2009/08/200984134334229388 .html (accessed January 9, 2010); Roselyn Costantino, "Femicide, Impunity, and Cit-izenship: The Old and New in the Struggle for Justice in Guatemala," *Chicana/Latina Studies*, 6 (1), Fall 2006, pp. 108–121.

99. Julie Bindel, "The Montréal Massacre: Can-ada's Feminists Remember," *The Guard-ian*, December 3, 2012, available at www .theguardian.com/world/2012/dec/03/mon treal-massacre-canadas-feminists-remember (accessed April 10, 2016); "The Manifesto of Elliott Rodger."

100. Ki Namaste, "Genderbashing: Sexual-ity, Gender, and the Regulation of Public Space," *Environment and Planning D: So-ciety and Space*, 14 (2), 1996, pp. 221–240; "Obama Signs Hate Crimes Bill into Law," CNN, October 28, 2009, available at www .cnn.com/2009/politics/10/28/hate.crimes /index.html Gregory M. Herek, "Hate Crimes and Stigma-Related Experiences among Sexual Minority Adults in the United States: Prevalence Estimates from a National Probability Sample," *Journal of Interpersonal Violence*, 24 (1), January 2009, pp. 54–74; FBI, "Hate Crime Sta-tistics 2014," available at https://www.fbi .gov/about-us/cjis/ucr/hate-crime/2014 /topic-pages/incidentsandoffenses_final Also Mary Allen, *Police-Reported Hate Crime in Canada, 2013* (Ottawa, ON: Min-ister of Industry, 2015).

101. FBI, "Hate Crime Statistics 2014," 93. On-tario Human Rights Commission, "Toward a Commission Policy on Gender Identity," (report) (Ontario Human Rights Commis-sion, October 1999), pp. 21–23; Rebecca L. Stotzer, "Violence against Transgender People: A Review of United States Data," *Aggression and Violent Behavior*, 14, 2009, pp. 170–179; Jim Spellman, "Transgender Murder, Hate Crime Conviction a First," CNN, 2008, available at www.cnn.com "US Marine Guilty of Killing Transgender Woman in Philippines," *The Guardian*, December 1, 2015, available at www.the guardian.com/world/2015/dec/01/us-marine -guilty-of-killing-transgender-woman -in-philippines (accessed December 2, 2015).

102. Myriam Miedzian, "Beyond the Masculine Mystique," *Gender Violence: Interdisciplinary*

Perspectives, Laura O'Toole, Jessica Schiffman, and Margie Kiter Edwards, eds. (New York, NY: NYU Press, 2007), p. 433.

103. John Ruskin, "Of the Pathetic Fallacy," *Modern Painters III* (1856).

Epilogue

1. See Judith Lorber, *Breaking the Bowls*: *Degendering and Feminist Change* (New York, NY: W.W. Norton, 2005). For a critique of state-led "degendering" efforts, see Holly Johnson, "Degendering Violence," *Social Politics: International Studies in Gender, State, and Society*, 22 (3), Fall 2015, pp. 390–410.

2. For an overview of some of these issues, see Barbara Ehrenreich and Arlie Russell Hochschild, eds., *Global Woman: Nannies, Maids, and Sex Workers in the New Economy* (New York, NY: Metropolitan Books, 2003).

3. Kate Millett, *Sexual Politics* (New York, NY: Random House, 1969).

4. Robert Jay Lifton, *The Protean Self* (New York, NY: Basic Books, 1994). See also Cynthia Fuchs Epstein, "The Multiple Realities of Sameness and Difference: Ideology and Practice," *Journal of Social Issues*, 53(2), 1997; and Floyd Dell, "Feminism for Men," *The Masses*, February 1917, reprinted in *Against the Tide*, M.S. Kimmel and T. Mosmiller, eds.

Index